Teacher Wraparound Edition

GLENCOE

The Basics of Speech

Learning to Be a Competent Communicator

KATHLEEN M. GALVIN
Professor and Associate Dean
Communication Studies Department
School of Speech
Northwestern University
Evanston, Illinois

PAMELA J. COOPER
Professor
Communication Studies Department
School of Speech
Northwestern University
Evanston, Illinois

McGraw Hill Glencoe

New York, New York   Columbus, Ohio   Chicago, Illinois   Peoria, Illinois   Woodland Hills, California

The McGraw·Hill Companies

Send all inquiries to:
Glencoe/McGraw-Hill
8787 Orion Place
Columbus, Ohio 43240

ISBN 0-07-861620-4 Student Editon
ISBN 0-07-861621-2 Teacher Wraparound Editon

1 2 3 4 5 6 7 8 9 058/055 09 08 07 06 05 04

Teaching and learning are both highly variable activities. They must be customized to the needs of both teachers and students. For this reason, it would be impossible for any rigidly prescribed approach to succeed in every case—or even in most cases. The following features of the *Teacher Wraparound Edition* for *The Basics of Speech* are offered as a starting point. Teachers are encouraged to choose information, features, and activities in this teacher edition, in the *Teacher Resource Binder* (a three-ring binder also referred to as the *Teacher's Resource Book*), and in *The Basics of Speech Workbook*. These materials will help teachers meet the needs of their speech classes.

The Prepare Pages

- The **Unit Planner** names each of the chapters included in the unit and provides the teacher with week-by-week time-management information. This planner also indicates that pages in the *Teacher's Resource Book* and Workbook are available for use with each of the chapters in the unit.

- **Unit Focus** gives an overview of the topics to be covered in the unit.

- **Unit Portfolios** icon indicates which products of individual, group, and class activities are suitable for inclusion in a portfolio.

- **Ability Key** indicates which activities and suggestions are especially suitable for a given ability group.

- **Ancillary Resource Key** indicates applicable materials.

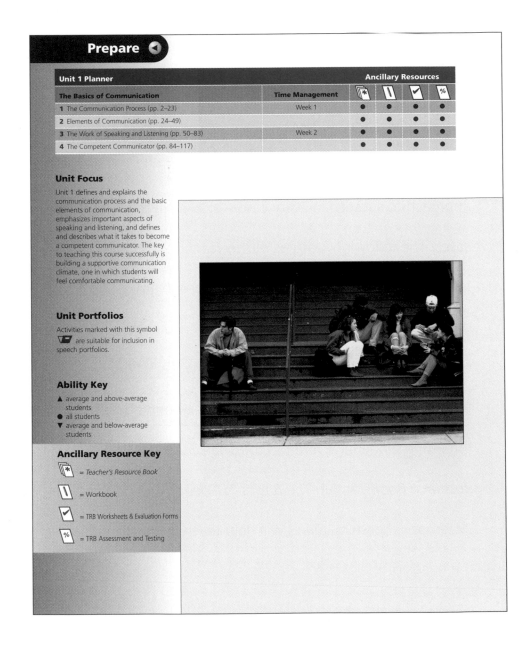

Prepare

Unit 1 Planner		Ancillary Resources				
The Basics of Communication	Time Management	📖*	❘	✔	%
1 The Communication Process (pp. 2–23)	Week 1	●	●	●	●
2 Elements of Communication (pp. 24–49)		●	●	●	●
3 The Work of Speaking and Listening (pp. 50–83)	Week 2	●	●	●	●
4 The Competent Communicator (pp. 84–117)		●	●	●	●

Unit Focus

Unit 1 defines and explains the communication process and the basic elements of communication, emphasizes important aspects of speaking and listening, and defines and describes what it takes to become a competent communicator. The key to teaching this course successfully is building a supportive communication climate, one in which students will feel comfortable communicating.

Unit Portfolios

Activities marked with this symbol 📖 are suitable for inclusion in speech portfolios.

Ability Key

▲ average and above-average students
● all students
▼ average and below-average students

Ancillary Resource Key

📖* = *Teacher's Resource Book*

❘ = Workbook

✔ = TRB Worksheets & Evaluation Forms

% = TRB Assessment and Testing

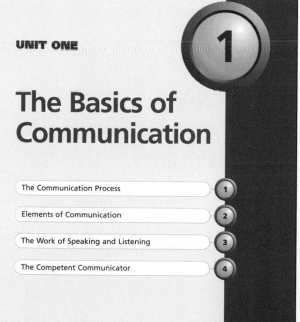

Performance Objectives

After completing this unit, students will be able to

1. define the communication process
2. describe how verbal and nonverbal communication are linked
3. describe the steps and types of listening
4. describe a competent communicator

▶ Prepare

UNIT ONE

1

The Basics of Communication

Bibliography

Print

Aitken, Joan E., ed. *Speech Communication Teacher: Ideas and Strategies for Classroom Activities.* Quarterly magazine available from National Communication Association, 5105 Backlick Rd., Building E, Annandale, VA. 22003.

Christ, William G., ed. *Assessing Communication Education: A Handbook for Media, Speech and Theatre Educators.* Annandale, Va.: National Communication Association, 1994.

Cooper, Pamela, ed. *Activities for Teaching, Speaking and Listening: Grades 7–12.* Annandale, Va.: National Communication Association, 1991.

Galvin, Kathleen M. and Cassandra Book. *Person to Person: An Introduction to Speech Communication.* 5th ed. Lincolnwood, Ill: NTC / Contemporary Publishing, 1994.

Galvin, Kathleen M. and Bernard Brommel. *Family Communication: Cohesion and Change.* 3rd ed. New York: HarperCollins, 1991.

Morreale, Sherwyn P. and Phil Backlund, eds. *Large Scale Assessment in Oral Communication: K–12 and Higher Education.* Annandale, Va.: National Communication Association, 1996.

1

- **Performance Objectives** clarify student goals for the unit.

- **Bibliography** suggests additional print and multimedia materials, including Web sites.

- The **Chapter Planner** provides a day-to-day description of the topics to be addressed in class. The bottom section of the planner lists the specific Worksheets and Evaluation Forms, Workbook pages, and Assessment and Testing materials that apply.

- **Motivation** provides suggestions for creating student interest in topics under discussion.

- **Links to Past Learning** relates speech concepts to prior knowledge.

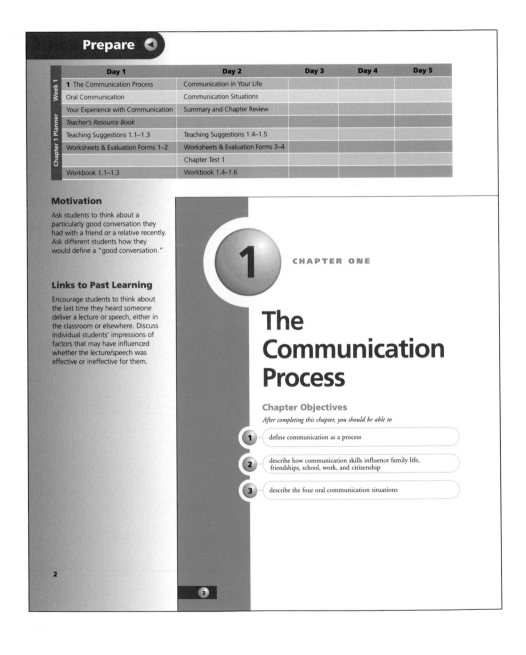

Prepare ◀

	Day 1	Day 2	Day 3	Day 4	Day 5
Week 1	**1** The Communication Process	Communication in Your Life			
	Oral Communication	Communication Situations			
	Your Experience with Communication	Summary and Chapter Review			
Chapter 1 Planner	*Teacher's Resource Book*				
	Teaching Suggestions 1.1–1.3	Teaching Suggestions 1.4–1.5			
	Worksheets & Evaluation Forms 1–2	Worksheets & Evaluation Forms 3–4			
		Chapter Test 1			
	Workbook 1.1–1.3	Workbook 1.4–1.6			

Motivation

Ask students to think about a particularly good conversation they had with a friend or a relative recently. Ask different students how they would define a "good conversation."

Links to Past Learning

Encourage students to think about the last time they heard someone deliver a lecture or speech, either in the classroom or elsewhere. Discuss individual students' impressions of factors that may have influenced whether the lecture/speech was effective or ineffective for them.

1 CHAPTER ONE

The Communication Process

Chapter Objectives

After completing this chapter, you should be able to

1 — define communication as a process

2 — describe how communication skills influence family life, friendships, school, work, and citizenship

3 — describe the four oral communication situations

2

Teach ◀

Amazing Fact!

The Mandarin language has the most speakers of any language in the world.

Substitute Teacher Tip

Students could role-play various speaking and listening scenarios. For example, one student might role-play a parent giving instructions to another student who is playing the role of a baby-sitter. Other students might role-play parents giving instructions to someone washing the family car, doing the family laundry, loading a dishwasher, sweeping the kitchen floor, ironing a shirt, and so on. Encourage the rest of the class to discuss what went well in each communication and which areas could use improvement.

Multicultural Learning

● Students could interview a person who has or had non-English-speaking parents. They might ask that person what it is like to translate information and ideas from one language to another, and whether that task requires special listening skills.

Good communication skills can help people deal with situations like these. The main goal of this book is to help you develop strong communication skills.

 INTERACT

With a partner, take turns describing a person who is the best communicator you know. Be specific in telling how the person acts and speaks and what situations he or she handles well.

COMMUNICATION IN YOUR LIFE

Communication affects every area of your life, now and in the future. Think of the various kinds of communication that took place today. Did your mother or father pat you on the back or smile good-bye? Did you talk to the bus driver, your friends, an acquaintance, or a stranger? How did you interpret the smile of a friend? the actions of a teacher standing up, pushing a chair in, and opening a book? the principal's voice over the public address system?

Every day you spend hours communicating. You may request help from a salesperson in a store. You may give directions to a visitor in your community. You may listen to your favorite music or to conversations among classmates. In addition to general, everyday situations, there are five areas of your life that require highly developed communication skills. These are the areas of family, friendship, school, work, and citizenship. In order to be a caring family member, a good friend, a good student, an efficient worker, and an involved citizen, you will need to develop and use specific communication skills.

Family

A person's ability to speak and listen carefully has a strong effect on life at home. Counselors report that some of the greatest

12

12

Unit 1 The Basics of Communication

The Teach Pages

- **Amazing Fact!** reveals fascinating bits of information related to the topics addressed in the text.

- **Substitute Teacher Tips** provide suggestions for class activities that require no preparation or planning.

- **Multicultural Learning** emphasizes ways to relate speech concepts to various cultures both within and outside the classroom.

- **Quotations** provide amusing or inspiring observations. These may be shared with students as conversation starters—or simply enjoyed.

- **Cooperative Learning** gives suggestions for activities or ideas to promote learning in pairs or small groups.

 Teach ◀

66 Words mean more than what is set down on paper. It takes the human voice to infuse them with shades of deeper meaning. 99
MAYA ANGELOU
I Know Why the Caged Bird Sings

Cooperative Learning

▼ Give students a few minutes to create tongue twisters like the ones shown on this page. Tell them to limit their tongue twisters to a maximum of ten words. When every student has come up with a tongue twister, collect their work. Then have individuals come to the front of the room, choose a tongue twister at random, and say it aloud for the class. After each tongue twister, allow the volunteer to explain why the tongue twister was or was not difficult to say. Encourage the rest of the class to comment and ask questions.

 INTERACT

With a partner take turns reading the following tongue twisters as clearly and quickly as you can.

A big bad bear bit a brown and black bug.

She sells seashells by the seashore.

In June the Jump Jazz group generates joyful tunes.

Vocal Quality This refers to the sound of your voice. Most people produce full sounds, which make their voices pleasant. Some speakers have a nasal voice, which makes them sound as if they are talking through their nose. Others have husky or raspy voices. Proper use of the voice is discussed in Chapter 12.

Importance of Vocal Production

Effective speech begins with good vocal production. It is important to develop correct habits for creating sounds so that you can make yourself understood in many situations. This is especially important when speaking with people from different areas of the country. When you travel across the United States, you find certain words pronounced in different ways. When you travel around the world, you find sounds in some languages that do not exist in the English language. You will hear clicks made in the back of the throat in some African languages and different tones in certain Asian languages. Most people take vocal production for granted. Skillful communicators learn how to improve their voices and make themselves more easily understood by listeners.

THE LISTENING PROCESS

What is listening? Is it the same as hearing? You may be surprised to learn that there is a difference. Hearing is the act of receiving sound. When you hear something, you are aware of sounds. Listening involves hearing, but it is much more complicated than just picking up sounds.

58

 Unit 1 The Basics of Communication

Teach ◄

Curricular Connection

Mathematics

● Using the metaphor that people "write a book a year, read a book a month, speak a book a week, and listen to a book a day," have students calculate how many books the average 75-year-old person would have written, read, spoken, and listened to.

Limited English Proficiency

Some students may be unfamiliar with the jobs listed under Apply. Ask for volunteers to explain, for example, what a Web master, aerobics instructor, or insurance agent does for a living. Ask for another name for *physician* (doctor), *chef* (cook), and *salesperson* (clerk).

read a book a month, speak a book a week, and listen to a book a day. Oral communication certainly affects every area of a person's life.

APPLY

Communication is part of almost every job. From the following list of career opportunities, try to select one in which communication skills would not be a basic job requirement. Explain your choice.

postal worker	salesperson	insurance agent
flight attendant	teacher	farmer
Web master	accountant	welder
actor	travel agent	driving instructor
reporter	truck driver	lawyer
child-care worker	store manager	machine operator
aerobics instructor	gas-station attendant	resort manager
physician	chef	police officer

INTERACT

In a small group, discuss the kinds of communication situations in which a person such as a principal, cafeteria worker, secretary, teacher, or maintenance staffer takes part. Does this person have to greet others, give directions, solve problems, give advice, or discipline others? Does this person listen or speak more frequently? What communication skills does this person need?

16

- **Curricular Connection** identifies ways to integrate speech instruction with other areas of the curriculum such as language arts, mathematics, social studies, and art.

- **Limited English Proficiency** provides help for integrating these students into the speech class.

- **Critical Thinking** suggestions help students build on what they have learned by analyzing, organizing, predicting, evaluating, and synthesizing.

- **Beyond the Classroom** suggests ideas to help students interact with the community.

Teach ◀

Critical Thinking

Evaluating

Ask students to talk in small groups for several minutes without looking at each other. Then ask them to talk about the result. How successful was the communication? How did this exercise make them feel?

Beyond the Classroom

● Have students think of jobs that use specific nonverbal signals. For example, a referee in a boxing match or a basketball game uses specific gestures to officiate at a fight or game. Airport signal personnel use important gestures to help pilots bring their aircraft safely from the runway to the terminal. Tell students to watch for instances in their daily lives where people communicate through gestures rather than, or in addition to, words. (They might mention crossing guard, traffic police, orchestra conductor, choir director, or choreographer.)

Nonverbal messages are expressed through facial expressions and body movements.

Verbal and Nonverbal Messages

A **message** is the way **meaning** is conveyed. Messages are at the center of the communication process. Without a message, there can be no communication. A message may be verbal or nonverbal. Verbal messages are spoken or written messages. They rely on words to carry the meaning. Nonverbal messages are those expressed without words. They rely on the use of facial expressions, vocal tone, body movements, and appearance.

Think about the verbal and nonverbal messages that you sent and received today. Do you know how much you communicated verbally through your words and how much you communicated nonverbally through your facial expressions or body movements? You probably haven't thought about these two areas separately because they usually work together.

Speakers and listeners share the responsibility for being good communicators. Communication works like a skilled tennis match. Both communicators are involved continuously in the process, just as both tennis players are involved constantly in the game. Once a good player hits the ball, he or she gets into

6

6

Unit 1 The Basics of Communication

Skill Development
On the Job
● Encourage those students who volunteer or have part-time jobs to share information about the various types of communication they receive from their supervisors, managers, and coworkers.

66That is the happiest conversation where there is no competition, no vanity, but a calm quiet interchange of sentiments.99
SAMUEL JOHNSON

Learning Styles
Audio-Visual Learning
Ask students whether they find it easier to learn by seeing or by hearing something explained. Ask for a show of hands. Emphasize that different people learn in different ways and that later in this class they will learn how to use audio-visual aids when they give a speech.

School

Your speaking and listening skills affect your school life in many ways. Often you are expected to give oral reports or explain your ideas to the class. You may be asked to give speeches or introduce speakers. You may lead a group project during class or organize group work for school charity drives or after-school events. In these situations, you need to feel comfortable speaking to a group of people. If you are not willing to ask and answer questions or share your ideas, you may feel like an outsider in class.

As a student you will spend between 50 and 90 percent of your class time listening, mostly to the teacher, but also to other students. Even on breaks from classes, you spend time listening to your friends. You might be surprised at how many hours a year you spend listening in school.

Work

The jobs you have after school or over the summer require good communication skills. If you baby-sit, you need to communicate with the parents, the children, and, in an emergency, doctors or the police. If you do yard work, you must talk with your neighbors. Maintaining Web sites requires dealing with customers. Employers were recently asked to rate the importance of communication skills for new workers. The skill receiving the highest rating was a listening skill—understanding directions. In a recent Junior Achievement survey of employers, researchers found that 27 percent of high-school graduates barely get by when communicating verbally. Eighty-five percent of employers believe verbal communication is very important, but they say that only one in ten high-school seniors shows real skill in communicating.

Almost every area of life requires some type of communication skill. Some listening experts estimate that 75 percent of a person's daily communication involves listening and speaking. We listen more than we speak, we speak more than we read, and we read more than we write. Some people say that we write a book a year,

15

- **Skill Development** ideas focus on media literacy, research, on-the-job skills, giving and receiving feedback, active listening, making conversation, vocabulary, and other skill opportunities.

- **Learning Styles** provides suggestions for using kinesic, visual, audio, or audiovisual ways of learning.

The Apply and Assess Pages

This section provides ways for students to show they have understood the material and for teachers to assess learning. It includes **answers** to end-of-chapter questions in the student book and a **Quick Check** section that highlights key terms used throughout the chapter.

Assess ◀

Answers

Think About It

Student answers will vary slightly. Here are sample answers:

1. Communication is a process because it moves forward from a beginning point.

2. Shared meanings allow communication. If two people have different meanings for the same words, they will confuse one another and be unable to communicate effectively.

3. Student answers will vary. Responses should include some of the following: Job—people have to communicate with coworkers, customers, and managers in order to be effective employees; family—good communication will prevent some arguments and reduce misunderstandings; community—as citizens people must be able to listen and speak to better serve their community, for example by voting; school—Students learn more if they listen, ask questions, and explain ideas, which are all qualities of good communicators.

4. Interpersonal communication—speaking to a friend; group communication—speaking as member of a planning team; public communication—giving a speech to an audience; interpretive communication—reading a story to a small child.

22

CHAPTER REVIEW

Think About It

1. Why is communication considered a process?

2. Why are common meanings important in communication?

3. In what ways can good communication skills help you in your job, in your family, in your community, and at school?

4. Describe the four communication situations and provide an example of each.

Try It Out

1. In a small group, brainstorm a list of guidelines for good family communication. Compare your list with those of other groups.

2. In small groups, think of some situations in which persons have problems communicating. Ask a few members of the group to role-play these situations for the class. Discuss these characters after the role-playing and explain how they could have communicated better. Examples: A tired parent and a spoiled child acting up at a supermarket; the first hours of a new student at school who does not speak much English; a popular group of students putting down other students in gym class; a shy student stumbling over a first oral presentation.

3. Provide your meanings for the following words or create your own list of words for classmates to define.

happiness	brother
war	rich
education	breakfast
honesty	popular
stepmother	extreme

Share your definitions with your classmates and discuss the similarities and differences in your meanings. Also discuss what happens to communication if your meanings are not the same as those of the persons with whom you try to communicate

Put It in Writing

1. Begin a communication journal and keep it during the entire course. In your journal, enter each assignment as it is given. You can also write in your journal about communication events you observe. You should also record changes and improvements in your communication skills. You may wish to include cartoons, poetry, quotations, and pictures or drawings that relate to the topic of communication. Describe in your journal why certain cartoons, poems, or other items had meaning for you. Try to use the key words at the beginning of each chapter when writing in your journal.

Skill Development
Media Literacy

● Interested students might create a newspaper ad for a job that requires a person with strong communication skills. They can designate job duties, salary, and necessary job skills. Encourage them to show in the job duties why communication skills are important for the position.

Try It Out

Many of the Try It Out activities involve role-plays. Role-playing enables students to experience the learning objectives rather than just reading and studying about them. Role-playing is, perhaps, one of the best instructional tools for helping students become competent communicators. Role-plays are more than entertainment. Students should not lose sight of the major purpose of role-plays-to act out real-life situations and analyze their own behavior and that of others.

2. Using the word *communication* as your topic, write a cinquain poem similar to the ones at the beginning of this chapter. Share your poem with your classmates.

3. Describe an experience in which you had to make a choice about how to treat another person. Select an experience that involved thinking about your values. Describe the way you analyzed the situation and the choices you made. Examples may include standing up for a friend, explaining a mistake, revealing your feelings, or agreeing to give a talk.

4. In your journal list three communication goals you have for yourself as you begin this course.

Speak About It

1. Choose any of the careers listed on page 16. Talk to a person in one of these careers. In a short presentation, explain to the class how the person uses communication in her or his career.

2. Choose an abstract word such as freedom, justice, friendship, or sadness. In a one-minute speech, define the word for your classmates. Use at least one example to clarify your meaning.

3. With a classmate, make a collage of pictures from magazines and newspapers that illustrate the ways people use communication. Make a list of all the different ways in which communication is used. Share your collage with the class.

Put It in Writing

Remember that students are not accomplished writers and that they are often writing on topics that they have never thought about previously. Give students an opportunity to rework the assignments based on your suggestions. Reworking an assignment they have not done well can aid their skill building.

Speak About It

The goal of activities included in these sections is to help students gradually build public speaking confidence and skills. Thus, by the time they reach the public speaking unit, they will feel quite at ease.

Quick Check

Ask students to find and define these Key Terms:

communication (5)
group communication (20)
interpersonal communication (20)
interpretive communication (20)
meaning (6)
message (6)
public communication (20)

23

GLENCOE

The Basics of Speech

Learning to Be a Competent Communicator

KATHLEEN M. GALVIN
Professor and Associate Dean
Communication Studies Department
School of Speech
Northwestern University
Evanston, Illinois

PAMELA J. COOPER
Professor
Communication Studies Department
School of Speech
Northwestern University
Evanston, Illinois

 **Glencoe**

New York, New York   Columbus, Ohio   Chicago, Illinois   Peoria, Illinois   Woodland Hills, California

To our children:
Matthew, Katie, and Kara
Jennifer and Jamie

The McGraw·Hill Companies

Printed in the United States of America.

Send all inquiries to:
Glencoe/McGraw-Hill
8787 Orion Place
Columbus, Ohio 43240

ISBN 0-07-861620-4 Student Editon
ISBN 0-07-861621-2 Teacher Wraparound Editon

1 2 3 4 5 6 7 8 9 058/055 09 08 07 06 05 04

Contents

4 UNIT 4 PUBLIC COMMUNICATION

SPECIAL FEATURES

To the Student

This book addresses a very important life skill—communication. Ever since birth you have been making contact with other people—your parents, brothers and sisters, other relatives, teachers, and the people in your community. Some of these contacts have been easy; others have been difficult. Your ability to communicate effectively touches every part of your life. Although you already have many communication skills, you can always become a more competent communicator.

In this book you will encounter many different ways of thinking about your communication skills. We hope you will understand the communication process and will learn to appreciate your communication strengths. We also hope you will develop greater strengths during the course. We believe that a competent communicator makes choices from a range of possible ways to act or respond in a situation. He or she (1) analyzes a situation, (2) chooses a way to deal with it, (3) acts on that choice, and (4) evaluates the results. Therefore a competent communicator is able to cope well in many situations. In addition, a competent communicator takes personal responsibility for the choices he or she makes.

The Basics of Speech has special features to guide you through understanding the communication process and improving your communication skills. Each chapter opens with a list of objectives and Key Words. Within the text, you will discover Speaking Of . . . pages, Journal Entries, and the Interact, Apply, and Observe features. The Chapter Reviews contain Think About It, Try It Out, Put It in Writing, and Speak About It sections.

Throughout the text are checklists, charts, evaluation forms, speeches, student comments, sample oral interpretation scripts, and many literature selections. This wide variety of materials will stimulate your interest and involve you in an enjoyable and rewarding learning experience.

CHAPTER OBJECTIVES

Good speakers and listeners need "road maps" or some way of knowing where they are going. The objectives give you a road map for the chapter and tell you what you should be able to do when you have completed the chapter.

KEY WORDS

A competent communicator has a large vocabulary and uses words correctly. In order to communicate about communication, you need to develop a proper vocabulary. The Key Words that appear at the beginning of each chapter are the most important vocabulary words in the text.

SPEAKING OF . . .

Many young people are expected to exhibit strong communication competencies as they take on serious responsibilities or leadership positions in their schools and communities. In each chapter you will encounter a description of how a teenager uses communication skills to achieve personal goals or to make a difference in the lives of others.

JOURNAL ENTRIES

Often, when a friend describes an experience or feeling, you may think, "I've felt that way" or "Something like that happened to me." Throughout the book you will find Journal Entries written by teenagers about the topics in the book. You may find that the Journal Entries help you understand someone else better. We are grateful to the teenagers who shared their entries with us.

OBSERVE

Seeing and hearing are important parts of understanding communication. The assignments in the Observe boxes are designed to help you really see and hear what is going on around you so you can respond in the best way. By doing these assignments, you should become a more careful observer of others' communication.

INTERACT

Reading and observing will tell you a great deal about communication. But talking about communication situations or trying out communication strategies can teach you a great deal as well. The Interact boxes contain directions to get you involved with other people in the class. You may be asked to share your ideas or to try out a specific communication skill.

APPLY

Within the text you will find sections that require you to respond actively to the text. Sometimes you are asked to complete a checklist, analyze an example, or find solutions to a problem. These sections are designed to help you apply the ideas you are learning.

THINK ABOUT IT

Before you can apply what you have learned, you need to understand the content. Questions and statements at the end of each chapter ask you to review what you have learned. If you can answers these questions correctly, you are well on your way to understanding communication principles.

TRY IT OUT

When people work together to solve a problem or to create something, they learn a lot in the process. The activity suggestions at the end of each chapter contain ideas for applying what you have learned.

PUT IT IN WRITING

Sometimes a good way to make sense of what you see, hear, or think is to write it down. Writing may help you clarify your experience. It may help you see how ideas go together. The Put It in Writing sections ask you to record ideas in a journal, analyze an event you observe, or describe what might happen in the future.

SPEAK ABOUT IT

The only way to develop your ability to speak in front of others is to practice your public speaking. The Speak About It activities will give you many opportunities to deliver short speeches to your class or to small groups.

BIBLIOGRAPHY

The Bibliography provides a list of sources for oral-interpretation material, for help in researching and giving speeches, and for answering questions about parliamentary procedure.

GLOSSARY

All the Key Words in this text, plus many other important vocabulary words, are defined in the Glossary. You will find it is a handy reference tool when you need to review word meanings.

Prepare ◀

Unit Focus

Unit 1 defines and explains the communication process and the basic elements of communication, emphasizes important aspects of speaking and listening, and defines and describes what it takes to become a competent communicator. The key to teaching this course successfully is building a supportive communication climate, one in which students will feel comfortable communicating.

Unit Portfolios

Activities marked with this symbol are suitable for inclusion in speech portfolios.

Ability Key

▲ average and above-average students
● all students
▼ average and below-average students

Ancillary Resource Key

 = *Teacher's Resource Book*

 = Workbook

 = TRB Worksheets & Evaluation Forms

% = TRB Assessment and Testing

Performance Objectives

After completing this unit, students will be able to

1. define the communication process
2. describe how verbal and nonverbal communication are linked
3. describe the steps and types of listening
4. describe a competent communicator

UNIT ONE

The Basics of Communication

1

The Communication Process ① 1

Elements of Communication ② 2

The Work of Speaking and Listening ③ 3

The Competent Communicator ④ 4

Bibliography

Print

Aitken, Joan E., ed. *Speech Communication Teacher: Ideas and Strategies for Classroom Activities.* Quarterly magazine available from National Communication Association, 5105 Backlick Rd., Building E, Annandale, VA. 22003.

Christ, William G., ed. *Assessing Communication Education: A Handbook for Media, Speech and Theatre Educators.* Annandale, Va.: National Communication Association, 1994.

Cooper, Pamela, ed. *Activities for Teaching, Speaking and Listening: Grades 7–12.* Annandale, Va.: National Communication Association, 1991.

Galvin, Kathleen M. and Cassandra Book. *Person to Person: An Introduction to Speech Communication.* 5th ed. Lincolnwood, Ill: NTC / Contemporary Publishing, 1994.

Galvin, Kathleen M. and Bernard Brommel. *Family Communication: Cohesion and Change.* 3rd ed. New York: HarperCollins, 1991.

Morreale, Sherwyn P. and Phil Backlund, eds. *Large Scale Assessment in Oral Communication: K–12 and Higher Education.* Annandale, Va.: National Communication Association, 1996.

		Day 1	Day 2	Day 3	Day 4	Day 5
Chapter 1 Planner	**Week 1**	**1** The Communication Process	Communication in Your Life			
		Oral Communication	Communication Situations			
		Your Experience with Communication	Summary and Chapter Review			
		Teacher's Resource Book				
		Teaching Suggestions 1.1–1.3	Teaching Suggestions 1.4–1.5			
		Worksheets & Evaluation Forms 1–2	Worksheets & Evaluation Forms 3–4			
			Chapter Test 1			
		Workbook 1.1–1.3	Workbook 1.4–1.6			

Motivation

Ask students to think about a particularly good conversation they had with a friend or a relative recently. Ask different students how they would define a "good conversation."

Links to Past Learning

Encourage students to think about the last time they heard someone deliver a lecture or speech, either in the classroom or elsewhere. Discuss individual students' impressions of factors that may have influenced whether the lecture/speech was effective or ineffective for them.

1

CHAPTER ONE

The Communication Process

Chapter Objectives

After completing this chapter, you should be able to

1. define communication as a process

2. describe how communication skills influence family life, friendships, school, work, and citizenship

3. describe the four oral communication situations

Motivation

The key to successfully teaching this course is building a supportive climate, one in which students will feel comfortable communicating. Encourage students to talk, and share your ideas and feelings with them. If you ask students to complete the checklist on page 10, complete it yourself and share your answers with the class.

66Perhaps of all the creations of man language is the most astonishing.99

LYTTON STRACHY

▼ Key Terms

communication	interpretive communication	public communication
group communication	meaning	
interpersonal communication	message	

Critical Thinking

Predicting

● Preview the chapter title and vocabulary words with students, and ask them to predict what specific information might be covered in this chapter. Challenge students to make distinctions between the various communication types in the Key Word list.

❝Sir, you have but two topics, yourself and me. I am sick of both.**❞**

SAMUEL JOHNSON TO JAMES BOSWELL

Skill Development

Quick Skill Opportunity

● Write this on the chalkboard: "My name is [blank]. I…." Ask students to take a few moments to consider an important aspect of themselves they would use to complete the sentence. Then ask for volunteers to complete the sentence in front of the class.

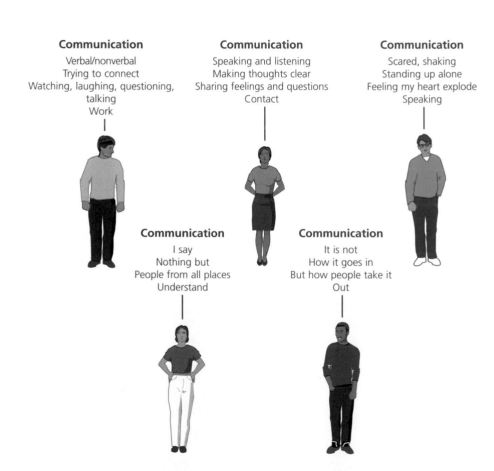

Communication
Verbal/nonverbal
Trying to connect
Watching, laughing, questioning, talking
Work

Communication
Speaking and listening
Making thoughts clear
Sharing feelings and questions
Contact

Communication
Scared, shaking
Standing up alone
Feeling my heart explode
Speaking

Communication
I say
Nothing but
People from all places
Understand

Communication
It is not
How it goes in
But how people take it
Out

Suppose you were asked, "What does the word *communication* mean to you?" How would you answer? You might respond by telling how you talk with friends or family members, how you speak in front of an audience, or how you relate to others in a group. Even before studying the subject you can explain what *communication* means to you now. The above cinquain poems represent five students' interpretations of the word *communication*. These may help you think about your meaning for this term.

ORAL COMMUNICATION

What is communication really? **Communication** is the process of sending and receiving messages in order to share meanings. The communication process involves two or more persons attempting to share their ideas, feelings, and attitudes. The process may be oral or written.

You may send letters or electronic-mail to friends to stay in touch. Frequently, relationships are maintained through both oral and written communication. Group functioning depends on oral interaction, and public speaking involves oral and written processes. Clearly, oral performance of literature relies heavily on the written as well as the spoken word. This book does not emphasize written communication, but it does discuss the interconnection between reading/writing and speaking/listening. Most of your previous course work highlighted reading and writing, whereas this text explores oral communication, which involves speaking and listening.

A Process

Communication is a process because it moves forward from a beginning point. In almost all communication situations, speakers and listeners interact with each other over a period of time, trying to understand what the others mean while trying to get their points across. Imagine the start of the communication process as being the first moment two people meet. The next minutes or hours continue the process. If these people come together again over weeks or years, the process continues.

For example, every conversation you have with a good friend reflects what you already know about that person. You know what kind of jokes your friend likes, what topics to avoid, and how to read your friend's moods. The communication process began the first time you and your friend met and continues throughout your relationship.

Curricular Connection

Language Arts

● Students could create their own cinquains similar to the ones on the first page of the chapter. Ask them to write the word *Communication* at the top of a sheet of paper and to continue the remaining four lines of the cinquain on their own. When students have finished, ask for volunteers to read their cinquains to the class.

5

Critical Thinking

Evaluating

Ask students to talk in small groups for several minutes without looking at each other. Then ask them to talk about the result. How successful was the communication? How did this exercise make them feel?

Beyond the Classroom

● Have students think of jobs that use specific nonverbal signals. For example, a referee in a boxing match or a basketball game uses specific gestures to officiate at a fight or game. Airport signal personnel use important gestures to help pilots bring their aircraft safely from the runway to the terminal. Tell students to watch for instances in their daily lives where people communicate through gestures rather than, or in addition to, words. (They might mention crossing guard, traffic police, orchestra conductor, choir director, or choreographer.)

Nonverbal messages are expressed through facial expressions and body movements.

Verbal and Nonverbal Messages

A **message** is the way **meaning** is conveyed. Messages are at the center of the communication process. Without a message, there can be no communication. A message may be verbal or nonverbal. Verbal messages are spoken or written messages. They rely on words to carry the meaning. Nonverbal messages are those expressed without words. They rely on the use of facial expressions, vocal tone, body movements, and appearance.

Think about the verbal and nonverbal messages that you sent and received today. Do you know how much you communicated verbally through your words and how much you communicated nonverbally through your facial expressions or body movements? You probably haven't thought about these two areas separately because they usually work together.

Speakers and listeners share the responsibility for being good communicators. Communication works like a skilled tennis match. Both communicators are involved continuously in the process, just as both tennis players are involved constantly in the game. Once a good player hits the ball, he or she gets into

Amazing Fact!

In 1492, there were some 2000 languages spoken in North America.

position to deal with the return shot. In communication, you send and receive messages simultaneously. This process is shown in the following diagram:

Person One
Speaking
Listening

Person Two
Speaking
Listening

Think about your own communication with others. Suppose you and your brother are discussing plans for Friday night. Even as you are speaking, he is frowning, smiling, looking puzzled, or muttering "Yeah, yeah. . . ." He might interrupt you or ask you a question. After you stop talking, he might tell you that he wants to borrow your favorite CDs or best sweater while you smile, groan, or look annoyed. You and your brother are equally involved and are constantly relating. It is important to realize that the listener is working just as hard as the speaker.

Meanings

Common meanings for words and nonverbal signals make it possible to communicate. Meaning is the interpretation you place on verbal and nonverbal messages. If you and another person do not have the same meanings for words such as *funny, borrow, help,* or *expensive,* you will have difficulty communicating. If you have different meanings for concept words such as *justice, friendship,* or *responsibility,* you will have even greater difficulties. If you do not have similar meanings for nonverbal messages such as thumbs down or a raised eyebrow, there will be total confusion.

Finding the meaning of a message requires more than understanding the individual words in the message. It also requires interpreting the message. For example, when Martina says a class is "hard," she means there is a lot of homework. When Philip says

Learning Styles

Kinesic Learning

▼ Call on volunteers to demonstrate for the class these words or situations.

Stop!

Go.

Turn left.

Come in.

That's great!

I don't care.

Get out of here.

Be quiet.

7

Multicultural Learning

● Discuss ways people can communicate with those who do not speak the same language. Ask for personal anecdotes from students about experiences they may have had in relating to people from other cultures. Ask what communication methods worked best in these situations.

Limited English Proficiency

Some students may need a little extra coaching when it comes to understanding the concept of homonyms. List the following word groups on the chalkboard and encourage students to distinguish among them.

to, too, two

there, their, they're

one, won

meet, meat

pour, poor

time, thyme

Encourage students to come up with a few more examples on their own.

a class is "hard," he means he finds the teacher's vocabulary unfamiliar and therefore difficult.

In the following journal entry, a student describes a typical communication problem:

JOURNAL ENTRY

After winning the second meet at 10:00 A.M., I heard that the track meet final for the district was at 2:00. The meet was actually at noon, and I had to forfeit because I had left for lunch. The director had said "In two" and I thought he said "At two."

Communication can also break down when common words that sound alike but have different meanings are mistaken for one another. For example, one student listened very carefully as her teacher discussed the next day's exam. The teacher said, "Know percentages." The student thought, "Thank goodness, no percentages." Needless to say, the student's grade suffered from this confusion over the meaning of *know* and *no!*

Meaning is affected by context, or the situation in which the message occurs. The jokes you tell or the private secrets you share are affected by time and place. You speak differently at your kitchen table, at a concert, or during a religious service. You are less likely to hold a serious conversation with someone if you are passing on the street than if you are together for an evening. Culture may serve as a context. If you live in a Hispanic neighborhood, or grew up in a Japanese family, you will use verbal and nonverbal messages that fit certain cultural norms when you are in those settings. Differences in culture may lead to communication breakdowns. The "OK" sign used in the United States (formed by making a circle with thumb and forefinger) is seen as an obscene gesture in parts of South America. In France the same gesture means that something is worthless.

8

Motivation

▼ Bring in the jobs section of a newspaper on which you have circled every employment opportunity that mentions communication skills as a job requirement. Display the newspaper to the students. Then choose a few of the listings at random and discuss with students why they think communication skills might be important in those particular jobs.

REMEMBER:
Three Main Ideas About Communication

The definition of communication includes three main ideas:

- Speaking and listening happen at the same time.
- Speakers and listeners must be aware of both verbal and nonverbal messages.
- Effective communication occurs when the speakers and listeners share common meanings.

OBSERVE

Observe two classmates having a typical conversation in the cafeteria. Pay careful attention to the behavior of each person when he or she is not speaking. Record the ways each person stays active in the conversation while listening.

Your Experience With Communication

You have been communicating with other people almost all your life. You have discussed plans, shared secrets, asked questions, given directions, and listened to problems. You have told stories, delivered oral book reports, argued about ideas, and role-played in skits.

Most people find that they are better in some communication situations than in others. They might argue well but be uncomfortable listening to others talk about their feelings. They may be great at social conversation but poor at speaking before a group. Everyone has strengths in communication and areas of needed growth. And with work, everyone can overcome fears or difficulties in communication.

Critical Thinking

Organizing

● Tell students to go over the checklist on this page, and select the statement that represents their biggest communication challenge. Students could create web diagrams of possible ways to combat their problem. Model the process for them by creating a partial web on the chalkboard.

CHECKLIST:
Personal Communication

Use this checklist to begin a study of your own communication strengths and weaknesses. Which statements never apply to you? Which statements sometimes or frequently apply? Which statements always apply?

1. When I'm introduced to people, I immediately forget their names.

2. I stumble over my words when I give an oral report.

3. I speak my mind when working in a group.

4. I tune out during a newscast or when hearing information I find boring.

5. I have trouble telling a friend that I'm upset or angry with him or her.

6. I have trouble carrying on a conversation with a person I just met.

7. I am uncomfortable when my friend expresses sadness or anger.

8. I find myself thinking about what I'm going to say instead of listening to other people.

9. I am afraid to join class discussion because I might say something silly.

10. I avoid making eye contact with people when I talk with them.

11. I tend to avoid taking a strong stand in an argument.

12. I wish I could find better ways to tell family members what concerns me.

13. I become uncomfortable when I have to relate to people from a cultural background different from mine.

14. I look forward to giving speeches on topics that interest me.

15. I find myself trying to structure the group tasks when we work on group projects.

Multicultural Learning

● Encourage students to examine the list on this page, and discuss whether traditional gender roles have any bearing on the way people communicate. For example, ask whether more men than women have trouble showing feelings of anger, hurt, concern, or love. Encourage students to come up with specific examples from their own experience and observations rather than depending on stereotypes.

Although you have a lifetime of experiences in communicating, it is unlikely that every interaction with another person was perfect. You may have come away from a discussion, argument, or conversation thinking, "Why couldn't we understand each other?" or "Why don't I feel good about how we talked to each other?"

Most likely you have had some difficulties talking to a parent or a friend. You may have felt unsure of yourself during a speech or performance. You may even have avoided talking to certain people who seemed different or difficult to understand.

APPLY

The following questions refer to situations with which people often have problems. See if you have ever found yourself in a similar situation. Do you ever have trouble

- telling a teacher that you do not understand the problem she just explained?
- talking to a friend about the problems you are having with your boyfriend or girlfriend?
- asking a stranger for directions if you are lost?
- convincing your parents to let you go out with friends even though you haven't finished your chores?
- explaining to your instructor or coach why you have to miss practice?
- expressing your opinion on a current-affairs topic?
- reading a poem or story aloud in class?
- understanding what a friend's facial expressions mean?
- telling a joke to a group?
- expressing feelings of anger, hurt, concern, or love?
- disagreeing with someone you like?
- looking people in the eye when you talk to them?
- arguing for your point of view?

Curricular Connection

Dramatic Arts

● Create an "open script." Write about five to ten lines of dialogue. It should not be on a particular topic or reveal any particular personality. Here's an example:

A: Hello.

B: Hi.

A: How are you?

B: Fine.

A: That's good.

B: How are you?

Invite students to perform the open script. When each pair of performers comes to the front of the room, whisper to them what their relationship is: good friends, acquaintances, boss and employee, siblings, or teacher and student. See if the rest of the class can guess the relationship by paying attention to the gestures, manners, voices, and facial expressions of the performers.

Amazing Fact!

The Mandarin language has the most speakers of any language in the world.

Substitute Teacher Tip

Students could role-play various speaking and listening scenarios. For example, one student might role-play a parent giving instructions to another student who is playing the role of a baby-sitter. Other students might role-play parents giving instructions to someone washing the family car, doing the family laundry, loading a dishwasher, sweeping the kitchen floor, ironing a shirt, and so on. Encourage the rest of the class to discuss what went well in each communication and which areas could use improvement.

Multicultural Learning

● Students could interview a person who has or had non-English-speaking parents. They might ask that person what it is like to translate information and ideas from one language to another, and whether that task requires special listening skills.

Good communication skills can help people deal with situations like these. The main goal of this book is to help you develop strong communication skills.

INTERACT

With a partner, take turns describing a person who is the best communicator you know. Be specific in telling how the person acts and speaks and what situations he or she handles well.

COMMUNICATION IN YOUR LIFE

Communication affects every area of your life, now and in the future. Think of the various kinds of communication that took place today. Did your mother or father pat you on the back or smile good-bye? Did you talk to the bus driver, your friends, an acquaintance, or a stranger? How did you interpret the smile of a friend? the actions of a teacher standing up, pushing a chair in, and opening a book? the principal's voice over the public address system?

Every day you spend hours communicating. You may request help from a salesperson in a store. You may give directions to a visitor in your community. You may listen to your favorite music or to conversations among classmates. In addition to general, everyday situations, there are five areas of your life that require highly developed communication skills. These are the areas of family, friendship, school, work, and citizenship. In order to be a caring family member, a good friend, a good student, an efficient worker, and an involved citizen, you will need to develop and use specific communication skills.

Family

A person's ability to speak and listen carefully has a strong effect on life at home. Counselors report that some of the greatest

Skill Development

Making Conversation

Since students often feel more comfortable talking to a single classmate than to the entire group, many of the Interact activities in this unit require students to pair off.

66Family jokes, though rightly cursed by strangers, are the bond that keeps most families alive.99

STELLA BENSON
Pipers and a Dancer

Curricular Connection

Language Arts

● Ask for volunteers to suggest stories, plays, or poems they have read in English class or outside of class that depict problems in family communication. (In many literature classes students begin the year or semester by reading short stories.)

difficulties in family life come from poor listening habits. A husband thinks he knows what his wife feels, and so he doesn't listen to what she actually says. A teenager thinks she knows what her parents will say and does not listen to them. Much of the arguing, blaming, and fighting in homes could be reduced if family members worked to communicate more clearly. Many family members feel misunderstood or ignored by those closest to them. Frequently these feelings reflect long-term communication problems.

INTERACT

With a partner, take turns recalling a past experience when you and a family member or friend assumed you knew what the other was thinking and caused a misunderstanding. Discuss how the problem could have been avoided.

Some of the best moments in family life occur when people feel connected to each other. This may happen when you and your mother or father have a good talk about something that is worrying you. Or it could happen when you are reading a story to your little sister or brother. It often happens when a family member tries to show caring directly. Statements such as "I missed you," "You are special," or "I'm proud of you" make people feel connected. Actions such as a hug or a pat on the shoulder have the same effect. Sometimes younger family members speak English when their parents do not, and they become the family's communication link to the community. Good communication gives family members a feeling of belonging.

Friendship

Good friends laugh with you, support you, listen to you, and tell you honestly what they think and feel. People often take friends for granted until a friend moves away or becomes a better friend to someone else.

13

66The best mirror is an old friend.**99**

GEORGE HERBERT

Critical Thinking

Evaluating

● Ask students to evaluate the statement "to keep a good friend, you have to be a good friend" and to give an example from their own experience to show how this might be true.

Curricular Connection

Art

● Some students might like to design a bumper sticker or poster about the values of friendship.

A strong friendship is based in part on loyalty, honesty, and keeping secrets.

Most strong friendships are built on clear communication and one-to-one sharing. As you will see later (Chapter 6), the qualities of good friendship are tied to communication skills. They include loyalty, warmth, supportiveness, honesty, the ability to keep secrets, and a sense of humor. If you think about your good friends, you will probably conclude that these are people you can talk with easily. Most of the time you may talk about sports or school or other people, but sometimes you can share a worry or problem. Communication in friendships is a two-way process— to keep a good friend you have to be a good friend.

JOURNAL ENTRY

My best friend heard from someone that I was talking about her behind her back when, in fact, I wasn't. We had a terrible fight, but when we talked it out we were friends again. If we hadn't been able to talk it out, our friendship would have been over.

Skill Development

On the Job

● Encourage those students who volunteer or have part-time jobs to share information about the various types of communication they receive from their supervisors, managers, and coworkers.

❝That is the happiest conversation where there is no competition, no vanity, but a calm quiet interchange of sentiments.❞

SAMUEL JOHNSON

School

Your speaking and listening skills affect your school life in many ways. Often you are expected to give oral reports or explain your ideas to the class. You may be asked to give speeches or introduce speakers. You may lead a group project during class or organize group work for school charity drives or after-school events. In these situations, you need to feel comfortable speaking to a group of people. If you are not willing to ask and answer questions or share your ideas, you may feel like an outsider in class.

As a student you will spend between 50 and 90 percent of your class time listening, mostly to the teacher, but also to other students. Even on breaks from classes, you spend time listening to your friends. You might be surprised at how many hours a year you spend listening in school.

Work

The jobs you have after school or over the summer require good communication skills. If you baby-sit, you need to communicate with the parents, the children, and, in an emergency, doctors or the police. If you do yard work, you must talk with your neighbors. Maintaining Web sites requires dealing with customers. Employers were recently asked to rate the importance of communication skills for new workers. The skill receiving the highest rating was a listening skill—understanding directions. In a recent Junior Achievement survey of employers, researchers found that 27 percent of high-school graduates barely get by when communicating verbally. Eighty-five percent of employers believe verbal communication is very important, but they say that only one in ten high-school seniors shows real skill in communicating.

Almost every area of life requires some type of communication skill. Some listening experts estimate that 75 percent of a person's daily communication involves listening and speaking. We listen more than we speak, we speak more than we read, and we read more than we write. Some people say that we write a book a year,

Learning Styles

Audio-Visual Learning

Ask students whether they find it easier to learn by seeing or by hearing something explained. Ask for a show of hands. Emphasize that different people learn in different ways and that later in this class they will learn how to use audio-visual aids when they give a speech.

15

Curricular Connection
Mathematics

● Using the metaphor that people "write a book a year, read a book a month, speak a book a week, and listen to a book a day," have students calculate how many books the average 75-year-old person would have written, read, spoken, and listened to.

Limited English Proficiency

Some students may be unfamiliar with the jobs listed under Apply. Ask for volunteers to explain, for example, what a Web master, aerobics instructor, or insurance agent does for a living. Ask for another name for *physician* (doctor), *chef* (cook), and *salesperson* (clerk).

read a book a month, speak a book a week, and listen to a book a day. Oral communication certainly affects every area of a person's life.

APPLY

Communication is part of almost every job. From the following list of career opportunities, try to select one in which communication skills would not be a basic job requirement. Explain your choice.

postal worker	salesperson	insurance agent
flight attendant	teacher	farmer
Web master	accountant	welder
actor	travel agent	driving instructor
reporter	truck driver	lawyer
child-care worker	store manager	machine operator
aerobics instructor	gas-station attendant	resort manager
physician	chef	police officer

INTERACT

In a small group, discuss the kinds of communication situations in which a person such as a principal, cafeteria worker, secretary, teacher, or maintenance staffer takes part. Does this person have to greet others, give directions, solve problems, give advice, or discipline others? Does this person listen or speak more frequently? What communication skills does this person need?

Motivation

● Remind students that almost every adult citizen of the United States is asked at one time or another to serve on the jury of a civil or criminal trial. Ask why strong listening skills are important to jurors.

If you need to organize volunteers for group work, you will require good communication skills.

Learning Styles
Audio-Visual Learning

● Show a videotape of part of the film *12 Angry Men*. Ask students to rate the characters' communication skills on a scale of 1 (the poorest communicators) to 10 (the best communicators).

Citizenship

Citizens are called upon to listen and speak as they serve their community, state, and nation. Citizens must make intelligent decisions in voting for local, state, and national candidates. Before making these decisions, they need to listen to speeches, debates, and political advertisements by the candidates. Responsible citizens use this information to help them decide for whom to vote. Thoughtful citizens must also be able to analyze the ways politicians communicate. Some active citizens serve as candidates. Others become campaign workers who try to persuade voters to vote for a certain candidate or to support a particular issue. Still others get involved on library boards, environmental control boards, scout troops, or parade committees.

A democratic government depends on the right of freedom of speech for its citizens. As a participating citizen living in a country with a government "of the people, by the people, and for the people," you must be prepared to practice this right. Responsible citizens have many opportunities to use their communication skills.

17

Cooperative Learning

▲ Students might enjoy performing a class talk show. One student could serve as the show's host and select other students to be the day's guests. Each should be chosen for a special "talent." That is, member of the speech team, basketball player, musician, science-fiction enthusiast, and so on. The host could ask the "guests" questions about school, local, or interpersonal issues. Allow the remainder of the class to serve as the studio audience. Afterward the audience members could offer feedback on the quality of the communication.

Many communities view their young members as assets who can contribute to the lives of other community members such as senior citizens or preschoolers. Countless hospitals, libraries, day-care centers, and nursing homes depend on teenage paid or volunteer staff who work with community members in these settings. In some communities younger members are employed to do research for community organizations and institutions, which often requires interviewing skills. In other communities teenagers run antidrug campaigns in elementary schools, speaking to children in fourth through eighth grades. In the student profiles in this text you will read about teenagers who are active in their communities and who use their communication skills effectively.

Communication is a critical life skill. You can use your communication skills to learn more about yourself and others, to sort out ideas and values, and to share ideas and feelings. To be most effective you need to exercise your ability to be fair, ethical, and honest as you deal with others. Well-developed communication skills enable you to make decisions, work in groups, create imaginative situations, and analyze arguments. Communication is the means by which you reach out to the rest of the world and by which the world reaches out to you.

COMMUNICATION SITUATIONS

There are several different oral communication situations. These include

1. Interpersonal communication
2. Group communication
3. Public communication
4. Interpretive communication

After completing the text, you should be able to understand how people communicate in each of these situations and how you can improve your communication in each area.

Skill Development

On the Job

If any students in your class are hospital volunteers, ask them to talk about their work and how it compares to that of Katherine Seitz. If students have other types of volunteer jobs, ask them to briefly tell where they volunteer and what their tasks are.

SPEAKING OF . . .

KATHARINE KIM SEITZ

Katharine Kim Seitz, known as Katie, is a student at New York's Newburgh Free Academy. During the summer, Katie works over eight hours a day as a volunteer at Columbia Presbyterian Hospital. Although she may be asked to do a variety of tasks, her main responsibility is to serve as a liaison between persons in the emergency waiting room and the patient being treated within the emergency room. In other words, she serves as the communication link between emergency room personnel such as doctors, nurses, and medical students, and the often nervous family members. Sometimes she is the link between the patient and his or her family.

Katie describes her communication tasks as talking to families of patients and indicating what the patient is doing at the moment. For example, she might report that "Maria is in bed waiting for a doctor to see her" or that "the doctors expect Sam to be in the emergency room for over an hour." In most cases, the family is feeling stressed and anxious. According to Katie, "Every aspect of communication is important in a job like mine. The way you talk to a family about the length of time their child will spend in the ER will affect their fears and worries more than you think. I try to convey a sense of calm, to soothe them." What makes this part of the job particularly difficult is when doctors are unwilling to communicate much about a patient and Katie has to persuade them to talk with her, or when the patient is seriously ill and Katie has to be the bearer of bad news. In this position, the nonverbal symbol of credibility comes from her volunteer jacket. "Wearing a volunteer jacket definitely gives you a sense of authority, and people tend to look up to authority and position," she says.

As Katie looks ahead to her future in the world of work, she can consider careers that would build on these communication experiences—hospital administraton, health communication, health insurance, and medicine.

"There is only one thing in the world worse than being talked about, and that is not being talked about."

OSCAR WILDE
Picture of Dorian Gray

Skill Development

Media Literacy

▲ Encourage students to view several different news shows over the course of a week. They can choose among nightly news programs, early morning shows, or news magazine shows. Ask them to take notes on the differences among the newscasters and to rate them as to their public speaking abilities. Students could then compare their observations as a class.

Interpersonal Communication

When you talk to a classmate on the telephone, meet someone at a party, or discuss your worries with your best friend, you are taking part in **interpersonal communication.** The word interpersonal means "between people." Much of your day is spent talking one-to-one with another person. Although you may not be aware of it, you follow certain norms when you talk with another person. A study of interpersonal communication will help you understand more about the communication process that occurs when individuals talk to each other.

Group Communication

When you meet in a committee such as the student council, work on a class assignment in a small group, or plan a youth group event with your friends, **group communication** is occurring. Throughout your life you will have to work in groups in order to solve problems or plan events. Group discussion works best when members follow certain rules or patterns and when leaders are prepared to help the members communicate well. A study of group communication will help you to become the best group member and leader you can be.

Public Communication

When you present an oral book report, make class announcements, or give a talk at a religious service, you are involved in **public communication**. Speaking in public requires you to be informed and organized. You must be able to connect with your audience. You may have to give different kinds of speeches, such as speeches to inform or to persuade. You may even have to debate with another person. A study of public communication will help you learn how to prepare a speech, practice your public speaking skills, and develop your analytic listening skills.

Interpretive Communication

When you read a story aloud to a child, recite a poem to the class, or quote a passage by a famous person, you are involved in

20

Amazing Fact!

Esperanto is a language that was invented in 1887 by Dr. Ludwik L. Zamenhof, a Polish oculist. It is based on word roots that are common to the chief European languages. Dr. Zamenhof was known as Dr. Esperanto ("one who hopes").

Cooperative Learning

If students were assigned the Observe activity, ask them to share their observations with the rest of the class.

interpretive communication. Interpretive communication involves bringing literature to life for your audience. You must understand the written material very well and know how to present it interestingly for the listeners. You may even write some of the material yourself, such as an oral history of a grandparent's life. A study of interpretive communication will help you learn how to prepare to interpret written material and to practice your interpretation skills.

OBSERVE

Observe people communicating in two of the four areas of communication. You might observe two friends talking, your family planning a trip, a pastor or rabbi giving a sermon to a congregation, a teacher listening to a class, or a television talk-show host addressing a studio and television audience. How does the communication process keep both speaker and listener involved? Give examples of the verbal and nonverbal ways both parties send and receive messages.

CHAPTER 1 SUMMARY

This chapter introduces the study of communication. Communication is a process of sharing meanings. It affects every aspect of daily life. It relates to your life as a family member, a friend, a student, a worker, and a citizen. This textbook discusses four major types of communication. They are (1) interpersonal communication, (2) group communication, (3) public communication, and (4) interpretive communication.

Answers

Think About It

Student answers will vary slightly. Here are sample answers:

1. Communication is a process because it moves forward from a beginning point.

2. Shared meanings allow communication. If two people have different meanings for the same words, they will confuse one another and be unable to communicate effectively.

3. Student answers will vary. Responses should include some of the following: Job—people have to communicate with coworkers, customers, and managers in order to be effective employees; family—good communication will prevent some arguments and reduce misunderstandings; community—as citizens people must be able to listen and speak to better serve their community, for example by voting; school—Students learn more if they listen, ask questions, and explain ideas, which are all qualities of good communicators.

4. Interpersonal communication—speaking to a friend; group communication—speaking as member of a planning team; public communication—giving a speech to an audience; interpretive communication—reading a story to a small child.

CHAPTER REVIEW

Think About It

1. Why is communication considered a process?

2. Why are common meanings important in communication?

3. In what ways can good communication skills help you in your job, in your family, in your community, and at school?

4. Describe the four communication situations and provide an example of each.

Try It Out

1. In a small group, brainstorm a list of guidelines for good family communication. Compare your list with those of other groups.

2. In small groups, think of some situations in which persons have problems communicating. Ask a few members of the group to role-play these situations for the class. Discuss these characters after the role-playing and explain how they could have communicated better. Examples: A tired parent and a spoiled child acting up at a supermarket; the first hours of a new student at school who does not speak much English; a popular group of students putting down other students in gym class; a shy student stumbling over a first oral presentation.

3. Provide your meanings for the following words or create your own list of words for classmates to define.

happiness   brother

war   rich

education   breakfast

honesty   popular

stepmother   extreme

Share your definitions with your classmates and discuss the similarities and differences in your meanings. Also discuss what happens to communication if your meanings are not the same as those of the persons with whom you try to communicate

Put It in Writing

1. Begin a communication journal and keep it during the entire course. In your journal, enter each assignment as it is given. You can also write in your journal about communication events you observe. You should also record changes and improvements in your communication skills. You may wish to include cartoons, poetry, quotations, and pictures or drawings that relate to the topic of communication. Describe in your journal why certain cartoons, poems, or other items had meaning for you. Try to use the key words at the beginning of each chapter when writing in your journal.

Skill Development

Media Literacy

● Interested students might create a newspaper ad for a job that requires a person with strong communication skills. They can designate job duties, salary, and necessary job skills. Encourage them to show in the job duties why communication skills are important for the position.

2. Using the word *communication* as your topic, write a cinquain poem similar to the ones at the beginning of this chapter. Share your poem with your classmates.

3. Describe an experience in which you had to make a choice about how to treat another person. Select an experience that involved thinking about your values. Describe the way you analyzed the situation and the choices you made. Examples may include standing up for a friend, explaining a mistake, revealing your feelings, or agreeing to give a talk.

4. In your journal list three communication goals you have for yourself as you begin this course.

Speak About It

1. Choose any of the careers listed on page 16. Talk to a person in one of these careers. In a short presentation, explain to the class how the person uses communication in her or his career.

2. Choose an abstract word such as freedom, justice, friendship, or sadness. In a one-minute speech, define the word for your classmates. Use at least one example to clarify your meaning.

3. With a classmate, make a collage of pictures from magazines and newspapers that illustrate the ways people use communication. Make a list of all the different ways in which communication is used. Share your collage with the class.

Try It Out

Many of the Try It Out activities involve role-plays. Role-playing enables students to experience the learning objectives rather than just reading and studying about them. Role-playing is, perhaps, one of the best instructional tools for helping students become competent communicators. Role-plays are more than entertainment. Students should not lose sight of the major purpose of role-plays-to act out real-life situations and analyze their own behavior and that of others.

Put It in Writing

Remember that students are not accomplished writers and that they are often writing on topics that they have never thought about previously. Give students an opportunity to rework the assignments based on your suggestions. Reworking an assignment they have not done well can aid their skill building.

Speak About It

The goal of activities included in these sections is to help students gradually build public speaking confidence and skills. Thus, by the time they reach the public speaking unit, they will feel quite at ease.

Quick Check

Ask students to find and define these Key Terms:

communication (5)

group communication (20)

interpersonal communication (20)

interpretive communication (20)

meaning (6)

message (6)

public communication (20)

Motivation

● People often make the mistake of assuming that everyone interprets events and people the same way they themselves do. Discuss with students the dangers of such an assumption. Ask them what kinds of problems could arise from this type of thinking.

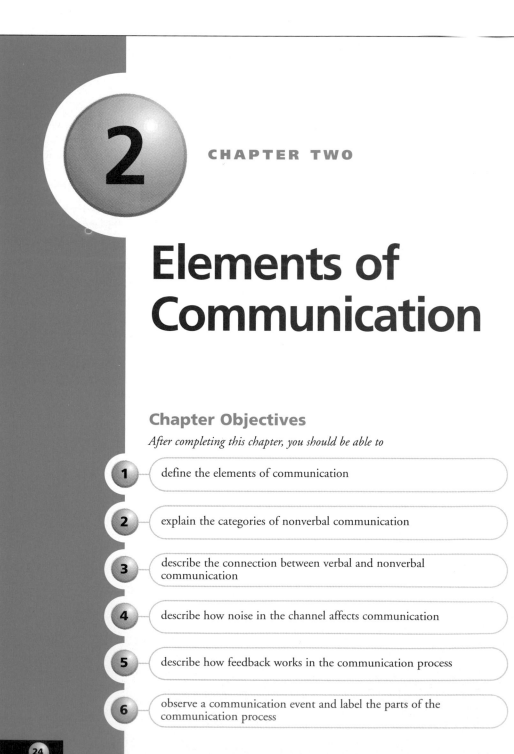

2

CHAPTER TWO

Elements of Communication

Chapter Objectives

After completing this chapter, you should be able to

1 — define the elements of communication

2 — explain the categories of nonverbal communication

3 — describe the connection between verbal and nonverbal communication

4 — describe how noise in the channel affects communication

5 — describe how feedback works in the communication process

6 — observe a communication event and label the parts of the communication process

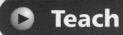

66Mastery of language
affords remarkable
power.99

FRANZ FANON

Key Terms

channel	denotative meaning	nonverbal messages	slang
connotative meaning	feedback	perception	verbal messages
context	noise		

Critical Thinking

Predicting

● Before students begin the chapter encourage them to predict what the various elements of communication might be. Write their predictions on the chalkboard.

Links to Past Learning

Remind students that they learned in Chapter 1 that effective communication occurs when speakers and listeners share common meanings.

❝I hear and I forget. I see and I remember. I do and I understand.**❞**

CHINESE PROVERB

Limited English Proficiency

Some students may recall and be able to share examples of American English idioms that have interfered with communication. The meaning of idiomatic expressions usually cannot be derived from the literal meaning of the words. Some examples are "take a walk," "keep tabs on," "beat the clock," "pull a fast one," "bite the dust," and "raise the roof." Encourage students to supply other examples that may have caused communication problems.

How often have you thought you explained something well only to discover that your friend did not understand? What silly conversational mistakes have caused some serious misunderstandings in your life? Can you identify exactly why the problems happened? Even simple misunderstandings cause embarrassment, as you can see from the following journal entry:

JOURNAL ENTRY

My cousin from Minnesota came to Phoenix for spring vacation, and we were talking about things to do. My mother asked her if she had seen the desert in bloom. She said she had not seen it, but maybe it had not played in Minneapolis yet. Imagine how embarrassed she looked when we told her it was not a movie or a play, but the local flowers in the desert, which bloom beautifully in early spring. Everyone in our family goes for rides in the desert just to see them.

My brother had an exchange student, Enrique, from Argentina with him for three weeks, and there were many communication confusions. The funniest one was when my brother was talking about a neighborhood kid as he made circles with his hand next to his ear. My brother was saying the guy was crazy, but the exchange student kept thinking there was a phone call for him. That's what Enrique said that sign means in Argentina.

As you know, communication is the process of sending and receiving messages in order to share meanings. All communication involves certain essential elements. If someone were to ask you, "What is needed in order for communication to occur?" your answer ought to include the following essential elements of communication: (1) verbal messages, (2) nonverbal messages, (3) perception, (4) channel, (5) feedback, and (6) context. The better you understand these elements, the more effectively you can communicate. In this chapter you will look at each element separately and then see how they work together.

26

VERBAL MESSAGES

Verbal messages are the spoken words you use when communicating. Verbal communication involves both the choice of words (*hungry, starved, famished*) and the order of the words in a sentence. For example, you can say, "Can you tell me how to get to the movie house?" or "The Cineplex, where do I find it?" Or you might even say, "Hogy tudok eljutni a moziba?" (Hungarian). All these verbal messages contain the same idea, but none would work equally well at all times.

Most children begin to use words by the time they are 10–14 months old, but there is no age by which people's use of words is "perfect." Words do not have the same meaning to everyone. Also, words change their meanings over time. Communicators need to know how to select the most exact words to get their messages across accurately.

Differences in Meaning

Different people may have difficulty understanding the same message even when all the words are English. Although words are an important part of communication, they do have certain limitations.

> **APPLY**
>
> Look at the following statements and predict what problems someone might have in understanding their meanings.
>
> "Don't have a cow, man."
>
> "Quit acting like a wannabe."
>
> "Take the scoop up and attach it to the batten."
>
> You probably understood the first two statements. But it is unlikely you understood the third statement unless you have worked backstage in a theatre.

Skill Development

Active Listening

To extend the Apply section, read the following sentences aloud, and ask for volunteers to tell who might best understand the meanings.

Whisk vinegar, olive oil, and shallots together. (chef/cook)

Write an equation for each problem. (math student)

Use a clove hitch to tie a line to a piling. (sailor)

Click the Start button in Windows 95. (computer user)

The switch-hitter is 5 for 21 with three home runs. (baseball fan or player)

The next five measures are andante. (musician)

27

Amazing Fact!

During World War II, a code based on the Navajo language was used by some 400 Navajo code talkers in the Marines. It enabled U.S. military commanders to issue orders and report on troop movements without fear of detection. The code was never broken by the enemy.

Critical Thinking

Organizing

▼ Write the following heads on the chalkboard: Positive, Negative, Neutral. Ask students to identify the following words or expressions according to these connotative categories. (Not every category is represented in each word group.)

thrifty / frugal / miserly

helpful / concerned / busybody

notable / celebrated / remarkable

poor / needy / down-and-out

well-to-do / rich / wealthy

Not all words mean the same thing to all people. In fact, no word means the same thing to everyone! Even a simple word like *right* has different meanings in different situations. It can mean correct, as in "I have the right answer." It can be a direction, as in "Take a right turn." It can also mean privilege, as in "I have a right to know."

INTERACT

With a small group of classmates, list the possible meanings of the following words and phrases.

expensive	party	See you later.
tall	hot	What a day!
free	bad	She is cool.

What's on Friday night?

That's an interesting video.

You can go to a dictionary for the definition of any word, and the definition you will find consists of other words or phrases that stand for the word you are looking up. The definition found in a dictionary is called the **denotative meaning.** However, some words may call forth an emotional response apart from a dictionary meaning. An emotional or personal response to a word is called **connotative meaning**. For example, most people would have positive emotional responses to the words *home, peaceful, cozy,* and *friend* and negative responses to the words *liar, anxious, filthy,* and *terrorist.*

Individual responses to a word like *marigold* might vary, depending on whether you were reminded of happy times in your grandmother's flower garden or an allergy to flowers. The denotative meaning of *cigarette* is a small roll of finely cut tobacco for smoking. Your connotative meaning may be distaste because your uncle developed lung cancer from smoking.

Learning Styles

Audio Learning

● Ask students to bring in tapes or CDs of music that has slang in the lyrics. Play some of the music in class and ask students to point out the examples of slang.

Curricular Connection

Language Arts

▲ To reinforce the idea that language changes, have students look through the annotated text of a play by William Shakespeare. They could choose a page at random and make a list of all the unfamiliar words or phrases and think of synonyms from modern usage.

❝A living language is like a man suffering incessantly from small hemorrhages, and what it needs above all else is constant transfusions of new blood from other tongues. The day the gates go up, that day it begins to die.❞

H. L. MENCKEN

Skill Development

Quick Skill Opportunity

▼ Give students the opportunity to do word association. Tell students to get out a sheet of paper and a pen and, when you say a word, to write the first thing that comes into their minds. Say the word *nice*. Give students no more than a few seconds to write their word association. Then go quickly around the room, and have them read off their answers. Point out how many different associations there are. Other words you might read for a word association exercise are *friendly, empty, rich,* and *loud*.

Changes in Language

Language changes constantly. Old words may disappear entirely, or their meanings may change. For example, the word *clepe*, meaning "to call" or "name" has disappeared from ordinary use. The word *score* dates from the 14th century, and one early definition of the word is "twenty." Abraham Lincoln used the word in his "Gettysburg Address." Today, *score* is seldom used to mean "twenty." Instead, it may mean the written form of a musical composition, a number of points attributed to a team, or a grudge or grievance. As life changes, words are created to name new objects, inventions, or experiences. Terms such as *e-mail, extreme sports, couch potato, designated driver,* and *snowboard* may be familiar to you, but when they were your age, your grandparents and parents would not have known these terms.

Slang is informal language that is unique to a particular group. Slang words are the words that change most often. They are used in informal conversations, often between persons within a certain age group. They fall out of favor very fast and are often understood only by a small number of people. The word *awesome* is such a word. Chances are that *awesome* will sound as strange to

Multicultural Learning

● Ask the class to name and define from 15 to 20 words that came into English from other languages. Ask students how they know these words. From hearing them spoken? seeing them in print? from taking a foreign language course? from learning them at home? Students will probably find it easy to think of words describing food: *blini, blintz, crepe, sauerkraut, taco, chili rellenos, sauerbraten, strudel, schnitzel,* and so on. They may go on to mention other words, such as *deja vu, arroyo, patio, kindergarten, mensch,* or *schlepp,* for example.

your children (or even to your younger brothers or sisters) as *keen* does to you. Look at the following words, which are used to indicate a positive reaction to something. Identify any you might use or mentally list the terms which would be used in your community. *Excellent, most excellent, dope, to the extreme, cool, phat, solid, groovy.* How many do you know or use? Some of these are words that came back into slang usage after a few decades.

As the United States population becomes more culturally diverse and the media reflects these changes, everyday language is enriched. Words from a variety of ethnic backgrounds are integrated into everyday vocabulary. For example, no matter what your cultural heritage is, you have picked up the ability to understand many words that reflect a Hispanic heritage. Many of these are related to celebrations, food, music, or entertainment. Such terms include *Cinco de Mayo, burritos, salsa beat,* or *tejanos.*

As a communicator, you need to be aware of the different meanings of words and how words change over time. The more carefully you choose your words, the more easily a listener can understand your message.

✳ INTERACT

Interview someone over the age of fifty. Ask the person to list ten words in use today that he or she did not know as a young person. Combine your list with the lists of three or four other classmates and share your findings with the class.

NONVERBAL MESSAGES

Nonverbal messages are messages expressed without words. Your appearance, facial expression, eye contact, posture, gestures, and voice affect how your words are understood. So do factors outside yourself, such as space, time, and place. Though you probably don't think about it often, you depend heavily on wordless communication.

30

Learning Styles

Visual Learning

● Bring in magazines and show students pictures of people in various advertisements or personality profiles. Ask volunteers to tell what kind of impressions of personality, occupation, wealth, or character they formed of the people in the pictures. Encourage them to analyze the pictures and provide details of why they formulated the judgments they did. Ask students to discuss whether first impressions are necessarily accurate.

❝The light bulb may appear over your head,… but it may be a while before it actually goes on.**❞**

FRANK CONROY

Skill Development

On the Job

● Ask students who do volunteer work or have joined the work force to address the issue of personal appearance on the job. Encourage them to discuss such possible requirements as issues of personal hygiene, dress, uniform maintenance, and so on. If possible, have these students bring in copies of their employee handbooks to show the class.

Exactly what fits under the label nonverbal communication? The next part of the chapter will help you understand the many ways you communicate with nonverbal messages.

Appearance

If you needed to ask someone for directions, who would you ask first: an old man in dirty clothes, a cute teenage boy or girl, a woman with an infant, or a woman in a sari? Clothes, body size, hairstyle, makeup, and decorations such as jewelry or slogan buttons all send messages about how a person sees herself or himself. You probably make quick first judgments about others based on appearance. So it stands to reason that others make first judgments about you based on your appearance. If you are shopping and need to know the time, your decision about whom to ask will be influenced by other shoppers' appearances. When a new student joins your class, you form a first impression that is often based on that person's appearance. In recent years some schools have begun to require uniforms in order to reduce peer pressure to dress a certain way and to limit the ways clothing can be used as gang symbols.

Facial Expression and Eye Contact

Smiles or frowns tell others a great deal about how a person is feeling. A person's face often reveals rather quickly that a person

Curricular Connection

Art

● Encourage students to think more about their facial expressions by having them draw a four-panel cartoon of their own face in different moods. Panel 1 could show extreme happiness; panel 2, extreme exertion or concentration; panel 3, sleepiness or exhaustion; and panel 4, frustration or anger. Display student drawings around the classroom.

is angry, happy, frustrated, or nervous. What is the look that tells you not to bother your parent? How can you tell whether a friend is tired or simply relaxed? Most people believe the eyes are the most expressive part of the body. Eyes show feelings that might be hidden otherwise. You can learn a great deal from a person's willingness or unwillingness to look at you. You can often read feelings such as anger, surprise, or delight by watching someone's eyes. According to an old expression, "The eyes are the windows of the soul."

Posture and Walk

Posture refers to your body's position as you sit, stand, or walk. The way you sit or stand communicates a great deal about your mood or feelings. If you are slouching, you create a very different image than if you are standing or sitting up straight. A person's posture often tells whether it is all right to start a conversation or make a request. If your mother is sitting slumped at the table with her head in her hands, then it's probably not the best moment to tell her that you need new shoes for gym class.

Posture can also send other messages. Models are taught to "walk tall" or "stand tall" to make a good impression. Persons interviewing for jobs are taught to stand and sit up straight because they will seem more confident. Interviewers usually notice people's posture while they talk with them about their qualifications.

The way you walk also sends nonverbal messages to others. Sometimes people slouch because they are uncomfortable with their height; others think slouching is the "in" way to walk for a certain group. When you watch people walking slowly and dragging their feet, you might decide they are reluctant to get to where they are going. When you see people walking briskly, you may conclude they are anxious to get somewhere or, if they are in athletic clothes, that they are exercising.

Beyond the Classroom

Invite an interpreter for the deaf to visit your class and demonstrate some of the basics of American Sign Language. Encourage students to ask the interpreter questions about individual signs and gestures.

66 Barring that natural expression of villainy which we all have, the man looked honest enough. 99

MARK TWAIN
A Mysterious Visit

Nonverbal communication includes gestures and facial expressions.

Multicultural Learning

Discuss whether or not women and men are held to different standards of appearance in school, the workplace, or in society at large. Compare these standards to those in other cultures, if there are students present who can explain and describe these standards. Encourage students to relate generalizations to specifics to avoid stereotyping.

Gestures

The way people move their arms, hands, and fingers plays a part in communication. Most good speakers use gestures to help make a point. The way gestures are used may also tell others something about a speaker's enthusiasm. Some people tend to talk with their hands constantly moving. You may have heard someone say, "If I tied your hands behind your back, you couldn't talk."

Besides the larger gestures, people use hand signals to communicate. Think of the different meanings of the peace sign, the OK sign, or crossed fingers. Can you think of other gestures that are used to send messages? As you read in Chapter 1, hand signals vary according to culture and community; what is meaningful in one culture may not be in another.

Voice

A person's voice, that is, not *what* is said but *how* it is said, conveys important messages. Voice includes

1. Pitch—how high or low the tone of voice is
2. Rate—how quickly or slowly something is said; the pace
3. Vocal quality—the tone or sound of a voice
4. Volume—the loudness or softness of a voice

33

Cooperative Learning

▼ Have students who are not friends stand facing each other as close together as they are comfortable. Measure the distance from toe to toe. Tell students that many people feel most comfortable when there is at least one arm's length between his or her body and that of another person. Students could talk about times when they felt that their personal space had been invaded. Encourage students to discuss their emotional reactions to these experiences.

Some voices can put the listener to sleep; others will make the listener pay attention.

Pitch, rate, quality, and volume are four elements of your voice that you can change for different effects when you communicate. If you always talk slowly, in a low-pitched, quiet, mellow voice, you probably will put your listeners to sleep. On the other hand, a rapid, high-pitched, loud, squeaky voice can be annoying. Either vocal pattern can be effective for a short time. But to hold people's attention and to emphasize points in different ways, you will have to vary your voice. Such changes make your voice interesting and help make your meaning clear.

OBSERVE

Observe several people in various situations. Try to guess their moods by observing their nonverbal cues. For example, you might notice the cafeteria workers smiling or frowning or rushing you through the line, your teacher standing behind you with arms folded, your best friend giving you a knowing look, or your sister's tone of voice when talking to someone on the phone. Record your observations in your journal or share them with the class.

Space, Time, and Place

The environmental factors of space, time, and place also affect communication. These serve as contextual clues. How close you stand or sit to someone says a lot about your relationship to that person. Friends often sit close together, while strangers keep a certain distance between them. In places such as crowded elevators or hallways, a group may be forced to bunch together, but if you watch people walking together on the street, you can often tell something about their relationship by noting the distances between them. In an uncrowded bus, strangers sit apart, while friends sit together. These differences in space send messages about the relationship.

Time also affects communication. If you are rushed, you will speak more rapidly than if you are relaxed. You may sound very different on the phone at 7:00 A.M. than at 7:00 P.M. Are you a morning person or a night person? How does this affect your communication? Time itself also sends messages. The amount of time you spend with someone may tell that person and other people that you are friends.

You probably notice the ways in which surroundings affect communication. If you are talking with a close friend, you may talk about different things in your kitchen than in the privacy of your room. If you are sitting in the principal's office, you may control your volume or choose words more carefully than you would at basketball practice. Different settings shape the way you communicate.

Feelings

You depend heavily on nonverbal messages to understand feelings and attitudes. When you exchange factual information, the words are of primary importance, as in this example, "The track meet will be Saturday morning at the school field." When you share feelings, the nonverbal part of the message becomes most important; for example, "When Susan said, 'No, I can't go,' she didn't need to say any more. Her eyes told me she was sad."

INTERACT

Form a small group of four or five people. Take turns describing how you are able to read the feelings of someone you know through their nonverbal communication. You do not need to identify the person you are describing. Comments may begin with examples such as "I have a friend who gets really quiet when he is angry, and he won't look at you" or "When my coach is excited, you can watch the arms wave."

35

Learning Styles

Kinesic Learning

● Many past and present performers are known for their nonverbal trademarks. Interested students might like to find videos of Charlie Chaplin, the Marx Brothers, John Cleese, or some of the Monty Python episodes. They might also look for videos of mime Marcel Marceau.

Good communicators learn to read nonverbal cues rather than relying only on the verbal message, because so much is communicated nonverbally. When Phil Jackson was coaching the Chicago Bulls he wrote *Sacred Hoops*, in which he described how he led the team: "When you're a leader, you have to be able to read accurately the subtle messages players send out. Over the years, I've learned to listen closely to players—not just what they say, but also to their body language and the silence between the words." Frequently actions speak louder than words.

APPLY

You may have found yourself in either of the following situations: Someone says, "Well, I've got to go," and continues to talk to you on the phone.
Someone says, "I like you a lot," but ignores you in the hallway when there are other people around.

How do you react when this happens to you? These people's actions communicated their feelings more clearly than their words. Even when words are spoken, the nonverbal message speaks louder than the verbal one.

Nonverbal messages differ according to culture. Many American business executives have to be taught how to understand the nonverbal messages of different cultures as they engage in international negotiations. Executives traveling to the Middle East have to learn to interact at much closer distances; when working in the Far East they learn that hand signals rather than head shaking may indicate a negative response. One way to gain a sense of the fascinating and complex world of nonverbal differences is to watch a subtitled foreign film to see how persons from different cultures use gestures, facial expressions, and space differently.

Verbal and nonverbal messages are central to the communication process. A good communicator sends and interprets both verbal and nonverbal messages skillfully. In addition, the communicator understands the vocal production process. Yet messages are only one element of the whole communication process.

INDIVIDUAL PERCEPTIONS

Perception

The process of giving meaning to information you learn through your five senses is called **perception.** Taste, touch, hearing, sight, and smell provide you with information about the world. When you perceive this information, you are making sense out of it for yourself. This perception process involves two steps.

1. Something affects your senses. (You see, hear, taste, smell, or touch something.)

2. You interpret and explain the sensation to yourself. (You give meaning to what you are seeing, hearing, tasting, smelling, or touching.)

For example, you may hear a friend say loudly, "It's about time you showed up." Seeing his tight mouth and wrinkled forehead, you get the meaning, "He is angry."

The meaning of a message tends to change as it moves from person to person. For example, what Tony thought was a joke, Aaron considered an insult. This explains many misunderstandings and conflicts that interfere with communication. The meanings change because the perception process can vary with the individual.

Every person views the world slightly differently, and therefore no two people interpret the same message in the same way. If you are angry at Laura, you may not see her smile as being friendly. If you just failed math, you may not want to listen to your older sister say, "When I had that class, I got an A." If Karen thinks Sandy doesn't like her, she may be careful about what she tells her. These little personal moods or prejudices are part of everyone's individuality. For this reason, communication depends on the perception of the people involved in the communication process. People may perceive the same sensory message differently for many reasons. Three major factors that influence perception are discussed next.

Motivation

▼ Help students understand how the senses affect one's information about the world. Hold up the following objects and ask students to tell what senses, *other than visual,* they could use to identify each item: half an onion, a pine cone, a dry leaf, a ticking clock or watch, a pebble, and a feather. Then give each student a lemon drop or a small slice of lemon to taste.

37

Curricular Connection

Science

Some students might like to do research to find out how sensory information makes its way to the brain where it can be processed. They might draw a cross-sectional view of the human eye and label the cornea, pupil, iris, optic nerve, and so on.

Although people perceive the world through their five senses, they do not all give the same meaning to the same sensory impressions.

Physical Differences Although most people have the use of all their senses, they may have very different abilities. For example, you might be farsighted, but your brother is nearsighted. You may have fine hearing, while your friend's ear infection may have reduced her ability to hear. As you sit in the back of the room, you may be able to see the handwriting on the board and your teacher's serious facial expression. You can hear the homework

Critical Thinking

Analyzing

Discuss with students how a speaker's language can influence listeners' beliefs, reactions, and perceptions. Skilled speakers select their language to fit their audience and purpose. For example, political candidates may alter their pronunciation, word choice, or examples depending on who their listeners are. Ask students to give examples of times they have used language selectively to influence their listeners' perceptions or to get a certain reaction.

assignment. Your brother and friend may miss part of the assignment because of their reduced ability to see or hear. Such physical problems may affect a person's ability to take in information through his or her senses.

Past Experiences Your past experiences add to differences in perception and to your ability to understand what you perceive. Past experiences may range from those that are considered general, to those shared by many people you know, to those that are unique or shared by few people you know. For example, depending on where you grew up, you might order a cold drink using the term *soda, pop,* or *soft drink.* If your family is Jewish, you know what happens at bar mitzvahs and bas mitzvahs, while other friends need a careful explanation.

Your past experiences will influence how you accept or reject a message. If you enjoy learning about outer space, you may be pleased to learn that the graduation speaker is a former astronaut. If you meet another gymnast at a party, you may talk to each other about kips and scales. Other people may not understand your conversation. If you have not seen certain films, you cannot really take part in a serious conversation about the acting of Jodie Foster or Samuel L. Jackson.

Past experience influences how people talk and how they listen. People with very different backgrounds may have to work hard to communicate well. It may be difficult to imagine how important a bas mitzvah is if you've never been to one. If your friend is a gymnast but you are not, you may get tired of listening to him use words you don't understand.

Present Situation How you feel mentally and physically also affects communication. If you are upset about an argument with your best friend, you may snap at your parent when asked to help in the kitchen. Your desire to make money may lead you to pay close attention to a radio ad for a summer job. If you have a headache or you are daydreaming about a person you like, it may keep you from paying close attention to a conversation.

Links to Past Learning

Students might like to share memories of times when their past experiences influenced how they accepted or rejected a message or caused difficulties in understanding. Factors that might influence these experiences include differences in family, social, and religious customs; dialects (including variant pronunciations); and unfamiliarity with jargon specific to certain occupations, sports, or hobbies.

Skill Development

Media Literacy

▼ Some students might like to check cartoon strips in the daily paper for instances of different ways people react to messages while they are communicating. They could post the cartoons on the bulletin board.

Curricular Connection

Art

● Students might create their own cartoons similar to the one on this page but with a different message and different reactions.

Mike says: I won't be going. I'm too upset to go to the party on Friday night.

Tom says: Oh, OK. Fine.

Tom might think: *I didn't hear him. Did he say he can't?* **or** *I'll bet he doesn't want to see Pat. They had a fight last time.* **or** *I'm too sick to argue with him.*

The cartoon gives an example of the different ways people react to messages while they are communicating.

CHANNELS OF COMMUNICATION

People need a way to send and receive their messages. Verbal and nonverbal messages are sent through a **channel** that uses the human senses. In communication terms, the channel is the means by which a message is transmitted. Suppose Susan tells you that she is very nervous about a test coming up tomorrow. You pat her on the shoulder and say, "Don't worry. You always do well in math." You have, even in this brief conversation, communicated through many channels:

Susan hears you speak. (sound)

Susan watches your facial expressions. (sight)

Susan smells your cologne. (smell)

Susan feels you pat her shoulder. (touch)

You watch her facial expressions. (sight)

You hear her speak. (sound)

You pat her shoulder. (touch)

Critical Thinking

Synthesizing

● Make sure that all students understand the idea that communication "noise" can be anything that stops the listener's ability to receive the message; it does not necessarily have anything to do with sound. Ask students to come up with at least five examples of silent "noise."

Like a television set or a radio, you have many channels and can switch them at will. If your parents are telling you something you don't want to hear, perhaps you tune out that channel and focus on their facial expressions or think about something else entirely, like the smell of dinner.

People tend to place greater importance on one channel than on another. For example, you may pay more attention to facial expressions or movements you receive through sight, emphasizing the visual channels. Someone else may pay more attention to words or tone of voice, emphasizing the channels of sound.

When a person has trouble understanding a message, there is said to be "**noise** in the channel." Perhaps the person was daydreaming and therefore didn't listen carefully. Or maybe the TV was on too loud, and he or she couldn't hear what was being said. These are examples of noise. Noise is anything that interferes with a listener's ability to receive a message. The noise can be outside the listener, such as loud stereo music, a freezing room, or a hard chair. The noise can also be inside the listener. A headache, worries, and boredom are examples of noise inside the listener.

Sometimes you can control the noise; at other times you cannot. You can turn down the stereo, but you can't turn up the school's heating unit. You may be able to force yourself to stop daydreaming, but you may start worrying about tomorrow's science test. Noise in the channel can lead to faulty perception and misunderstanding.

"Noise," whether inside or outside the listener, can prevent someone from receiving a message.

Skill Development

Vocabulary

Ask for volunteers to define *mediation,* and ask whether any of them have been involved in the mediation process.

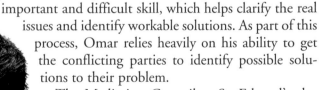

SPEAKING OF . . .

OMAR SIDDIQ

As schools become more racially and ethnically diverse, issues arise that must be addressed, and conflicts develop that must be managed or resolved. Omar Siddiq, a student at St. Edward's School in Ohio, spends much of his time dealing with these concerns. He serves on his school's Mediation Council on Human Relations. According to Omar, the population of St. Edward's consists of a ". . . white majority in which 80 percent of the kids fall. I fall in the other 20 percent." As part of his responsibility in school, Omar serves on the council that addresses ethnic conflicts and misunderstandings, usually relying on mediation to resolve these issues.

As part of his work in mediation, Omar needs strong listening skills, specifically reflective listening. Reflective listening depends on each party's ability to paraphrase the other's points and feelings before attempting to respond. It is an

important and difficult skill, which helps clarify the real issues and identify workable solutions. As part of this process, Omar relies heavily on his ability to get the conflicting parties to identify possible solutions to their problem.

The Mediation Council at St. Edward's also sponsors dialogue days in which students discuss the differences in ethnic groups and their stereotypes. Omar reports that in both the mediation sessions and the dialogue days, the discussion of feelings is critical. These experiences provide Omar with a set of skills that will serve him in the future. He may use such skills if he works in law enforcement, international relations, community relations, or arbitration and mediation.

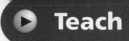

Learning Styles

Audio Learning

Students might role-play a telephone conversation in which they use tone of voice to convey feedback. If they have trouble coming up with a topic, suggest that they discuss a movie that both have seen, strategies for getting an increase in allowance, or a cancellation of an outdoor game (baseball, soccer) because of rain.

FEEDBACK

How do senders and receivers know if they are communicating effectively? To communicate successfully, Person A must interpret Person B's **feedback** accurately. When you are communicating, the person you are talking with responds to you verbally and nonverbally. Feedback consists of the verbal and nonverbal messages that tell speakers how they are being perceived.

Positive and Negative Feedback

Feedback may be positive or negative. Positive feedback tells you that you're doing fine. A smile, nod of the head, and laughter at your joke all indicate that you are "getting through" as you intended to. The feedback is negative if you see a frown, a questioning look, or hear a mutter or grumble. These responses help you realize that you need to change your communication. Positive feedback tells you to continue what you are doing. Negative feedback tells you there is a problem to deal with or lets you know the listener does not agree with your ideas. It is important to recognize whether a listener is confused or whether a listener is disagreeing.

Feedback may differ across cultures. In some cultures it is impolite to indicate directly that you disagree with a speaker's ideas. In this way, neither the speaker nor listener is embarrassed or "loses face." In these situations the polite feedback does not really tell the speaker there is a problem.

Self-Feedback

Feedback also may come from yourself. Self-feedback is the message you give yourself as you pay attention to your own behavior. Although you may not be getting much external feedback, you may say to yourself, "I think I'm talking too much. I'd better be quiet for a while" or "I can feel myself getting too silly. I'd better calm down." Sometimes you may tell yourself to keep going even though the feedback is negative. Perhaps you are saying to yourself, "I'm finally saying what I really want to, so I will keep on talking."

66 The teacher should never lose his temper in the presence of the class. If a man, he may take refuge in profane soliloquies; if a woman, she may follow the example of one sweet-faced and apparently tranquil girl—go out in the yard and gnaw a post. 99

WILLIAM LYON PHELPS
Teaching in School and College, 1912

Skill Development

Feedback

● Tell students that negative self-feedback can sometimes be distortive to the point that it becomes noise in the channel. Remind them that depending on mood, situation, and a variety of other factors, their "little voice inside" can overreact. Students might want to keep a feedback journal for a few days. In their journals they can explore whether or not they overreacted to certain stimuli and analyze reasons why this may have happened.

Skill Development

Quick Skill Opportunity

● Go around the room and ask for volunteers to improvise a brief conversation where one person speaks and the other listens. The rest of the class could write down instances of both negative and positive feedback. Encourage them to watch for body language, facial expressions, gestures, and so on. Discuss students' overall impressions. Topics might range from the intrinsically uninteresting to controversial ones. For example, speakers might talk about the weather, pets, school uniforms, curfews, homework, or foreign language requirements for graduation.

43

Links to Past Learning

Ask whether any students have ever played charades. You or a volunteer could explain how to play, and tell what part context plays in the proceedings. For example, show students the pantomimed actions to illustrate book, film, television show, or song. Discuss how players' knowledge of which media is being portrayed provides context that is vital to guessing the charade. Students might enjoy playing a few rounds of the game.

Multicultural Learning

● Encourage students to discuss customs that reflect cultural values. Ask students whether they have noticed any difference between the way men and women communicate. Lead the discussion to focus on specific behaviors and avoid overgeneralization and stereotyping.

Communication goes smoothly when speakers and listeners pay attention to feedback. You may see some puzzled looks and think, "I'm going too fast, so I'll slow down." Without feedback, speakers and listeners would not be able to adapt to each other.

OBSERVE

Select a communication situation in which one person is an active speaker and the others are listeners. Carefully note the kinds of feedback the listeners give the speaker, such as questions, smiles, and yawns. Describe any ways the speaker shows that he or she is paying attention to the listener feedback.

CONTEXT

Finally, all these essential elements of communication come together within a context. A **context** is the setting and people that surround a message. Context provides the background that helps reveal the message's real meaning. Good communicators are similar to detectives. They look for clues that tell them how to interpret and understand a message.

Setting is the first part of context. It involves time, place, and occasion. You may say something at a certain place or time that you would not say at another place or time. You may be more honest about your feelings in your room than in a crowded restaurant during a birthday party. If your coach is rushing to an important meeting, you probably should not stop him to talk about last week's soccer game.

The people in the setting influence what is said and what is not said. You may decide not to talk about your bowling trophy when a member of the losing team is sitting at the next table. You probably will not make fun of the talent show in front of the director's son.

The way you see the setting and the other people involved will affect how you handle certain topics. The basketball game may not be the place to discuss your sister's serious illness.

As communities and schools become more multicultural, you will continue to have friends and classmates from different ethnic backgrounds, and this will affect your communication. In some cultures you are expected to look at the person you are addressing; in other cultures it is polite to look down or avoid staring during a conversation. Speech in some cultures is characterized by excited and loud vocal tones; other cultures value soft vocal tones. In highly individualistic cultures it is appropriate to talk about yourself and to ask others personal questions; in more communal cultures, people see themselves as members of a group and are uncomfortable being singled out as individuals.

All human communication takes place within an overall context. This context is an essential element of communication that touches all the other elements, influencing the messages, people, feedback, and channels people use to communicate.

Read the following paragraphs from an article on how communication at Central Florida University has been affected since Coach Alan Gooch recruited Dwight Collins to play tailback on their football team. As you read this, think about situations in which you and another person had to rely heavily on nonverbal symbols in order to communicate.

A Coup for the University

Lisa Guernsey

. . . Beneath dusty photographs of football teams past, Mr. Gooch is talking football with Dwight Collins, the team's new tailback. Neither man utters a sound, but using sign language, they manage to understand each other perfectly.

The coach bends forward, looks down at the papers in his lap, makes the sign for "zone defense," and points to the message board at the front of the room. His recruit nods, pauses, and scribbles a response. Their movements are quick and intense, punctuated by the soft thump of the pen's felt tip on the board's slick surface.

The muscular 5-foot-9, 210-pound Mr. Collins lost his hearing after contracting

45

Critical Thinking

Synthesizing

● Ask students to describe what benefits and possible disadvantages Mr. Gooch, Dwight Collins, and the rest of the team could experience as a result of having Collins on the team.

Skill Development

Research

▲ Students could look into recent advances in technology that aid the deaf or hearing impaired. Encourage them to check into the various facilities some auditoriums, churches, synagogues, museums, art galleries, and theatres offer the deaf or hearing-impaired, including supertitles and audio-enhancement headsets, computer and telephone technology, and so on. Interested students could report their findings to the class.

meningitis when he was eleven months old. But his deafness did not stop him from becoming an all-state running back in Louisiana last season, or from attracting the attention of football scouts from around the country. . . .

But achieving success on the field will be complicated by the fact that the nineteen-year-old Mr. Collins cannot hear. Or, as Mr. Gooch prefers to put it, that he is a coach who can barely sign.

In April, a few months after Mr. Collins agreed to come to Central Florida, Mr. Gooch signed up for his first class in American Sign Language. By the time this July afternoon rolled around, he was becoming adept at signing some of the most common words in the football vocabulary, and Mr. Collins was recognizing most of them right away.

These were words that, in many cases, were new even to Mr. Collins. In Louisiana, he and his high-school coaches had come up with a simplified signing system, because the coaches didn't know American Sign Language. But Mr. Gooch and Mr. Collins decided early on that it would be best if they used as much sign language as possible. "I wanted to do this right," the coach says.

That afternoon, Mr. Gooch had participated in a two-hour sign-language class, as he does three times each week. . . .

Mr. Gooch also will have help from Alissa Nicholson, the team's student trainer, and Jason Thorpe, the reserve quarterback, who are taking the sign-language class with the coach. By summer's end, several people will have put in hundreds of extra hours . . . to make sure that Mr. Collins and his teammates can communicate easily.

But personal interaction is only the first of many challenges confronting the team. When the Knights begin practicing this month, the coaches and quarterbacks will test a new system for sending plays into the game. Standing on the sidelines, Mr. Gooch will send one signal to the tailback and the quarterback. As a result, Mr. Collins will not need to know what's said in the huddle.

Nor will he need to know the count on which the ball is snapped. While most players take their cue from the quarterback's voice, he will take his from the movement of the center's hands. . . .

Interpreters in the area say people in Orlando's deaf community are buying season tickets to see Mr. Collins play. And the cheerleading squad is planning to teach hearing fans how deaf people signal applause: hands above the head, waving vigorously and waggling the fingers.

Skill Development

Vocabulary

▲ Ask for volunteers to define the six elements of communication and provide an example from their own lives.

People and setting affect what and how messages are sent and received.

REMEMBER:
The Elements of Communication

verbal messages	perception	feedback
nonverbal messages	channel	context

CHAPTER 2 SUMMARY

This chapter discussed the essential elements of communication. Good communicators pay attention to verbal and nonverbal messages. Communicators must be aware of how people's perceptions affect communication. Finally, communicators must be aware of the importance of channel, feedback, and context in communication.

Answers

Think About It

1. verbal messages, nonverbal messages, perception, channel, feedback, and context

2. appearance; facial expression/eye contact; posture/walk; gestures; voice; space; time; and place

3. Noise in the channel negatively affects communication because it can distract a person from speaking and/or listening effectively.

4. Communicators depend on self-feedback and feedback from others to show them how effectively they are communicating. If they interpret from the feedback that they are not communicating well, they can adjust.

Put It in Writing

The booklet suggested in number 2 could be a part of a student's portfolio.

CHAPTER REVIEW

Think About It

1. What are the six essential elements of communication?

2. Give an example of each of the categories of nonverbal communication.

3. How does noise in the channel affect communication?

4. Why is feedback important in communication?

Try It Out

1. Role-play various stereotypical nonverbal messages that you associate with the following people. Show how each person would walk or stand. See if other students can identify the role you perform. (It may help you to imagine these persons doing specific things when you role-play them.)

football coach	politician	large person
two-year-old	smart six-year-old	old person
burglar	police officer	ballerina
teacher	street person	principal
wrestler	student	chef

2. Observe a speaker addressing an audience. Record the kinds of positive and negative feedback the audience members gave the speaker.

Note how the speaker responded to the feedback. Describe any noise in the channel that interfered with the sending and receiving of messages.

3. In a small group, redesign your school to make it more comfortable for you. Consider the spatial arrangement and environmental factors. How would you change the cafeteria and classrooms? What rooms would you add, and what would the purpose of each added room be? How might these nonverbal changes affect verbal communication?

Put It in Writing

1. Record the slang words or expressions you hear throughout one day. Tell whether the words are familiar to everyone or to just a few.

2. Create a body language booklet. Find pictures in magazines, newspapers, and comic books to illustrate ten of the following emotions or attitudes:

happiness	fear
disappointment	surprise
fatigue	anger
love	boredom
hurt	irritation
relaxation	excitement
compassion	conflict
approval	disgust

sadness	emphasis
grief	affection
joy	confidence
shyness	disapproval

Use a page for each emotion or attitude. Label the picture. Then write a brief explanation of the facial expressions, posture, and gestures that indicate which emotion or attitude is expressed. Share your booklet with your classmates. Do your classmates perceive the pictures in the same way you do? Why or why not?

3. Watch fifteen minutes of a subtitled foreign film and describe four examples of nonverbal communication that appear to be different from your experience. Be specific about the nonverbal signals and what they appear to mean.

Speak About It

1. Create your own communication model. Use a collage, mobile, or poster. Explain it to the class.

2. Describe a situation in which you were involved where actions spoke louder than words. Carefully describe the verbal messages expressed during the situation. Then describe the nonverbal messages that seemed to carry the real meaning.

3. Interview someone who has lived in another culture for part of his or her life and discuss differences in the ways people in that culture communicate. Describe your findings to the class.

Speak About It

The key to effective assessment in a speech class is to use a variety of assessment procedures. Certainly, a student's knowledge of content can be assessed using a paper-and-pencil test. That is why these kinds of tests are included in the *Teacher's Resource Book*. However, assessing student performance also requires observation. Assessment instruments for listening, interviewing, group discussion, oral interpretation, group interpretation, and public-speaking skills are all included in the *Teacher's Resource Book*.

Quick Check

Ask students to find and define these Key Terms:

channel (40)

connotative meaning (28)

context (44)

denotative meaning (28)

feedback (43)

noise (41)

nonverbal messages (30)

perception (37)

slang (29)

verbal messages (27)

49

		Day 1	Day 2	Day 3	Day 4	Day 5
Week 2		**3** Vocal Production	The Listening Process	Guidelines for Good Listening		
			Barriers to Listening	Summary and Chapter Review		
Chapter 3 Planner	*Teacher's Resource Book*					
	Teaching Suggestions 3.1–3.3		3.4–3.8	3.9–3.14		
				Worksheets & Evaluation Forms 3–6		
				Chapter Test 3		
	Workbook 3.1–3.3		3.4–3.5	3.6–3.8		

Motivation

Encourage students to think of the human voice as a communication tool. Remind them that a strong, well-modulated voice can make an enormous difference in how a person is perceived by the rest of the world, including potential employers.

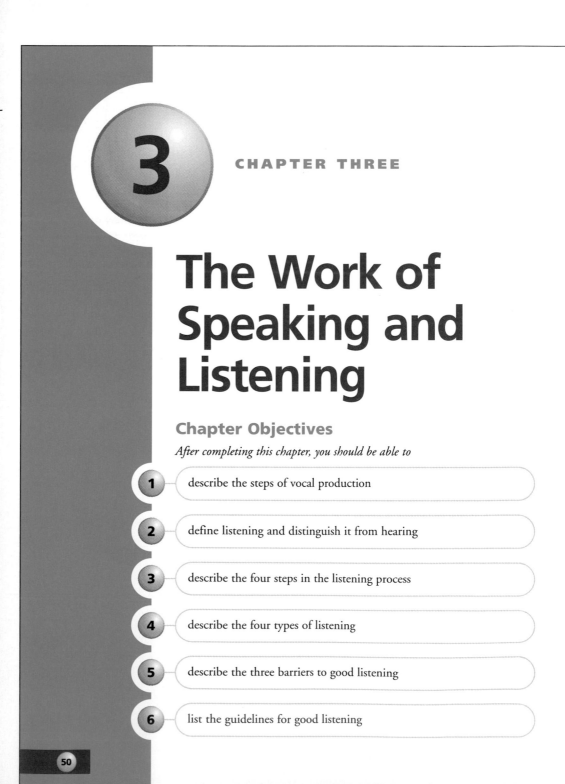

3

CHAPTER THREE

The Work of Speaking and Listening

Chapter Objectives

After completing this chapter, you should be able to

1 — describe the steps of vocal production

2 — define listening and distinguish it from hearing

3 — describe the four steps in the listening process

4 — describe the four types of listening

5 — describe the three barriers to good listening

6 — list the guidelines for good listening

Critical Thinking

Predicting

● Read the chapter title aloud and ask students to predict what information the chapter might contain.

❝Remember that you are a human being with a soul and the divine gift of articulate speech: that your native language is the language of Shakespeare and Milton and the Bible: and don't sit there crooning like a bilious pigeon.**❞**

HENRY HIGGINS
Pygmalion, Act I

▼ Key Terms

articulators	larynx	pitch	thought speed
diaphragm	listener barriers	resonators	trachea
external barriers	pharynx	speaker barriers	vocal cords

Links to Past Learning

You might ask whether anyone in the class has ever "lost" his or her voice because of laryngitis. Tell them that laryngitis literally means inflammation of the larynx. Have students place their hand over their own larynx and say a few words. They should be able to feel the vibration.

Limited English Proficiency

The Key Words in this chapter may present problems for some students. Have each word pronounced aloud and ask students to practice saying these words.

> **❝**I don't want to talk grammar. I want to talk like a lady.**❞**
>
> **ELIZA DOOLITTLE**
> *Pygmalion, Act 2*

Curricular Connection

Music

● Bring in a recording of an aria from an opera. Encourage students to take note of where the singer takes a breath. Tell them that an opera singer has a very strong diaphragm, which allows the singer to push the sound out more forcefully.

According to a French proverb, "The spoken word belongs half to those who speak, and half to those who hear." This is another way of saying that speaking and listening are two parts that form the whole—communication. To become skillful at communication, you need to know how to create sound properly and how to give meaning to the sounds you hear. In short, you need to know about the work of vocal production and listening.

VOCAL PRODUCTION

Every day you get out of bed and begin to make an amazing number of different sounds. You may yawn, grumble, giggle, talk, yell, or sing. But do you know how your voice makes these sounds? To do their work well, singers, actors, teachers, and politicians learn how their voices produce sound. Most other people know little about vocal production.

▶ **Teach**

66For my voice—I have lost it with hallooing and singing of anthems.**99**

FALSTAFF
King Henry the Fourth, Part Two,
Act I, Sc. 2

When a friend telephones, you can usually tell instantly who it is by listening to his or her voice. Even if three friends were to call and say the exact same words, you would recognize each speaker's voice. How do people produce the sounds that become vocal tones and words? Why does each person sound slightly different? The production of sounds and speech is a complicated process. It is so automatic that people are usually unaware of it. The four major elements in vocal production are (1) breath and sound, (2) pitch, (3) resonance, and (4) articulation. The first part of this chapter will look at each element separately.

Breath and Sound

The production of sound begins with the breathing process. The breathing process provides the air needed for sound production. Besides the lungs, the process involves the **diaphragm,** a muscle that separates the chest from the abdominal cavity. When you fill your lungs with air, or inhale, the diaphragm expands. When you let air out, or exhale, the diaphragm contracts and forces the air from your lungs into your windpipe, or trachea. Most of the time you perform this process without thinking about it.

Beyond the Classroom

▲ Doctors have long known that the positive effects of deep breathing can help a person to relax and reduce stress. Students could find out more about relaxation techniques that involve breathing exercises by calling yoga and meditation centers or health clubs and sports medicine facilities. Encourage students to share their findings with the class.

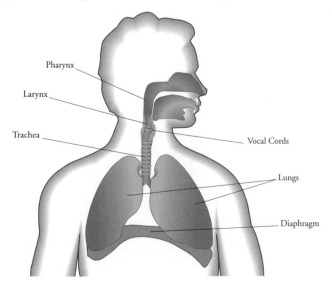

Pharynx

Larynx

Trachea

Vocal Cords

Lungs

Diaphragm

Breath, sound, resonance, and articulation all affect vocal production.

53

Skill Development

Quick Skill Opportunity

● Ask students to take a deep breath and, using the diaphragm to push the sound forward, produce a single extended note. Encourage students to hold onto the note for as long as they comfortably can. Remind them not to overdo it to the point where they feel weak or faint. Afterward, elicit responses from students about any physical sensations they may have noticed during the exercise.

Breath Control What do you find yourself doing when you need to hold a musical note for a long time during choir practice? Or when you have to give a speech to a large group without a microphone? Usually you try to take in a large amount of air. You then control the flow of air from your lungs to create a sound that lasts for the right length of time.

Most people try to take in a deep breath and let it out slowly. Often they do it incorrectly and waste a lot of energy with poor results. When some people hear "Take a deep breath," they suck in their stomachs and raise their shoulders. But this does not get more air into the lungs. When inhaling, the diaphragm needs to move down and out as the air fills up the lungs. The shoulders should remain level. Also, it is more effective to breathe through the nose to avoid gulping air.

Links to Past Learning

▼ Students might like to share anecdotes about speeches or other performances they have given or witnessed where they or the speaker exhibited poor vocal production. Encourage students to describe the experience. Remind them that any number of elements can affect vocal production, for example, poor breathing, dry mouth or throat, improper posture, and so on.

Amazing Fact!

Sound loudness is measured in units called bels, named after Alexander Graham Bell, who invented the telephone.

BRIAN R. WARD
The Ear and Hearing

Beyond the Classroom

● When rehearsing on the stage, actors are often directed to "hit the back wall of the theatre." This means that they must project their voices to fill the entire theatre. Have the class visit the school's auditorium or a theatre in your neighborhood. Give each student the opportunity to hit the back wall vocally.

INTERACT

Choose a partner and stand face-to-face. Watch each other take in deep breaths (inhale) and slowly release the air (exhale). If you see your partner's shoulders rising, say so. Press gently on your partner's shoulders while he or she inhales. Place your fist above your own belly button as you inhale. As you exhale, you should feel your hand being pushed out as your diaphragm moves down and out. Do this only three or four times because it can make you feel faint. Try breathing properly a few times each day until this process becomes more natural for you.

Sound Production As you exhale, air leaves your lungs and passes into the windpipe, or **trachea.** The trachea is the tube that carries air, just as the esophagus carries food. At the top of the trachea, air passes into the **larynx,** also called the voice box. The larynx contains your **vocal cords**, which are two elastic folds with a slit between them. As air is pushed upward through this slit, the cords vibrate to produce sound. When you hold the neck of a balloon before knotting it, you can hear slight noises as air escapes. Your fingers act very much like the folds of the vocal cords, opening and closing to regulate the air flow.

Not all speech sounds depend on the vibration of the vocal cords. For example, some consonant sounds, such as *p, s,* and *ch,* have no voiced tone. When you make them you allow air to pass through your vocal cords without vibration. However, when you make voiced sounds, your vocal cords vibrate. Voiced sounds include *b, z,* and *j.* You can try making these sounds to see how this works. Be sure you make the sound rather than say the letter.

OBSERVE

Place your three middle fingers gently across your throat. Make the *p* sound and repeat it. You should not feel any vibration in your throat. Now repeat the experiment with the following pairs of sounds: *b/p, g/k, v/f.*

55

Multicultural Learning

● Encourage students who speak a language in addition to English to go through that language's alphabet, producing the sound of each letter aloud for the rest of the class. Discuss the way in which pronunciation of letters such as *j* can differ from one language to another.

Pitch The length of the vocal cords affects the **pitch**, or highness and lowness of sound. The longer the cord, the lower the voice; the shorter the cord, the higher the voice. Men usually have longer vocal cords than women, which is why their voices are lower.

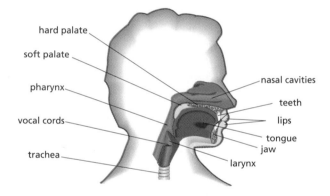

Tension also can affect the length of the vocal cords. When you are very nervous, your neck area becomes tense and your vocal cords tighten up. This tension may create a higher pitch or a more strained sound. If you are relaxed, the sound will be lower and less strained.

Singers, actors, and speakers are very aware of how they use their vocal cords. They wish to produce the proper sounds and keep their voices relaxed. They are careful not to strain their voices through yelling or speaking too long or too often.

Resonance The sound produced by the vocal cords moves upward in the throat to resonating chambers. The **pharynx**—the muscular sac between the mouth and the esophagus—or the back part of the throat, the mouth, and the nasal cavities act as hollow chambers, or **resonators**, to increase the sound. (If you have ever been in a cave, you know how a sound increases as it bounces off walls.) The thin soft sound that comes from the vocal cords becomes louder as it moves through the resonators. Many wind instruments such as a bassoon and French horn are actually complex resonators for the air flow produced by the player.

56

Skill Development

On the Job

● Invite individual students to tell about aspects of their jobs or volunteer work that require them to make use of their vocal skills. They might mention talking to visitors, speaking over a public address system, reading to children, and so on.

Just as an instrument creates different notes when the player changes the shape of the resonator (by covering and uncovering holes or pushing keys), the sound of the human voice is affected by the size of the resonating chambers and by the tongue, lips, and jaw. For example, if you do not open your mouth wide enough and if your jaws are tense, the sound may not be relaxed or pleasant.

Articulation Speech occurs when articulators form sounds into words. The **articulators** are the tongue, teeth, jaw, hard and soft palate, and lips. These parts of the vocal mechanism affect the final formation of words. Try forming the sounds *s, d, v,* and *r,* and pay careful attention to the position of your lips, tongue, and teeth.

JOURNAL ENTRY

I have a friend who is hearing impaired and who had to learn to read lips. It's amazing to see how Charlie can figure out some very complicated words just by watching my lips and face. I know it must be hard when he is first introduced to someone and has to read that person's lips.

Most articulation errors occur because of laziness or carelessness. You may hear *jest* for *just*, *git* for *get*, *ax* for *ask*, *comin'* for *coming*, and *Linder* for *Linda*. Some people substitute one sound for another. They may substitute *t* for *th* as in *nort* instead of *north*, or substitute *in* for *ing* as in *goin'* instead of *going*. Other people may leave sounds out, dropping the *g* in *recognize* or the *d* in *friend*, for example.

Articulation is very important to making sure that your message is understood. While listeners usually can figure out what you mean, they may get tired or distracted if they have to work hard to understand you. Careful, accurate articulation is easier for listeners to follow.

Learning Styles

Audio-Visual Learning

● If the class is not familiar with Shaw's *Pygmalion* or the musical based on it, give a short description of the thesis of the works—that one's station in life is determined by how one speaks—and play "The Rain in Spain" from *My Fair Lady,* or show appropriate brief clips from the original film or the film of the musical. Ask students to comment on the idea of dialect as a determiner of class or status.

66Words mean more than what is set down on paper. It takes the human voice to infuse them with shades of deeper meaning.99

MAYA ANGELOU
I Know Why the Caged Bird Sings

Cooperative Learning

▼ Give students a few minutes to create tongue twisters like the ones shown on this page. Tell them to limit their tongue twisters to a maximum of ten words. When every student has come up with a tongue twister, collect their work. Then have individuals come to the front of the room, choose a tongue twister at random, and say it aloud for the class. After each tongue twister, allow the volunteer to explain why the tongue twister was or was not difficult to say. Encourage the rest of the class to comment and ask questions.

INTERACT

With a partner take turns reading the following tongue twisters as clearly and quickly as you can.

A big bad bear bit a brown and black bug.

She sells seashells by the seashore.

In June the Jump Jazz group generates joyful tunes.

Vocal Quality This refers to the sound of your voice. Most people produce full sounds, which make their voices pleasant. Some speakers have a nasal voice, which makes them sound as if they are talking through their nose. Others have husky or raspy voices. Proper use of the voice is discussed in Chapter 12.

Importance of Vocal Production

Effective speech begins with good vocal production. It is important to develop correct habits for creating sounds so that you can make yourself understood in many situations. This is especially important when speaking with people from different areas of the country. When you travel across the United States, you find certain words pronounced in different ways. When you travel around the world, you find sounds in some languages that do not exist in the English language. You will hear clicks made in the back of the throat in some African languages and different tones in certain Asian languages. Most people take vocal production for granted. Skillful communicators learn how to improve their voices and make themselves more easily understood by listeners.

THE LISTENING PROCESS

What is listening? Is it the same as hearing? You may be surprised to learn that there is a difference. Hearing is the act of receiving sound. When you hear something, you are aware of sounds. Listening involves hearing, but it is much more complicated than just picking up sounds.

The listener must share the responsibility for effective communication.

Skill Development
Active Listening

● Ask students to sit quietly and write down every sound they hear. After a minute has passed, have each student read his or her list to the class. Point out that even though the students were sitting in the same room, they didn't all hear or pay attention to the same things. Encourage them to recognize that they were actively listening to things they would normally just hear.

Listening is the four-step process of receiving, interpreting, evaluating, and responding to messages. Hearing is only part of the first step in the listening process. Although you may listen to non-human sounds such as car motors, air conditioners, or singing birds, the focus in this chapter is on listening to other people. This includes messages sent by people to other people in face-to-face situations and messages sent through the media.

Receiving

The first step of the listening process is receiving. It involves hearing and seeing. You use your ears and eyes to gather information, or sense data. Your ears take in the vocal tones and words, such as, "Did you know about the party at Jenny's house?" or "There will be a final band rehearsal at 3:30 this Friday." Your eyes read the nonverbal signals to get the full message. You watch facial expressions, gestures, and eye movements.

Interpreting

Once you have received a message through your ears and eyes, you have to use your own experience to interpret what you just heard. An effective listener tries to interpret the speaker's message to truly understand what the speaker intended to say.

59

Learning Styles

Visual Learning

▼ Ask students to illustrate graphically the four steps in the listening process. They can draw a diagram or a cartoon or construct a model.

Skill Development

Making Conversation

● Encourage students to talk with a partner about the different kinds of feedback they receive on a daily basis. Students should discuss their emotional reactions to such events and describe what they did to make sure their messages had been received.

Suppose you hear the question, "Did you know about the party at Jenny's house?" You may interpret it as meaning "Did **you** know there was a party? No one told me about it." Or you may interpret it as meaning "Did you know what **really** happened at that party?" Or you may understand it as "Did you **know** about the party since I didn't see you there?" There may be still other meanings. Nonverbal cues will give you helpful information in figuring out the meaning.

Evaluating

After you have interpreted the message, you need to evaluate it carefully. You have to connect that message to your ideas or feelings about the subject of the message. You have to decide if you agree or disagree, or if you need more information.

For example, depending on how you interpreted the message about Jenny's party, you may need to consider whether or not you should tell the other person why he wasn't invited, or you may want to know exactly why he is asking. While each person is talking, you begin to think, "So what?" You will ask yourself, "What do I think?" or "How do I feel?" or "What do I need to know?"

Responding

Almost all messages require some type of response. A lack of response frustrates most speakers. The listener who gives no verbal or nonverbal feedback makes a speaker feel invisible. Sometimes this is called a disconfirming message or a message that carries the meaning "I do not recognize your existence." Speakers expect a verbal or nonverbal signal that you "got" the message. Without such a sign speakers are left wondering if they should try again with a similar message.

As a listener you are faced with sending a response. You may say, "She only had the basketball team members over," or you may nod your head to indicate you knew about the party. Whatever your response, it tells the speaker that the message

Taking notes in class requires listening for information.

Curricular Connection

Mathematics

● Encourage students to use the information about thought speed on this page to calculate the number of words a lecturer would speak during a 55-minute presentation. Once they have calculated the speaker's thought speed, have them calculate the average listener's thought speed.

reached you. The listener's response is important for effective communication. If the speaker gets no feedback, he or she has no connection to you and no sense of whether the message was received.

Listeners have one advantage over speakers. This advantage allows them to be active while listening. It is called **thought speed**. Most people can speak at a rate of 120 to 180 words a minute. Yet people can listen at a rate of up to 400 words a minute. That's a big difference! Thought speed refers to the extra time listeners gain because they can process words faster than speakers can produce them.

TYPES OF LISTENING

An effective listener uses four types of listening. They are informational, empathic, critical, and creative listening. Each type of listening requires effort and awareness. A competent listener is comfortable using all types.

Critical Thinking

Evaluating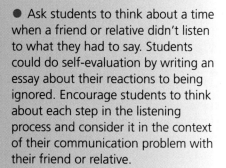

● Ask students to think about a time when a friend or relative didn't listen to what they had to say. Students could do self-evaluation by writing an essay about their reactions to being ignored. Encourage students to think about each step in the listening process and consider it in the context of their communication problem with their friend or relative.

Informational Listening

An important purpose for listening is to get information. Many people have problems at home, work, or school because they do not listen carefully for information they need. Often they do not ask the right questions to find out what they need to know.

Informational listening involves listening to information such as directions, explanations, or news. You are listening for information when you take notes in class, when you take telephone messages for another family member, or when you pay attention to a demonstration speech on how to make vegetarian pizza. During television or radio broadcasts you also listen for information about weather, news events, and sports.

Informational listening is the basis for the other types of listening. Unless you understand a message accurately, you cannot analyze another person's ideas or respond to another person's feelings.

Tips for Note Taking

Competent communicators listen with their ears and their eyes to take classroom notes effectively. Following are some guidelines for note taking:

1. *Decide what kind of notes you need to take.* Think about the teacher and the subject. Do you need only a few key words on each topic because the material is also in your history book? Do you need to write down much of what the teacher says because you have no textbook or because the material is not covered in your book?

2. *Pay special attention to what the teacher highlights.* Look at what the teacher writes on the board or overhead, since this is a clue to what is important. Listen carefully to what the teacher emphasizes or repeats. Example: "So by this time there were thirteen colonies. Not eight, not seventeen, but thirteen." Also listen carefully to what the teacher says is important. Example: "Remember this formula because you will need to use it again."

continued

"He listens well who takes notes."

DANTE ALIGHIERI
The Divine Comedy, XV

Beyond the Classroom

Invite a newspaper reporter or a police officer or both to talk about the importance of critical listening. Students might prepare a list of questions to ask the speakers. Remind them that they themselves will be critical listeners as they hear answers to their questions.

3. *Follow the teacher's outline format.* Try to get the whole picture before you start to take notes. Example: "There are six steps in this experiment" or "We will review the criteria for becoming a senator." Use clues the teacher gives. Example: "So the second step is the addition of salt."

4. *Make your own comments as you write notes.* Tie the points to your own life or your opinions. Star or circle ideas you think are important.

5. *Review your notes after class.* Correct your spelling or clean up messy handwriting. Underline or circle ideas you think are important. (Colored pencils might help with this.) Write down any reactions you have to the material or clues to help you to remember. Examples: "similar to Brazil" or "gopher story." Draw arrows or lines to connect related points.

6. *Remember the "don'ts."* Don't try to write down every word. Don't try to write down the stories and examples, just label them. Example: "Kentucky Derby horse story."

7. *Ask for more information.* Ask the teacher to summarize the main points. If you don't understand an idea, ask the teacher to elaborate, or give more details. You may also ask the teacher to repeat points that went by quickly or to repeat the name of a person or place that was hard to understand.

Critical Listening

Critical listening means examining an informative or a persuasive message and making decisions about your findings. After examining a message, you need to respond actively. Perhaps you need to ask questions to obtain further information, or you may need to think about the reasons someone is trying to persuade you to do something.

Critical listening involves separating fact from opinion and checking out the source of a message. A fact is a statement that

Critical Thinking

Evaluating

● Remind students that it isn't always easy to distinguish facts from opinions. You might share with them examples of so-called experts who dispense information that sounds like fact in order to promote their own opinions or to sell products. Use examples from advertisements or infomercials to illustrate your point, or ask students to bring in some examples.

Skill Development

Quick Skill Opportunity

▼ Go around the class, pointing to students at random. As you point to each student, say "Fact" or "Opinion." The student then has five seconds to make a fact or opinion statement, depending on what you designate. The rest of the students can decide whether or not their classmates answer correctly.

Before deciding to buy, critical listeners learn to ask questions in order to distinguish between facts and opinions.

can be proved or disproved. An opinion is a statement that is based on a belief or feeling. It is a judgment. For example, you can prove that the temperature in Dallas, Texas, was 95 degrees yesterday. Yesterday's Dallas temperature is a fact. You may also believe that it was a beautiful day in Dallas yesterday, but that is an opinion. You cannot prove the opinion. Someone else might feel that 95 degrees is too hot to be considered a beautiful day.

A critical listener hears the other person's ideas first; looks for facts, opinions, disagreements, confusion; and then figures out how to respond effectively. Whether you are an audience member during a persuasive speech or a participant in a debate, your mind should be working constantly.

What questions might a critical listener ask when responding to the following statements? (Keep looking for facts and opinions.)

Remi says there will be only two slots open on the track team and one is already promised to Darren.

The election was a joke. Forty-five percent of the citizens did not know who was running.

The Hatfields have three cars. They are very rich.

You should buy this hiking boot because it has an extended PU stabilizer and an extended toe bumper.

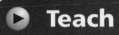

All these statements should be questioned by a person interested in how true they are. Critical listeners always keep alert and ask questions. It's hard work, but it's worth it.

APPLY

Listen to a political advertisement on the radio. Identify two ways the commercial attempts to discredit the candidate's opponent. How did you recognize this bias? What strategies are used to "sell" the candidate?

Creative Listening

Creative listening means using your active imagination as you interpret a message. This is sometimes called recreational listening. You probably enjoy listening to music. Your imagination may create pictures or stories to go along with the music. Often when you listen to others, your mind docs similar things. A talented storyteller helps you create mental pictures. You can find yourself in a medieval castle or on a new planet in just a few seconds. A comedian makes you see the world in new and surprising ways. You use your imagination when you watch a play or listen to a comedy tape. In all these cases the speakers stir up your creativity while you listen.

You may become more actively involved in other kinds of creative listening. If you have done role-playing, you know how carefully you have to listen to respond to the other people in the scene. Whether you and a friend are working on a science project or creating a computer game, listening to each other makes the work more imaginative. As you listen to your friend's ideas, you may find new solutions to problems that come up.

Sometimes you can see new ways to do things in response to what other people say. Suppose you are building a model of the planets and one group member wants to glue the rings around Saturn. Another person wants to create a complicated hanger so the rings can come off. If you take the time to discuss your ideas

Skill Development
Media Literacy

● Remind students that while newspapers and television news shows purport to be objective, almost all media are subject to editorializing. Explain that one of the most common types of editorializing has to do with inflammatory or emotion-based language. Use the following examples:

heinous crime

tragic accident

beautiful and talented child

vicious killer

popular entertainer

remarkable athlete

Encourage students to come up with several more examples.

❝The analysis of verbal behavior, particularly the so-called discovery of grammar, came very late. For thousands of years no one could have known he was speaking according to rule.❞

B. F. SKINNER
About Behaviorism

Learning Styles

Audio Learning

● Bring in recordings of natural sounds, such as bubbling streams, crashing waves, frog and cricket calls, and whale songs. Before you play a recording, tell students to use their imaginations to visualize where the sounds are taking place. Then encourage them to write a descriptive poem or paragraph about the place they envisioned.

and hear each other out, you may come up with a third approach—using magnets or hook and loop fasteners to make the rings detachable. Creative problem solvers have very fine listening skills.

✳ INTERACT

Try out creative listening by doing a soap opera role-play. With a partner, try to portray two imaginary characters in a particular situation. Act out the situation so the class can understand who the characters are and what is going on.

As a class, you might try a role-play tag. Start with two characters and a particular situation. After a couple of minutes, someone from the class tags one of the characters and steps into the role-play. After a couple more minutes, someone else tags the other character and steps into the scene. Continue the role-play tag until everyone has had a turn being an actor. Afterwards, discuss the role that listening played in the role-play tag, as people created characters or had to adapt to new characters.

When a friend is angry or sad, eye contact or touch is often a better response than words.

66

Unit 1 The Basics of Communication

Empathic Listening

Empathic listening involves listening to another's feelings. This is a very difficult type of listening. It is not easy just to listen when others are talking about feelings. Sometimes you want to solve their problems. Sometimes you want to interrupt with questions or ideas. Sometimes you just want to get away from the conversation because the strong feelings make you uncomfortable.

Listening to negative feelings requires patience and caring. Talking to a friend who is angry or sad can be difficult. Eye contact, head nodding, or touch are often better responses than words. As a camp counselor, baby-sitter, or hospital volunteer, you may hear many people talk about their feelings. These situations will give you the opportunity to engage in empathic listening.

APPLY

Read the following comments and identify the feeling being expressed in each. Then imagine how you might respond if a good friend made these comments to you.

"What do you do when your folks get in a fight? Do you just pretend you don't hear anything? I never know whether to hide in my room or just help by cleaning up."

"Hey! Guess what! I came in first in the 440."

"What did I ever do to Lee? That whole group isn't talking to me. I don't even know what is going on. It makes me so mad!"

OBSERVE

Think back to the last time you listened to someone's feelings. What kinds of feelings do your family and friends ask you to listen to? How do you respond? When is it easy to respond? When is it difficult? Share your stories with your classmates and listen to their stories too. Have you all had similar experiences or problems?

Skill Development
Making Conversation

● Students could work together in pairs to discuss examples of empathic listening in their own lives. Each could describe a situation and describe what they did to fulfill the role of listener. Partners should offer input about what went right in the communication, as well as those areas where the listener could have used some improvement.

Critical Thinking

Organizing

▼ Students could create pie charts to show what percentage of their listening time is spent doing informational, empathic, critical, and creative listening. They could label the pie slices and give a few examples of each type of listening.

SPEAKING OF . . .

NATALIE DIGATE

If you call the Fox Valley, Illinois, crisis line you might find yourself talking with Natalie Digate, a crisis line volunteer. Natalie explains her responsibilities in this way: "My job is to take calls from people who call the line because they are having a difficult time dealing with certain problems and people in their lives, or people who just need someone to talk to." She reports talking with people who are mentally ill, emotionally disturbed, depressed, or who have experienced a recent crisis. Natalie does not try to solve their problems. Rather, she says her job is to "guide them to realize that they can help themselves." Sometimes Natalie serves as an educator, informing callers about local resources they could turn to for help or assisting them in creating a plan of action to deal with their problem.

Natalie's training for this volunteer position involved extensive practice in listening and speaking. Most important, she learned to be an empathic listener. On many calls she relies on phrases such as "I understand" or "That must have been terrifying." These responses show caring but do not attempt to solve the problem. She received specialized training to handle a major crisis, such as a suicide call. According to Natalie, "A volunteer needs to be empathic to the caller, listen well, and have good judgment on what to say." This experience could serve as basic preparation for a number of future careers, including psychologist, reporter, teacher, communication consultant, or director of customer relations.

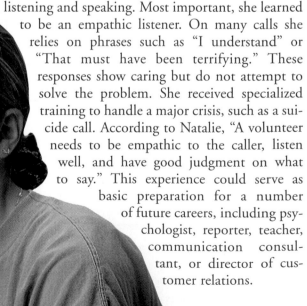

Substitute Teacher Tip

Encourage students to think about past times (in the classroom, while listening to a radio, or at other times) when they "tuned out" a speaker. Ask whether their inattention stemmed from within, from something the speaker was or wasn't doing, or from an external barrier such as background noise or extreme heat. Try to get students to connect their personal experience to the barriers to listening.

> **❝**Bore, *n.* a person who talks when you wish him to listen.**❞**
>
> **AMBROSE BIERCE**
> *The Devil's Dictionary*

Curricular Connection

Social Studies

▲ Encourage students to look into the problem of noise pollution. They could do research on the effects of noise pollution on the populations of large cities or within certain high-risk workplaces, such as construction sites, factories, airports, and so on. Some students may wish to present their findings to the class.

Someone who is upset may just need another person to be there. The listener does not have to solve the problem. The listener simply has to respond in a way that demonstrates understanding of the problem and the feelings it is creating. For example, you can't solve your friend's family problems, but you can listen and show you care about your friend.

BARRIERS TO LISTENING

A person with normal hearing is not necessarily a good listener. Many different things can prevent a speaker's message from being received. These are called barriers to listening. The three major barriers to listening are external barriers, speaker barriers, and listener barriers. A discussion of each barrier follows.

External Barriers

External barriers are situations in the environment that keep you from paying careful attention to the speaker. Such distractions may include a bee flying around your head, an ambulance siren wailing outside, or a beeper going off. Coughing, whispering, or giggling can distract you in the classroom. (These are examples of noise in the channel discussed in Chapter 2.)

External barriers can be temporary and unusual, but they also can be ongoing or permanent. If you go to school near a busy airport, you may hear the sound of jets passing over your classroom every afternoon. This is a temporary distraction. If you live near a noisy factory, this may be a long-term or permanent distraction. Sometimes you can change the distractions by shutting the windows. Other times you have to learn to listen in spite of them.

External barriers exist outside the speakers and listeners but can greatly interfere with communication. Good listeners recognize the distractions and ignore or remove them. Usually good speakers try to adapt to them in order to help the listeners.

69

Amazing Fact!

Gallaudet University, in Washington, D.C., is the only university in the world exclusively for deaf people. It is named for Thomas Hopkins Gallaudet (1787–1851), who was a founder of the first U. S. school for the deaf in Connecticut.

Critical Thinking

Analyzing

● Remind students that while the use of filler words may be a part of their daily conversations, it has no place in public speaking. Encourage them to pay attention to their use of filler words throughout the day. Students may be surprised by how often these words are used, both in their own conversation and in the conversations of others, particularly on radio and television.

Speaker Barriers

Speaker barriers are characteristics of the speaker that interfere with listening. They include appearance and manner, prejudice, and believability.

Distracting Appearance and Manner Some speakers turn off their audiences through their appearance or by their manner of speaking. Appearance may interfere with the message. If you are distracted by a speaker's clothes, jewelry, or hairstyle, you may miss the main point of the message.

Some people constantly use filler words such as "you know," or "like." Others look at the floor or tap their fingers during a conversation. These habits distract listeners, who remember the annoying habit rather than the message.

Prejudice Speakers who appear narrow-minded or prejudiced also turn off listeners. Listeners are not likely to concentrate on the message when they are upset. They may get angry at a speaker who says that female sports teams should not receive the same amount of money as male teams, for example. You may remember occasions when you judged a speaker too quickly, however, and later discovered how much you missed. Usually these experiences help you to keep an open mind.

Lack of Believability Listeners need to believe that the speaker knows his or her subject well. A speaker with low believability may create barriers to listening. A speech on "How Karate Can Change Your Life" should not be given by a student who has taken only three karate lessons. A seriously overweight doctor is not an ideal person with whom to discuss weight loss. Listeners may not respect these speakers' opinions.

What makes people believable when they are talking? In some cases, a person's formal or informal reputation precedes a message. A speaker may be introduced like this: "Dr. May Falk, a specialist in sports medicine, will talk about how athletes stay healthy. Dr. Falk is head of the sports medicine program at Fairlawn

Skill Development

Media Literacy

● Discuss how advertising depends on endorsements by famous people to sell certain products. Encourage students to cite examples of spokespersons who inspire belief in certain products. Start them off with the example of a professional basketball star's endorsement for a particular sports drink, car, or athletic shoe. You may want to assign students to keep a log of all advertisements they see on TV in a given week that depend on famous spokespersons.

Appearance and manner greatly affect how a speaker is received.

Beyond the Classroom

Invite a psychiatric social worker, rabbi, pastor, or some other professional whose job requires strong listening skills to speak to your class. Encourage your students to ask the visitor questions related to speaking and listening. You may want to start the questioning off by asking, "Why is listening important in your line of work?" Students could take notes on the visitor's responses.

University." This formal introduction makes the speaker believable. Informal reputations also serve to influence believability. You may think of someone as a bigot, liberal, burnout, or brain. Such labels tend to influence how you react to what they say.

Sometimes a speaker establishes believability during a conversation. Comments such as, "When I ran the marathon . . ." or "When I play the saxophone . . ." show knowledge about the subject. When you hear two people trade baseball statistics or argue skillfully about computers, you begin to see them as believable speakers on their subjects. On the other hand, people who talk about topics they know little about tend to create a barrier between themselves and their listeners.

Listener Barriers

Listener barriers are personal attitudes or behaviors that interfere with listening. You can keep yourself from being a competent communicator. Internal distractions, lack of knowledge, personal prejudices, and your desire to talk may get in the way of listening.

Critical Thinking

Evaluating

● Ask students what type of person would most likely be an expert on the following topics:

science fiction

keeping your cat healthy

figure skating

building model airplanes

how tornadoes are formed

Curricular Connection

Language Arts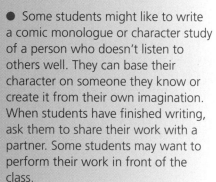

● Some students might like to write a comic monologue or character study of a person who doesn't listen to others well. They can base their character on someone they know or create it from their own imagination. When students have finished writing, ask them to share their work with a partner. Some students may want to perform their work in front of the class.

Curricular Connection

Art

Some students might like to show listener barriers, perhaps drawing a strip of cartoon figures suffering from internal distractions, lack of knowledge, or personal prejudices. Ask students to try to avoid using words but to rely on facial expressions, question marks, exclamation points, actions, and so on.

If you believe a subject is not interesting, this will keep you from being an effective listener.

Internal Distractions Your thoughts, feelings, or physical conditions can interfere with listening. If you failed a test last period or just had a fight with a friend, you may be unable to pay attention. Thinking of next weekend's party can also cause you to tune out a speaker. Physical distress may also interfere with your ability to give full attention to someone else. Headaches, toothaches, stomach cramps, or lack of sleep are internal distractions. If you are in pain, will you be able to give full attention to a friend's conversation with you?

Lack of Knowledge Sometimes you will find that no matter how hard you try to listen, you cannot understand what the speaker is saying. Your past experience or classes may not have prepared you for a discussion of straight-edge vegans, rock collecting, or gospel music. Sometimes a speaker uses a special language that you cannot understand. For example, if you do not understand terms such as *fadeaway, dunk, assist, lane violation, traveling,* or *pump* you will have trouble understanding a basic discussion of last night's basketball game.

Skill Development
Vocabulary

Remind students that the word *prejudice* is made up of a prefix and a Latin word and that it literally means to judge before hearing or to judge with insufficient knowledge.

Good listeners take the risk of asking questions to clear up what they cannot understand. They also try to learn to interpret new words and nonverbal symbols to be more effective listeners in the future. Sometimes you may have to say, "I don't understand now, but I'll try to learn more about it."

Personal Prejudices Personal beliefs may also keep you from really hearing what another person has to say. People have their own beliefs on certain subjects. These beliefs may reflect a listener's studies or upbringing and can be difficult to change. Some people believe they know everything about a certain topic. They don't think they can learn anything new by listening carefully to others. This attitude leads to closed minds and creates barriers to communication.

APPLY

Sometimes you create a barrier just because you believe a subject is uninteresting. Which of the following subjects is likely to cause you to close down mentally?

modern poetry	the NWBA playoff schedule
recent Broadway shows	the space program
rodeo riders	badminton
modeling careers	country and Western music

Some of these topics may meet with a ho-hum from you. Yet many people are fascinated by these topics and enjoy listening to a discussion of them.

Sensitive topics can cause barriers to good listening. Each of us has strong feelings about discussing values with anyone, particularly with people we don't know well. If a person you just met asks you about your religion, you may put up a barrier. But with a trusted friend you may feel very comfortable talking for hours about your religious beliefs.

73

66People who know little
are usually great talkers,
while men who know much
say little.99

JEAN JACQUES ROUSSEAU

Links to Past Learning

Ask students to give examples of how watching for nonverbal clues is important to empathic listening.

Sometimes you will tune out after hearing a speaker take a particular position, saying to yourself, "I hold the opposite view. Why should I bother to listen?" This often happens with national political topics, such as nuclear energy, affirmative action, or welfare. But it can also happen on issues of personal taste, such as choice of clothes, sports teams, or music. If you don't listen to points of view different from your own, you may learn more and more about one point of view (yours!) but remain unaware of others.

Desire to Talk Many people would rather talk than listen, especially if they have to listen carefully. You probably know someone who may appear to be listening but is really waiting to talk. And you can probably remember arguments in which all you could do was wait for the other person to finish. In these situations, very little listening is going on. When people with this attitude finally get to talk they usually just repeat their own position because they did not listen to the others' ideas.

People who find themselves always trying to get in the next word need to learn the value of controlling their talking. Good listeners try to listen until a speaker is finished. Then they start to respond.

Sometimes people compete to "top" another person's joke or story. You can recognize such a listener in the person who says, "You think that's bad, wait till you hear this. . . ." Usually this competition takes the fun out of a conversation because the speakers seem to be listening only to themselves.

Every speaker and listener has the responsibility to try to communicate with the other. Communication breaks down when barriers go up and one or both persons stop trying to reach each other.

OBSERVE

Listen to your classmates at the lunch table for fifteen minutes and record all the barriers that keep them from listening to each other. For example, list the distracting noises that compete for attention. Or note how certain people tune out when a particular subject is mentioned.

Links to Past Learning

Ask students to give examples of how trying to see things from the speaker's point of view could be important when listening to an informational talk on use of pesticides by fruit and vegetable growers, for example.

Listening to news or weather forecasts on radio or television is listening for information.

GUIDELINES FOR GOOD LISTENING

The following guidelines are used by people who work at their listening skills. These guidelines can help you develop your own listening skills.

1. *Watch for nonverbal clues.* Often speakers tell us what is important through nonverbal messages. A speaker's hand gestures may stress a point. A speaker's face reveals his or her feelings about a subject. When a speaker's voice gets louder or softer, it may be a signal to pay special attention. Good listeners look for nonverbal clues.

2. *Try to see things from the speaker's point of view.* Whether or not you agree with another person, you will be a better listener if you try to understand what is going on inside the other person. If your friend is angry at people who were calling her names, you need to imagine why it makes her so upset or how you would feel if someone called you those names. If you are listening to a speech on outdoor adventure activities, you might try to imagine how exciting it would feel to ride a motorcycle or climb a mountain. Good listeners try to put themselves in the speaker's shoes.

Learning Styles
Audio Learning

● Bring in an audio recording of *Romeo and Juliet,* and play one of the soliloquies for students as they follow the text in their literature book. Discuss how the actor used pace and volume to express meaning and maintain listener interest.

Skill Development

Feedback

● Have students take turns reading the excerpt from Martin Luther King, Jr.'s "I Have a Dream" speech. Encourage the class to respond to each reading by pointing out instances where the speaker did or did not use pace and volume to heighten listener interest. Model the criticism process for students by telling each speaker something positive in addition to any negative criticism you may have.

3. *Avoid distractions.* When you enter a classroom, you may have a choice of whether to sit at a window seat or next to your best friend. If you really wish to pay attention to the teacher, you may avoid both your friend and the window. You may choose to sit close to the front of the room. In many settings you can choose to pay attention to distractions, or you can choose to avoid or ignore them. Believe it or not, you can even choose to ignore the loud music, the crawling spider, the noise in the hall. Good listeners do!

4. *Listen for the new and unusual idea.* What makes you pay special attention to a speaker? Something that forces you to take notice. It may be a funny story or it may be the way your name is said. Any change will tell you, "Pay attention!"
   Good speakers change the pace. They may switch from facts to stories, put up a chart, or tell a joke. Even in everyday conversation, change will force you to take notice. If your friend normally calls you "Katie," but suddenly you hear her call loudly, "Katherine!" you will pay closer attention. If your friend changes to a higher voice or a funny accent to tell a story, it will grab your attention and make you listen. As a listener you will remember the unique and creative.

5. *Listen for repetition.* If information is repeated several times, you are more likely to remember it than if you hear it only once. From conversations to formal speeches, repetitions send the signal "Important!" Many famous speeches use repetition. Martin Luther King, Jr., used repetition effectively in his famous "I Have a Dream" speech.

   So let freedom ring from the prodigious hilltops of New Hampshire.

   Let freedom ring from the mighty mountains of New York.

   Let freedom ring from the heightening Alleghenies of Pennsylvania.

   Let freedom ring from the snow-capped Rockies of Colorado.

   Let freedom ring from the curvaceous slopes of California. But not only that.

   Let freedom ring from Stone Mountain of Georgia.

   Let freedom ring from Lookout Mountain of Tennessee.

● Students might enjoy creating a song, poem, or speech using the repetition technique shown in the "I Have a Dream" speech. You may wish to discuss with them the differences between senseless repetition, repetition for dramatic effect, and repetition for the sake of clarity.

Martin Luther King, Jr., who won the 1964 Nobel Peace Prize, mastered his speaking skills as a preacher.

Let freedom ring from every hill and molehill of Mississippi, from every mountainside, let freedom ring.

You use repetition in everyday life as well. If someone making cookies says, "When making gingerbread cookies, use light molasses. Remember, light molasses," you are more likely to remember the correct kind. If it is important for a sweater to be washed in cold water, repeating that fact draws attention to it.

Good listeners create opportunities for repetition. They may prompt the speaker to repeat by asking, "Where did you say I turn for the hobby shop?" They may even say, "Tell me that again" or "Would you mind repeating the directions?" Hearing information more than once helps fix it in your mind. Ask for repetition if you need it.

77

Cooperative Learning

Groups of students could analyze the types of announcements delivered over the school public address system and the barriers to listening. Groups might brainstorm ways in which the announcements could be improved.

6. *Get prepared.* People have something on their minds at all times. Many good listeners make a deliberate effort to clear their minds so they can concentrate on a conversation. For example, you may have to stop thinking about your English test in order to be able to listen to your friend's description of a fight with her sister. If you can't clear your mind, you will either miss important information or keep asking questions such as, "What did you just say?"

    When you are about to listen in a formal situation, such as a class or a speech, you can prepare by arriving on time, sitting where you can see and hear the speaker easily, and getting your notebook ready ahead of time.

7. *Respond to the speaker.* Nothing is worse than talking to someone and getting no reply. It makes the speaker feel invisible. Good listeners find a way to show the speaker that they received the message. It may be in the form of a nod of the head, a laugh, or a comment. Sometimes a listener will respond by doing what the speaker requested, such as taking out the garbage.

Responding nonverbally to a speaker is one way to show that you're getting the message.

APPLY

How might you find a way to apply three of the following topics or issues to your life?

Raising dogs for fun and profit

How music videos are made

Gangs in our high schools

Why people get divorced

Buying athletic shoes

Brothers: how to cope with them

Summer programs in theatre and dance

It's not always easy to find the connection, but any idea you can apply to your own life will make it easier for you to listen to that topic.

Limited English Proficiency

Some students may be embarrassed to ask for information to be repeated because they feel that such a request will make them appear unintelligent. Reinforce the idea that asking questions and requesting repetition or clarification is a very large part of being a good listener. It may be helpful for students if you write these active listening tips on the board.

• Put the speaker's message into your own words. Then ask the speaker whether you've understood correctly.

• Ask the speaker to repeat any part of the message that went by too quickly.

• Ask the speaker to explain any point that is unclear to you. Ask for more details or additional examples.

8. *Apply the ideas to yourself.* As a listener you should try to answer the question, "How does it relate to my life?" If you can apply information to yourself, you are more likely to remember and use it. Usually you have to do the work of connecting the information to yourself. If the speaker is discussing jewelry making, you may think, "I could make something like that for birthday presents." A speaker discussing training for cross-country runners may provide you with information you could use on a diet.

9. *Listen for structure.* Most speeches follow a definite structure or order: "First point, second point, third point, fourth point." The structuring and ordering of information keeps the listener from getting lost. The structure helps good listeners look for clues that indicate where the speaker is. A listener may say, "That's the end of that story" or "Now she's heading for the punch line." If you listen for the speaker's clues, you can follow what is said more easily.

10. *Review and preview the points.* Careful listeners review in their minds the points a speaker has made. For example, you might think, "Roberto has talked about the history of Alaska

79

Teach

Curricular Connection

Language Arts

Ask students to write a short paragraph describing the best listener they know and giving an example to support their opinion. Some students might like to read their work aloud in class.

and the geography of Alaska. Now he seems to be getting into the major industry there." This kind of thinking keeps you in touch with what was said and what is to come. In some cases a speaker will tell what the next points will be.

The good listener uses thought speed. This provides the extra time to practice the listening guidelines that are appropriate. Better listening is a very important part of better communication.

JOURNAL ENTRY

I find it easy to talk to my older brother because he listens and doesn't say anything until I ask him a question. I can talk or ask him anything, and he will give me an answer if he knows it. If he doesn't know the answer, he finds one and then tells me.

REMEMBER:
GUIDELINES FOR GOOD LISTENING

1. Watch for nonverbal clues.
2. Try to see things from the speaker's point of view.
3. Avoid distractions.
4. Listen for the new and unusual.
5. Listen for repetition.
6. Get prepared.
7. Respond to the speaker.
8. Apply the ideas to yourself.
9. Listen for structure.
10. Review and preview points.

80

Multicultural Learning

Some students may come from a culture in which listening in school is valued more than contributing one's own ideas. You might ask these students to say a few words about their former school experiences with listening.

CHAPTER 3 SUMMARY

This chapter covers vocal production and listening. Vocal production involves breath and sound, resonance, and articulation. Skillful communicators learn how to use their voices properly and carefully. Listening involves a four-step process: (1) receiving, (2) interpreting, (3) evaluating, and (4) responding.

Thought speed gives a listener time to process what a speaker is saying. There are four types of listening: informational, empathic, critical, and creative. Good communicators avoid the three barriers to listening (external, speaker, and listener barriers) and use the guidelines for good listening.

Answers

Think About It

1. breath and sound, resonance, and articulation

2. Keep shoulders level; swell diaphragm upon inhalation; breathe through the nose.

3. Steps: receiving, interpreting, evaluating, and responding. Student examples will vary. Here is a sample answer: You receive a message when you hear your friend greet you and see that she is smiling; you've seen her smile that way before, so you interpret that she has some good news; you know that she was trying out for the school play, so you evaluate what her getting the part would mean to her and to you; you respond by smiling back at her and asking about her audition.

4. Informational, critical, creative, and empathic. Informational listening is the basis for other types of listening. Critical listening involves examining a message and making decisions about your findings. Creative listening means using your imagination to interpret a message. Empathic listening involves listening to another's feelings.

CHAPTER REVIEW

Think About It

1. What are the three elements of vocal production?

2. Describe the proper way to breathe.

3. What are the four steps in the listening process? Give an example of how one message goes through these steps.

4. Describe the four types of listening and their importance.

5. Describe the three barriers to listening. Give examples of each.

Try It Out

1. Role-play examples of barriers to listening. Try to act out these situations and others:

   A teenager who has distracting habits tries to talk to some friends.

   Two students are talking about what a good time they each had at the dance, but neither is responding to what the other is saying.

   A young person is talking about music videos to an older relative.

2. Say each of the following sentences aloud and change the meaning by emphasizing different words.

   I thought not. (surprise)

   I thought not. (agreement)

   I thought not. (sarcastic)

Did you get a B in English? (Thought you'd get a D.)

Did you get a B in English? (Thought it was math.)

Did you get a B in English? (Thought you'd get an A.)

3. Listen to conversations on television or radio or in public places. Record examples of five articulation errors you hear. Also find two or three variations in pronunciation that occur because the speakers are from different parts of the country.

Put It in Writing

1. Think about the different places in which you need good communication skills in your own life (home, school, work, sports events, clubs, church). Choose one of these places, and think back to when good listening was an important part of your activity there. Describe one time when the listening was effective and one time when it was not. Then explain why good listening did or did not take place.

2. Keep a listening log for twelve hours. Keep track of how much time you spend listening to TV, radio, your parents, your friends, and your teachers. Then write one paragraph for each of the following questions.

   How much of what you heard in those hours can you actually remember?

Skill Development

Active Listening

Play an instructional video for the class. As students watch, have them take notes about the process being demonstrated. Then have students discuss the process and share the comments and observations they wrote while watching the video. Ask them to explain how taking notes helped them understand the instructions.

What did you really listen to?

Why did you listen to these things and not to others?

How might you listen better, so that you can remember more of what you hear?

How did you use thought speed to improve your listening?

Speak About It

1. Describe to your classmates an incident in which a barrier to listening caused problems for you.

2. In small groups, take turns presenting short speeches that give instructions. The listeners should be able to follow the instructions as they are being presented. (Example: how to do a dance step) At the end of each speech, check how closely the directions were followed. Then analyze who was responsible for the successes and failures—the speaker, the listener, or both.

3. Work with a partner to explain the plot of your favorite movie or book. As you listen, respond to what your partner says. Make comments, ask questions, or paraphrase main points to check your understanding. When it's your turn to speak, answer your partner's questions and clarify or restate information as necessary.

5. External barriers, speaker barriers, and listener barriers. Examples will vary. Here is a sample answer: External barrier: someone is talking and laughing loudly while you're trying to listen to a lecture. Speaker barrier: You don't believe the speaker knows what he or she is talking about. Self-barrier: You are hungry or sleepy or too warm or cold.

Quick Check

Ask students to find and define these Key Terms:

articulators (57)

diaphragm (53)

external barriers (69)

larynx (55)

listener barriers (71)

pharynx (56)

pitch (56)

resonators (56)

speaker barriers (70)

thought speed (61)

trachea (55)

vocal cords (55)

Motivation

Encourage students to think about the best communicator they have ever known. Ask what made this person so special. What communication tools did he or she use? Ask students to take note of any information the responses might have in common. Then ask whether anyone can give an example of a social ritual.

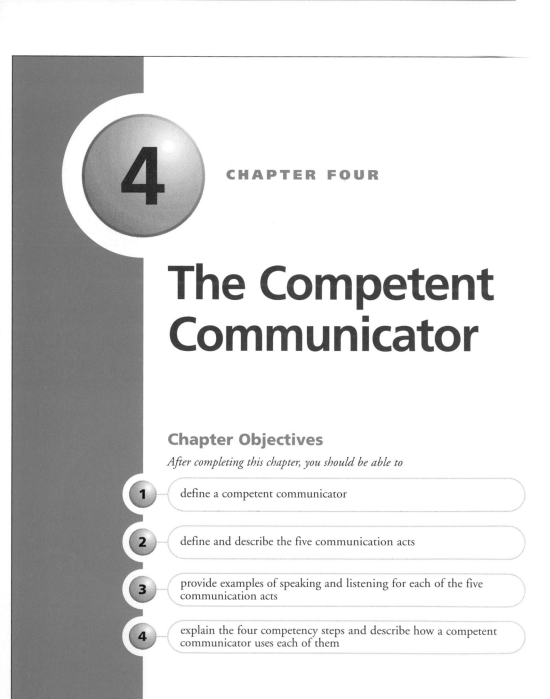

4

CHAPTER FOUR

The Competent Communicator

Chapter Objectives

After completing this chapter, you should be able to

1 — define a competent communicator

2 — define and describe the five communication acts

3 — provide examples of speaking and listening for each of the five communication acts

4 — explain the four competency steps and describe how a competent communicator uses each of them

Teach

"There is no pleasure to me without communication: there is not so much as a sprightly thought come into my mind that it does not grieve me to have produced alone, and that I have no one to tell it to."

MICHEL DE MONTAIGNE
Essays, 1588

Links to Past Learning

Tell students to read the definition of the word *competent* and then write down several areas of life where they have shown competence. Remind students that competence in a variety of different areas is one of the keys to becoming a well-rounded person.

Key Terms

communication acts
communication strategies
competency steps
competent communicator
social rituals
visualize

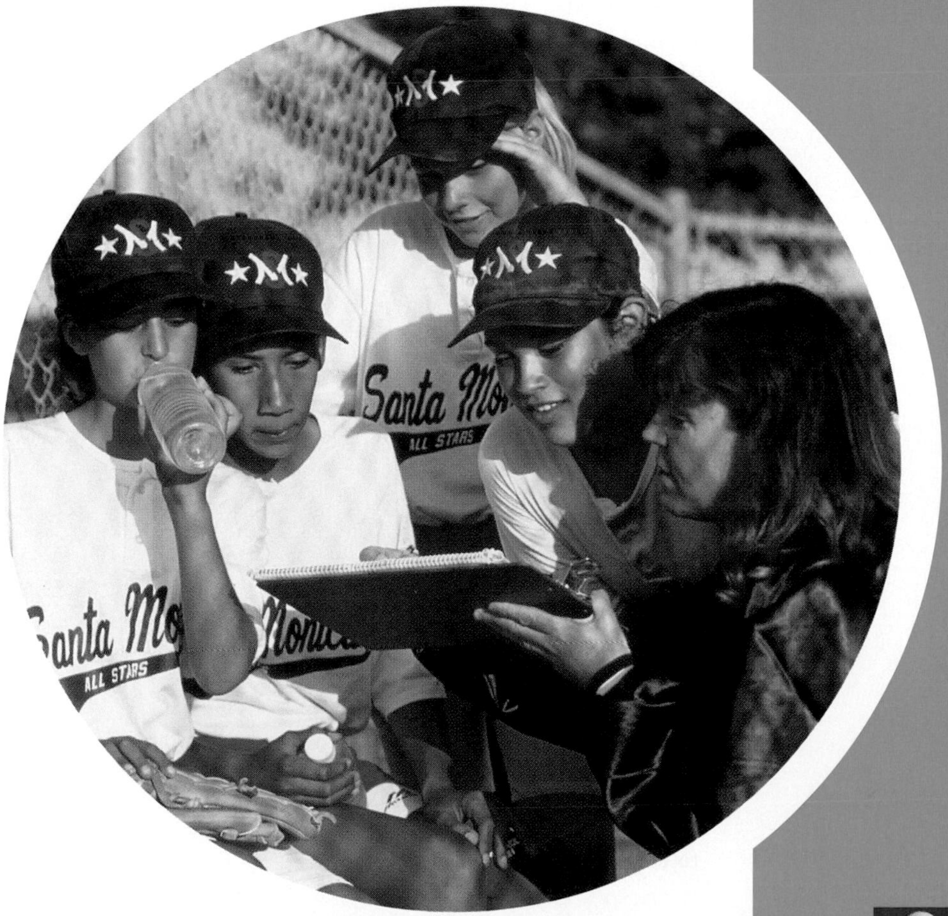

> "Communication is the most complete when it proceeds from the smallest number of words, and indeed of syllables."

JACQUES BARZUN
Simple and Direct

Skill Development

Quick Skill Opportunity

● Tell students that they are going to use the list of communication acts on this page and the next as a reference point for their own experience. Read one of the items aloud, and ask for a volunteer to relate a conversation or an experience that illustrates that particular communication act. Continue on through the list.

Almost everyone can talk and hear, but effective communication takes effort. People who communicate well are called **competent communicators**. The word competent means "well qualified and capable." Competent communicators have knowledge and skills in the area of communication. You recognize these people because they seem to know what to say or do in any situation. They also know how to improve their knowledge and communication skills.

The communication competence model described in this chapter provides the framework for developing communication knowledge and skills. It shows you that good communication is not the result of good luck or natural talent. Rather, it is the result of working to apply this model. The model applies to both speaking and listening.

Competent communicators do not have a secret formula. Rather, they do two things: they develop a number of ways to deal with new communication situations, and they follow certain steps in order to reach their communication goals.

Model

Communication Acts	Competency Steps
+ sharing information	+thinking of strategies
+discussing feelings	+selecting a strategy
+managing persuasion	+acting on the strategy
+following social rituals	+evaluating the strategy's effect
+using imagination	

COMMUNICATION ACTS

If someone asked you "What are the reasons you communicate?" which of these reasons would you give?

to get information I need

to tell someone something

86

Curricular Connection

Science

Some students might like to explain a simple scientific process they have recently learned. Conversely, they might be encouraged to share their confusion about a process they haven't fully understood and to analyze why they haven't.

to find out how to do something

to learn things I didn't know before

to persuade someone to do, or believe, something

to show someone I care about him or her

to make up my mind on a debatable subject

to enjoy myself by talking with others

to test new ideas

All of the above statements express good reasons for listening or speaking to other people. They are **communication acts**.

There are five communication acts that describe the major reasons for communicating. The five acts are (1) sharing information, (2) discussing feelings, (3) managing persuasion, (4) following social rituals, and (5) using imagination.

These communication acts involve you as a speaker and as a listener. For example, as a speaker you may act as a persuader, and as a listener you may try to analyze the persuasive message directed at you. Competent communicators are skilled in using all the communication acts. In this section of the chapter, you will look more carefully at each one.

Sharing Information

As you know, an important part of communication is sending and receiving information. Many people take this communication act for granted. Then they find themselves with problems at home, at their jobs, or in school, because they did not present their information well or listen for information carefully. They may mix up the steps or omit important information when giving directions for things like making chili or describing the location of a movie theatre. Perhaps they do not ask the right questions to find out what they need to know.

Often speakers assume, "I told you. Therefore you should understand." Yet, if the speaker is disorganized in presenting information, the listener may not get the right message. If the

87

> 66Whatever you do, do it to the purpose; do it thoroughly, not superficially. Go to the bottom of things. Anything half done, or half known, is, in my mind, neither done nor known at all. Nay, worse, for it often misleads.99
>
> LORD CHESTERFIELD

Critical Thinking

Organizing

▲ You may wish to have students create flow charts or process diagrams illustrating a simple process such as how to prepare popcorn, play dominoes, set a VCR to record two programs on successive days, or plant a tree.

Competent communicators try to present information in an organized fashion.

speaker uses words the listener cannot understand, the meaning is not conveyed. Competent communicators organize their information and choose their words very carefully to help their listeners get the main points.

In so many areas of your life, you need to share information. Incorrect or unclear information can result in frustration or serious confusion. You know how frustrating it is to get the wrong order in a restaurant or to wait outside the wrong store for a friend.

You probably experience many little communication breakdowns each week because of careless speaking or listening. Communicating to share information serves as the basis for all speaking and listening. Unless you send a message accurately, you cannot get your point across, and you cannot truly understand another person's ideas.

Skill Development
Feedback

▼ Have students work in pairs. One student gives verbal directions on how to get from one location to another. The other person creates a map according to the verbal directions. Encourage the students who are drawing maps to ask for clarification any time their partners' directions are unclear.

APPLY

Read the following short example in which the same ideas are presented in two different ways.

Imagine that you are a student in a first-aid course. Someone is explaining how to help a choking victim by using the Heimlich maneuver. Decide which explanation you would prefer to follow if you had to save a life.

A

If you have a friend who is choking, you can help him. You have to get behind him and put your arm around him. It doesn't matter if you are taller or shorter than he is. Then make a fist and push the fist inward under the ribs. Use the fist thumb side in, and be sure to push upward also. Keep doing this until he stops choking.

B

If you have a friend who is choking, you can help the person by following some simple steps. I will now describe what to do if the victim is standing up. First, get behind the victim and place your arm around the victim's waist. Second, make a fist with that hand and place it, thumb side in, below the bottom of the victim's ribs and just above the navel. Third, grasp your fist with your other hand and press inward with a quick upward motion. Fourth, keep repeating this movement several times until the object comes out of the victim's mouth.

Although both explanations contain similar information, explanation B is clearer. It presents the information in steps and includes all important information, such as where to put your arm around the victim. Explanation A is unclear, disorganized, and omits important information.

Skill Development

Media Literacy

● Ask students to comment on the use of emotional content in television news shows or documentary drama such as court TV. Encourage them to think about the questions that newscasters ask of disaster victims, family members of murder or kidnap victims, and so on. Do they ask about feelings? Ask: Why do people agree to be interviewed on television? How does the questioning style affect those being questioned? How do the interviewees' reactions affect the viewing public?

INTERACT

Prepare a set of verbal directions telling how to do a task, how to get to a certain location, or how to prepare something. You might consider examples such as how to perform a dance step, how to get to the sports arena, and how to make a peanut butter sandwich. Present the directions to the class. Check how well your classmates listened to the directions by asking them to repeat what you said or perform the action. Note any problems that arise and try to see if the problem lies with the directions you gave.

Read the following directions, and anticipate how someone might have trouble with them.

> To get to Gene's go down Sheridan Road until you pass the big chapel and then make a right. Follow that street for about six stop signs and you should be at Crawford. There's a gyros place on the corner. Go past the gyros sign, turn left, and immediately turn into the alley. This will lead you to a small field where you can leave the car. Gene's is the house with all the flowers on the back porch.

Depending on your familiarity with the area, you might have an easy or a difficult time getting to Gene's.

Discussing Feelings

Discussing feelings involves personal effort and risk for both speaker and listener. Talking about feelings requires you to reveal information about yourself. When you share your feelings with a friend, you might gain a stronger friendship, or your friend might try to change the subject or avoid you. Often people become uncomfortable and do not know how to respond when a conversation moves into a discussion of feelings. Yet sometimes a person who is talking about his or her feelings does not need a response but just needs someone to listen.

Most people are not used to saying "I feel. . . ." They may have learned to talk about ideas and to keep feelings to themselves. Even many adults cannot communicate that they are proud, happy, sad,

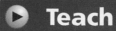

Multicultural Learning

Do girls discuss feelings more than boys do? Ask for some comments on this. Then ask how often films include dialogue between men discussing feelings. What can students conclude from their answers?

Links to Past Learning

Ask students to recall the four kinds of listening they learned about in the previous chapter. Which kind is involved in listening to someone express feelings? (empathic)

A person who wants to talk about feelings needs a listener who will not try to change the subject.

angry, or disappointed because they have learned to control their emotions and cannot talk about them. When asked "How do you feel about the accident?" a person might answer, "I think it is terrible" or "I feel that we need to take a tougher stand on drinking and driving." These are not really statements of feeling, since a feeling has not been expressed. A person who is comfortable talking about feelings might say, "I feel angry" or "I feel sad."

The following journal entry shows how hard it is to communicate feelings when a person does not try to respond.

91

Critical Thinking

Analyzing

Ask students to comment on whether they think there could be a connection between violence in our society and people not discussing their feelings. If there is a link between the two, how might that link be broken?

JOURNAL ENTRY

When I feel that I have hurt my dad's feelings and I want to say I'm sorry, he just sits there in silence. He won't tell me what he's feeling. That gets me mad, and by this time I don't care if he is hurt anymore.

APPLY

Complete the following sentences for yourself and see how easily you can connect a feeling with an event.

I feel excited when. . . .

I feel happy when. . . .

I feel embarrassed when. . . .

I feel frustrated when. . . .

I feel angry when. . . .

I feel scared when. . . .

I feel disappointed when. . . .

I feel jealous when. . . .

I feel silly when. . . .

Think about how you respond when someone else talks about feeling happy, sad, angry, or frightened. Do you let the person talk, or do you try to change the topic? Some listeners who get uncomfortable say, "Oh, you don't really feel that way" or "You shouldn't feel like that." These kinds of responses do not allow the speaker to talk freely. Other listeners take over the conversation by immediately responding with their own feelings instead of letting the other person speak. Competent communicators are able to talk about their feelings and to listen to other people's feelings.

Substitute Teacher Tip

Ask students whether they have tried to persuade anyone to do something in the last 24 hours and if so, to tell what it was.

Managing Persuasion

In our society it is not enough to exchange information or to share feelings. You must be able to manage persuasive messages. There are times when you need to listen carefully to the persuasive messages you receive. There are times when you need to persuade others. One student listed the following as examples of her own use of persuasion:

I try to persuade my
brother or sister to drive me places.

friends to go to a certain movie.

teacher to let me turn a paper in late.

best friend to visit my dad and stepmother with me.

uncle to take us camping.

coach to let me go to Saturday's meet.

parents to increase my allowance.

brother to go bicycle riding with me.

Persuasive messages are a part of everyday life. You need to be able to present information persuasively, to argue, and to come to agreement with other people. You may wish to change another person's beliefs or actions. For example, you may want to talk a friend into quitting smoking or persuade him or her not to shoplift or skip school anymore. You also need to evaluate persuasive messages, such as deciding whether to loan a friend money or your favorite CD.

To become a competent communicator, it is very important to analyze persuasive messages directed at you so that you can make careful judgments about how to respond. You may need to question or argue with the speaker. Analyzing the message requires thinking about it, sorting out points, and looking for both good ideas and problems. The competent communicator understands the power of persuasive messages.

Critical Thinking
Synthesizing

● Encourage students to synthesize the chapter so far. Ask them to choose one of the situations from the list of communication acts on pages 86 and 87. Tell them that they will use what they have learned about sharing information and discussing feelings to role-play a scene that requires persuasion. Students could perform their role-plays in front of the class and receive feedback on things they did well and areas where they may need improvement.

93

Skill Development

Media Literacy

Ask students to watch their usual television programs for one hour and to write down the number of times that an advertisement tries to persuade them to buy something. Ask them to record each time and tell what the product was. If money were no object, could they be persuaded to buy any of the things advertised? Why or why not?

Persuasive messages are intended to influence beliefs, attitudes, and behavior.

OBSERVE

Think of five kinds of persuasive situations that you have observed or experienced in the last week. Did a fast-food sales-person try to persuade you to buy one more item? Did your sister offer to do your homework for a week if you would lend her your music for a party? Were you persuaded to buy a product or make a decision? Why or why not? Did you try to talk someone into driving you somewhere? Discuss your situations in class. How might a competent communicator act in these situations?

Following Social Rituals

Each culture or society has its own **social rituals**, or rules for interaction. There are rituals for greetings, for saying good-bye, for small talk, and for telling secrets. There are also rules for talking. For example, in a conversation you should not do all of the talking or stand very close to the other person. Neither should you talk or listen with your eyes staring away from the person. You should look at the person with whom you are communicating.

People follow many informal rituals every day. Your mother may have a certain way of waking you up. You and a friend may have a secret handshake or code words you use to communicate. If you play a team sport, your teammates may use rituals to get each other mentally prepared for a game. If you are in a performing group, you may have rituals of support before the performance begins.

Some rituals for communicating apply only to certain settings. In a classroom, students usually raise their hands when they wish to talk. One student does not answer all the questions. The teacher usually talks to start and to end the class. Very personal information is discussed with the teacher in a one-to-one situation. These are only a few of the classroom rituals. You can probably list many others.

In a store, customers can ask questions about a product but not personal questions of the salesperson. It is unacceptable for salespeople to shout at or express anger to customers. Both customers and salespeople are expected to say "Thank you" when the sale is completed.

Different cultures have different social rituals. Americans tend to expect listeners to maintain eye contact or look at them most of the time. They also expect listeners to respond by nodding, smiling, frowning, or by other similar means. These signals show that the listener is thinking about what is being said. In other cultures, good listeners do not look at the speaker's eyes; instead, they look down as a sign of respect. Their faces may not show much emotion because it is not expected. In some cultures people stand almost nose to nose when conversing or bow when

Cooperative Learning

Tell students that many social rituals stem from a need to create order and to make life more pleasant. Have students work in small groups to analyze the social needs that brought about rituals such as raising your hand in class to ask or answer a question, or various table manners such as asking to have something passed instead of reaching for it, not talking with one's mouth full, and not leaving the table until all have finished eating. Encourage students to come up with other examples of social rituals and to discuss their possible beginnings and purposes.

95

❝There is always a best way of doing everything, if it be to boil an egg. Manners are the happy ways of doing things.**❞**

RALPH WALDO EMERSON
The Conduct of Life

Multicultural Learning

Social customs differ around the world. For example, in Japanese homes and even in some restaurants, one removes one's shoes upon entering and changes to slippers. If there are students from other countries in your class, ask them to mention and/or demonstrate a social custom in their home country that is not observed in the United States or Canada, or one that *is* observed in the United States and Canada and that they find different or odd.

greeting another person. People who use the social rituals they learned in one culture may find these rituals unacceptable in another culture.

Although most people learn their society's rituals at home and in school, some people never do learn them. When a person acts differently from the rest of the group, other people may make fun of him or her. Often the student who stands too close to others, shouts out in class, constantly interrupts, or discusses very personal information in public gets teased or avoided. If that person really understood the unspoken social rules, he or she might choose to stop breaking them.

APPLY

Think about the following communication rituals and decide how you would explain them to a person unfamiliar with them:

introducing a stranger

asking to talk in class

ending a friendly conversation

telephoning to talk to a friend

asking for the time of day

bidding in an auction

asking someone to dance

leaving a friend's party

Formal social rituals in a society are highly predictable. They are repeated over and over again in the same way. When you recite the Pledge of Allegiance or when you recite familiar prayers during a religious service, you are taking part in a formal social ritual. Groups that use parliamentary procedures to run their meetings are participating in a formal social ritual. What other formal social rituals can you think of?

Multicultural Learning

Daily newspapers often publish photographs of diplomats, heads of state, and other dignitaries greeting each other. Appoint a small group of students to bring in such examples from five issues of a daily paper or from a weekly newsmagazine.

In every society, people are expected to act in certain ways and to avoid other actions. Competent communicators understand the social rituals and usually follow them. If they do not follow a ritual, it is because they choose to be different. Competent communicators are alert to new rituals and know when to follow them. Although engaging in social rituals may not appear to be the most critical area of speaking or listening, the person who is effective in social rituals may develop relationships that lead to more important conversations. If a communication breaks all the social norms, others may avoid the person or cut their interactions short. In such cases more meaningful conversations may not develop.

Saying "hello" and "good-bye" involves certain social rituals and nonverbal communication.

OBSERVE

Choose a social ritual and observe some people engaging in it. Predict ahead of time the communication you expect to see. After watching the ritual, describe in detail two or three examples of predictable communication. Also, describe any communication you found surprising or inappropriate.

> 66 Let no one who wishes to receive agreeable impressions of American manners, commence their travels in a Mississippi steamboat. 99
>
> **FRANCES TROLLOPE**
> *Domestic Manners of the Americans*
> *(1832)*

Skill Development
Media Literacy

Emily Post (1872–1960) was the first authority on manners to write for the ordinary person instead of the socially elite reader, which she did in a syndicated newspaper column. A recent successor, Miss Manners (also known as Judith Martin), writes a similar newspaper column today. Her daily column may also be found on the *Washington Post* Web site.

> 66 You mentioned your name, as if I should recognize it, but I assure you that, beyond the obvious facts that you are a bachelor, a solicitor, a Freemason, and an asthmatic, I know nothing whatever about you. 99

> **SIR ARTHUR CONAN DOYLE**
> *The Memoirs of Sherlock Holmes*
> ("The Norwood Builder")

Beyond the Classroom

Protocol is a form of etiquette observed in diplomatic, military, governmental, and court circles. For example, there are protocol rules for how people are to be seated at a formal dinner according to rank, who precedes whom into a room, and so on. Invite someone from the military or government to talk to the class about protocol.

🍎 Substitute Teacher Tip

Have students practice making formal introductions with partners. Remind them to take notice of social rituals such as shaking hands, saying full names, mentioning the name of a girl or woman first, and using language appropriate for the situation. When students have perfected their greetings and introductions, you may wish to have them demonstrate for the class. These introductions might be audiotaped or videotaped.

Making and Acknowledging Introductions Social rituals involve making formal introductions. Many people avoid this ritual because they are afraid they do not know the correct way to introduce someone. If you remember some simple rules when introducing someone, then you can use these rules for all introductions.

Remember to speak clearly. If you have an interesting remark about the person you are introducing, include that in the introduction since it may help the people find something to talk about. The key to making formal introductions is to remember age, gender, and position.

Rule 1: Always mention the name of the oldest person first, then the name of the person you are introducing. Then introduce the youngest person to the oldest.

Example: "Mrs. Van Eyck, this is my sister, Natalie. Natalie, this is my algebra teacher, Mrs. Van Eyck."

You could then add: "Mrs. Van Eyck is the coach of the soccer team. Natalie will be in your math class next year and hopes to be on the team. She has played since kindergarten."

Rule 2: Mention the name of a woman or girl first.

Example: "Mrs. Coleman, I'd like you to meet my dad, Edward McKinney. Dad, this is my English teacher, Mrs. Coleman."

or: "Katy, I'd like you to meet my brother, Thomas Gordon. Thomas, this is my good friend, Katy Gavin."

Rule 3: Mention the name of the person who has a higher position of authority first.

Example: "Dr. DiCarlo, this is Ms. Knight our new student teacher. Ms. Knight, this is our principal, Dr. DiCarlo."

Formal introductions should be handled with politeness. Older people should be addressed by their title, and not by their first name. In a social situation, women initiate the handshake, if they choose to shake hands. (They are not required to do so.) In a business

Motivation

Write this on the chalkboard: "You never get a second chance to make a first impression." Discuss the significance of this adage as it regards making and acknowledging introductions. Remind students that the way a person comes across within the first few minutes of meeting someone new creates the foundation for future communication between them.

An introduction is one way of helping people to become acquainted.

Limited English Proficiency

Students could talk about how it feels to be the new person in a group. They could address the various ways in which a good introduction might make a new person feel more comfortable.

situation, the person with the higher or senior position extends the hand first. Introductions can be awkward, but, with confidence and a friendly attitude, you can master this social ritual.

> **REMEMBER:**
> **GUIDELINES FOR INTRODUCTIONS**
>
> 1. Mention first the name of the oldest person. Introduce the youngest person to the oldest person.
>
> 2. Mention first the name of the woman or the girl.
>
> 3. Mention first the name of the person who has a higher position of authority.

Making and Receiving Telephone Calls One ritual that is important in our interpersonal skills is making and receiving telephone calls. Many times, people do not know the person to whom they are talking on the phone. Therefore, impressions depend entirely upon the voice and manners of the person speaking. There are several key things you should remember for courteous and effective phone conversation.

Amazing Fact!

Alexander Graham Bell's telephone was patented and displayed in Philadelphia in 1876 at the Centennial Exposition. Just two years later, the first telephone was installed in the White House. By the early 20th century, Bell's company was the largest in the United States.

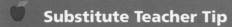

Substitute Teacher Tip

Work with students to create a list of jobs that require employees to have strong telephone skills. To get students started, mention telemarketers, travel agents, and auditorium box-office personnel. Encourage students to think of as many different jobs as possible.

Skill Development

On the Job

● Ask students who work as baby-sitters or volunteers to tell the class about any telephone duties they have on the job.

Making Personal Calls

1. Call at a convenient time. Try to avoid mealtimes and late-night calls.

2. Identify yourself to the person who answers the phone, and then ask for the person you are calling.

   Example: "Hello, Mrs. Wilkinson, this is Jamie Hall. May I speak to Kara?"

3. Keep the conversation short and try to get to the reason for calling. If it is a social call, chat for a brief time and then end the conversation. Remember that there are others who may need to use the phone.

4. If details are given, you may wish to repeat these details or have the receiver recite the information back to you to make sure all information is clearly understood.

5. End the conversation. Remember, if you made the call, it is generally up to you to end the call.

When talking on a pay phone, you should try to keep your conversation brief if someone is waiting.

100

Receiving Personal Calls

1. When receiving a call, answer quickly and pleasantly. "Hello" is a pleasant way to answer the phone. "Yes," "What," and "Yeah" are generally considered poor manners.

2. Listen attentively and avoid interrupting or being impatient. If you cannot talk at that time, ask the caller if you can return the call at a later time. Example: "I am sorry, but we just sat down for dinner. May I call you back in a half hour?"

3. Speak clearly and use verbal responses such as "yes," "no," or "I understand." Grunts or phrases such as "uh-huh" are considered impolite.

4. If the caller wants to speak to someone who is either not home or is unable to come to the phone, ask the caller if he or she would like to call back or leave a message. It is discourteous to say "Who is this?" or "What do you want?" It is courteous to say "May I take a message or say who called?"

5. Thank the person for calling.

Making Business Calls

If you have to make a business call or formal call, you need to make a good impression. Keep the conversation short, to the point, and courteous.

1. Identify yourself and state your business. If you are trying to raise money or arrange for an interview, state the purpose clearly.

2. Have all information at hand so that you can refer to your notes if needed.

3. Be brief and polite.

4. If you have a complaint, be specific with your facts and reasons. Do not be impatient or irritable. If you do not receive satisfaction, ask to speak to a supervisor and then begin again.

5. End with a thank you or some statement of appreciation for the person's time.

Cooperative Learning

▼ Have students work in pairs to role-play various telephone situations. For example, one person could role-play a restaurant host while the other person role-plays a customer making a reservation. Ask students to suggest various situations, and after students have performed their role-plays in front of the class, solicit audience feedback.

Curricular Connection
Dramatic Arts

● Bring in a copy of Viola Spolin's book *Improvisation for the Theater,* and select from it a game students can play as a group. There are many different games and exercises that will allow students to use their imaginations in creative—and communicative—ways.

Learning Styles
Audio Learning

● Play a tape of a storyteller telling a familiar fairy tale or fable. One source is an Ella Jenkins recording titled *Holiday Times,* which offers songs, chants, rhymes, and stories related to Chinese New Year, Christmas, Hanukkah, and Kwanza. (Folkways SF 45041). After students have listened, ask them to analyze how Jenkins successfully creates an imaginary situation.

Leaving a Voice Mail Message

1. Identify yourself and your intended listener first.

2. Be brief, and make your point clear.

3. Indicate what response you wish such as "Call me today at 555-4783" or "You don't need to call back unless you need a ride."

Remember, telephone interactions are important to communication. Be polite, brief, and organized.

Using Imagination

A very important area of communication involves using your imagination. One way of creating through imagination is through dramatic situations. Older brothers and sisters may tell stories to a toddler. Actors and actresses create roles in plays by using their imaginations. When you role-play in a historical debate, you are creating an imaginary situation. The person who describes a scary situation communicates the fear to the listeners. You have probably entertained your friends by telling humorous tales of your family vacations. Or you may have entertained your family by telling stories about funny events in school. You may also have read poetry at a school assembly or recited the words of a famous speaker in a camp program.

As a listener you often enjoy speakers using their imaginations. Examples might include listening to your father telling his corny jokes, your grandmother telling her stories of the old country, or your friends playing verbal games. You might also listen to actors performing in your favorite TV show, friends reciting their own poetry, or the community theatre putting on a production. Although you need the same skills for any other listening situation, you may be more relaxed if you are listening for enjoyment.

Skill Development
Quick Skill Opportunity

Tell students that, just like Tiffany Black, they probably change their language to be formal or informal depending on the speaking situation. Have students discuss the following questions. In what settings do you use formal language? In what settings are you comfortable using informal language? How do you adjust your language and your nonverbal messages for the setting? Why is it important for speakers to use language that is appropriate to the setting and the audience? Encourage students to share their answers and experiences with the class.

Skill Development
Vocabulary

Be sure students know what NAACP (line 6) stands for and what its purpose is.

SPEAKING OF . . .

TIFFANY BLACK

This young New Jersey woman must adapt to many different audiences—student groups, parent organizations, and community officials—as she gives presentations on a range of topics. As vice-president of SAVVY (Students Against Violence and Victimization of Youth), Tiffany organizes performances and workshops to raise awareness of violence and to teach ways to deal with it. As the secretary of the Bergen Council NAACP Youth Council, she deals with many community members, both in person and on the phone. In addition, Tiffany is captain of the cheerleading squad, a position that requires her to create cheers, run practices, oversee the group at games, and serve as a communication link among the cheerleaders, coaches, parents, and the administration.

One of Tiffany's strengths is her ability to tailor messages to make them appropriate to her different listeners. When Tiffany describes adapting her vocabulary and nonverbal messages to each group, she says, "If I'm talking to my principal I won't dress up, but I will be sure my clothing is neat and clean . . . I will make a lot of eye contact and not slouch, but sit or stand confidently." When talking to peers, she may use slang expressions such as "You're playin' yourself," which means "You are allowing, doing, or saying things that you know aren't right" or "I'll be straight," which means "I'll be OK." When talking with parents' groups, however, she avoids slang and tries to use more sophisticated language. If she is talking with sports groups, she uses the technical terms of basketball or football, the teams for which she cheers.

Tiffany is proud of her communication skills and her ability to select the most appropriate message for a particular listener or audience. This skill will serve her well in any career that involves active contact with people. For example, her communication skills would serve her very effectively in a business, such as sports marketing; in medicine, such as a liaison between patients and the hospital; or in community relations.

Cooperative Learning

▼ Encourage students to brainstorm about life in the 21st century. Appoint one student to take notes on the brainstorming session. Remind students that the object of brainstorming is to hear everyone's ideas, even those that do not sound practical. At the end of ten minutes, stop the session and have the person taking notes read back all the ideas.

Let students discuss which ideas have the most merit.

Critical Thinking

Evaluating

● Encourage students to keep a communication journal for two or three days. They could write about every communication act they remember performing for each day. Then they could tell which category each communication act falls into. Students should be able to come up with at least ten communication acts per day.

> ### APPLY
>
> When do you find yourself in situations involving dramatic imagination? Do you enjoy telling jokes or stories? Do you like to do magic or watch TV comedians? Add to the list of examples that follow:
>
> doing puppet shows
>
> reading for the blind
>
> telling a scary story to campers
>
> describing a rock concert
>
> joking with friends
>
> talking about a TV show
>
> imitating your favorite comic

Imaginative communication occurs in many other situations besides storytelling or drama. When you and a friend are working together to solve a problem, creative communication occurs. You may suggest one idea, and your friend may use your idea to create a second, which then leads to a third idea. In this way you may be feeding each other's imaginations. When you make predictions, you are using your imagination too. You can make predictions about transportation in the year 2020, or about the clothes of the future. Good listeners like to hear how other people put ideas together. It stimulates their thinking.

Imagination allows you to entertain, to create new worlds, and to predict. It is a special part of your communication abilities. Competent communicators value their own imaginative ability and that of other persons.

The five communication acts are important because effective speakers and listeners are skilled at each of them. In the following section you will see how you can develop your communication competence by following four key steps.

Telling a story requires using imagination.

Limited English Proficiency

Make sure that these students understand that a strategy is a plan or method devised to achieve a goal.

COMPETENCY STEPS

Competent communicators work to gain knowledge and skills to become effective at communicating. They grow in competence through meeting other people, dealing with new situations, and watching others interact. Over time, they develop plans of action for dealing with various situations. Competent communicators follow four specific **competency steps**:

1. Thinking of strategies

2. Selecting a strategy

3. Acting on the strategy

4. Evaluating the strategy's effect

Thinking of Strategies

A competent communicator has various communication strategies that can be applied to one situation. **Communication strategies** are the verbal and nonverbal messages created to reach a specific goal.

105

Critical Thinking

Evaluating

● Ask students to discuss which strategies listed in the Apply section would be the most and least effective.

Critical Thinking

Organizing

● Have students create web diagrams to show various strategies they could use to reach a long-term goal. You could assign a goal such as getting into college or finding the ideal job or career, or students might enjoy coming up with their own long-term goals.

The older you get, the more ways you have to cope with communication difficulties. Each year you have learned new strategies for handling certain events or problems. For example, when you were a three-year-old and your parents told you it was bedtime, what did you do? You may have cried, begged for a nighttime story, or asked for a drink of water. By the time you were ten, you had added more strategies. You may have reasoned with your parents, "I don't have to get up early tomorrow." You may have compared yourself to your friend, saying "J. P. doesn't even have a regular bedtime." You may even have tried persuasive strategies, arguing, "I have to study for a history test. You don't want me to flunk, do you?"

By now you have developed even more strategies, although you probably don't disagree about bedtime as frequently. Your strategies now may involve extending your curfew.

APPLY

To gain a later curfew, which of the following strategies have you used?

1. I plead for an extra half hour.
2. I inform my parent(s) I'm too old for this type of curfew.
3. I explain that my friend's parents do not give her or him a curfew.
4. I try to convince my parent(s) that this is a very special occasion.
5. I volunteer to help around the house tomorrow.
6. I promise I will never ask for a curfew change again.
7. I threaten to go live with my best friend's family.
8. I remind my parent(s) how responsible I have been in the past.
9. I stop speaking to my parent(s).
10. I slam doors and sulk around the house.

Did the strategies you used leave both you and your parent(s) satisfied?

Most teenagers have more than one strategy for getting the keys to the car.

▲ Ask students to think about the last time they consciously formulated a strategy to achieve something such as mastering a piece on the piano, getting in shape, overcoming shyness, or becoming better at playing chess. Encourage them to give brief oral explanations of the problem or situation and the strategy they used to handle it.

Strategies do not apply just to your relationships with adults. You can be a more effective communicator with your friends if you have a number of different ways of handling difficult situations. For example, if you have a friend who gets laughs by making fun of you, how could you handle it? You could ignore the situation and hope it will go away. What else could you do if that doesn't work? You might try the silent treatment, but your friend might not understand your silence. You might say, "Quit making fun of me in front of other people. I don't think it's funny." Or you might say, "It hurts my feelings when you make fun of me. I wish you would stop it." You might consider threatening a loss of your friendship: "If you don't stop making fun of me I'm going to stop being your friend." Finally, you might consider how to tease your friend back and hope that this will solve the problem.

The competent communicator thinks up a number of possible ways to deal with a situation. The greater the number of strategies, the more choice there is in dealing with a problem.

107

Curricular Connection

Language Arts

▲ Interested students could create a script for the discussion between the mother and the son or daughter in the curfew example. Their scripts should designate the two characters and the time and place setting. Script writers could choose two classmates to perform the work.

Critical Thinking

Analyzing

● Write the Chesterfield quote on page 88 on the chalkboard and discuss with students how this relates to the idea of selecting and acting upon strategies. Encourage students to discuss the importance of follow-through in the strategic process.

Selecting A Strategy

Once you have thought of a few ways to handle a problem, consider the specifics of that problem situation. Think about the who, what, where, and when:

Who—When considering "who," you need to think about what you know about the person. You also need to think about your past relationship and possible future relationship with this person.

What—When considering "what," you need to think about the importance of the problem to you and to the other person and how much each of you knows about the situation.

Where—When considering "where," you need to think about how the place or setting will affect your discussion of the problem situation.

When—When considering "when," you need to think about whether this is a good time to discuss the topic.

All these add up to how you act or use the best strategy for a person, topic, place, and time.

Now look at how these factors might affect a curfew discussion between you and your mother after you have moved to a new city. The situation is that you want to come home one hour later than your usual curfew from a trip to the amusement park.

The "who" is your mother. You know the following about her: She often gives you rules similar to those of your friends; she is not acquainted with many adults in this neighborhood; she has been flexible about curfew for special occasions.

The "what" is a trip to the amusement park. It's not a once-in-a-lifetime experience, but it's not an everyday event either. This amusement park is in a safe area, and it can be reached by a train that runs into the evening.

The "where" and "when" are not fixed, and you have control over them. For example, you might be able to talk in the car on a weekend or in the kitchen after dinner. You would need to consider whether you want to be alone with your mother or in a group of your friends. You might also consider when your mother is likely to be in a good mood.

Cooperative Learning

Additional Interact situations might include these:

1. (Between classes) Asking a teacher to explain his comments on your English paper.

2. (At home before dinner) Asking your mother to iron a shirt.

3. (At the video store) Telling a clerk that you lost a tape.

Now that you have thought about the who, what, where, and when, you are ready to make a plan. Because your mother likes to know what other parents do, you might make the comparison. "Janella's and Sally's parents let them stay out an hour later than I'm allowed. You can call and check this." Because you know she can be flexible about special events, you could call this a special trip. You might consider briefly telling her that you will move in with a friend's family if she doesn't let you do what you want. But you then may decide that your mother will find this funny rather than realistic. Of course, you could promise never to ask for a curfew change again, but that may also be unrealistic.

You may decide that "where" should be the car and "when" should be a time you are alone together and your mother is cheerful, probably in the morning.

INTERACT

Examine the following situations and think about the who, what, when, and where that would affect the communication strategies you choose to use. Discuss these in a group of four.

1. (Walking home after school)
Responding to a stranger who wants you to search for a lost dog

2. (In the hall between classes)
Asking a friend to lend you five dollars

3. (At the day care center)
Telling a parent that his child hits some of the other children

4. (In school cafeteria line)
Finding out why a friend has not talked to you for a week

5. (As bell rings for class)
Explaining to a teacher why your homework is late

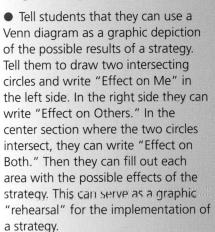

Critical Thinking
Organizing

● Tell students that they can use a Venn diagram as a graphic depiction of the possible results of a strategy. Tell them to draw two intersecting circles and write "Effect on Me" in the left side. In the right side they can write "Effect on Others." In the center section where the two circles intersect, they can write "Effect on Both." Then they can fill out each area with the possible effects of the strategy. This can serve as a graphic "rehearsal" for the implementation of a strategy.

109

Skill Development

Research

● Ask if any of your students have ever heard of creative visualization. Explain that some people use this technique to help themselves accomplish goals, understand new material, and even battle major illness. Some students might be interested in doing research to find out more.

When developing a communication strategy, think about the best setting for your conversation.

Remember that after you consider the circumstances—the people involved, the topic, and any other important facts—you will select a specific strategy from those you thought about.

Acting on the Strategy

Do you ever know exactly what you should say or do but fail to go ahead and say or do it? Most people find they do not carry out all their plans. They may think of some good strategies and even select the one they consider the best. And then they stop.

Selecting the strategy doesn't do much good until you act on it. It is one thing to plan to tell a friend that he or she hurt your feelings and another to actually say, "You hurt my feelings" or "I want you to stop teasing me."

Many Olympic champions report that they **visualize**, or picture in their minds, every single move before actually performing. Swimmers see every stroke in their minds and imagine a perfect, winning race. Basketball players visualize perfect foul shots, experiencing each muscle movement in their minds. Just as athletes use visualization to practice before competitions, competent communicators often rehearse in their minds what they will say.

110

Beyond the Classroom

Students might enjoy inviting a member of the school swimming or diving team to talk about how he or she uses the technique of visualization to help perfect his or her execution. Students can then discuss how to apply this technique to various communication situations.

APPLY

Which of the following actions have you planned to do but failed to carry out?

volunteer in class

ask a sales clerk for more information

tell your mother or father how wonderful she or he is

compliment a friend for something well done

thank a teacher for a good term

apologize for talking badly about someone

ask a teacher for extra help

invite a new student to join your lunch group

Competent communicators learn to follow through with their plans.

Many athletes visualize performing every move perfectly before competing.

111

Motivation

Some students might like to role-play one of the situations under Apply on page 111. For example, complimenting a friend for something done well or inviting a new student to join the lunch group.

For example, you can rehearse what you will say to someone else and try to imagine how the other person will respond. Many fine public speakers visualize delivering their whole speech, over and over again, imagining each word and gesture. Many debaters plan each response they will give to an opponent's argument. Visualization is a kind of mental rehearsal.

Active rehearsal occurs when you role-play a situation or practice a speech out loud. You and a friend may practice ways to apologize for forgetting to invite a friend to a party. You may practice your sales pitch for selling candy bars to raise money for the school trip. The speaker who practices the persuasive speech out loud is rehearsing. But until the speaker talks to the audience, it is only planning.

At some point you must take the final step and act on the plans. Until you talk to your mother about curfew or apologize to your friend, it's all imagination and rehearsal. Acting on the strategy means speaking and listening in the real situation—when it counts. Remember that nothing will happen unless you act on the strategy.

OBSERVE

Record two experiences of hearing people discuss what they should have said or done. Very often people will say, "I should have told him no," or "I wish I had asked about the price."

Describe two situations in which you or a friend knew what strategy to select but didn't act on it. Describe what kept you or your friend from acting on the strategy.

Evaluating the Strategy's Effect

Now that you have carried out a strategy, can you relax? The answer is no. The final step is to make a judgment—to decide how well the strategy worked. Basically, you have to reach a conclusion. You can think in terms of the following: the effect on you, the effect on others, and the result.

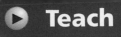

66Mend your speech a little,
Lest you may mar your fortunes.**99**

SHAKESPEARE
King Lear, Act I, Sc. 1

Even though you do not evaluate every word or action, you need to evaluate important communication events. For example, if you had three different strategies for an apology and chose one, did both you and the other person feel good after the apology? If you chose a joke to introduce your speech, did the class find it funny? When you communicate in important situations, you need to look at the effects and the results. Then you can decide if you would repeat the strategy in a similar situation or if you would do something else the next time.

JOURNAL ENTRY

I am always embarrassed when my father calls me by nicknames in front of my friends. They always tease me about it after he leaves. I used to give him a dirty look, but he never seemed to get it. I thought I could get my sister to talk to him about it, I could leave him a note, I could yell at him in front of my friends, or I could talk to him directly. I decided on the last choice. One night when he was alone, I told him some friends were coming over soon and asked him not to call me by my nicknames. He did not really understand until I told him they kept teasing me and I didn't like it. Nicknames are private. He said he would try, and he did. He slips once in a while, but I don't get too mad because he is really trying. This was better than having my sister do it for me.

You need to consider your beliefs about right and wrong when choosing, using, and evaluating a strategy. A competent communicator does not hurt another person on purpose. Sometimes the first strategy does not work well and then you need to try another one. The following advice is a variation on this method. The evaluation step is missing, but it gives you a sense of how these ideas are applied.

Critical Thinking
Evaluating

Ask students to discuss the difference between a hasty "excuse me" or "sorry" from someone who steps on your foot and runs out the door and an apology from a friend who seeks you out to say he regrets a hurtful remark. Is the first instance really an apology?

113

Substitute Teacher Tip

Use the boxed copy about Peer Pressure Reversal to spur a student discussion of peer pressure. Ask whether any students have tried the techniques mentioned in the text (or techniques like them) for avoiding poor decisions related to peer pressure. Encourage students to respond to the text by agreeing or disagreeing with specific points.

Preparing to be a Competent Communicatior

This simple three-step skill called Peer Pressure Reversal* will get you out of tough situations and still let you be part of your peer group.

1. *Check out the scene.* Checking out the scene involves two steps. First, look and listen for anything unusual or strange in the way your friends are talking or behaving. Are they in an off-limits place, or are they trying to bribe you into doing something wrong? Second, ask yourself: "Is this trouble?" If the situation would break a law or get someone in charge mad, you are facing a trouble situation.

2. *Make a good decision.* To make a good decision, you need to think about two things. First, weigh both sides. Your friends will tell you about the positive consequences: you must rely on yourself to consider the negative consequences. The risks involved are usually not worth it. Second, you must make a firm decision so that the pressure won't cause you to act weak. If you take a risk, be prepared to accept the consequences. If you decide against the trouble, you might just convince your friends not to take the risk either.

3. *Act to avoid trouble.* There are many ways to refuse a friend's suggestion including saying no politely and firmly, leaving, or giving a true excuse. You can suggest a better idea and walk toward it and your friend will often follow you! Some people can say "No" in joking ways, such as "I wish I could, but it's my night to walk the goldfish." And if a friend dares you, learn to return the challenge, "Are you scared to do it by yourself?"

When using Peer Pressure Reversal, remember to stay in control, look the person right in the eyes when talking to him or her, and get out of the trouble in 30 seconds or less.

*Scott, Sharon. *Peer Pressure Reversal, How to Say No and Keep Your Friends.* Amherst, MA: Human Resource Development, 1986.

APPLY

As you consider your own communication competence, identify two areas where you wish to improve. Describe carefully in your journal how you act in each of these situations at the present time. Then write a description of what you would say or do if you were very satisfied with your communication. This last description represents your competence goals. Identify some behaviors you will have to exhibit as you try to move from your current situation to your ideal situation. Once a week make an entry in your journal indicating what progress you are making toward your goal.

CHAPTER 4 SUMMARY

This chapter discussed the competent communicator, a person with the knowledge and skills to communicate well. Competent communicators can use their knowledge and skills to (1) share information, (2) discuss feelings, (3) manage persuasion, (4) follow social rituals, and (5) use imagination. To use these communication acts well, competent communicators follow four steps: (1) thinking of strategies, (2) selecting a strategy, (3) acting on the strategy, and (4) evaluating the strategy's effect.

Limited English Proficiency

Students with limited English proficiency might work with a partner to discuss and clarify any potential problems that might arise from the journal writing activity in Apply. You may want to encourage these students to use graphic organizers and other ways of processing and recording information.

115

Answers

Think About It

Student answers will vary. Here are sample answers:

1. A competent communicator is a person with knowledge and skills in the area of communication, someone who always seems to know what to do and say in any situation.

2. (1) Sharing information—sending and receiving information; (2) discussing feelings—revealing emotional or personal information about yourself and receiving such information from others; (3) using persuasion—the ability to present information persuasively and come to agreement with others; (4) following social rituals—participating in standard customs and rules for societal order; (5) using imagination—using techniques for presenting or enjoying dramatic situations, brainstorming, or listening for enjoyment.

3. (1) Thinking of strategies—To effectively handle a problem it is often necessary to think of a variety of possible strategies. (2) Selecting a strategy—After a person has thought over the possible strategies, he or she must choose the most effective one. (3) Acting on the Strategy—Once the strategy has been selected, the person must put it into effect.

CHAPTER REVIEW

Think About It

1. What is a competent communicator?

2. Define and describe the five communication acts.

3. What are the four competency steps used by competent communicators? Give a one- or two-sentence description of each step.

4. When selecting a strategy, what four specifics of the situation do you need to take into consideration? Write a sentence or two explaining each.

Try It Out

1. To help you enhance the imagining function of communication, picture yourself in the following situations and answer the questions.

   You are walking through the woods on a spring day. The sun is shining. What do you see and feel?

   You have done poorly on an exam. Your teacher asks to see you. You open the door to the classroom and walk in. The teacher is sitting at the desk. What happens next? Describe the classroom. How hot is the room? Where do you sit? What does the teacher say? What do you say? How do you feel?

   Your best friend returns home after living in another community for three months. As soon as you see each other, what do you say? How do you feel? How do you act?

2. Interview a classmate about how he or she handled a problem communi-

cation situation. Ask that person to describe what he or she did at each of the competency stages. Then have your classmate interview you while you describe a problem communication situation.

3. Describe two communication rituals you observe as part of your daily life. Describe the setting and the words people speak or the nonverbal messages they send. For example, you could describe how your coach speaks to the team before a game; how you say good-bye to your best friends on the phone; how your club meeting starts each week.

Put It in Writing

1. Giving or getting information is an important communication act. Using the questions below, interview your grandparent or an older member of your community. Write two or three paragraphs describing what you learned from the interview.

   What was the world like when you were growing up? For example, how much did a candy bar cost? What did teenagers do for fun? What were the rules your parents set? What was school like? What world events were occurring? Who was president of the United States?

   If you could live your life over, what would you change? Why?

2. Describe a persuasive communication situation in which you believe you

could have been more effective—for example, a situation in which you tried to persuade a friend to do something, such as lend you CDs or money. Then write a sample dialogue in which you act as a competent communicator and are persuasive.

Speak About It

1. Using the information you gained from interviewing your grandparent or an older member of the commu-

nity, present a short speech to your class in which you share the most interesting piece of information you gained.

2. Go to the library and find information about rituals of other countries. Choose a ritual and describe it to your class. For example, in China and Japan the concept of "face" (respectability) is of vital importance, and codes of behavior to avoid "losing face" are also important.

(4) Once the strategy has been implemented, the person must evaluate the result.

4. (1) The effect on you—Ask yourself how you feel after the strategy has been implemented. (2) The effect on others—How did other people respond to your strategy? (3) The result—What was the overall result of your strategy? (4) The conclusion— Would you use the same strategy the next time?

Quick Check

Ask students to find and define these Key Terms:

communication acts (87)

communication strategies (105)

competency steps (105)

competent communicator (86)

social rituals (95)

visualize (110)

117

Unit 2 Planner

Communication with Self and Others	Time Management				
5 Communication and Yourself (pp. 120–147)	Weeks 3 and 4	●	●	●	●
6 Communication with Others (pp. 148–179)	Weeks 5 and 6	●	●	●	●

Ancillary Resources

Unit Focus

Unit 2 explains self-concept and self-esteem as they affect the communication process, defines interpersonal communication and friendship, and describes communication skills that are necessary in human relationships.

Unit Portfolios

Activities marked with this symbol ▱ are suitable for inclusion in speech portfolios.

Ability Key

▲ average and above-average students

● all students

▼ average and below-average students

Ancillary Resource Key

= *Teacher's Resource Book*

= Workbook

= TRB Worksheets & Evaluation Forms

= TRB Assessment and Testing

Performance Objectives

After completing this unit, students will be able to

1. explain the relationship between self-concept and self-esteem and communication skills

2. list their communication strengths and weaknesses

3. describe ways to improve their self-concept

4. define interpersonal communication

5. describe characteristics, stages, and components of friendships

66The battles that count aren't the ones for gold medals. The struggles within yourself—the invisible, inevitable battles inside all of us—that's where it's at.**99**

JESSE OWENS

UNIT TWO

Communication With Self and Others

2

| Communication and Yourself | 5 |
| Communication with Others | 6 |

Bibliography

Print

Brown, Lyn Mikel and Carol Gilligan. *Meeting at the Crossroads: Women's Psychology and Girls' Development.* New York: Ballantine, 1992.

Cassagne, J. M. *101 Spanish Idioms: Understanding Spanish Language and Culture Through Popular Phrases.* Lincolnwood, Ill.: Passport Books, a division of NTC / Contemporary Publishing Group, 1995.

Dillon, J. T. *Using Discussion in Classrooms.* Philadelphia: Open University Press, 1994.

Measday, Ellen and Lisa F. Knight. *Speak Out! Authentic Communication Activities for the Intermediate & Advanced ESL Student.* Dubuque, Ia.: Kendall-Hunt, 1994.

O'Keefe, Virginia. *Speaking to Think Thinking to Speak.* Portsmouth, N.H.: Heinemann, 1995.

Pipher, Mary. *Reviving Ophelia: Saving the Selves of Adolescent Girls.* New York: Grosset/Putnam, 1994.

Williams, Bard. *The World Wide Web for Teachers.* Foster City, Calif.: IDG Books, 1996.

Web Site

Dave's ESL Cafe
http://www.eslcafe.com

For teachers and students of ESL and EFL.

	Day 1	Day 2	Day 3	Day 4	Day 5
5 Communication & Yourself					
Self-Concept	Self-Concept	Self-Concept	Self-Concept	Communication and Self
Teacher's Resource Book					
Teaching Suggestions	5.1	5.2	5.3	5.4	
Workbook	5.1	5.2	5.3		

Chapter 5 Planner Week 3

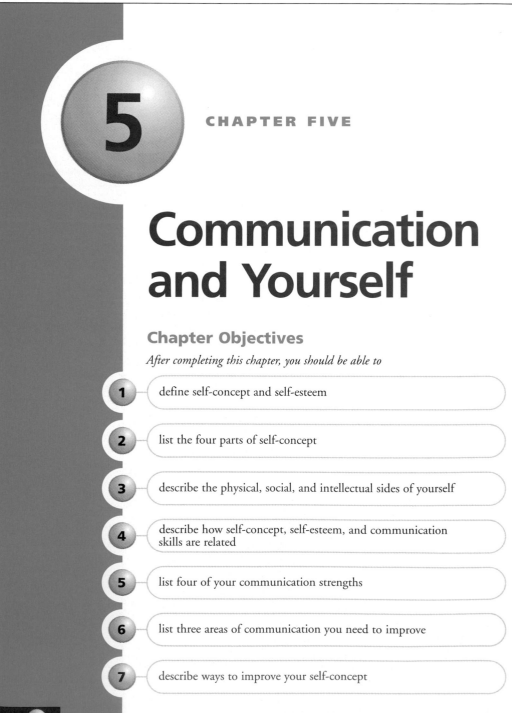

CHAPTER FIVE

Communication and Yourself

Chapter Objectives

After completing this chapter, you should be able to

1. define self-concept and self-esteem

2. list the four parts of self-concept

3. describe the physical, social, and intellectual sides of yourself

4. describe how self-concept, self-esteem, and communication skills are related

5. list four of your communication strengths

6. list three areas of communication you need to improve

7. describe ways to improve your self-concept

	Day 1	Day 2	Day 3	Day 4	Day 5
5 Communication & Yourself					
Improving Self-Concept	Improving Self-Concept	Improving Self-Concept	Improving Self-Concept	Summary & Chapter Review
Teacher's Resource Book					
Teaching Suggestions	5.5	5.6	5.7		
					Worksheets & Eval. Forms 14
					Chapter Test 5
Workbook	5.4	5.5	5.6		

Week 4 — Chapter 5 Planner

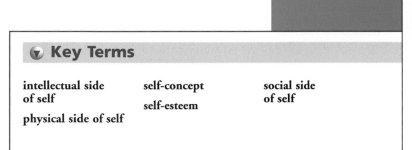

Key Terms

intellectual side of self

physical side of self

self-concept

self-esteem

social side of self

Motivation

Write this on the blackboard: "To think well of others you must first think well of yourself." Ask for volunteers to explain the meaning of this adage and to tell whether they agree. Discuss the importance of a strong self-concept in every area of life, including school, work, and play.

Critical Thinking

Predicting

● Preview the chapter title and Key Words with students. Encourage students to predict what they might learn in this chapter and to think about how the vocabulary words might apply to their daily lives.

121

Links to Past Learning

If students are keeping a journal, ask them to write a paragraph or two about a time in their lives when they felt they did not fit in. Encourage them to describe what made them feel the way they did. Ask, "Were your feelings based on the way you were treated or the way you *assumed* people felt about you?" When students have finished writing, ask for volunteers to share their work with the class.

If you were asked to compare yourself to something, how would you respond?

I am an old-looking bicycle.
I can do more than people give me credit for.
—Frank

I am a knife.
I can be sharp and witty at times.
At other times, I can be
dull and boring.
—Richard

I am a chameleon.
I am constantly changing colors. One
minute I'm pastels and very happy;
then the next minute
I'm red and angry.
—Debbie

The way you see yourself affects every part of your world, especially the way you communicate. To help you understand the connection between how you see yourself and your own communication skills, in this chapter you will consider (1) your self-concept; (2) how self-concept, self-esteem, and communication are connected; (3) your communication skills; and (4) ways to improve your self-concept.

SELF-CONCEPT

Almost everyone wishes he or she were different and better. Few people are satisfied with the way they are. Most people think, "If I could only be smarter, thinner, funnier, better looking, or richer, my life would be happier." Most people also want to be better at doing things: "If I could dance more gracefully, talk more easily to new people, score more baskets, have more money, or get more A's, life would be terrific." Often it boils down to "If I could only be like so-and-so, my life would be wonderful."

Critical Thinking

Analyzing

● Have students read the self-comparisons on page 122. Ask what each of the comparisons has in common. (They are all metaphors.) Then ask students to write self-comparisons of their own. Students might share their work with a partner and ask for feedback about how their self-comparisons relate to their partner's perceptions.

Limited English Proficiency

Some students may need extra help understanding metaphors. Tell them that the first writer might have compared himself to a bicycle by saying, "I am *like* an old bicycle." Explain that a metaphor is a comparison without the use of the word *like.* Point out that each student writer has started with a comparison of two basically unlike things and then gone on to explain the comparison. Ask students to tell which of the following sentences contains a metaphor:

I am a shy person.
I am a tall tree in the wind.

Considering who you are requires a lot of time and thought.

You are not alone in having these thoughts. Many people look at their lives and ask questions such as these:

Who am I anyway?

Why can't I fit in?

Why can't I be like so-and-so?

Why am I the only one who seems to feel like this?

You may have other questions you could add to this list. You spend a great deal of time thinking about yourself and how you fit into your world, your family, school, religious organization, or community. These are important thoughts. They help you decide who you are. These thoughts help form your self-concept.

What is self-concept anyway? Your **self-concept** is your picture of yourself, formed from the beliefs and attitudes you have about yourself. Your self-concept is composed of how you see yourself;

> **"I seem to have an awful lot of people inside me."**
>
> DAME EDITH EVANS

how you would like to be; how you think others see you; and how others actually see you. Some students answered these questions by spelling out their names with adjectives that applied to them.

Silly
Yahoo
Laughing
Venturous
Impartial
Appreciative

Rowdy
Attentive
Mischievous
Outgoing
Sensitive
       —Sylvia Ramos

Rough
Outgoing
Gifted
Extraordinary
Ridiculous

Dashing
Amiable
Vivacious
Intricate
Lazy
Artistic
       —Roger Davila

How You See Yourself

Although you can use words such as *smart* or *dumb* and *happy* or *sad* as labels for your whole self, they are very general. Instead you may say things like, "I'm good at sports but lousy at math" or "I'm usually cheerful except when my mom and dad fight." Or perhaps, "I'm lazy except when I can earn money from working."

Amazing Fact!

After English, Spanish is the most common language spoken at home by Americans. It is followed in order by French, German, Italian, and Chinese.

As you probably know, you have many different sides. Each affects your answer to the question "How do I see myself?" You may like some parts of yourself better than others. How coordinated are you? How attractive are you? How do you see yourself as a friend? as a son or daughter? Are you a hard worker? What kind of math or English student are you?

If you were to compare thoughts with your friends, it is likely that you'd come up with many similar ideas. You share similar ideas and concerns because you are all living your teenage years. That means a lot of self-exploration is going on. When a group of students was asked what it's like being a teenager, here is what some of them said:

"Being a teenager is like being David when the whole world is Goliath."

"Being a teenager is like walking a tightrope without a net."

"Being a teenager is like jumping into the sea and not knowing how to swim."

"Being a teenager is like skydiving without a parachute."

A little praise goes a long way toward improving someone's self-concept.

Learning Styles

Kinesic Learning

● Ask for volunteers to create nonverbal portraits of a person with a very strong self-concept and a person with a very weak self-concept. First encourage volunteers to sit, stand, and walk around the room in the manner of a person who does not feel good about himself or herself. As students are walking, instruct them to "become" a person with a strong self-concept. Ask the class to take note of how posture, gait, and facial expression change. Ask volunteers to describe how it felt to transform from one type of person to another.

❝Each of us has a mental picture of himself, a self-image which governs much of his conduct and outlook. To find life reasonably satisfying you must have a self-image that you can live with.❞

DR. MAXWELL MALTZ

Critical Thinking

Organizing

● Encourage students to organize their self-concept in a web diagram. For each adjective they come up with to describe themselves, they could create a web that shows why. For example, if a student writes "funny" as one of her adjectives, her web might contain examples such as, "I make people laugh at parties," "I can imitate almost anyone," and "My friends say I'm the funniest person they know."

Cooperative Learning

▼ Ask students why some people seem to do nothing but talk or brag about themselves. Encourage students to discuss the idea that sometimes behavior that seems arrogant may actually be evidence of a weak self-concept.

APPLY

Look at the following list and pick out the sentences that express how you see yourself most of the time.

I am sad.	I am helpful.	I am a mess.
I am lovable.	I am smart.	I am loud.
I am lazy.	I am capable.	I am talented.
I am energetic.	I am dumb.	I am friendly.
I am clumsy.	I am happy.	I am attractive.
I am honest.		

How satisfied are you with your answers? There are sixteen descriptions, some positive, some negative and some neutral. Did you pick out more positive or more negative statements? What kind of picture do you have of yourself?

OBSERVE

On a separate piece of paper, list six to ten adjectives that you would use to describe yourself. Try not to use the adjectives that appear in the sentences above. Complete the sentence, "I see myself as . . ."

Sides of Self

Questions regarding how you see yourself are important to answer as you try to understand more and more about yourself. Most of the questions you ask about yourself can be put into three areas related to your physical, intellectual, and social sides.

Physical The **physical side of self** includes how you look and how you use your body for physical activities such as sports, work, or creative movement like dance or mime. As you consider

Skill Development

Quick Skill Opportunity

● Go around the classroom calling on various students to finish the sentence that begins "Being a teenager is like...."

your physical self, think about your height, weight, hair color, voice quality, body build, ease of movement, and facial features. Television, movies, and magazines send powerful messages about physical attractiveness, often causing persons who do not fall into those narrow ideals to feel unattractive.

Read the following journal entry and identify the parts of this writer's physical self-concept:

JOURNAL ENTRY

I think that my overall personality is pretty good. I'm usually in a good mood. On first impression, I think I wear pretty nice clothes and look pretty nice. I have been listening to myself while I write this entry and I sure sound stuck up! One thing I don't like about myself is that I wear braces and have freckles and wear glasses. I know how "your looks don't count, it's what's inside that does," but sometimes I don't believe that. After writing this, I have come to the conclusion that I have both bad and good points. After all, no one is perfect!

Intellectual The **intellectual side of self** includes how you handle ideas, values, and beliefs. Your intellectual side is your thinking and analytical self. As you consider your intellectual self, think about such things as school work, honesty, religious beliefs, reading and study habits, and curiosity.

Multicultural Learning

▲ Students might want to research how people from various cultural groups view self-concept. Ask interested students to look into and compare, for example, the average American student or worker to the average Japanese student or worker.

Skill Development

On the Job

▼ Ask students to give examples of
how self-concept may influence a
person's work life. Encourage them to
discuss self-concept as it relates to
volunteer or part-time job
experiences. Ask what they can tell
about someone's self-concept by the
way that person dresses, accepts
criticism or praise, or treats others on
the job.

Skill Development

Media Literacy

▲ Encourage students to write an
assessment of the old adage "beauty
is only skin deep." What does the
adage mean? Do students agree with
it? Tell them to compare their
assessment with advertisements they
see on television or in newspapers
and magazines. What, in general, is
society's view of this adage?

In the following journal entry, a student describes his love for new knowledge, a part of his intellectual self.

JOURNAL ENTRY

I was talking with a friend the other day, and he asked me why I like to experiment in model rocketry. Ever since the beginning of time, man has thirsted for knowledge, and some scientists even think that's why man has his appearance, and such a large capacity for his brain. People also ask me why I read so much and so fast. Books open a whole new world and usually give a thought or a question to ponder when you finish.

Sometimes it is not seen as "cool" to show your intellectual side. Peer pressure can be difficult for teenagers who enjoy reading literature, discussing ideas, or doing science. Yet this is an important part of personal development and is central to how many people see themselves. For some people, having just one friend with similar intellectual interests is exactly what they need.

Social The **social side of self** refers to how you relate to other people. As you consider your social self, think about how comfortable you are in large groups or in small groups, your concern for other people, and your ideas about popularity or friendship.

In this short entry a student writes about a major social problem.

JOURNAL ENTRY

I don't consider myself popular, and right now I'm having lots of trouble finding out who my *real* friends are and where I should be. Should I be with the popular group? Right now there are really two popular groups, and I don't know if I want to belong to either of them.

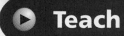

Beyond the Classroom

Invite a psychologist or psychiatric social worker to speak to your class about eating disorders and their relationship to self-esteem and self-concept.

Critical Thinking
Evaluation

● Ask students why self-concept is often tied to specific kinds of clothing, shoes, and other possessions. How do people acquire the idea that certain labels on clothing can improve one's self-concept?

66My one regret in life is that I am not someone else.99

WOODY ALLEN

Critical Thinking
Analyzing

▼ Encourage volunteers to give their definition of a "cool" person. Write students' definitions on the chalkboard. When you have written five students' definitions, encourage the rest of the class to agree or disagree with each one. If students disagree with a definition, encourage them to explain their reasoning.

Critical Thinking
Organizing

▼ Some students might use the model on this page to create a diagram that illustrates their personal example.

The physical, social, and intellectual parts of one's self are very important to self-concept. In addition to a view of "who I am," everyone also has an idea of "who I would like to be."

How You Would Like To Be

If you are like most people, you have dreams or desires about how you wish to be. You may wish you were a famous person such as Tiger Woods, Winona Ryder, Angela Bassett, Leonardo di Caprio, Sheryl Swopes, Denzel Washington, Tracy Chapman, Stephen Hawkins, or Rosie O'Donnell. You may even wish you were one of your friends or classmates. Do you dream about being like someone else, famous or not? Who would that person be?

You may wish to reach a goal. What are some goals you have for yourself? You may wish to act differently: "I wish I could be friendlier, smarter, funnier." "I wish I could make Mom's life easier." "I wish I could be more organized and less lazy." "I wish I could make the all-state team." What things do you hope to be able to do?

Very few people are satisfied with the way they are. Most people think, "If I could only be like so-and-so, my life would be so much better." What's often surprising is that so-and-so also wishes to be like someone else.

Look at the following model and try to think of similar examples that apply to you and your friends.

Tamika wants to be popular and cute like her classmate Marissa.

Marissa wants to be more intellectual and get better grades in school like José.

José wants to be athletic and strong like Tom.

Tom wants to be wealthy and have expensive clothes like Bill.

Bill wants to be easygoing and carefree like Tamika.

Chapter 5 Communication and Yourself

Teach ◄

❝Just remember, we're all in this alone.❞

LILY TOMLIN

Substitute Teacher Tip

Encourage students to create lists for themselves like the one shown on this page. They might create a four-column list with at least five adjectives for each of these four categories: Best Friend, Parent, Teacher, and Classmates. When students have finished their lists, have them discuss whether they ran into any problems as they compiled their lists and what those problems were.

Although you may have dreams, goals, or plans for things to be different, it's nice to feel good about who you are now. As you know, each day and each year you become slightly different. Perhaps you are like the following student who seems quite satisfied with who he is but hopes for a few changes.

JOURNAL ENTRY

If I could be anyone in the world, I would probably want to be me, still. I would just want to have more "in" clothes and be able to play in the band. That would be OK with me. I would never want to be a popular person because they never have any privacy to do what they want to do. I would still like to be myself because I like the way I am.

How You Think Others See You

If you asked your best friend, mother, and math teacher to list four adjectives that describe you, what would each say? Here's what one student expected:

best friend	mother	teacher
worried	popular	friendly
caring	attractive	silly
smart	active	average
funny	forgetful	athletic

You will never know exactly how others think of you. Yet most people are affected by what they *think* other people think of them. How often have you heard someone say, "Oh, so-and-so doesn't like me"; "So-and-so thinks I'm really cool"; "So-and-so acts like I'm dirt"; or "Did you see how so-and-so smiled at me?"

If you think that a certain person is terrific and you hear that he or she likes you, how do you feel? How do you feel about yourself if you discover that this person doesn't like you?

130

❝We would rather speak ill of ourselves than not talk about ourselves at all.❞

LA ROCHEFOUCAULD

Thinking someone likes you can make you feel happy. Thinking someone dislikes you can upset you.

Often people guess about the meaning of the messages others send them. Look at the following journal entry in which the writer does just that.

> ## JOURNAL ENTRY
>
> My biggest fear is people making fun of me. I can't stand being laughed at. I really want people to like me. I guess that's kind of insecure. I don't know. I just can't stand it if a girl refuses to dance with me. I'm sure she doesn't like me.

This student assumes that, because a girl refuses to dance with him, she does not like him. This is possible, of course, but there are other reasons why a girl may refuse to dance. She may be afraid of being teased or of making her boyfriend angry. She may not know how to dance to the kind of music being played, or she may be ill and not want to dance at all. If the boy assumes he is being refused because he is not liked, his self-concept may be affected. But it's not always necessary to assume the worst!

How Others Actually See You

The student who made out a list predicting how others viewed her decided to see if she was right. She actually asked her best friend, her mother, and one of her teachers to list four adjectives describing her. The following are the results of the survey:

best friend	mother	teacher
funny	friendly	studious
caring	sloppy	cheerful
pretty	moody	creative
sincere	nice-looking	polite

Cooperative Learning

Students might create comic skits about the different ways people second-guess messages they receive from others. Have students work in small groups to brainstorm scenarios involving this type of guesswork. Then encourage students to work improvisationally to build their skits.

131

Multicultural Learning

▲ Encourage students to find out more about direct personal feedback in other cultures. They might try to find out about the ways various cultures give and take compliments, how they give and accept presents, how they display anger or resentment, and so on.

How you think others see you can have a strong effect on your self-concept.

Compare this list with the girl's own predictions. (See page 130.) How accurate were her original ideas?

Sometimes you know exactly what others think of you because they have told you. You may have asked for their opinions, or they may have told you voluntarily. Here are two examples of such comments:

My friends have told me I have a bad temper. I've gotten better at controlling myself. When people insult me, hurt me, or cheat on me, I just laugh it off. If it's really bad, I just go home and cry, then forget about it. I wish I could talk with some of them about the comments.

One thing that is really getting me down is my ex-best friend. Last year we were the best of friends. The only thing I didn't like about her was she always told me what she didn't like about me. So one day I told her what I was mad at her about. She got real upset and hasn't talked to me since.

In these two cases, people were direct about their thoughts. It wasn't hard for the students to know what these people thought of them.

Skill Development

Vocabulary

● Have students discuss the difference between self-concept and self-esteem. Encourage volunteers to give examples of each.

There are times when you may need to separate comments about yourself from evaluations of your work or ability. For example, getting a bad grade in history does not make you a bad person, nor does having your friends tell you that you have a bad temper. But it may mean that you have to work on your grades or learn to control your temper. Often one person's ideas about you are completely different from another's because not everyone will see you the same way. Below are examples of how Juan sees himself and how he is seen by several others who know him:

Juan thinks of himself as being witty and outspoken.

His friends think Juan is humorous and talkative.

The teacher thinks Juan is disruptive.

Your self-concept reflects your picture of yourself. You may decide it is a very positive picture or a very negative picture. This affects your self-esteem.

Self-Esteem

Self-esteem is your opinion of yourself, which is based on your self-concept. Depending on your opinion of yourself, you may have high self-esteem or low self-esteem. You may like the person you think you are, or you may wish that person were different.

For example, if you see yourself as popular and you like being popular, you will feel good about yourself and have high self-esteem. If you don't believe you are popular but want to be, you may have low self-esteem. If you are popular but don't think it is important, this will not affect your self-esteem. People who like themselves, that is, who have high self-esteem, feel productive, capable, and likable. Those who have low self-esteem feel worthless, incompetent, and unlikable. Low self-esteem can cause a powerful negative cycle which can be very destructive unless it is turned around.

Links to Past Learning

Encourage students to think about what they may already know about self-esteem. For example, ask them what types of behavior they believe are linked to low self-esteem.

133

Limited English Proficiency

Keep in mind that issues of self-esteem have special relevance to students with limited English proficiency. While it is important to keep these students involved in the discussion, it may not always be a good idea to ask them to provide examples from their own lives.

Skill Development

Feedback

▼ Have students work in pairs to discuss their personal self-esteem checklists (but see above). Students may want to talk about areas of the checklist where they could use improvement. Encourage students to use their listening and speaking skills to support one another and to offer constructive feedback.

CHECKLIST: Self-Esteem 1

Use this checklist to assess your self-esteem. Which statements never apply to you? Which statements sometimes or frequently apply? Which statements always apply?

1. I am comfortable with my appearance.
2. I welcome new experiences.
3. I am satisfied with my ability to make friends.
4. I am able to talk about my feelings with some other person.
5. I can handle helpful criticism.
6. I stand up for important beliefs.
7. I learn from my mistakes.
8. I welcome new challenges.
9. I can laugh at myself when I do something foolish.
10. I can be proud of a job well done.

Try this checklist again, but this time think in terms of how you are changing rather than how you are at this moment.

CHECKLIST: Self-Esteem 2

1. I am becoming more comfortable with my appearance.
2. I am able to welcome new experiences more easily.
3. I am developing my ability to make friends.
4. I am getting better at talking about my feelings with someone else.
5. I am becoming better at handling helpful criticism.
6. I am more willing to stand up for important beliefs.
7. I am improving at learning from my mistakes.
8. I am more willing to try new challenges.
9. I am more likely to laugh at myself when I do something foolish.
10. I am getting better at being proud of a job well done.

Links to Past Learning

Tell students to recall what they know about "noise" in the communication channel. Tell them to think about situations where one's self-esteem level might provide such noise. For example, imagining that someone is critical of your answers may prevent you from volunteering to answer questions in class. Encourage students to come up with other specific examples.

This may seem like a silly distinction but it is really very important. If you are willing to say you are "improving" or "getting better" or "more likely" to do something, this indicates a positive change and should be reflected in an increase in self-esteem.

COMMUNICATION AND THE SELF

Communication, self-concept, and self-esteem are closely related. Communication affects your self-concept and self-esteem, and your self-concept and self-esteem affect how you communicate. Look at this statement from both sides.

How Communication Affects Self-Concept and Self-Esteem

From the moment of your birth, people started talking to you and about you. Their conversations sent you messages about how others saw you. After many years of receiving messages from other people, you have developed an idea of how you think other people see you and how they actually see you. Therefore, much of your self-concept has been built on verbal and nonverbal messages from others. A good self-concept and high self-esteem are created through positive messages; a poor self-concept and low self-esteem are created through negative ones.

APPLY

Look at the following comments. Decide which might lead toward a good self-concept and which to a poor one.

"What a fine piece of poetry!"

"He has his father's ears, poor thing."

"I can always count on you to complete your work on time."

"Gerry is very irresponsible."

"She thinks she's so smart!"

continued

135

Teach

66Three things are important in this world: good health, peace with one's neighbor, friendship with all.99

TRADITIONAL AFRICAN SAYING

Learning Styles
Audio-Visual Learning

● Ask students to watch a favorite television drama and evaluate it for any content that relates to issues of self-esteem and self-concept. Encourage students to see that concern over these issues is central to the human condition.

Skill Development
On the Job

● Tell students to imagine that they have a volunteer job at a hospital and that their duties involve welcoming new young patients. Ask them what techniques they would use to make these young people feel relaxed, comfortable, and confident. Discuss why making patients feel comfortable and confident aids their healing.

Motivation

After students have looked over the list of positive and negative messages, encourage them to come up with more examples of their own. Call on students at random to encourage participation.

APPLY *continued*

"Where did you get that shirt?"

"You're on the team? They must take anyone."

"Try out for the talent show. We need a good pianist."

"I really missed you when you were sick."

Messages like these tell how others see someone. If most of the messages are negative, the listener might develop low self-esteem. If most are positive, he or she is likely to develop high self-esteem.

Read the following self-description and notice how encouraging comments affect the writer of this journal entry:

JOURNAL ENTRY

I am the dew on the grass. People don't notice me much, but I am always there, listening. Sometimes, when I have encouragement from my friends, I shine.

When this young woman feels noticed, she has a positive self-concept and she "shines." She may talk more, smile more, perhaps even argue more. This change leads to the second point.

How Self-Concept and Self-Esteem Affect Communication

If your self-concept is positive and your self-esteem is high, how are you likely to communicate? What kinds of messages do you send when your self-concept is poor and your self-esteem low?

Critical Thinking
Analyzing

● While students are involved in the Interact activity, encourage them to analyze the list of words and phrases to see if there are any behaviors listed that could, depending on the situation, indicate either a strong self-concept or a weak one. As an example, point out the word *apologizes.* A person who is capable of apologizing when he or she is wrong could have a very strong self-concept. A person who apologizes constantly, even when not at fault, probably has a poor self-concept.

INTERACT

Look at the following words and phrases. Which do you think describe someone with a good self-concept? Which describe someone with a poor self-concept? Discuss your ideas in a small group.

gives compliments

interrupts

teases

acts rude

smiles

complains

agrees with everyone

avoids direct eye contact

speaks very softly

always stops talking when someone interrupts

apologizes

Communication is so complex that a single type of behavior cannot be matched with a particular level of self-esteem. Someone who avoids people, apologizes constantly, and seems uncomfortable sharing ideas probably has low self-esteem. If you have a good self-concept, you may risk trying new things, talk more in class, or try to meet new people. You probably have confidence in your ability to do well.

The point is simple. If you believe you are dumb, unattractive, or unfriendly, your poor self-concept and low self-esteem may make you avoid many social situations. The expression "having a bad hair day" does not refer just to how you look. It refers to how you are feeling about yourself and the ways negative feelings can create negative moods. If you see yourself as smart, attractive, and friendly, you will be comfortable speaking and listening in different situations. Usually your self-esteem remains the same over

137

Substitute Teacher Tip

Ask students to write a one-sentence self-compliment about something they feel they do particularly well. Those who would like to read their sentences aloud should be encouraged to do so.

Curricular Connection

Language Arts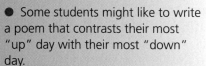

● Some students might like to write a poem that contrasts their most "up" day with their most "down" day.

a long period of time. But on some days you may feel better about yourself than on others. You notice those days, and people around you do too.

The link between self-concept and communication is very important. Remember that communication from others affects your self-concept and self-esteem, and your self-concept and self-esteem affect how you communicate.

OBSERVE

Select a person you know well, perhaps a family member or close friend. Describe how you know when this person is feeling "up" or "down." How does this person's communication change as his or her self-esteem changes?

Johari Window

One way to consider what you are communicating to others is to use the Johari window. This four-part box diagram, created by psychologists Joseph Luft and Harry Ingham, represents the awareness people have of themselves and others. The diagram may be developed in stages.

In the first stage, imagine (1) what you know about yourself and (2) what you are not aware of. For example, you know your personal history, your likes and dislikes, your dreams and fears. But you may not know what a particular person thinks of you. You may not know your scores on certain tests or that your friends describe you as moody and smart.

Then imagine a second stage, including (1) things about you that are known to others and (2) things about you that are not known to others. For example, many people may know your nickname, your favorite foods, your

interest in animals and computers. No one may know that you worry about your mother's health, or that you would love to be a famous singer.

Now, put these stages together into the full Johari window.

THE JOHARI WINDOW

Quadrant 1. The open area refers to behavior and motivation known to an individual and others.

Quadrant 2. The blind area, where others can see things in an individual of which that person is unaware. This is sometimes called the "bad breath" area, but it also refers to positive things.

Quadrant 3. The hidden area, which represents things the individual knows but does not reveal to others (for example, a hidden agenda, matters about which the individual has sensitive feelings, or private and very personal information).

Quadrant 4. The unknown area represents what the individual does not know about himself or herself and what others do not know about the individual, at least not yet.

Your Johari window sections change shape depending on the person or pressures to which you are responding.

Beyond the Classroom

Ask for volunteers to tell where they go to talk with someone about something personal. Do they go to a certain room in an apartment or house? a restaurant? a park? How important is setting to having a personal talk?

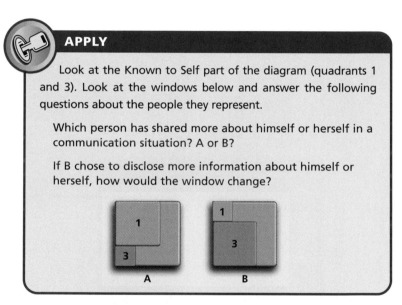

APPLY

Look at the Known to Self part of the diagram (quadrants 1 and 3). Look at the windows below and answer the following questions about the people they represent.

Which person has shared more about himself or herself in a communication situation? A or B?

If B chose to disclose more information about himself or herself, how would the window change?

Here are some other windows with the Known to Self and Not Known to Others sections filled in.

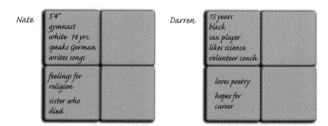

You can think about your window in relationship to people in general or in relationship to certain persons. Your self-esteem affects how much you are likely to share about yourself with others. People who feel good about themselves may share more with others.

How much are you willing to share about yourself? How much do you allow others to probe you about yourself? Take a few minutes to analyze your self-disclosure—how much personal and private information you are willing to reveal in order to improve communication. Draw your own Johari window and think about how you share information with others and how others see you. Think about your self-disclosure behaviors and the things that affect your communication about yourself.

SPEAKING OF . . .

ANGIE RODRIGUEZ

This video director is receiving rave reviews for her piece, *Puerto Rican Pride,* which showcases the culture of Puerto Rico through music, dance, and a sense of spirit. As part of the piece, Angie speaks directly to the camera about her love for her culture.

This young woman uses her multiple communication skills in her daily life. A student at Chelsea High School in Massachusetts, Angie has worked with many organizations that promote self-esteem and cultural diversity. For three years Angie has worked with a peer leadership group called Health Is Power (HIP), which is dedicated to improving the self-esteem of youth through a healthier body, mind, spirit, and community. This position requires her to use many group communication skills as she facilitates meetings, provides technical support for meetings, and serves as a mediator for group problems. She uses public communication skills when she runs workshops on drug abuse, teen pregnancy, and respect for Puerto Rican culture. She has spoken at community festivals, in schools, and in the State House of Massachusetts. Some of her presentations have been seen on local television channels.

In her own words, "My mission is to replace the feeling of hopelessness with empowerment and opportunity. I have trained and carried the skills I have learned from Teen Voices and other organizations to other projects that help the community people develop their own positive visions on certain issues."

Angie has developed communication skills that will serve her well as a community leader, a member of government, or an educator.

Skill Development

Making Conversation

● Encourage students to form discussion groups to discuss the ways that the self-concept improvement guidelines on this page can be related to becoming a better public speaker.

Links to Past Learning

Encourage students to think about any unrealistic goals they might have set for themselves in the past. Have volunteers share their experiences with the class.

IMPROVING SELF-CONCEPT

One thing in life you can be sure of is change! You will continue to change, as will your friends, family, and other people around you. Some changes you can control; others you cannot. For example, your mother or father could receive a job transfer to another state, and your family would have to move. Or you might grow two inches next year and become a better basketball player as a result. These changes are not under your control, but they may affect your self-concept. You can make some deliberate changes to improve your self-concept. You may decide to work very hard in math to receive a better grade. You may get a new haircut and buy new clothes to change your appearance. If a change in self-concept is desired, you may wish to consider the following guidelines:

1. Evaluate yourself honestly.
2. Set realistic goals.
3. Support yourself.
4. Support others.

Evaluating Yourself Honestly

Improving self-concept starts with an understanding of the physical, intellectual, and social areas of the self. A realistic understanding involves looking at both personal limitations and strong points.

All people have to learn to live with some limitations. Look at the following lists one student made of her personal limitations and personal strengths:

Limitations

1. I have exercise-induced asthma.
2. I have to study hard even to get a passing grade in science.
3. I have a hot temper and get angry quickly.
4. I am shy at parties.
5. I can't afford the kinds of clothes other people have.

Skill Development

Feedback

● Encourage students to make lists of their own strengths and limitations. When they have completed their lists, have them compare lists with a partner, if they feel comfortable doing so. Each partner can determine whether they agree or disagree with the other's self-evaluation.

66 If I am not for myself, who will be for me? And if I am only for myself, what am I?... And if not now—when? **99**

HILLEL

Strengths

1. I am loyal to my friends.
2. I find it easy to work with computers.
3. I can draw very well.
4. I listen well to my friends' problems.
5. I can talk easily in front of groups of people.

A realistic evaluation of self is the first step in improving self-concept. Remember these mottoes: "Know your limits but don't let them control you" and "Know your assets and value them."

Skill Development

Research

▲ Interested students might like to research a well-known sports figure or an Olympic gold medalist to find out more about the tough goals athletes often set for themselves. Students could present their findings to the class.

Setting Realistic Goals

Once a person has a realistic picture of himself or herself then it is possible for that person to decide on one or two things to change. Not twelve things, but one or two! Not fix, but change. It's important to be realistic.

If Max is five feet, ten inches tall, he cannot be a successful jockey, but he can ride horses for fun. If Benita can't carry a tune, she is not likely to get the lead part in the school musical, but she can sing with her friends. Setting realistic goals saves unnecessary self-criticism. For example, if you have a bad temper, a goal such as "I will never lose my temper again" would be unrealistic. But a goal such as "When Ravi bothers me again, I will leave the room or change the subject" may be realistic because it is specific. You could do it.

If someone is nervous about giving speeches in class it would be unrealistic to set a goal of never being nervous again. Instead the person may say, "I'll prepare my speeches more carefully, and I'll try not to be so nervous."

Read the following example of one student's goal setting:

Limitation:
When I meet other people, I have trouble remembering their names.

Unrealistic Goal:
I will concentrate on names of new people and never forget anyone's name.

143

Critical Thinking

Evaluating

● Tell students to give a few of their friends or relatives the positive verbal feedback these people deserve. Encourage students to keep a log of the different kinds of responses they receive for their efforts. Then work as a class to evaluate those responses.

Possible Realistic Goals:

I will try to say a person's name out loud when we are introduced to help me remember.

I will try to find a way to connect a new person's name to something else to help me remember it.

INTERACT

With a partner, look at the following unrealistic goals and decide how each could be changed into a possible goal.

I'll never fight with my brother again.

I will not be shy anymore.

I will get 100 percent on all my English tests.

I'm going to win the next science fair.

Sometimes you don't appreciate your strengths until you have lost your edge. A *New York Times* article recently profiled Erin Davis of Saratoga Springs, who was the first freshman runner to win a national high-school cross-country title sponsored by a chain of shoe stores. She was 15 at the time and it had seemed pretty easy. Her victory, however, was followed by illness, injury, bodily changes, and athletic defeats. She needed to set new goals and find renewed commitment. During the summer after junior year, Erin trained at the Olympic Center in San Diego, got into good shape, and found support from other athletes who had faced physical illnesses. She began to run 50 miles a week and won all three of her early races in the fall. Erin set tough goals and worked hard to reach them.

Supporting Yourself and Others

Have you ever heard the expressions "Don't blow your own horn" or "Don't brag about yourself"? Many people find it difficult to praise themselves. Yet people need to pat themselves on the back when they do things well. Most people are good at finding all the bad things about themselves, but they have to learn to recognize the good things as well.

144

Amazing Fact!

Emoticons or smileys are typed characters that are often used on the Internet to express an emotion. For example, {*} means a hug and a kiss.

People need to support or praise themselves for making small steps in the right direction. For example, someone might say, "Well, I still got angry at Andy, but I didn't swear at him as I would have a few months ago" or "I got three of my foul shots, although I missed four. Last year, I could hardly ever make one. I'm getting better." Self-praise takes practice, but it's worth learning.

People who accept themselves also tend to accept others. When people feel good about themselves they are able to be positive and helpful to others. Yet often people don't tell others the good things they are thinking. For example, you may notice that someone is smart, helpful, funny, or good at something. You may think "Conrad gave a great speech" or "Sumi is such a good artist" or "If I have a problem I can always talk to Janice." But do you ever tell Conrad, Sumi, or Janice? People need to be supported when they have done something well or been helpful.

There is an adage that says "We are not another's keeper, but another's maker." Each person has the ability to influence how others see themselves. Each person has the power to help or hurt others. Praising others may help them improve their own self-concepts.

As you work to improve your own self-concept and that of others, remember the words of the Greek writer, Epictetus, "First say to yourself what you wish to be; and then do what you have to do."

CHAPTER 5 SUMMARY

Curricular Connection
Language Arts

Ask students to write their own biographical entry as it might appear in *Who's Who* 20 years from now, and post the entries on a bulletin board. Alternatively, students could work in pairs and write each other's entry.

Throughout this chapter you have looked at the role of the self in communication. Self-concept is made up of four parts: (1) how you see yourself; (2) how you would like to be; (3) how you think others see you; and (4) how others actually see you. Self-esteem is your opinion of yourself based on your self-concept. Your self-concept and self-esteem affect communication and vice versa. To improve your self-concept, you should follow these four guidelines: (1) evaluate yourself honestly; (2) set realistic goals; (3) support yourself; and (4) support others.

Answers

Think About It

Answers will vary. Here are sample answers:

1. Self-concept is based on one's perceptions of how he or she fits into the world, family, school, community, and church, synagogue, or temple. Self-esteem is a person's opinion of himself or herself based on his or her self-concept.

2. (1) How you see yourself, (2) how you would like to be, (3) how you think others see you, and (4) how others actually see you.

3. Low self-esteem and a poor self-concept may keep a person from participating in many social situations or to keep quiet at those in which he or she does participate. It may also result in anti-social behavior.

4. To improve self-concept a person should (1) evaluate himself or herself honestly, (2) set realistic goals, (3) support himself or herself, (4) support others.

CHAPTER REVIEW

Think About It

1. Describe the difference between self-concept and self-esteem.

2. What are the four parts of self-concept?

3. Give an example of how self-concept and self-esteem affect communication.

4. How can one's self-concept be improved?

Try It Out

1. Make a collage using various words, pictures, and slogans to represent your communication strengths and weaknesses. Share your collage with a partner. Describe at least one strength and one weakness as represented on your collage.

2. Suppose you were to bury a time capsule about yourself to be opened ten years from now. Make a list of the things that are representative of you at this time. In a few sentences explain what these things would tell about you ten years from now to someone who didn't know you.

3. Write a bumper sticker that describes how you see yourself. Place all the bumper stickers written in your class on one desk and ask someone to read them aloud. Have classmates guess who wrote each one.

Put It in Writing

1. Write a three-paragraph journal entry describing your physical, social, and intellectual sides.

2. Keep a daily diary for a week. Write about how the following topics affect your self-concept.

   Popularity

   Proud moments

   Conflicts with teachers or parents

   Peer pressure

   Fears

3. Examine your reading preferences and determine what this says about you. List your five favorite books with a two- or three-sentence description of why each text is important to you. Then begin a four-week reading log in which you list the materials you read outside of class assignments. This should help you identify your personal preferences regarding fiction and nonfiction. (It will also help you with your oral-interpretation assignments later in this book.)

Speak About It

1. Present an impromptu speech in a small group of five to six students. Tell about one of the following:

   My most embarrassing moment was when . . .

The happiest day of my life was when . . .

My proudest day was when . . .

My most valuable possession is . . .

My favorite toy as a child was . . .

If I could get enough money, I'd . . .

My children will never have to . . .

2. Present to your class one of the incidents you wrote about in number 2 of "Put It in Writing."

Quick Check

Ask students to find and define these Key Terms:

intellectual side of self (127)

physical side of self (126)

self-concept (123)

self-esteem (133)

social side of self (128)

147

Motivation

Ask students to estimate how much time during a weekday they spend alone, with family, with friends, with other people who are not friends. Ask them to jot down their estimates; then compare the various estimates. On the average, how much time is spent with friends?

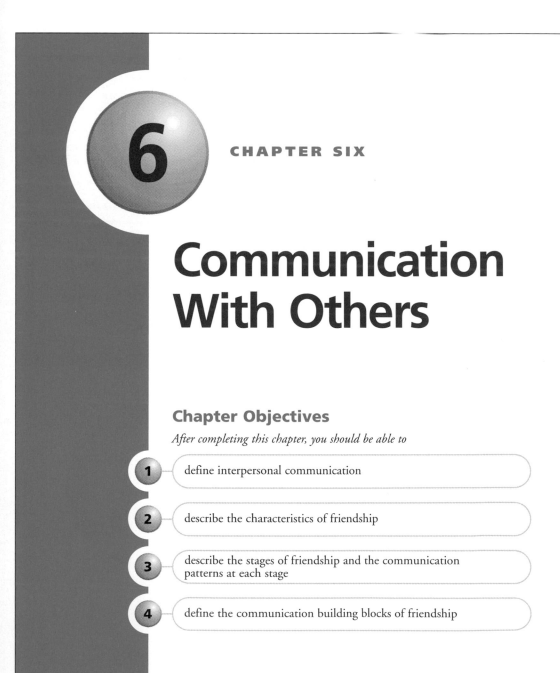

6

CHAPTER SIX

Communication With Others

Chapter Objectives

After completing this chapter, you should be able to

1 define interpersonal communication

2 describe the characteristics of friendship

3 describe the stages of friendship and the communication patterns at each stage

4 define the communication building blocks of friendship

	Day 1	Day 2	Day 3	Day 4	Day 5
Chapter 6 Planner Week 6	**6** Communication with Others				
	Interpersonal Communication Skills	Interpersonal Communication Skills	Interpersonal Communication Skills	Interpersonal Communication Skills	Summary and Chapter Review
	Teacher's Resource Book				
	Teaching Suggestions 6.8	6.9	6.10	6.11	
					Chapter Test 6
	Workbook 6.4	6.5	6.6	6.7	

Critical Thinking

Predicting

● Ask students how the Key Words *constructive criticism, empathy,* and *stereotyping* might be related to communication with others.

⊽ Key Terms

constructive criticism

empathy

first meetings

interpersonal communication

stereotyping

149

Amazing Fact!

One researcher discovered that listeners can tell, 80 percent of the time, whether an unseen speaker is smiling.

ALVIN AND VIRGINIA SILVERSTEIN
Wonders of Speech

Curricular Connection

Language Arts

● Read through the list of similes, and ask for volunteers to define the word *simile*. Then have students write a few similes of their own on the subject of friendship.

Multicultural Learning

● Write the following German, French, and Spanish words for "friend" and "friendship" on the board. If there are students who know equivalent words in other languages, ask them to write them on the board.

Ger.—Fruend (m) / Freundin (f) / Freundschaft

French—ami (m) / amie (f) / amitié

Sp.—amigo (m) / amiga (f) / amistad

Ask students which language the English words for "friend" and "friendship" most closely resemble.

A competent communicator uses a variety of interpersonal communication skills to build and maintain relationships with others. As you interact with community members, teachers, neighbors, family members, and friends, you develop interpersonal relationships with many different kinds of people. Friends learn how to speak and listen to each other in order to strengthen their relationship. This chapter focuses on the special interpersonal communication skills that build friendships.

FRIENDSHIPS

What would life be like without friends? Friends are people with whom you share things and develop a special kind of communication. People often take friends for granted until a friend moves away or becomes a better friend to someone else. The students who wrote the following statements capture the importance of friends and friendships in their lives.

> Friendships are like seeds. When nurtured they grow; when neglected they die.

> Friends are like rubber bands. If you stretch them too far, they'll snap back at you.

> Friends are like crayons. They come in all colors.

> Friends are like mirrors. You can see your true self through them.

Interpersonal Communication

Friendship requires a special type of communication called **interpersonal communication**. Interpersonal communication refers to the voluntary, ongoing interaction that takes place between individuals who want to create and maintain long-lasting relationships. Merely communicating with persons such as the grocery store clerk, bus driver, or neighbor is not interpersonal communication. Although you must communicate with many different people during a day or week, the term "voluntary" implies that you wish to build a relationship with the other

> **❝**I always felt that the great high privilege, relief, and comfort of friendship was that one had to explain nothing.**❞**
>
> KATHERINE MANSFIELD

person. Although you may have friendships with your parents, other family members, or various adults, in this text, friendship and communication with people close to you in age will be emphasized. It is through communication that friends share their joys and problems while building a stronger friendship.

Skill Development

Quick Skill Opportunity

● Ask students to call out all the words they can think of in association with the word *friend* while a student writes the words on the board. Limit the activity to from three to five minutes.

CHECKLIST:
Friendship Communication

Use this checklist to help you think about how you talk with your friends. Which statements never apply to you? Which statements sometimes or frequently apply? Which statements always apply?

1. I am comfortable talking to other people about personal things.

2. I often ask others how they feel about what I'm saying.

3. I am often able to put myself in the other person's place, and I imagine what he or she is feeling.

4. I often check to see if others really understand what I'm saying.

5. I can be trusted with other people's secrets.

6. When I feel hurt, I tell others how I feel.

7. I am usually able to say what I mean.

8. Other people come to me with their problems.

9. I try to be honest with my friends.

10. I stick up for my friends when others make fun of them.

11. If friends criticize my actions, I think seriously about their comments.

12. I am sure to find time to spend with my friends.

151

"One friend in a lifetime is much; two are many; three are hardly possible."

HENRY BROOKS ADAMS
The Education of Henry Adams

Curricular Connection
Social Studies

▲ Interested students might want to conduct a class or schoolwide survey asking about important qualities in a friend. They can use the list of qualities on this page and add any other qualities they can think of. When they have collected the data, ask them to present their findings in class.

Curricular Connection
Mathematics

● Ask some students to put the results of the survey on this page in the form of a bar graph. If a similar survey is conducted in your class or school, students could prepare a bar graph for the results of that survey as well.

When you think about your responses to the previous checklist, you realize that good friends don't just happen. People learn to be good friends.

Characteristics of Friendships

What qualities do you look for in a friend? A magazine survey asked people to tell how important the following qualities are in a friend. The percentages next to the quality show the number of people who said that the quality was important or significant. All of these qualities are tied to communication.

Qualities	Percent responding
Ability to keep secrets	89
Loyalty	88
Warmth, affection	82
Supportiveness	76
Honesty	75
Sense of humor	74

Communicating honestly and warmly with a friend is one of the most rewarding experiences in life.

Links to Past Learning

Encourage students to think back to times when their friends did or did not keep a secret. Ask individual students how their experiences affected the friendship afterward. Encourage class discussion of the various responses.

Ability to Keep Secrets To keep a secret, or a confidence, you must know which messages are private or confidential. Keeping a friend's confidence says you are a friend. Here is what one student wrote in her journal about the importance of keeping a confidence:

JOURNAL ENTRY

I have found one friend I can trust. I can tell Bruce anything, and he will never tell anyone. Last year someone I thought was my friend told half the school about my problems. Bruce would never do this. He is a true friend who listens well and knows how to keep a secret.

Loyalty A good friend does not ignore old friends after making new friends. There is an old song with the following lines, "Make new friends, but keep the old. One is silver and the other gold." Through loyalty you can develop many long-term friendships. The journal entry below describes a friend who was not loyal.

JOURNAL ENTRY

I thought that Liz would be my friend forever. We had such great times together. I told her everything. I thought that she told me everything too. Recently, I have been noticing a change in her feelings toward me. She doesn't want to talk as much. She seems almost embarrassed to be around me. It has been getting worse. I feel so cheated. Is there something wrong with me? Why has she suddenly become tired of being my friend? I don't understand how she could do this to me.

Skill Development

Making Conversation

● Students new to the school might be assigned to small groups with students who have attended the school for some time to discuss how one can make friends in new surroundings.

Warmth Nonverbal clues tell you a lot about which people are friends. Usually you can sense warmth between friends. They may look pleased to see each other, sit close together, tease each other, do things together, or share food. The way they include each other or talk about each other tells you they are good friends. Usually you can sense the warmth in a relationship by paying close attention to nonverbal messages.

Support Good friends support each other. Support refers to messages that make people feel good about themselves. Friends may support each other in arguments. They may help each other with homework, worry when the other one is sick or stick up for each other. If one wins a prize, the other is happy. When asked how friends support each other, some students replied:

> My friend Eric always congratulates me when I beat him in basketball. He is pleased that I'm getting better.

> I always encourage my friend who gets upset with herself when she can't do something. I tell her she can do it. The last time she tried out she got a part in the school chorus!

Friends can tease each other, but they know when to stop.

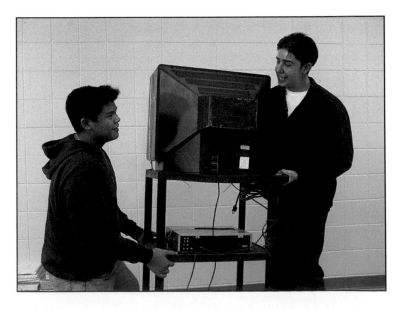

Unit 2 Communication with Self and Others

Curricular Connection

Art

● Students with artistic talent might like to create posters or greeting cards about friendship.

Cooperative Learning

▼ Encourage a class discussion on the subject of honesty among friends. Do students want friends to be honest? Are they comfortable being honest with friends?

Honesty "Friends are like pins. They are pointed and sharp." Sometimes only a friend will tell you the truth. If you are being a snob, you may need a friend to set you straight. If you tease too much, a friend may tell you it hurts. Your friend may tell you that you are too stubborn, selfish, careless, or getting into the wrong crowd. A good friend tells you for your own good and sticks with you as you change. A poor friend criticizes you to hurt you and then disappears.

Although good friends are honest, they are sensitive and careful with their words.

Humor Being a friend may mean putting up with bad jokes. Friends can laugh with each other and sometimes at each other. They enjoy having fun together. They act silly, kid around, and tell funny stories about their times together. Friends cannot be serious all the time.

Friends are many things to each other. They contribute to each other's self-concept and self-esteem. Friends show each other loyalty, warmth, supportiveness, and honesty. They keep secrets and laugh together. Friends make you feel good about yourself, which helps build a strong self-concept and high self-esteem. If you have a friend with some of these qualities, you are very lucky. Not all people have all of these qualities, but most of those who do are capable of being true friends.

INTERACT

Read the following student essay on "The Friendship Game." With a partner discuss what, in your opinion, characterizes a good friend. Describe one frustration you experienced in a specific friendship and how you learned to be a better friend to that person.

155

Critical Thinking

Synthesizing

● After reading Julie Buchwald's essay "Knowing How to Play the Friendship Game," students might write their own essays on the subject of friendship. First, encourage them to come up with a strong analogy like Buchwald's card-game metaphor.

Knowing How to Play the Friendship Game

by Julie Buchwald

Friends come in a variety package; we all have our different kinds of friends, school friends, non-school friends, work friends, older, younger friends, your parents' friends, "Hi, how are you?" friends, be-nice-to-somebody-if-you-want-something friends, other friends …the list could scientifically reach eternity. Of all the friends in the world, however, the rarest and most hard to come by are true friends.

How do you know who your true friends are? Realistically you don't. You can't see into the future (unless you pay a visit to a psychic Gypsy), and a real friend is one who will be there for you for the rest of your life. But that's just the fun of it: you don't know what's going to happen, so you take chances. Gambling always has risky implications, especially with friends, but then again, so does life.

Playing your cards right is often very tricky, most importantly after you've just made a bad move. Friendship conflicts are the absolute epitome of fights. They usually start over a very trivial issue, such as returning books to the library, and end up getting blown up as big as the national debt. Of course, "the ideal friendship law," which states that friends must always live under perfect conditions, does not realistically exist. Fighting is a natural phenomenon when it comes to friendship, but be careful not to take it too far; otherwise, you'll be out of the game instantly.

You could actually end up having nothing and losing everything. Learning that someone is not who you thought them to be is a very difficult realization to accept. But don't back off from this someone so quickly; give the person a chance for redemption. You don't really want to walk away from a friendship you thought would last a lifetime, because if you did, you'd live to regret the decision you made. Losing a friend for any reason at all is a tragedy, and will leave you with your cards chaotically splattered all over the floor in a huge mess.

A true friend is an ace of hearts—right up there at the top of the stack. This person would stand up for you through thick and thin. This person would fight for you, lie for you, walk the wire for you, die for you . . . You will keep in touch with the person over the next twenty-five years. With luck, you will get an ace of hearts. With even more luck, you could get a full house, and end up with an over-abundance of true friends.

The friendship game takes both patience and initiative. Friends, true and real friends, must endure complete honesty and trust. If your friendships can survive the test of time and will, the good times will definitely outshine the rough ones.

Skill Development

Media Literacy

▼ If students do not already do so, ask them to read the comics section of a newspaper for several days and cut out or copy cartoon strips that deal with characteristics of or problems in friendship. Post all submissions on the bulletin board.

Learning Styles

Visual Learning

● Bring in photos from magazines or newspapers that show a wide variety of types of people. Display the pictures for the class and ask for feedback about which people different students think they would like to know. Encourage them to consider how expression, dress, and general appearance, as well as reputation (if known) can negatively or positively influence their first impressions of people.

STAGES OF FRIENDSHIP

Think about your friendships. How did each begin? What made you decide to continue a friendship after your first meeting? Generally, friendships progress through fairly predictable stages. These stages are first meetings, becoming acquaintances, becoming friends, and sometimes becoming best friends. Friendships move gradually from stage to stage. You are not acquaintances one day and best friends the next. A detailed discussion of friendship stages follows.

First Meetings

Any of the following statements might be the beginning of a friendship between two people.

"Dad, I'd like you to meet my coach, Mr. Darrel."

"Hi. Are you new here?"

"Excuse me. Can you tell me how to get to room 201?"

First meetings are the beginning stages of relationships. They can be compared to auditions or tryouts for a play or music group. New people go through tryouts to see if they want to get to know each other.

Physical appearance and any previous knowledge you have about a person affect first meetings. It's unfortunate but true that people pay close attention to appearance in first meetings. Certain clothes, hairstyles, or shoes may help you decide whether to talk to someone. You may never know who ignored you or approached you because of how you looked. College counselors have many stories of seniors who went on college visits and chose their school because of the shoes or clothes worn by students on the campus.

Sometimes you know about a person before you have met that person. You may have heard that Antonio is funny and smart. When you meet Antonio, you may make time to talk with him. If you heard that Heather is stuck up, when you meet her you may not waste your time trying to talk with her.

Links to Past Learning

Have students give examples of times in their lives when they misjudged another person based on his or her appearance. Encourage class discussion about the importance of looking beyond physical appearance to understand the whole person.

Skill Development

Media Literacy

● Encourage students to analyze television programs for use of stereotypes. They might keep a log of every stereotype they see on television over the course of an entire week. Have students compare their examples in class.

When you meet someone for the first time, you probably follow some social rituals. The rituals may include

sharing your names, schools, and classes

talking about interests, such as music and concerts

making small talk about the place where you are meeting

avoiding arguments

avoiding sharing very personal information

Communication at first meetings is often based on stereotypes. **Stereotyping** is labeling people as part of a group and treating them as if they possessed only the characteristics of that group. For example, if you meet a person at a party who belongs to a group different from yours, you may evaluate that person according to what you know about the group, rather than as an individual. People evaluate others on the basis of their social or cultural groups. The following comments show how hard it can be to be judged according to a stereotype:

JOURNAL ENTRY

Just because I'm on the football team people think all I can talk about is sports. Whenever I meet new people, they always want to talk about playing football.

I have to be very careful about what I eat because I have diabetes. As soon as other people find this out, they think I'm weird or something.

You know stereotyping is going on when you hear phrases such as "Oh, you know, she's one of those _____" or "All you _____ are alike" or "She's not really like all the other _____." These messages focus on the differences between groups, not on what an individual is really like.

❝If a man does not make new acquaintances as he advances through life, he will soon find himself left alone. A man, Sir, should keep his friendship in constant repair.❞

SAMUEL JOHNSON

Skill Development

Making Conversation

● If some students have pen pals or other long-distance friends that they keep in touch with only through phone, letters, or e-mail, assign these students to a small group to talk for from five to seven minutes about these friends and friendships.

The first time you meet someone, you form an impression or picture of that person. This picture helps you decide whether you wish to get to know the person better. If both of you have positive first impressions, you may be on your way toward a friendship.

> **INTERACT**
>
> In small groups, discuss which stereotypes are sometimes applied to
>
> | | |
> |---|---|
> | cheerleaders | female athletes |
> | straight-A students | drama-club members |
> | football players | teachers |
> | chess-club members | wealthy students |
> | student-council members | poor students |
> | dancers | |
>
> Add examples from the types of groups found in your school or community. Discuss how these stereotypes affect the way people relate to members of each group.

Becoming Acquaintances

You relate to most people you know at the acquaintance level. Acquaintances are not strangers, but they are not really friends. You may say hello in the school hall, you may play together on the softball team, or you may sing together in the chorus. Some family friends, teachers, or store clerks may be your acquaintances.

Your communication with these people follows a set pattern. Comments such as, "How's it going?" or "Hi, how are you?" may begin your interactions. After that you may have very predictable conversations. Often you discuss the same things each time you meet. The same questions may be asked, such as, "Which team is going to win the championship?" or "How's

Links to Past Learning

● Almost everyone has been the victim of stereotypical thinking. Discuss with students why stereotypes about groups or types of people such as Native Americans, honor-roll students, poor people, blondes, athletes, lawyers, Asians, and many others persist. Is it because people who perpetuate the stereotypes really don't know individual members of these groups or types of people? Or do some people believe that stereotyping doesn't matter? Are people who believe they are the victims of stereotypes too sensitive? Urge each student to try to imagine why someone unlike them might feel hurt by remarks that reflect stereotypical thinking.

your sister's new baby?" or "Have you been to any good movies lately?" These conversations are pleasant but not very personal.

You may know something about the person's family, school activities, or hobbies. You may know, for example, that the person in the "jock" group is also a good musician. The "rich" person may be an expert at bicycle repair. Because you know more about an acquaintance than someone you meet for the first time, you don't rely on stereotyping as much.

Although acquaintances may not share very personal information, they may discuss opinions on many subjects. Comments like the following keep the conversation going: "I'm sure glad Pat won the student council election" or "This is going to be a great weekend for racing. I can't wait."

People at the acquaintance level have few ties to each other. If you run into an acquaintance, you will probably have a pleasant

Sharing activities or hobbies is one way for people to move from acquaintances to friends.

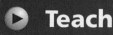

❝I don't know the key to success, but the key to failure is trying to please everybody.**❞**

BILL COSBY

Curricular Connection

Language Arts

▲ Interested students might like to present oral reports on books that deal with the subject of friendship or that portray an especially close friendship between two people. Many young-adult novels deal with this theme.

conversation, but neither of you will make an effort to spend time together. Sometimes acquaintances move on to become friends. Then the relationship and level of communication change.

Becoming Friends

Friends have a special relationship. Friends talk to each other more often than do acquaintances. They talk for longer periods of time and about many different topics. Friends share personal information with each other. You know what makes your friend angry, sad, or frustrated. You discuss your friend's family, interests, and past experiences. You share worries and happiness with each other.

Friends develop special communication abilities. Sometimes they finish each other's sentences. They may have code words or nonverbal signals that only the two of them understand. For example, a certain look may mean "Let's get out of here." Friends can talk about experiences that other people may not share with comments such as, "Remember the night your brother . . ." or "That's like the time at the dance when . . ." Sometimes friends use a short version of a message because they don't have to explain very much to each other. The statement "My Dad says we can go 'trouting' on Saturday!" may not mean much to most people. But to two friends it could mean "My Dad says he will take us up to the lake cabin next Saturday, let us go fishing in his boat, and he'll cook the catch for dinner." Friends can change their communication rapidly. They may be silly one minute and serious the next.

Many times friends will talk to each other about being friends. Each may say how important the other is with comments such as "You can't move. Who will I talk to?" or "It's great we are in four of the same classes" or "If you're not invited, I'm not going either. Friends stick together." Most outsiders know when two people are friends. They see and hear messages that tell them that two people have a close relationship.

Teach

Links to Past Learning

As an extension to the Observe activity on page 162, suggest that students think about good friendships they have enjoyed in past years. What characterized those friendships? How did students behave with their friends? In what way was their behavior similar to the behavior they observe today in other pairs of friends? Have students share their observations with the class.

Best friends spend many hours in each other's company.

OBSERVE

Describe a good friendship between two people you know. As an outsider how can you tell these two are friends? How do they talk to each other and about each other? What nonverbal messages show they are friends?

Becoming Best Friends

If friendships are special, best friendships are very special. Usually a person has one best friend, although sometimes a person may claim two or three people as best friends. It is impossible to have many best friends because friendships need privacy and time. You

Critical Thinking

Analyzing

● Ask students to discuss whether people who join gangs are looking for friendship. What do gangs provide in the way of friendship?

tell your best friend secrets. You share deep feelings and worries with each other. You are able to read your friend's nonverbal messages very well. One look at your best friend's face and you can tell if he or she is angry, upset, or excited.

Best friends do all the things friends do with verbal and nonverbal messages and more. They can often predict what the other will do or say and are right 90 percent of the time! Sometimes people say that two friends look or sound alike. They may use the same gestures or expressions, or laugh the same way. Comments such as, "You sound just like (your best friend)" make you feel good.

Best friends spend many hours together. They may talk on the phone every day and may spend hours at each other's houses talking or shooting hoops. They develop a history in their relationship. They may share possessions such as clothes, tapes, or jewelry.

Best friends look out for each other. They do things for each other that they would not do for someone else. One student's journal entry described how best friends solved a problem of winning and losing.

JOURNAL ENTRY

My brother Matt and his best friend Mike both entered the Arbor Day Five-Mile Race last year. They were in the same age category. They got out in front early and ran together. I could see that they were still together when they got near the finish line. I kept waiting for one to break out ahead. Instead they just kept coming together. As they ran up to the line they both stopped. They looked at each other, laughed, and both stuck one foot across the line at exactly the same moment. The park district had to plant a tree to honor each of them because they both won.

Often other people recognize a pair as best friends. You hear comments like, "If you want Ed to come, you'd better invite Marco also" or "Vicki says she's going. That must mean Becky will be there too."

Amazing Fact!

Peter Ilyich Tchaikowsky and Madame Nadejda von Meck had one of the most celebrated friendships in history, but though they corresponded for 13 years, they never met.

Critical Thinking

Predicting

● Have students read the heading "Changes in Friendship" and use examples from their own experience to predict what changes might occur in a friendship and why.

A family member sometimes feels like a best friend. You might be able to talk with your mother, father, or brother about what is important to you. Sometimes you may not have a best friend, but a few months later you may have two.

Best friendships take effort. You have to make time to see each other and to talk to each other. Each of you has to be willing to listen when the other needs to talk. You have to reach compromises on many plans or ideas.

Changes in Friendships

Just as you and another person can move forward through the four stages of friendship, you also can move backward. You may know someone at school who used to be a close friend, but now you hardly even speak to each other. You may say "I don't know

Friendships can change when one person finds new relationships.

Students who sing or play guitar or piano might like to compose a song about some aspect of friendship and play it for the class. Or they may already know a song about friendship that they can perform.

Jessica anymore" even though you spent five years in the same grade-school classroom and were good friends once.

As the quotation at the beginning of this chapter says, "Friendships are like seeds. When nurtured they grow; when neglected they die." Sometimes people neglect a best friendship. They get involved in new activities, find new groups, or join new clubs. As the relationship changes, the verbal and nonverbal messages change. While you once shared secrets, you may now talk about the math test. You ignore each other's nonverbal clues. You don't spend much time together. The relationship becomes more distant. Best friends become just friends. Friends become acquaintances. People around you sense the change. In some cases the two people can move their relationship up through the stages again, but in other cases neither person wants to bother. Sometimes friendships change when people drift apart because of different interests. Sometimes they change when someone moves away and it's hard to stay really close.

Most relationships remain at the acquaintance stage. A few lucky people get to be best friends. Some friendships don't last very long; others last far into adulthood. The friendships that endure over time are characterized by effective communication.

OBSERVE

Select a friendship from a novel, short story, or television show and decide at what stage the friendship appears to be. Describe the communication behavior of each person, and use this behavior to explain why you think they are at that stage.

INTERPERSONAL COMMUNICATION SKILLS

Some people seem to make friends easily. Others see friendship as a mysterious thing. Using your communication skills can help you build friendships. There are six building blocks or communication

165

Curricular Connection
Mathematics

▼ Ask a student to read aloud the six building blocks of interpersonal communication. Encourage interested students to create pie charts to show the relative importance of each area to a typical friendship in their lives.

Links to Past Learning

Encourage students to think about a talk, lecture, sermon, or speech they have heard recently. Ask whether the speaker shared any personal information during the presentation. Ask also what effect this information—or lack of it—may have had on their enjoyment or understanding of the presentation.

skills you can use to construct a strong friendship. These skills include: (1) sharing personal information, (2) sharing feelings, (3) empathizing, (4) listening, (5) supporting, and (6) constructive criticism. A discussion of each follows.

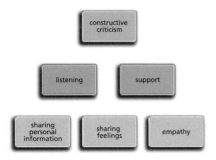

Sharing Personal Information

Sharing personal information means telling someone private information about yourself. You choose to share this information; no one forces you to do so. You also take a risk, because if your friend told other people your secrets, you might be hurt or embarrassed.

Many people wear masks much of the time. They appear happy, tough, or unfeeling when they really feel sad, scared, or upset. When people slowly drop their masks for one another, they get to know each other well. True friendship does not require masks, because friends accept each other. There is a sense of being oneself with another person. People sometimes hesitate to drop their masks, fearing that, "If you really know who I am, you won't like me anymore." One student describes the problem in putting on a social mask:

JOURNAL ENTRY

If you put on a false front, you may find some friends, but you'll always have that question in the back of your mind if they like you or if you like yourself. I don't think it's worth it.

❝Words are gifts, our grandparents say, and they give us many words so we will remain a nation, a circle of people.❞

DEBRA CALLING THUNDER (ARAPAHO)

Links to Past Learning

Some students, like Brad Auerbach, may have been involved in a peer mediation process. If so, ask them to tell about it.

SPEAKING OF . . .

BRAD AUERBACH

If you "drop in" to the drop-in center at Stevenson High School in Lincolnshire, Illinois, you might find Brad Auerbach in the middle of a serious conversation with some of his peers. Although he may be holding a discussion with friends, it's more likely that he is mediating a dispute between students at the school. Brad helped to found a peer mediation program and serves as a director of the center where any of the 3,000 students are welcome to come and discuss anything. Students talk with him about disputes with friends as well as arguments with parents. Brad and the other mediators have prepared for this task through intensive training seminars and courses on how to help others resolve serious disagreements. In short, he has developed expertise in conflict resolution, an important interpersonal skill.

Brad relies on a five-step mediation process. His task is to help the disputants find ways to solve their own problems. "During the mediation process I'm allowed to ask questions of each disputant," Brad explains, "but offering suggestions is not allowed. Each disputant's goal is to come up with suggestions on how to work the problem out."

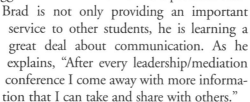

Brad is not only providing an important service to other students, he is learning a great deal about communication. As he explains, "After every leadership/mediation conference I come away with more information that I can take and share with others."

The dispute resolution skills Brad is practicing will serve him well in the future, both in his personal relationships and in his career. He may become a lawyer with a specialty in mediation, a family therapist, a labor negotiator, or a business consultant. He may also work as a volunteer court or community mediator.

Skill Development
Media Literacy

▼ Tell students to watch a local or national news program. Encourage them to distinguish thought statements from feelings statements. Have students share in class their thoughts about remarks made by elected officials, community leaders, and other people being interviewed.

When good friends share personal information, their relationship usually gets stronger. They usually share this information carefully and slowly, with both persons being actively involved.

Guidelines for Sharing Personal Information

These guidelines help many friendships develop slowly and well:

1. *Don't overtalk.* The person who tells all and tells it quickly can ruin a possible friendship. If the first time you meet someone, you hear all about his or her troubles, old best friends, travels, and so on, you will be uncomfortable. People who talk about themselves too much and too quickly will have trouble making friends.

2. *Don't undertalk.* The person who listens to everyone else but never says anything personal can also ruin a possible friendship. You may realize that a new person knows all about your family and friends, your interests, and your plans for the future. If you know almost nothing about this person, you need to ask yourself, am I talking too much? Is this person unwilling to talk to me? Undertalking keeps the relationship from continuing through the friendship stages.

3. *Choose the information you wish to share wisely.* Even best friends do not have to share everything. You do not have to answer every question someone asks you. You can decide when and with whom you wish to talk about personal things.

It's up to you to decide when and with whom you wish to share personal information.

Unit 2 Communication with Self and Others

Skill Development

Vocabulary

▼ Encourage students to work together to list 20 emotion-based words that might be used in statements of personal feelings. Start them off with examples such as *envious, thrilled, amazed, hurt,* and *angry*.

Sharing Feelings

Feeling statements describe your emotions, a very personal part of you. Many people cover up their feelings with thought statements, because a thought statement is less personal. For example, it is less personal to say, "I think the director cast a good show" than "I'm so glad I got a part in the show." Often people hide their sadness, anger, or jealousy by talking about a subject but never sharing their feelings about it. Feeling statements let your friends see parts of you that you don't often share. As people get to know each other better, they share their feelings more openly.

APPLY

From the following quotations, pick out those you think are feeling statements and those you think are thought statements:

1. "I'm so happy I'm going to be in the all-state orchestra. I really wanted to make it."

2. "It seems like the auditions were fair. I'm going to play first chair violin."

3. "I get so jealous when I see how easy it is for Stephanie to sight-read music."

4. "It seems that some people have a natural talent for reading music. Not me."

The first and third statements are feeling statements. The second and fourth are thought statements.

It is surprising to realize that many people do not really talk about feelings at all. They will say things like "I think that was a dumb thing to do" instead of "I was really scared when he did that." Or they might say, " It's stupid for Angela's family to move at this time" rather then "I'm sad that Angela is moving away."

Limited English Proficiency

Have students with limited English proficiency work with other students to understand the difference between sharing feelings and making thought statements. Tell students to come up with feelings statements for each of the following thought statements:

My mother won't let me go to the show tonight.

My younger brother got a car for his birthday. I got a video game.

He's a nice guy.

She's very talented.

Amazing Fact!

In the first edition of Emily Post's book on etiquette in 1922, one chapter was titled "Chaperons and Other Conventions." In the 1937 revised edition, the chapter became "The Vanished Chaperon and Other Lost Conventions."

Critical Thinking

Evaluating

● After students have read the journal entry on this page, ask them to think about the generalization that adults keep their true feelings inside. Have students use real-life examples to agree or disagree with the journal entry.

Skill Development

Vocabulary

● Ask students to use a dictionary to find out the difference between empathy and sympathy. Ask volunteers to provide real-life examples of experiences they may have had with feeling, or being given, empathy and sympathy.

🔍 OBSERVE

In your journal, keep a record for three days of feeling statements you hear. For example, if you hear someone say "I'm so angry at the bicycle repair shop," write "I'm angry." After three days count how many feeling statements you actually heard and describe the types of feelings you heard expressed most often, such as sadness, joy, fear, or anger.

Sometimes your good friends use nonverbal clues to show how they are feeling. Suppose you ask your friend, "How are you?" and your friend looks away and quietly says, "Fine." If you are paying attention to your friend's voice and eyes, you will know he or she is not really fine. If you pay attention to nonverbal clues, you can help your friend put into words what is going on. The better you know people, the easier it is to find out how they are feeling by reading their nonverbal cues.

JOURNAL ENTRY

A lot of adults seem to have trouble talking about feelings. We used to have a joke in our family about "Are you mad, glad, sad?" but only the kids really used feelings words. Most adults I know keep their real feelings inside.

Empathizing

Recently a newspaper columnist discussed the story of a twelve-year-old seventh-grader. The boy returned to his desk after lunch one day to find a printed card that said "Most Unpopular Student Award." Some classmate had filled in the boy's name under the title.

Think about this situation for a minute. If this happened to your best friend, how would he or she feel? How would you feel

Cooperative Learning

● Encourage students to discuss how audience empathy might help a speaker make a point.

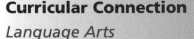

Curricular Connection

Language Arts

▲ Does the situation described in the Journal Entry on page 171 strike a sympathetic chord with some students? Can they think of a similar situation in which one special friend came through for them at a time when others let them down? Challenge interested students to retell their experiences in a one- or two-paragraph account. Volunteers can read their paragraphs to the class.

if it happened to you? After the newspaper article was published, many adult readers wrote in to say they felt bad for the boy. The article reminded them of when they or their children were teased in school. Because they could still remember their own feelings when this happened, these adults had empathy for the student.

Empathy is the ability to put yourself in another person's place and understand what that person is feeling. You can show empathy for a friend when you have had a similar experience or when you understand the feelings your friend is having. Good friends try to put themselves in the other person's shoes and empathize. In the following journal entry, one student describes just such a situation.

JOURNAL ENTRY

I would have lost my mind without Jay last summer. After I broke my leg, I lost my place on the soccer team, and I was stuck home for most of the summer. Everyone else told me how lucky I was the car accident didn't kill me. Only Jay seemed to know how really sad and angry I was. Jay always made me feel he understood what I was feeling.

A skillful communicator tries to see the world from a good friend's point of view and then tries to show the friend that he or she is not alone in those feelings, that someone else understands. This does not mean you must have had the same experience in order to empathize. It means you can imagine what it would be like to be in this situation and how it would feel. Frequently this is very difficult.

Listening

The student who wrote "Sometimes the best thing a friend can do is just sit and listen" discovered something important about communication in friendships. Good friends should be able to

171

Skill Development

Active Listening

● Bring in a book of poems by Robert Frost, and read one or two of the poems aloud, perhaps "Mending Wall" and "A Time to Talk." The former is about fences and neighbors; and the latter, about stopping work to talk to a friend. Ask students whether they think it is important to stop work or another activity when a friend wants to talk. Are there times when it's necessary to postpone such a talk?

count on each other to listen to feelings and personal information. As you learned in Chapter 3, listening takes effort and empathic listening takes effort and commitment.

Sometimes good friends have to listen to the same story or the same problem over and over again. Other times they have to help a friend sort out feelings or figure out how to deal with a problem, without telling the friend what to do. This type of listening takes patience.

You may have heard the expression, "You have to read between the lines," which means figuring out what is implied but not actually stated in a written text. The same idea can be applied to spoken words. It's called "listening between the words," and it means hearing what is implied but not actually said.

Many people do not say what they mean, particularly when they are talking about negative feelings. As a listener, you hear a part of what is in the speaker's mind. But you don't get the whole story directly. The better you know someone, the easier it is to put his or her remarks into context. For example, if you heard someone say, "I'm certainly not up for spending Thanksgiving at my father's. I wish the day would just disappear," you might interpret the remark in a number of ways. Below are several interpretations.

I'm jealous of my father's time with his new wife.

I feel guilty leaving my mother on Thanksgiving.

I feel uncomfortable in their house. I just don't fit in.

I feel sad not spending Thanksgiving with my mother and grandmother.

Only if you knew the speaker well would you be able to interpret the correct feeling. You would know that the original statement about Thanksgiving was a surface statement. The strong feelings were below the surface and could only be understood by "listening between the words."

"What is lofty can be said in any language, and what is mean should be said in none."

MAIMONIDES

Recognizing the difference between what a friend says and what he or she means may require listening to feelings.

Cooperative Learning

Have students work in pairs to make a list of put-downs they commonly hear among their peers. Pairs can share their lists with the class, and students can discuss the reasons why people use put-downs in everyday conversation.

INTERACT

Write three messages that contain implied meanings. In a small group read your statements to each other and discuss the context in which these might be said. Each person should try to identify possible meanings by "listening between the words."

Supporting

Your hair always looks so nice. I hate you.

How come your brother is the only coordinated one in your family?

These and other put-downs are heard every day. Some people think it's clever to make fun of others. Some people seem to feel better about themselves when they cut down someone else. Often such messages hurt friendships, as shown in this journal comment:

173

Curricular Connection

Art / Language Arts

Students might work in pairs to design greeting cards or self-stick removable notes expressing congratulations, good wishes, good luck, or appreciation.

JOURNAL ENTRY

Just this morning Carlos and I were insulting each other, and I really hate it when he gets me worked up like that. When he insults me, I try to defend myself, but I guess that's only natural. I don't know if he's trying to get back at me or at someone else, but it seems like he loves to call people names and tries to cut them down. People who belittle others are just insecure themselves, but their comments still hurt.

The opposite of cutting down is providing support. Supportive messages make people feel good about themselves. These messages may include compliments, praise, good wishes, appreciation, or congratulations on a job well done. They may be directed to the person, or they may be said about the person when he or she is not there. Look at the following examples:

Your hair always looks great.

I heard you got the only A on the history test. You deserved it.

I appreciated your help on the pep rally.

Although some friends enjoy themselves by kidding around, there are times when a direct message of support is important. Good friends are willing to give direct compliments or recognize a friend's achievements.

What friends say about each other to different people is a real test of friendship. What do you say if you hear someone cutting down your good friend? Do you ignore it, or do you defend your friend? Do you ever cut down your friends when they are not with you? When friends support each other, they help build each other's self-esteem. When they cut each other down, they may lower each other's self-esteem. Friends have a great deal of power over each other.

Constructive Criticism

All friends must deal with differences between them. No one is perfect, and people will upset each other by things they say or do.

Some friends never really say what is bothering them and keep annoying each other until the friendship dies. Other friends are able to tell each other what they do and don't like.

APPLY

Look at the following conversations and decide in which case Susan is acting as a better friend to Brittany.

Susan to Consuelo

Brittany makes me so mad. She borrows my sweaters and ruins them. She's always asking if she can wear my earrings or use my bags. Then she forgets to return them. She's a real slob, and I'm not letting her use my things again.

Susan to Brittany

I don't want to hurt your feelings, but I need to tell you something. I get upset when you borrow my sweaters and return them with stains. And I don't like it when I have to remind you to bring back stuff, like my earrings. I would appreciate it if you would clean things that get messed up and return the other stuff when you said you would.

In the first case Brittany may never know how she upsets Susan. Susan is complaining to Consuelo about Brittany. Brittany has no reason to change unless Susan tells her how she feels. In the second case Susan has told the right person. Brittany now knows there is a problem. Susan has told her what to do to solve the problem.

Guidelines for Constructive Criticism

Good friends need to give and receive constructive criticism from each other. **Constructive criticism** involves stating what is bothering you and making suggestions for change. The purpose of constructive criticism is to remove the problem and make the relationship stronger. The following guidelines can help you give constructive criticism.

175

"He was wont to speak plain and to the purpose."

SHAKESPEARE
Much Ado About Nothing, Act II, Sc. 1

Skill Development

Active Listening

You might read at least the first stanza of William Blake's poem "A Poison Tree" aloud and ask students to comment.

> I was angry with my friend:
> I told my wrath, my wrath did end.
> I was angry with my foe:
> I told it not, my wrath did grow.

Cooperative Learning

Students role-playing the Interact activity might develop scenes based on the following suggestions:

One student has borrowed a jacket and not returned it.

One student has not telephoned the other at the agreed-upon time.

One student offered to return a videotape for the other but forgot about it and a large fee is due.

One student borrowed five dollars from the other and has not repaid it, even after repeated requests.

1. Talk in terms of "I." Tell others how their behavior affects you. Think how you feel when someone says, "You were very rude to me." Do you feel differently if the person says, "I felt ignored when you kept interrupting." In the earlier example Susan told Brittany she got upset about certain behavior. She did not say, "You are a real slob," or "You ruin my stuff."

2. Describe the behavior; don't label the person. Rather than saying someone is "lazy" or "mean" or "dumb," describe the behavior that upsets you. Comments such as the following tell your friend exactly what is upsetting you: "You said we would go to a movie Friday night, and then you made plans to go over to Terry's house"; "When we were at the party, you did not talk to me."

3. Avoid name calling. Calling people names or giving them negative labels does not help solve a disagreement. If you call people names, they do not hear your true message. Also, it's hard to forget the names you were called even long after a disagreement is over. Name-calling shuts out any constructive criticism or communication.

4. Stick to the present. Don't criticize by dragging in past history. If you are upset about how someone treated you last weekend, don't remind that person of what made you angry last month or last year. Storing things up and then telling someone everything at once is not fair. No doubt, when someone does this to you, you get quite angry. No one likes to find out that a friend has been holding a grudge.

INTERACT

Work with a partner and develop two scenes based on a single interpersonal situation, for example, a friend who is angry at another friend for breaking weekend plans. First, play out your scenes using "you" messages and labels. Then replay the scene using "I" messages and descriptions. Each participant should describe how he or she felt in each scene.

176

Encourage pairs of students to write short scripts for two people about friendship. Scripts might involve giving criticism, being empathic, giving support (or not giving support), or they might be a dialogue between acquaintances who are gradually becoming friends. Scripts could then be performed for the class.

Name calling may appear funny but can be hurtful.

All these guidelines and ideas depend on time. If you don't spend much time with your friend, it will be harder to share feelings and ideas with him or her. Too many people place other things above their friendships. For example, you might want to visit your sick friend, Joe, but also want to see a movie with other friends the same night. You have to make a choice. Your friend Celina may want to talk with you about a problem after school on the day you had planned to go shopping for new clothes. Again, you have to make a choice. Making time for your friends is important. It's hard to share personal things with people you see once in a great while.

CHAPTER 6 SUMMARY

This chapter defines and discusses interpersonal communication and relationships. It looks at (1) some characteristics of friendships, including the ability to keep secrets, loyalty, warmth, support, honesty, and humor; (2) stages of friendship, including first meetings, acquaintances, friends, and best friends; (3) communication skills of friends, including sharing personal information, sharing feelings, empathizing, listening, supporting, and offering constructive criticism.

177

Answers

Think About It

Student answers will vary. Here are sample answers:

1. Six qualities of friendship: (1) Ability to keep secrets. A person needs to know that he or she can trust a friend. (2) Loyalty. This is what leads to long-term friendships. (3) Warmth. This quality is often expressed nonverbally by facial expressions, sitting very close to one another, etc. (4) Support. Good friends help each other in many ways; for example, they give each other positive reinforcement, are happy for one another if something nice happens to one of them, etc. (5) Honesty. A good friend tells you the truth, even when it hurts. But a good friend is also careful to make sure the honesty is helpful, not hurtful. (6) Humor. Friends can't be serious all the time. They need to be able to laugh and kid around with one another.

2. Students should come up with personal examples of the following: (1) first meetings, (2) becoming acquaintances, (3) becoming friends, (4) becoming best friends.

3. As an example: "Sue failed math. She must not study."

CHAPTER REVIEW

Think About It

1. What are the six characteristics of friendship? Briefly describe each in one or two sentences.

2. What are the four stages of friendship? Describe and give an example of a relationship you have observed at each stage.

3. Give an example of stereotyping.

4. Describe the six communication building blocks, or skills, of friendship.

5. Define and describe interpersonal communication.

Try It Out

1. In groups of three or four classmates, discuss your beliefs about friendship. Use the following questions to guide your discussion: What is the importance of friendship? What qualities should a close friend possess? What actions can ruin a friendship?

2. In groups of three or four classmates, describe situations in which you or a friend have been stereotyped. Discuss how the stereotyping affected communication between the stereotyped person and others.

3. In a group of four or five students, discuss one of the following statements in relation to the key word that precedes it.

Empathy: Do not judge a person until you have walked a mile in his or her shoes.

First Meetings: It's unfortunate that you only have one chance to make a first impression.

Listening: Listening between the words helps you find the real meaning of the message.

4. Using the statements at the opening of the chapter as a guide, create three two-sentence statements about friendship. Each one should start "Friendships are . . ."

Put It in Writing

1. Pretend you have a pen pal in a foreign country who will come to live in your community for a year. Write your pen pal a letter describing how good friends communicate with each other in your culture.

2. Look at some want ads in your local paper. Write a want ad for an ideal friend.

3. Write a paragraph describing a time when constructive criticism given by a friend helped you or someone you know make a friendship stronger.

4. Write a paragraph describing a time when sharing information with a friend improved your friendship.

Speak About It

1. In a one- or two-minute speech, describe your ideal friend.

2. Find a poem about friendship, or write one of your own. You might use the form of a cinquain poem. Read your poem to your classmates.

3. Tell the class a short story about a turning point in a friendship. You may use your own experience or describe an incident from a friendship you read about or heard about.

4. (1) Sharing personal information, (2) sharing feelings, (3) empathy, (4) listening, (5) support, (6) constructive criticism.

5. Interpersonal communication is the type that goes on between friends and in close relationships. It is built on trust and sharing.

Quick Check

Ask students to find and define these Key Terms:

constructive criticism (175)

empathy (171)

first meetings (157)

interpersonal communication (150)

stereotyping (158)

Unit 3 Planner		Ancillary Resources				
Group Communication	**Time Management**					
7 Communication in Groups (pp. 180–219)	Week 7	●	●	●	●	
8 Forms of Group Discussion (pp. 220–253)	Week 8	●	●	●	●	

Unit Focus

Unit 3 introduces and explains the characteristics of small groups, presents steps in group problem-solving, elaborates on a number of different discussion formats, and introduces parliamentary procedure.

Unit Portfolios

Activities marked with this symbol are suitable for inclusion in speech portfolios.

Ability Key

▲ average and above-average students
● all students
▼ average and below-average students

Ancillary Resource Key

 = *Teacher's Resource Book*

 = Workbook

 = TRB Worksheets & Evaluation Forms

 = TRB Assessment and Testing

Performance Objectives

After completing this unit, students will be able to

1. explain the characteristics of groups

2. describe steps in group problem-solving

3. evaluate group discussion

4. understand various group formats

5. participate in parliamentary procedure

UNIT THREE

Group Communication

Bibliography

Print

Carr, Marjorie Mitchell and Marjorie Mitchell Cann. *Point of Order: The Ready Reference for Simple Rules of Order and Parliamentary Procedure.* New York: Berkley Publishing Group, 1993.

Fox, William M. *Effective Group Problem Solving.* San Francisco: Jossey-Bass, Inc., 1987.

Muir, Janette Kenner, ed. *C-Span in the Communication Classroom.* Annandale, Va.: National Communication Association, 1992.

Pohl, Alice N. *Formal Meetings: How to Preside and Participate.* Lincolnwood, Ill.: NTC/Contemporary Publishing, 1990.

Web Sites

Aardvark's EFL Resources
http://www.ilc group.com/aardvark

ERIC Clearinghouse on Reading, English, and Communication
http://www.indiana.edu/~eric_rec

National Communication Association
http://www.natcom.org

U.S. House of Representatives
http://www.house.gov

U.S. Senate
http://www.senate.gov

White House
http://www.whitehouse.gov

Motivation

Ask students to think about the various groups to which they belong. Ask them how often they participate in group discussions. Remind them that, although one-on-one communication is important, knowledge of how to participate in a group is also important, especially in school, work, and extracurricular settings.

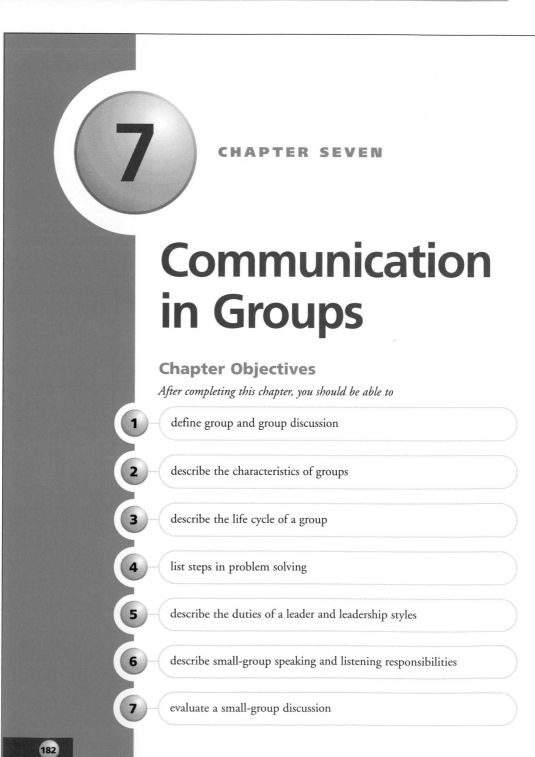

7

CHAPTER SEVEN

Communication in Groups

Chapter Objectives

After completing this chapter, you should be able to

1 — define group and group discussion

2 — describe the characteristics of groups

3 — describe the life cycle of a group

4 — list steps in problem solving

5 — describe the duties of a leader and leadership styles

6 — describe small-group speaking and listening responsibilities

7 — evaluate a small-group discussion

▶ **Teach**

Critical Thinking

Predicting

● Encourage students to read the chapter title and predict the chapter content. Ask them what *group communication* means to them. Elicit responses from several volunteers. Tell these volunteers that by answering your question they are exhibiting group communication skills.

Links to Past Learning

Encourage students to think about the many kinds of groups they have participated in or seen in action. Students might mention classes, scout troops, bands and orchestras, committees, clubs, choirs and choruses, and so on. Ask whether the people in these groups were congenial. Were any of these groups formed to solve problems? Ask students to give some reasons why groups are formed.

⦿ Key Terms

brainstorming	group	group purpose	role
clique	group norms	moderator	storming
criteria	group problem solving	norming	subgroup
forming		performing	

183

183

"Men are never so likely to settle a question rightly as when they discuss it freely."

THOMAS BABINGTON MACAULEY

Substitute Teacher Tip

Ask students to think about two or three problems in their neighborhood, school, town, or city. Have groups been formed to deal with these problems? If so, what are these groups? If not, could the problems be alleviated or solved if groups *were* formed to deal with them? Ask what the advantages are to problem-solving as a group.

Skill Development

Quick Skill Opportunity

▼ Ask for volunteers to tell you some factors that make a person a good leader.

All your life you have been part of different groups. You may have belonged to 4-H, a track team, speech team, student council, volunteer tutors, or swing chorus. Some of these groups may have worked well together and accomplished a lot. Others may not have worked well together. The following comments describe students' experiences in groups.

> We talked for an hour and we didn't get anything decided.

> Everyone was talking all at once and no one wanted to listen to anyone's ideas.

> We were supposed to cover several agenda items at the student council meeting, but we got in a disagreement over the dress code and pretty soon we ran out of time.

> At the Scout meeting last night, we made several major decisions about our troop's goals for the year.

Groups do not automatically work well together. Members and leaders need to be competent communicators in order to act effectively in groups. This chapter introduces the characteristics of groups, describes effective problem solving in groups, discusses communication skills needed by group members and leaders, and shows you how to evaluate groups.

CHARACTERISTICS OF GROUPS

What makes a bunch of people a group? Are people in the school hall a group? Are servers in a soup kitchen a group? Are holiday shoppers in the mall a group? There is a difference between crowds or bunches of people and groups. A **group** consists of people who

> share an interest in the same things or share a common purpose

> communicate regularly among themselves

> participate in planning and decision making

> feel connected to the other members

Do people always know how to act within a group? Are there rules or guidelines for members? In most cases, members have to figure out how the group works while they are part of it.

Cooperative Learning

● Ask students if, after reading the characteristics of groups, they feel that this class is a group. Encourage students to discuss the four characteristics and to form a consensus about the nature of the class as a group

Learning Styles

Visual Learning

● Encourage students to bring in newspaper or magazine pictures of groups (class pictures, sports teams, Supreme Court, U. S. Congress, local committees and clubs, partygoers, or protest groups, for example). Ask students to display their (unlabeled) pictures and ask others to identify the groups. Do students know the purpose of each group? Are there any things that identify these people as a group besides the fact that their pictures were taken together? Are the people in each group of similar age or height? Are they all the same sex? Do they dress alike? Are they doing or holding similar things?

Competent communicators consider the following characteristics: structure, purpose, norms, roles, and subgroups.

Group Structure

Group structure is the amount of organization a group needs to carry out its business. There are two basic types of structure, formal and informal. You may have already noticed that there is a difference between the way a student council meeting is conducted and the way a Halloween dance committee meeting is conducted or between a meeting of the basketball team and the meeting of the police youth-advisory board.

Groups with set rules for communication are highly organized and have what is called a formal structure. You know which persons will take certain responsibilities and you know the order of meetings. In most cases, groups such as student council are governed by a constitution, rules, or procedures. There are established procedures for speaking to the group. Usually one person runs the meeting, and each meeting follows the same general pattern. As you will see in the next chapter, groups that run their meetings according to parliamentary procedure have a formal group structure.

Groups with an informal structure are less organized and do not follow set rules. Each meeting might be organized differently. These groups find ways to run a meeting without many rules and regulations. Friendship groups or groups that organize quickly for a specific purpose, such as a school dance or community picnic, may not need much formal structure.

JOURNAL ENTRY

Two of the students in our school were burned out of their home. A group of teachers, parents, and kids got together to raise money and collect food, clothing, and furniture for the family. We operated as a group for about three weeks but no one really took over. Everyone called each other and took on certain projects. In three weeks they were in a nice apartment and the group stopped working together.

APPLY

Read the following conversations and decide which group has a formal structure and which has an informal one.

A. **Travis:** The agenda for tonight's meeting will follow the usual order. We will hear the secretary's report, the treasurer's report, and the social committee's report. Then we will finish old business and move on to new business.

   Aimee: What about the fund-raising for the spring trip?

   Travis: That comes under new business. We will get to it later.

B. **Travis:** Well, we better get started. What do we want to talk about first?

   Aimee: I think we need to get started on raising money for the spring class trip. We have to plan car washes, popcorn sales, and a mini-marathon.

   Travis: That's a good idea. Let's get a committee organized today in order to divide up the work.

As you can tell, conversation A had a formal structure. There was a very specific way to carry on the meeting and Travis insisted that the order be followed. Conversation B illustrates the informal structure, which is more unpredictable.

Many groups have neither a totally formal nor a totally informal structure. If you think of a line that runs from formal to informal, you might place some groups in the middle. Also, groups that are usually formal may become more informal at times and vice versa. For example, as the date for the dance gets nearer, the dance committee may become very structured in order to get its work done on time.

Group Purpose

A **group purpose** is the group's reason for existing. Just as group structures range from formal to informal, group purposes range from all work to all social activity. Groups with a work purpose attempt to complete a task or reach a goal. The main purpose of a social group is for the members to enjoy one another's company and have fun. Many groups are a combination of both purposes. Think about the purposes of groups to which you belong. Are the meetings set up for members to work, socialize with friends, or do both?

Although many groups involve some work and some play, groups faced with a problem have little time for socializing. For example, if your school athletic program is going to be dropped because of lack of money, some parent-student groups might try to raise money quickly. These people would come to meetings to work hard and fast.

Other groups encourage members to enjoy each other's company. Although the group members may do work, there is social time to laugh, talk, or have fun together. For instance, a swim team or marching band may involve fun and work. A Scout troop works on badges and has fun on camp-outs. Spanish club members work to improve their ability to speak the language, but they also enjoy parties with Latin music and food. What groups have you joined mainly because you wanted to be with the other people?

Links to Past Learning

Ask for volunteers to try to state the purpose of some of the groups below.

- Campfire Girls
- 4-H Clubs
- Big Brothers and Sisters
- National Future Farmers of America Organization
- Make-a-Wish Foundation
- PTA
- soccer or basketball teams
- orchestra and/or band

Putting out a school publication is the specific purpose of one type of group.

66In general those who have nothing to say continue to spend the longest time in doing it.99

JAMES RUSSELL LOWELL

Substitute Teacher Tip

Encourage students to think of the school as a vast group. Ask individual students to name some of the norms that all group members (students and teachers) are expected to follow.

Skill Development

On the Job

● Encourage students who volunteer to share with classmates some of the group norms and behavior they encounter on the job. They might discuss such issues as uniforms, arrival and departure times, communication with others, and so on.

Group Norms

Certain behaviors are expected in some groups. Each of the following statements describes the way members of a group know how they are expected to act:

When we have a swim-team meeting, the coach locks the door as soon as we start. If you're late, you don't get in.

When you criticize someone else's performance on the speech team, you have to discuss exactly what the performer did. You can't just say 'I liked it' or 'I didn't like it.'

Group norms are the standards for action within the group. In other words, norms establish a model for the behavior of group members. All groups have norms. Most groups have both general norms and communication norms. General group norms might include these:

how to act or dress

whether it's OK to arrive late or leave early

how hard to work

whether taking a break is acceptable

who can be part of the group

Groups also have norms for speaking and listening. Particular communication norms within a group might include these:

whether it's OK to disagree

how to disagree

what topics are safe to talk about

how much to talk

how to talk about certain people

who to talk to on certain subjects

how to talk about the group to outsiders

For example, the school newspaper staff may expect members to meet all deadlines. Group members who wish to talk loudly may be expected to move to another room if others are working on

188

Beyond the Classroom

● You may wish to take your class to visit a local city-council meeting, school-board meeting, or other public meeting. Encourage students to take note of the group dynamic and the various roles the members fulfill.

Motivation

After students have looked over the list of communication roles on this page and the next, ask them to think about which role they find themselves in most often, and which role they most enjoy. Encourage class discussion of the part personality plays in communication roles.

stories. People may not be allowed to leave until the plan for all the pages is finished, even if it gets late. Members will learn how to disagree with another's idea for an article. There may be inside jokes about people who are involved with the paper or about people in the school, but these jokes are seldom shared with outsiders.

OBSERVE

Spend an hour with a group you know. Try to identify some of the general norms and the communication norms followed by members of the group.

Group Roles

A **role** is a pattern of communication that characterizes one's place in a group. Think of a group in which you often find yourself. How would you describe yourself in that group: funny, serious, helpful, shy, angry? People tend to behave in fairly predictable ways within groups.

There are many roles people can take on in a group. These roles may be helpful or harmful to the group. The following list includes the most common communication roles.

1. *Experts.* These people know a great deal about a subject and are willing to share their knowledge with the group. If the experts start to take over and force ideas on other members, they may be looked on as "know-it-alls."

2. *Supporters.* These people support and defend the ideas of others in the group. Sometimes they help a shy person's ideas to be heard and may encourage him or her to speak again. If supporters never offer their own ideas, however, they often become known as "yes-people" or "head-nodders."

3. *Questioners.* These people raise important points about ideas. They make everyone think twice before rushing into decisions. They may spark discussion and new ideas. However, if the questioners raise issues about every topic, they slow down the group's progress and become "question hounds."

189

Skill Development

Media Literacy

● Encourage students to look for the different group communication roles in the television programs they watch. Students could try to find at least one example of each communication role over the course of a weeks' viewing. They could keep a log of their findings. Encourage students to discuss their findings as a group to ascertain which communication roles are most popular on television.

4. *Compromisers.* The compromisers can see how ideas could be combined into even better ideas. This is valuable because it uses other members' ideas creatively. However, compromisers also need to produce their own new ideas.

5. *Challengers.* These people are willing to argue or debate ideas rather than just accept them. They force the entire group to think more carefully. When they challenge everybody just for fun, they annoy other group members and slow the group's progress.

6. *Moderators.* These people keep the group process moving and try to see that everyone gets involved. They may remind the group of deadlines or help quiet members to participate. They may bring up group rules. When they try to police the group at all times, however, they lose their effectiveness.

7. *Tension Relievers.* These people keep things from getting too serious or boring. They may crack jokes, tease a member of the group, or make funny, supportive remarks. When they can't do anything but act silly, however, they are known as "clowns."

8. *Observers.* These people prefer to watch and listen during group meetings. They may feel uncomfortable in the group. They may be shy or they may just feel that they don't have anything to add.

INTERACT

In a group of six to eight classmates, each person should choose a role from the list of group roles. (Every role need not be chosen, and more than one person may choose the same role.) The group should then select a school-related topic and discuss it in front of the class. After the discussion, the class should identify the role or roles each group member played. The identification should include examples of the comments that indicated the role, such as "Lisanne seemed to be a challenger because she asked members hard questions about their points and asked them to link their points to the ideas expressed by others. She even told Josh he was 'waffling' and said he should 'take a stand.'"

Subgroups

Not all groups remain one single unit. Many groups form into subgroups. A **subgroup** is a smaller unit within a group. The rhythmic gymnastics team may have beginning, intermediate, and advanced subgroups. The student council may have a projects committee, a social committee, and a finance committee. Large social groups may include smaller groups of friends. These people may be closer friends because they live near each other, take the same classes, or have the same interests.

Subgroups sometimes allow people to work on specific jobs or to use special talents. For example, the finance committee can manage the student council budget. Sometimes the subgroup can become more important than the larger group. Members may feel more attached to the subgroup and forget the goals of the larger group. For example, the social committee of the student council may get so involved in planning fun activities that members may lose sight of the larger group's governing goals. Think about a large group of which you are a member. Does it have subgroups? What are its subgroups? How well do the subgroups contribute to the large group's overall goals?

A special kind of subgroup is called a clique. **Cliques** are subgroups of people who tend to associate with each other and avoid others. They consider themselves a closed group or an "in" group. Usually clique groups make non-members feel like outsiders. Cliques always raise issues of insiders and outsiders. One student expressed negative feelings about popularity and "in" groups in the following way:

> **JOURNAL ENTRY**
>
> Okay, I know I'm not popular. I'm sort of glad I'm not. Popularity does sort of make you a snob, because everybody not in your clique is supposed to be a nerd or stupid or any negative name they can classify you by.
>
> *continued*

Critical Thinking
Organizing

▼ Have students create graphic organizers that show the subgroups of a major group. They might choose a government body such as the U.S. Senate, a club, the student council, or any large, multifaceted membership organization. (Senate and House committees are shown in *The World Almanac*)

Motivation

▼ Ask students to think about any groups they may have belonged to but quit in the past. Encourage group discussion about what types of problems can interfere with a person's enjoyment or participation in a group.

continued

When new people come to our school, the popular group tries to become their friend in order to prove to each other that they have a lot of friends. As soon as the new person has become their friend, they start to ignore that person. Sometimes they "accept" people into their group and then try to make them feel out of place.

OBSERVE

Observe a group in your school. Describe in your journal the communication behaviors that indicate who is "in" and who is "out." Look at language, use of space, appearance, common interests, and how "outsiders" are treated.

As a competent communicator you need to be aware of a group's structure, purpose, norms, roles, and subgroups. As you learn about each of these group characteristics, you will be able to select the best communication strategies to make your group work well.

GROUP PROBLEM SOLVING

Although some groups get together just to have fun, most groups have a task purpose. Very frequently the task involves problem solving. As a group member or leader, you need to understand the process of **group problem solving** so that you can work effectively in different types of groups.

According to an old expression, two heads are better than one. If this is true, do you think six heads are better than five, or seven better than six? Although there is no perfect number for a small group, several people can often solve a problem better than one person. But sometimes a group is unable to solve problems

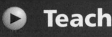
because members disagree, become lazy or stubborn, or spend too much time on one point. If a group does not work well, the situation may become frustrating. One student describes the possible difficulties of working in groups in the following way:

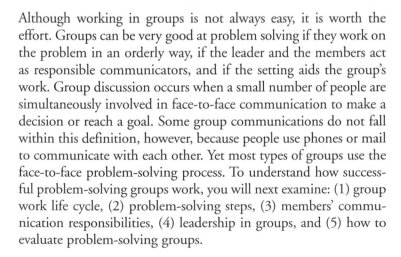

JOURNAL ENTRY

Sometimes you may never know what kind of a predicament you can get into when you're in a group. If everyone is shy, it's hard to communicate. If they don't work, you get stuck with all the work. If everyone wants to lead, there will be lots of arguments. Sometimes it's very hard for a group to work together unless the members can communicate in an orderly way. That means people have to have self-control. That's not always easy!

Although working in groups is not always easy, it is worth the effort. Groups can be very good at problem solving if they work on the problem in an orderly way, if the leader and the members act as responsible communicators, and if the setting aids the group's work. Group discussion occurs when a small number of people are simultaneously involved in face-to-face communication to make a decision or reach a goal. Some group communications do not fall within this definition, however, because people use phones or mail to communicate with each other. Yet most types of groups use the face-to-face problem-solving process. To understand how successful problem-solving groups work, you will next examine: (1) group work life cycle, (2) problem-solving steps, (3) members' communication responsibilities, (4) leadership in groups, and (5) how to evaluate problem-solving groups.

Group Work Life Cycle

Sometimes groups are formed to deal with a particular problem or issue. In most cases, some or all of the members may not have worked together before. Therefore, the group members are trying

Links to Past Learning

Share with students the adage, "Too many cooks spoil the broth." Ask for commentary about situations students know of where too many leaders and not enough supporters or followers created problems for a group project.

193

Cooperative Learning

▲ Invite students to work in small groups to present skits about one of the stages in the group life cycle of discussion. See if classmates can guess which stage is being presented.

Critical Thinking

Organizing

● Encourage interested students to draw process diagrams that illustrate the group life cycle of discussion.

to figure out how to work together at the same time that they are trying to deal with a problem. Most groups experience a predictable life cycle of development and most groups follow a specific problem-solving process. The group life cycle of discussion includes four stages: **forming**, **storming, norming,** and **performing.**

Forming: This is the stage when members come together, size each other up, try to figure out where everyone fits, and try to find some sense of leadership. It is similar to the first meeting stage in friendship development (Chapter 6) when you try to be polite, avoid strong disagreements, and find some similarities.

Storming: This stage occurs after some similarities have been established and members have become more comfortable in the group. It is the time when differences begin to surface and members start to assert their individual positions and goals. Some members try to seize power, others try to be persuasive, while others begin to wonder if they belong at all. Frequently frustrations and differences are aired. The group is struggling to create some sense of order. This is often an uncomfortable period when some members will consider leaving or wonder if the problem can be solved.

Norming: At this stage members begin to function effectively together and to develop a sense of group identity because they have worked through the struggles about influence and process in the storming stage. Group norms have been established, and members have a sense of the rules and limits. Group roles are also established, and members follow the expected problem-solving steps. Members tend to trust each other more easily and feel more confident that they can reach some solution.

Performing: The task is the key point at this stage, and work is accomplished without much interpersonal difficulty. Members feel like part of a working team as they continue to solve the problem. They can predict others' responses and know how to avoid certain pitfalls. Energy is focused on the problem, group tasks, and solutions. Eventually the task is completed. As you

Limited English Proficiency

Be sure students understand the idiom "Size each other up" (under "Forming"), and ask someone to define *pitfalls* (under "Performing").

might imagine, each stage has certain predictable communication patterns. The following are examples of typical comments:

Forming

"Has anyone been involved with something like this before?"

"What are we supposed to do exactly?"

"I'm not sure why I'm in this group."

"Shouldn't we get more information or get a leader?"

Storming

"This is getting to be a waste of time."

"It feels like we are just going around in circles."

"Let's just get off dead center."

"Some people talk too much, and others just sit there."

Norming

"If you look for more historical information, I'll do the two interviews."

"Everyone agrees to be back with a report in six days."

"Who did we agree would write the three alternatives?"

"Let's be sure anyone with an objection gets a turn."

Performing

"So we all agree to the three-part solution?"

"What's the best way to report our conclusions?"

"After Dawn presents the needs, Jay can talk about fundraising."

"Are we ready to write this report?"

As the group goes through these stages, the problem is being worked out. Many groups try to use a formal problem-solving model to keep them on task. The most commonly used model is discussed in the next section.

195

Links to Past Learning

▲ Ask for volunteers to come up with at least one more typical comment for each of the four stages of the life cycle of group discussion, and write the comments on the board.

🎙 **SPEAKING OF . . .**

FRANK SMITH

Many Kansas City adult community leaders are surprised to encounter the skills and knowledge displayed by Frank Smith, a local teenager who designs communication workshops and training programs for adults and young people. For four years Frank has volunteered at the Promise Project, a non-profit organization that works to build healthy youth-adult partnerships and to strengthen the voice of youth in the community. The project is formed by cooperation between Kansas City Consensus and the Junior League of Kansas City, Missouri. As cochair of the Training Committee, Frank frequently is responsible for managing meetings, a role in which he facilitates discussions, encourages contributions, supports new ideas, and moves the group toward a solution.

Frank reports that he sees himself as a "trustee" rather than a traditional leader. In his opinion, a trustee is someone who, before she or he can influence the community in any way, must win the community's trust. Trusteeship implies a partnership; trustees have strong personal commitments to be group members and always try to work for the group's benefit. Frank also tries to be a good facilitator. He tries to encourage many different types of ideas and also encourages group members to "piggyback" or expand upon the idea of another person. One of his greatest challenges is to convince adults to listen carefully to teenagers' ideas and to learn to work on an equal basis with young people.

Frank will find that these group communication skills serve him well in college and that they will benefit him in many careers that involve training, such as business, educational psychology, recreation, and government.

Curricular Connection

Language Arts

Interested students might like to write a "Speaking Of..." feature about someone in their class, school, or community who is a competent communicator.

Five-Step Model of Problem Solving

Group solutions don't happen by accident. They should represent the best thinking of the group members. Problem solving follows a series of steps.

1. Identify the problem

2. Analyze the problem

3. Set criteria for a solution

4. Develop solutions

5. Select a solution

To help you see how the problem-solving process works, a problem related to extracurricular speech activities will be discussed at each step of the process.

Identify the Problem

To hold an effective problem-solving discussion, you first have to identify a specific problem. This first step has two parts. The first part requires narrowing the topic, and the second part requires phrasing it into a question.

Successful problem solving requires contributions from all members of a group.

66The biggest problem in the world could have been solved when it was small.99

WITTER BYNNER
The Way of Life According to Lao Tzu

Skill Development

Media Literacy

● Tell students to keep the five-step model of problem solving in mind while they watch television or films. See how many students can cite an example of group problem solving they have witnessed on a favorite show. Encourage students to chart the steps they saw.

Skill Development

Research

▼ Encourage students to think about career options that require group communication skills. Make a list of their suggestions on the chalkboard, and encourage them to research one of those careers and report to the class.

Cooperative Learning

● Set the class a problem and ask them to work as a group to come up with a solution. Student discussion should cover each of the five steps in the problem-solving model. Topics might include graffiti on school buildings, improving cafeteria food, improving on-time class attendance, or making the neighborhood safer.

Narrow the Topic Topics like "Bicycle Safety" and "Lack of Involvement in Speech Activities" are unclear because they are too broad. For example, what would be included under "Lack of Involvement in Speech Activities"? Would you discuss types of activities? values of speech and drama clubs? finding new members? The words of a discussion topic must be clearly defined, and everyone must understand what they mean. The topic must also be limited to an area the group can manage. For example, the group may decide to discuss types of activities one week and values of drama activities another week.

Phrase the Topic as a Question A topic must be phrased carefully so that everyone understands the exact problem. It should be phrased as a question and expressed simply, clearly, and fairly, and it should be phrased to avoid getting only yes or no answers. Usually problems are phrased as questions of fact, value, or policy:

1. *Questions of fact* ask about what is. They require people to find the answers. The solution to the problem is found in the information contained in the answer. The answer should be the end of the discussion. These are examples of questions of fact:

   What are the bicycle laws in this county?

   What extracurricular speech activities exist in this school?

2. *Questions of value* concern issues of good or bad, right or wrong. They ask if ideas for things are valuable or not, useful or not. They depend on facts plus opinions. The answers to questions of value are based on facts and opinions. These are examples of questions of value:

   How good are the bicycle safety laws in our community?

   How valuable are the school's extracurricular speech activities?

3. *Questions of policy* ask what should be done. They are designed to examine change. These are examples of questions of policy:

   What bicycle safety laws should be enforced by the school?

   What should the school do to promote speech activities?

The discussion will depend on how the question is phrased. If the speech activities topic is phrased as a question of fact, the group has to decide exactly what is classified as a speech activity and how many there are in the school. The group might discuss whether forensics should be called a speech activity, and they might list the Kiwanis Club Oratory Contest as a speech activity.

If the topic is phrased as a question of value, the group has to decide how valuable speech activities are. Members may speak from their own experiences or from the experiences of others in the school.

Finally, to answer a question of policy, the group would have to consider ways to promote the speech activities and then choose the best ideas. The policy question "What are the best ways to promote the school's speech activities?" will be used as the rest of the problem-solving steps are discussed.

INTERACT

In pairs or small groups, evaluate the following discussion questions. Identify each question as a question of fact, value, or policy. Then decide whether each question is acceptable or unacceptable. If it is unacceptable for discussion, rewrite it on a separate sheet of paper as an acceptable question.

1. How can we improve the grading system in the school?
2. Should students be allowed to leave school during their free periods?
3. Should extra credit be available to all students?
4. What should be done to reduce school absences?
5. How effective is the school absence policy?
6. How many students take part in the school lunch program?
7. What can the school do to improve cafeteria food?
8. What should the school do to promote respect for student diversity?

Limited English Proficiency

Have students work with others to distinguish between fact-, value-, and policy-based questions. Students might work with flashcards with various sentences written on the front and the designation *fact, value,* or *policy* written on the back.

Links to Past Learning

Students will probably identify 1, 5, and 6 as fact; 2 and 3 as value; and 4, 7, and 8 as policy.

Analyze the Problem

As a group member you need to understand the history, causes, and current state of a problem. When discussing the problem of promoting interest in speech activities, the group would need to collect information such as what activities exist; how many students are involved; why these students are involved; how many students take speech classes; why other students do not get involved; and what attempts have been made to involve more students.

Perhaps the group did research and discovered the following information: Many students do not even know the speech program exists; those who are aware of the program are unclear about the amount of work involved; some students say the speech activities conflict with sports activities or take too much time. Having made these discoveries, the group may decide that some students do not choose to be involved but that others simply do not know enough about the speech activities. After analyzing the problem, the group needs to set up ways to find a solution.

Set Criteria for a Solution

As a group moves toward solutions, its members have to consider what would make a solution workable. In other words, they have to decide what **criteria,** or standards, a good solution has to meet. In value and policy issues, the criteria must be defined for terms such as effective, valuable, or useful. In the example given, the group must decide what makes a speech activity valuable.

Policy questions usually involve criteria for setting up a program. These may involve money, time, people, or regulations. For example, when discussing the best ways to promote the school's speech activities, a good solution may have to meet the following criteria:

1. *Money.* The activity can cost no more than $300.

2. *Time.* The activity must be done in the spring to create interest and build the activity for the fall.

3. *People.* The activity should reach all students.

When trying to solve a problem, ask someone to record ideas suggested in a brainstorming session.

Motivation

Encourage students to consider the various ways in which they analyze problems during their everyday lives. Have them describe their process for solving problems such as how to make money for a specific item, or how to improve their grade in a certain class.

Develop Solutions

At this point group members try to find all kinds of possible solutions. This can be done in a number of ways. Members may suggest ideas and then discuss them as they are suggested. Or members may brainstorm to uncover as many solutions as possible.

Brainstorming is a process of listing aloud as many ideas as possible before discussion. In brainstorming, it is perfectly all right to add to someone else's ideas. There are two main rules for a brainstorming session:

1. Do not criticize or evaluate any of the ideas until the brainstorming session is completed.

2. Write down all ideas as they are given—even ideas that are similar.

After the brainstorming session is finished, the group should evaluate all of the ideas. Solutions to the speech activities problem might include these:

a letter to parents describing the activities and their benefits

a school assembly demonstrating the activities

after-school speech demonstrations showing teams and performers in action

201

Cooperative Learning

● Encourage students to use brainstorming to find a viable solution to a current school problem. Remind students to write down every idea, even those that seem silly or that are similar to other ideas already stated. Give the group 8 to 10 minutes for this activity. Then allow them to choose the best solution from the discussion.

Beyond the Classroom

You might want to invite a union arbitration expert or other person experienced in problem solving to speak to your class. Encourage students to ask questions and take notes about the arbitration process. Later they might use their notes to carry out short arbitration scenes.

a school tournament that involves participation by many classes

speech activity representatives talking to each class

a parent-student meeting one evening

giving speech activity members permanent hall passes

Select a Solution

To decide which of the solutions should be adopted, a group needs to ask three major questions:

1. Which solutions meet the criteria the group set up?

2. What are the weaknesses of each solution?

3. What are the strengths of each solution?

Some solutions are unworkable, impractical, or unfair. For example, the last solution given above is unfair. Few schools would give permanent passes to the members of one activity group without giving them to all students.

Some of the other solutions do not meet the criteria. The letter to parents may not reach the students and would be costly to mail. The tournament could not be held in the spring because it would take too much planning time. The after-school and evening activities would only be available to a small number of students, those who do not ride buses or have jobs. The group may reject all solutions except those involving the assembly and room representatives.

When examining the criteria, both the assembly and the room representatives solutions fit the criteria. The solution involving room representatives might have the disadvantage of only one person talking about the activities. The solution involving the assembly, on the other hand, would enable many students to demonstrate debates, give speeches, or perform group interpretations. Therefore, the group may decide to plan an assembly for the entire school.

A lot of effort goes into reaching a workable solution. Group members must be prepared to give time and energy to go through the steps correctly.

OBSERVE

Within the next week, observe a small group trying to solve a problem. It could be your friends deciding what to do Friday night, or it could be your club deciding how to spend money. Try to identify the five problem-solving steps. Describe the comments people made at each step.

GROUP MEMBER COMMUNICATION

I have a problem working with people in a group. Most of the problem involves communication. People won't be quiet, and so others around them can't hear what is being said. Everyone wants to voice his or her opinion at the same time.

All in all I think that the biggest problem with working in groups is that some people do not respect and listen to others' suggestions. If everyone is polite and gets along, your group project will be successful.

The previous comments indicate the struggles that arise as people try to work together. Group members' communication can support the group goals and help the problem-solving process, or it can slow down the process. To be a competent communicator in a problem-solving group, you have to act as both a responsible speaker and a responsible listener.

Speaker Responsibilities

Problem solving will be easier if speakers fulfill their responsibilities at all times. The following are effective speaking skills for group members.

Be Prepared Nothing slows a problem-solving discussion more than unprepared members. Just showing up with pages of material may not be helpful. You have to know what points you wish to share and have the important material in one place. Unprepared members not only waste their own time at the meeting, but they are a burden to the other members.

Have students write one paragraph that describes their own group-communication skills. At the bottom of the page, have them rate themselves as group communicators on a scale from 1 (expert communicator) to 10 (poor communicator).

Skill Development

Feedback

● Have students share their findings from the Observe exercise with a partner. Encourage both partners to analyze each other's information to figure out how well the person adhered to the problem-solving steps.

203

Links to Past Learning

Ask students to think of times in their lives when a member of a team or group talked nonstop. Encourage feedback on how this type of behavior affected them as individuals and the group as a whole.

Skill Development

Making Conversation

● Encourage students to share their experiences of having been unprepared for a presentation, class, or event. Get them to analyze the reasons for their lack of preparation and what, if anything, they might have learned from the experience.

When you are prepared and organized, your efforts can contribute greatly to solving a problem.

Share Your Ideas Thoughtfully Take your share of the responsibility in the group. No matter how informed you are, you will be of no value to the group unless you share your information and ideas. You need to contribute as much and as often as necessary to help the group solve the problem. Make sure, however, that you do not talk too much or stray from the subject.

Speak with Self-Respect Sometimes a member complains, "No one ever likes my ideas." This may occur because no one hears these ideas. Don't mumble! Be direct and clear. When you disagree with someone, don't make fun of his or her idea. Indicate that you have a different position or an alternative suggestion. Present your ideas in a firm and organized manner. Be willing to repeat your ideas to make your point.

APPLY

   Read the following dialogue of a group discussion. Can you identify the speakers' mistakes? Who is the competent group communicator?

Jennifer: Here's my idea for the theme of our social dance this spring. I talked to several people, and we all agreed that we should use a Renaissance theme. Everyone could make costumes or rent them, and we could have lords and ladies as the favorites. It's the perfect solution, and everyone I've talked to agrees with me.

(*Karen and John nod at her in agreement.*)

Anne: Well, that sounds great for people who can get their parents to rent or make costumes for them. But, my mom can't sew and we really can't spend money on renting a fancy costume. Maybe a '70s dance would be better. We could use our parents' clothes or go to a thrift store.

Will: I think Jennifer's idea is great. If students don't want to wear a Renaissance costume they don't have to. They can just wear school clothes. Let's vote on Jennifer's super idea.

(*Karen and John look puzzled.*)

Anne: I don't think it would be much fun coming to the dance unless you feel a part of it. I remember once not feeling a part of a party I went to, and then I felt left out. It's kind of like that episode of *The Simpsons* when Homer told Bart about the time he was left out as a kid.

Jennifer: Look, if you want to wear a Renaissance costume, do it. If not, don't. Everyone agrees except a couple of people. Let's vote.

Thomas: Excuse me, Jennifer. We need to listen to everyone's opinion before we vote. I think a Renaissance idea is different and clever, but I like Anne's idea too. I'd like to hear what Karen and John think before we make a decision.

You probably decided that Thomas is the only competent communicator in the group. He states his opinion and also encourages others to share their ideas.

Ask Questions Knowing how to ask the right questions is as important as knowing the answers. Too often people don't ask questions when they need to—when something is unclear or when they need more information. For example, saying "What's the point?" is less helpful than asking "How does that idea tie into the solution we are discussing?" Competent communicators know when to ask questions and act on that knowledge.

Support Others Encourage other members of the group to contribute and share their ideas. Offer nonverbal support by smiling, nodding your head, or giving other signs of approval. When you support others, they feel good about themselves. If they feel that their contributions are worthwhile, they will want to continue to help the group reach its goal.

APPLY

Look at the following quotes and decide which come from competent communicators and which come from group members who need to develop better communication skills.

Speaker 1: Ingrid, that's the dumbest idea I've heard today.

Speaker 2: We're running out of time. I'm leaving. Bye.

Speaker 3: We need to look at the cost of this plan more carefully.

Speaker 4: I forgot my notes. I think we have to tell the principal by November 20. No, maybe it's November 15.

Speaker 5: I think Bradley's idea could save us at least $50. We need to consider it carefully.

If you recognized that speakers 1, 2, and 4 need to develop their group communication skills, you're correct.

Listeners can give nonverbal feedback by making eye contact with a speaker.

Multicultural Learning

▼ Interested students might want to speak or write about times in their lives when they have not been listened to because of their youth. Encourage students to think about other factors that might keep a person from getting a fair hearing in a group setting.

Listener Responsibilities

Remember the quotation from Chapter 3, "The spoken word belongs half to those who speak and half to those who hear." Often group members forget the second half of this bit of wisdom. Many times while one person is speaking, other people can't wait to begin talking themselves. They think about what they are going to say instead of listening to what is being said. Or they interrupt the speaker. Effective listening skills are just as crucial as effective speaking skills. Some important listening skills for group members are discussed below.

Practice Good Listening Remember that good listening takes work. Apply the listening guidelines you learned in Chapter 3 to your group communication.

Avoid Barriers Although many people may be trying to talk and things may be moving quickly, try to overcome speaker barriers and self-barriers.

Use Your Thought Speed Remember that while other members are speaking at 120 to 180 words a minute, you can listen at a rate of 300 to 400 words a minute. Use this extra time to think about the ideas you are hearing.

207

Learning Styles

Audio Learning

● Encourage students to make a recording of the next meeting they attend. (Make sure that they get permission in advance from the participants.) Students might play their recordings for the class and point out examples of effective and ineffective speaking and listening skills.

Skill Development

Media Literacy

● Assign groups of students to watch various local or national news programs (one program for each group) in which several people, led by a discussion leader, talk about current events. Ask students to think about the purpose of the program, whether the leader was effective, and whether the participants were organized and articulate.

> ### OBSERVE
>
> Watch a small group operate and record the behaviors of the people who are not speaking. Are they remaining alert and involved? Are they giving positive or negative nonverbal feedback?

Listen for Connections As you listen to Leo argue for one solution and Marita for another, see how their ideas might be similar. Check out suggestions as they are made to see which ones might fit within the group's criteria.

Give Nonverbal Feedback Don't shut down when you are not talking. Look at the person who is talking and give nonverbal support to ideas you find interesting. Make other members feel as if someone is listening. For example, make eye contact, nod your head, or smile.

LEADERSHIP ISSUES

Some people fight to become leaders in groups. Others try hard to avoid leadership responsibilities. Both of these behaviors interfere with successful group communication. The quality of leadership strongly affects a group's ability to solve problems. Good leaders are competent communicators. They have ways to speak and listen responsibly. They select the best strategy for each problem and act on it. Then they see how the members of the group act. Good leaders keep thinking, "How can I help this group do its best work at problem solving?"

Becoming a Leader

There are several ways a group member might become a leader. Leaders may be appointed or elected, or they may gradually emerge from the group.

Appointed Leaders Sometimes one person in authority chooses group leaders. A teacher may appoint leaders for classroom

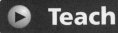
Motivation

Encourage students to assess their own leadership skills. Make sure they discuss the things they do competently as well as areas where they could use improvement.

❝You don't lead people by following them, but by saying what they want to follow.❞

ENOCH POWELL

Links to Past Learning

Encourage students to think of an example of each of the leadership types from their own experience: appointed leaders, elected leaders, and emerging leaders.

discussion groups. The president of an organization may appoint another officer, such as the vice president, to head a committee. When a leader is appointed, the group has no control over the choice. Sometimes appointed leaders have trouble because they are not the group's choice.

Elected Leaders Often sports teams elect their own captains, and extracurricular clubs elect their officers. It is common for groups to elect their leaders. The job of elected leaders is often easier because they have the group's support. On the other hand, if the group elects the most popular person, but not a strong and organized leader, there could be problems. One student describes the cooperation an elected leader might expect:

> Our football team elects its captain, or leader, because the coach believes the team members will work best with someone they elected. Every week we have an hour in which the players and the captain discuss the team's problems. The captain encourages all players to talk about their feelings and share their ideas for new plays.

Emerging Leaders. Sometimes a group starts out without an appointed or elected leader, but over time a leader arises from the group because of how he or she has acted. A member may start to take charge and act as a leader. If the other members do not object, he or she may emerge as that group's new leader. If you emerge as a leader, it could mean you are the only one willing to do the work. Or it could mean you have leadership skills that others respect.

If an appointed or elected leader is not strong, someone else may emerge as the actual leader, even if there is no change in title. Groups members may turn to the emerging leader for support and guidance because he or she displays the qualities needed by the group to lead the group.

Leadership Responsibilities

Some people like the title of leader but not the work that goes along with the title. Being a responsible leader takes effort.

209

Leadership responsibilities fall into the general areas of (1) beginning the discussion, (2) acting as moderator, and (3) closing the discussion.

Beginning the Discussion The leader will begin by introducing the topic, introducing the members, or beginning the discussion. To introduce the topic, the leader may state the question or explain to the group or audience why the discussion is taking place. If group members do not know each other well, the leader can spend part of the first meeting helping members to get acquainted.

In beginning the discussion, the leader may suggest who will speak first or what part of the topic will be discussed as the meeting opens. For example, "First we'll discuss the problem of playground destruction and then possible ways to stop it." Usually, appointed or elected leaders get things started. If there is no such leader, someone may emerge as a leader by taking over some of these duties.

Acting as Moderator Leaders act as moderators for the discussion. **Moderators** are people who keep a discussion moving and see that everyone's ideas are heard. Leaders are concerned with the group process and will try to keep the discussion on track. It is important that members make comments that relate to the topic under discussion. If the group is analyzing the problem and someone suggests a solution, the leader could say, "That's an interesting point, Jack. Maybe you could bring that up again when we get to solutions."

Leaders also make sure everyone contributes. The leader should prevent one or two members from talking all the time and encourage quiet members to share their ideas. The leader may encourage quiet members who speak up by saying, "I'm really glad you said that. We hadn't thought of that idea."

Leaders also must watch the clock so the task can be completed before the group runs out of time. It's frustrating to spend forty minutes discussing all the problems and only ten minutes solving them.

Skill Development

Media Literacy

● Encourage students to analyze the ways leaders are portrayed in recent films. Have students create a list of leadership qualities from life and compare it with lists of leadership qualities as illustrated in films. For example, are leaders in films violent? abusive? loud? armed? Or are they firm, fair, quiet, good listeners, and able to compromise?

Closing the Discussion Leaders end the discussion by summarizing the main points and announcing any conclusions that were reached. They also thank the members for their contributions.

Improving Leadership Skills

A good leader can always become a better leader. Competent leaders evaluate their own performances in order to improve their skills. You can use the following checklist to examine your leadership skills. Do not write in your book.

**CHECKLIST:
Leadership Skills**

Use this checklist to assess your leadership skills. Which statements never apply to you? Which statements sometimes or frequently apply? Which statements always apply?

1. I try to include everyone in the discussion.

2. I guide the group through problem-solving steps.

3. I try to help members compromise.

4. I am able to control excessive talkers.

5. I am able to draw out quiet members.

6. I watch the time.

7. I keep the group on the topic.

8. I encourage members to express different opinions.

9. I avoid talking too much.

10. I bring up the topic and close the discussion.

211

Cooperative Learning

● Have students work together in groups of four or five. One person will act as moderator and the others will serve as members of a panel. Encourage them to address a topic of their choice. The moderator's task is to keep the discussion moving and on track. The panel members' task is to address the specific issue as fully as possible, while utilizing the rules of good group communication.

INTERACT

In a small group, discuss possible ways a group leader could handle the following situations:

1. Abdul, who has not done any research on the topic, constantly criticizes what other group members say.

2. Rosa shows interest in the discussion nonverbally but hasn't said anything.

3. Rebecca talks constantly. It is difficult for other members to get their ideas out.

4. Everyone is getting frustrated, although for varying reasons. Everyone is arguing. No one seems willing to listen to anyone else. If their grade didn't depend on this project, group members would never meet together again.

Although most leaders follow certain guidelines, more experienced leaders may take risks and involve group members in different ways. In his book *Sacred Hoops*, basketball coach Phil Jackson says he finds ways to motivate the Bulls players "in the moment." He reads the situation and then responds to whatever he believes is going on. Because he is an experienced leader he can think of creative leadership strategies on the spot.

EVALUATING GROUP DISCUSSION

Decide whether the following statement is true or false:

The more small groups you are in, the better you become as a small-group communicator.

If you said false, you are correct. Having been in ten or twenty group discussions does not necessarily mean you are a better communicator. All it means is that you have been in more groups! Do you remember the steps a competent communicator follows? Competent communicators (1) think of communication strategies, (2) select a strategy, (3) act on the strategy, and

▼ Encourage students to think of examples of moderators they have seen on television. Have students analyze these moderators' skills by determining if they (1) keep the discussion on track and moving forward and (2) make sure that all viewpoints are heard. Students could rate the moderators numerically.

(4) evaluate the strategy. Competent communicators must evaluate their group discussions. Careful evaluation allows members or leaders to retain helpful behaviors and change behaviors that do not work well.

The purposes of the evaluation are to (1) strengthen good points, (2) correct weak points, and (3) reduce mistakes. If you don't evaluate your group discussion by giving and receiving feedback with other group members or group observers, you will never know how well you are communicating.

Guidelines For Evaluation

The following comments were offered after a group discussion:

Martina was good.

J. P. could have done more.

These kind of comments do not help group members. They are too general. When giving feedback to others, remember the following guidelines:

1. *Describe what you saw and heard.* Instead of saying "Martina was good," say, "Martina asked three good questions and made two useful suggestions to solve the problem." Don't say, "J. P. wasn't a good group member." Instead, say, "J. P. talked to the person next to her instead of to the whole group. She made three jokes but did not make any suggestions for a solution."

2. *Limit your comments.* Don't try to evaluate everything. For example, say, "Jake contributed two or three things, yet didn't dominate," or "Samara listened carefully and encouraged others." Do not make eight or nine comments. The person will never be able to keep track of what you are saying.

3. *Include strong points, weak points, and areas for improvement.* When giving feedback, do not limit yourself to one type of comment. It is not useful to say, "I could not hear Kara." It is more helpful to say, "Kara came with lots of good information. It was hard to hear everything she said. Next time, Kara

213

Critical Thinking

Synthesizing

▲ Call on interested students to show their understanding of the material by summarizing the main points of the class so far. They could mention the main ideas that were discussed and point out any conclusions that were reached.

Skill Development

Feedback

● Students might want to share their group participation checklists with a partner. Students can work together to think of strategies to improve their weakest communication areas.

should speak more loudly and clearly. Then everyone can benefit from her good ideas."

Your group discussion should improve as you evaluate your own work and that of others. As a competent communicator, you should strive to improve each time.

CHECKLIST:
Group Participation

Use this checklist to assess your participation in group communication. Which statements never apply to you? Which statements sometimes or frequently apply? Which statements always apply?

1. I worry about being wrong.

2. I ask questions to get attention.

3. I avoid interrupting speakers.

4. I am prepared with the necessary information.

5. I look at people when I speak to them.

6. I listen carefully to others' ideas.

7. I avoid disagreements.

8. My mind wanders when I'm not talking.

9. I try to include people who don't say much.

10. I am too willing to compromise.

11. I stick to the topic of the discussion.

12. I try to support others.

13. I am conscious of whether the others like me.

14. I tend to accept the first good idea I hear.

214

Beyond the Classroom

Some students might enjoy reading Phil Jackson's book *Sacred Hoops*. Encourage interested students to do an oral or written book report that details some of Jackson's ideas on leadership.

Base your feedback on what you saw and heard.

Providing Feedback

You can give feedback to yourself and to others to improve communication competence in groups. In order to examine your own behavior, you can create a checklist to chart your skill development. You might want to copy the Group Participation Checklist in the book or develop your own form. Evaluate your own communication each time you participate in a group discussion. Your feedback to others should be based on a description of what you saw and heard. You can create forms to help you observe members in a group discussion. The sample feedback form on the next page shows one way of recording group members' communication behavior. Each time a contribution is made, a check is placed in the appropriate space for each member.

Teach ◄

Critical Thinking

Organizing

● Encourage students to create evaluation forms for themselves, using the model on this page as a jumping-off point.

Evaluation Form—Group Communication

Directions: Place a check in the appropriate column each time a group member contributes to the discussion. Add comments below.

Group Members	Agreeing	Disagreeing	Seeking information	Giving information	Seeking opinion	Giving opinion	Asking for solutions	Giving solutions	Encouraging others	Summarizing
_____										
_____										
_____										
_____										
_____										

Comments: _____

_____

_____

_____

216

CHAPTER 7 SUMMARY

This chapter introduces characteristics of small groups and problem solving. Five important small-group characteristics are structure, purpose, norms, roles, and subgroups. Group members should be able to recognize these characteristics. Most groups experience a four-stage life cycle of forming, storming, norming and performing. Group discussion is most effective when the five steps of problem solving are followed: (1) identify the problem; (2) analyze the problem; (3) set criteria for a solution; (4) develop solutions; and (5) select a solution. Effective group problem solving means that leaders and members must be responsible for the group's work and follow guidelines for responsible speaking and listening. Each member needs to know how leaders are chosen and what the leaders' responsibilities are. Finally, evaluation of the group can tell you a lot about how well the group performed.

Cooperative Learning

There are several standard activities for having students role-play to solve problems in a group. For example, they could tackle the problem of whom to save in a small sinking lifeboat. Passengers could include a young husband and wife with an infant, an elderly minister or rabbi (male), a middle-aged doctor (female), a young college student (male) majoring in astronomy, and a wealthy movie actress. One person must leave to save the others. After a leader is chosen, the remaining group of six people must decide who to sacrifice. Students should role-play according to what they learned in this chapter. Variations on this activity are numerous.

Answers

Think About It

Student answers will vary somewhat. Here are sample answers:

1. A group consists of people who share interest in the same things or share a common purpose; communicate easily and regularly among themselves; participate in planning and decision making; and feel connected to other members.

2. Forming, storming, norming, and performing

3. (1) Identify the problem. (2) Analyze the problem. (3) Set criteria for a solution. (4) Develop solutions. (5) Select a solution.

4. Be prepared; share ideas thoughtfully; speak with self-respect; ask questions; support others.

5. Practice good listening; avoid barriers; use thought speed; listen for connections; give nonverbal feedback.

6. Beginning the discussion; acting as moderator; closing the discussion.

CHAPTER REVIEW

Think About It

1. Define group and list the characteristics of groups.

2. What are the four stages of a group's life cycle?

3. What are the five steps in problem solving?

4. What are speakers' responsibilities in groups?

5. What are listeners' responsibilities in groups?

6. What are the responsibilities of group leaders?

Try It Out

1. In a group of six or seven classmates, talk about cliques. Use the following questions in your discussion:

Are there cliques in your school that are subgroups of other groups?

Is it possible to belong to more than one clique?

What are the different images various cliques have?

How accurate are the images?

How does it feel to be with members of a subgroup different from the one you usually spend time with?

What are the advantages and disadvantages of cliques or subgroups?

2. In a group of five to seven members, discuss either a topic of your choice or the topic, "Should the Student Council Be Given More Power in Determining School Policy?" At the end of fifteen minutes, discuss the following questions: (1) What role did each group member perform? (2) To what extent did your group follow the five problem-solving steps? (3) To what extent did your group follow the four stages of a group's life cycle?

3. Assume that your school is up for re-accreditation this year and that the principal has asked students to write a one-paragraph description of student-related school problems that should be addressed. In small groups brainstorm a list of student-related problems. After listing the problems, prioritize them in order of importance. Select the one most people see as most serious. Your overall goal will be to develop a carefully written two-paragraph statement describing a key problem and making one or more suggestions to solve it. After completing your overall goal, analyze the process the group went through to get from the brainstorming to the written page. Discuss the group leadership and evaluate the effectiveness of your group's meetings and your own work in the group.

4. Evaluate a small-group discussion in which you took part. Use the

evaluation form included in this chapter or make up one of your own. Then write a one-page paper discussing the strengths, weaknesses, and ideas for improvement of the group communication or of your own communication in that group.

Put It in Writing

1. Select one of the following topics and write two or three paragraphs describing the topic.

   The Group That Left Me Out

   The Group That Took Me In

   The Group I Didn't Want to Join

2. Select one group to which you belong. Describe the group's norms and explain how they developed in the life cycle. Give an example of

what might happen if a member of the group does not follow the norms.

Speak About It

1. Present a two- or three-minute speech in which you give three reasons why group discussion is important.

2. Phrase three discussion topics—one of fact, one of value, and one of policy. Make sure these three topics meet the criteria on page 198. Present the three topics to your class, explaining why you think they are good topics.

3. Describe to your class a particular group that you think is an important part of the nation or the community. Explain why you consider this group effective.

Quick Check

Ask students to find and define these Key Terms:

brainstorming (201)

clique (191)

criteria (200)

forming (194)

group (184)

group norms (188)

group problem solving (192)

group purpose (186)

moderator (210)

norming (194)

performing (194)

role (189)

storming (194)

subgroup (191)

219

		Day 1	Day 2	Day 3	Day 4	Day 5
Week 8	**8** Forms of Group Discussion					
Chapter 8 Planner	Discussion Formats		Discussion Formats	Parliamentary Procedure	Parliamentary Procedure	Summary & Chapter Review
	Teacher's Resource Book					
	Teaching Suggestions 8.1–8.3	8.4–8.6	8.7	8.8		
	Worksheets & Eval. Forms 25	26–28			29	
						Chapter Test 8
	Workbook 8.1	8.2–8.4			8.5	

Motivation

Ask students to name as many groups in the school that they can think of while one student writes them on the board. Ask which group is probably the largest and which the smallest.

Links to Past Learning

Encourage students to think about what they learned in the last chapter about group life cycles and leadership. Ask which activity or discussion stands out most strongly when they recall Chapter 7, "Communication in Groups." Have a discussion about the kinds of groups most students belong to.

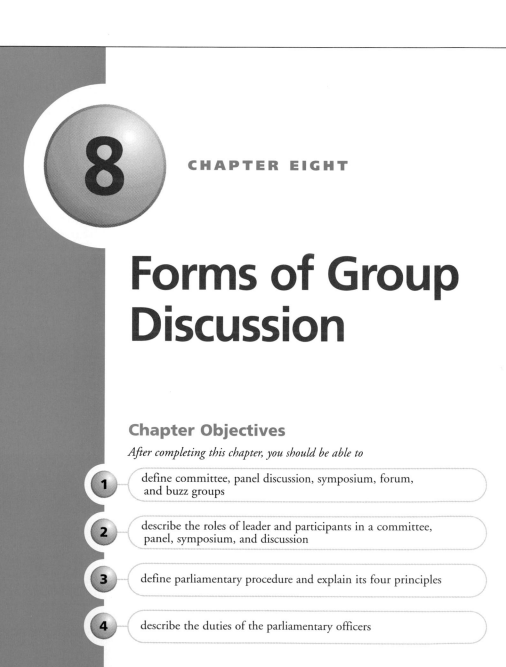

8 CHAPTER EIGHT

Forms of Group Discussion

Chapter Objectives

After completing this chapter, you should be able to

1. define committee, panel discussion, symposium, forum, and buzz groups

2. describe the roles of leader and participants in a committee, panel, symposium, and discussion

3. define parliamentary procedure and explain its four principles

4. describe the duties of the parliamentary officers

Substitute Teacher Tip

Quiz students to see whether they can name the groups that made the following decisions or took the following actions.

Called for civil disobedience against the British (First Continental Congress)

Passed the Social Security Act (U.S. Congress)

Ruled that racial segregation in public school was unconstitutional (U.S. Supreme Court)

Nominated Governor Bill Clinton of Arkansas as its candidate for president in 1992 (Democratic Party)

Nominated former senator Bob Dole as its candidate for president in 1992 (Republican Party)

Hired the school principal (varied answers)

Ask how students think their lives have been changed by these groups and these acts.

Critical Thinking

Predicting

● Encourage students to predict what they are about to learn in this chapter. You might ask them to write at least one question that they would like the chapter to answer for them.

▼ **Key Terms**

abstain	forum	motion	second
agenda	majority	panel discussion	symposium
buzz groups	minority	parliamentary procedure	
committee	minutes		

Group discussion is important in our community. Several community members met with the city council, parks and recreation department, PTA members, and interested kids from all our schools. The goal was to build Kids' Place (a large playground) in the largest park in our city. Everyone was allowed to express their opinions about the design and fund raising, even the kids. The Kids' Place would have playground equipment for kids of all ages. One of the decisions was to make it look like a large castle. The community children held discussion sessions in their schools and collected pennies from students in kindergarten through twelfth grade. Once the money was collected, volunteers from all over the city held discussions to arrange the work schedule to complete their plans. The community worked together around the clock for several days. We accomplished something very wonderful for our city. What was even more exciting, after we finished, several of the kids at our local schools got to be on *Good Morning, America.*

This student understands the importance of group discussion. Group discussion is used by school and community groups to examine issues and make decisions. Your life may be changed greatly by the group decisions. Think about the decisions of groups in your school and community that affect your life. Examples of such decisions may involve rules for inline skating in public places, county funding for summer jobs for teenagers, or establishment of curfew policies.

The success of groups depends on the communication competence of the group members. Group members must use their communication skills effectively if the group is to complete its job. Group members must know the topic area well, decide on their views, listen carefully, and speak responsibly. As you read this chapter, think about speaking and listening responsibilities and why they would be important in each of the groups discussed.

Although most problem-solving groups follow the steps described in the last chapter, other groups use different ways of conducting their business. This chapter discusses various group formats for addressing issues or confronting problems. These include special types of groups, such as committees, panels, symposiums, and groups that use parliamentary procedure.

Skill Development

Quick Skill Opportunity

▼ Ask students to tell in what cities Congress, the state legislature, and the United Nations meet.

DISCUSSION FORMATS

Group members can use various formats to discuss, share ideas, and reach conclusions. These include committees, panel discussions, and symposiums.

Committees

At some time you've probably been a member of a committee. A **committee** is usually a subgroup of a larger group, and it is formed to study or manage a specific task. If a large group has a problem or is discussing a topic on which it needs more information, the group may form a committee of a few members to study the problem further.

Suppose your class is planning a class trip. A committee could look into possible places the class could go, figure the cost, find chaperones, and report its findings to the class. This committee could recommend an action for the group to approve. Other committees have the power to make decisions for the larger group.

Often participants in a committee meeting sit at a round table so that all members face one another. Although occasionally an audience may be present, audience members do not take part in the discussion. At some meetings each committee member gives a report on the topic area. Following the reports, all participants discuss the topic. For example, suppose you are a member of a committee discussing course changes in your school district. First each committee member would report on the courses he or she thinks are necessary. Discussion following the reports might focus on specific courses and the steps necessary to introduce the new courses.

At other meetings, committee members do general business or discuss proposals. They may use the steps of problem solving or do some brainstorming. Sometimes the leader will "run the group" to ask for short responses or one idea from every member. This involves going around the circle and having each person speak in turn. Each person is limited to one or two sentences.

Frequently group discussion is only part of an overall set of committee responsibilities. Suppose your school sponsors car

Cooperative Learning

● Encourage students to work in committees of four or five. Assign them a task such as raising money for school band uniforms or cleaning up an area near the school. Ask them to work together to plan how long the task will take, the best way to organize volunteers, and how much it will cost to put the plan into effect. Have each committee present its finished plan to the class.

223

Beyond the Classroom

Invite a city council person or other city or town official to speak to your class. Encourage students to ask him or her questions about various committees and the purpose of each.

Committees are subgroups of larger groups and are formed to deal with specific tasks.

washes to raise money for community charities. As a committee member, you might be involved in planning and publicizing the day's events, making car wash signs, and deciding which charities should be supported this year.

JOURNAL ENTRY

At our school we have a committee made up of students who are against drugs. This is a subcommittee of our student council. We are allowed to plan a week called "Red Ribbon Week," in which red symbolizes being drug free. We plan activities and events for every day of this week. Our group usually has fifteen members, and often we have more ideas than we can use. When we gather all our ideas together, we take them back to the student council and vote on which activities we will use. We really enjoy sharing our ideas with each other.

Your work in groups and committees does not exist only in school. More and more communities are beginning to use "asset based community development," a program to identify and use the gifts and skills of all members of the community.* This approach specifically relies on the strengths of young community members who may work on housing rehabilitation, paint murals, form a "crime watch patrol," serve as volunteer mentors and tutors for children, or visit elderly community members.

🔌 APPLY

Imagine that you have been assigned to one of the following committees. What kinds of tasks would you and the other committee members discuss and carry out?

Special Olympics Track Events Subcommittee

Volunteer Firefighters' Auction Committee

Parents' Night Entertainment Committee

Mayor's Downtown Beautification Organization

County Drug Prevention Week Committee

As part of your involvement in such groups you may find yourself taking part in discussions that are held in front of an audience.

Panel Discussions

During a **panel discussion** a subject is explored by the group members in front of an audience. A panel discussion format allows the speakers to inform or influence the audience. Most panels have four to eight members. The members should be seated so that they can see and be seen by the audience. Members of a panel make statements, ask questions, and comment on what other panel members have said. Most panel members refer to notes with information on them.

Usually a panel discussion has a leader, called a chairperson, whose job is to (1) introduce the panel members and the subject,

---

* Kretzman, John, and John McKnight. *Building Communities from the Inside Out.* Chicago: ACTA Publications, 1993.

(2) define important terms, (3) call on speakers during the discussion, (4) review points during the discussion, and (5) summarize the main ideas. Most panelists remain seated so that they can communicate with each other easily and informally.

Panel members are expected to be well informed about their subject areas. Preparation is important to successful panels. Usually the panel members and chairperson meet to discuss who will speak about certain ideas. Panelists try to reach some agreement on their ideas before the end of the discussion.

Panel discussions are popular in history and English classes because students can consider topics from different points of view. Many governing bodies use panel discussions to inform community members about issues of local concern. These panel discussions often occur before citizens vote on an issue. The following is an example of a panel discussion about course changes.

A panel discussion takes place in front of an audience.

Bob: Good afternoon. Welcome teachers, parents, and students. As you know, the officers of the student council have been asked to discuss what new courses are needed at our school. Each panel member will give his or her suggestions. Let me introduce the panelists. To my far right is Maria Vasquez, vice president. Next to her is John Holmes, treasurer. And next to me is Soon-ja Park, secretary. To my left is Mark Levy, social committee chair. Next to him is Nancy Henderson, service committee chair. I am Bob Marks, student council president.

As most of you know, every ten years the school district reviews all the courses in the curriculum. The school board looks for feedback from anyone interested in curriculum. Therefore they appointed a committee of students and a committee of teachers to look at our courses and recommend changes. At this meeting we will share with you some of the student committee's ideas. John, since you suggested this panel discussion, why don't you begin?

John: I've talked to a lot of students, and they think we need a course in video production. Since most students have VCRs at home, they're interested in learning how to make videos. This course would also teach us what to look for as we watch videos at home.

Bob: Maria, you look like you want to say something.

Maria: How many students did you talk to, John? I talked to more than fifty and none mentioned video production. Most of the students I talked to wanted an additional class in computers that would focus on the Internet. I know that would help me. I'll have to do Web research for my American History term paper. My dad just bought our family a home computer, and he wants me to look up all kinds of topics and help him get into chat groups on diabetes. The Introduction to Computers class just teaches word processing.

John: Hey, that's a good idea. Mr. Finley says we should do health education research using the Internet but I don't know much about the search engines or how to evaluate the information I find.

Skill Development

Feedback

● Select five students to perform the panel-discussion script on pages 226–228. Encourage the rest of the class to listen and give feedback about the quality of the discussion. They could discuss such factors as vocal production, posture, concentration, and so on. The first five students could read part of the script and another five students could be selected to read the rest of it.

227

Teach ◀

Critical Thinking
Synthesizing

▲ Encourage one of the students who read the role of Bob in the student-panel script to summarize for the class the main ideas of the discussion.

Bob: John, please raise your hand when you want to speak. Mark has his hand up. Mark, go ahead.

Mark: I think both John and Maria have good ideas. I'd like to have more art courses besides painting or drawing. The people I talked to wanted computer graphics and photography.

John: I like those ideas also.

Bob: Fine, but let's hear Nancy's ideas, since she's been waiting to speak.

Nancy: I talked to about fifty students and about ten suggested a course in woodworking. About twenty-five wanted more variety in English, such as classes in science fiction or mysteries. The rest had lots of different ideas.

Mark: Could an Internet course teach you how to make your own Web page?

(*. . . The discussion continues.*)

This panel has made some good points. Bob will summarize the ideas near the end and ask for final comments from the panelists. Notice that, instead of formal speeches, a panel discussion is more like a conversation led by a chairperson.

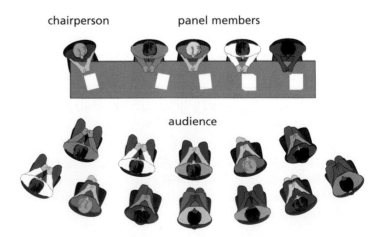

chairperson   panel members

audience

228

> “More and more, I used the quickness of my mind to pick the mind of other people and use their knowledge as my own.”
>
> ELEANOR ROOSEVELT

Skill Development

Feedback

- Take some time to discuss students' reactions to their classmates' panel discussions suggested in the Interact section. Encourage students to be specific with their feedback. Model good feedback procedure by first telling what students did well and following with any negative criticism you might have.

INTERACT

Set up a practice panel that uses your own classmates' opinions. Four or five students will act as panel members, and the rest will act as interviewees. Have each panel member take ten minutes to interview a small group from the rest of the class about one of the following subjects or another subject of your choice. Give the panelists an extra five minutes to get organized and select a chairperson. The panel discussion should last for ten to fifteen minutes. Possible subjects appear below:

making curriculum changes at your school

installing a new snack bar in the cafeteria

improving the school grounds

raising money for new computers for the library

After the panel discussion, answer the following questions:

1. How well were your classmates' opinions represented?
2. How well did the chairperson direct the panel?
3. How well did the panel members express their ideas?

Symposiums

A **symposium** is a discussion during which members give short speeches to an audience. A symposium is similar to a panel discussion. The main difference is that a symposium is more formal. Frequently a symposium is a way to hear several experts on a subject present their views to an audience. Each person gives a speech representing a different point of view on the subject being discussed. Unlike a panel, speakers usually don't talk with one another unless there is a question-and-answer period following each speech. As in a panel, the leader introduces the symposium members and the topic. The leader also closes the symposium by briefly summarizing the speeches.

Teach

Links to Past Learning

Encourage class discussion of students' experiences with audience participation. They may mention anything from theatrical performances they have given or witnessed to buzz groups in which they have participated. Ask what factors they think might link all forms of audience participation.

Each symposium member gives a speech expressing a different point of view on a subject.

Suppose the panel discussion on course changes had been a symposium. Each participant would have spoken for the types of courses they supported. John would have given a short talk on a video production course; Maria, on the need for a computer course on the Internet; Mark, on art classes; and Nancy, on woodworking and various English classes. The speakers would present reasons why the courses they suggested are needed. They would also give facts, such as how many students requested a certain course.

Audience Participation

Sometimes audience members take part in panel discussions or symposiums. When the audience becomes involved, the discussion is called a **forum.** There are panel-forums and symposium-forums. Audience members can ask questions of the persons presenting the information. Usually the questions are asked at the end of the panel discussion or symposium, but sometimes there is a question-and-answer period after each speaker's comments.

When the speakers use only half the scheduled time, audience members are sometimes asked to get into small groups, called **buzz groups**. Buzz groups are expected to discuss the ideas presented by the speakers and decide on some solution to the problem.

Links to Past Learning

If students have completed the Observe activity, ask what the chairperson's responsibility is toward helping to maintain the self-esteem of others. Should the chairperson be concerned about this? Why or why not?

The entire audience comes back together, and a representative of each buzz group reports on the group's solution. After a summary by the chairperson, the audience and symposium members discuss the proposed solutions and try to decide on the best.

JOURNAL ENTRY

Recently at one of the local schools, a forum was presented to discuss changing our school district from a nine-month school year to a year-round school year. The panel consisted of school board members from our school district and panel members from school districts in our state that had already changed to year-round schools. The forum was very informative, and parents and students had many questions that were answered.

OBSERVE

Attend a panel discussion or symposium in your school or community, or watch one on TV. Pay careful attention to the role of the chairperson. How well did this person keep the speakers in line? How well did he or she introduce speakers and summarize points? If audience members got involved, how well did the chairperson handle the audience participation?

PARLIAMENTARY PROCEDURE

Federal, state, and local governments use parliamentary procedure to conduct their business. **Parliamentary procedure** is a set of rules for running large group meetings. Groups, especially large ones, need rules to work effectively. Most large groups follow the parliamentary procedure rules found in *Robert's Rules of Order Revised* by Henry Robert or in *Learning Parliamentary Procedure* by Alice Sturgis.

231

Limited English Proficiency

Be sure students understand the terms *minority* and *majority*. Ask how many members would make up a majority in the class.

> ### JOURNAL ENTRY
>
> During our Washington trip the class observed a session at the House of Representatives. The members of Congress run their meetings according to parliamentary procedure. The Speaker of the House chairs the meeting, and the members follow set rules for how to talk. It was complicated but interesting.

Parliamentary procedure began in the English Parliament many years ago as members tried to gain fair and equal opportunities to speak. American governmental groups use these rules to protect the democratic rights of all members to be heard. Today most student governments and large community organizations run their meetings according to parliamentary procedure.

Principles and Process

Parliamentary procedure is based on the following principles:

1. The right of the majority (more than half) to decide

2. The right of the minority (less than half) to be heard

3. Decisions made according to a one-person, one-vote rule

4. The right of absent members' opinions to be included

Parliamentary procedure is used by state legislatures such as this one.

66Be sincere; be brief; be seated.**99**

FRANKLIN D. ROOSEVELT'S
ADVICE TO HIS SON JAMES

SPEAKING OF . . .

BJ COLEMAN

If you are in Washington, D.C., and tune in to Black Entertainment Television's *Teen Summit,* you will see BJ Coleman actively interviewing a celebrity, fielding a question from an at-home caller, or arguing with another member of the *Teen Summit* "posse." The show is shot live every Saturday at noon. BJ must arrive at 9:00 A.M. to meet with the director, crew, and other posse members. At that meeting the discussion is filled with technical terms such as "shoot," "TelePrompTer," "miked," "key light," "rundown," and "on-location."

Teen Summit is a talk show aimed at helping teenagers across the nation deal with problems or confront issues. BJ and seven other posse members, as well as hosts and special guests, appear on the show. The host and posse members interview the guests and, with an expert, try to suggest solutions to the problems. BJ reports, "It gets difficult because a lot of research must be read in order to be prepared to interview or question a particular guest." The show has addressed topics such as AIDS, sibling rivalry, and celebrity news.

The posse members need to use a range of communication skills. They must be prepared to interview guests with thoughtful questions, to get their points across in heated discussions, and to answer questions from callers. According to BJ, "Group discussions are difficult. One has to have complete control over the situation and learn how to interrupt people at the appropriate time so you are able to say what you have to say." Sometimes posse members go on location and tape part of the show in malls and schools. All posse members must be able to work from scripts and read from a TelePrompTer.

This experience prepares BJ for many careers—some in the media, such as a television talk show host or commentator, some in politics, and some in business, particularly the entertainment industry.

233

Critical Thinking

Analyzing

Put a vote to the class over some silly issue such as whether all students should be required to wear red on Wednesdays, clean out their lockers every Friday afternoon after school hours, or all attend the same feature film at their own expense on Thursday afternoon at a local theatre. Have students express their votes first by a show of hands and then by a voice vote. Encourage students to discuss with a partner the possible reasons someone might abstain from voting, either in the classroom or in a presidential election.

According to parliamentary rules, the decision of the majority is accepted for the whole group, hence the expression "majority rules." A **majority** is more than one-half of the votes. Even though the majority may win, the **minority,** or the group with less than half the votes, always has a chance to express its views. The leader of the group is elected by a majority vote and is expected to be fair and objective in running the meeting.

A vote can be taken by a ballot, by a show of hands, or by voice vote. In a ballot vote, each person receives a ballot and writes his or her vote on the ballot. Absent members may vote if they have previously turned in a ballot according to the group's rules. To vote by a show of hands, people raise their hands to indicate support for their position. If the show of hands seems close, there will be a count of the hands raised for each position.

In a voice vote, the chair says, "All in favor, say yes; All those opposed say no." If the majority of votes are yes, then the chair says, "The yeas have it," and the motion passes. If the majority of votes are no, then the chair says, "The nos have it," and the motion fails. If it is not possible to determine whether there were more votes for yes or for no, the chair may call for a show of hands. Those who do not wish to vote may **abstain** and the number of abstentions will be counted and reported along with the yes and no votes.

The parliamentary process helps people work in an orderly way because

only one topic is considered at a time.

all group members have a chance to speak their minds.

all sides of a subject are heard.

one or two people cannot shut off or dominate the discussion.

If a meeting is run according to parliamentary procedure, discussion of one topic must be completed before discussion of another topic can begin. Under parliamentary procedure, all members are given a chance to speak. This means that all sides of a topic will be heard. Members may move to end discussion, but two-thirds of the group must agree to do so. Therefore, one or two people cannot take control of the discussion.

66Words set things in motion. I've seen them doing it. Words set up atmosphere, electrical fields, charges.**99**

TONI CADE BAMBERA
The Writer in Her Work

Multicultural Learning

▲ Some students might want to find out about legislative assemblies in other countries. Encourage them to choose one nation to research and report their findings to the class.

JOURNAL ENTRY

Our community is debating whether to change the school attendance policies. A group of student representatives attended the last school board meeting, which was run according to parliamentary procedure. If you didn't understand the rules it was very hard to know exactly what was going on. We did get to talk for a short time, but we could have had more influence if we had known how to work according to parliamentary procedure.

Order of Business

Most formal group meetings follow the same unchangeable order. Some groups print an **agenda,** a list of topics to be discussed, to make the order clear. This standard order of business usually involves the following set procedures:

1. *Call to Order.* The call to order begins the meeting. The chair says, "The meeting will come to order."

2. *Approval of Agenda.* The chair asks the group to review the agenda, or plan for the meeting, and determine if there are other topics to be considered, or if it is necessary to alter the order of business. Any necessary changes are made and the agenda is approved as corrected.

3. *Reading of Minutes.* The **minutes** are notes taken at the previous meeting of the group. The chair asks the group's secretary to read the minutes. After the secretary reads the minutes, the chair asks, "Are there any additions or corrections?" If there are no additions or corrections, the chair asks for a motion to approve the minutes. The chair indicates the minutes are approved or approved as corrected.

4. *Reports of Other Officers.* Besides the chairperson and secretary, many organizations have a treasurer and other officers. The chair says, for example, "The treasurer will give us a treasurer's report." The treasurer then reports the group's financial balance and accounts for money that was received or expended. The chair then calls for the treasurer's report to be received by the group. Each officer provides a report on his or her area of responsibility.

235

Limited English Proficiency

Ask one or two students to write and/or say the possible dialogue among the people in the photograph.

5. *Committee Reports.* The chair asks each committee chair if the committee has a report to make. Each committee chair then gives a brief report of the group's work or indicates the group did not get together since the last meeting. Organizations with a large number of committees may request brief written committee reports to be passed out. The oral presentations may reflect only debatable topics.

6. *Old Business.* Old business includes any issues that were not resolved at the last meeting or any updates on ongoing business. The chair asks, "Is there any old business from the previous meeting?" In large groups, the old business may be listed on the agenda. In this case, the chair says, "Let us turn to the old business."

7. *New Business.* New business is any topic that has not been discussed previously. After completing the old business, the chair asks, "Is there any new business?" Any member is free to introduce new business. A member may raise his or her hand and state an issue for discussion. For example, a student council representative may say, "Our school is the only one in this area without a video yearbook. I wish to bring this issue to the student council's attention."

The meeting chair asks for reports from committee chairs.

Amazing Fact!

The parliament of Norway is the Storting, meaning "great assembly."

8. *Announcements.* The chair or other designated speaker announces future events, including news about members. These announcements may be comments such as, "The science fair has been rescheduled for April 10" or "Mrs. Hiller is out of the hospital."

9. *Adjournment.* The chair closes the meeting by saying, "The meeting is ended" or "This meeting is adjourned."

Motions

A **motion** is a proposed action. A motion should be brief and clear, propose a specific action for the group to take, and state only one idea.

APPLY

Compare the following motions. Which ones are well-stated?

I move our club have a skating party, sell candy, and have a bake sale to raise money.

I move the hockey club have a picnic on the last day of school.

I move the art club sponsor a contest for the poetry book cover.

I move the soccer team get involved in a community project.

You're correct if you think that the second and third motions are the better motions, because they propose specific actions.

There are four types of motions: (1) main, (2) subsidiary, (3) privileged, and (4) incidental. Main motions introduce the topic that members wish to discuss. Subsidiary motions modify the content of a main motion or change the way a main motion is dealt with. Privileged motions are concerned with the immediate needs and comforts of the members; therefore, once a privileged motion is made, it is considered before any other motion.

Skill Development

Quick Skill Opportunity

● Go around the room and call on several students to state a motion that is brief and clear and proposes a specific line of action. Encourage feedback from the class about why each motion was or was not well stated.

237

Cooperative Learning

● Have students work together in groups of four. Encourage each group to come up with a meeting topic and four motions: main, subsidiary, privileged, and incidental. Have them write out their motions for comparison with motions of other groups.

Limited English Proficiency

Encourage these students to work with a partner to make sure they understand the meanings of terms like *motion, minutes,* and *second* in the parliamentary process.

Finally, incidental motions deal with procedures involved in running the meeting. The following are examples of such motions:

1. Main

   I move we give $500 to the "Mathletes" for their trip to Washington.

   I move the adoption of the following resolution: "We the students of North High urge the school board to establish a policy on school uniforms."

2. Subsidiary

   I wish to amend the motion to change $500 to $800.

   I move to postpone this discussion until the results of the survey on school-uniform policies at neighboring schools is completed.

3. Privileged

   I have a motion of privilege. I move that we ask Mr. Sherman to go get a copy of the budget from last year.

   We have been discussing this for two hours. I move to recess for a half-hour.

4. Incidental

   I move we suspend the rules and discuss new business now since Catherine has to leave in ten minutes.

   Point of order! Zak was recognized on a point of order but he is now talking abut the main motion.

Before a main motion can be discussed, at least one other member must **second** it, or support it. After a motion is proposed, another member says, "I second the motion." If no one volunteers, the chair asks if there is a second to the motion. If no one will second the motion, there is no discussion of that motion.

To pass, a motion must be accepted by the majority of the voters. If members wish to change the main motion, they can make a subsidiary motion to amend it. If the members wish to discuss it at a later time, they can make a subsidiary motion to table the main motion. When a motion is tabled, it is usually put on the

Amazing Fact!

Iceland's Althing, or assembly, is the world's oldest surviving parliament.

Skill Development

Quick Skill Opportunity

Ask students to suggest what a president or chair might say to a group member who wanders off the subject under discussion. How should group members handle the problem of a chair who wanders off the subject?

The chair is responsible for managing the group's interaction.

next agenda as part of old business. If the members want to have the main motion studied further, they can make a subsidiary motion to send it to a committee.

Only one motion can be considered at a time. If a member believes discussion has gone on long enough and he or she wants the motion voted on, he or she would say, "I call the previous question." If there are no objections, the chair calls for a vote on the motion. Two-thirds of the group must agree to close discussion.

Duties of Officers

When parliamentary procedure is used, each officer performs certain duties. The officers serve to keep the organization alive and responsible. Each position requires time and energy. Effective officers are competent communicators who understand the rules of parliamentary procedure.

President or Chair If you are the president or chair of a club or organization, parliamentary procedure can help you lead the group effectively. It's your job to make sure the group accomplishes something. The president's duties include these:

1. *Keeping the meeting under control.* The president has to keep the members on the subject, make sure that everyone has an equal opportunity to be heard, and budget the time so that the group can complete its tasks.

239

Motivation

Remind students that the duties of various officers require people with particular skills. Ask them to name what skills the president, secretary, treasurer, and historian would most likely need in order to fulfill their duties.

2. *Making sure each main motion is finished.* The president is responsible for making sure each motion is voted on or set aside before a new one is introduced.

3. *Explaining the points if some members don't understand.* One of the president or chair's main duties is repeating questions and information so that everyone in the group can hear and understand them. If there are any questions about procedure, the president is responsible for answering them, or for asking the group's parliamentarian to answer them.

4. *Moderating the discussion.* The president does not participate in the discussion, but he or she makes sure that all the members know what is going on. The president recognizes and introduces speakers and makes sure that discussion continues in an orderly manner.

5. *Voting in case of a tie.* The president or chair only votes in order to break a tie. The reason for this policy is so that members won't feel pressured to support the president's side of an issue.

Vice President or Vice Chair The vice president or vice chair assists the president or chair. The vice president's duties include these:

1. Chairing the meeting when the president is absent

2. Chairing certain committees as an assistant to the president

3. Substituting for the president whenever necessary

4. Completing any vice presidential tasks listed in the group's constitution

Secretary Most organizations or clubs have a secretary to keep records. The secretary's duties include these:

1. Keeping the minutes or records of meetings

2. Checking the attendance at meetings

3. Sending out notices about future meetings

4. Sending out letters as directed by the president or chair

240

Amazing Fact!

The national legislative assembly in Japan is called the Diet. The word is derived from Middle English *diete*, meaning day's journey or day for meeting, and from Medieval Latin.

Keeping the minutes is an extremely important duty. Minutes include the date, time, and place of the meeting; the person who ran the meeting; the main points from the reading of the last meeting's minutes; all main motions presented at the meeting and what happened with them; and what time the meeting was adjourned.

Treasurer The treasurer is the group's financial officer. The treasurer's duties include these:

1. Keeping records of all expenses and incoming funds

2. Paying the bills

3. Collecting dues or other money

4. Giving a financial report when required

Parliamentarian The main duty of the parliamentarian is to advise the president or chair on parliamentary procedure. Whenever questions arise about parliamentary procedure, the parliamentarian's job is to provide the correct answer. If any violations of parliamentary procedure occur, the parliamentarian is responsible for pointing them out.

One of the secretary's duties is keeping the records of meetings.

241

Skill Development

Vocabulary

● Encourage students to study the glossary of key parliamentary terms. Divide the class into two teams and have the teams compete to define all the terms in the list without looking at their books.

Curricular Connection

Social Studies

● Encourage students to read their reports from the Observe activity aloud. Ask whether or not the meeting could be called successful.

Historian The historian keeps records of the group's history. Often this record takes the form of a scrapbook that includes the group's special events and projects, past officers, awards, and so on.

Committee Chairs Some groups may have committee chairs in areas such as publicity, fund-raising, or long-range planning. Each person's duties are spelled out in the constitution.

OBSERVE

Attend a school or community meeting in which parliamentary procedure is used. Write a report on the effectiveness of the chairperson and how the use of parliamentary procedure helped the meeting run smoothly.

Key Parliamentary Terms

adjournment	closing of the meeting
agenda	list of subjects to be discussed at a meeting; often indicates order of reports as well as topics of old business and new business to be considered
amendment	a proposed change in a motion. It is stated as "I move to amend the previous motion by. . . ."
by-laws	list of rules governing the procedures to be followed by the group
call previous question	move to an immediate vote. Example: "I call the previous question on this motion." Sometimes just stated as "question."

continued

❝With the sense of sight, the idea communicates the emotion, whereas, with sound, the emotion communicates the idea, which is more direct and therefore more powerful.❞

ALFRED NORTH WHITEHEAD

chairperson	person who leads the meeting (or president)
constitution	document that describes nature and purpose of a group
floor (to have the)	to have been granted the right to speak. Example: "I'm sorry, Tamara. Kyle has the floor right now. You may speak when he has finished."
incidental motion	motion dealing with procedures involved in running the meeting
main motion	proposed item of business or action for the group to consider. It is stated as "I move. . . ."
minority	one less than one-half of those people voting
minutes	written report of what happens at a meeting; usually prepared by the secretary. Minutes are considered for approval at the following meeting.
order of business	the sequence or order in which matters will be discussed; usually established in an agenda, but group may decide to change the order of business through a vote
parliamentarian	person responsible for making sure parliamentary procedure is followed; usually uses *Robert's Rules of Order Revised* or *Learning Parliamentary Procedure* for reference.
point of order	objection to the discussion on the floor. Reasons for a point of order include a speaker moving to an unrelated topic, telling an inappropriate joke, and so on.
privileged motion	motion to deal with immediate need of members
quorum	number of members who must be at the meeting in order to conduct the business and make binding decisions

continued

Limited English Proficiency

Students could work in pairs to create flashcards with the parliamentary procedure terms on one side and short definitions on the other. Students could then use the flashcards as an informal drill.

243

Links to Past Learning

Encourage students to discuss times when they have had to vote on issues in school or during extracurricular activities. Determine which method of voting is most often used: secret ballot, show of hands, or voice vote.

continued

recess	to take a break from the meeting for a set period of time
request for information	question asked of the speaker or chair in order to clarify a point
second a motion	show of support for a motion. Example: "I second the motion."
secret ballot	written vote used for nominations and controversial topics
subsidiary motion	motion to change the main motion or way of dealing with main motion
table a motion	to put a motion aside to be discussed at another, usually specified, time. Example: "I move we table the motion until the next meeting." A motion cannot be tabled without a second.
two-thirds rule	rule that states two-thirds of the group must be in favor to close debate

Parliamentary Procedure in Action

The following script follows a meeting in which parliamentary procedure was used. Notice how parliamentary procedure is followed by the different group members.

call to order

    Chair: The meeting will come to order.

approval of agenda

    May I have an approval of the agenda?

    Kirsten: So moved.

    Jack: Second.

Chair: Any objections? (*Pause.*) There being no objections we will follow the agenda as proposed. Our secretary, Nancy, will present the minutes of the last meeting.

reading of the minutes

Nancy: The monthly meeting of the Community Service Club was called to order by President Mary Jones on Tuesday, March 9, at 3:15 in Room 102 of Highland School. The minutes of the last meeting were read and approved. Treasurer Jeff Nielsen reported that the club has $87.12 in the treasury. Under old business, the group reviewed the problem of attendance at the soup kitchen. Under new business, Jeff moved that the Community Service Club sponsor a child in Colombia. The motion was passed. Jeff is looking into the arrangements. The group also discussed fund-raising for the Thanksgiving food baskets that we give out at the soup kitchen.

Paul Valenzuela moved to adjourn the meeting. The meeting was adjourned at 4:45.

Chair: Thank you, Nancy. Are there any corrections or additions to the minutes? (*Pause.*) If not, the minutes are approved. Jeff will read the treasurer's report.

treasurer's report

Jeff: We spent $48 on food and table decorations for Parents' Night. We took in $165. Our current cash balance is $204.12.

Chair: Thank you, Jeff. May we have the committee report for our Student Council Banquet? Julissa?

committee report

banquet planning

Julissa: The best place we could find that is within our budget is McKinney's Alpine House. The dining room is large enough for all of us. The banquet dinners are $12 a person. We will report back to you next week on the date. The restaurant is checking its calendar for May. We hope to have a date by next week's meeting.

Cooperative Learning

● Assign roles and have students perform the script of parliamentary procedure in action. To give more students a chance to read, you might have them switch roles about halfway through the script. Encourage students to listen actively and to take notes about what they see and hear.

old business

Chair: Thank you, Julissa. On to old business. At our last meeting we discussed the need for a fund-raising project for our Thanksgiving food baskets. Does anyone have any ideas? Margie, your hand was up first.

main motion

Margie: I move we sponsor a track run.

Chair: John.

second the motion

John: I second the motion.

discussion

The chair or president can vote only to break a tie.

Chair: It's been moved and seconded that we have a track run to raise money for our Thanksgiving food baskets. Is there any discussion? Sara.

Learning Styles
Kinesic Learning

Remind script readers that they are role-playing. They should not be afraid to use body language and other nonverbal signals.

amendment

Sara: Every other group does track runs, and people are getting tired of them. I would like to make this one different. I move to amend the motion by changing "track run" to a "triathlon," which would include track, cycling, and inline skating.

Chair: Jeff.

Jeff: I second the amendment.

Chair: It's been moved and seconded to amend the motion by changing "track run" to "triathlon." Is there any discussion? Jack.

discussion on the amendment

Jack: I really like that idea, but I think we have to do some careful planning to set up three events in the same day. It will be a lot more work than a track run.

point of information

Sue: Point of information.

Chair: Sue.

Sue: What exactly is a triathlon?

Chair: Sara.

Sara: A triathlon is an athletic event with three parts. In this case each participant would have to run the track for so many laps, ride a bike through some blocked off streets, and then skate for three miles.

Sue: Excellent. Thanks.

discussion

Chair: Is there any further discussion? Kirsten.

Kirsten: I think Jack's right. It would require a lot of volunteers and planning to make this work. It's complicated.

Chair: Is there further discussion of the amendment? (*Pause.*) Does anyone have any objections? Donna.

Donna: Yes. I'm worried that we don't have time to get this organized. This would take the help of the police department to block off streets and to patrol the skating route.

Chair: Any response? Jack.

247

Jack: Although I think this will be tough, I think it would get a lot of attention and we could raise lots of money. I think we could get lots of people involved.

Chair: Donna.

Donna: No, that's not exactly my objection. I don't mind trying to get people to work. I just don't think we can get the police department and the school administrators on board fast enough.

Chair: Sara.

Sara: I see what you mean, Donna. But I think that this special twist might really interest community members, and we could get someone to talk with Chief Montgomery about helping us out.

vote

Chair: Any more comments? (*Pause.*) Since there is no further discussion, all those in favor of amending the motion by changing the word "track run" to "triathlon" say yes. All opposed say no. (*Pause. Scans room.*) The amendment is approved.

Chair: Any discussion on the motion? Michael.

Michael: I don't think we should have an athletic event at all. Everyone is sick of sponsoring runners or whatever these super athletes do. There's something like this almost every week during the fall. I think we should think of something totally different.

Chair: Other ideas? Sara.

Sara: Well, I think this is new and fun enough. A lot of people will get into the event since the bikers and skaters will move through the neighborhoods, and we can make a lot of money for the Thanksgiving baskets, which is what we're supposed to do anyhow.

Chair: Michael.

Michael: I don't mean to offend you. I'm sure we can make some money at an athletic event. I just wish we could find a more creative way to do it. I don't have any ideas yet, but if we defeat this motion, I'll work to come up with something better.

Chair: Kurt.

Kurt: We could always have a filmfest. People could sponsor us for watching movies all weekend. We could make a fortune!

Chair: Is that another amendment?

Kurt: Well, what do you think?

point of order

Kirsten: Point of order. This is getting us off the real issue.

Chair: I have to agree. Kurt, we will not talk about the film-fest.

calling the question

Chair: Gail.

Gail: I think we should vote on the motion. I mean, I call the previous question.

Chair: Any objections to calling previous question on the motion? *(Pause.)* If there are no objections, let's vote. Any objections? *(Pause.)* None. It has been moved that we hold a triathlon to raise money for the Thanksgiving baskets. All those in favor say yes.

Group voice: Yes

Chair: All opposed say no. *(No sound.)* Abstentions?

Ralph: I came in late. I'll abstain.

Chair: The motion passes. Rachel, I'll recognize you.

adjournment

Rachel: It's getting late; I move that we adjourn.

Chair: Chris.

Chris: I second that motion.

Chair: It is moved and seconded that we adjourn. All those in favor say yes. All opposed, say no. *(Pause.)* The meeting is adjourned.

As you can tell from this sample meeting, effective parliamentary procedure depends on the group members' knowledge of the rules and their good communication skills. Group members must listen carefully to the chair and other speakers, or else they

Teach ◀

Skill Development

Quick Skill Opportunity

Answers to Interact:

1. G

2. A

3. E

4. C

5. F

6. D

7. B

may become confused and unable to contribute. Speakers must form their ideas quickly and stay on the point in order to address a large group effectively.

INTERACT

Work with a partner to match the following situations to the standard parliamentary phrase used in a meeting:

Situation	Phrase
1. Postpone the vote on a motion	A. I move we adjourn the meeting.
2. End the meeting	B. I move this motion be amended by _____.
3. Limit discussion of a motion	C. I call the previous question.
4. Vote on a motion	D. The meeting will come to order.
5. Take a break	E. I move debate on this motion be limited to 15 minutes.
6. Start the meeting	F. I move we recess until 2:15.
7. Change a motion	G. I move we table the motion.

Cooperative Learning

Since the best way to remember parliamentary procedure is to use it, conduct the class as a meeting following the basic parliamentary principles.

CHAPTER 8 SUMMARY

This chapter describes various discussion formats and parliamentary procedure. There are a number of formats in which groups can share ideas: (1) committee, (2) panel discussion, and (3) symposium. Members are expected to communicate in certain ways. Large groups often use a set of rules called parliamentary procedure to govern their meetings. Parliamentary procedure, which is based on certain rules and principles found in *Robert's Rules of Order Revised,* helps keep order in large group meetings. It uses specific terms and a specific order of business. Officers have certain duties, and it assigns specific duties to officers.

251

Assess

Answers

Think About It

Student answers will vary. Here are sample answers:

1. A committee is a subgroup of a larger group and is formed to study or manage a specific task. A panel discussion is one in which a subject is explored by a group of members in front of an audience. A symposium is a discussion in which each member gives a short, formal speech in front of an audience and answers questions afterward.

2. In a panel discussion the chairperson's job is to introduce the panel members and the subject, define important terms, call on speakers during the discussion, and summarize the main ideas. In a symposium the leader introduces the symposium members and the topic and closes the discussion by briefly summarizing the speeches. In a committee a leader may ask for short responses or one idea from every member.

3. A forum signifies audience participation in a group discussion. A buzz group is a small group of audience members who gather to discuss ideas presented by speakers and come up with some solution to a problem.

4. Parliamentary procedure is a set of rules for running large group meetings. Its principles are (1) the right of the majority to decide, (2) the right of the minority to be heard, (3) decisions made according to a one-person, one-vote rule, and (4) the right of absent members' opinions to be included.

5. President or chair: Keep the meeting under control, explain the points if some members don't understand, moderate the discussion, and vote in case of a

252

CHAPTER REVIEW

Think About It

1. Describe a committee, a panel discussion, and a symposium.

2. Explain the role of the leader in each of the following group formats: panel discussion, symposium, and committee.

3. What is a forum? What is a buzz group?

4. Define parliamentary procedure and explain its four principles.

5. What are the duties of each of the parliamentary officers?

Try It Out

1. Attend a meeting of a student club or the city council. Take notes to describe (1) the type of rules or procedure followed by the group (2) the effectiveness of the group in completing its work, and (3) any problems that arose. As a class, discuss your findings and make suggestions for how the group could have used parliamentary procedure.

2. Select a possible school event, such as a talent show, fund-raiser, or dance. List possible committees that would plan and carry out the event. In small groups, select one of these imaginary committees. Then plan your committee tasks and create a planning report. Meet as a large group to share your planning reports.

3. Invite a school administrator to your classroom to discuss the importance of small groups in school life. Before he or she arrives, brainstorm a list of questions you might ask the administrator. Select the best question to begin your discussion.

Put It in Writing

1. After observing a classroom panel discussion or a symposium, write a two- or three-paragraph paper in which you summarize the panel's main points and evaluate the role of the leader and participants.

2. In many schools around the world, students do not get a chance to work in groups. Rather, they sit and listen to a teacher speak for most of the day. Write a letter to a pen pal from another country telling that person about the kinds of classroom and extracurricular group activities that are part of your education.

Speak About It

1. With five to seven classmates, select a discussion topic. Present your discussion to the entire class in a panel or symposium format. After the discussion is completed, conduct a forum based on the discussion.

2. Hold a symposium to discuss one of the following topics:

    Eliminating Cheating in the Classroom

tie. Vice president or vice chair: Chair the meeting when the president is absent, chair certain committees as an assistant to the president, substitute for the president whenever necessary, and complete any vice presidential tasks listed in the group's constitution. Secretary: Keep the minutes of meetings, check the attendance at meetings, send out notices about future meetings, send out letters as directed by the president or chair. Treasurer: Keep records of all expenses and incoming funds, pay bills, collect dues or other money, give a financial report when required. Parliamentarian: Advise the president or chairperson on parliamentary procedure. Historian: Keep records of the group's history. Committee chairs or other officers: May run special areas of the group such as publicity, fund-raising, or long-range planning.

Providing Better Food in the Cafeteria

Making the School More Attractive

After the discussion, divide into buzz groups. A representative from each buzz group should report the group's findings to the class.

3. After learning the rules for parliamentary procedure, pair up and instruct other classes or groups in the practice of parliamentary procedure.

Quick Check

Ask students to find and define these Key Terms:

abstain (234)

agenda (235)

buzz groups (230)

committee (223)

forum (230)

majority (234)

minority (234)

minutes (235)

motion (237)

panel discussion (225)

parliamentary procedure (231)

second (238)

symposium (229)

253

Unit 4 Planner | Ancillary Resources

Public Communication	Time Management	*	🖊	✓	%
9 Introduction to Public Speaking (pp. 255–275)	Week 9	●	●	●	●
10 Finding and Using Information (pp. 276-311)					
11 Constructing the Speech (pp. 312–339)	Week 10	●	●	●	●
12 Delivering the Speech (pp. 340–375)	Week 11	●	●	●	●
13 Creating the Informative Speech (pp. 376–405)	Week 12	●	●	●	●
14 Creating the Persuasive Speech (pp. 406–441)	Week 13 & 14	●	●	●	●
15 Learning About Debate (pp. 442–469)	Week 15	●	●	●	●

Unit Focus

Unit 4 introduces public speaking, examines sources of information and how to evaluate and record these sources, explains how to construct and deliver a speech, focuses on creating the informative and the persuasive speech, and describes debate.

Unit Portfolios

Activities marked with this symbol are suitable for inclusion in speech portfolios.

Ability Key

▲ average and above-average students
● all students
▼ average and below-average students

Ancillary Resource Key

 = *Teacher's Resource Book*

 = Workbook

 = TRB Worksheets & Evaluation Forms

 = TRB Assessment and Testing

Performance Objectives

After completing this unit, students will be able to

1. describe and evaluate research sources

2. demonstrate how to record information

3. define the main organizational patterns of a speech

4. outline and deliver a speech to inform and a speech to persuade

5. take part in a debate

UNIT FOUR

4

Public Communication

Introduction to Public Speaking	9
Finding and Using Information	10
Constructing the Speech	11
Delivering the Speech	12
Creating the Informative Speech	13
Creating the Persuasive Speech	14
Learning About Debate	15

Bibliography

Print

MacArthur, Brian, ed. *The Penguin Book of Twentieth-Century Speeches.* London: Viking, 1992.

Naegelin, Lanny. *The Book of Eulogies: A Collection of Memorial Tributes, Poetry, Essays, and Letters.* New York: Scribner, 1997.

Safire, William. *Lend Me Your Ears: Great Speeches in History,* rev. ed. New York: W.W. Norton, 1997.

Wood, Roy and Lynn Goodnight. *Strategic Debate,* 5th ed. Lincolnwood, Ill: NTC/Contemporary Publishing, 1995.

Video

Great Speeches Video Series. Educational Video Group, 291 Southwind Way, Greenwood, IN 46142.

Successful Speaking: Delivery Techniques, 22 min. Cat #2520. Educational Video Group.

Successful Speaking: Conquering Communication Anxiety, 24 min. Cat #2510. Educational Video Group.

	Day 1	Day 2	Day 3	Day 4	Day 5
9 Introduction to Public Speaking					
Public Speaking and You	Audience Goal				
Purpose of Public Speaking	Summary and Chapter Review				
Audience Analysis					
Teacher's Resource Book					
Teaching Suggestions 9.1–9.6	9.7				
Worksheets & Evaluation Forms 30					
	Chapter Test 9				
Workbook 9.1–9.3	9.4–9.5				

(Week 9 / Chapter 9 Planner)

CHAPTER NINE

Introduction to Public Speaking

Chapter Objectives

After completing this chapter, you should be able to

1. define public speaking

2. give examples of situations in which people give public speeches

3. describe the two main purposes of public speaking

4. describe the guidelines for selecting a topic

5. explain the importance of audience analysis

6. list various types of information needed for an audience analysis

7. define and create audience goals

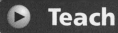

Motivation

Encourage students to discuss times in
their lives when they may need to be
capable public speakers, and ask them
to share anecdotes about public
speaking opportunities they may have
already had.

Critical Thinking
Predicting

● Ask students to predict why
audience analysis is important in
giving a speech.

 **Key Terms**

audience analysis	social-ritual speech
audience goal	speech to inform
public speaking	speech to persuade

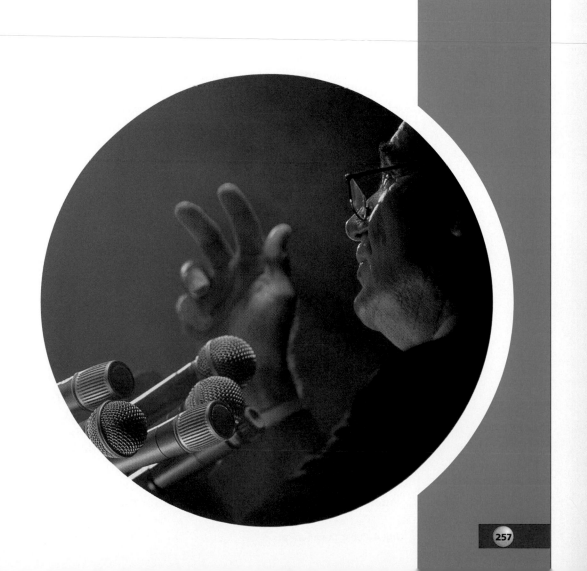

> ❝Never let the fear of striking out get in your way.❞
>
> GEORGE HERMAN (BABE) RUTH

Curricular Connection

Language Arts

● Have students write poems about what it's like for them to give a speech. Encourage them to be honest and to use descriptive language. You might have students exchange their finished poems with a partner or you could read several of the strongest examples aloud to the class.

Curricular Connection

Mathematics

▼ Encourage students to figure out how many people it would take to make up 60 percent of the 500 mentioned in the information about the public-speaking survey.

Skill Development

Quick Skill Opportunity

▼ Have volunteers say the four statements on this page the way they would if they were addressing a large crowd. Encourage feedback from the class.

Vote for Corelle Brown for Treasurer. She will keep good records of expenses. . . .

I am pleased to welcome the players and parents to the fifth annual baseball league dinner. Tonight we will honor two retiring coaches. . . .

As festival volunteers, you will need to know how to apply make-up to children. There are four basic steps. . . .

The Mars Pathfinder mission provided the world with information about a planet that had been a mystery. . . .

These opening statements could be spoken by young people or adults to listeners who were voting in an election, attending an awards dinner, helping with a community festival, or considering scientific discoveries. You may find yourself speaking to large or small groups many times in your life. In a recent survey of five hundred adults, over 60 percent said they had given at least one speech to an audience of more than ten people. Most had given four or more speeches over the past two years. Most of these speeches were presented on their jobs. Some were given in activity or community groups.

There will be many times in the future when you will have to stand up and talk to an audience. The more knowledge you have about the speaking process and the more practice you have had, the easier it will be. This chapter discusses the purposes of public speaking, topic selection, audience analysis, and audience goals. Later chapters will describe how to create and deliver different types of speeches.

PUBLIC SPEAKING AND YOU

Public speaking occurs when one person addresses a group for a specific purpose. You may find yourself delivering a message to audience members, or you may be an audience member listening to a speaker. In both cases you are an important part of the public-speaking process.

You might think you will never have to give a speech. When you think about the many situations that involve public speaking, however, you may change your mind. There are many situations in which one person stands up and talks to a group of people. Speeches may be short or long, formal or informal, funny or serious. Keep your eyes and ears open. You may be surprised to discover how many times people are called upon to speak in public.

Teenagers often find themselves in public-speaking situations. Look at the following situations in which a student is asked by the principal to speak to an audience:

It's your job to introduce the football team at the sports banquet.

As part of the English Honors evening, you will be expected to give a short presentation to the parents on the author you studied.

During the assembly, you will give a short thank-you speech for the math award.

You are one of three students asked to address the school board on the new student discipline code. Will you do it?

Many of the students featured in the "Speaking Of . . ." features in each chapter spend part of their time giving speeches in schools and in their communities.

Giving short presentations is as much a part of public speaking as giving long, formal speeches.

Skill Development

On the Job

Ask whether there are any students who, as part of their volunteer work, have to speak to groups of people. Encourage these students to share some anecdotes with the class.

JOURNAL ENTRY

We have a small zoo in our town, and I am a volunteer who works with the animals. I never thought I would have to give a speech, but in the summer when the camps come to the zoo on field trips, I have to talk to the children about the snakes. I explain the types of snakes we have, I show them many of the snakes, and then I answer questions while some of the children pet the snakes. I used to be terrified when I had to speak, but now it's just part of my job.

Some people think public speaking consists of long formal speeches delivered to large audiences. Although this is one type of public speaking, other situations call for speakers to talk to small, informal groups of people. As you grow older, you will find even more situations that involve talking to an audience. Look at the following comments that adults might make about public speaking. Some apply to work life; others to community groups adults join.

This looks like a tough jury. My closing arguments better be persuasive or my client will be in trouble.

The boss wants me to talk at the union meeting about the new safety regulations.

I'm talking to the Rotary Club tomorrow night about how I got started in sports medicine. I have to give the report to the PTA on next year's budget.

OBSERVE

When do people you know make speeches? For one week list all the situations that involve a person you know talking to an audience of ten or more people. Note the ages of the speakers and the reasons for their presentations. Here are some examples:

1. My teenage brother has to do an oral report in class next week.

continued

66 Talking and eloquence are not the same: to speak, and to speak well, are two things. 99

BEN JONSON

OBSERVE

2. My dentist will give a speech about clear braces at the next dental convention.

3. My grandmother talks to senior-citizen groups about volunteer opportunities.

In addition to giving speeches, a competent communicator must evaluate speeches. Almost every day you are an audience member for a speaker. You listen to teachers, political speakers, religious speakers, and many others. You use your listening skills to evaluate these speakers and their messages.

PURPOSES OF PUBLIC SPEAKING

The main purposes for public speaking are to inform and to persuade. Other reasons to give speeches are to entertain and to inspire. This text focuses on the two main purposes, informing and persuading.

Speaking to Inform

A **speech to inform** is designed to increase the knowledge of the listeners. The speech may introduce the audience to a new subject or present an in-depth look at a familiar topic. It may describe or demonstrate. A speech to inform tries to be fair and objective. Here are some sample titles of speeches to inform:

How to Make Tacos

What Did the Mars Pathfinder Mission Tell Us?

How to Play a Saxophone

How Do Electrical Circuits Work?

Putting On Clown Makeup

Making Your Own Web Page

Fossils of Arizona

Basic Bicycle Repairs

261

Limited English Proficiency

Ask those students with improving English skills to work with a more proficient partner to prepare to introduce each other in front of the class. Partners should take from three to five minutes to learn a little about each other before making the introductions. They might assume that each person is a guest speaker.

Links to Past Learning

Ask students if any of them have ever given a speech to persuade. Do an in-class survey of whether or not students were or were not allowed to choose their own speech topics.

For each of these topics, the speakers describe or demonstrate something. Listeners would expect to learn new information or new skills.

A special type of speech to inform is the **social-ritual speech**. Social-ritual speeches are short and follow a set pattern. The following situations may involve social-ritual speeches:

introducing the acts in a talent show

announcing awards

nominating a candidate for a school office

introducing a guest speaker

making announcements at meetings

Listeners expect social-ritual speeches to follow certain patterns and may become annoyed or confused if the patterns are not followed. For example, a speech introducing a guest speaker is expected to be very brief. If the person introducing the guest speaker gives a fifteen-minute introduction, the audience will become annoyed. After all, the audience came to hear the speaker, not the person introducing the speaker!

Speaking to Persuade

A **speech to persuade** is designed to convince the listeners to hold a certain belief or to act in a certain way. It may include new information if the speaker needs to increase the audience's knowledge as a means to move the audience to some belief or action. The speaker's main purpose, however, is to get the listeners to think or act differently. The following are titles for speeches to persuade:

Protect Our Children: Fingerprint Them!

Drunk Drivers Deserve Tougher Punishments

Homelessness Is Everyone's Problem

Using E-mail to Create International Understanding

Anorexia and Advertising: Is There a Connection?

Skill Development

Research

● Students might choose one of the topics on page 262 as a basis for further research. They could either submit a written report or deliver a speech to persuade the rest of the class.

66Language is the road map of a culture. It tells you where its people came from and where they are going.99

RITA MAE BROWN
Starting from Scratch

In each of these speeches, the speaker would try to convince the listeners to agree with him or her or to take some action. Listeners must be aware of the strategies that speakers use to persuade them.

TOPIC SELECTION

Every speaker is faced with the question of what to talk about. You might ask yourself, "Should I describe my rock-climbing experiences, or should I demonstrate how to make hair wraps? Should I persuade class members to join the walk for handgun control?" For most classroom speeches, you can choose your own topic.

In other school-related situations, you may be asked to speak on an assigned topic. If your school has assemblies related to various holidays, you may be asked to speak on social, religious, or political subjects related to the holiday. Or you may be asked to talk with parents about the school trip to the Ellis Island Immigration Museum.

In most speaking situations, you can choose a topic that is related to your interests or to a certain occasion. If the school board is considering changing the school discipline code, you may need to prepare a persuasive speech on the discipline topic for the school-board meeting. To introduce the bands in the Battle of the Bands Night, you might be expected to give short descriptions of how each band was formed.

When you choose a classroom speech topic, use the following guidelines: (1) select a topic that interests you and (2) select a topic that will interest your audience.

Personal Interests

As a speaker, you must select a topic that interests you. If you are not excited about a topic, it will be hard for you to get your audience interested. If you are bored, you are going to bore your listeners! If you are excited, your audience will probably get excited too.

Curricular Connection

Social Studies

Ask each student to introduce a famous historical figure. Each student should supply some background about the person, after which the class should try to supply the famous person's name.

263

Learning Styles

Kinesic Learning

● Tell students to pay attention to their bodies the next time they are reading a newspaper, textbook, comic book, or novel. Have them write their bodily reactions to material that holds great interest, that holds little interest, and that holds no interest. Encourage students to share their reactions with the class.

SPEAKING OF . . .

CHRISTINA ELIZABETH VASQUEZ

The entire business community of Mercedes, Texas, knows Christina Vasquez because she is serving for one year as "Miss Mercedes." A student at Mercedes High School, Christina spends much of her time representing her community at business events such as ground-breaking ceremonies and grand openings of stores. She also acts as a host at major regional events such as auctions, parades, and the Rio Grande Livestock Show.

Her position requires Christina to deliver many social-ritual speeches at special community events. In addition, she presents motivational and persuasive speeches to younger community members in the Boys and Girls Club and at municipal public-library events. According to Christina, "Representing my community as Miss Mercedes actually requires excellent communication skills. For the most part, speaking for different audiences requires the ability to identify with them. For example, when I talk with the youth of my community, I refer to the empirical experiences in my life, and when I talk to the leaders of my community, I talk to them about my career goals and ideals." In addition to giving speeches, Christina is frequently interviewed by local media representatives, an experience she believes improved her "thinking-on-the-spot skills." Christina reports that, in order to create a professional image, she tends to wear a business suit or a conservative dress when giving formal presentations. On the other hand, when Christina appears at informal events such as National Trash Bash Day and benefit golf tournaments, her attire is quite different.

Someday Christina may use her communication skills as a television host, a convention planner, a politician, or a member of community government, such as mayor.

Motivation

Ask students how they can tell when an audience is interested in what a speaker is saying. Encourage them to note physical as well as verbal audience reactions.

APPLY

Make a list of ten possible topics that interest you. You need not know much about the topic right now. If you actually use the topic for a speech, you will do research. As you think of each topic, ask yourself, "Can I get excited about this subject?" Before you begin your list, think about questions such as these:

What are my future goals?

How do I like to spend my weekends?

What is interesting about me?

What do I worry about?

What is unusual about my hobbies and interests?

These questions will help you determine what interests you.

Audience Appeal

The second thing you must do as a speaker is select a topic that will interest your audience. Ask yourself if your listeners would find this subject interesting. After you find two or three topics that interest you, think about how your audience might react to each. One student considered the following topics interesting: diets, camping, music, baseball, astronomy, magic, and animals. This student based her final decision on the topic she thought the class members would find most interesting:

> I could talk on any of the seven subjects, but I decided to speak about music because most of the other students in the class are interested in music. I limited myself to guitar music. I decided to describe how I compose simple songs on the guitar and play some examples.

AUDIENCE ANALYSIS

A good speaker always considers how to connect the audience and the message. **Audience analysis** is any information about the

265

Amazing Fact!

With the advent of William Caxton's printing press in 1476 in London, English spelling was essentially standardized, no matter how strange it may seem today in words such as *knight* and *knife*.

Links to Past Learning

Remind students that in addition to knowing something about an audience, to communicate effectively they must keep in mind the importance of good vocal projection, pitch, and rate. (See Chapter 3.)

audience that helps the speaker communicate effectively. The analysis includes basic data, beliefs, and attitudes.

How often have you heard someone say, "The speaker was telling us things we already know" or "After five minutes most of the audience was half-asleep because the topic was so boring." To communicate well you must know your audience well. This knowledge will help you select the right topic or the right words to keep their attention.

In a classroom situation you speak to the same group of students a number of times. Ask yourself what might interest them. In speaking situations outside of class, you may talk to many different audiences that you don't know as well. You will need to know something about each one in order to communicate effectively.

APPLY

If you were to talk to an audience you did not know well, what information would you try to learn about the members? Look at the two lists of audience characteristics and decide which contains the more important information.

List 1	List 2
gender	hair color
age	mother's first name
educational level	favorite color
cultural background	shoe size
religious views	phone numbers
political views	square-dancing ability
income level	car model
reason for attending	scuba-diving experiences

If you concluded that the information in List 1 would be more helpful, you are correct.

266

In the next few pages, you will look at the kind of information that could be helpful as you do an audience analysis. This information includes basic data, beliefs or opinions, knowledge of topic, and expectations.

Basic Data

Often you need to know basic information about your listeners, such as age, gender, occupation, educational level, and income level. If you were talking about fossil hunting to second graders, for example, you would not use terms such as *sedimentary* or *trilobites*—at least not without carefully explaining them. Information about the audience's age would help you choose the right level of scientific language and technical information. The more you know about your audience, the more ways you will find to connect the audience and your topic. Use examples and language that the audience will understand.

JOURNAL ENTRY

I am part of a team of students that talks to community groups about helping our school. When we talk to business groups, we ask for money or equipment. When we talk to senior-citizen groups, people who don't usually have much money, we ask them to volunteer their time. Because we are talking with adults, we tend to dress formally and present our message in a serious tone.

Beliefs and Opinions

It is important to know whether most audience members hold specific beliefs or values related to your topic. Being sensitive to an audience's political views or religious beliefs can help speakers avoid offending the audience by accident. Some hunters will not appreciate a speaker who supports gun control. People who believe in government spending to support the poor will not listen kindly to a speaker who wants to cut welfare programs.

Beyond the Classroom

● Encourage students to think about the speeches they have heard at school over the years. Ask what speakers did or could have done to make sure their speeches were connecting with the audience. Encourage students to give specific examples.

267

❝A problem is a chance for you to do your best.❞

DUKE ELLINGTON

Critical Thinking

Analyzing

Ask students to suggest ways of finding out about the audiences for topics such as the ones listed in the Apply activity.

Once you know basic information about your audience, you can connect the audience to the message.

APPLY

Look at the following and decide which audience beliefs or opinions a speaker should try to learn about before giving a speech on these subjects.

divorce

homelessness

school dress codes

children's rights

MTV

smoking

immigration restrictions

career planning

the Middle East

open adoption

Many of these topics can be controversial. It is important to know how the majority of your listeners might feel about such topics so that you know how to develop your speech. This does not mean you have to tell the listeners what they want to hear. It means you need to select the speaking strategies that will keep your audience involved and listening.

Knowledge of the Topic

It is important to ask yourself, "Am I introducing this audience to a new subject, or do most people know a lot about this topic already?" If you plan to talk about a topic that is new to most audience members, you need to start with the basics. You may have to define words or terms, discuss unfamiliar ideas, or explain how something works. If most of your audience is familiar with the topic, you may need to take a new approach or go into great detail in order to provide fresh information.

APPLY

Look at the following topics and think about whether most of your classmates would be familiar with them.

gun control   the history of radio

prison reform   South African music

NWBA   The Real World

the impact of tornadoes

Expectations

At a sports award dinner, what would you expect the main speaker to talk about? What would you expect from a speaker at a funeral service? Most of the time audience members expect a speaker to do or say certain things, depending on the occasion or on their knowledge of the speaker. The speaker needs to know what the audience expects.

Critical Thinking

Evaluating

Encourage students to write a list of five of their opinions and beliefs about such topics as the death penalty, juvenile crime, salaries for professional athletes, gun control, or any school-related topics they feel strongly about. They need not share their lists; however, ask them whether they think they could be persuaded to change their mind about any of these topics.

269

Skill Development

Making Conversation

● Students might enjoy comparing their journal entries from the Apply activity.

Multicultural Learning

If you have a student or students who have spend time abroad, ask them about any experiences they might have had speaking publicly about the trip.

Audience expectations may affect your choice of topic or how you talk about your topic. An audience that expects you to talk about your experience as a student in Spain may be surprised to hear a speech on soccer. An audience that expects you to give a humorous speech may be disappointed when you give a serious one. As a speaker, you don't have to do exactly what the audience expects, as long as you do something appropriate for the occasion. But if you are going to do something different, you may wish to prepare your audience with a comment such as, "You are used to my humorous approach to speech topics, but today I want to tackle a serious subject."

APPLY

After returning from a year of study abroad, most students are asked to speak with different audiences about the experience. Using the following audiences (who are frequently included on a returning student's speech agenda), conduct the following analysis task: (1) identify the basic data characteristics of each audience, (2) note your beliefs about their expectations for such a speech, (3) explain what the student speaker should do to adapt the presentation to each audience. (You may wish to identify a country or area in which the student studied for the year.)

1. Local Rotary Club members who provided scholarship support for part of the trip

2. Parents of students who are considering spending a year abroad during the next school year

3. Students who are considering studying abroad for the following school year

Write the results of your analysis in your journal.

Skill Development
Media Literacy

● As most students know, advertisers of products are usually quite clear in deciding on specific audience goals. Ask what advertisers of cars, toothpaste, dog food, or shampoo want an audience to do or to believe and how they determine whether their audience goals have been met.

Announcing awards is a common social-ritual speech.

AUDIENCE GOAL

Although you know the two general speech purposes—to inform and to persuade—one question remains. Why does the individual speaker actually give a speech? A few people give speeches to get attention or to prove how smart they are, but most give speeches to change their listeners in some way. The change may be very small, but good speakers want something to be different by the time the speech is finished. They want their audiences to do something or to believe something. They have a specific goal for the audience.

After you think about your purpose for giving a speech and consider your audience, you must decide on your specific **audience goal**. An audience goal describes what the listeners should be able to do after the speech is completed. A speaker might phrase an audience goal in the following way: "After my speech is over, I want my listeners to . . ." For example, if Tina is

271

Amazing Fact!

Noah Webster's *American Dictionary of the English Language* (1828) was the first dictionary to distinguish American from British usage.

Learning Styles

Visual

- Ask students to suggest the kinds of visual aids that could help support audience goals 2 and 4. They might suggest photographs of the school grounds and photographs or graphs and charts showing effects of acis rain.

giving a speech on the value of playing sports, her audience goal may be stated in this way: " I want my listeners to understand three reasons why playing sports is important: (1) developing physical coordination, (2) learning about teamwork, and (3) getting exercise." An audience goal is always worded in terms of what the listeners should be able to do, NOT what the speaker will do.

Which of the following are stated as audience goals?

1. I will describe my trip down Grand Canyon.
2. The listeners will donate one Saturday morning a month to clean up the school grounds.
3. The listeners will hear about this year's top country singers.
4. The listeners will understand the problem of acid rain and know two possible ways to reduce it.

Numbers 2 and 4 are correctly-stated audience goals. They describe what the audience members should be able to do after listening to the speech.

The audience goal helps a speaker decide what should be included in the speech and what parts of the speech should be given the most attention. For example, if you are giving a speech on "Halloween Safety," your audience goal might be stated in this way: "I want my listeners to be able to list six ways to make Halloween safer in our community." With this goal, your speech should focus on the ways to make Halloween safer, rather than on the history of Halloween or how to sew costumes.

Public speaking is a very special way to reach many people with ideas you believe are important. Developing your public-speaking skills will help you now and in your future careers.

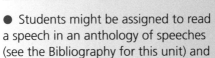

INTERACT

In small groups, select three of the following topics and create one correctly worded audience goal for each topic. Remember to write the goals in terms of what the listeners should be able to do.

chocolate-chip brownies	Yoruba ritual dance
stepfamilies	backpacking
lake pollution	healthy hearts
student government	collecting as a hobby
jazz	the economy of India

CHAPTER 9 SUMMARY

Public speaking is a two-way process that involves speaking and listening. There are two main purposes for public speaking—to inform and to persuade. Public speakers follow three important steps in preparing to speak. They select a topic, analyze the audience, and set an audience goal.

Critical Thinking
Evaluation

● Students might be assigned to read a speech in an anthology of speeches (see the Bibliography for this unit) and evaluate it in writing.

273

Answers

Think About It

Student answers will vary. Here are sample answers:

1. A student giving an oral report in class, a lawyer giving a speech to the jury, a scientist speaking to a group about recent scientific discoveries

2. Choose a topic that interests the speaker and one that will interest an audience.

3. Speaking to inform, social ritual speech, speaking to persuade

4. Try to establish the audience's basic data (e.g., age, gender, etc.), their beliefs and opinions, their knowledge of the topic, and their expectations.

4. Try to establish the audience's basic data (e.g., age, gender, etc.), their beliefs and opinions, their knowledge of the topic, and their expectations.

5. An audience goal helps focus the speech in a way that will change the listener in some way. For example, a speaker might have as his or her audience goal: "The listeners will seriously consider donating blood at the bloodmobile the next time it comes to their area."

274

CHAPTER REVIEW

Think About It

1. Name at least three situations in which people you know give speeches.

2. What guidelines should a speaker use to select a topic?

3. What are the main purposes of public speaking?

4. What things should you look for when analyzing your audience?

5. Explain the importance of an audience goal and give one example.

Try It Out

1. With two or three classmates, complete an audience analysis for your class. Be sure to consider basic data, beliefs and values, knowledge of the topic, and expectations.

   What are the future goals of your classmates?

   How do class members like to spend their weekends?

   What do classmates worry about?

   What kind of television shows or books do your classmates enjoy?

   What is unusual about your classmates' hobbies and interests?

   What do your classmates do during summer vacations?

   What languages other than English do your classmates speak?

2. List four topics on which you might like to speak. Write an audience goal for each. Ask two or three of your classmates if they are interested in the topics. Have them explain why or why not.

3. For one week keep a list of all the situations in which you have been an audience member. Describe two situations when you thought the speaker analyzed the audience poorly. Explain why you did not believe the speaker was well informed about the audience.

Put It in Writing

1. Interview three persons who give speeches regularly. Were the speeches most often related to the person's job or to a social situation? Write a few paragraphs in which you analyze the importance of public speaking in these individuals' lives.

2. Pretend you are about to give a speech on a controversial topic. Imagine two different audiences. Describe each audience's basic data, knowledge of topic, beliefs and opinions, and expectations. Then write a specific audience goal for each audience on the basis of your analysis.

Speak About It

1. Attend a public speech. Briefly describe to your classmates the public-speaking event—who the speaker

was, where the speech took place, and so on. Then share one thing you learned about public speaking from attending the event.

2. Present a one- to two-minute description of the most effective speaker you have ever heard. Tell your class about the setting and the audience. Describe the speaker's topic and delivery style. Explain why this person was an effective speaker.

Quick Check

Ask students to find and define these Key Terms:

audience analysis (265)

audience goal (271)

public speaking (258)

social-ritual speech (262)

speech to inform (261)

speech to pursuade (262)

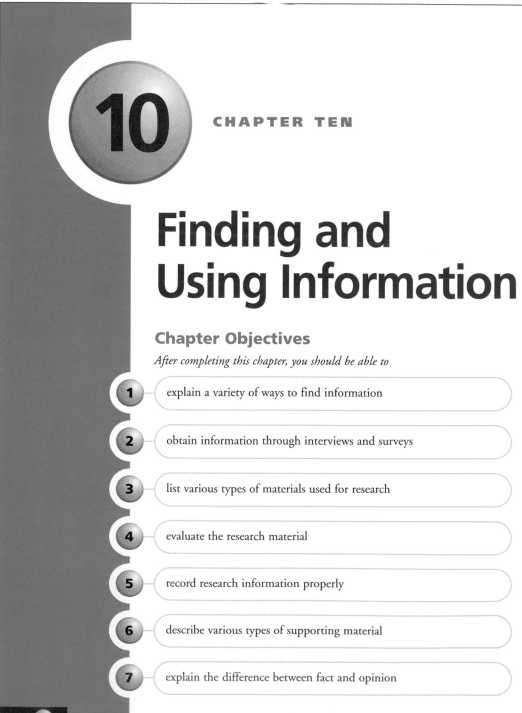

10

CHAPTER TEN

Finding and Using Information

Chapter Objectives

After completing this chapter, you should be able to

1 — explain a variety of ways to find information

2 — obtain information through interviews and surveys

3 — list various types of materials used for research

4 — evaluate the research material

5 — record research information properly

6 — describe various types of supporting material

7 — explain the difference between fact and opinion

Motivation

Encourage students to think about the various ways they use research in their daily lives. Remind them that research is also a common task in many jobs.

Critical Thinking

Predicting

● Encourage students to scan the chapter title and the Key Words and to predict what this chapter has to do with public speaking.

⊙ **Key Terms**

cyberspace resources	opinion	research
fact	plagiarism	supporting material
interview	PowerPoint	survey

Links to Past Learning

Ask students to tell whether they have done research on the Internet, in a library, or through interviewing and surveying and whether the research was required for a class or was independent research.

Student A: I'm talking about students' views on cafeteria food.

Student B: I'm explaining the need for a crossing guard.

Student C: I'm discussing the history of karate and demonstrating kicks.

Although it may come as a surprise to students A, B, and C, each of their speeches will require research. Student A will have to survey students to get their opinions on the cafeteria food. Student B will have to observe student traffic to find out how many students cross the busy intersections. Student C may have already done most of the research by taking karate lessons. Since student C plans to include the history of karate, some Internet research or a trip to the library may be necessary.

RESEARCH SOURCES

Effective speeches are built on a foundation of solid ideas and information. After you have a topic and an audience goal, you need to find the best materials to help your audience reach that goal. These materials are found through careful research. In this chapter you will learn how to use research skills to find and record the materials you need to support your speech.

What comes to your mind when you hear the word *research*? **Research** is a process of investigation that you use every day. For example, how do you buy a skateboard? You might ask your friends questions about the boards they own. You may check the size of their boards and see if they have soft or hard wheels. You might look at ads in the paper or talk to a salesperson in the sports store. You might read a magazine article in *Transworld Skateboarding* or *Consumer Reports* that rates skateboards. You may even try out your friends' boards. That's research!

The public speaker goes through a similar process. Imagine that you have decided on the topic and purpose of your speech and that you have analyzed the audience. Now it's time to research the topic to find the supporting material you need. To gather information, you may turn to (1) your own experience,

278

❝Knowledge is of two kinds. We know a subject ourselves, or we know where we can find information upon it.❞

SAMUEL JOHNSON

A typical Web site.

Critical Thinking

Analyzing

▼ Encourage students to analyze speeches they have heard in the past by discussing whether the speaker brought himself or herself into the discussion. Remind students that speakers often use personal pronouns, such as *I, me,* and *mine,* to personalize the content of the speech. Encourage students to listen for the personal information in speeches.

(2) interviews and surveys, (3) written or printed materials, (4) electronic media materials, or (5) cyberspace resources. A discussion of each of these sources follows.

Personal Experience

Competent public speakers often start their research by using their own experience. This is similar to what writers do. When you have to write an essay, you begin by examining your connection to the topic. Writers may consider what experience they have had with the topic, what they know or think about the topic, who they have listened to on the topic, or how this topic relates to another topic with which they are familiar. Public speakers also start with the connections they already have and then move on to other sources for information, ideas, and issues.

Suppose you are giving a speech on playing the drums. Your speech could include a description of how you became interested in percussion instruments and how you learned to play. All of that information comes from you.

279

Beyond the Classroom

▼ Bring in several copies of *Consumer Reports* magazine, and allow students to look up comparative reports on various products. Remind them that doing research is a part of life, even when it comes to such things as buying a new television set or camera.

Cooperative Learning

● Have students continue working with their partners from the Interact activity. Encourage each person to speak to his or her partner about several topics. Have partners give one another feedback about which topics seemed to excite both listener and speaker most.

Skill Development

Research

● Have students choose one of the topics listed on this page and think of three or four good interview candidates for those topics. Students could write a paragraph about why they chose the interview subject they did.

Your own experience also includes what you have observed. For instance, if you have seen people flying kites at the city park every evening between 7 P.M. and 9 P.M., you can describe what you observed. If you decide to give a speech on the violence in prime-time television shows, you would watch some shows and use examples of violence from them to support your point.

If you are speaking about the difficult life of many foster children, you may draw on your own feelings when your father was hospitalized for two months or the experiences of a friend who volunteers in a children's home. These may help you identify issues to research.

INTERACT

With a partner, brainstorm ideas for topics that come from your own experiences and that might be used for class speeches. When you are finished, you and your partner should have an interesting list of possible speech topics. While brainstorming consider subjects such as favorite authors, movies, or music, as well as special travel experiences, school activities, and hobbies.

Interviews and Surveys

Who would you talk to if you wanted to know more about these topics?

How the Human Heart Pumps Blood	Saudi Arabia
America's Twentieth-Century Presidents	1970s Music
Dyslexia	History of MTV
Getting a Job as a Caddie	Interracial Adoption
Old Superhero Comic Books	Movie Critics

Other people are valuable sources for research. You can quote other people during your speech. For example, you can say, "I talked to my grandmother about World War II, and she said . . ." or "I asked 36 people where they would like to have the spring dance. The results were 19 for the community center; 10 for the

Substitute Teacher Tip

Have a class discussion about television interview programs. Encourage students to identify manipulative or invasive interviewing techniques common to exposé shows and some talk shows. You might start them off with the example of a surprise interview in which the interviewee is accosted by a reporter and forced to speak impromptu in front of the cameras. Have students discuss their reactions to such interviews.

school; and 7 didn't care." If you talk to other people, you will learn a lot. Two common ways to use people as sources are interviews and surveys.

Interviews Sometimes the best way to get information on a topic is to interview an expert. An **interview** is a conversation designed to obtain specific information. Good interviewers are well prepared. Here are some guidelines for conducting a good interview:

1. *Study your topic before the interview.* When you are familiar with the topic, you know what information you need from the expert. You should also know the vocabulary related to the topic. Unless you are familiar with the technical terms, you might misunderstand them or interpret them incorrectly.

2. *Prepare specific questions before the interview.* The people you interview don't have time for you to make up the questions as you go along. Prepared questions will help you get the specific information you want. Although you can certainly ask some questions that occur to you during the interview, you should have at least ten to twelve questions ready ahead of time.

3. *Set up the interview.* Don't drop in on your expert. Call ahead and arrange a definite time and place to meet. When you call, tell the expert what you wish to discuss. You might reveal some of the questions ahead of time so that he or she can think about them before you meet.

4. *Handle questions carefully.* When you ask a question, allow the person time to answer. If the answer does not seem complete, ask for more information or ask a more specific question. Avoid asking questions that can be answered by a "yes" or "no." Try to ask questions that allow the person to display his or her special knowledge and not information you could find easily in print.

5. *Keep a record of the information.* During the interview take notes or record the conversation on tape. The disadvantage of taking notes is that you cannot look directly at the expert while writing. Taping the interview will provide you with a record of the expert's exact words. Be sure to ask permission to use a tape recorder when you make your appointment.

6. *Express your thanks.* Thank the expert for his or her time and send a thank-you note after the interview.

Beyond the Classroom

● Have students use the six pointers for good interviewing to interview a family member. They might consider topics such as family history, the person's job, the happiest experience the person ever had, what period in history that person would like to have lived in and why, a place the person would like to visit and why, or a secret ambition the person would like to fulfill. Interested students could present their findings in a speech to the class.

Links to Past Learning

Ask students who have been interviewed to share their experiences. Encourage them to rate their interviewers' skills.

Cooperative Learning

● Have students work in pairs to perform the dialog in the Apply activity. Then encourage them to come up with ways that Jay might salvage the interview. For example, as Rod Solomon starts to explain what a person who wants to be a writer should do, Jay might turn off the tape recorder, begin taking notes, and ask questions related to the information Solomon is giving him. Students could perform these continuations of the dialog in front of the class.

Prepare your interview questions ahead of time.

APPLY

Below are the opening remarks of Jay's interview with Rod Solomon, a mystery writer. Read these remarks and pick out the problems Jay is going to have.

Rod Solomon: Hello, Jay. Come on in.

Jay: Hi, Mr. Sullivan. Thanks for letting me talk to you. I'm going to tape this.

Rod Solomon: I guess that's OK. Sometimes it makes me uncomfortable.

Jay: I want to know about the books you write.

Rod Solomon: Any one in particular you want to discuss? Did you read *The Pocket Watch Mystery*?

Jay: No. Did you write it?

Rod Solomon: Yes, it was my first book. Which of my books did you read?

continued

Beyond the Classroom

▲ Encourage students to find out about the U.S. Census, one of the largest and most detailed surveys in the country. They might find out how it is conducted and what questions are asked.

APPLY

Jay: Well, I didn't read any, but my teacher says you are a good writer. Do you think I could be a good writer?

Rod Solomon: That's hard to answer since I have never seen your work but anyone who really wants to write should . . .

You can probably tell that Jay is in trouble. He called Mr. Solomon by the wrong name. He didn't ask ahead of time for permission to tape. His first question was much too general, and he hasn't even read any of Mr. Solomon's books! Finally, Jay shifted the topic to his own writing —a bad move.

Surveys A **survey** is a method of gathering information and opinions from a large number of people. In doing research through a survey, you ask many people the same questions. You can ask about their experiences or their opinions on a specific topic. For example, you could ask, "What is your favorite vacation spot?" or "What changes, if any, should be made in the school's disciplinary policies?" People who call you at home to ask you what TV shows you watch or what radio stations you listen to are taking a survey.

JOURNAL ENTRY

Instead of doing library research, my friend and I decided to do a survey. We created a list of questions about how people our age get and spend money. We asked questions such as "Do you get an allowance?" "If so, how much do you get?" "Do you have a job?" "If so, how much do you make a week?" "What things are you expected to buy with your own money?" We surveyed 40 students and did a big report with charts. It was a lot of work, but we had a good time doing it, and I learned enough to convince my grandmother to raise my allowance.

283

Critical Thinking

Evaluating

● Ask interested students to evaluate and rewrite the cafeteria survey. They can take on whatever cafeteria issues they find interesting. They might also write survey questions on another topic and ask classmates to fill out the survey forms.

Use these guidelines for your survey questions:

1. Ask only a few questions and talk briefly. More people will be willing to respond if you ask for only a few minutes of their time.

2. Ask questions that can be answered simply. Use questions that require either yes or no answers or short statements.

3. Ask everyone exactly the same questions in the same order. In order to compare answers, you need to be sure everyone heard the same message from you.

4. Record your answers carefully. Don't try to remember what people tell you. Check boxes or write down the suggestions so that you are able to count and organize the responses.

This sample survey shows how one student arranged her survey questions about the types and quality of food bought in the school cafeteria.

Survey Form

How do students use the school cafeteria and rate the cafeteria food?

1. What kinds of foods do you buy at most meals? Check all that apply.

    _____ Drink

    _____ Dessert

    _____ Salad

    _____ Sandwich

    _____ Chips/snacks

    _____ Hot main dish

2. How often do you buy something besides a drink and dessert?

continued

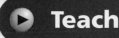
66I often quote myself. It adds spice to my conversation.99

GEORGE BERNARD SHAW

_____ 4 or 5 times a week _____ 3 times a week

_____ 2 or fewer times a week

3. Given this week's menu, rate the food. Use 1 for the meal you enjoyed most and 5 for the meal you enjoyed least.

_____ Cheeseburger

_____ Taco plate

_____ Spaghetti

_____ Hot dog

_____ Veggie sandwiches

4. How would you rate the cafeteria food? (Check one.)

_____ Very good

_____ Good

_____ Average

_____ Bad

_____ Very bad

APPLY

Look at the following speech topics and pick out those you might use in a survey of students and teachers in your school:

Job Opportunities for Teenagers

The Need for Computers in All Classrooms

Pros and Cons of the TV Rating System

Language Requirements for Honor Students

How to Start a Coin Collection

Unless you are at an unusual school, it would be hard to do a survey on coin collecting. Few people know much about this topic.

Critical Thinking

Analyzing

● Encourage students to think about survey results they have read or been familiar with in the past. Mention statistics such as "four out of five dentists surveyed recommend [a certain brand of chewing gum] for their patients who chew gum." Discuss how such "statistics" may not be as significant as they initially sound. Ask, for example, how many dentists were surveyed all together? When students say they do not know, tell them, "If only five dentists were surveyed, this is not a particularly viable statistic. However, if 100 dentists were surveyed, and 80 of them made the same recommendation, the data could be considered viable." Encourage students to analyze the statistics they hear and read to be sure they are not being misled.

285

Cooperative Learning

● Tell students that surveys are part of corporate market research. For example, a magazine might conduct a survey to find out the age, gender, occupation, race, and approximate income of its readership. A resort might create a survey to find out what amenities patrons might feel are lacking. Encourage students to work in small groups to create surveys about market-research topics of their choice.

The following is an example of survey research collected by a student for her speech on "Teenage Attitudes Toward Fashion":

> After taking a survey of 45 classmates, I found that 17 like to dress in the latest style, 14 like to dress in a traditional fashion, and 13 said they don't care about fashion, as long as they are comfortable. One person said he hates to think about clothes. My survey showed the average student changes clothes 782 times a year.

Print Materials

When you do research with print materials, you are doing library research. There are many kinds of printed materials that you can use. They include books, magazines, journals, pamphlets, newspapers, and general information sources such as encyclopedias and

❝Books think for me.❞
CHARLES LAMB

If possible, arrange to have your class visit a regional or city library and take a guided tour. With the help of a librarian or trained library assistant, students could learn to use the computer catalog, microfilm or microfiche, and other information resources.

dictionaries. You can locate these materials through computer searches or in a card catalog.

Books To do research in books, you must know how to use the card catalog or the library computer system. These catalog systems list every book in three different ways: according to the subject or topic area, according to the title, and according to the author's last name. The filing system will tell you the book's library number, which will help you locate the book on the shelves. A computer system may also tell you whether the book has been checked out. Be sure to note the book's title, author, date of publication, and publisher, as well as the page numbers where you found your key material.

Magazines and Journals Magazines and journals are types of periodical literature. Periodicals are published at regularly scheduled times. These include publications ranging from popular magazines to specialized journals on unusual topics.

If you are looking for general magazine articles, you can use the *Readers' Guide to Periodical Literature* (*Readers' Guide* for short). This guide lists articles in 180 of the most popular magazines in the United States. The articles are listed alphabetically according to subject, title, and author. When you locate an article in the *Readers' Guide*, you will also find the date and volume of the magazine and the page numbers of the article you wish to read.

✳ **INTERACT**

Working with a partner, pick a speech topic that interests you both. Using an index such as the *Readers' Guide to Periodical Literature* or a computer search engine such as Yahoo! or Web Crawler find the titles of ten articles or resources that might relate to your topic. Look up at least five of them. List the title of each article or resource and give a short description of it.

287

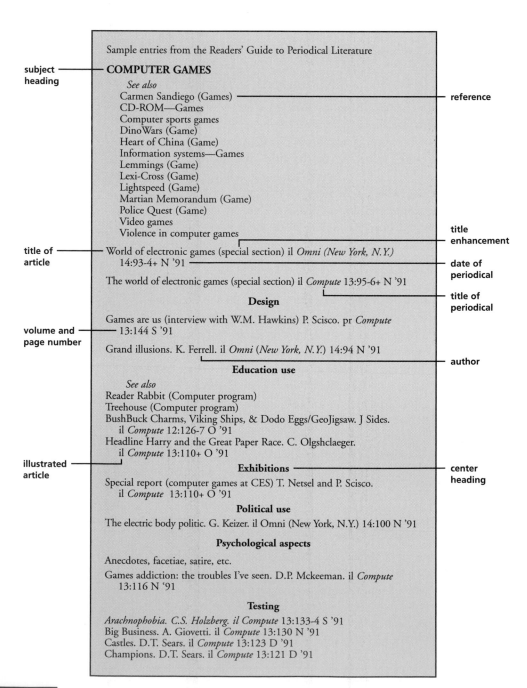

Beyond the Classroom

Mention to students that copyright laws allow some photocopying of material in libraries without permission or payment of fee to the copyright holder, provided the copying is not substantial and an obvious attempt to avoid buying published materials.

Sample entries from the Readers' Guide to Periodical Literature

subject heading → **COMPUTER GAMES**

See also
Carmen Sandiego (Games) ←————————————— **reference**
CD-ROM—Games
Computer sports games
DinoWars (Game)
Heart of China (Game)
Information systems—Games
Lemmings (Game)
Lexi-Cross (Game)
Lightspeed (Game)
Martian Memorandum (Game)
Police Quest (Game)
Video games
Violence in computer games ←————— **title enhancement**

title of article → World of electronic games (special section) il *Omni (New York, N.Y.)* 14:93-4+ N '91 ←————— **date of periodical**

The world of electronic games (special section) il *Compute* 13:95-6+ N '91 ←————— **title of periodical**

Design

Games are us (interview with W.M. Hawkins) P. Scisco. pr *Compute*
volume and page number → 13:144 S '91

Grand illusions. K. Ferrell. il *Omni (New York, N.Y.)* 14:94 N '91 ←————— **author**

Education use

See also
Reader Rabbit (Computer program)
Treehouse (Computer program)
BushBuck Charms, Viking Ships, & Dodo Eggs/GeoJigsaw. J Sides.
   il *Compute* 12:126-7 O '91
Headline Harry and the Great Paper Race. C. Olgshclaeger.
   il *Compute* 13:110+ O '91

illustrated article → **Exhibitions** ←————— **center heading**

Special report (computer games at CES) T. Netsel and P. Scisco.
   il *Compute* 13:110+ O '91

Political use

The electric body politic. G. Keizer. il Omni (New York, N.Y.) 14:100 N '91

Psychological aspects

Anecdotes, facetiae, satire, etc.
Games addiction: the troubles I've seen. D.P. Mckeeman. il *Compute*
   13:116 N '91

Testing

Arachnophobia. C.S. Holzberg. il Compute 13:133-4 S '91
Big Business. A. Giovetti. il *Compute* 13:130 N '91
Castles. D.T. Sears. il *Compute* 13:123 D '91
Champions. D.T. Sears. il *Compute* 13:121 D '91

Limited English Proficiency

Some students may not be certain of the differences between encyclopedias, dictionaries, almanacs, and so on. Show examples of each, and have students explain what they are and what their purpose is. You may also want to show examples of newsmagazines.

Weekly newsmagazines such as *Time, Newsweek,* or *U.S. News and World Report* cover the major news events of the past week.

To find magazines on very specific topics, ask your librarian for help. Another way to locate special articles is by finding an index that lists articles on certain topics. Examples of such indexes are the following:

Social Sciences Index (sociology, psychology, criminology, and so forth)

Humanities Index (English and American literature, history, music, speech, theatre, and so forth)

Education Index (elementary, secondary, special education, and so forth)

Be sure to note the article's title, the magazine or journal's title, the author, the date of publication, and the page numbers.

Pamphlets Pamphlets and public documents are also valuable sources of information. For example, government pamphlets on health may tell the kinds of medicines to use for different illnesses. In most libraries, pamphlets are kept in a vertical file index. Your library may also have a *Monthly Catalog of U.S. Government Publications;* the *United Nations Documents Index,* which lists what the U.N. prints; and the *Public Affairs Information Service,* which names special books and articles on different topics. Be sure to note the title, date, and publisher of pamphlets.

Newspapers Daily newspapers are good sources of information when you are studying your local government or a famous person in your town or city.

Sometimes you need to use old newspapers or a major out-of-town paper to research your topic. Some of these newspapers have their own indexes. By using a microfiche reader, you can see what the *New York Times* headlines were on your date of birth or how the paper covered the Gulf War or the return of Hong Kong to China. Some libraries subscribe to current newspapers from major cities. Be sure to note the title, author (if noted), newspaper name, date, and pages of the article.

Skill Development

Quick Skill Opportunity

● Ask students to name which references they would use for

information on past Academy-Award winners

finding the population of Utah

finding the origin of a word

finding the death date of Thomas Jefferson

learning about the Constitution

finding the height of the world's tallest building

finding current mayoral candidates

finding out about recent medical advances

If you are investigating a current topic, you may wish to examine recent newspaper articles. You may find recent copies of your hometown newspaper or major papers such as the *New York Times* in your school or local library. You can also use electronic sources to examine the newspaper on-line. Sometimes you will not find the full text of an article, but you should always be able to locate an abstract.

General Information Sources Suppose you want to know something about songbirds, World War II, or the human skeleton. To get this information, you could turn to sources that give you factual information on a wide range of topics. These sources include various encyclopedias, *Facts on File*, and the *Information Please Almanac*.

Dictionaries of the English language can give you background information on words you want to use. Some of the most commonly used dictionaries are *The American Heritage Dictionary*, *Merriam-Webster's Collegiate Dictionary*, the Thorndike-Barnhart dictionaries, and the *Random House Dictionary*.

If you need information that deals with numbers, you can check the *World Almanac*. It contains good statistical information. It includes, for example, how many people are born each year in India, how much beef the United States sells to Japan, how many cars are made in Detroit factories, and other similar types of information.

You can also contact government offices and local or national organizations. For example, on the subject of prospecting for gold or exploring caves, you can get free literature from the U.S. Department of the Interior. To get information on how to help accident victims, you could write to the Red Cross. In addition, you may find pamphlets on health-related issues at the local pharmacy.

Suppose your teacher asks you to give a speech on Paul McCartney, Oprah Winfrey, Albert Gore, Winston Churchill, or Harriet Tubman. Where would you start? There may be books on

The Internet provides vast resources for research.

each person in your library, but you could also turn to the following indexes of famous people:

Who's Who in America

Dictionary of American Biography

Webster's Biographical Dictionary

Electronic Media Resources

Electronic media resources include radio, television, video, and audiotapes. To use information from radio and television, you need to include the name of the program, the name of the speaker, and the date on which you heard it. For example, if you were

Skill Development

Research

● Remind students that for information about distances and geographical areas they could check map and atlas resources. Bring in a U.S. atlas and display it for students. You may wish to have them calculate the distances between several major cities, or have them find where a major river or mountain range begins and ends.

291

Beyond the Classroom

▲ Encourage students to find out more about the legal guidelines for using televised or written materials in research projects. Interested students could interview a copyright lawyer or contact the following address.

Copyright Office
Information Section, LM-401
Library of Congress
Washington, DC 20559

Here is the Copyright Office web site.

http://www.loc.gov/copyright

Skill Development

Media Literacy

● Remind students that many video stores have large documentary sections that contain videos on an array of subjects. Tell students that as they watch a documentary, they should try to figure out the filmmaker's purpose. Often the creators of documentaries have a particular point of view to impart. Students should be aware of how the documentary's facts are presented and take note of any bias on the part of the filmmaker.

speaking on the development of the Chicago Bears football team, you might say "On August 8, 1997, sportscaster Chris Bowdon announced on WBBM News Radio that Chris Zorich will be back with the Bears sooner than expected following thumb surgery." Radio and television information cannot be rechecked easily unless you can replay the program. Therefore you have to take careful notes. Because radio and television information usually cannot be rechecked, many speakers use these media for stories, examples, and background information only. Frequently they turn to other sources for direct quotations, facts, and figures. Often researchers try to find a second print source on the topic. Occasionally printed copies or transcripts of radio and television programs are made available on written request. If you tape television shows, you must follow the legal guidelines for using such copies.

When you enter your local video store you may find an entire section of videos with information on travel, self-help, health, and hobbies. If you are giving a speech on San Francisco or on bird watching you could refer to the information on a videotape, indicating its title and publisher. In addition many stores and libraries have audiotapes which you can use for information on many topics.

Cyberspace Resources

The Internet provides you with an extraordinarily wide range of resources, which are sometimes referred to as **cyberspace resources**. Sites such as Yahoo! or Web Crawler are search engines that will uncover more material than you could possibly use. For this reason, you will have to use specialized key words to find what you need. Sometimes a Web site address allows you to find information quickly or track a current event unfolding. For example, when the Mars Pathfinder mission began, NASA established a Web site that could be reached through its home page (http://www.nasa.gov). Millions of students, science researchers, and interested citizens followed the mission daily on their computers.

If you need information about the FBI, such as agent qualifications or the ten most wanted criminals, you would turn to (http://www.fbi.gov) In addition, the Web can provide you with

Motivation

Students who do not have home access to a computer might enjoy learning about Internet cafes. These are facilities that act as combination cafe and computer access shops. Patrons can use the computer and Internet facilities for free or for a small fee. Remind students that libraries and some universities also offer free on-line services.

Links to Past Learning

Ask students to discuss any Internet problems or suspicious information they may have encountered in their research so far.

access to newspapers and magazine sites that will give you current articles and stories. Suppose you wished to talk about touring the nation's capital. You could go to the White House home page (http://www.whitehouse.gov) and click on "White House History and Tours." This would give you the most up-to-date information on tour plans and schedules.

Net researchers must be careful to evaluate their sources since anyone can create a Web page of information on a particular topic. Researchers need to ask questions such as the following:

Is the Web site source credible? Is it, for example, a government or university site?

Can I find any other source to support this claim?

What are the credentials of the person developing this individual Web site?

Careful researchers record the data on electronic sources such as discussion groups, bulletin boards, and e-mail. To refer to a specific Internet site, such as one for the Junior Great Books program, you would record http://www.greatbooks.org on your note card. To refer to an e-mail interview, indicate the e-mail address of your source, his or her name and title, and the date of the interview.

INTERACT

With a group of three classmates, decide on the source or sources you might use to find information on the following topics:

The increase in the U.S. population since 1970

Last year's major forest fires in the Western states

Hong Kong's turnover to Chinese rule

Guidelines for CPR

Survival stories of the Holocaust

Community reaction to year-round schools

The author of *A Wrinkle in Time*

293

Beyond the Classroom

Remind students that they too can become involved in doing volunteer community work just like Kavitha Kareth does. Suggest that students think about community activities that they might be motivated to undertake. What communication skills would be helpful for them to develop in order to participate in the activity they choose?

SPEAKING OF . . .

KAVITHA KARETH

Many of the elementary-school students in Springfield, Illinois, know Kavitha Kareth as the person who guides them through the discovery room of the Illinois State Museum and who comes to their schools to talk about epilepsy. Middle-school and high-school students know her as a member of P.E.A.C.E. or Peers Educating Against Chemicals Effectively. This young woman reaches out to many different youths of her community through her informative and persuasive speeches.

Kavitha has a powerful effect on young people with epilepsy because she talks to them about how to deal with their lives and how to handle the questions their friends ask. She creates a safe and informed place to talk about specific kinds of medications for epilepsy, petite-mal seizures, and other types of seizures. She talks with young people about driving rules, reminds them not to drink, and tries to predict other things they should be aware of. Most importantly, she says, "I tell them that you are a normal kid, you are not different from the rest of them." Although she has epilepsy, she explains that, when she talks with young people, "I have to relate to their lives, not mine." Sometimes she has to listen to some painful feelings these children express. She reports at those times, "I sit down calmly with them and listen to what they have to say. Then I think about what I can say to make them feel better or safer. I tell them it's OK to express your feelings and that I'm always there for them." Kavitha must constantly research changes in epilepsy treatments and medications so she can be current and accurate. She dresses "basically like an ordinary kid" when meeting with these groups so that she can appear to be similar to them.

Kavitha's strong interpersonal communication skills, as well as her public-speaking skills, will prepare her for many careers. She might become a counselor, a doctor, a teacher, or a religious leader.

Curricular Connection

Mathematics

▼ Have students use the information from the text to figure out how many index cards they would need for a 40-minute speech.

RECORDING YOUR INFORMATION

Perhaps you've been in the library for an hour and found an encyclopedia article and two books on your topic. Or you have found two helpful Web sites and an audiotape. What do you do next? After finding the information, you must take notes carefully. This requires time and effort, but doing it correctly can save you a repeat trip to the library.

If you are using information based on observations, you also need to keep records. For example, if you are growing plants from seeds, write down how many sprout and how tall they are every three days. You will need this exact information for your speech.

Research Cards

Use 3 × 5 or 4 × 6 index cards to record information. Cards are easy to sort, file, and organize. Keep your cards in a file box with dividers and arrange them according to areas of information. Put stories, problems, solutions, quotations, and so on into separate categories.

The more cards you have, the better informed you will be on your topic and the more choices you will have when selecting the information most appropriate for your occasion and audience. For example, to give a two- or three-minute speech, you should have 20–35 cards. For a four- or five-minute speech, you should have 30–70 research cards.

What To Record

Each research card, often called a content card, should contain only one quotation, fact, or example. It should have a heading of one or two words that states the card's content. In addition, it should include the source of the information, complete with the publication date and the page number. If you are going to have many cards with information from the same source, put the source information on a numbered key card and then place the key card number on all cards containing information from that source.

295

Learning Styles

Audio Learning

● Encourage interested students to listen to a radio news or talk show and take notes as if they are going to give a speech on the show's content. They could then create a series of note cards for the speech. Students could present the speeches based on their note cards if they wish; otherwise, check over the cards for completeness and for synthesis of the chapter content.

Key Card

"The High Frontier of the Rain Forest Canopy."

By Edward O. Wilson

National Geographic

December 1991 (vol 180 #6)

pp. 78–107

Source 2

Content Card 1

Source 2   p. 102

Life is piled upon life in the tropical rain forest. "But this great edifice is all a house of cards. Most of the millions of species are so highly specialized that they can be quickly driven to extinction by the disturbance of their forest homes."

Content Card 2

Source 2   p. 104

1979—rain forest and monsoon forest were destroyed at a rate of 29,000 square miles a year. 1990—Figure doubled to 55, 000 square miles (larger than the state of Florida).

Teach

Amazing Fact!

The Library of Congress, which serves as the national library, has more than 80 million items in 470 languages.

Most research cards fall into three types: information summary, direct quotations, or specific facts or examples. Information summary cards contain a short summary, in your own words, of the main ideas of an article or section of material. Direct quotation cards give the exact words of an author, which are put in quotation marks. Cards that contain specific facts or examples may simply list the important facts that will help you make your points in your speech. Look at the following examples to see what kind of information is contained on each type of research card.

Information Summary

Coast Guard Work — heading

The Coast Guard Service employs cutters, ice breakers, patrol buoy tenders, helicopter pilots, and many more who can work in air stations and navigation stations that circle the globe. About 5,000 officers are needed to command vessels and stations. — information summary

"Always Prepared" Boy's Life May 1986, p. 22 — complete source information

Direct Quote

Gettysburg Address — heading

". . . That this nation, under God, shall have a new birth of freedom, and that government of the people, by the people, and for the people shall not perish from the earth." — direct quote

Dedication of the National Cemetery
Gettysburg, Nov. 19, 1863 — complete source information

Critical Thinking

Evaluating

▲ Challenge interested students to expand the assignment given in the Apply activity on page 298. Have them create a fact note card for each of the main facts presented in the article on pages 299–300.

Critical Thinking

Organizing

● Explain to students that another useful tool for collecting information is a spreadsheet. Spreadsheets are used to show financial data. Students may use a spreadsheet when collecting and presenting information on a club's finances, the results of a fund-raiser, or a company's bottom line. Encourage students to use a spreadsheet to organize information on a topic of interest to them.

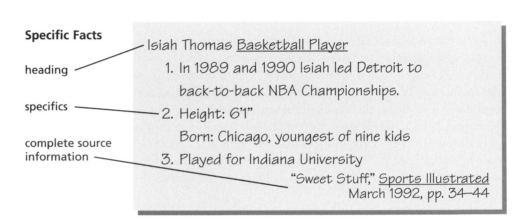

Specific Facts

heading

specifics

complete source information

Isiah Thomas <u>Basketball Player</u>
1. In 1989 and 1990 Isiah led Detroit to back-to-back NBA Championships.
2. Height: 6'1"
   Born: Chicago, youngest of nine kids
3. Played for Indiana University
   "Sweet Stuff," <u>Sports Illustrated</u>
   March 1992, pp. 34–44

Perhaps you have access to computerized note card programs in which you enter the same information. These note cards are not portable, but you can search for information more easily by using a search feature. Another advantage is that you do not need to retype a quotation into your speech manuscript or outline since you can transfer it.

APPLY

Using the following news article, create three cards: one on which you summarize the entire article, one with a quote, and one with a single fact.

The reference section of a library contains dictionaries, biographical indexes, atlases, encyclopedias, and, often, computers to help you into cyberspace.

CHA KIDS FOLLOW A PATH OF SAFETY

by Jerry Thornton

Gang activity isn't as prevalent, fighting is down, and the word "safety" has a real meaning for pupils whose parents belong to a volunteer tenant patrol in the Chicago Housing Authority's Ida B. Wells development.

A hundred men and women at the Darrow Homes extension of the Wells complex have taken to ensuring safe passage for their children to and from Einstein Elementary School by posting themselves at the school and along the way. They take turns patrolling the area.

"It's safer to come to school now," said LaShanda Beal, 12, a 6th grader at the school at 3830 S. Cottage Grove Ave. "There used to be a lot of fighting. Now there's not as much, and the patrol breaks them up."

LaShanda's words were backed Thursday when raucous play and a few scrimmages were quickly stopped by parents, who identify themselves by dark blue jackets and caps with the words "Tenant Patrol" in bright yellow letters.

"The patrol was started last June because of rumors of a child molester being in the area," said Robert Byas, captain of the patrol.

"We started out with just the kids in my building," added Byas, a resident of the Wells project for 25 years.

Soon, other children were meeting at Byas's building at 706 E. Pershing Rd., and the tenant patrol started placing members at various points along the routes to school.

"We try to set a positive image in front of the kids," Byas said. "We respect them, and they give us that respect back."

Patrol members concede that the children known for fighting haven't turned into angels, but things are quieter.

"A lot of the fighting has died down since we've been on patrol," said member Dwayne Al-Amin. "Kids come to us if there is a problem, and we escort them home."

To keep older gang members away, the patrol got help from the Chicago police, who have patrol cars at the school two days a week, and from CHA police, who are there the rest of the week.

So far, there has been no problem with gangs, patrol members said. "But we are letting them know we are not going to tolerate that kind of activity around our school, and when they gather we are going to report them," Byas said.

The morning patrols begin at 8:30 A.M. and last until 9:15 A.M. "for stragglers," Byas said.

Patrollers are back at the school when classes let out at 2:30 P.M. and remain until 3 P.M. They return at 4:30 P.M. Tuesday, Wednesday and Thursday, when late classes are held.

"Tenant patrols were formed by the CHA and are in operation at CHA sites through

Links to Past Learning

▼ Ask students how the feature writer obtained the information he needed to write the article. (The chief source seems to be interviews.)

Beyond the Classroom

● Encourage interested students to choose a subject that a member of the local police force or a member of a community action group would be knowledgeable about and to interview that person. Students could create note cards of their interviews and present their findings to the class. Encourage them to use quotes, facts, and examples.

Skill Development

Research

● Students may wish to do research for a speech on gang activities and citizen response in their own area.

the city, but the school patrol was an initiative of the parents at Wells," said CHA spokesman Andre Garner. "They are the eyes and ears of the community."

Those eyes and ears belong to members like Betty Reynolds, who volunteered six months ago "because I wanted a safe environment for my kids and grandkids."

"We have our eyes on everything for the protection of the children," Byas added.

The CHA provided members of its tenant patrol with walkie-talkies and space in buildings from which to operate, Garner said.

"It has been very effective," said Phyllis Tate, principal of Einstein School, which has an enrollment of 551 pupils.

"Before the patrol, there were more incidents and problems," Tate said. "In fact, one of the children was raped in a building after school."

"Before, there was a higher incidence of fighting. When that happened, the confrontations outside the building would be brought inside, disrupting the whole class. The patrol has helped to stop that, and in turn create a more conducive climate for learning."

Some members of the patrol are members of the local school council, Byas said.

"Since the patrol formed, the kids seem to want to go to school," Byas said. "They feel safe that the gangs won't bother them, and the gangs have shied away."

Accuracy and Ethics

As a researcher, you have a responsibility to work with integrity. This means you work within a personal code of honesty to do the most accurate research possible and give credit when you refer to the work or ideas of others. Unethical communicators deliberately fabricate information or commit plagiarism, two kinds of behavior you wish to avoid.

Fabrication involves inventing or making up information as part of the research process. Although you might be tired or frustrated in your search for appropriate information, as an honest researcher you cannot create an interview quotation or article title. This point should be obvious.

Plagiarism involves representing the words or ideas of others as your own. The most obvious case is handing in or performing work written by someone else and claiming that you wrote it. Sometimes students who do not take careful notes run the risk of plagiarism by carelessness. This can happen when you take notes

300

66Plagiarists are always
suspicious of being stolen
from.**99**

SAMUEL TAYLOR COLERIDGE

from a source but you don't record the title, author, or date and just use the notes as your own. Or it can happen when you forget to put expert statements in quotation marks so you do not cite your source later in your speech. Even when you pretend you thought of a great idea when you actually heard about it during a newscast, you are involved in plagiarism.

These ethical concerns are based on the belief that the works created by a person belong to that person. In our society people have legal ownership over what they create and others must obtain permission before using these creations. There are copyright laws that explain how one may legally use the work of others. Those laws are intended to protect creators such as writers, artists, and musicians.

USING INFORMATION TO SUPPORT YOUR SPEECH

Effective speeches are built on a foundation of solid ideas and information. Main points in a speech must be explained or defended with additional information. This information is called **supporting material.** Supporting material develops the main point. As you prepare your speech, you will use the information you find through your research as supporting material.

APPLY

One student used the following statement as the main idea of a speech: Drunk drivers must be kept off the road. What might the speaker say next to support the point?

1. An average of 50,000 persons are killed by drunk drivers each year.

2. My best friend's aunt was killed by a drunk driver last winter.

continued

Links to Past Learning

Ask students if someone else has ever taken credit for their ideas. Elicit comments about how students reacted when this happened.

Skill Development
Media Literacy

● Students might be unfamiliar with one area of copyright law concerning the use of popular music in films or plays. Encourage students to watch the entire credits section at the end of the next film they see. No doubt they will notice careful documentation of the songs and incidental or background music used in the film.

301

Skill Development
Research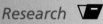

▲ Have students conduct library research to find an audio- or a videotape of a speech on a topic of interest to them. Ask students to listen to the speech and determine the speaker's main points and types of support. Students could then write a short report on the speech and explain whether they think the speaker's message and supporting material are effective.

APPLY *continued*

3. Police Chief McMasters says, "Drunk drivers claim more lives than any other type of criminal."

4. Another national problem is gang crime.

5. We must get drunk drivers off our roads.

The first three statements support the main idea. Number 4 does not relate to the topic of drunk driving. Number 5 should not be used because it only restates the sentence in different words.

Types of Support

Effective speakers find a number of ways to make their points. They support ideas with different types of information in order to reach all their listeners and to keep them involved. Materials that can be used to support speeches include description, examples, quotations, statistical information, personal experience, and visual supports.

Description Description can be used to help listeners picture a person, place, or thing. It can also be used to illustrate how something works or how something is done. Here is part of one student's informative speech with the following audience goal: *Listeners will appreciate the importance of the arts in elementary education.*

> The first thing you see is color—there are children's pictures hanging on every wall. Some are combinations of shapes in bright colors. Others show the trees and flowers the children saw on their nature walk. From the ceiling hang Halloween mobiles— ghosts, black cats, and skeletons. . . .

In another example, a speaker gave an informative speech in which the audience goal was this: *Listeners will be able to apply basic clown makeup to preschool students.*

Media Literacy

Ask students to read a daily newspaper for several days or a Sunday newspaper and to find examples of material that could be used to support a speech. For example, they might find descriptive or example material in a travel or entertainment section, quotations in news or feature stories, and statistical information in the sports or transportation section.

1. Cover face and eyebrows with white face paint.

2. With bright red lipstick, draw triangle shapes above each eye, at corner of each eye, and on chin.

3. With same lipstick, draw a circle around the nose and fill in with color.

4. For a laughing clown, draw mouth curving up at the ends. For a sad clown, draw mouth with ends pointing down.

5. With eyebrow pencil, draw brows following the shape of triangles. For the final touch, draw a teardrop on each cheek.

Examples Examples help an audience remember the main point and make the speech come alive. They help listeners picture what the speaker is discussing. This makes the speech more interesting and memorable.

When you use examples, you are telling a story or narrative about a person, place, or thing. The example may be based on facts or it may be fiction. One speaker used the following fictional example in a speech about rudeness, which had the following audience goal: *Listeners will recognize some of their own rude behaviors and try to change one of them.*

303

Critical Thinking

Analyzing

● Ask students to assume that they are preparing a speech on the need for more national parks to be created. What kind of people might prove good sources for quotations to support such a speech?

The scene is rush hour in a city train station. A woman is on her way home from work. As she enters the subway station, she is pushed against the stairway wall by three well-dressed business-men running for a train. As she opens her purse to buy her token, the woman behind her snaps, "Hurry up, lady." When the train arrives, people are packed together like sardines. She is thrown against a pole while someone steps on her foot.

Quotations When you use quotations, you are presenting another person's words on a subject. Usually, you quote persons who are experts in the topic area. For example, Dr. John Gottman, psychologist and author of *The Heart of Parenting*,* writes about the importance of emotion in raising children:

> I call the parents who get involved with their children's feelings "Emotion Coaches." Much like athletic coaches, they teach their children strategies to deal with life's ups and downs. They don't object to their children's displays of anger, sadness, or fear.

Sometimes a speaker has to select certain ideas from a direct quotation to help the listeners understand. For example, a student speaking on crime had this audience goal: *Listeners will recognize that poverty coupled with a difficult home life can put a young person on the road to crime.* She used the following statement by a school security chief:

> Social and cultural deprivation also play a significant role in the individual's predisposition to violence. While poverty does not cause crime, poverty coupled with an impoverished home life— unhappy family relations, lack of moral values and education, lack of opportunity—can lead a young person into crime.

The student paraphrased the chief's statement this way:

> It is Chief Goggins's belief that poverty and a home life without moral values, family support, and education can lead young people into crime.

---

* Gottman, John. *The Heart of Parenting.* New York: Simon and Schuster, 1977.

When you use quotations, be sure to double-check your information. Be careful not to put your own words into someone else's mouth!

Statistical Information. Statistical information, or numbers, can be used to support a point. Often the numbers show the importance of a topic or the size of a problem. In a speech on pollution, one student used the following statistical information in his speech, which had the following audience goal: *Listeners will be able to describe two ways that ordinary citizens can fight pollution.*

> In Houghton, Michigan, a park was named for Verna Mize, who struggled for 13 years to prevent a mining company from dumping 67,000 tons of waste matter a day into Lake Superior.
>
> It takes but one gallon of solvent to make 20 million gallons of groundwater unfit for drinking; it will take 10 years and $1 billion to clean up Chesapeake Bay.

Personal Experience When you use personal experience in a speech, it can provide a special kind of support, because it shows a personal connection to a topic. For example, if you are talking about a hobby such as raising rabbits, you can talk about your own rabbits. If you are talking about pollution, you might describe the smog you saw when you visited Los Angeles. When you can give personal examples, you show that you have knowledge based on firsthand experience.

In the following statement a student describes her personal experience as a zoo volunteer:

> I have volunteered at the Parkside Zoo for the last two summers. At first, I just worked on the line for the pony rides. Near the end of last summer I was asked to work in the small-animal section of the children's zoo. I hold mice and guinea pigs so the children can pet their fur.

As you might imagine, this was her audience goal: *Listeners will volunteer to work at the Parkside Zoo one afternoon a week.*

Visual Supports In addition to using verbal supporting material, a speaker can use nonverbal materials, such as pictures,

Critical Thinking
Analyzing

● Have students continue to assume that they are looking for support for a speech on the need for more national parks. Ask what kind of statistical information they think they would need and where they would find it.

305

Critical Thinking
Organizing

▼ Have students create web diagrams of the various kinds of visual support that can be used during public speaking.

Links to Past Learning

Remind students that when using personal experience to illustrate a point, they must be careful to distinguish between facts and opinions. Illustrate this concept with the following example:

Fact: "We noticed brown smog along the horizon line as our plane was landing at the L.A. airport."

Opinion: "L.A. has got to be the smoggiest city in the world."

charts or graphs, objects, or video clips. For example, you might use a graph to show the increase in sports injuries over the past decade. If you were demonstrating how to make shell jewelry, you could show examples of pieces you have made. Speakers can also use sight and sound media to give a technical presentation on a topic. For example, you might play a video you made to show the changes in the community after a flood. If you have access to a **PowerPoint** computer program, you could create graphics to use during your speech. These graphics may include words and phrases, graphs and charts, and clip art.

All these types of supporting material explain or defend the speaker's points. They also make a speech more interesting and effective. Finally, they serve as evidence to prove a point.

Evaluating Supporting Material

When evaluating supporting material, competent communicators assess five factors: (1) whether the evidence is fact or opinion, (2) whether it is from a credible source, (3) whether it is relevant to the goal of the speech, (4) whether it is timely, and (5) whether it is a representative example.

Fact or Opinion A **fact** is information based on evidence that can be proved or disproved. Facts are concerned with the truth or certainty of a statement. Some examples of facts are the following:

Sharon Lytle has three red-headed brothers.

The first A-bomb test occurred on July 16, 1945.

The chairs were turned over, and paint was splattered on the walls.

An **opinion** is a judgment based on belief or feelings. It cannot be proved. Some examples of opinions are the following:

Sharon Lytle dislikes her brothers.

The first A-bomb destroyed the world's hope for peace.

The chairs were thrown by a very strong person.

Facts and opinions are both necessary and helpful. Neither is better than the other, but problems arise when people confuse statements of opinion with statements of fact.

INTERACT

With a partner, discuss the following announcement and identify the sentences that contain facts and those that contain opinions.

The Northfield Soup Kitchen needs your help. We serve 140 to 160 people every Tuesday night with a staff of 10 to 12 people. The lines are too long, and people have to wait for tables. This is disgraceful. The staff begins cooking and setting up at 2 P.M. We need people to shop and clean up. If we don't get enough volunteers, we'll have to close down. This would tell needy people that we just don't care.

Source Credibility Evidence should come from a believable source. For example, if you are trying to persuade your audience to use seat belts, you could use an expert on traffic accidents or the chief of police as a credible source. You would not want quotations from a fire inspector or a carpenter, because they are not experts on the subject of seat belts and auto safety.

Many magazines and newspapers give an author's name and occasionally, their experience or titles, at the end of an article or editorial. On a radio and television talk show, the host usually gives the background of the guests. For example, you will hear their title, their college degrees, their years of experience working in an area. This will help you decide if they seem believable on that topic. Sometimes famous people will speak out for a cause that is unrelated to their area of experience. They may have sound opinions as individuals, but they should not be regarded as experts. Because someone is a movie star or famous athlete does not mean that person is a credible source on AIDS treatment or acid rain.

Information found on the World Wide Web can create concerns about source credibility. Whereas books, newspapers, and magazines usually have trained writers or provide the credentials of their

Critical Thinking

Evaluating

Make sure students understand that people's personal values may influence their opinions and conclusions. A person who speaks passionately about a subject is not necessarily an expert on the subject. Remind students that they should look at a person's credentials before deciding whether he or she is a credible source.

66What I want is Facts. Teach these boys and girls nothing but Facts. Facts alone are wanted in life. Plant nothing else, and root out everything else.99

CHARLES DICKENS
Hard Times

Critical Thinking
Evaluating

▼ Tell students that when they are evaluating whether information is relevant to their topic, they also need to determine how well the information supports their topic. You might suggest that students ask themselves: Does this information present a strong argument for my point?

authors, information on the Web includes material written by very fine sources as well as information provided by any individual who wishes to post a home page. For example, in 1997 the Web included over 90,000 documents that matched the word *asthma* and over 89,000 that matched *multiple sclerosis*. You would have to look at the credentials of the persons, their titles or degrees, or their connection to a medical center to decide whether a source is credible. Sometimes you will find information on the Web in a discussion group or on a home page where you have little or no information about the source. Then you have to be careful not to build an argument based entirely on that person's information.

Relevance The evidence must relate, or connect, to the exact point you are making. If you are talking about the books Judy Blume writes for teenagers, you should not quote sections of her books for adults. If you are describing the causes of the Civil War, you should not go into the development of railroads in that era.

It's easy to get off track during research time. For example, while preparing a speech on athletic training, one student got so involved in recording the types of jumps Tara Lipinski performs that she never collected material about Lipinski's training.

Timeliness Your evidence must be up to date. If you are using statistics on drunk driving, you don't want to use figures from 1992. Figures on drunk-driving deaths are now much higher. If you are using a quotation from an expert, be sure the person still has the same title and holds the same opinion. A person who thought pollution was the nation's greatest problem in 1989 may not hold that view ten years later.

Representativeness Don't describe a very unusual situation as if it were typical. If you use an example, a number, or a quotation that is the exception to the normal pattern, you aren't being honest. If you decide to speak on the major problems in your school and can only find one example of recent vandalism, the example is an exception. Obviously vandalism is not one of the major problems in your school. Be sure your supporting material does not describe a once-in-a-while happening.

308

Cooperative Learning

▲ Have students work in pairs to research one of the topics listed in the Research activity below. Then encourage them to use the checklist on the student page to evaluate the sources they find. Ask pairs to identify the information that presents the strongest support for their topics and to decide whether the sources they have found will be enough support for their speeches. If not, what additional source material will they look for? Interested students may wish to continue working as partners to write and present a speech on the topic.

CHECKLIST:
Evaluating Supporting Material

1. Is it fact or opinion?

2. Is it credible?

3. Is it relevant ?

4. Is it timely or up to date?

5. Is it representative?

CHAPTER 10 SUMMARY

This chapter provides the foundation for creating a speech. The research process is described, including using personal experience, interviews and surveys, and print and electronic media materials. Guidelines for recording information are included, as are samples of supporting material. Finally, the chapter discusses the five ways of evaluating supporting material.

Skill Development

Research

Ask students which of the following topics would require the most up-to-date support information or which ideas might have been altered over the years.

organ transplants
space exploration
music teaching in the public schools
women's roles in medieval France
silent films of the 1920s
building model airplanes
the influence of unions today

Skill Development

Writing

▲ Interested students could use the information that they gathered in the first Put It in Writing activity to develop their topics further and write an informative or persuasive speech. Suggest that they choose their audience—either the class or a parents' group. Remind students to write in language that is appropriate for the purpose, the occasion, and the audience. Have students present their speeches.

Answers

Think About It

Student answers will vary. Here are sample answers:

1. (1) Personal experience. Competent public speakers can relate their personal observations and experiences to a topic about which they are speaking. (2) Interviews and surveys. These information-gathering techniques allow the speaker to get firsthand information, reactions, and statistics. (3) Print materials. These include references such as books, magazines and journals, pamphlets, newspapers, and general information sources such as encyclopedias, dictionaries, almanacs, and atlases. (4) Electronic media, including radio, television, video, and audiotapes. (5) Cyberspace resources; that is, anything that can be accessed through a computer.

2. (1) Study your topic before the interview. (2) Prepare specific questions before the interview. (3) Set up the interview. (4) Handle questions carefully. (5) Keep a record of the information. (6) Express your thanks to the interviewee.

3. (1) Description. Used to help listeners picture a person, place, thing, or process. (2) Examples. Used to help listeners remember the main points of the speaker's

---

CHAPTER REVIEW

Think About It

1. Describe four sources of research information.

2. If you had to help a friend prepare to interview someone, what guidelines for good interviewing would you share?

3. Give examples of each of the various types of supporting materials.

4. What five questions should you ask when evaluating supporting materials?

5. What is the difference between fact and opinion?

Try It Out

1. Which research sources might you use to find out the following information?

   The average annual rainfall in Ethiopia

   The grain production in the United States over the past ten years

   The structure of the British Parliament

   The best way to set up a dark-room

   The average weekly allowance of American fourteen-year-olds

2. Choose a speech topic and a purpose for your speech. Interview a person who is an expert on this topic. Follow all the guidelines for good interviewing. Describe the information you obtained through the interview.

3. Choose a speech topic and a purpose for your speech. Write three survey questions. Conduct a survey using the guidelines outlined in this chapter. Share the results of your survey with your classmates.

4. Bring to class a recent editorial from your local newspaper. With a partner, analyze the supporting material in the editorial, using the criteria discussed in this chapter.

Put It in Writing

1. Choose a speech topic and a purpose for your speech. Assume that your audience will be your class. Begin researching your topic by listing your own experience and observations on the topic, the people you should interview, possible print materials, electronic media sources, Internet resources, and two questions you could ask in a survey. Describe in a paragraph how you would change this presentation if the audience members were members of the Parent Advisory Council.

2. Select a speech topic and find three written sources of evidence on that topic, such as a magazine article, a pamphlet, and a chapter in a book. Record two evidence cards for each source using the correct form.

Skill Development

Research

▲ Tell students that conducting research is a skill that is useful both in school and in the real world. Ask students to work with a partner to decide on a topic for an informative speech that would be educational for members of their class or community. Have students use a variety of reference material—magazines, newspapers, journals, computer catalogs, or the Internet—to gather information that supports their topic and point of view.

3. Select a topic which can be explored using quantitative visual displays such as graphs or charts. Sample topics might include drunk driving, the stock market, population changes, or sports statistics. Develop this material in two visually appealing formats, such as computer graphics, overheads, or poster displays.

Speak About It

1. Choose a speech topic and a purpose for a speech. Think of how you can use a personal example in the speech. Share the personal example with your classmates.

2. For the same speech topic, decide on two other types of support. Share these with your classmates.

3. Choose a school-related topic. With a partner, role-play an interview between an expert on that topic (for example, a principal, cafeteria worker, bus driver, or teacher) and a student reporter from another school. Ask for feedback from your classmates on the effectiveness of the questions used in the interview.

4. Choose a speech topic and a purpose for a speech. In small groups, share your topic and purpose with your classmates, discussing possible Internet resources you could use and potential problems you might encounter.

message. (3) Quotations. Speakers can use quotes from experts to back up their own points. (4) Statistical information is used to support a point. Often the numbers show the importance of a topic or the size of a problem. (5) Personal experience. Used to show the speaker's connection to the topic. (6) Visual support. Gives a graphic depiction to support verbal material.

4. (1) Is it a fact or opinion? (2) Is it credible? (3) Is it relevant? (4) Is it timely or up-to-date? (5) Is it representative?

5. A fact is based on evidence that can be proved or disproved; an opinion is a judgment based on belief or feelings that cannot be proved or disproved.

Quick Check

Ask students to find and define these Key Terms:

cyberspace resources (292)

fact (306)

interview (281)

opinion (306)

plagiarism (300)

PowerPoint (306)

research (278)

supporting material (301)

survey (283)

	Day 1	Day 2	Day 3	Day 4	Day 5
	11 Constructing the Speech	Patterns of Organization	Language	Introductions, Conclusions, & Transitions	Summary
	Purpose Statement	Outlining			Chapter Review
	Teacher's Resource Book				
	Teaching Suggestions 11.1	11.2–11.4	11.5–11.6	11.8–11.9	
	Worksheets & Eval. Forms	34			
					Chapter Test 11
	Workbook 11.1–11.2	11.3–11.5		11.6	

(Week 10 / Chapter 11 Planner)

Motivation

Suggest that students work in small groups to listen to an audiotape or view a videotape of one or more short historic speeches. Ask them to take notes and analyze the purpose and organization of the speech.

Links to Past Learning

Have students tell about speeches they have heard in the past that may have confused them. Encourage them to analyze the reasons for their confusion. Was the speaker the source of the confusion, or was the listener? Tell students that many people who know a subject well do not necessarily know how to present the material to an audience. This chapter will help students learn how to construct a speech to avoid confusing listeners.

11

CHAPTER ELEVEN

Constructing the Speech

Chapter Objectives

After completing this chapter, you should be able to

1. define purpose statement and give an example

2. describe the main organizational patterns for speeches

3. create a sentence outline and a word outline

4. list the characteristics of language that help get the meaning across

5. identify and give examples of figures of speech

6. develop introductions and conclusions for your speeches

7. develop transitions to connect main ideas

66 A speech is poetry: cadence, rhythm, imagery, sweep! A speech reminds us that words, like children, have the power to make dance the dullest bean bag of a heart. **99**

PEGGY NOONAN
What I Saw at the Revolution

⊙ Key Terms

chronological order	introduction	purpose statement
conclusion	metaphor	simile
hyperbole	personification	transition

Critical Thinking

Analyzing

● Have someone read the chapter objectives and Key Terms aloud. Ask students to tell why the construction of a speech is important to giving an effective speech.

Substitute Teacher Tip

Ask for volunteers to suggest reasons why they, as listeners, might have difficulty paying attention to what a speaker is saying. If they mention that the topic is boring, ask for volunteers to suggest how the following topics could be made interesting:

the history of dentistry
why oatmeal is good for you
wind patterns in the upper Midwest
understanding 19th-century poetry

Then mention that the organization of a speech can also cause problems for listeners. Ask how a speech on the first topic above might be effectively organized.

How often has a speaker made you feel frustrated because the speech was confusing or disorganized? What does a good speaker do to help you follow along? The following comments of student speakers and listeners describe the difficulties.

Speakers
The hardest part of preparing a speech is getting all the pieces to fit together and make sense.

When I try to write a speech, I can't figure out how to begin it or how to organize my points.

Listeners
That speaker is jumping all over the place. I still don't know what his point is.

I still don't get the connections between the first part of the speech and the conclusion. It's not clear what kind of change the speaker wants.

The outline and organization of a speech are very important because the audience has only one chance to understand the information and get the point. A person reading a newspaper or book can go back to reread the parts that were unclear or to figure out the connection between a story and a main point. But an audience member doesn't get a second chance. When giving a speech, you have to present clear and organized ideas or your audience will get confused.

This chapter covers the five major steps to organizing a speech: (1) creating a purpose statement, (2) finding the right organizational pattern, (3) outlining the speech, (4) choosing the language, and (5) creating introductions and conclusions.

PURPOSE STATEMENT

The first step in organizing the speech is to write a **purpose statement**. A purpose statement summarizes the main idea or purpose of your speech. The purpose statement in a speech is similar to the thesis statement in an essay. Some speakers use one carefully-worded sentence as a purpose statement, while others

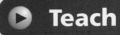

❝Nothing is so unbelievable that oratory cannot make it acceptable.❞

CICERO

use two or three sentences. These statements are included in the introduction to the speech.

A good purpose statement (1) tells the audience the topic of the speech, (2) provides a guide to the organization, or main points, of the speech, and (3) gives the audience goal for the speech. For example, if a speaker begins a speech by saying that soccer is a valuable extracurricular experience because it teaches athletic skills, keeps you in condition, and gets you involved with friends, you can be almost certain that the speaker will give a three-point speech on the topic of the school soccer team. The speaker will describe the values of soccer as (1) teaching athletic skills, (2) keeping you in shape, and (3) involving you in an activity with friends. As you will probably guess, this speaker's audience goal is that listeners will be able to explain the three values of soccer.

When it is well written, the purpose statement indicates the pattern of organization or the logical progression of ideas. Listeners use this as their first clue about the main ideas or points.

Cooperative Learning

● Give students two minutes to come up with a purpose statement for a speech on "Why Oatmeal Is Good For You."

Getting organized is a key step in preparing a speech.

Curricular Connection

Language Arts

● Mention that the three-part structure of a speech is similar to the structure of a written essay and that essays are also organized in one of the patterns of organization described here.

INTERACT

With a partner, identify the three parts of the following purpose statements.

1. There are eight safety rules that careful bikers should follow.

2. There are three reasons why helping to resettle refugee families is a worthwhile use of your time.

3. To appreciate Hopi kachina dolls, you need to know their history and what types of kachinas there are.

4. Raising sheep can bring you fun and profit.

5. Hosting an international high-school student from Latin America will increase your world awareness, improve your Spanish, and possibly give you a friend for life.

PATTERNS OF ORGANIZATION

Most formal speeches have a general three-part structure—an introduction, a body, and a conclusion. This structure is similar to that of a composition. The **introduction** gains the audience's attention and tells the listeners about the topic and purpose of the speech. The body contains the main points. The **conclusion** summarizes the message and ends the speech in an interesting way.

The body of the speech contains the structure, or organizational pattern. Good speeches are not random ideas that the speaker strings together on the spot. Good speeches have a clear structure to guide the speaker's points. The purpose statement and the audience goal help a speaker create the organizational structure.

There are a number of common organizational patterns that speakers can use. These include time order, space order, process order, topic order, and problem-solution order. There are also two persuasive speech patterns, which will be discussed in Chapter 14.

Curricular Connection

Social Studies

Students could do library research to find out about a subject in American history that interests them and that would be a possible topic for a speech organized in time order. Ask them to create a time line of events relating to that subject and based on their research. Possible topics for time lines might be Negro baseball leagues, history of jazz, development of the blues, the Cherokee Removal, or United States flags.

Time Order

Time order refers to arranging the points of a speech into a time-related pattern. The speaker may talk about time in terms of the past, present, and future. Time may refer to predicting the future or placing historical events in sequence. Time may also refer to smaller segments such as morning, noon, and night. This time-oriented pattern is easy to use because you are able to see the logical movement. Some topics that might be time oriented include the history of air travel, the past and future of the Olympics, and plans for building the community center. The following is a sample purpose statement for a time-order speech:

> For the next few minutes I would like to describe the seven days of the Outward Bound program that you will attend.

Often a story or narrative follows a **chronological order**. This means that events are presented in the order that they happened. You can imagine the time order a speaker might use in telling stories about the following events:

> The Day I Almost Drowned
>
> Our Trip to the Grand Canyon
>
> My Brother's Big Car Wreck

Space Order

Space order refers to organizing a speech on the basis of physical relationships between people, places, or objects. A speaker may talk about experiences or people in one place and then move on to another place. Some topics that might be organized according to space include historical sites in New England, the neighborhoods of San Francisco, and the regions of India. The following is a sample purpose statement for a space-order speech:

> As an exchange student I had the opportunity to live three months in three different cities—Munich, Hamburg, and Berlin. Let me tell you a little about each of them.

Skill Development

Quick Skill Opportunity

● Ask students to tell which of the following topics would be suitable for a speech arranged in time order:
identifying birds
the wives of Henry VIII
making masks
lighthouses on the Great Lakes
how hurricanes form

317

Skill Development

Quick Skill Opportunity

Ask students to tell which of the following topics would be suitable for a speech arranged in space order:

major desert areas of the world
how to refinish a table
the life of Jackie Robinson
a trip to the Everglades
the Lewis and Clark expedition

Process Order

Process order refers to explaining the way something works or the way something is made. The speaker explains the steps in a process from beginning to end. A process speech describes the steps that the listener needs to understand in order to use the information. Some topics that might be organized in terms of process include screening your own T-shirts, filming music videos, and making pizza. Here is an example of a purpose statement for a process-order speech:

> There are five easy steps to taking great pictures with a 35mm camera.

Topical Order

Topical order refers to dividing a speech topic into its natural parts. There is no specific sequence. Any point could be first or last. Yet together these points will tell the listeners a great deal about the entire topic. Some subjects that may be organized by topic are types of video games, the paintings of Picasso, and understanding the library. Here is a sample purpose statement for a topical-order speech:

> To fully appreciate your visit to historical Williamsburg, you need to experience the historical buildings, the craft demonstrations, the historical performances, and the restaurants.

Problem-Solution Order

Problem-solution order refers to organizing information around two major areas—the problem or set of problems and the possible solutions. This order is often used in a persuasive speech, when the speaker is trying to persuade the listener to believe or do something. The listener needs to understand the problem fully and to grasp the connection between the problem described and the suggested solutions. Examples of speech topics that could use the problem-solution order are world hunger, school cliques,

318

Critical Thinking

Organizing

One method of organization not mentioned here is comparison-contrast. Topics that might lend themselves to this organization include medical treatments in the early 20th century contrasted with those today; assumptions about the moon's surface prior to the late 20th century; rural pastimes before the electronic age.

There are at least five speech organizational patterns.

and acid rain pollution. The following is a sample purpose statement for a problem-solving speech:

> In order to reverse the pollution from acid rain, we need to understand the extent of the damage and to mount a three-pronged attack to prevent more extensive pollution.

INTERACT

With three or four classmates, decide which patterns of organization might work for the following topics:

Fashion in the Twentieth Century

Sections of the Orchestra

Drugs in the Junior High Schools

Violence on Kids' TV

The Bermuda Triangle

Teenage Alcoholism

How to Start Your Own Summer Business

The Poetry of Nikki Giovanni

Select one topic and create three purpose statements that would result in three different organizational patterns.

Curricular Connection

Social Studies

● Have students write a purpose statement for a speech on soil erosion or air pollution using problem-solution order.

Cooperative Learning

● Have the groups formed for the Interact activity present their purpose statements to the class. Allow the rest of the students to question each group's methods and provide feedback.

Teach ◀

❝I start at the beginning, go on to the end, then stop.❞

ANTHONY BURGESS

Critical Thinking

Analyzing

▼ Tell students that textbooks are outlined before being written. Have them skim Chapter 11 and write down the chapter title, main headings, and subheads. Lead them to see that this information provides an outline of the chapter material.

An outline helps you keep your main points in mind.

OUTLINING

A very important step in speech preparation is outlining. The purpose of an outline is to help you organize your speech. Besides helping you order the material, it helps you identify major points and supporting points. An outline is useful both in preparing and in presenting a speech which is easy for listeners to follow. A good outline provides you with a map. If you follow the map, you won't get lost during the speech and—of equal importance—your listeners won't get lost either.

Creating an outline takes work, but when you are delivering the speech, you will be able to keep your points straight. You will also be more relaxed and sure of yourself. Your audience will be able to follow your ideas, and your speech is likely to be more effective.

Types of Outlines

There are two basic types of outlines:

1. A sentence outline shows the relationship of information and the development of arguments or ideas.

2. A word outline lists only key words and divisions.

If you are a beginning public speaker, you should use the sentence outline. A sentence outline lets you use more detail and forces you to think about each main point and supporting point. This gives you more confidence while learning the topic. Once you have practiced and gained confidence, you may wish to use a word outline while actually delivering the speech. Word outlines permit you to have greater eye contact with your audience.

The following examples present the first point in both a full-sentence outline and a word outline for a speech titled "Our Dying Planet":

Sentence Outline

Our Dying Planet

I. Pollution is a significant threat.
   A. Sulfur emissions from power plants return to earth in acid rain.
      1. It deadens lakes.
      2. It kills fish.
      3. It destroys forests.

   B. Carbon dioxide builds up from the use of coal, oil, and gasoline.
      1. New deserts are forming in Africa.
      2. Floods are created.
      3. Farmland is diminishing.

Word Outline

Our Dying Planet

I. Pollution Problem
   A. Sulfur and acid rain
      1. Lakes
      2. Fish
      3. Forests

   B. Carbon dioxide
      1. Deserts
      2. Floods
      3. Farms

Skill Development

Media Literacy

▲ Assign students an outlining task. Ask them to try outlining a television documentary, newspaper or magazine article, or book from one of their other classes. Have them use one of the standard outlining formats.

321

Teach

Curricular Connection

Math

● Encourage interested students to tell the class what they know about Roman numerals. Ask these students to write Roman numeral equivalents for fifty and one hundred on the board.

Learning Styles

Visual Learning

● Write the outlining format shown on this page on the chalkboard. Ask students to suggest topics they would be interested in working on. Choose one of their suggestions as the outline title. Then ask for volunteers to come up and write heads and subheads that might apply to the title.

Guidelines for Outlining

Most outlines follow a detailed form. They use numbers and letters to show the importance of each idea. Roman numerals (I, II, III) show the main points. Capital letters (A, B, C) show subpoints. Arabic numerals (1, 2, 3) show specific details about, or support for, the subpoints; and small letters indicate support for, or information about, those specific details.

I. _____
   A. _____
      1. _____
      2. _____
         a. _____
         b. _____
   B. _____
      1. _____
      2. _____
II. _____
   A. _____
      1. _____
         a. _____
         b. _____
      2. _____
         a. _____
         b. _____

You need to remember that the type of symbol you use shows the level of importance of an idea. I, for example, is more important than A, because A is included under I. The numeral 1 is included under A since it is a subpoint to A, and so on throughout the outline.

Cooperative Learning

● Encourage students to share their outlines from the Apply activity with another student. Ask students to provide one another with feedback about the completed outline.

❝Eloquence is the power to translate a truth into language perfectly intelligible to the person to whom you speak.❞

RALPH WALDO EMERSON

Links to Past Learning

Lead a class discussion about people who use language particularly well. Ask what these people do that sets them apart from other speakers.

All roman numerals should be lined up under one another, as should all capital letters, and so on. The symbols should be used consistently to indicate main points, subpoints, and supporting statements. When a new Roman numeral is used, begin the subpoints with a capital A. Whenever a new capital letter is used, begin subpoints with the numeral 1, and so on. Every point must be divided into two or more subpoints. No point should have just one subpoint.

Most speakers work from their outline, but they have usually memorized most of it so that they can keep the speech flowing in a logical manner. Before a speech, most speakers could tell you their main points, such as "My first point deals with teenage drivers, my second point discusses the ways communities are trying to reduce the number of accidents caused by teenage drivers, and my third point offers one successful solution."

APPLY

Using two of the purpose statements you just created in the last Interact, create model outlines. You just need to name the categories since you will not have researched the topics yet.

LANGUAGE

Competent communicators take pride in their use of language. They work to create a message that is meaningful and memorable. Speakers are concerned with getting the meaning across in a vivid way. For example, in his speech at a political convention on the need for stronger leadership, Senator Bill Bradley said:

People are angry, and so am I.

For twelve years, I've seen kids kill kids in our cities and people sleep in the streets.

For twelve years, I've watched workers lose their jobs, our land further poisoned, and government yield again and again to the special interests.

323

Critical Thinking

Analyzing

Have students analyze what makes Bradley's words effective. Note his use of repetition and alliteration.

Skill Development

Active Listening

Read the following words and phrases aloud and ask students to identify them as abstract or concrete. A volunteer might record the words on the board in the following categories:

- abstract
  breakfast
  car
  small
  house

- concrete
  orange juice and corn flakes
  Honda Civic
  the size of a button
  white house with green trim

For twelve years, I've heard our leaders say, "Nothing can be done."

For too long, American leadership has waffled and wiggled and wavered.

These words were more effective than if he had simply said, "Everyone is angry about the lack of leadership in this country for the past twelve years."

Getting the Meaning Across

To make sure the audience understands the message, speakers try to use language that is accurate, clear, appropriate, and original.

Accuracy As you learned earlier, people interpret messages differently. Words such as *liberal, expensive, friendly, large,* and *attractive* have different meanings to different people. Your meaning will be more accurate if you use words that are concrete and specific, rather than abstract and general. Define any words that might be unusual or unfamiliar to your audience.

Defining unfamiliar words helps the audience understand your topic.

SPEAKING OF . . .

REID MATSUOKA

As a senior member of a local Boy Scout troop in the Seattle area, Reid Matsuoka contributes actively to his community. Two years ago he served as the Senior Patrol leader in charge of the management of the troop. Success in this role depends on his strong communication skills, which enable him to deal with the everyday concerns of running the troop, dealing with interpersonal and personal problems of troop members, and conducting meetings.

Reid had to take a leadership role for decision making within the troop and for planning events. He also had to help troop members resolve personality conflicts. Currently he deals with younger scouts who are confronting the issues of gangs, drugs, and divorce, attempting to help them by listening to and discussing their concerns. As he says, "Leadership in the Boy Scouts is huge. All the younger Scouts look up to me and expect me to know what to do all the time."

Reid is also a trained member of his local Explorer Scout Search and Rescue division, a role that sends him into medical emergency situations. He reports that a large part of dealing with the injured "includes communicating with them and assuring them that everything is OK." As an extension of this role, Reid teaches first aid to junior members of his troop and answers medical questions the boys raise.

Such experiences will serve Reid well in the future, both in terms of a career and in terms of family and community life. Reid might use his strong communication skills in a range of medical careers, in corporate management, in health or outdoor education, or in counseling.

Motivation

Make a videotape of parts of several interviews from various types of television shows. Play the tape for the class, stopping between segments, and ask students to evaluate the speakers on clarity, appropriateness, and originality (discussed on pages 326–327).

Motivation

Tell students that, while it is a good idea to keep language simple if possible, many speakers must use technical language. Emphasize that someone speaking to an audience of volleyball players, as in the example in the first paragraph, would not need to define the terms. An audience who had never played or seen a volleyball game would need definitions or examples.

Links to Past Learning

Tell students that even people who use very simple language can be unclear when making a speech. Remind them that for maximum effectiveness, speakers must get and keep their thoughts in order and speak at a rate that is neither too fast nor too slow.

If you talk about volley ball, be sure your audience understands the terms *spike, block,* and *kill.* If you talk about attending a *quincenera,* be sure you explain this traditional Latin American custom if your audience is not familiar with it.

> ### JOURNAL ENTRY
>
> When I gave my first demonstration speech, I was pretty confident. I am a brown belt in karate, and I knew the class would be interested in my demonstration of karate moves. What I did not realize was how many technical terms I used that confused them. I talked about *kata* and *kumite* and synchronized *kata* without explaining the names. I mentioned a roundhouse kick and a block. Unfortunately, even though the class liked the karate moves, I didn't do well on the speech, because no one really knew what I was referring to.

Clarity Words with four and five syllables or less frequently used terms are not automatically better than one- or two-syllable ones even though a few speakers seem to think they are. In a recent presentation, a speaker kept referring to a cemetery as a "garden of memories" and to a funeral director as a "mortician" and to the dead person as "the deceased." Although these words are not incorrect, the audience had to work harder to listen than if the speaker had used more direct language. In today's business world, individuals are not "fired" or "laid off," rather they are "selected out" or "redeployed" and the work force is "downsized." Such language is an attempt to cover a painful reality. Imagine a speech in which the boss says "Due to suboptimal market conditions sizable numbers of personnel face redeployment for a quarter." A clear statement would be: "Because of stock market losses, we have to lay off one-third of the employees for three months." Lee Iacocca, former head of

326

the Chrysler Corporation, is known as a very successful speaker. According to him, the secret of his success is talking "plain and simple." Remember: Don't use fifty-cent words when a nickel word will do!

Appropriateness Speakers must use language that is appropriate to the topic, the listeners, and the occasion. The statement "Hi, y'all. I sure am glad you could stop by to see us in our fancy threads" is not the best way for a speaker to address an audience at a graduation ceremony. Your language should be formal and dignified when the occasion is formal (such as a graduation ceremony). It should be informal when the occasion is casual; for example, if you are telling the Scout troop about the coming camp out, your language would be informal and personal.

Whether your language is formal or informal, your speech gives you an opportunity to practice both correct grammar and articulation. When you mispronounce words or speak with grammatical errors, the audience members lose their focus because your speech patterns distract them.

Originality Competent communicators find original ways to say something familiar. They are creative without being unclear. One student decided the sentence "I had to feed the cat" sounded dull. Instead, she said, "I could no longer ignore the outraged cry. It was time to fill the stomach of the gray meowing beast." Another student spoke about volunteerism by opening with a quotation from John F. Kennedy, "Ask not what your country can do for you—ask what you can do for your country." The more effort you put into finding the best language for your speech, the greater your chance of reaching your audience goal.

Using Figures of Speech

Figures of speech help a speech come alive. They appeal to listeners' imaginations and help them remember what was said.

Curricular Connection

Language Arts

● Encourage students to think about and discuss clichés they may be using unknowingly. Tell them that clichés are overused expressions, just the opposite of original language. For the most part, they should be avoided. Give examples such as "good as gold," "happy camper," "busy as a bee," and others. Have volunteers come up with original ways of stating the thoughts expressed by these clichés.

327

"Why shouldn't we quarrel about a word? What is the good of words if they aren't important enough to quarrel over? Why do we choose one word more than another if there isn't any difference between them?"

G. K. CHESTERTON

Curricular Connection

Language Arts

● Students might like to try their hand at making simile pictograms. You can set up the format for them by writing "_____ is as _____ as_____" on the chalkboard. Instead of writing words in the blanks, students could draw pictures.

APPLY

Choose the sentence from each of the following pairs that would be more likely to get your listeners' attention.

The sky was dark and the stars were out as we hurried home on our bikes.

The sky was black velvet sprinkled with stars. Our bikes flew across the bridge when we saw the lights of home.

I used a computer to do my book report.

That computer saved my life! My book report was done in one-third the usual time.

In each pair, the second sentence contains figures of speech and would be more likely to gain attention.

Figures of speech are ways of making language more imaginative and more memorable. There are many different kinds of figures of speech. Four of the most commonly used are simile, metaphor, personification, and hyperbole.

Similes A **simile** is a comparison of two things that are not alike but that have some similarities. A simile includes the words *like* or *as*. For example, a speaker might say, "The frozen hiker was shaking like a leaf when the safety patrol reached him." Or, "I entered the subway as cautiously as a jungle fighter, watching every shadow." One student speaker used a simile to describe his time in a foreign country.

Living in the Spanish countryside was like going through a time warp. People still used horses to pull their ploughs. The teenagers met at special parties chaperoned by older community members. . . .

Metaphors A **metaphor** is also a comparison of two things that are similar but basically not alike. The comparison is implied. The words *like* and *as* are not used. For example, a speaker might say, "My family is a rock. It makes me feel secure" or "Rivers of ice cream flowed

Skill Development

Vocabulary

▼ Be sure that students pronounce *personification* and *hyperbole* correctly.

Skill Development

Media Literacy

● Encourage students to look for examples of figures of speech in the television programs they watch or in television or print commercials. Have them write down examples to read to the class.

from the cone, splashing to the sidewalk." One student effectively used metaphors to describe a city cleanup campaign:

> We are the urban pioneers. We circle our wagons around the city lot. We reclaim the wilderness, clearing away the jungle. We sow new seeds of life. At harvest we see green grass and flowers.

Whether you know it or not, you use metaphors every time you talk about surfing the net or riding the information superhighway. Computer experts sometimes debate the value of these metaphors; many believe the surfing metaphor makes computer competence appear too simple and playful.

Personification A figure of speech that gives human characteristics to nonhuman things is called **personification**. For example, a speaker might say, "The graffiti mocks me as I turn the corner" or "The tree comforted the child in the embrace of its branches."

Often speakers use talking animals or talking objects as a humorous part of their speeches. Comments such as "Did you hear what the apple said to the banana?" or "The mountains shrugged off the clouds" lets you know objects are being given human characteristics.

Hyperbole An intentional exaggeration is called **hyperbole**. For example, a speaker might say, "This computer saved my life!" or "The fish I caught would have fed an army." One student used hyperbole to describe a baseball hit:

> The bases were loaded. It was the bottom of the ninth. Simmons came to bat. I was on second base ready to go. The pitcher wound up, let go, and Simmons swung. He hit that ball to the moon!

Cooperative Learning

● Encourage students to go over their work from the Apply activity with a partner.

Critical Thinking

Synthesizing

● Encourage students to write an introduction that they might use in an actual speech and that fulfills the three general purposes.

APPLY

Identify the figures of speech in the following statements. Some of the statements may contain more than one figure of speech.

Alone, my life is just a sketch. With friends, my life becomes a masterpiece.

That puppy took off like a rocket when the cat snarled back.

The silent telephone mocked me as I sat waiting and hoping.

Life is a shoe. Friendships are the laces.

Life is like a swamp filled with dark and dangerous critters.

His face was a mask of hate.

INTRODUCTIONS, CONCLUSIONS, AND TRANSITIONS

The effect of a speech depends heavily on how you greet the audience, how you leave the audience, and how your speech hangs together. Therefore you must put time and effort into introductions, conclusions, and transitions.

Introductions

There is a piece of metaphorical advice that says, "If you haven't struck oil in two minutes, you'd better stop boring." For the speaker this means that if you don't grab the audience in the introduction, you might as well make it your conclusion! An introduction should serve three general purposes:

1. *Gain attention.* This is your big moment! You need to get the group interested. Find a way to make people say, "This is going to be good!"

2. *Present your topic and purpose.* Before your introduction is completed, your audience should know your topic and the purpose of your speech. Your introduction should preview your main points.

Substitute Teacher Tip

Have each student choose one of the eight types of introductions described on this page and the next. Tell them they are going to write the introduction to a short speech using the introduction type they choose. Give students some time to collect their thoughts and write their ideas. Then have individuals present their introductions for the class. Stress that speakers who use a story to begin a speech must be sure that the point of the story is relevant to the speech.

66Once you get people laughing, they're listening and you can tell them almost anything.99

HERBERT GARDNER

---

3. *Connect with your audience.* You must come across as a person who is interested in the topic and in your listeners. Show your listeners that you recognize any connection they might have to the topic. Your ideas and your delivery will help you make these connections.

REMEMBER:
Elements of an Introduction

1. Gain attention.

2. Present your topic and purpose.

3. Connect with your audience.

There are many ways to introduce a speech. Here are some of the most common types of introductions:

1. *Startling statement* A startling statement presents information that surprises the audience.

    Jessie is a normal three-year-old child except for one thing—she is the victim of child abuse. She has already been hospitalized with broken bones four times in her short life.

2. *Rhetorical question* A rhetorical question requires no answer from the audience. It challenges the audience to think. It should not be answered by a simple yes or no.

    What do Albert Einstein, Cher, and Tom Cruise have in common? They have all overcome dyslexia, a learning disability that interferes with the ability to read.

3. *Humor* A joke or funny statement serves to relax an audience. Yet humor should relate to the topic.

    What ten-letter word starts with G-A-S? It's automobile. And this year we may run short again.

4. *Quotation* A quotation from a famous person can interest an audience.

Skill Development
Feedback

▼ Ask students what risks speakers might run using a humorous introduction. Encourage individuals to tell a joke to the class. (You might find it necessary to remind these students to keep the jokes clean.) Then have the class discuss their reactions. Did everyone understand the joke? Had some people heard it before? Did listeners find it amusing?

331

Skill Development

Active Listening

● Encourage students to read aloud their introductions from the Apply activity. Have the class listen and then ask volunteers to guess which method of introduction was being used in each case.

Abraham Lincoln once said, "You can fool some of the people all the time and all of the people some of the time; but you can't fool all the people all the time." We can no longer be fooled by the newspapers in this city.

5. *Story* A story involves the audience in the topic.

   Many years ago, a stranger arrived in our town. He wore ragged clothes and carried a walking stick.

6. *Personal experience* A personal experience gets the listeners' attention and helps the audience connect with the speaker.

   Who would want to spend hours in the blazing sun digging carefully in the dirt with a small spoon? I did. Last summer I spent two weeks at the Kampsville dig doing archeological research. And I have the calluses to prove it.

7. *Example.* An example gives a vivid picture of the topic.

   Anne Graves, age four, died from a gunshot wound to the chest. Her killer was shocked and heartbroken. He was her six-year-old brother, who had found a loaded gun.

8. *Reference to occasion, audience, or topic.* A reference to the reason for the speech lets the listeners know what is going on.

   I am very pleased to present this award for the Outstanding Student Leader of West High School. Rhonda Washington has maintained an almost perfect record in math and science while taking part in many school activities.

APPLY

Using what you know about introductions and language, rewrite the following introduction to make it more effective. Create a possible purpose statement to conclude the introduction.

I'm going to talk to you today about something I find interesting. I've been interested in this for a long time. Most of you should find it interesting, too. You may have seen dolphins at the zoo. My topic today will be on communication with dolphins.

Conclusions

During the conclusion of your speech, you need to remind your listeners of what you told them and give them a final thought. A conclusion has three purposes:

1. *Summarize your main points.* Listeners can forget your main points because they cannot go over them again. Therefore, you need to remind them. Summarize the main points so that they stay in your listeners' minds.

2. *Repeat your main goal.* Get your audience set to reach the audience goal.

3. *Provide a clear ending.* Don't leave the listeners wondering whether the speech is over. Give a decisive final statement.

There are many types of conclusions. Here are some of the most common:

1. *Summary.* A summary consists of a restatement of the main points of your speech.

   When you see a shark in the aquarium or in a movie, remember these points: (l) Humans have little to fear from sharks, (2) sharks provide us with material for medicines, and (3) sharks keep aquatic wildlife in balance.

Critical Thinking
Organizing

▼ Encourage students to create graphic organizers that illustrate the three purposes of conclusions. Remind students that even if a speech is interesting and entertaining, a poor conclusion can make it seem a poor speech. Stress that each part of the speech is important to the whole.

Ending your speech with a challenge can stir an audience to action.

333

66Always be shorter than anybody dared to hope.**99**

LORD READING

Skill Development

Media Literacy

● Ask students to think about courtroom dramas or court TV they have seen and to describe the various types of conclusions lawyers and judges seem to use most often in the courtroom.

Skill Development

Quick Skill Opportunity

● Call on individuals to come up with an impromptu conclusion that adheres to one of the conclusion styles in the text. You may wish to give the student a speech topic. For example: "Summer School: Yes or No?"

2. *Quotation.* A quotation summarizes your speech or suggests the action or attitude you want your audience to have.

   I leave you with the words of the Hopi leader Polingaysi Qoyawayma, "Evaluate the best there is in your own culture and hang on to it, for it will always be foremost in your life; but do not fail to take also the best from other cultures to blend with what you already have."

3. *Appeal.* An appeal asks the audience to do something for themselves or someone else.

   Please remember that seat belts save lives and prevent serious injury. Buckle up. Wear your seat belt!

4. *Challenge.* A challenge serves to motivate an audience to action. It is a bit like a dare.

   Who in this room will be the first to go up to a lunch table of students, different from yourself, and say "May I sit here?"

5. *Story.* Just as a story can be used to introduce your speech, it can also be used to end it.

   I opened my speech with the story of my grandfather's arrival as a boat person from Vietnam. Whenever I get really down or frustrated, I close my eyes and picture the waves, the hunger, and the fear. I imagine myself trying to comfort and protect five terrified children for two full weeks, and I think, "This is nothing. If he could do that I can go forward with my little problems for another day."

REMEMBER:
Elements of a Conclusion

1. Summarize your main points.

2. Repeat your main goal.

3. Provide a clear ending.

Connecting the Introduction and Conclusion

When possible, tie the introduction and conclusion together by referring to your introduction in your conclusion. This is sometimes called a turnaround. It reinforces your purpose and gives your speech closure and balance.

For example, suppose you introduce your speech with the startling statement, "Jessie is a normal three-year-old child, except for one thing—she is the victim of child abuse." You might conclude your speech with a sentence such as, "We must create a future world in which children like Jessie will be safe and happy."

Whatever form of introduction and conclusion you choose, make sure each is appropriate to your audience, purpose, and topic. Some topics don't lend themselves to humor. Some audiences will enjoy humor; others will not. Persuasive speeches often begin with a startling statistic or startling statement. Speeches of social ritual frequently use a reference to the occasion as an introduction.

Linking Ideas Through Transitions

You have probably noticed the key sentences that move a speaker from point to point or from introduction to conclusion. Below are two examples:

Now that you've seen the problem, let's move on to a solution.

My second point is that underdeveloped nations need help.

These statements link, or connect, parts of the speech and help listeners follow the flow of ideas. **Transitions** are words, phrases, or sentences that form links between ideas. After a speaker has made a point, he or she usually indicates that a new idea is coming and that it is connected to the earlier idea. In the next example, a speaker concludes a point on the recent growth of radio and moves into discussing cable television:

Radio has found a place in the sun again. In addition, we are witnessing the tremendous growth of cable television, which. . . .

Limited English Proficiency

Have students work in pairs. More-proficient students should create an introduction to a speech topic of their choice, and less-proficient students should create a conclusion with a turnaround to the introduction.

Skill Development

Vocabulary

● Ask students to read the definition of the word *transition* and to tell you what the word part *trans-* means.

335

Critical Thinking

Analyzing

Ask students to suggest a transition word or phrase as you read the following:

1. Statistics show that women buy more greeting cards than men. [For example] in 1998 greeting card companies reported that women bought. . . .

2. In many countries there is a huge food surplus every year. [In contrast] many people on the African continent go hungry.

3. You have heard some of the reasons why volunteers are needed. [In conclusion / therefore] I ask you to consider helping these unwanted pets.

In this case, the phrase *in addition* indicates a shift, linking the previous idea of radio to the new discussion of television. Here are some other examples of transitions:

> The third dance company I wish to discuss is the Joseph Holmes dance company.

> We've looked at ratting and roping. Now let's look at rappelling.

> Jessie is only one case. Let me now summarize several others.

The following words are simple transition words or phrases. They serve as verbal clues, showing that the speaker is moving from one point to another.

meanwhile	moving to	in contrast
first, second	for example	in conclusion
also	on the contrary	in the second place
next	to sum up	furthermore
as a result	another point	finally
in addition to	on the other hand	therefore

Transitions are important because they help your listeners stay with you. Transition words tell the audience that you are linking parts of the speech together as you move to a new idea. If you plan your introduction, conclusion, and transitions carefully, they will become the structure that helps the audience follow your speech.

CHAPTER 11 SUMMARY

Constructing a speech requires planning and following organizational patterns. It takes time and effort. This chapter discusses purpose statements, organizational patterns, outlining, language, and introductions, conclusions, and transitions. All of these are necessary in building a speech. Taking the time to construct your speeches carefully will help you become a successful speaker.

Critical Thinking
Synthesizing

Ask students to critique a videotaped speech, a speech on television, or a live speech based on what they learned in this chapter. They should name the speaker, describe the setting for the speech, and state whether the speech was live or taped before they begin their written critique.

337

Answers

Think About It

Student answers will vary. Here are sample answers:

1. A purpose statement is the first step in organizing a speech. It is similar to a thesis statement in an essay in that it summarizes the main idea or purpose of the speech.

2. (1) Time order. This method places points of the speech into a chronology. (2) Space order. This method organizes the speech based on physical relationship of people, places, or objects. (3) Process order. This method organizes the speech through the steps of a process. (4) Topical order. This method divides the speech into its natural parts. (5) Problem-solution order. This method organizes the speech around two major areas—the problem and the solution to the problem.

3. (1) Sentence outlines show the relationship of information and the development of ideas or arguments. They are used by beginning public speakers because they allow for more use of detail. (2) Word outlines show key words and divisions. They permit more confident public speakers to maintain better eye contact with the audience.

CHAPTER REVIEW

Think About It

1. What is a purpose statement?

2. Describe the five patterns of speech organization.

3. Describe two types of outlines and give reasons for the use of each one.

4. What are the characteristics of language that help get meaning across?

5. What are the three purposes of an introduction? of a conclusion?

Try It Out

1. Choose a speech topic and write a purpose statement. Develop an introduction and conclusion and choose an outline structure for the speech. Possible topics are shown below:

space travel	missing children
today's fashion	teenage life
adoption	roller blading
patriotism	sports in school

2. Choose a different speech topic and write a purpose statement. Explain which organizational pattern should be used for the topic. Provide reasons for your decision.

3. Find two examples of each of the following figures of speech: simile, metaphor, personification, and hyperbole. Include these examples in your communication journal.

4. Select two main points in the body of a speech you plan to give. Develop a sentence outline and a word outline for these points.

Put It in Writing

1. Listen carefully to the beginning of three presentations, such as political speeches on TV, class lectures, or sermons. Record the way each speaker opens the presentation. If the speaker does not use an effective method to gain your attention, write a sample introduction the speaker might have used to interest the listeners. Share your introduction with your classmates.

2. Using one of the topics you chose in the Try It Out activities, write two transitions of two or three sentences each to link the three main points in the body of your speech.

3. Begin a portfolio for your public speeches. This is where you should place

   articles, references, or lists of ideas for speeches

   drafts of your manuscript material

   any supporting material that may be incorporated in your speeches, such as quotations, statistics, or stories you find in newspapers

   critique sheets you receive from your teacher and classmates.

4. (1) accuracy, (2) clarity, (3) appropriateness, (4) originality

5. Introduction: (1) gain attention, (2) present topic and purpose, and (3) connect with the audience. Conclusion: (1) summarize main points, (2) repeat main goal, and (3) provide a clear ending.

Speak About It

1. Present to your class the purpose statement, introduction, and conclusion you wrote for activity 1 in Try It Out. Then ask for feedback from the class.

2. Choose four topics for speeches. Write a purpose statement for each. After presenting all four purpose statements to your classmates, find out which topic they'd like to hear more about.

3. Imagine that a club or a group you are in is planning a fund-raiser. You are on the organization committee. Prepare a formal speech in which you ask school officials for permission to hold the event on school grounds. Then prepare a short informal speech in which you ask classmates to volunteer at the event. In each speech, be sure to state your purpose, explain the event, and indicate what you need. Use language that is appropriate to each audience and occasion.

Quick Check

Ask students to find and define these Key Terms:

chronological order (317)

conclusion (316)

hyperbole (329)

introduction (316)

metaphor (328)

personification (329)

purpose statement (314)

simile (328)

transition (335)

Motivation

Encourage a student discussion of the factors that go into the preparation of a strong speech. Ask students to think of ways they could prepare both mentally and physically before giving a speech.

Links to Past Learning

Ask students to cite personal examples of experiences they may have had with stage fright. Ask for reasons why stage fright might occur.

12

CHAPTER TWELVE

Delivering the Speech

Chapter Objectives

After completing this chapter, you should be able to

1 — define stage fright and describe ways of developing speech confidence

2 — describe the four methods of delivery and explain when each might be used

3 — list the nonverbal factors in delivery and explain their importance

4 — explain how to rehearse a speech

5 — describe guidelines for making and using audiovisual aids

▼ Key Terms

clarity	gestures	memorized method	vocal quality
delivery	impromptu method	pitch	volume
extemporaneous method	manuscript method	rate	
	media aids	stage fright	

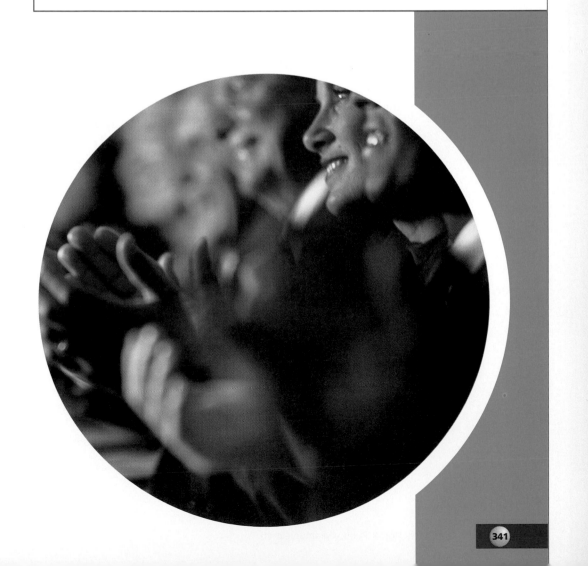

Critical Thinking

Analyzing

● Have a student read the chapter objectives and Key Words aloud. Ask students how they would define stage fright and to think about how it could be an advantage.

Skill Development

Media Literacy

● Ask students to name various comedians they have seen. Encourage them to analyze and compare each comedian's delivery. Ask how delivery may have made the comedians' material more (or less) humorous.

Critical Thinking

Organizing

● Have students create web diagrams using the five aspects of delivery (speaker confidence, methods of delivery, personal delivery, rehearsing the speech, and use of media aids). They can fill out each part of the web as they continue reading and discussing the chapter.

The success of your speech depends on what you say and, also, how you say it. The following comments indicate how delivery can affect your audience.

> Mr. Anderson gave a great lecture on his trip to China. He showed slides of Chinese students in elementary classrooms.

> I could listen to Maya talk about gospel music for hours. She gets so excited about it that I catch her enthusiasm.

> Last week we had a speaker who lived in Grand Forks during the Red River flood. We heard all about their weeks of sandbagging and how the levees finally gave way. His appearance showed how people got worn down and exhausted. It was really sad.

This chapter will present information about **delivery**. Delivery is the way you use your voice and body to present a speech. Delivery includes (1) speaker confidence, (2) methods of delivery, (3) personal delivery, (4) rehearsing the speech, and (5) use of media aids.

SPEAKER CONFIDENCE

Two students expressed their feelings about public speaking in this way:

> When I get up to give a speech, I wait until people are looking at me before I start. I try to stand balanced on both feet so I don't sway. I try to remember why I am there and tell myself the listeners will be interested in what I am saying.

> When I get up to talk to a group of people, I feel really nervous. I get really very shaky. My hands shake and get sweaty. I also sway and shift my feet.

Most people worry about delivering their speeches. Some people worry about giving speeches because they experience stage fright. **Stage fright** is nervousness when talking to an audience. Being nervous, or having stage fright, is very common. Even the best speakers experience it sometimes. For example, singer Barbra Streisand suffers from severe stage fright.

Substitute Teacher Tip

Ask students to write one paragraph about a time when they had to perform in front of an audience, perhaps reciting a poem, playing a musical instrument, or competing as part of a sports team. After they have finished, ask for volunteers to read their paragraphs in front of the class.

Skill Development

On the Job

Ask students who work as volunteers to share with the class any recent experiences they may have had speaking in front of a group of coworkers. Remind students that public speaking is a part of many jobs.

You can build confidence by memorizing the first two or three sentences of your speech.

What happens when you have stage fright? People have various experiences with stage fright. Some signs of nervousness while speaking include these:

dry mouth	fast breathing
tense voice	"butterflies" in the stomach
sweating palms	hands in pockets
shaky legs	pounding heart
eyes looking down	shifting from foot to foot

Although you may not like the way you feel when you are nervous, stage fright can have an advantage. If you can turn the nervous energy into speaking energy, you can make the speech better. You can make your nervousness work for you. Having stage fright shows you care enough about speaking in public to want to do a good job.

> **❝**Our doubts are traitors,
> And make us lose the good
> we oft might win,
> By fearing to attempt.**❞**
>
> **WILLIAM SHAKESPEARE**
> *Measure for Measure*, Act I, Sc. 1

Motivation

Encourage students to take a mental tally of how many of the Tips for Developing Confidence they already use. Tell them to figure out which of the seven tips relates to the area in which they need the most work.

Links to Past Learning

Tell students that one technique for remaining calm while giving a speech is to remember past public performances that went well. Remembering a success can help pave the way for more success.

344

Most speakers feel more confident about their ability to handle stage fright when they keep in mind that stage fright becomes easier to control with practice and that nervous people usually look much better than they feel. One student dealt with her stage fright in this way:

> Every time I get up to speak my knees knock against each other. I was sure everyone could see my legs shaking. Now I wear a longer skirt when I have to speak. It makes me feel more comfortable and more confident.

Tips for Developing Confidence

Here are some suggestions to help you use stage fright to your advantage as you develop confidence as a speaker.

1. Prepare thoroughly. The more prepared you are, the more poised or self-confident you will feel.

2. Take a few deep breaths before you begin to speak. Deep breathing helps you relax.

3. Remind yourself of your audience goal. You are not there to perform. You are there to make a change in your audience.

4. Start strong. Have your first two or three sentences memorized so you can say them without mumbling or stumbling over your words. There is nothing like making a good start to build your confidence.

5. Reduce signs of nervousness, such as playing with a pencil or with your hair. Plan ahead so you will not have those distractions. For example, leave the pencil on your desk and push your hair back.

6. If a media aid, such as a slide, is helpful, use it. The energy you need to display your media aid will help use up some of your nervous energy.

7. Pay attention to your listeners' nonverbal feedback. If you focus on your listeners, you will pay less attention to your own nervousness.

Cooperative Learning

▼ Have students work together in groups to suggest some other useful tips to follow before giving a speech. They might suggest eating a good breakfast, getting plenty of sleep the night before, and realizing that the audience is not an enemy, since almost everyone in the audience has also had experience with public speaking.

Beyond the Classroom

Ask students if they have ever seen a play where the actors obviously missed lines of dialog or made similar mistakes. Ask how the actors handled the situation. Tell students that most good actors know how to cover their mistakes so that the audience remains unaware of the error. They do this by remaining calm and thinking on their feet. Ask if any students have ever had this experience themselves.

Confident speakers are able to think on their feet. Most confident speakers have high self-esteem and know that if something goes wrong they will adjust and make the best of it. If they recognize a problem, they find a way to cope with it. Some speakers worry that a problem will happen during their speech and they won't know what to do. If you are prepared, even if a problem occurs during your speech, you will be able to cope with whatever happens.

APPLY

Look at the following situations. What would you do if one of them happened to you?

1. You are in the middle of your speech when an announcement comes over the loudspeaker.

2. You stumble and nearly fall down on your way to the front of the room.

3. Halfway through your speech, you realize that your remaining note cards are out of order.

4. The computer program locks during your PowerPoint presentation.

5. Your audience bursts out laughing because you have said "hoppimess" instead of "happiness."

6. You forget your next idea.

If any of these situations ever happens to you, you must, above all else, remain calm. In situation 1, stop speaking, wait for the announcer to finish, and then continue your speech. In situation 2, you should stand up and continue walking to the podium. In situation 3, you could stop for a few seconds to put your note cards back in order. In situation 4, you might say, "My equipment is broken, so I'll explain the process as clearly as I can," or you could draw a basic diagram on the board. Situation 5 could be a good chance to use humor. You might say, "Let me untie my tongue and try that again." In situation 6, you might admit you

345

forgot and pause until you remember, or you could check your notes and then continue.

A key to handling all problems is to deal with them and move on. The less upset you are, the less your audience will notice the problem. Don't make a face, roll your eyes, or do anything that calls attention to your problem. Keep your audience goal in mind and move ahead.

METHODS OF DELIVERY

> Whenever I give a classroom speech, I speak from note cards. I memorize the ideas but never say the speech exactly the same way each time.

> When I introduced the speakers at the sports banquet, I wrote out each introduction and read from my paper. I had practiced enough so I could look up at the audience.

> When I go to a speech contest, I have to deliver a speech I memorized. I may give the exact same speech three or four times in one day.

> At Scout meetings we practice giving speeches without real preparation. We draw topics from a hat and get one minute to think before we have to talk. My last speech was on bowling balls.

As shown by these comments, public speakers use four methods for delivering a speech: extemporaneous, manuscript, memorized, and impromptu. Each has different strengths and weaknesses. Each works better in certain situations. In this section you will look at each of the four methods.

Extemporaneous

When using the **extemporaneous method**, speakers use a prepared outline but do not plan each word or sentence. Therefore, if a speech is delivered more than once, the ideas remain the same each time but the words change. For an extemporaneous speech, speakers usually put the speech outline on note cards or a single sheet of paper, using key words or phrases. The notes contain

Skill Development

Media Literacy

● Students who have watched Oprah Winfrey's television show might be encouraged to comment on her performance. Ask: Is she a good interviewer? Does she show any signs of nervousness? How does she use nonverbal language? Does she dress appropriately? Does she speak clearly? Does she use voiced pauses ("umms" and "ers")? How do the performances of various guests compare with her performance?

Oprah Winfrey, host of her own television show, is an expert at public speaking, both formally and informally.

names of people, or statistics, or a descriptive word to help the speakers remember an example or story. That way, when they are talking they can carry the card in one hand and read it easily. The example on page 349 shows notes for an extemporaneous speech on stepfamilies.

Good extemporaneous speakers prepare their introductions and conclusions carefully so they are very strong. Often they memorize them. Extemporaneous speakers also practice aloud to rehearse key phrases and ideas from the body of the speech.

Skill Development

Media Literacy

● Ask students to cite examples of extemporaneous speeches they have seen on television. Tell them that often what looks like extemporaneous speech in a variety show or news show is actually being read from a TelePrompTer or a cue card held off-camera. Have students watch specifically for actors or news personnel who are reading from a TelePrompTer or from cue cards. Have students analyze the techniques these performers use to make their speech look natural.

Good extemporaneous speakers know how to adapt key ideas to different audiences. For example, the student who returns from a year of study abroad and is expected to talk to community groups is going to tell each group about the values of the experience. Each group may hear some of the same stories, examples of communication breakdowns, and discussion of family life in a new culture. Yet the speech will vary depending on the audience characteristics and the occasion.

Extemporaneous delivery can be very effective because it leaves you free to respond to audience feedback. You can rephrase or repeat ideas if necessary. In addition, your tone will be more conversational, since you must think about your ideas as you phrase them.

One disadvantage of the extemporaneous method is that it may give you false confidence. Many beginning speakers think that by using this method they will not have to prepare very carefully. They assume that grand ideas will come as they talk. If you have this idea, you may be in for an unpleasant surprise when you get up to give your first speech! Good extemporaneous speakers practice the speech many times so that they are sure to make all their points with clear and interesting language, examples, stories, and statistics. You should not sit down and suddenly think, "I forgot about the crime statistics or the helicopter story." Practice also keeps speakers from using too many voiced pauses, "umms" and "ers," as they try to find the next words.

Manuscript

When using the **manuscript method**, a speaker writes out the entire speech and delivers it from the typed or written paper. Effective speakers know the content of their speeches so well that they can look at the audience often enough to establish effective eye contact.

It is important to use this method of delivery when you must be sure to say exactly what you mean, when you have very detailed information to present, or when you have a very tight time limit. Politicians use this method when they want to make very specific

Amazing Fact!

Marcus Fabius Quintilianus
(Quintilian) (A.D. c.35–c.100)
stressed the importance of good
character in his textbook on the
art of oratory.

Beyond the Classroom

Invite someone who speaks regularly
before the public to talk to the class
about which methods they use for
delivering a speech, to whom they
deliver speeches, and whether they
have tips for conquering anxiety. They
might also relate any unusual
incidents that occurred while they
were speaking.

Sample Notes For Extemporaneous Speech

Communicating in Stepfamilies

Intro: "No small child ever pushed a doll carriage and dreamed of
    being a stepparent."
  — surprise for many
  — 1/3 of families in this school
  — year 2000—most common family type in America

Purpose: Describe the steps of blending families, the problems
       and the advantages.

 I. Steps
  A. Try it Out
    1. Hopes
      a. solve old problems
      b. get great brothers or sisters (Alice and Tamara)
    2. Differences
      a. way people fight (Dad and Liz)
      b. habits and ways to do things (eating, bed times)
  B. Confronting Problems
    1. Admitting them (summer vacations)
    2. Negotiating time together, discipline
  C. Resolving Problems
    1. Trusting each other
    2. Being open (Dad and fishing trip)

II. Problems and Advantages
  A. Problems
    1. Holidays
      a. mixing traditions
      b. travel schedules
    2. School Events
      a. who to invite
      b. names and introductions
  B. Advantages
    1. New sisters or brothers (Reggie)
    2. Part of big family (stepgrandparents, parties)

Conclusion: Pretty soon everyone will be a step-relative!

349

Limited English Proficiency

Encourage these students to tell about any times they have introduced a guest speaker or been invited to talk to a group, perhaps in their first language.

points. Reading the manuscript keeps them from saying something they might regret later.

Often people who give a speech on radio or television use a manuscript to be sure they stay within certain time limits. For example, an editorial may run thirty seconds. If the speaker's speech is not fully written and timed, he or she may get cut off before finishing.

You may want to use this method when you introduce a guest speaker, because you may need a manuscript to make sure you have the correct information. One student described her experience introducing a speaker this way:

JOURNAL ENTRY

The senior-high group at our church took responsibility for all church activities one Sunday. I had to introduce the guest speaker for education hour. I had to write it all out because I had to give her title, the schools she attended, and the organization where she worked. I never could have remembered all the correct names.

Critical Thinking

Evaluating

The full text of the final football speech appears on pages 404–405 at the end of the next chapter.

Curricular Connection

Language Arts

▲ Encourage interested students to present an essay or report they have written for an English or social studies class as a speech. Then have a question-and-answer session about the differences between presenting something as an essay and presenting it as a speech.

STAGES OF MANUSCRIPT DEVELOPMENT

Creating a manuscript speech is similar to creating a fine essay. A first draft is written and then edited. A speech may go through three or four drafts before the speaker is satisfied that the language captures the appropriate mood and tone and "sounds like me." Look at the stages of one paragraph of a student's speech on football. How would you describe the differences between draft 1 and the final draft?

Stages of Manuscript Development

DRAFT 1

The quarterback sends the football in my direction. I'm open and dragged out of bounds after a gain of 40 yards. This is the best part of the game for me. I love catching passes. I wish there was a pass machine that would throw passes all day so I could practice. Catching a pass takes all my troubles away.

DRAFT 2

The quarterback drops back to pass and I'm open down the sidelines. "Wilkinson catches the ball and he's dragged out of bounds after a gain of 40 yards." Catching a ball is like hitting a home run. I love to catch passes. I wish there was some kind of a machine that could throw passes to me all day. Every time I catch a pass, my troubles are all gone.

FINAL DRAFT

". . . the ball is snapped. Reeder drops back to pass. There's Wilkinson down the sidelines; he has his man beat. The ball is caught by Wilkinson and he's dragged out of bounds after a gain of 40 yards."

To me, catching a pass is like hitting a home run and trotting around the bases; it's my time to shine. I love to catch passes. I want some kind of machine that could throw passes to me every day, but I have to wait until the football season starts to do it. Every time I catch a ball all the bad things that happened are all gone. I get high catching passes.

351

Links to Past Learning

Ask students to think about material they have memorized in the past, such as song lyrics, dramatic or comic monologues, and jokes. Ask why they think some things seem easier to memorize than others.

Most manuscript speeches go through two or three drafts as speakers write their ideas, read them out loud, and then revise their language. The previous example shows how the text became more specific, descriptive, and personal.

Manuscript delivery has two possible problems. First, you might read the whole speech and never look at the audience. Second, you might never move because you can't leave the manuscript. You cannot adapt to audience feedback or maintain eye contact if you just read to your audience.

President Bill Clinton encountered a very unique problem with his manuscript speech during a major speech to Congress on his health plan. His speech was on the TelePrompTer and all he had to do was read it. The problem was, someone put an old speech into the TelePrompTer. Fortunately, President Clinton spotted the mistake quickly and he had to deliver an impromptu speech for *nine* minutes while his staff located and inserted the correct manuscript. Speakers can take nothing for granted.

Memorized

When using the **memorized method,** speakers write out a manuscript and memorize it word for word. This takes a lot of work, but it leaves the speaker free to move and look directly at the audience because there is no need for notes. Often speech contest rules state that contestants must deliver memorized speeches. You may wish to memorize your speech for a formal occasion such as a school assembly or a religious program.

Speaking completely from memory can be a problem. You might end up memorizing the exact words but not the ideas. If your words are not attached to the main ideas you'll have a difficult time thinking on your feet if you forget even one word. Good speakers memorize the order of ideas and the words. Then, if they forget the next word, they can use an extemporaneous method to talk about the idea. Usually after a moment or two, they will remember where they were in the speech.

Sometimes speakers memorize some key stories or examples which they use in a number of different presentations and that

Skill Development
Feedback

● Have students exchange their final edited descriptions from the Apply exercise with a partner. Encourage partners to discuss each work's positive and negative points.

are central to their main points. Charles Wilkinson, a family therapist who speaks regularly to community and parent groups, uses a jazz metaphor to describe well functioning families. He wrote a number of drafts of his metaphor and settled on the one below, which he memorized and which he works into most of his speeches.

> I like to think of the well functioning family as a jazz ensemble, where members move with the flow of what's happening around them, looking for a harmony of sorts, playing off one another, going solo at times, always respecting the talents and surprises provided by the musicians around them.

> Standards,—yes. Expectations,—always. But everyone moving with the feel of the moment and of one another. At any time anyone can stop and say "This isn't working" and can challenge other members to pick up the beat, go on a riff, or settle in to a necessary silence. We know that "family" isn't a lonely drum in the distance or a plaintive flute within hearing. Family is found in the creative energy and interplay of its members.

APPLY

Select a concept that may be central in a speech that you will deliver, and create a carefully worded description. This should be five to seven sentences. Keep copies of your drafts. Check your final draft for correct spelling, punctuation, and capitalization by using a spellchecker computer program or asking a friend to edit it. You may use concepts such as health, family, love, success, wealth, or faith.

Impromptu

When using the **impromptu method** of delivery, speakers talk without notes and with very little preparation. An impromptu speech is a spur-of-the-moment presentation. The speaker may have a few seconds or a minute to prepare a short talk. The time

Beyond the Classroom

You might invite an improvisational comedy group to perform for your class. Remind students that many improvisers work from audience suggestions and without a script—the ultimate in "thinking on their feet." Some students might like to try their hand at improvising a scene in front of the class.

it takes the speaker to rise from a seat and walk to the front of the room may be his or her preparation time.

Generally, the best way to organize an impromptu speech is to look at the audience and

tell them what you're going to tell them

tell them

tell them what you've told them

In real-life situations people often are called on to say a few words. A teacher may ask you to say a few words about how the soccer tournament went on Saturday or about an upcoming event. For example, your English teacher might say, "Tim, why don't you take a minute and tell us about this year's freshman play?" If Tim is not able to think on his feet, he might say, "Um, well, this weekend there'll be a play about a stepfamily. It's, um, funny and you should see it." However, if Tim has had practice giving impromptu speeches, he might say, "This weekend the freshman class will present the play *Step On a Crack*. It's about a young girl's life in a stepfamily. It's very funny but very realistic. Audrey Jackson will play the part of the girl. I play her father. The curtain goes up on Friday and Saturday night at eight. It's free. I think you'll all enjoy *Step On a Crack*."

As you might guess, the impromptu method is a difficult type of delivery to use. However, it is useful to practice it, since you will be asked frequently to speak on the spur of the moment at a meeting or before a small group of people. One thing good impromptu speakers do is to take a minute to collect their thoughts. They think about their two or three points before saying anything. These 15 seconds improve their chances of being effective and of avoiding voiced pauses. The more you practice giving impromptu speeches, the more comfortable you will be when you have to think on your feet.

Madeleine Albright, former United States Ambassador to the United Nations and later Secretary of State under President Clinton's administration, is frequently called on for impromptu speeches.

Skill Development

On the Job

You might ask a manager from a local business to talk to the class about times when employees might have to speak in public as representatives of the company they work for.

⚹ INTERACT

In small groups of six or eight, divide into pairs. Each pair should submit three topics for an impromptu speech. Place the topics facedown on a desk. Have each pair pick a topic. One person in each pair will have only 30 seconds to prepare an impromptu speech on the topic. The other person will have five minutes to write notes for an extemporaneous speech. Do this for each pair. Each pair should give its speeches to the others in the group. Compare the differences in the speeches on the same topic.

355

Critical Thinking

Evaluating

● Before a day when you plan to assign impromptu speeches, privately ask three or four students to wear clothes or jewelry that they think others would find distracting. (Or, you might dress in an unusual manner yourself.) Ask the speakers and the rest of the class what they learned from this experience.

Critical Thinking

Evaluating

● Encourage students to evaluate their own appearance as if they were about to give a speech today. Ask whether they would change their appearance, and if so, how. If they were giving a speech to the whole school, to students in another school, to a few friends, or to a community group of adults, how would they change their appearance?

PERSONAL DELIVERY

Personal delivery involves your nonverbal messages, or how you use your appearance, voice, facial expression, eye contact, gestures, and body movements during your speech. Your nonverbal messages may support your spoken message, or they may prevent your listeners from getting your message. In some cases personal delivery involves using a microphone to convey your message more easily to a large audience.

Appearance

I kept getting distracted by all her shiny, sparkling jewelry.

Wearing shorts and a ripped T-shirt to talk to the school board did not make a good impression.

Have you ever had reactions like these when listening to a speech? Appearance does matter when you are giving a speech! Remember, you are communicating with your audience from the moment you rise from your seat to give a speech. The audience looks at your clothes, hair, posture, movements, and mannerisms and creates an impression of you. Listeners expect you to be dressed appropriately for the occasion. You may dress differently for a classroom speech, a speech contest, and an awards assembly. Your appearance needs to support your message and not distract the listeners.

Your personal delivery can add to or detract from the message you want to communicate.

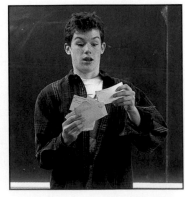

Skill Development

Quick Skill Opportunity

● Give volunteers a few moments to prepare a one-sentence introduction for a speech they might like to give. Tell them to walk to the front of the room and present their introduction in as confident a manner as they can. Encourage feedback from the class.

> **66**Her voice is full of money.**99**
>
> **F. Scott Fitzgerald**
> *The Great Gatsby*

Motivation

Tell students that you are going to read aloud to them for a short time. Choose a short short story that has interesting language and a strong plot line. Begin reading to the students in a monotone. Read a page or two, and then ask students for their reactions. Next, have a student continue the story with full vocal energy.

A speaker also needs to appear confident. If you project an image of confidence and enthusiasm as you walk to the front of the room, your listeners will think, "This speaker will be interesting." Don't let your appearance keep your listeners from getting the message!

Voice

I can't listen to him for more than two minutes before I fall asleep.

She gets nervous and talks so fast I cannot understand what she is saying.

How often have you felt like this about a speaker or left a speech feeling frustrated because you couldn't hear the speaker or because the speaker's voice was annoying? The vocal characteristics of volume, rate, pitch, quality, and clarity all affect a speaker's delivery.

Volume Volume refers to the loudness or softness of a speaker's voice. Very often beginning speakers whisper or shout at their listeners. Competent speakers change their volume as their content changes. For example, when you are talking about something that excites or angers you, your voice may get louder. When you are describing something sad, scary, or peaceful, you may use a soft voice. You will adjust your voice to the feedback you receive from your listeners. If you see people in the back straining to hear, it's time to speak louder.

Rate Rate, or pace, refers to the speed at which you speak. Rate also includes your use of pauses. Frequently beginning speakers talk as quickly as possible in order to finish and sit down. When this happens they leave their listeners confused or frustrated. Remember, a normal speaker talks at a rate of 120 to 180 words a minute. If you speak too slowly, your audience's attention will wander. If you speak too quickly, the audience will get confused. Experienced speakers vary their rate of speech. They adapt their rate to the topic, the feedback, and the occasion.

When you are making an important point, you may slow down in order to emphasize each word. This allows your listeners

357

to understand your main points. If your listeners look bored, you may speed up your rate to get their attention. If they appear confused, you may wish to slow down to give them time to use their "thought speed" properly.

Pauses must be silent. A voiced pause, such as "ah," "um," or "you know," is distracting to listeners. When too many vocal pauses are used, listeners stop paying attention to the speaker's message. Sometimes they even start counting the "likes" or "you knows."

Pitch Pitch refers to the highness or lowness of the voice. Nervous speakers frequently tense their vocal cords and speak in a high voice. This may distract the audience or make the speaker sound boring. In everyday conversation, you change your pitch naturally. If you can think of public speaking as a type of conversation, your pitch will change naturally.

It's time to speak up if people in the audience seem to have trouble hearing.

A speaker's pitch should help support the meaning of the message. For example, when speakers express pleasure or excitement, their pitch rises. When speakers express sadness or seriousness, their pitch tends to get lower.

Vocal Quality **Vocal quality** refers to the sound of a voice. Poor vocal quality can distract from the speaker's message. For example, if a speaker has a nasal voice that sounds like a whine, the listeners may become annoyed. If the speaker's voice is raspy or throaty, it will distract from the message. The best way to know how your voice sounds to others is to record yourself on tape. You may be surprised by what you hear.

APPLY

Working in pairs, record your voices and analyze them. Stand up and pretend you are speaking to an audience. Tell a short, funny story and then talk for a minute about a serious topic, such as child abuse or homelessness. Listen to how your voice reflects the different moods. See if your pitch and rate change as you move from funny to serious. Examine how you use volume to make a point. Pay attention to voiced pauses. Finally, listen to your vocal quality to see if you have a full tone, a nasal tone, or a raspy tone. Share your opinions with each other; sometimes it is hard to analyze your own voice because you are so familiar with it.

Clarity **Clarity** refers to the clearness of a speaker's words. A competent speaker tries to say words carefully and correctly. Pronunciation can affect a speaker's image. For example, a speaker who says "gode" for *gold,* "candate" for *candidate,* or "eatin'" for *eating* projects a careless image.

In addition, a speaker who mispronounces words does not appear to know the topic well. For example, a speaker who says "nucular power" instead of *nuclear power* or "amonia" rather than *pneumonia* sounds unprepared. Constant mispronunciation distracts audience members from the message. If you know you have difficulty remembering how to pronounce a certain word, write its pronunciation on your note card. Then you can refer to the card when you need it.

Motivation

Tell students that one way to ensure clearer speech is to concentrate on pronouncing the final *d*'s and *t*'s in words that end in these letters. As an exercise, call on individuals to say the words *did, went, had, treat,* and *could.*

359

Cooperative Learning

Have partners compare their lists from the Observe activity.

Skill Development

Active Listening

Other frequently mispronounced words could be added to the list.

probly	for	probably
should of	for	should have
Febuary	for	February
athuhletics	for	athletics

Links to Past Learning

Remind students that they react to people's facial expressions every day. Encourage a discussion of how they know, without being told, when a friend, parent, or teacher is happy, sad, ill, nervous, and so on.

The following words are frequently mispronounced. Some people say:

yutes	for	youths
natcherl	for	natural
eggsept	for	accept
axed	for	asked
acshul	for	actual
tree	for	three
Settemba	for	September
flustrated	for	frustrated

If you practice your speech out loud for someone before your actual presentation, that listener can give you feedback about words that you may be mispronouncing.

OBSERVE

Listen very carefully to speakers for a week. Record the words that they mispronounce. Make a list of the six most commonly mispronounced words.

Facial Expression

If speakers are interested in their topics, they show this in their facial expressions. A deadpan face, or a face without expression, sends a message that the speaker thinks the topic is boring. An excited or animated face sends a message the speaker thinks the topic is important and interesting.

INTERACT

Say the following sentences first with facial expressions that match the idea and then with facial expressions that contradict the idea. Have listeners describe their reactions to each.

continued

▼ Ask someone in the class to videotape short segments from one or two television soap operas. Show the tape to the class without the sound. Discuss what the class can tell about the characters from facial expressions and gestures.

INTERACT

I promise you the best summer of your life if you work at Adventureland.

It is a great honor to speak to this group today. I could hardly wait to get here.

I want to talk about one of our country's most serious problems—the future of the small farmer.

It is time to welcome our winning basketball coach, Leslie Mannix. Let's give our favorite coach a great big Wilmington welcome!

Eye Contact

The eyes have been called the windows of the soul. People use eye contact to indicate their involvement with others. If the speaker looks over your head or at the floor, you may not feel connected to the person or the topic. The speaker who looks at you makes you feel recognized and important. After hearing a speaker talk about the need for students to tutor in an elementary reading program, one student wrote, "I signed up to work as a reading tutor because, when he asked for volunteers, I felt like Mr. Horshak was talking just to me."

Good speakers also use eye contact to get feedback. Confused looks, angry glances, or friendly smiles from the audience tell you how you are doing. As a speaker, you use your eyes to find the answer to the question "What do you think of what I'm saying?"

When you are speaking, concentrate on your audience members. Look at them and read the feedback they give you. Remember the diagram on page 7 (Chapter 1) which shows how you send and receive messages simultaneously. Your eyes tell you how you are doing at reaching the audience. Try to look at each audience member during the talk. Do not rush from one face to the next. Be careful not to look only at one side of the room or only at the people in the front or back. Don't just look at your audience, really concentrate on what they are telling you through their feedback.

Skill Development

Quick Skill Opportunity

● Students might like to perform the statements from the Apply activity. Remind them that not all information requires a gesture. Gestures should be used only when needed to illustrate a point.

Gestures

Gestures are movements of the head, shoulders, hands, or arms that speakers use to describe or emphasize a point. A speaker may describe how to shoot a basketball by going through the motions. A speaker may place emphasis on an idea by pointing at the audience or pounding a fist on the podium. Speakers may use their hands and arms to help the audience envision something.

> **APPLY**
>
> How do you predict a speaker would gesture or move while saying the following statements?
>
> There are three—only three—major issues in this campaign.
>
> When the pond was stocked with fish, most of them were about six inches long. Now we are catching trout that are two feet long.
>
> As the earth moves around the sun, we experience night and day.
>
> The center crouched, and then exploded with a winning three-point basket.

When you talk to your friends or family, you use gestures naturally. Don't change when you speak to an audience. It's easy to say gestures should appear natural, but what does this mean for the public speaker? Gestures must be large enough to be seen and understood by the audience. Hand gestures must be made above the waist, and they must move out and away from the body.

Beginning speakers often wonder what to do with their hands. Remember that the things that feel like watermelons at the end of your arms do not look as large and awkward to your audience as they feel to you! Let your hands hang easily at your sides or hold your note cards in one hand and let the other stay near your side until you gesture.

Enlarge your gestures when you have a large audience.

Limited English Proficiency

Ask these students to suggest gestures that might accompany the following statements:

Each insect is about a half inch long.

Stir the flour into the egg mixture.

He wrote on the board with great big letters.

The teacher told the children to "please be quiet."

Good speakers adapt their gestures to the size of the audience. If you are talking to ten people, your gestures can be quite small. If you are talking to a group of sixty, you will need to use larger gestures.

Movement

Good speakers do not move constantly, nor do they stand perfectly still. They use movement to make their message clearer to the audience. Here are some simple do's and don't's for movement and gestures:

Do

1. take a few steps during the major transitions in the speech.

2. when you move, face in the same direction you are moving.

3. stand balanced on both feet, with your weight forward.

363

Motivation

Have students make a list of jobs that might require employees to use a microphone or public address system.

Don't

1. pace back and forth. Stay in one place when discussing a main point.

2. gesture all the time. It is fine to stand with your hands at your sides.

3. rest your weight on one foot. You can lose your balance.

4. play with a pen or with keys or loose change in your pocket.

APPLY

Assume you are watching a speaker. What might the following body movements signal to you?

1. The speaker pauses, takes two steps forward, and starts to speak again.

2. The speaker shrinks back and then returns to a normal speaking position.

In both examples a speaker is using movements to send a message. In example 1, the speaker may be telling the listener, "This is a transition" or "I'm moving on to a new point." Good speakers often use movements to get their listeners' attention. In example 2, the speaker may be acting out a story. Perhaps it is the story of a child afraid of a circus clown. Perhaps it is someone hiding until other people pass. The body movements support the speaker's message.

Speaking with a Microphone

In some cases you will have to deliver your speech using a microphone. You may have a choice of a stationary microphone, such as one attached to a podium; a hand mike, which you have to hold; or a lavaliere mike, which is attached to your clothing. Each affects your delivery. The stationary mike limits your ability to move or make gestures the audience can see. The hand mike means you have to hold it near your face and can gesture with

Learning Styles

Kinesic Learning

Ask volunteers to act out 1, 2, 4, 5, and 6 on the list of don'ts on this page. Ask other volunteers to act out correct behavior for 1, 4, and 5. Students could use a hairbrush to represent a microphone.

66Don't be so loud all the time as to make it impossible to raise the voice to drive home a point.99

STROM THURMOND

Beyond the Classroom

If possible, invite a local disk jockey or radio announcer to visit your classroom. Encourage students to ask the guest questions about microphone techniques and potential problems.

only one hand. The lavaliere mike gives you the greatest freedom of movement.

If you are going to use a microphone, check to see that it is working properly before you start your speech. If, while you are speaking, you suspect the speaker system is not working, stop speaking until it has been fixed. There is little sense in continuing to speak when perhaps 50 percent of the audience cannot hear what you are saying. If the group is small and you have good volume, don't use the microphone.

Tips for Using a Microphone

1. Don't tap on the microphone to test it. Say, "Test one, two, three." Tapping is harmful to a microphone and annoying to audiences.

2. Don't stand too close to the microphone. It magnifies each sound.

3. Don't yell or raise your voice when using a microphone. Check the volume of the microphone while you are testing it, and then decide how close you need to stand in order to be heard clearly.

4. Don't look at the microphone while speaking. Speak to your audience.

5. Don't let the microphone block your face as you speak.

6. Don't swing the microphone on its cord. This can break the cord.

REHEARSING THE SPEECH

Just as in basketball, tennis, skating, or any other activity that involves skill development, competent speechmaking requires practice. Rehearsing your speech is one of the most important parts of speech preparation. As you rehearse, you can try out

365

Skill Development

Quick Skill Opportunity

● If possible, bring in a microphone that students can use to practice. You could have each student state his or her name and give some personal information. Encourage students to follow the tips for using the microphone.

Critical Thinking

Predicting

● Encourage students to think about times in their lives when they have rehearsed something. They might think of sports events they've practiced for, musical or dramatic material they've rehearsed and so on. Have students use their own experiences as a guideline to predict what the heading "Rehearsing the Speech" might entail.

Rehearsing in front of a mirror can help you practice gestures and movements.

different delivery techniques, just as you try out various ways to do a jump shot or play a jazz piece. If you think you will use a microphone, this is the time to practice doing it properly.

In this section, you will examine ways to rehearse an extemporaneous speech. You can use many of the same techniques for other delivery methods. You will find that your words will change each time you practice, but your ideas should remain in the same order. Rehearsing involves ordering the ideas in your mind and polishing the delivery of your speech.

Ordering the Speech in Your Mind

As you prepare to speak, you must be sure to fix in your mind the main ideas in the correct order. The following simple steps will help:

1. Read over your entire outline silently two or three times. Go straight through without going back over any section.

2. Repeat step 1, but this time aloud.

3. Try to give your speech without looking at your outline or note cards. Stand up and practice gestures and movements. Even if you can't remember certain points, go on and try to complete the entire speech. Remember, this is a rehearsal, so it doesn't matter if you make mistakes. It is important to go through the entire speech without stopping.

4. Reread your outline silently as in step 1.

5. Reread your outline aloud as in step 2.

6. Try again to give the complete speech.

7. Continue steps 4 through 6 until you can complete your speech without any errors. Remember, in this part of your rehearsal, you are working on getting a grasp of the order of ideas in your speech.

8. Practice the visualization technique you learned in Chapter 4. This technique allows you to rehearse anywhere you can concentrate.

This work is well worth the effort. When the ideas are fixed in your mind, you will not get confused during the actual speech.

Polishing Your Delivery

After you are able to deliver the main ideas of your speech aloud in the correct order, you can pay attention to your delivery. Following these steps can help you with the delivery:

1. Imagine your audience in your mind. Set chairs up in front of you, talk to a mirror, or have one or two friends listen to you. If you are using visual aids, be sure to practice with them.

2. Try to communicate with your real or imaginary audience. Be enthusiastic both verbally and nonverbally. If you are not excited about your topic, how can you expect anyone else to be?

3. If your audience is real rather than imaginary, adapt to your listeners. Watch for cues indicating that you need to change your delivery. Ask your audience for feedback.

4. Give special practice to the introduction, conclusion, and any stories, examples, or jokes. You may wish to memorize these parts so that they will sound exactly as you imagine them.

5. Spread your rehearsal time over three or four days. If you wait until the last minute, you will only increase your nervousness. Allow enough practice time so you will be able to rehearse your speech until you are comfortable with it. You may want to rehearse six to eight times.

6. Don't let your speech become stale.

Cooperative Learning

● Have students select a short speech from the pupil text or from another source of famous speeches. Then suggest that students work in pairs, using the speeches they have selected to practice delivery techniques on one another. Have students focus on steps 2 and 3 under "Polishing Your Delivery" on page 367.

367

Curricular Connection

Curricular Connection

Language Arts

● Encourage students to keep a journal throughout the Observe activity. Students might like to exchange their journals with a partner to compare experiences and reactions.

Motivation

Have students name various media aids they have seen speakers use. Have volunteers explain the function of media aids in specific speeches.

🔍 **OBSERVE**

As you give two or three speeches, try to rehearse in slightly different ways. Work in front of a mirror one time. Try the speech out on your family or friends another time. Practice while moving around and gesturing. Describe the ways that work best for you. As a variation on this, videotape yourself using a family or school videotape recorder. Play your speech back and decide how effective your movement, gestures, facial expression, and appearance are in conveying your message.

MEDIA AIDS

Media aids, sometimes called presentation or audiovisual aids, are supporting materials, such as graphics, diagrams, and tapes. In many speeches to inform or to persuade, speakers use media aids to make their points more clearly and to interest the audience, as demonstrated by the following comments:

> On the graph you can see the number of teenagers who smoked in 1988 compared to 1998.

> Here you can see the four chambers on the model of a human heart.

> Listen to this tape of the last two minutes of Martin Luther King's "I Have a Dream" speech. This speech changed the lives of many Americans.

Think about speeches you have heard and try to remember what media aids the speakers used effectively.

Types of Media Aids

Speakers may support their ideas with objects, visual aids, or technology presentations. Below are some examples.

Actual Objects	musical instrument, a completed needlepoint project, a lacrosse stick
Pictures	photographs or drawings of an object, event, or person

Models	miniatures of an actual object, scale models of houses, railroads, the human heart
Diagrams	simplified representations of an area, a process, or a situation
Graphs and Charts	visual comparisons of information, such as bar graphs or pie charts
Visual Materials	slides, videotapes, overhead transparencies
Audio Materials	records, cassette tapes, sound effects
Computer Graphics	charts, cartoon figures, graphs

Students in one school reported the following examples of media aids for public speaking assignments:

I showed pictures by Frieda Kahlo, my favorite artist, for my speech.

My family's home videos provided great images of white-water rafting.

I used PowerPoint on the computer to create a persuasive message on school fundraising drives.

My tapes of Tito Puente helped support my argument about the value of Latin jazz.

Preparing Media Aids

Media, or audiovisual aids can ruin a speech if used improperly. They can distract the audience or cause the speaker to lose focus. Audience members are familiar with overhead transparencies and flip charts but some speakers find their fancy PowerPoint presentation tends to shift the focus from their message to their hardware. Competent speakers think carefully about preparing and using media aids. These guidelines will help you prepare media aids for your speeches:

1. Create audiovisual aids that can be seen or heard by all audience members. People who have to strain to see a chart or to hear a tape might get frustrated and tune out.

Links to Past Learning

Encourage individual volunteers to discuss their own past use of media aids in speeches. Ask each student why his or her media aid did or did not work well for the speech.

369

Cooperative Learning

● Have students work in pairs to create media aids. Let them choose their own topics. Then allow them to discuss their options and come up with the media aids best suited to their topics. If they cannot create an actual aid (for example, a videotape or film strip), allow them to write about their ideal media-aid option.

Learning Styles

Audio-Visual Learning

● Bring in or borrow a VCR or video camera from the audiovisual department, and show students how to use the equipment.

2. Make visual aids clear and readable. Use dark, heavy lines on white paper. Don't draw complicated, hard-to-interpret designs. Use colors to emphasize words.

3. Be sure your visual aids are simple to use. The easier they are to hold, tape up, or prop up, the easier they will be to handle.

4. Practice using your media aid. Be sure you know how to operate the necessary equipment. Don't hope a technical expert will be sitting in your audience.

5. Check out the equipment before the speech. If you need a stand to display charts or posters, be sure you have one. You may discover you need a special plug or a new light bulb for an overhead projector.

Graphs and pictures are just two common visual aids.

6. Be sure to reserve the equipment, such as a laptop computer, ahead of time instead of hoping it will be available when you need it.

Critical Thinking

Analyzing

● Ask students to think about the kind of volunteer work that Atley Chock performs. If he were asked to give a speech to community leaders to make them aware of the needs of the annual Thanksgiving Turkey Drive, what media aids would help Atley with his presentation? What media aids would help him with a presentation on the children at the battered women's shelter?

SPEAKING OF . . .

ATLEY CHOCK

As an active member of the Key Club in Michigan's Lahser High School, Atley Chock encounters many different people in his community and the surrounding area. Every year he helps coordinate the annual Thanksgiving Turkey Drive, which involves planning the fund-raising effort, the food collection, and the delivery of food to needy families. Because Atley enters the homes of many people, he needs to relate to them and make everyone feel comfortable. He tries to be friendly and open, greeting each family member, asking where the food should be unloaded, and, after the work is completed, wishing them a happy holiday. Throughout the year he is active in the local food bank, which collects and distributes food within the community.

Atley also makes regular visits to a battered women's shelter to talk and play with the children who are temporarily living there. He reports, "I am quite moved when I see these kids. They have already lost so much in their lives, but then they also have that sparkle in their eyes." Many of these children are glad to have a young person who will listen to them and whom they can trust. Atley reports that he has learned to keep their confidences and not to tell others what the children tell him. As he explains, "I am there to listen, to be supportive, to help others." As he goes about his work, Atley says he tries to "look presentable and have a smile on my face." He believes these nonverbal cues are important.

Regarding his efforts to serve children, Atley says, "I always try to teach others to help themselves. I never tell them the answers straight out. I want to show them a method to solve the problem and to get them thinking for themselves." These attributes and experiences will serve Atley well in many careers. He would be effective as a school administrator or psychologist, personnel director, charity director, or community leader.

Skill Development

Research

● Interested students might want to find out more about Lee Iacocca. Encourage them to research the story behind this American business icon.

Skill Development

Media Literacy

Bring in a videotape of segments of television cooking, gardening, or craft shows. The segments should show someone actively using a media aid. Ask students to evaluate how skillful the speaker is at using the aid.

Using Media Aids

Remember that media aids should support you, not replace you. Media aids should never become more important than your content. One student, who was giving a demonstration speech on caring for snakes, brought his boa constrictor to class. His audience members were so frightened, they could not concentrate on what he was saying. Be sure the audience remembers the message, not the media aid. The following guidelines will help you make sure your media aids work for you, rather than against you:

1. Speak to the audience, not to your media aid. Sometimes beginning speakers talk to their object or overhead. This makes it difficult for an audience to hear the speaker. Also, when you focus on your audiovisual aid and not on the audience, you cannot read the feedback your audience sends.

2. Don't show media aids until you are ready to use them. When an object or picture is visible, your audience will focus its attention on the visual aid rather than on what you say. Once you have used the media aid, remove or cover it. Turn off the computer or tape recorder.

3. Don't play with the media aid. Pick it up or point out the various parts of it while you are talking about it. Otherwise, don't touch it.

4. Do not pass objects around. This is distracting. When audience members take time out to examine an object, they lose what you are saying at that moment.

5. Don't hide behind your aid. Stand next to your aid, not behind it or in front of it. You are giving the speech, not your tape recorder or your computer. Don't hold charts in front of your face or allow tapes to run for long periods during your speech.

The main thing to remember is to focus on your audience goal. Make all your decisions about your media aids based on the question, "To what extent will this material help me reach my audience goal?"

The ability to deliver a fine speech will serve you well for the rest of your life. According to Lee Iacocca, former head of the Chrysler Corporation and nationally known businessperson, his

Critical Thinking

Synthesizing

● Have students close their books, and then ask several volunteers to tell one thing he or she learned in this chapter.

business success was directly related to his speaking ability. In his autobiography he writes: "I've seen a lot of guys who are smarter than I am and a lot who know more about cars. And yet I've lost them in the smoke. Why? Because I'm tough? No . . . You've got to know how to talk to them, plain and simple."

CHAPTER 12 SUMMARY

This chapter provides the important points in presenting a speech. Every speaker needs to develop self-confidence. This can be gained by avoiding stage fright and thinking on your feet. As a speaker, you may use one of four methods for delivery: extemporaneous, manuscript, memorized, or impromptu. Speakers also need to control the nonverbal aspects, or personal delivery, of their speaking. As a final step in speech preparation, speakers must rehearse their presentation. If the speech requires media aids, a competent speaker plans ahead to create and use these aids effectively.

373

Answers

Think About It

Student answers will vary. Here are sample answers:

1. Stage fright is a condition of nervousness related to public speaking or performance. Symptoms of stage fright include, among others, dry mouth, sweaty palms, shaky legs, and pounding heart. Ways to combat stage fright and achieve speaker confidence are: (1) prepare thoroughly; (2) take deep breaths; (3) remind yourself of your audience goal; (4) start strong; (5) avoid fiddling with pencil, playing with hair, and other distracting behavior; (6) use media aids; (7) pay attention to nonverbal feedback from the audience.

2. (1) Extemporaneous: This type of delivery can be very effective because it leaves the speaker free to respond to audience feedback. (2) Manuscript: This type of delivery is used when a specific piece of information has to be delivered in a relatively short amount of time. (3) Memorized: While completely memorized speeches involve a lot of work, they do allow the speaker the freedom to move around and make eye contact with the audience. This type of delivery is most effective for formal speaking occasions such as religious programs or school assemblies. (4) Impromptu: This is a spur-of-the-moment presentation where the person is asked to say a few words about a certain subject, with little or no time to prepare.

3. The nonverbal elements of personal delivery are appearance, vocal characteristics, facial expression, eye contact, gestures, and body movements.

4. To rehearse a speech one must order the ideas and polish the delivery.

Skill Development

Presenting

▲ After completing the first Put It in Writing activity, some students may be interested in presenting their own demonstrations for the class. Have students prepare an informative speech in which they explain how to do something, such as a sports activity, game, or craft. Tell students to plan how they will use gestures, movement, eye contact, vocal techniques, and facial expressions in their delivery. Then have students present their speeches to the class. Provide feedback.

CHAPTER REVIEW

Think About It

1. Define stage fright and describe ways to develop speech confidence.

2. List the four methods of delivery and explain the use of each.

3. What are the nonverbal elements of personal delivery?

4. Describe ways to rehearse your speech.

5. What are the guidelines for preparing and using media aids?

Try It Out

1. In order to get comfortable with gestures, practice your speech and exaggerate the gestures you plan to use. Make them much bigger and stronger than you would in a real speech. Then work to tone the gestures down and make them presentable. This exercise may help you to become more comfortable with gesturing.

2. Listen to a recording of a famous public speaker (Martin Luther King, Jr., John F. Kennedy), a comedian (Lily Tomlin, Robin Williams), or a great storyteller (Orson Welles, Jackie Torrence), and pay attention to the way the person changes volume, rate, pitch, and vocal quality to keep the delivery interesting. Report your observations to the class.

Put It in Writing

1. Observe a cooking demonstration in a department store or on television. Write a paragraph that describes how the speaker used gestures, eye contact, and vocal variety to hold audience interest. If the speaker used an audiovisual aid, describe how it was used.

2. In your journal, write about your own speech confidence. How confident do you feel when speaking in public? What signs of nervousness do you have? Do you use the guidelines for overcoming stage fright? Do you have other techniques for reducing nervousness?

3. Select a topic and write a carefully crafted manuscript introduction, including a purpose statement, two pieces of supporting material (story, example, description), and a conclusion. Do at least two drafts, until you are satisfied with your language. Memorize the draft you will use as you deliver an informative or persuasive speech.

Speak About It

1. Create an introduction for a speech and practice giving it using a variety of delivery methods. Write out the full introduction and deliver it to the class twice—once using the memorized method and once using the manuscript method. Ask for feedback on the effectiveness of each method.

5. Preparing media aids: (1) Make sure the aids can be seen or heard by all audience members. (2) Make visual aids clear and readable. (3) Make sure the visual aids are as simple as possible. (4) Practice using the media aid. (5) Check the equipment before beginning the speech. (6) Reserve the equipment in advance. Using media aids: (1) Speak to the audience, not the visual aid. (2) Don't show a media aid until you're ready to use it. (3) Don't play with the media aid. (4) Do not pass objects around the audience. (5) Don't hide behind the media aid.

2. To practice using media aids, make a visual about yourself and present it to the class. The visual (collage, drawing, PowerPoint figure) should contain at least three things that are part of your life or your personality that most people do not know about. These need not be highly personal. You can think about the hidden area of the Johari Window to do this.

3. Practice developing your extemporaneous style. Choose one of the following topics and take fifteen minutes to prepare an outline with an introduction, at least two main points, some supporting material, and a conclusion.

   Something that should be invented (and why)

   The person I would most like to meet (and why)

   If I have children some day, I will be sure to . . .

   When people get angry, they should . . .

   Some day I would like to help solve the problem of . . .

   The famous person I'd most like to be (and why)

   The most pressing problem America is facing today

4. Tape three or four minutes of your speech and listen for any voiced pauses, such as, "um," "uh," "you know," or "like." Note when you tend to use them. Practice this section at least three times trying to reduce the number of voiced pauses in each version.

5. Present an informative or persuasive speech to the class. Use technology to include both audio and visual supporting materials. Before you give your speech, practice it and practice using any equipment that you need for the technical presentation.

Quick Check

Ask students to find and define these Key Terms:

clarity (359)

delivery (342)

extemporaneous method (346)

gestures (362)

impromptu method (353)

manuscript method (348)

media aids (368)

memorized method (352)

pitch (358)

rate (357)

stage fright (342)

vocal quality (359)

volume (357)

Motivation

Ask students to brainstorm for topics they would like to know more about. Suggest they think about general areas such as space travel, the arts, history, mathematics, medicine, or government and then think of some specific topics. Have them each write one idea on a slip of paper. Collect the ideas and save them for possible speech topics, either for students or for speakers who might be invited to talk to students.

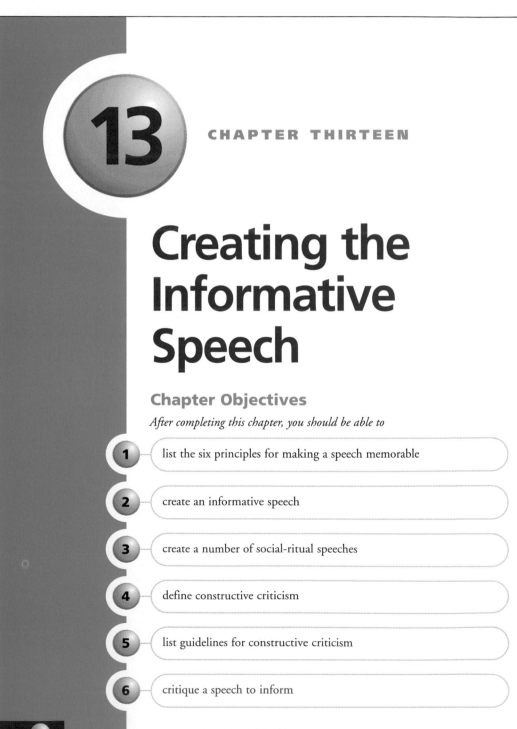

13

CHAPTER THIRTEEN

Creating the Informative Speech

Chapter Objectives

After completing this chapter, you should be able to

1 — list the six principles for making a speech memorable

2 — create an informative speech

3 — create a number of social-ritual speeches

4 — define constructive criticism

5 — list guidelines for constructive criticism

6 — critique a speech to inform

⊙ Key Terms

connected information	critic	formal feedback	informative speech
	critique	informal feedback	social-ritual speech
constructive criticism	eulogy		

Links to Past Learning

Some students will already know what constructive criticism is. Ask a volunteer to define the term and give an example.

Critical Thinking

Evaluating

Ask students which of the following topics would most likely be the title of a speech to inform:

- Georgia's Famous Gardens
- Changing the Way You Eat
- Five Steps to a Great Self-Image
- The Films of Francis Ford Coppola
- Designing and Making Woven Baskets
- Traveling in Quebec
- You *Can* Organize Your Time!

Every day you listen to speeches to inform. Your history teacher may describe the Middle Ages, your religious leader may talk about young people who reach out to others, or your Scout leader may explain how to build campfires. Each day you also hear social-ritual speeches, such as school announcements or the introductions of speakers. Social-ritual speeches are informative speeches that follow a formula or pattern. You might evaluate informative speeches by saying "This is boring" or "That sounds excellent." This chapter discusses how to give informative speeches, including social-ritual speeches, and how to evaluate these speeches effectively.

SPEAKING TO INFORM

Speaking to inform is the most familiar type of public speaking. An **informative speech** is a speech that presents or describes information. Your days are filled with informative speeches—those that you receive and those that you give. You listen to teachers' lectures, which are a type of informative speaking. You might announce to your classmates the date and time of the music department's winter concert. You might give a report on author Maya Angelou in English class. You might teach your Spanish club a song you learned in Mexico.

Listeners are more likely to pay attention to an informative speech when they can connect what is said to what they already know.

Beyond the Classroom

▼ Work with the class to come up with examples of the "need to know" in their personal lives. Examples might include weather information, deadline for a paper to be turned in, location of a meeting or rehearsal, or the items on a loved one's gift list. Encourage students to think creatively and come up with as many examples as they can within a three- to five-minute period.

Principles for Informing

When you create an informative speech, think of the speech as a form of expository writing. Your purpose is to inform and explain. The audience goal is to increase the listeners' knowledge. When you speak to inform, remember these principles about sharing information. Audiences are more attentive and receive information better when (1) they have a need to know; (2) the information is connected to something they know; (3) the information is well organized; (4) the information is repeated; (5) the information is tied to feelings, and (6) the information is focused.

The Need to Know People who feel a "need to know" receive information more easily. When your teacher tells you what to study for an important test, you listen closely. Your audience, too, will listen closely if it has a need to know. Thus, one of your first duties as an informative speaker is to analyze your listeners' needs or interests and create a need to know.

Connections Connected information is more easily received than unconnected information. **Connected information** is new information that is related to information an audience already knows. If your teacher speaks to your class about persuasion, you may simply tune out. On the other hand, if your teacher connects that information to television ads and explains how you are personally affected by persuasion in advertising, you will become more interested in the information. Competent speakers use information that connects to what the listeners already know.

Organization Well-organized information is more easily understood. If you are describing a process, for example, you must start at the beginning and discuss each step in sequence until you reach the end of the process. If you skip around instead of presenting the steps in order, your audience will become confused and may not understand you. Process, time, space, and topic order are organizational patterns that work well in informative speeches. You learned about them in Chapter 11.

Skill Development
Media Literacy

● Ask students to recall watching local news programs on television. Ask how news programs seem to create a "need to know." Students might mention seeing weather bulletins, information on health, and warnings about various hazards. Ask: How much of this news do people really need to know? Do news programs sometimes create unreasonable fears? Let students take a few minutes to discuss these questions.

379

Learning Styles

Audio Learning

● Play an excerpt from Martin Luther King, Jr.'s, "I Have a Dream" speech. Discuss with students why they feel the repetition of the phrase "I have a dream" is or is not effective.

Skill Development

On the Job

Encourage students who are volunteers to comment on the six principles of informing as they relate to their own volunteer-training programs. Encourage them to cite which of the principles relate most specifically to their own experiences.

Multicultural Learning

Remind students that different audiences experience varying levels of information overload. As an example, encourage them to think about how they respond to the following: repetitious commercials, discussions about feelings they may not want to acknowledge, or talks that contain more than they need or want to know about a topic.

Repetition Repeated information is more easily understood and remembered. Choose two or three of the most important ideas in your speech and use repetition to emphasize those points. You may not repeat the exact same words each time but you need to repeat the ideas. But be careful not to overuse repetition. Too much repetition in a speech can become as tiresome as too many reruns of a television show.

Feelings Information tied to feelings is more easily remembered. Think about the past week. What event stands out in your memory? Was it when you tripped and were embarrassed because you felt half the school was watching you? Perhaps it was a difficult exam or a compliment paid to you by a classmate. Probably it was an event that involved your feelings. When giving an informative speech, use memorable examples, illustrations, and stories to involve your audience and help them remember your main ideas.

Focus Too much information reduces understanding. You need to focus your speech so that you cover only a few main points. When your teacher lectures and covers too much material, you will probably remember very little because of information overload. Information overload should be avoided in all types of speaking, because most people can understand and remember only five to nine pieces of key information at one time.

INTERACT

With a partner, brainstorm ways in which one of the following topics could be developed, using four of the six principles discussed:

buying a video camera   MTV

guidelines for baby-sitters   raising pigs for profit

baseball's greatest pitchers   women in popular music

Amazing Fact!

One popular type of demonstration speech today is the television "infomercial." An infomercial is a program that combines entertaining information about a product with advertising to sell that product. Infomercials dominate late-night programming on many TV stations.

Cooperative Learning

▲ Interested students could continue work on one of the speech topics they selected and brainstormed during the Interact exercise on page 380.

Types of Informative Speeches

There are many forms of informative speeches. The following are the most common ones.

Description A speaker attempts to describe a person, place, thing, or experience. One person may describe what happens at a weekend forensics tournament, another may describe the experience of roller blading, while a third may describe his feelings for his grandfather. These speakers attempt to create mental pictures for audience members.

Sample titles

ALS: A Progressive Disease

The Festival of Kwanza

The Grand Canyon Sunrise

Architectural Wonders of Boston

Definition A speaker may use this type of speech to explain a word or concept in great detail. For example a speaker may attempt to define what the terms *family* or *friendship* mean to him or her. Civic groups often sponsor contests that require speakers to define terms such as *freedom* or *democracy*. Most speakers talk about dictionary meanings, general understanding, and personal meanings of words or concepts.

Sample titles

Grounded: The World's Worst Word

What Liberty Means to My Family

Swamp Is Not a Dirty Word

Demonstration A speaker uses a media aid to explain or demonstrate a particular concept or thing. You may use a large poster of a motorcycle to explain the Harley Davidson's parts, their names, and how they work. You may demonstrate through gestures the correct form for various sports activities such as

Curricular Connection

Science

● Encourage students to think of a scientific process about which they could speak. Instead of writing an outline for the speech topic, have students create process diagrams that they could use as both an outline and a media aid.

swimming the butterfly stroke, pitching a fast ball, or riding on a horse. You may bring in a chessboard to demonstrate moves.

Sample titles

Recognizing Hopi and Navajo Jewelry (pictures or examples)

Spinning Wool on a Drop Spindle (wool and drop spindle)

Basic Chess Moves (chessboard)

Process A speaker explains the step-by-step process by which something is created or operated. The speaker may or may not use a visual aid. For example, you may show how to create buttons with slogans by using the button-punch machine in class. You may explain the process of making double chocolate-nut brownies by writing each step on the board and sharing an example of the final product with the class. Or you may talk about the steps in conducting an interview or running a meeting according to parliamentary procedure.

Two men demonstrating basic karate moves.

Sample titles

How to Draw Faces

How to Pitch Curve Balls

How to Create French Braids

As you may have noticed, there may be some overlap between the demonstration and the process type of informative speech. It is possible to include a demonstration as part of a process speech.

APPLY

Read the following example of an informative speech. Try to identify the outline pattern. Find examples of definition and description.

Stardust: The Adopted Wild Horse

We adopted a new family member last summer. No, the latest member is not a brother or sister. It's a wild horse named Stardust. Stardust came to us through the U.S. government Adopt-a-Horse Program. The U.S. government is giving away wild horses to people who prove they can take care of the animals. I'd like to tell you about the American wild horses and how we went about getting Stardust.

In the western part of the United States wild horses roam free on the open ranges. Spanish explorers brought the horses to America hundreds of years ago. For centuries they ran wild in large herds. By the 1960s most of the horses were gone because ranchers killed them to keep the horses from grazing on their land.

In 1971 Congress passed a law to protect these horses. Now there are so many wild horses that the government must take some off the range each year. Since 1973 the government has used helicopters to round up 64,000 horses. Cowboys rope the horses or helicopters drive them into corrals. These horses are then sent across the United States to families who will provide them with good homes.

How did our family get Stardust? My sister, Gretchen, has always loved horses. She has ridden since she was four and

continued

Skill Development

Vocabulary

● To help increase students' powers of description, ask them to call out descriptive words for the following scenes. Urge them to use their five senses in imagining the scenes and to stretch their vocabulary.

- a basketball game with the score tied during the last three minutes
- a green park with benches and flowering trees in the middle of a city block
- a trash-strewn area under a viaduct
- a windy, cool day on a deserted beach
- time travel back to 1776 in Boston

Critical Thinking

Analyzing

● Have students make a two-column list of examples of definition and description in the speech in the Apply activity. Then have students compare their work with a partner.

APPLY *Continued*

always helps out at the Crossroads Stables. My parents said she could have a horse, but they could not afford to buy one. When Gretchen heard about this program from a friend at the stables, she begged my parents to get a horse and keep it in the old barn.

My father called the Bureau of Land Management and found out that anyone can adopt a horse if the person has enough land for the horse to live on and pays the $125 adoption fee. We all went to the adoption center and helped Gretchen pick out Stardust. She liked Stardust because of her black and white color. She has a race, or a narrow white stripe down the center of her face, and a star, or a white patch, on her forehead. When we got Stardust she was undernourished and sad. Now she is fattened up and friendly.

Everyone in our family enjoys our new member. Now I want to adopt a wild horse of my own!

SOCIAL-RITUAL SPEECHES

> It's a pleasure to see you all here tonight . . .
>
> I am here to nominate . . .
>
> Thank you for this award, which . . .

Introductory comments such as these signal a social-ritual speech, which is a common speaking-listening experience. A **social-ritual speech** is a special kind of speech to inform. It follows a set formula or pattern. Although you may never campaign for president of the United States or accept an Oscar for your movie roles, you will probably give some social-ritual speeches, and you will no doubt listen to many of them.

Some of the common social-ritual speeches are introducing a speaker, welcoming the audience, presenting awards, accepting awards, nominating a person, making announcements, relating stories, and delivering eulogies. Success in giving each of these speeches depends on your ability to be brief, clear, and enthusiastic or sincere.

JOURNAL ENTRY

I am working toward becoming an Eagle Scout and, as part of my preparation, I must lead many meetings and act as the chairperson of many big troop events. I am often called upon to announce upcoming events, introduce a Court of Honor, thank a speaker, or tell a story about our camping trip. I used to be very nervous, but after you have to keep repeating these short speeches you become much more comfortable. These experiences also helped me earn the public-speaking badge.

A discussion of each type of social-ritual speech follows.

Curricular Connection
Language Arts

Ask students to write a journal entry, similar to the one on this page, in which they describe a social-ritual speech they may have given. Alternatively, they might describe a social-ritual speech they have heard or that they will soon have to give.

385

Learning Styles

Audio-Visual Learning

● If you have access to audiovisual equipment, record any student social-ritual speeches on videotape. Student speeches may consist of any type of social-ritual speech, not to exceed one minute. After each student has taken his or her turn in front of the camera, play back the speeches for the class and encourage class and self-feedback about the presentation.

Introductions

The goals of an introduction speech are to give the audience information about the speaker and to create a positive attitude about the speaker. When introducing a speaker, you need to give the speaker's name and title, tell something about the speaker's experience, and describe why the listeners will find the speech interesting or valuable. The following is an example of an introduction:

> Today we have with us one of the most outstanding doctors in our community, Dr. Jerry Wilson. Dr. Wilson has practiced medicine in Riverdale for fourteen years. He has a special interest in nutrition, and he volunteers at a drop-in center for teenagers. He is here to discuss with us the problem of starvation diets—a problem that is increasing among young people. It is with a great deal of pleasure that I present to you Dr. Jerry Wilson.

Welcomes

The goal of a welcoming speech is to make audience members feel comfortable and prepared for what is to follow. When giving

A student speaker may welcome parents to graduation.

Unit 4 Public Communication

Substitute Teacher Tip

Have students work in pairs. One student should write an Academy-Award presentation speech for the partner. The award can be for any category usually honored at the Academy Awards, and the speaker should make up the name of the film. Tell the presenters to limit the speech to a minute. The recipient of the award should then give an acceptance speech limited to 30 seconds. Give students some time to rehearse their speeches, and have them present their speeches to the rest of the class during the course of several days.

Amazing Fact!

At the 1998 Academy Awards show in Hollywood, Oscar winners were asked to restrict their acceptance speeches to 30 seconds or less in order to keep the show moving along quickly.

this speech you need to express pleasure at seeing the listeners, and briefly describe the event to come. The following is an example of a welcoming speech:

> Good evening and welcome to the Hennepin School's Annual Musical Review. This year it is titled, "Songs Across the States." We have enjoyed preparing this show for you and hope you will have a wonderful evening. Sit back and enjoy the show!

Award Presentations

The goal of an award-presentation speech is to honor someone who has done something special. When giving an award you must describe the award, tell why the winner deserves it, name the winner, and hand out the award.

If the audience knows who is going to receive the award, you can name the winner early in your speech. If the winner is a surprise, name the person at the end of the speech. The following is an example of a surprise award-presentation speech:

> It seems right that we should be presenting the award for Outstanding Speech Student of the Year today on the birthday of John F. Kennedy, one of the greatest speakers in our country's history. The Forensics Team presents this award every year to the student who has contributed the most to the team in terms of team spirit as well as success at tournaments. Our award this year goes to Eduardo Romero.

If you hand out the award, shake the winner's hand with your right hand and present the award with your left hand.

Acceptance Speeches

Expressing appreciation at receiving an award or honor is the goal of an acceptance speech. When delivering this speech, you need to thank the person or organization who gave the award, tell why the award is important to you, and express how you feel about receiving it. You also should thank anyone who helped you attain the award and then receive the award; that is, pick

Learning Styles

Kinesic Learning

▼ Have students work in pairs to nonverbally model presenting and accepting an award. They should first decide what the award is (big check, little check, plaque, key to the city, statue, knighthood, and so on) and then decide who is giving the award (England's queen, a president of a country, a celebrity, a religious leader, school principal, and so on).Have each partner take a turn playing both the recipient and the presenter.

Skill Development

Making Conversation

● Encourage students to share any experiences they have had in giving or accepting awards. Ask students to describe how their emotional reactions affected their speeches.

387

Skill Development

Feedback

● Encourage students to present their revised speeches from the Apply activity to the rest of the class and ask for listener feedback.

up the trophy or certificate. The following is an example of an acceptance speech:

> It is an honor to receive the Liberty Essay Award. I wish to thank the members of the Kiwanis Club and my English teacher, Mrs. Evelyn Klein. My grandfather came here as an immigrant from Hungary in 1943. I am pleased to have the chance to share his life story through this essay. Thank you.

Nominations

The goal of a nominating speech is to support someone running for office and to convince the listeners to vote for this person. The person may be running for an office in school, in a club, or in a social organization. When making a nomination, you must name the candidate and the office, describe the candidate's qualifications for the office, and express your hope that the listeners will vote for this person. The following is an example of a nominating speech:

> It is my pleasure to nominate Megan Murray for class treasurer. Megan has worked on the school athletic committee. She was in charge of the money for the Haywood School Car Wash last spring. She is also a good math student. I know Megan Murray is honest and will be accurate in keeping accounts. I hope you will support Megan at election time on Tuesday.

APPLY

Select one of the previous types of social-ritual speeches and imagine a situation in which you might deliver such a speech. Write a version and deliver it out loud to a partner. Ask for feedback on how the language could be clearer or stronger, or more effective. Rewrite the speech making these changes.

6 6A story must be
exceptional enough to
justify its telling.**9 9**

THOMAS HARDY
entry in notebook, 1893

Skill Development

Active Listening

● Have students write and deliver
announcements on topics of their
choice. Ask the class to write down
the information relating to who,
what, when, where, and why.

Links to Past Learning

Have volunteers talk about the last
time they told a story in front of a
group of people. Ask: What, if
anything, would you do differently if
you were to tell the story again?

Announcements

When making announcements, the goal is to give important
information or directions to the audience. When you make an
announcement you usually give information about who, what,
when, where, or why. The following is an example of an effective
announcement:

> Hungry? Come to the Wallace School Student Council bake sale
> on Saturday, February 16, from 9:00 A.M. to noon, in the Commons.
> We will use the money we raise for the Homecoming Dance.

Stories

A speaker may be asked to relate a story in order to give the
audience background on a certain occasion or to capture a
funny, moving, or important moment from a larger experience.
A speaker may be asked to tell the story of the founding of an
organization or program, or to tell the story of something funny
or important that happened during a school trip or an event.
When telling a story, you need to describe the background of the
event, relate the main points in order, and create a clear and
memorable ending. The following is an example of a story that
relates background:

> In 1954 this land was cornfields, but there was a vision in the eyes
> of Elinor and Asher Levinson that said this land could be a special
> place for families to come together for fun and for growth. This
> couple began a community campaign to build a recreational and
> educational center that would house athletic events, theatre pro-
> ductions, and classes. By 1956 a gymnasium was built and the first
> basketball games were played. My father was on that first team.
> Every few years a new wing was added to this building, which has
> become the heart of our community. Tonight we honor the
> Levinsons who have contributed so much to all of our lives. And I
> wish to add that in this gym, last week, I beat my father at basket-
> ball for the first time. Great things have happened in this building!

Limited English Proficiency

Mention that sometimes social-ritual speeches turn out to be impromptu speeches, especially if a scheduled speaker does not appear. Ask students what steps they would follow if they had to make an impromptu announcement or present an award to fill in for an absent speaker.

Curricular Connection

Language Arts

▲ Some students might like to try their hand at writing a eulogy. They could choose as the subject of the eulogy a family pet. They should write about a recently deceased friend or relative only if they feel able to do so.

Sometimes a person is called upon to entertain an audience by telling original or fictional stories. This type of storytelling is discussed in Chapter 17.

Eulogies

A **eulogy** is a speech given to honor a person who has died. Even as a young person you may find yourself at the funeral or memorial service of someone you cared deeply about and you may be asked to say a few words about that person. This may be a friend who died at a young age or a grandparent who died. Eulogies usually include a description of how the speaker knew the person who died and a positive description of the person's life and actions. When Yhitzak Rabin, Prime Minister of Israel, was killed in 1995 many world leaders spoke at his funeral. But the most moving tribute to his life came from his 17-year-old granddaughter, Noa Ben-Artzi Philosof, who spoke the following words:

> Grandfather, you were the pillar of fire in front of the camp and now we are left in the camp alone, in the dark; and we are so cold and sad. I know that people talk in terms of a national tragedy, and of comforting an entire nation, but we feel the huge void that remains in your absence when grandmother doesn't stop crying . . .

> Others greater than I have already eulogized you, but none of them ever had the pleasure I had to feel the caresses of your warm, soft hands, to merit your warm embrace that was reserved only for us, to see your half-smile that always told me so much, that same smile which is no longer, frozen in the grave with you . . .

Although these are very difficult speeches to deliver, the speaker may find it is an important way to say good-bye to a special person and to deal with the grief.

Social-ritual speeches tend to be brief and patterned. It is important to be familiar with the expectations of each type so that you can develop an appropriate and effective speech for a particular occasion.

Evaluating

● To illustrate the point about how listeners can affect a speaker, ask whether any students have had the experience of telling a joke at which no one laughed. Have them compare this experience to that of telling a joke and having everyone respond by laughing appreciatively. What was the difference in how the speakers felt?

Skill Development

Media Literacy

Ask: Why do television situation comedies sometimes have recorded audience laughter? Is it intended to make the comedy seem funnier? Does it?

INTERACT

In a small group, prepare an imaginary social-ritual speech. The situations listed below may help you choose a situation. Now create two presentations—one on video and one as a speech to an audience. Ask class members to serve as the audience for both formats.

Nominate someone for president of the French club.

Accept an award for outstanding speech student.

Introduce the mayor at a school assembly.

Announce the school musical, *Oklahoma!*

Welcome parents and community members to the school science fair.

After the presentations compare the two formats. Ask questions such as the following:

Which format conveyed the information most accurately? Why?

Which format had more audience appeal? Why?

Under what future conditions would you choose to use video rather than a direct speech?

EVALUATING INFORMATIVE SPEECHES

Public speaking is two-way communication. Although you may not talk much, as a listener you do affect the speaker. Have you ever watched a performer respond to the audience? When the audience claps or laughs, the performer seems to get more energy. When the audience does not respond, the performer seems to have less energy. Listener feedback can change a speech.

A listener may give informal or formal feedback to a speaker. **Informal feedback** consists of verbal and nonverbal messages given spontaneously to the speaker. The listener is giving the

391

❝Never demean yourself
by talking back to a critic,
never. Write those letters to
the editor in your head, but
don't put them on paper.❞

TRUMAN CAPOTE

Curricular Connection

Art

● Students might enjoy working
together to create comic strips
illustrating formal and informal
feedback.

Skill Development

Feedback

Tell students that what seems like
informal feedback may not be true
feedback at all but the result of a
poor audience. Listeners who think
they do not want to hear what the
speaker has to say, who talk to each
other, appear to be asleep, read, do
homework, or make comments while
a speaker is talking are exhibiting
poor audience behavior. Many
speakers encounter this type of
audience behavior with young people
as well as with adults. Ask students to
suggest some causes for this behavior
and to imagine how they would feel if
they encountered this type of
audience when they were speaking.
What would they do?

speaker a personal response. **Formal feedback** consists of planned
written or oral comments. They are intended to affect the speaker's
next speech.

Informal Feedback

How does a teacher in a large class know whether the students are
bored or interested? How does someone speaking to a group of
ten know how the audience members feel? Audience feedback tells
speakers how they are doing. This feedback may come during or
after the speech. There are various kinds of positive and negative
feedback a speaker may receive from groups of different sizes.

Speakers try to read the audience's feedback during the speech.
In a small group, they may be able to see all the faces clearly.
When speaking to a large group, they may see only blurred faces
in row after row of seats. The size of the audience affects the
kinds of positive and negative feedback a speaker receives.

Feedback during a speech affects what speakers do next. If audience members look bored, yawn, or squirm around, a good speaker
will make a change. He or she may speak more loudly, ask a question, or start to use more gestures. A poor speaker will not change
anything. If the poor speaker gets nervous, he or she may use
more "ums" and "ahs" and try to finish the speech quickly.

Informal feedback
may come
immediately
after a speech.

392

Amazing Fact!

The Chautauqua movement, which was founded after the Civil War at Chautauqua Lake in southwestern New York state, sponsors informational lectures and other adult educational programs in the U.S. In 1924, at the height of its popularity, the movement boasted over 400 "Chautauquas" across the country that played host to visiting lecturers.

SPEAKING OF . . .

REBECCA CARLTON

After 72 hours of Red Cross training in peer education, Rebecca Carlton took her place as an instructor for the AIDS Coalition. As a student at New Trier High School in Illinois, Rebecca now co-chairs this group, which is dedicated to AIDS education in the schools. Although some of Rebecca's time is spent planning fund-raisers and food drives or recruiting adult speakers, most of her efforts are directed toward speaking to gym classes about AIDS. Peer educators like Rebecca present scenarios in which the AIDS infection risk is present. In addition, they answer factual questions about AIDS and HIV. Some of the students think they know all about AIDS or think that AIDS would not affect "our community." They wonder why they need to listen to another presentation. Rebecca responds that "AIDS/HIV is spreading, and if people knew how bad it was, AIDS wouldn't be spread anymore."

Recently Rebecca had to address the local Rotary Club to ask them for support for outside speakers. This occasion meant dressing up in more formal clothes, maintaining good eye contact with the audience members, describing the importance of the group's mission, and talking informally with members after the speech. In order to maintain a high level of group effort, the members meet regularly to discuss their current activities, to plan for future projects, and to consider suggestions for improving the program. Rebecca frequently chairs these meetings.

Rebecca uses a range of communication skills in her work as co-chair of the AIDS coalition. She may use these skills in her future career, especially if she finds her future in medicine, pharmaceuticals, health education, or community development.

66I like criticism, but it must be my way.**99**

MARK TWAIN

Cooperative Learning

● Encourage the class to discuss their impressions from the Observe activity.

Skill Development

Feedback

Correctly identifying an audience's need to know will have a direct effect on the feedback one receives. Ask students how they might present a topic such as nutrition, AIDS awareness, or another topic that might personally affect audience members and about which they probably *should* know but feel no need to know.

If, on the other hand, the members of an audience look interested, smile, or nod, a good speaker will respond by becoming more relaxed. He or she may look directly at the audience more often or tell an extra joke or story. A poor speaker will not use the feedback.

Sometimes the feedback after a speech affects the speaker's next speech. A comment such as "I enjoyed the poetry you included in the speech" may encourage a speaker to use poetry again. If someone said, "You used so many statistics I thought I was in math class," the speaker may try to cut down on the use of numbers in future speeches.

Sometimes feedback comes in the form of questions or comments about the topic. For example, a question like "Where can I learn more about magic?" tells the speaker the audience member was interested in the speech. Some comments will tell a speaker that the audience goal was reached. For example, the speaker's goal might be for listeners to learn the three things to look for when buying sport shoes. If a listener says, "My new shoes fit your three requirements of cost, support, and strength," the speaker knows the goal has been reached. Competent speakers pay close attention to the feedback they receive during and after a speech. They use the feedback to become even better speakers.

OBSERVE

Watch someone giving a talk or lecture for fifteen minutes. Record in detail the verbal and nonverbal feedback the audience gives the speaker. Note yawns, smiles, and groans. Describe what changes, if any, the speaker made as a result of the feedback.

Formal Feedback

I enjoyed your stories, but I had trouble finding your main points.

You looked directly at the audience, so I felt as if you were talking to me.

There were times when I got lost because I did not understand some of the words you used.

394

Motivation

Have students bring in some newspaper reviews of movies, plays, books, or concerts, and have the class analyze these materials. Do they contain any constructive criticism? You may want to help students make a distinction between reviews and critiques.

These are the words of a critic. What does the word *critic* mean to you? Many people think a critic is someone who finds fault. They see a critic as someone who only looks for problems or negative things. Actually a **critic** is a person who judges or evaluates. As a critic, you make judgments of both strengths and weaknesses and look for ways to improve a speech. In other words, you give speakers feedback. The formal feedback given by a critic is called a **critique**. A competent critic gives helpful, useful critiques of speeches.

Learning to Critique

There are four reasons for learning to be a competent critic. As you learn how to be a competent critic you will (1) develop appreciation for speechmaking, (2) become a better listener, (3) improve your own speaking, and (4) help others become better speakers.

A competent critic develops appreciation for speechmaking and knows there is a difference between just talking and talking with a purpose. It takes skill to gather information, organize it, analyze an audience, and adapt the materials to fit that audience. It also takes skill to deliver the speech and adapt to audience feedback.

A competent critic becomes a better listener. As you develop your ability to analyze and critique speeches, you will become a smarter consumer of speeches. You will listen to public speeches more carefully in your everyday life.

You can improve your own speaking by observing the strengths and weaknesses of other speakers as well as your own. Suppose you say to a classmate, "You never looked at us." This comment reminds you to work on eye contact in your own public speaking.

As you give feedback to speakers, you can help them improve their performances. You may make comments such as, "I could not tell when you moved to the third point" or "I thought your gestures helped show what you thought was important." Your feedback tells the speaker what could be improved and what worked well.

Links to Past Learning

Ask students to talk about times when they have received feedback that was not helpful. Remind them that positive feedback is not always constructive.

Beyond the Classroom

Tell students that when comedians perform but can't make an audience laugh, they call the experience "dying." Ask the class why this expression most likely came into being. Continue the discussion by asking students if any of them have had the experience of "dying."

Formal feedback should focus on strengths as well as weaknesses.

Becoming a Constructive Critic

Constructive criticism tells the speaker what worked well, what could be improved, and how to improve. The following are some guidelines for giving constructive criticism:

1. *Be specific.* Don't say, "Your speech was good." Instead, tell the speaker exactly what was good—the evidence, the organization, the visual aids, or the delivery. Use specific examples from the speech.

2. *Establish some criteria.* Consider the speaker's purpose. That will help you focus your comments. If the speech is a type of social-ritual speech, you can begin by asking yourself whether the speech contained the necessary parts.

3. *Describe what you saw and heard.* Don't jump in with comments such as "Your eye contact was great." Say instead, "You looked at everyone in the audience. It made me feel like you were talking to me." Don't say, "The ending was bad." Say instead, "There was no conclusion. The speech stopped at the last point. You need to remind us of the main points at the end."

4. *Limit your points.* Don't tell the speaker five things you liked, eight things you did not like, and six ways to improve. Select only the most important things.

5. *Discuss both strengths and weaknesses.* Critics too often focus on the negative. You need to point out what worked. This tells the speaker to continue doing what worked. In giving a balanced critique of the speaker's voice, you could say, "I could hear you easily in the back of the room. Keep up the good volume. However, you did not use pauses when you moved from one point to another. Stop at the end of an idea to let the audience think about it before you move on." Avoid making someone feel bad.

6. *Suggest improvements.* Suggest what the speaker could do to make the next speech better. Remember to be specific. You might say, "In your next speech, use more variety in your voice. Changing your rate or pitch might help us stay interested" or "Try not to lean on the desk. It's distracting to the audience."

> **REMEMBER:**
> **Guidelines for Giving Constructive Criticism**
>
> 1. Be specific.
>
> 2. Establish criteria for criticism.
>
> 3. Describe what you saw and heard.
>
> 4. Limit the points of criticism.
>
> 5. Discuss strengths and weaknesses.
>
> 6. Suggest improvements.

A critic's feedback is intended to help the speaker. As a critic, you should be supportive and note the strong as well as the weak points in a speech. Always discuss the weak points in a constructive way. Some critics like to follow this pattern: (1) describe what worked well, (2) describe one or two problem areas, and (3) make a suggestion for improvement of the next speech.

Critical Thinking
Evaluating

● Have students use the guidelines for constructive criticism to evaluate their own critiques of others' work. Each student should select the guideline that refers to his or her area of greatest weakness. Students can write a goal for acquiring more skill as a critic.

Skill Development
On the Job

Have students work together as a class to create a list of jobs that require a person to give feedback much of the time. To start the discussion you might mention teachers, coaches, construction bosses, orchestra conductors, and directors of plays.

397

Skill Development

Feedback

● Some people have a hard time accepting even the most constructive criticism. Tell students that the more often they are in a position to hear feedback and criticism, the easier it will be for them to respond in an effective, positive manner.

APPLY

Read the following feedback comments and decide which ones a speaker would not find helpful.

1. I liked your speech a lot.

2. I could not hear you when you described the painting. Be sure to talk loudly enough.

3. It was boring.

4. You looked at everyone in the audience, so it felt like you were talking to us.

5. You were really great.

As you might guess, comments 1, 3, and 5 really do not help a speaker. Although number 1 and number 5 are positive, they are not specific. The speaker might ask, "What did you like?" or "What was great?" A comment such as "It was boring" leaves a speaker feeling bad. If you could give some suggestions to make the speech more interesting, these might help the speaker.

Accepting Constructive Criticism

In addition to giving feedback, competent communicators accept and use feedback from others. Accepting constructive criticism is not easy. Speakers need to think about what was said, decide if the comments are valid or useful, and then reply. Frequently speakers just defend what they said or did and do not hear the suggestions for improvement. These guidelines can help speakers benefit from constructive criticism:

1. *Listen carefully.* Find out what specific points of your performance the other person is criticizing. Don't start planning your reply while the other person is talking.

2. *Get tips.* Ask the other person for specific suggestions for improvement.

3. *Think before defending yourself.* Do not immediately defend your actions. You do not need to make excuses. It is all right to

Learning Styles
Kinesic Learning

● Remind students that when they are in the position of accepting constructive criticism, body language is an important part of the process. Have individual students model open, accepting body language and closed, defensive body language.

66A critic is a necessary evil, and criticism is an evil necessity.**99**

CAROLYN WELLS

make mistakes, because mistakes help you learn. If you have been acting according to certain rules or standards, you should explain those. Otherwise, stay silent for a moment and think about whether the criticism is true. You might say you will take time to think about an idea or suggestion.

4. *Try it out.* Try to correct key points in your performance according to the critic's suggestions. Then ask in a friendly way whether you are doing what he or she suggested. For example, ask "Is this closer to what you had in mind?"

5. *Double-check the criticism.* If you have real doubts about whether a person's criticism is justified, check it with someone else. This second person should understand the problem and be objective. Don't ask a friend who will tell you only what you want to hear.

6. *Practice the whole speech.* Work in the changes and create a smooth presentation. Ask for feedback on the new version of the speech.

Skill Development
Feedback

● Tell students that when they have prepared and rehearsed a speech, it is sometimes a good idea to create a list of questions they would like the audience to be able to answer as a result of having heard the speech.

REMEMBER:
Guidelines for Accepting Constructive Criticism

1. Listen carefully.

2. Get tips.

3. Think before defending yourself.

4. Try out suggestions.

5. Double-check the criticism.

6. Practice the entire speech with changes.

The feedback process is a critical part of communication. If you want to reach your audience goals, you have to know how you are doing. Formal and informal constructive feedback helps you reach these goals.

399

Curricular Connection

Language Arts

● Have students respond to the journal entry on this page by writing a journal entry about their own experiences with various forms of rehearsal. Encourage them to write about what technique works best for them, as well as those techniques that they have found to be less successful.

Accepting constructive criticism is an important part of learning to be an effective speaker.

JOURNAL ENTRY

I used to practice my speeches in front of a mirror, but I never really finished the speech and I never saw many problems. Now I do my speech in front of my mother. She is able to give me some helpful suggestions and point out places where I am not clear. You really need feedback from an audience member to know how you are coming across.

Feedback Forms

Sometimes it's hard to remember what you want to tell a speaker. At other times it is hard to remember what others tell you. During speeches many listeners use feedback forms, or critique forms, to give information to a speaker. The sample forms on pages 401 and 402 can help you give useful feedback to a speaker. Form A allows you to describe the parts of the speech that worked well, the parts that did not work as well, and provides an

"A good critic is the sorcerer that makes some hidden spring gush forth unexpectedly under our feet."

FRANÇOIS MAURIAC

Beyond the Classroom

▲ Some students might enjoy tailoring the evaluation forms on pages 401 and 402 to fit other forms of criticism such as film, music, and book reviews.

area for improvement. Form B allows you to rate each area of the speech on a scale of 1 to 3. One means excellent, 2 means good, and 3 means improvement is needed. Explanations for your ratings can be written in the Comments section.

When you evaluate a social-ritual speech, you may use the same type of feedback form that you use for the speech to inform. You can add the very specific parts of the set pattern for the social-ritual speech. For example, when evaluating a speech to introduce a speaker, include the following on your form: (1) the speaker's name and title, (2) a description of the speaker's experience, and (3) an explanation of why listeners should be interested in the speech.

Pay careful attention to the feedback process in public speaking. Responding to feedback can make the difference between a good speech and a great speech.

Evaluation Form: Informative Speech Feedback (A)

Speaker's Name _____

Speaker's Topic _____

The parts of your speech that worked were:
  Example: The introduction got my attention.

The parts of your speech that did not work as well were:
  Example: The speech ended with the last point. There
      was no conclusion.

In your next speech, I'd like you to:
  Example: Tie your conclusion to the introduction.

401

Evaluation Form: Informative Speech Feedback (B)

Speaker's Name _____

Speaker's Topic _____

Factors	Excellent	Good	Needs Improvement	Comments
1. Clear Purpose Statement	1	2	3	_____
2. Introduction				
Gained attention	1	2	3	_____
Appropriate to audience and occasion	1	2	3	_____
3. Body				
Main points well organized	1	2	3	_____
Supporting materials varied	1	2	3	_____
Transitions clear	1	2	3	_____
4. Delivery				
Eye contact with audience	1	2	3	_____
Movement, gestures supported ideas	1	2	3	_____
Voice clear and loud enough	1	2	3	_____
5. Language				
Difficult words explained	1	2	3	_____
Appropriate use of repetition/figures of speech	1	2	3	_____
6. Conclusion				
Summarized ideas	1	2	3	_____
7. Visual Aids				
Visual aids support purpose	1	2	3	_____

● Students could show their understanding of the chapter content by making short informative speeches. Listeners should fill out evaluation forms for each classmate's speech.

CHAPTER 13 SUMMARY

This chapter described the principles, presentation, and evaluation of speeches to inform, including social-ritual speeches. Set patterns for eight social-ritual speeches were presented: (1) speaker introductions, (2) welcoming an audience, (3) award presentations, (4) acceptance speeches, (5) nominations, (6) announcements, (7) relating stories, and (8) eulogies. Also discussed was the importance of giving and accepting feedback, including some specific ways to provide formal feedback by using critique forms.

403

Answers

Think About It

Student answers will vary. Here are sample answers:

1. Need to know, connections, organization, repetition, feelings, and focus

2. (1) Introductions: give the speaker's name and title, tell about the speaker's experience, and describe why the listeners will find the speech interesting or valuable. (2) Welcomes: express pleasure at seeing the listeners and briefly describe the event to come. (3) Award presentation: describe the award, tell why the winner deserves it, name the winner, and hand out the award.

3. Informal feedback can be verbal or nonverbal. It might consist of listener reactions such as laughing, yawning, and slouching. Or, it might come in the form of questions to the speaker about certain aspects of the content of the speech. Formal feedback is a judgment or evaluation of a speech. It is given in the form of a critique.

CHAPTER REVIEW

Think About It

1. What are the six principles for informing?

2. Describe the steps of three social-ritual speeches.

3. Distinguish between informal and formal feedback.

4. Describe constructive criticism and list guidelines for giving criticism.

5. List guidelines for accepting criticism.

Try It Out

1. Bring a magazine advertisement to class. Explain how your advertisement uses principles of informing.

2. Critique a classmate's informative speech, using a feedback form. In addition, give an oral evaluation following the guidelines for constructive criticism. Then ask for feedback on your critiquing skills.

3. Read the speech titled "533-12 Freeze," parts of which you read in Chapter 12. Answer the following questions:

    How did the speaker attempt to get the listeners' attention?

    How effective was his introduction?

    What feelings were conveyed through this speech?

    How do you imagine this speech was delivered in the classroom?

    How did the speaker use his language to help create mental pictures in the listeners' minds?

533-12 Freeze
Matt Wilkinson

". . .the ball is snapped. Reeder drops back to pass. There's Wilkinson down the sidelines; he has his man beat. The ball is caught by Wilkinson, and he's dragged out of bounds after a gain of forty yards."

To me catching a pass is like hitting a home run and trotting around the bases; it's my time to shine. I love to catch passes. I want some kind of machine that could throw passes to me every day, but I have to wait until the football season starts to do it. Every time I catch a ball all the bad things that happened are all gone. I get high catching passes.

When it comes game time, all I think about is catching passes. The pre-game routine points toward the next three hours of competition. Ten minutes of catching footballs gets me ready for my chance to get in the game. I try to get the fundamentals oiled, so right from the opening kickoff, I'm ready to do my part. Once the game starts I'm totally into it. After seemingly hours of anxious waiting the coach calls, "Wilkinson, get over here," and tells me to get ready to go in. The play: 533-12 Freeze. As I tell the quarterback, he smiles. He loves pass plays. When I run up to the line of scrimmage, I notice that the defense is playing perfectly to our advantage for this play. My confidence grows as our quarterback barks, "Set." The instant after the ball is hiked I begin my journey between the opposing jerseys that stand between me and my goal. I go around the outside linebacker and start up field into the stretch of green grass between the cornerback and the free safety. There are no more opposing jerseys in my way, just me and the ultimate prize: six points. I turn my head but I see nothing but a little piece of leather on the horizon. As the ball comes over the skyline of linemen and into clear view, my legs shift into cruise-control. My eyes lock onto the perfectly spinning oval as it reaches the height of its flight, and my arms become hard driving pistons pushing me closer to where the tight spiral will make its floating descent out of the sky and into my hands. I lick my lips and smile as I watch the ball into my hands, right on stride! All I hear is myself repeating, "Yes, Yes, YES!" The ball feels warm to the touch. The words WILSON PRO 2000 engraved in the cowhide and the eight white laces send a tingling to my fingers as I pull it in and tightly tuck it under my arm.

After I've got the ball where I want it, my body turns toward the majestic goal posts that sit in the middle of where I'd most like to be, the place on the field that will pay me back for all the time I've spent practicing. Getting there just once would make all that hard work, sweat, and pain worthwhile. Although I've caught many passes, I still haven't made it into the end zone. So, I will be working hard until that day comes when the perfect spiral will guide me into the center of where my dreams will become a reality. But until then, the night before every game

will be spent dreaming about those few seconds of complete joy I will feel when I finally step across the goal line and hear the announcer bellow, "Touchdown, Evanston!"

Put It in Writing

1. Think of an occasion when you benefited from constructive criticism. This criticism may have been given to help you improve a sports skill, study habits, your performance in a group, or your appearance. Write three paragraphs describing the criticism, your reaction to it, and the ways in which you changed your behavior in response to it.

2. In your journal, keep track of the informative speeches you hear during a week. Note the speaker's name, the topic of the speech and a brief description of the speech. Write a two-paragraph evaluation of one of the informative speeches, using the guidelines of constructive criticism.

Speak About It

1. In a group of four students, have each person deliver a different social-ritual speech. The specific parts of the speech should be distinct enough for listeners to recognize. Listeners should identify any missing parts and help that speaker develop information for those parts.

2. Prepare and deliver a presentation speech for one of the following:

    The trophy for the varsity football team's most valuable player

    A certificate for first prize in your school's science fair

4. Constructive criticism tells the speaker what worked, what didn't, and how the speech might be improved. Guidelines: (1) Be specific. (2) Establish some criteria. (3) Describe what you saw and heard. (4) Limit your points. (5) Discuss both strengths and weaknesses. (6) Suggest improvements.

5. (1) Listen carefully. (2) Get tips. (3) Think before defending yourself. (4) Try out suggestions. (5) Double-check criticism.

Quick Check

Ask students to find and define these Key Terms:

connected information (379)

constructive criticism (396)

critic (395)

critique (395)

eulogy (390)

formal feedback (392)

informal feedback (391)

informative speech (378)

social-ritual speech (385)

Motivation

Ask students to think about the times in their lives that they try to persuade someone or that someone tries to persuade them. Write some examples on the chalkboard.

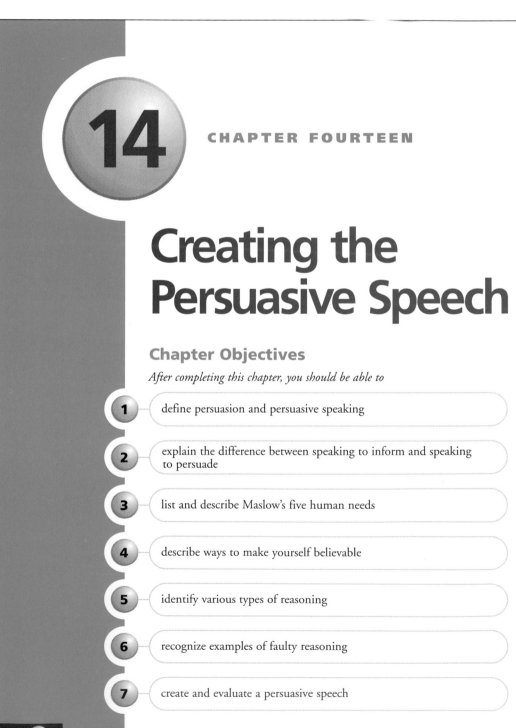

14

CHAPTER FOURTEEN

Creating the Persuasive Speech

Chapter Objectives

After completing this chapter, you should be able to

1. define persuasion and persuasive speaking

2. explain the difference between speaking to inform and speaking to persuade

3. list and describe Maslow's five human needs

4. describe ways to make yourself believable

5. identify various types of reasoning

6. recognize examples of faulty reasoning

7. create and evaluate a persuasive speech

	Day 1	Day 2	Day 3	Day 4	Day 5
Chapter 14 Planner Week 14	Organizing a Persuasive Speech	Organizing a Persuasive Speech	Evaluating Persuasive Speeches	Chapter Review	Chapter Review
			Summary		
	Teacher's Resource Book				
	Teaching Suggestions		14.8		
	Worksheets & Eval. Forms		45		
					Chapter Test 14
	Workbook 14.6				

Links to Past Learning

Ask students to tell which type of speech—informative or persuasive—is more likely to require sound reasoning.

⊙ Key Terms

bandwagon appeal

card stacking

cause-effect reasoning

deductive reasoning

ethical decisions

faulty reasoning

glittering generalities

impact

inductive reasoning

name calling

persuasion

persuasive speaking

testimonials

unrelated testimonials

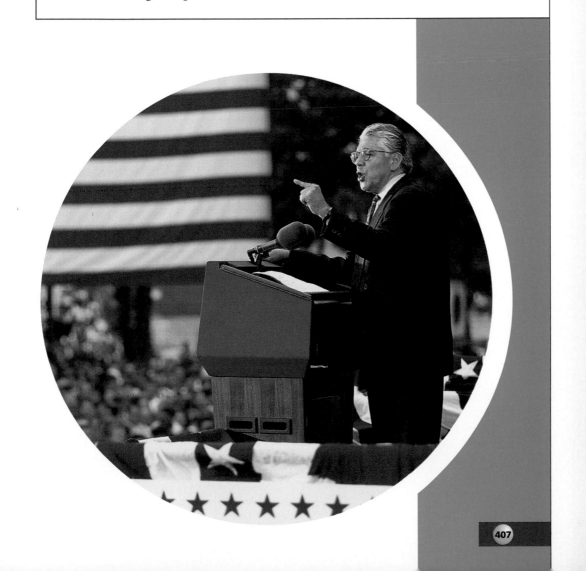

Skill Development
Quick Skill Opportunity

● Ask volunteers to make brief persuasive statements like those on this page on a topic of their choice. Have the class give feedback as to which statement was the most persuasive.

Skill Development
Media Literacy

● Remind students that all media rely to some extent on persuasion. Tell them that one succinct form of persuasive tactic is the bumper sticker. Have students create their own bumper-sticker slogans that they think would persuade people to take a stand on a topic that students feel strongly about.

What is similar about each of the three following messages?

Ms. Garcia, may we have another day to study for the history test? We already had an English and math test today.

I ask all of you to be non-smokers. Give it up if you've started; avoid it if you've never started. The life you save will be your own.

The book *Beyond the Classroom*, based on a study of 200,000 students, reports that nearly 20 percent of students said they do not try as hard as they could in school because they are worried what their friends might think. It's time for this kind of attitude to change!

Each of the statements above involves persuasion. **Persuasion** is the communication process of changing a listener's beliefs or moving a listener to action. Every day, you send and receive persuasive messages in conversation and in speeches. You receive a large number of messages through the media. You may be trying to influence someone else, or someone may be trying to influence you. Persuasion is a complicated process. Some people are easily persuaded while others are not.

SPEAKING TO PERSUADE

Whenever you try to convince others of certain beliefs or of the need for certain actions, you are using persuasion. Whenever you talk to an audience to convince the listeners of certain beliefs or of the need to take certain actions, you are involved in persuasive speaking.

Much of what you learned about informative speeches also applies to persuasive speeches. This chapter focuses on **persuasive speaking** and covers these subjects: (1) selecting a persuasive topic; (2) adapting to the audience; (3) making yourself believable; (4) using reasoning; (5) organizing a persuasive speech; and (6) evaluating persuasive speeches. Each of these subjects is part of a process of ethical decision making.

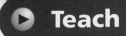

Skill Development

Media Literacy

● Bring in a copy of the local newspaper. Display the front page and ask students which story's headline has the most impact from a visual standpoint. Then ask which story has the most impact from a content perspective.

The Ethics Issue

A persuasive speaker is often faced with decisions that have to do with questions of right and wrong. These are known as moral or **ethical decisions**. Persuasive speakers attempt to change the listeners' minds or move the listeners to action. A persuasive speaker may be tempted to talk about only one side of an issue in order to persuade the listeners to think or act in a certain way. In order to build a strong case, unethical persuaders ignore or avoid information that does not support their point of view. They do not conduct research that will help them see the whole picture. Ethical persuaders, however, do not ignore one side of an issue. Instead they consider both sides, acknowledge what might be important points on the opposing side, and then try to convince the listeners of why their position is stronger.

In every step of the persuasion process you will be faced with an ethical issue. You will have to ask yourself whether you have looked at all sides of the issue, whether you've given your listeners all the information they need to make a good decision, and whether you have been fair in your speech development and presentation.

The Impact Issue

Persuasive speeches are intended to have a specific **impact** or major effect. You can see examples of such attempts in national and international situations. Addresses by the presidents of the United States and other world leaders are often intended to change policies or to gain support for a new legislative program. Frequently the president's annual, State of the Union address can be seen as a persuasive speech since the president tends to lay out plans for the future in order to gain support for these efforts.

President John F. Kennedy's Inaugural Address called for a new world role for the United States and contained many specific action steps. He concluded his list of challenges saying, "All this will not be finished in the first 100 days. Nor will it be finished

Critical Thinking

Analyzing

● Ask students to react to the following statements. What would they want to ask each speaker?

The new Squirrel has the largest trunk capacity of any U.S. car on the market.

Dazzle toothpaste cleans your teeth whiter.

This running shoe will provide greater support.

Shouldn't you be eating Country Corn, the number-one rated cereal in the nation?

If it's good enough for the U.S. Squid team, it should be just the right burger for you.

409

Learning Styles
Audio-Visual Learning

● Bring in videotapes of famous persuasive speakers (see the bibliography for this unit), or urge students to look for them. Excerpts from speeches by John F. Kennedy, Barbara Jordan, and Jesse Jackson would be a good starting point.

Multicultural Learning

▼ Students who have not heard Queen Elizabeth II, Winston Churchill, or Tony Blair might like to view videotapes of these or other British speakers, noting voice quality, articulation, and pronunciation.

in the first 1,000 days, nor in the life of this Administration, nor even perhaps in our lifetime on this planet. But let us begin."

Sometimes a speech that appears to have a different purpose is actually persuasive in intent. For example, after the death of Princess Diana of Britain the Royal Family was severely criticized by British citizens for remaining in seclusion and not sharing in the grief of their subjects. Many in Britain seriously questioned the importance of the monarchy. Eventually the Royal Family made a public appearance, and Queen Elizabeth delivered a televised speech, an extraordinary event in itself since it was only her second personal address to the country in 45 years.

Although the speech contained tributes to Princess Diana, the overall intent was to persuade the British people that the Royal Family felt the loss deeply and that the monarchy was in touch with the immense grief felt by the mourning citizens. The nonverbal aspects of the speech were important. The Queen delivered the speech on television in front of a window of Buckingham Palace, which overlooked the mourning crowds and mounds of flowers. This setting created a visual connection to the people outside. The verbal and nonverbal messages were intended to persuade television viewers that the queen was in touch with her subjects. The press reported that most Britons changed their negative attitudes about the Royal Family after the speech.

Your speeches may not have an impact on large numbers of people, but they have the potential to significantly affect your listeners. Profiles of effective teenage persuasive speakers are found within this text. They speak on topics such as AIDS awareness, cultural identity, and community concerns—and they have an impact.

SELECTING A PERSUASIVE TOPIC

When selecting a topic for a persuasive speech, you should find a topic that is personally important to you and about which there is disagreement. If you don't care about a topic, you will

410

❝A companion's words of
persuasion are effective.❞
HOMER

have a difficult time persuading other people that it is important. If the topic is not controversial, there is little need for a persuasive message.

Skill Development
On the Job

▼ Encourage students to think of occupations that would entail persuasive speaking. They might mention lawyers, salespeople, advertising copywriters, teachers, coaches, ministers, rabbis, and so on.

APPLY

Look at the following titles and decide which are more likely to be speeches to inform and which speeches to persuade:

1. Music Censorship: Who Is Behind It?

2. We Need to Rate Music As We Do Movies

3. The Legal Rights of the Adopted Child

4. Adopted Children Should Be Able to See Their Birth Records

5. The Rise in Missing Children

6. Children Must Be Fingerprinted for Their Safety

7. The State of America's Blood Banks

8. Every Healthy Teen Should Donate Blood

You probably named items 1, 3, 5 and 7 as possible informative topics because they suggest the speaker will present facts about the subject. Topics 2, 4, 6, and 8, on the other hand, suggest the speaker will give reasons why listeners should do something or believe something. The speaker on item 3 might inform the audience about the rights of an adopted child, without giving his or her opinion on the subject. The audience goal might be that listeners be able to explain the three main legal rights of an adopted child. The speaker on item 4, on the other hand, has taken a stand. This speaker is trying to persuade the listeners that adopted children should be able to see their birth records. This speaker is planning a persuasive speech. Thus the odd numbered topics appear informative; the even numbered topics appear persuasive. However, you would have to hear the actual speech to make final judgments.

411

Critical Thinking

Organizing

● When students have chosen a topic from the list on this page, encourage them to create a web diagram that addresses various aspects of the topic.

Learning Styles

Visual Learning

● Once students have chosen their topics, encourage them to think of visual aids they might use to make their speeches more persuasive.

Skill Development

Research

▲ Many people in the United States are employed to find out what consumers own, eat, believe, and want so that products can be targeted to specific audiences. Ask students what kind of research they could do to find out how to persuade an audience listening to a speech on a topic from this page.

A topic such as music censorship might be informative or persuasive; however, you would have to hear the actual speech to know for certain.

Here are some sample topics you might consider for persuasive speeches:

neglect of the elderly	capital punishment
school reforms	drug abuse
standardized testing in schools	missing children
nuclear weapons	vandalism
illiteracy	body piercing
fad diets	pollution
teenage alcoholism	animal rights

After you have chosen a topic for a speech, you may decide your position on the topic right away, or you may need to do research to decide what stand to take. No matter what topic you choose, be sure you and your listeners can get excited about it.

✺ INTERACT

Brainstorm as many speech topics as possible with your classmates. Then decide which topics on your list are controversial and therefore might make good persuasive speeches. Note any topics you believe will present an ethical problem.

❝A good play is a play which when acted upon the boards makes an audience interested and pleased. A play that fails in this is a bad play.**❞**

MAURICE BARING

ADAPTING TO THE AUDIENCE

How do you persuade someone to accept or consider your point of view? Look at the following situations and think of convincing arguments you could use:

1. The big party of the year is Friday night at a classmate's home. It will last long past your curfew. How can you persuade your parents to let you stay out late?

2. As chair of the social service club, you have to ask the student council for $16 a month to support a needy child in South America. How will you convince the council members to provide the money?

After thinking about these situations, what strategies did you decide to use?

In the first situation, you probably have to convince your parents that you are responsible enough to stay out late. If you describe several instances when you were responsible and trustworthy, they may be persuaded. However, your parents may have valid reasons for not letting you stay out late. Therefore, they may try to persuade you to do things their way this time.

In the second situation, you would have to convince the group that supporting the South American child is a better social project than others the club has considered. You may have to explain how the money would help the child. You could explain that the money would go to one special child whom the school would sponsor for the year. The group would receive letters saying how their child is doing.

In both situations you have to figure out how to reach your listeners. The more you know about your listeners, the easier it is to find the right messages. To become a competent persuader, you must analyze your listeners and identify their needs.

Listeners' Needs

Persuaders try to learn about their audiences so that they can appeal to needs the listeners find important. This helps speakers to plan audience goals. All human beings have similar needs.

Motivation

Before students read about Maslow's hierarchy of needs, ask them to give examples of human needs that are common to one and all. Write their examples on the chalkboard.

413

Substitute Teacher Tip

Encourage students to discuss what they feel to be their most important personal need beyond the basic needs such as food, water, clothing, and shelter.

Critical Thinking

Organizing

● Draw a copy of Maslow's pyramid of needs on the board or on an overhead. Ask students to give at least five examples of each type of need and fill in each part of the pyramid. For example, under physical needs, they might write *heat* and *water,* in addition to the things named in paragraph 2. Point out to students that as they go higher up the pyramid, the needs will become much more specific to each individual.

Psychologist Abraham Maslow created a list of human needs ranging from the most basic to the least basic. According to Maslow, people must meet their most basic needs before they are interested in satisfying higher-level needs.

Maslow's Pyramid of Needs

Physical Physical needs include basic things such as food, clothing, and housing. People need to satisfy these basic physical needs before they can worry about anything else. For example, if parents are worried about feeding their children, they probably won't be concerned about buying a laptop computer or belonging to a certain social group. Physical needs are critical to basic survival. A persuasive speaker may try to get community residents to work for a political candidate who supports community shelters or job-training programs.

Safety Safety needs include security and a belief that one's friends and family will be safe from physical harm. People need to feel safe and able to protect themselves and those they love. Insurance companies often appeal to the parents' desire to protect their child's future when trying to sell insurance. A persuasive

❝I wouldn't want to belong to any club that would accept me as a member.❞
GROUCHO MARX

speaker may try to persuade you to take a self-defense course to protect yourself. Street gangs may try to persuade people to join for safety reasons.

Belonging These include the human needs for affection and a feeling of belonging. Most people value having friends or being part of a group. Often persuaders will send the message that if you want to appear to be part of a certain group, you should dress or act like people in the group. A persuader may tell you that loyal friends never tell on each other. You may be persuaded to go to the amusement park instead of studying because you want to be part of a group.

Self-Esteem Self-esteem needs refer to the desire to feel good about yourself. These needs are met by feeling worthwhile or feeling satisfied with your accomplishments. You may be persuaded to work on the Special Olympics because you feel good about yourself when you help other people. You may be persuaded to compete in a race or a dance contest to prove how fast or how graceful you really are. Persuaders try to discover what makes listeners feel good about themselves, and they appeal to those self-esteem needs.

Cooperative Learning

● Encourage students to break into discussion groups to talk about the effect of peer pressure on the need to belong and on the desire for self-esteem. Ask students to relate the discussion to reasons why people join gangs.

Self-esteem and self-actualization are higher-level needs in Maslow's hierarchy.

Multicultural Learning

● Mention that the pressure to conform is greater in some societies than in others and greater among certain groups of people than among others. Ask students how people conform at the basic needs level. Ask whether they think people are better able to achieve self-esteem when they conform or when they don't. Then ask how they can apply their observations to persuasive speaking.

Self-Actualization The need to be creative and true to yourself is a self-actualization or self-fulfillment need. A self-actualization need is the need to be the best person you can be. Persuaders try to convince people to take risks in order to become the best they can be. One may be persuaded to work at poetry, art, or sports. People may also reach self-fulfillment through their religious beliefs or by living according to certain values.

Order of Needs

The needs at the base of Maslow's pyramid have to be met before people can worry about the needs higher in the triangle. It may be hard to persuade you to go to the mall with your friends (belonging need), if you are afraid of walking home in the dark (safety need). You may be persuaded to go, however, if you can ride home with a friend. When you create a persuasive message, choose the right listener need for your appeal.

JOURNAL ENTRY

In our community senior citizens are always trying to persuade the police chief to provide more police protection at night. People are not willing to take night classes, visit friends, or go to church activities until they can walk safely to these places. Their basic need is safety.

INTERACT

Divide into small groups. Match each persuasive statement to one of the needs on Maslow's pyramid. Each need is used once.

1. Always walk to and from school with other people. Do not go near strangers' cars if they try to talk to you.

continued

416

66 Believe one who has proved it. Believe an expert. **99**

VIRGIL

Links to Past Learning

Ask students to think about speakers they have heard in the past who exhibited more emotion than they provided information. Ask why these speeches were or were not effective.

INTERACT

2. If you join the band, you'll get to know all the people in the band and a lot of the athletes too.

3. Don't quit playing the piano. It's one of the things you do very well, and you can play better than most other pianists your age.

4. Since you lost your backpack, I'll give you half my sandwich if you let me use your radio.

5. There's a light in you that can grow brighter. Help others and continue to grow into a stronger human being.

Now have each one in the group write statements appealing to three needs. Share the statements with the class.

MAKING YOURSELF BELIEVABLE

Why should anyone listen to you? What qualifies you to talk about homelessness, drunk driving, or animal rights? Why should someone be persuaded by you to attend a school play or donate to the community food drive?

The best persuaders are people who know a great deal about their subject and appear to care about it. In other words, persuaders must be believable. You can become believable by demonstrating your knowledge of the topic, connection to the topic, and interest in the topic.

Knowledge of the Topic

You can become an expert on a topic through firsthand experience or through study. For example, if you have gone camping with your family for several summers, you have firsthand experience about camping safety. If you have no camping experience, you could read books and government publications on safe camping. Or, you could interview a local Scoutmaster. If you give a persuasive speech titled "Camp Safely This Summer," and demonstrate that you know your topic, you will be believable.

Motivation

Encourage students to think of the various kinds of evidence they have heard in past speeches. List these forms of evidence on the chalkboard.

Links to Past Learning

● Students might skim Chapter 10 to refresh their memories about how to research supporting materials and evidence.

417

Skill Development

Media Literacy

● Encourage students to keep a log of every television commercial they see for one day. Encourage them to analyze which needs the commercials appealed to.

The more a speaker knows about his subject, the more believable he is.

Connection to the Topic

Tell your listeners why you are able to speak on a certain topic. You might say, "I became interested in this topic of poverty because of my volunteer work at the Haven House Soup Kitchen." If you do not have firsthand experience, explain how you obtained your information. You might say, "A recent article in *Newsweek* magazine estimates that 10 percent of Americans go to bed hungry each night."

Interest in the Topic

Persuasive speakers appear believable if they are excited or enthusiastic about their topic. Their enthusiasm tells the listeners they really care. Use gestures and vary your voice to avoid appearing bored. If you are enthusiastic about your topic, you will have a greater effect on your listeners. You are living proof that you really care about animal rights, CPR courses, or a smoke-free environment. Your enthusiastic delivery will convince your listeners that your ideas are important.

Critical Thinking

Evaluating

● Ask students to use the five questions at the bottom of this page to test the following statements:

Classical music is boring.

Although the murder rate has gone down in some cities, cities are still unpleasant places to live.

Statistics from 1995 show that Americans are getting fatter and fatter.

Only a few people really believe that space research is necessary or desirable.

INTERACT

In a group of three or four, list ways that teenagers can become believable experts on five of the following subjects:

bicycle safety	forest-fire dangers
air pollution	support for cancer funds
school honor codes	individuality
space research	classical music
fair-housing laws	food labels

REASONING

There are thirty-two reasons why this school needs a swimming pool. I don't have time to list them, but I hope you will support the swimming pool campaign.

Senior citizens are lonely. We need to create a new senior-citizens' center in town.

If you read these arguments carefully, you found that both contain problems in reasoning. In the first argument, the audience is not given any of the thirty-two reasons, only a general statement that there are numerous reasons. In the second argument, the problem-solving link is missing. No reason is given to show that a new senior-citizens' center will help stop loneliness.

To make a strong argument, you will need to use evidence to support your ideas. You can use the suggestions given in Chapter 10 on how to research and find supporting materials for evidence. Remember that you can test your evidence and the evidence of other speakers with the following questions:

Is it fact or opinion?	Is it timely?
Is it reliable?	Is it representative?
Is it relevant?	

Critical Thinking

Analyzing

Ask students to give three reasons why Jennifer Cornfeld is believable as a speaker for the Israel Quest Program. Have students support their reasons with evidence from the article about Jennifer.

SPEAKING OF . . .

JENNIFER CORNFELD

Jennifer Cornfeld, a high-school student in Washington, D.C., is committed to the Israel Quest Program, a teen Jewish identity project based on the belief that Jewish education and an international experience in Israel will create a strong identity among Jewish youth. When Jennifer was in tenth grade, she received financial support from this organization to travel to Israel and explore her heritage. Now she serves as an ambassador for the program. In this role Jennifer gives speeches about her trip and the goals of the Israel Quest program.

Frequently Jennifer is asked to speak to parent groups about the program, hoping to convince them that such an experience would be educational, safe, and enjoyable for their children. In order to be persuasive, Jennifer carefully analyzes her audiences and adapts to them. Describing a recent presentation, she says, "I spoke to these parents as if I were their age, and I always maintained eye contact in order to express how invested I am in this program." She once spoke to over 300 people at the Mayflower Hotel in Washington, a gathering that included politicians and members of the press. Jennifer explains her speaking success: "It is absolutely imperative that I speak with enthusiasm and engage my audience. I accomplish this by maintaining eye contact, gesturing, and changing the tone of my voice. . . . I always dress for the occasion. If the meeting is informal, I would wear khaki pants and a collared shirt. If the meeting is formal, I would wear a tailored suit." While her speeches are delivered extemporaneously, after each presentation Jennifer directs a question-and-answer period when she provides impromptu responses.

Her public-speaking experiences provide Jennifer with a set of skills that will serve her well in college and in a career. She may want to become a leader in college student government and eventually take on a position such as a lawyer, politican, international business leader, or religious leader.

Limited English Proficiency

Encourage limited-English-proficient students to work with more-proficient students to master the differences between inductive and deductive reasoning. If possible, have the more-proficient students provide examples that the LEP students can identify as either inductive or deductive reasoning.

As you consider possible evidence, you must remember that an ethical persuader looks at all the evidence, not just the evidence that supports his or her idea. If you are trying to persuade your parents to let you have a party, you cannot just talk about how much fun the last party was. If someone broke a lamp at the last party and someone else dumped potato chips into the fish tank, this evidence must be considered, too, even if it does not support the idea of having another party.

Types of Reasoning

Once you have supporting materials, or supporting evidence, how do you use them? In most cases you use them to make your point clearer or to build your argument. You have to make all the supporting material fit together to help you reach your audience goal. In other words, supporting evidence is the raw material of your speech. A speaker uses reasoning to show listeners the logical connection between ideas. When you use reasoning, you develop arguments based on evidence. There are three major types of reasoning: inductive, deductive, and cause-effect.

Inductive Reasoning **Inductive reasoning** involves using specific pieces of information to reach a general conclusion. When using inductive reasoning, a speaker lists many pieces of evidence to help listeners draw their conclusions. The following are examples of inductive reasoning:

Fourteen children in our community received state writing awards. Our schools train good writers.

In our class, Sandra, Pam, Dirk, and Rodney have the chicken pox. Chicken pox is running through the school.

It is important to test inductive reasoning by looking at the connection between the evidence and the conclusion. Look at the following example:

Evidence: I met five unfriendly people in the town of Lionsville.

Conclusion: Lionsville is a very unfriendly town.

Cooperative Learning

● Divide students into two teams, and have each team come up with five examples of valid inductive reasoning and five examples of valid deductive reasoning. Have the teams present their statements and answer the opponent's questions. For each statement, rate the teams from 1 (excellent) to 5 (needs a lot of improvement). Whichever team has the highest number of points at the end wins.

Skill Development

On the Job

● Encourage students who volunteer or work at part-time jobs to discuss examples of on-the-job problem solving in which they called upon inductive or deductive reasoning skills.

What kinds of questions might you ask about the connection between the evidence (five unfriendly people) and the conclusion (the town is unfriendly)? First, you might ask whether there are enough examples. Have enough people been observed? Second, you might ask whether the examples are typical. Is there anything unusual about these people? Finally, you might ask if there are important exceptions or considerations. Would it make a difference in the conclusion if it turned out that all five unfriendly people had just come from the dentist's office?

When reasoning through induction, you need to ask the following questions:

1. Are there enough examples?
2. Are the examples typical?
3. Are there important exceptions or special cases?

Deductive Reasoning **Deductive reasoning** involves using a general idea to reach conclusions about specific instances. When using deductive reasoning, a speaker states a conclusion which is then applied to individual cases. The following are examples of deductive reasoning:

People in Advanced Algebra are smart. Tom is in Advanced Algebra. Tom must be a great student.

Debaters like to argue. Carolyn is a debater. Get Carolyn to argue for permission to hold a class party.

Each of these examples represents three steps of reasoning. Although you may think through the three steps, most people actually talk in terms of two steps. For example, "Debaters like to argue. Let's get Carolyn to argue for permission for a class party."

As with inductive reasoning, it is important to test deductive reasoning. Look at the following example:

Evidence: Connie is a cheerleader. Cheerleaders are very popular.

Conclusion: Connie is very popular.

Curricular Connection

Science

▲ Ask students to give an example of scientific inductive reasoning. For example, when archeologists find evidence of pottery in one village that they know was made in another site far away, inductive reasoning tells them that the two peoples traded goods.

Motivation

Ask students to come up with personal examples of cause and effect. Write their examples on the chalkboard.

Skill Development

Quick Skill Opportunity

● Ask for volunteers, and go around the room calling on them to come up with possible valid effects based on the following causes.

Kit chipped a tooth; therefore . . .

Manuel made more money this year than last year; therefore . . .

Tamara is quite tall; therefore . . .

Abe's cat is missing; therefore . . .

Some parts of the nightshade plant are poisonous; therefore . . .

Questions: a. Is the general statement true? Are cheerleaders popular?

b. Is the specific example true? Is Connie a cheerleader?

c. Does the specific example apply to the general statement? Is Connie very popular? Might Connie be popular for other reasons, such as friendliness? After you answer these questions, you can decide if you agree with the conclusion that Connie is very popular.

When reasoning through deduction, ask yourself:

1. Is the general statement true?

2. Is the specific example true?

3. Does the specific example apply to the general statement?

Cause-Effect Reasoning **Cause-effect reasoning** suggests that one event produces a second event. In other words, it suggests that an effect (what happens) can be tied to a specific cause. The following are examples of cause-effect reasoning:

The federal government has cut its contributions to local charities; therefore, people in our town are going hungry.

The 55-mph speed limit saved many people from dying in traffic accidents.

To test cause-effect reasoning, you need to look carefully at the relationship between the first and second events. Consider the following example:

Evidence: Jane studied for four hours.

Conclusion: She will get a good math grade.

Questions: a. Is the cause connected to the effect? Will studying for four hours necessarily result in a good math grade?

Cooperative Learning

● Have students work in small groups to create radio ads for common household appliances. Each group should choose one appliance and write two ads for it. In the first ad, students should use logical arguments to persuade consumers to buy the appliance. In the second ad, students should use emotional appeal.

b. Is the cause capable of producing the effect by itself? Studying may not be enough. Jane also needs to attend school regularly and listen in class.

c. Could some other cause produce the same effect? Has Jane worked with a tutor outside of school?

When reasoning from cause to effect, you need to ask the following questions:

1. Is the cause connected to the effect?
2. Is the cause capable of producing the effect by itself?
3. Could some other cause produce the same effect?

Faulty Reasoning

Persuasive speakers must choose their evidence and types of reasoning carefully. Sometimes speakers use incorrect or false reasoning, called **faulty reasoning**, to try to persuade their audience members. Listeners must be prepared to recognize poor evidence and false reasoning so that they are not misled by it. Examples of false reasoning include emotional appeal, glittering generalities, card stacking, bandwagon appeal, unrelated testimonials, and name calling.

Emotional Appeal An **emotional appeal** arouses the feelings of audience members. The appeal may arouse positive emotions, such as the desire for good health or success; or it may arouse negative emotions, such as fear or greed. In an emotional appeal, the speaker stresses feelings over logic. The speaker bases his or her argument on emotions, not reasoning. Speakers choose specific words and images to stir up the audience's emotions. Look at the following examples.

Are you embarrassed when you lose or forget your school assignments? Our new binder contains an assignment notebook, subject notebook, and folders. Buy it and get organized!

If your child's safety is one of your top concerns, you'll make sure your child wears a helmet while riding a bicycle.

Substitute Teacher Tip

Give students a few moments to think about glittering generalities and to come up with two or three of them.

Glittering Generalities **Glittering generalities** are vague general statements. These generalities are not supported with specific information and are not linked to the main point. Below are some examples of glittering generalities and questions that may be asked about them:

General Statement: Men make poor drivers.

Questions: Did the speaker see a male driver cut in front of another car this morning, or did the speaker look at accident reports to make this statement? What is the evidence for this general statement?

General Statement: Emily Bashnagel is a wonderful mother. Vote for her for PTA president.

Questions: Did the speaker link Emily Bashnagel's ability as a mother to her ability to run the PTA? What abilities does she need to lead the PTA? Does she have these talents?

Remember that the goal of a speaker who uses glittering generalities is to get listeners to accept an idea without examining any supporting material. To avoid making glittering generalities, check to see whether your general statements are supported by specific information. Then double-check to make sure your supporting material is linked to the main idea. A listener who looks for supporting evidence will be able to recognize a speaker's weak arguments.

Card Stacking **Card stacking** refers to piling up information in favor of an idea with very little backing. The speaker gives examples or reasons for one side of the issue without explaining them carefully. Look at the following example of card stacking.

Join the Urban Youth Corps. You will make friends, learn new skills, get to know the city, and make money. It's a great way to spend your summer. Sign up today in the counseling office!

Critical Thinking
Evaluating

What examples of card stacking can students find in television commercials or radio commercials? Let volunteers share a few with the class.

425

Amazing Fact!

Beanie Baby dolls offer a potent example of the effect that a bandwagon appeal can have. In 1997, a major fast-food chain's promotion of these dolls was so successful that they ran out of dolls long before the promotion was scheduled to end. The demand for the dolls became so great that unscrupulous marketers tried to smuggle hundreds of thousands of fake Beanie Babies into the United States.

Skill Development

Media Literacy

● Have students create their own product advertisements using unrelated testimonials. Allow them to use any medium they like. For example they might create a print ad, a radio ad, or a television commercial. Encourage them to use the techniques they have seen in the media but to use their own ad copy and slogans.

What more would you like to hear about each of these points? So far you don't even know what kind of work teenagers do in the program, nor do you know how much you could earn. Each of these points needs to be explained.

As a listener you need to ask yourself these questions: Is the speaker just piling up points? Are the reasons that are given carefully explained? If the answer to the first question is yes and the answer to the second question is no, then you may be listening to card stacking, another type of faulty reasoning.

Bandwagon Appeal A **bandwagon appeal** suggests that you should jump on the bandwagon or do something because everyone else is doing it. You may hear arguments with opening statements such as, "Everyone has one" or "We're all going to go. You don't want to be left out." Often you will hear commercials containing bandwagon appeals such as "People in the know buy their clothes at Bergoff's" or "Athletes who care about their feet buy Rabbit running shoes."

As a listener ask yourself: Am I getting pushed into something before I think about it? Going along with a crowd should be your choice; don't let someone else push you into it.

Unrelated Testimonials A **testimonial** is an opinion expressed by a well-known person on a particular subject. **Unrelated testimonials** try to link things that are not related. Valid testimonials try to persuade listeners by linking positive feelings for one person, thing, idea, or event to a related person, thing, idea, or event. For example, a film star may urge parents to take children for eye exams because the celebrity has a child with serious vision problems. An athlete may convince listeners to avoid high fat foods.

When unrelated testimonials link things that are not related, you should wonder about the connection. If there is no obvious or valid connection between the person and the thing receiving the testimonial, you need to be careful. For example, what is the real connection between eating Great Grain Cereal and a football touchdown by a sports hero who endorses the product? Not all testimonials involve faulty reasoning, but you need to recognize those that do.

Name Calling Name calling attacks a person rather than the person's ideas by using unpopular names or labels. Below are several examples:

> It is true that many people support a 75-mph speed limit, but these people are dangerous fools.

> How can you listen to a guy who flunked math tell you how to use a computer?

> I wouldn't pay attention to anything that airhead said.

Competent listeners are not fooled by the negative feelings created by name calling. Be sure to ask yourself: What evidence did the speaker present in addition to name calling? Can I check out this evidence? For example, did the person actually flunk math? How is flunking math related to teaching about computers?

All these types of faulty reasoning can be used to persuade listeners, especially listeners who are uninformed about the topic. An ethical persuader avoids using faulty reasoning.

INTERACT

With a partner, analyze the following appeals and identify the problems in reasoning. Then write two short sample paragraphs explaining the faulty reasoning.

1. There are some narrow-minded people who cannot look toward a better future. But I say to you that if I am elected president of this student council I will make changes. The halls will be cleaner, the cafeteria food will be better, there will be more sports events, and there will be a change in the homework policy.

2. This is going to be the best dance our school has seen. Our favorite assistant principal, Ms. Wilier, says she has never seen such an organized group. Ms. Hong, the gym teacher, says the decorations are fantastic. Everyone is going to be there. You can wear whatever you want. Just come and have a good time.

Learning Styles
Audio-Visual Learning

● If possible, bring in recordings of several recent political campaign commercials. Have students identify examples of name calling, card stacking, bandwagon appeal, or glittering generalities.

427

Beyond the Classroom

Remind students that public speaking is not the only arena in which people sometimes resort to faulty reasoning. Have students keep a journal of listening experiences in which they are made aware of another person's faulty reasoning.

Although it is tempting to use some of these faulty reasoning approaches to convince your listeners, the ethical speaker selects material honestly. This means the speaker does not exaggerate, use misleading statistics, rely on unrelated testimonials, resort to calling names, or hide contradictory information. The speaker tries to create the best case with accurate information, careful reasoning, and ethical strategies.

ORGANIZING A PERSUASIVE SPEECH

What is similar about the following statements?

> Once you hear how serious the problem is, you will agree that we need to put a stoplight at Cook Avenue and Main Street.

> You can't learn soccer in this community because there is no place to play. Once we build a new soccer field, eight teams will be able to play on Saturday, and many more kids can learn to play.

Each of these statements mentions a problem and proposes a solution. Although you can use many different organizational forms in a persuasive speech, the most commonly used form is the problem-solution method.

The Problem-Solution Form

When using problem-solution organization, the speaker describes a problem and then describes a way to solve the problem. He or she tries to convince the listeners that the problem is serious and that the given solution is the best way to solve the problem. The following outline shows how one student prepared a persuasive speech on organ donation.

I. Introduction
  A. Opening—An average of sixteen people die in the United States each day awaiting organ transplants.
  B. Goal—Listeners will believe lives can be saved through organ donation.

II. Problem
  A. There is a shortage of organ donations.

Motivation

Remind students that problem solving is a skill they will use in many areas of life and work. Students might discuss the various problem-solving situations they are involved in every day.

    1. More than 80,000 people are waiting for transplants.
    2. More than 100 people are added to the transplant list each day.
  B. Many people do not understand organ donation.
  C. Families may not give consent if they do not know their loved one's wishes.

III. Solutions
  A. Become an organ donor.
  B. Talk to your family about your decision.
  C. Educate others about organ donation.

IV. Conclusion
  A. Summary of argument and ideas
  B. One organ and tissue donor can save and enhance the lives of twenty-five people.

Notice that the speaker included everything necessary for good problem-solution organization. The outline includes four points explaining why the problem is serious and presents solutions to solve the problem.

A persuasive speech is commonly organized by describing a problem and proposing a solution.

Critical Thinking

Organizing

● Encourage students to think about what type of graphic organizer or visual aid might effectively illustrate parts of Kenyatta Wilson's speech. Interested students might like to create such a visual aid.

Curricular Connection

Language Arts

● Have students write a paragraph describing which aspects of Kenyatta Wilson's speech they found most persuasive.

✖ INTERACT

In a group, read the following short speech given by a junior-high-school student who addressed the problem of missing children. Identify the following:

1. The audience you think she addressed

2. Parts of the organizational pattern

3. Three pieces of evidence

4. One of the appeals to an audience need

5. The solution

I Think The Best—I Expect The Best

Kenyatta Wilson

On the morning after Christmas of 1974, thirteen-year-old Janna Chanson went to a friend's house. A short time later Janna's mother drove by to pick up her daughter; Janna wasn't there. On February 27, 1983, Jeana Rodriguez, an eleven-year-old sixth grade student in San Jose, California, got off her school bus and began her walk home, which was only one hundred yards away. Jeana never made it home. These are but two of thousands of children who are reported missing each year.

I think the best, I expect the best of society to help in the search for children who are missing. Missing children are a national problem that has to be solved. A missing child is defined as a child whose whereabouts are unknown. It is estimated that 1.8 million children are missing each year in the United States.

Many times the question is asked, Why are these children missing? About 1.3 million are runaways. Usually these children leave home because of social, school, or family problems. Runaways often end up in gangs and get involved in drugs, prostitution, and theft.

One hundred thousand children are abducted by strangers. Usually they will be taken while alone in places thought to be safe, such as parks and movie theatres. These children may be used in pornography, prostitution, and shoplifting.

Fifty thousand children are taken by divorced parents who did not receive custody of their child. Because there are so

Beyond the Classroom

Encourage a class discussion of the possible audiences to whom Kenyatta Wilson might deliver her speech. Ask what type of audience would be most likely to take action based on what they heard.

Curricular Connection
Social Studies

● Encourage students to make a list of social problems—both local and nationwide—that would be well served by a Hey/You/See/So speech form. Students could then create posters about an issue of their choice.

many reasons for missing children, the answer to why there are so many missing children remains complex.

There are agencies that aid in the search for missing children. These include the police, FBI, Missing Children Centers, and Child Find. However, these agencies are understaffed and lack the financial resources to be highly effective. For example, Missing Children Centers and Child Find send out flyers, posters, and pamphlets on missing children and take information from persons who think that they may have seen missing children. Yet the success rate is low when only five hundred children are located each year by the combined efforts of these agencies.

What then is the solution to this problem? I believe that the solution lies within you and me. Not only must we advocate that more governmental funds be made available to adequately finance our law enforcement agencies in the search for missing children,

but we must volunteer our time and creative ideas to solve this problem. For example, we can get more media exposure to publicize missing children and establish a network system where pictures and information about missing children would be more visible. If you, the community, will give not only your money but your time as well, maybe this problem will be resolved.

Remember, missing children is a problem that causes many lives to be totally destroyed. The missing child is often faced with a life of cruelty and crime. The parents suffer many worries because of this. With the help of Missing Children organizations, parents, and you, perhaps this terrible problem will someday be just an awful memory of the past.

As for the two girls, Janna's body was found two days later in a trash can near an alley, and Jeana was safely returned home. But not all children are as lucky as Jeana.

The Hey-You-See-So Form

Although the form title seems silly, the words *Hey, You, See,* and *So* create an easy but effective speech outline. This model is based on a more elaborate persuasion model called Monroe's Motivated Sequence. The outline works like this:

Hey Pay attention! Something important is happening and you need to be aware of it. For example, children are becoming sick, national forests are being burned, drunk-driving accidents are increasing, or few people voted in the last election. This step says, "Hey, there's something going on," or "There's a problem and you should pay attention."

431

Cooperative Learning

● Have students work together in groups of four and brainstorm ideas for a Hey/You/See/So speech. Each member of the group will take one of the four parts in the actual presentation of the speech.

You This situation affects you! You have some stake in making things different. A child you care about could get sick, the national parks won't be beautiful without trees, you won't be safe on the road, or only the few people who vote will determine government policies for everyone. This step emphasizes that the listeners are directly connected to the problem.

See See how things could be different! Imagine or visualize the good things. Picture happy and healthy children, beautiful national parks for citizens, safe highways, or full participation democracy. This step involves painting a picture of a wonderful world so that the listener can visualize it without the problem. This provides a goal.

So So what are you going to do about it? You can contribute to the positive change. You can lobby for nutritious school meals, practice careful camping, support MADD (Mothers Against Drunk Driving), or persuade your parents to vote. This step explains the specific action a listener can take to address the problem that was presented in **Hey** and **You** and to reach the good situation described in **See**.

APPLY

Using the simple four-step Hey-You-See-So persuasive-speech form, write an opening sentence for each step for one of the following problems:

Leaks in nuclear reactors

The increase in lake pollution

The rise in rudeness among strangers

The increase in anti-immigrant hostility

High rates of media violence

Rising illiteracy

continued

Links to Past Learning

Remind students of what they have learned about giving and receiving constructive criticism. If necessary, have them skim the last part of Chapter 13.

🔑 APPLY

This four-step format also could be used for more interpersonal persuasion situations such as convincing a parent to change a rule, selling raffle tickets in the neighborhood, persuading a friend to go to a concert with you, or persuading a friend to smoke less.

EVALUATING PERSUASIVE SPEECHES

You seemed convincing.

I don't care what you say; it's a dumb idea.

I couldn't agree with you. I'm a Democrat.

Critical reactions such as the above do not really help a persuasive speaker. The comments are not specific. The critics either made general responses or decided that the speech could not apply to them and closed their minds.

As a critic, you must remain open-minded and judge a speech on its merits. You should not make up your mind on the topic before you hear the speech. You should listen carefully for evidence, appeals, and speaker believability. Then you can decide how well the speech worked.

Feedback forms can help you to evaluate your own speeches and those of others. Chapter 13 contains examples of feedback forms for speeches to inform. Forms A and B in this chapter are examples of forms that are useful for evaluating persuasive speeches. Form A allows you to rate parts of a speech as poor, fair, good, very good, or excellent. Comments can be written on the bottom of the sheet. Form B allows you to describe the parts of the speech that worked well, the parts that did not work as well, and an area for improvement. You can also create your own forms for persuasive speeches by adding certain sections to these forms.

Skill Development

Making Conversation

▼ Encourage students to share their work from the Apply activity on page 432 with a partner. Partners could assess which opening sentences work best and which could use improvement.

433

Teach ◀

🍎 Substitute Teacher Tip

Have students create self-evaluation forms for their speeches. Tell them that they can use these forms to document how effective they felt the speech was. They will be able to compare their self-evaluations to the feedback they receive from others.

Skill Development

On the Job

Students might talk about evaluations they have received from supervisors or managers. Lead a class discussion on how the use of such forms can help job performance.

Evaluation Form: Persuasive Speech Feedback (A)

Speaker's Name _____

Speaker's Topic _____

	Poor	Fair	Good	Very Good	Excellent
Clear audience goal	1	2	3	4	5
Use of material to support points	1	2	3	4	5
Valid reasoning	1	2	3	4	5
Topic appropriate to audience and occasion	1	2	3	4	5
Language appropriate to audience and occasion	1	2	3	4	5
Use of persuasive appeals	1	2	3	4	5
Speaker is believable	1	2	3	4	5

Comments: _____

_____

_____

_____

_____

_____

_____

_____

434

434 Unit 4 Public Communication

Critical Thinking

Synthesizing

● Ask individual students to tell what parts they found the most and least interesting in the study of this chapter. Ask whether other students generally agree or disagree.

Evaluation Form: Persuasive Speech Feedback (B)

Speaker's Name _____

Speaker's Topic _____

The parts of your speech that were most persuasive:
  Example: I was concerned by the description of the
      methods of capital punishment. You seemed
      excited about the topic. I thought you cared.

The parts of your speech that were least persuasive:
  Example: You did not tell us the titles or
      qualifications of the people you quoted,
      so I questioned your evidence.

To make the speech stronger you could:
  Example: Explain who you are quoting. Look up at the
      audience as you pause while reading the quotes.

CHAPTER 14 SUMMARY

Persuasion is a complicated process. To give a fine persuasive speech, you must select the topic carefully and adapt it to your audience in terms of listener needs and beliefs. You must make yourself believable by showing your interest in, and connection to, the topic. Your reasoning should be clear. Then you need to fit your evidence and reasoning into a workable organizational pattern. Finally, you need to know how to evaluate persuasive speeches given by yourself and by others. At each point, ask yourself if you are making ethical decisions as a communicator. Persuasion is a powerful tool. Competent communicators use it wisely.

Answers

Think About It

Student answers will vary. Here are sample answers:

1. Persuasion is the communication process of changing a listener's beliefs or moving a listener to action. Doing this in front of an audience is called persuasive speaking.

2. The purpose of a speech to inform is to let the audience know about a subject. The purpose of a persuasive speech is to convince the audience of a particular point of view or need for action.

3. Physical—a persuasive speaker might appeal to the audience's basic needs for shelter, food, and so on. Safety—a speaker could attempt to convince the audience of the need to protect themselves or their families. Belonging—the speaker might appeal to the audience's status as members of a certain group. Self-esteem—the speaker might attempt to make the audience feel good about themselves in relation to the topic. Self-actualization—the speaker could appeal to the natural human desire to be the best possible person.

> ### CHAPTER REVIEW

Think About It

1. What is persuasion? What is persuasive speaking?

2. What is the difference between a speech to persuade and a speech to inform?

3. List Maslow's five levels of human needs and explain how a persuasive speaker could use these needs.

4. How can you make yourself believable for an audience?

5. List and describe the various types of faulty reasoning.

Try It Out

1. During a trip to the grocery store, examine the various persuasive messages you find there. Check out promotional material, slogans, and information on boxes, store posters, and bulletin boards. List three different types of faulty reasoning used in this persuasive material. Note these in your journal.

2. In groups of five or six, brainstorm ways to handle certain persuasive situations. Below are some situations you might discuss:

   Getting a parent to raise your allowance

   Asking a teacher for an extension on a paper

   Gaining votes for a student-body president

   Selling raffle tickets to raise money for sports team equipment

3. Analyze the persuasive speech titled "Meeting America's Challenge," and answer the following questions:

   What is this speaker's goal?

   What steps does she say our nation must take?

   How does she support her argument about each step?

   What does she say are the benefits of following her proposal?

   What questions would you like to ask this speaker?

Meeting America's Challenge
Aliya Esmail

What are the challenges America faces as she moves toward the year 2000? What do we as Americans wish to stand for? Do we want to simply be a highly technological, intellectual society? Or do we wish to see America as a nation of cooperation, respect, motivation, diversity, culture, and encouragement? To create the latter, America faces a great challenge—that of creating a national unity. Recently in America, there has been emphasis on the power of the individual. America's power, her greatness, will originate within the power and the greatness of the individual, of course. However, we must never let the individual come before the family, and we must never let the family come before the American family.

To first create a powerful individual, we must educate. According to Vartan Gregorian, an educator, "Education has to teach us not only what we can know, but also what the limitations of our knowledge are—what we don't know." Once we have identified what we know, we must inspire our children—our future to forge forth. We must motivate them. We must make them want to learn. Education is simply an introduction to learning. Only by finding our own curiosity will we truly seek to learn. We must create this curiosity in every American.

Our next progressive challenge is to create strength within the family. Many members of the families in America have become too concerned with the individual. We must learn to strengthen our families. We must make an effort to not only live together and eat together, but to truly be together—to learn together and to grow together. By strengthening our individual families, we will create a powerful base upon which we must create an American family. And this, the creation of an American family, is our greatest challenge.

Ralph Waldo Emerson said, "What lies behind us and what lies before us are small matters compared to what lies within us." Our individual duties as Americans are to find that which lies within us and utilize it, make it grow, put it into our country. We are often

worried about what we can extract from certain people, certain things—like a democratic nation. Now we must learn to concern ourselves with what we can put into our nation. We must be willing to come together with the other people of this country to unify. To become a true nation. To forget our minor differences and realize our similarities. Our diversity will not destroy the unity. It will but make us stronger and more powerful. People should be in America to create a better society. Not just a better living. America must find this American family. This is our challenge. The Founding Fathers did not create a land of opportunists. They created a land of opportunity.

America's challenge today is to strengthen the individuals of this nation with education. But it is also to use these strong individuals as a foundation for a stronger American community. Our challenge is to seek and to find national unity. To do this, we must show Americans that America's future is their future. It is their children's future; their grandchildren's future. America has graciously accepted challenges to help people, militarily or otherwise, in every corner of the world. Today we must not shy away from our own challenge. Just like previous goals, a goal of national unity may seem unattainable. Perhaps even impossible. However, as George Bernard Shaw once said, "Some men see things as they are and say 'Why?' I

4. Speakers can make themselves believable to the audience through knowledge of the topic, connection to the topic, and interest in the topic.

5. Glittering generalities—vague, general statements that are unsupported by specific information and are not linked to the main point. Card stacking—piling information up in favor of an idea with little or no backing. The speaker gives one-sided reasons and does not explain them fully. Bandwagon appeal—a form of faulty reasoning that suggests an idea is sound because "everyone is doing it." Unrelated testimonials—try to link things that are not related. For example, if an athlete promotes a certain kind of toothpaste, the testimonial is linked to the athlete's fame, not to his or her knowledge of toothpaste. Name calling—this form of faulty reasoning attacks a person rather than the person's ideas. It does so by using unpopular names or labels.

437

dream of things that never were and say 'Why not?'" Today, America's challenge, national unity, will begin to become a reality when each American looks inside himself or herself and asks, "Why not?"

Put It in Writing

1. Choose a topic for a persuasive speech. Write a one-paragraph introduction for each of three different audiences—an audience that agrees with you, an audience that disagrees with you, and an audience that holds a neutral position.

2. Select a problem you have with a friend, parent, brother or sister, or teacher. Using the problem-solution organizational pattern, write out two paragraphs that outline (a) what you see as the reasons for the problem, and (b) your ideas for solutions to the problem. Include the paragraphs in your journal.

3. Watch or listen to a political advertisement on radio or television and write a paragraph that describes the persuasive appeals that were included. Indicate any bias or prejudice that seems to be contained in the message.

4. Analyze the speech, "It's All Arabic to Me" by Mona Abo-Zena on the next three pages. Indicate what you believe is her audience goal, her organizational pattern, and her use of persuasive strategies.

Speak About It

1. Prepare two possible introductions for a persuasive speech. Present each one to a small group. Ask for feedback about which introduction gains greater audience interest and why.

2. Create a three- to four-minute persuasive speech and present it to your class. Before you begin, research your topic and select your evidence carefully. Develop arguments based on your evidence using at least one of the following types of reasoning: inductive, deductive, or cause-effect. As you listen to your classmates' speeches, try to identify the types of reasoning they included in their speeches.

3. In small groups create a thirty- to sixty-second commercial to sell an idea, a product, or a service. You may wish to create an audiotaped (radio) commercial or a videotaped commercial. If you use media, pay attention to the background, including such things as music and pictures. Present the commercial in class. Be sure to

   see that your introduction includes a device or gimmick for getting the audience's attention

   see that your conclusion includes a final appeal or sales pitch (The body of the presentation is up to you.)

   have a specific purpose for your commercial and a specific goal for your audience

4. Give a four-minute presentation in which you analyze a persuasive speech and try to determine its impact on the listeners. Describe the circumstances in which the speech was given, the reason for the speech, and the reaction to the speech. You can find examples in national newspaper files using a library index or the Internet.

It's All Arabic to Me
by Mona Abo-Zena

Ata mana ina gamel oumro yi tof fil zabada bi ta yack win ni hayatac daman ti koon saaida.

What? Why do you have that lost look on your face? It's not like I'm speaking a foreign language, is it?

Languages are foreign only when you don't speak them. Too many Americans find themselves only acquainted with English and have thus closed their lives to culture and closed their minds to knowledge.

The melting pot that the United States has based our country and our society on seems like a fraud. The American dream appears little more than a nightmare when we realize the general disdain that exists for bilingualism and language education. Our definitions of assimilation have changed from contributing to a cultural tradition to a society of complete conformity. Survival of the fittest now means survival of the American way and the termination of all other ideas.

The United States needs to leave behind the thoughts of a monolingual society and face the challenge of the future. The only way for us to do so is to make the United States a bilingual culture by encouraging the use and practice of foreign languages.

Do not be confused. I am not suggesting that the United States adopt two official languages such as English and Swahili. That would leave us in the same predicament as Canada where it seems that their bilingual culture is more of a hindrance than an asset. Instead I am encouraging the bilingualism or multilingualism of individuals. They should be given the opportunity to study the languages of their choice at young ages. In order to better understand this necessity, we should consider

why languages are not presently being emphasized

the reason we should encourage languages

how we can improve this system

The United States is a leader in technology, politics, industry, and economics. Yet, many students graduate from high school without ever having taken a foreign-language course. Simultaneously, students in third-world schools on the other side of the world are studying up to five different languages and are reaching some level of proficiency in them.

James Follows, author of the article "Viva Bilingualism," explains the logic in this as a type of polygamy: "According to Western standards, it just doesn't work to have two wives. Partners in a marriage require a certain exclusive commitment from each other. If a man gives it to one wife, there's not enough left over for the other. The same is true with languages; there is only so much space in the brain before it gets used up. And if his brain were not the problem, his heart would be since he can be truly loyal to only one language."

Since it is not the person's inability to master languages, we have yet to determine why the United States almost ignores bilingualism. The answer lies in the insecurities that are present here. The United States has no official language, but English has unofficially taken that role. Linguistic uniformity in the United States helps keep our society together and we are agreed that pressures from non-English speaking people will tear our society apart. Results of these fears can be seen everywhere, such as when California passed an amendment making English their official state language in December of 1986.

Actually, though, according to Geoffrey Hunberg, a linguistic professor at Stanford University, "The English language needs about as much official protection as the Boston Celtics need elevator shoes."

They say that a mind is a terrible thing to waste. Additionally, there is no such thing as wasted knowledge. There is nothing that can be lost by learning a second language, only things to gain, for there is no end to what can be accomplished by mastering another language.

Job opportunities related to languages do not end with the car manufacturer who realized that Chevrolet's Novas were not selling in Mexico because "no va" means "no go." Positions in the area of business and politics need to be filled by Americans overseas. These jobs cannot be given to only English-speaking citizens. Even back home, bilingual job applicants are generally given the edge.

A language student is a world student. Bilingual people are generally more well-rounded. They have a better understanding of their own language in addition to the other because similarities are always present. Finally, a bilingual person is generally more communicative because a study of a language goes hand in hand with the study of the culture. This leads to understanding and acceptance.

The student is not the only one who would benefit from a multilingualism. A knowledge of another language would encourage overseas employees to bargain more with the natives and would give us a more balanced position with our foreign competition. With a little time, the United States' intractable trade deficit may finally be on the road to recovery.

There is one more facet of possibilities that we have not yet explored. In this sense, the fringe benefits of mastering a language are literally endless. Just think, you can talk behind someone's back right in front of their face. You can comment to your girlfriend about how gorgeous the waiter is, tell your boyfriend that his zipper is undone, and tell your physics teacher that he is an ibn el kalb. That will be my little secret.

The United States must be given some credit, for they have not fully ignored their responsibilities to languages. According to [former] Secretary of Education William Bennett, approximately 75 percent of funds for languages are given to transitional bilingual programs. Bennett has proposed an amendment to give more flexibility to the local government to determine how these funds are appropriated. One program should not be improved at the cost of the other, they both need attention.

Colleges are restoring their language requirements, but Marguerite La Follotto of Alliance Française finds that it takes at least 600 hours of study to be fluent in French. If proficiency is the goal, then languages should be introduced at a very young age, especially since studies have found preadolescent children learn a second language more easily than adults.

Finally, the methods in which languages are taught need to be evaluated. After four years of studying Spanish, I am proud to say that I can finally tell a native speaker that I have to use the bathroom. Unfortunately, I don't think I would understand their response. Students are being taught to copy sentences out of books and repeat phrases after the teacher hundreds of times. It seems that languages are being taught so we can say we are teaching languages, rather than with the ultimate goal that we are learning languages.

The United States may be one of the leading countries in the world, but our advancements will halt if we do not address issues such as bilingualism. I am not suggesting that the United States adopt two languages, for that would cause only more problems. I am encouraging the bilingualism or multilingualism of the individual. There is nothing that can be lost by learning a language, only things for the society and the individual to gain. In order to achieve this level, foreign-language requirements need to be increased, and they should be introduced at a young age so proficiency can be gained. But before this can be done, before the United States can become bilingual, individuals must make their stand, for there is no such thing as a bilingual country, only a bilingual individual.

Oh, by the way, "Ata mana ina gamel oumro yi tof fil zabada bi ta yack win ni hayatac daman ti koon saaida" is a simple wish from me to you. I hope that your life is always filled with joy and that a camel never spits in your yogurt.

Quick Check

Ask students to find and define these Key Terms:

bandwagon appeal (426)

card stacking (425)

cause-effect reasoning (423)

deductive reasoning (422)

ethical decisions (409)

faulty reasoning (424)

glittering generalities (424)

impact (409)

inductive reasoning (421)

name calling (427)

persuasion (408)

persuasive speaking (408)

testimonials (426)

unrelated testimonials (426)

		Day 1	Day 2	Day 3	Day 4	Day 5
Week 15		**15** Learning About Debate				
		The Values of Debate	Creating the Proposition	Researching the Topic	Debate Formats	Summary
		The Debate Process				Chapter Review
Chapter 15 Planner		*Teacher's Resource Book*				
		Teaching Suggestions 15.1	15.2	15.3	15.4	
		Worksheets & Evaluation Forms				
						Chapter Test 15
		Workbook 15.1	15.2	15.3	15.4–15.5	

Motivation

Ask students to talk about various ways people try to settle differences of opinion. After students have mentioned fights, wars, terrorism, arguments, and, probably, debates, read aloud the words of French essayist Michel de Montaigne: "He who establishes his argument by noise and command shows that his reason is weak." Tell students that they will learn what part reasoning plays in debate.

Links to Past Learning

Ask the class what they know about different kinds of debate. Ask whether anyone has seen a debate and to tell about it if so.

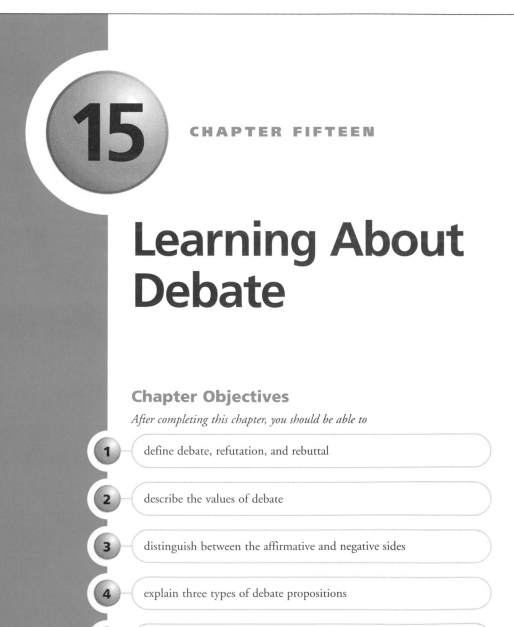

CHAPTER FIFTEEN

Learning About Debate

Chapter Objectives

After completing this chapter, you should be able to

1. define debate, refutation, and rebuttal

2. describe the values of debate

3. distinguish between the affirmative and negative sides

4. explain three types of debate propositions

5. describe ways to create arguments

6. describe two debate formats

❝Give me the liberty to know, to utter, and to argue freely according to conscience, above all liberties.**❞**

JOHN MILTON

▼ Key Terms

affirmative	Lincoln-Douglas debate	proposition of fact	rebuttal
brief	negative	proposition of policy	refutation
case	policy debate	proposition of value	
debate	proposition		
flow sheet			

Critical Thinking

Predicting

● Ask students to predict what the text will tell them about how debate differs from argument. Write student predictions on the chalkboard.

443

443

66It is better to debate a question without settling it than to settle a question without debating it.99

JOSEPH JOUBERT

Beyond the Classroom

Invite a member of the legal profession or a member of a high-school or college debate team to speak to your class about how debate skills have helped in his or her professional or academic career. Encourage students to take notes and ask questions.

Chris: The science fair should be a competition. The best three exhibits should win the top prizes.

Jaime: No. It should be a time when everyone shows what they created. We shouldn't be competing against each other.

Chris: How are you going to get people excited unless there are prizes for the best exhibits?

Jaime: A science fair should not be a contest. It should be a time for people to show what is interesting to them. Competition only makes it tense.

Chris: If you want people to do their best work, you have to . . .

The conversation above is an argument. Two people are expressing opposite points of view on the topic of running a science fair. Arguments begin when there is a difference of opinion between two or more persons and each person tries to persuade the other person to change his or her ideas. Arguments have no time limits or rules, and anyone may join in.

Formal arguments that operate according to an organized set of rules are called **debates**. You may be part of a debate in an English or history class. You may be a member of the school debate team that competes with other schools. You may listen to politicians or lawyers holding formal debates.

This chapter describes the values of debate and how debate works. Debate involves creating a proposition, researching the topic, and arguing the issues. This chapter also discusses the two most common formats for school debates.

THE VALUES OF DEBATE

Why would people wish to learn to argue with each other? Debate helps people to develop valuable skills. The ability to do effective research, to organize well, to listen critically, and to speak with confidence helps you now and in the future. Many lawyers, businesspersons, politicians, and teachers say their debate training helps them in their careers.

444

Research Skills

The research skills you learn in debate will help you find information and evidence. You can use your research skills to do your English or history assignments. Your research skills could help you work on a community history project or study your family tree.

Organizational Skills

The organizational skills you learn in debate will help you plan speeches or write papers. You will be able to decide quickly what are main points and what are supporting points. You will be able to organize a large amount of information quickly and clearly, using various organizational patterns.

Critical-Listening Skills

As a debater, you will develop your critical-listening skills. When another person presents an argument, you will be able to analyze it quickly. You will learn to examine the quality of the evidence and reasoning. You will learn to ask probing questions to get more information.

Skills learned in debate, such as critical listening, can be helpful in future jobs and careers.

Learning Styles
Audio Learning

Tell students that being a critical listener in a debate means being an active listener. Ask for some ideas on how to be an active rather than a passive listener.

445

Limited English Proficiency

The vocabulary of debate is often a stumbling block for many students but particularly for LEP students. Write the boldfaced terms on the chalkboard, along with brief definitions, as students learn them. Then students can quickly refer to the board for review.

Motivation

Ask students whether they have ever had to defend themselves against a schoolyard accusation or had to convince, with evidence, one or both parents of their trustworthiness. Tell them that debate is a formalized version of these experiences.

Speaking Skills

As a debater, you will also learn to create arguments for your case and to defend them aloud. The more you debate, the more confident you will become in presenting your ideas and standing up for your beliefs in front of a group. Debate is a valuable speaking experience.

In a recent article on debate in schools one student explained the value of debate in the following words: "It broadens your perspective on a lot of issues that you don't get in a classroom. . . . It's good to be in mental competition."

THE DEBATE PROCESS

Debate is a contest of spoken argument between individuals or teams. It is a contest that has rules, time limits, and a winner and loser. One side, the **affirmative**, speaks in favor of an issue or change. The other side, the **negative**, speaks against the issue or change.

Debates center around a problem or issue that is contained in a **proposition**. A proposition is a statement of a problem that is worded so that there are clearly two sides to the argument. For example, the proposition "Resolved: That the federal government should guarantee comprehensive medical care for all U.S. citizens" is debatable. The affirmative might argue that private insurance is too expensive and that people who don't have full-time jobs are left without insurance coverage. The negative might argue that a federal insurance program would cost even more money than private insurance and that the government already protects people who are unemployed. Each side would have to use evidence and reasoning to support its arguments.

A debate is won by the side that presents the best arguments and evidence in the opinion of the listeners or judges. There are time limits and rules that state which speaker can talk and what types of things the speaker can talk about. At the end of the debate, a judge names one side as the winner.

Skill Development

Feedback

● If students can see and hear debates by debate-team members, have them discuss their observations from the Observe activity.

❝Facts do not cease to exist because they are ignored.❞
ALDOUS HUXLEY

Cooperative Learning

Have students come up with an informal list of pros and cons regarding the issue of a twelve-month school year before they read pages 447–448. Write their ideas on the chalkboard.

🔍 **OBSERVE**

Listen to examples of debates. Record the debate topic and the points made by each side. Decide which side won and which side lost the debate. Give reasons for your decision.

One of the best ways to understand debate is to look at a sample situation involving a debate. In some suburbs and cities, people are considering starting a twelve-month school year. This subject would lend itself to a formal debate for community members to hear. A proposition for this topic might be stated in the following way:

Resolved: That the Glenriver school system should establish a twelve-month school year.

The Affirmative Position

The affirmative team would argue for a change in the current situation. They would try to point out the problems with the current nine-month school year. The affirmative team might argue that students lose important learning time and that, during a three-month summer vacation, students forget much of what they learned. As proof, the affirmative team could show low test

Debaters for both sides need good evidence.

Substitute Teacher Tip

Divide students into two groups—one on the affirmative side of the school-year issue and the other on the negative. Ask them to brainstorm ideas for how to research their arguments. Have at least one member of each group take notes on what is said.

scores for students in nine-month programs compared to students in twelve-month programs. An affirmative speaker might say, "Summer vacations were started because farm families needed their children to help on the farm. Today children in this suburban community do not work on farms." An affirmative speaker might also describe the trouble students get into because of all the free time.

After describing the problems, the affirmative team might suggest a plan for a four-term school year with a ten-day vacation after each term. They might list some advantages of the twelve-month school year, such as higher test scores and better salaries for teachers.

The Negative Position

The negative team would defend the present situation—the nine-month school year. The negative team would argue that there is nothing seriously wrong with the nine-month school year. They would also argue that spending more months in school may not automatically result in higher test scores. The team would describe the benefits of summer vacations when students learn different skills, travel, and enjoy nature. The negative team could also show that it would be hard to find teachers willing to work twelve months of the year.

The negative team would attack the affirmative team's plan for change. The negative team might say, "Working parents could never get child care for ten-day periods every three months" or "Family life would be hurt because families spend more time together in the summer." In addition, the negative team might argue that the community would be hurt because camps and summer programs would have to close down.

During the Debate

The debaters for both sides would need good evidence and logical arguments to convince the audience and judges that they are right. They might quote famous experts on how people learn, and use articles from education magazines that support their

When debate judges rate delivery, they are concerned with whether the debaters' effectiveness adds to or detracts from the case. Tell students that debaters are not performers; they are persuaders. Then ask them to recall what they have learned about effective delivery.

points. They could also report the results of surveys of teachers' and parents' opinions.

In most debates there is time for each side to build a case and time to respond to what the other side said. Each speaker on a team knows the kinds of arguments or points that will be raised by other team members. Most teams follow an organizational pattern that helps divide up the responsibilities between the speakers on that side. In some formal debates, the members of each team may question, or cross-examine, speakers from the other team.

During the debate the judge usually takes notes. The judge tries to summarize the main points, the kinds of evidence used, and objections each team raises to the other side's ideas. These notes provide a map of what was said in the debate. The judge uses these notes about what was said and his or her judgment about each speaker's delivery to decide which side won. In a good debate the listeners should have heard strong arguments for both sides of the proposition.

Debaters usually take notes as their opponents speak.

Chapter 15 Learning About Debate

Cooperative Learning

Encourage groups of students to share their findings from the Interact exercise with the rest of the class.

Cooperative Learning

Encourage groups of students to share their findings from the Interact exercise with the rest of the class.

Beyond the Classroom

Encourage students to bring in newspaper or newsmagazine stories about current court cases. Discuss what possible types of arguments the lawyers for each side of a case might make.

In order to argue against opposing team members' ideas, you must have a good record of what they said. Most debaters take notes when their opponents are speaking. These notes are called a **flow sheet**. The flow sheet is a diagram of the arguments, listed in parallel columns across a page.

INTERACT

Good debaters begin their preparation by thinking of all the possible arguments, affirmative or negative, that could be raised on a topic. In groups of four, brainstorm as many affirmative and negative arguments as possible on two of the following broad topics:

Required community-service hours for high-school students

Required B grade average for participation in extracurricular school activities

Mandatory uniforms in public schools

Required foreign-language instruction in elementary grades

CREATING THE PROPOSITION

A good debate starts with a good proposition. A proposition begins with the word *resolved,* and should be worded so that there are two clear sides to the debate. Sample propositions are shown below:

Resolved: That smoking in public restaurants should be prohibited.

Resolved: That all elementary schools should provide time for daily prayer.

Resolved: That the Utah Jazz is a better basketball team than the Seattle Sonics.

Teach

Skill Development

Media Literacy

Ask what current competing values students have read or heard about recently. (Often there are publicized disputes between neighbors; for example, those who want a natural lawn versus those who want a manicured one; or those who have differing definitions of "junk.")

Critical Thinking

Evaluating

Ask students to suggest three more propositions of fact, remembering that they must be debatable. "Resolved: That the world will come to an end next year" is not debatable.

Curricular Connection

History

▲ Interested students might want to research and write a report about debate situations from America's past. For example, it took much debate to get the U.S. Constitution ratified. Students might look into what types of questions were being debated during that time and find out how such questions were finally resolved.

Types of Propositions

Just as groups may discuss questions of fact, value, or policy, debaters may argue propositions of fact, value, or policy. Most formal debates center on propositions of value or policy.

Propositions of Fact A **proposition of fact** is a statement that something is or is not true. Propositions of fact center on statements with answers that can be discovered. You may debate with a friend over when the English assignment is due. You may argue over who directed the movie *Batman Returns*. You can check out a proposition of fact. You can ask your English teacher the correct date or do research to find the name of *Batman*'s director.

Often, propositions of fact are argued in courts of law. Lawyers may argue about whether Mark Jones cheated Lee Smith or about who stole money from the grocery store. The following are two examples of propositions of fact:

Resolved: That schools with vocational programs have lower student dropout rates.

Resolved: That more than half of America's children will live in single-parent homes before they turn 18.

Propositions of Value A **proposition of value** is a statement that something is good or bad, right or wrong, useful or useless. The teams debate which idea, thing, or person is better or more valuable. A good example of competing values may be seen in the clashes between those concerned with the environment and those concerned with the economy. There are struggles over which is more important, the habitat of the spotted owl or the jobs in the local lumber industry. Many communities must face struggles between the value of protecting the environment and protecting the value of the economy of the region. The following are two examples of propositions of value:

Resolved: That one course in health education is adequate for high-school students.

Critical Thinking

Evaluating

● Ask students to list five good strong policy propositions. Then have each student choose his or her best proposition and state it in front of the class. Encourage class feedback on why each proposal is or is not a good one based on the qualities on page 453.

Resolved: That an oppressive government is better than no government at all.

Propositions of Policy Propositions of policy center on change. A **proposition of policy** is a statement that says something should or should not be done. The following are examples of propositions of policy:

Resolved: That all eighteen year olds should be required to perform a year of community service.

Resolved: That the United States government should adopt more aggressive policies to reduce the rise in juvenile crime.

✸ INTERACT

In groups of three or four, read the following propositions and identify which are propositions of fact, value, or policy.

Resolved: That the death penalty should be abolished.

Resolved: That violent TV programs are harmful to children.

Resolved: That seniors with a course grade of A should be excused from taking the final exam.

Resolved: That over twenty percent of high-school freshman in the district fail algebra.

Resolved: That the federal government should guarantee health care coverage to all citizens.

Most debate contests and many public debates center on propositions of policy. The success of such debates partly depends on the careful wording of the proposition. A carefully worded proposition sets the stage for a good debate.

Beyond the Classroom

Invite a city-council person or member of the state legislature to speak to your class about proposals currently being debated in the council or legislature. Your guest could describe for the class a typical day when members are in session.

Propositions of fact are often argued in court before a jury.

Qualities of a Good Proposition

The following are four qualities of a good policy proposition:

1. *The proposition should be debatable.* It should have two sides, no more, no less. The proposition "Resolved: That our streets should be made safe," is poor. There may be disagreement about how to make streets safe, but everyone agrees that streets should be safe. There is only one side to this proposition.

2. *The proposition should be worded so that the affirmative supports the change.* The affirmative team must argue for a change. If the proposition is stated, "Resolved: That the federal government should not establish a required seat-belt law," the affirmative team would be supporting a negative proposition. This could make the debate very confusing.

3. *The proposition should be worded as a statement, not a question.* The proposition should be worded to call for a change in the present system. Do not present the proposition as a question, such as "Should Congress establish a required seat-belt law?" or "How should a required seat-belt law be established?" These are not easily debated. The statement might be "Resolved: That Congress should enact a mandatory seat-belt law for all citizens."

4. *The proposition should contain only one issue.* The exact issue of difference should be clear. A statement such as "Resolved: That Hennepin County should start a free lunch program for senior citizens and a full-day kindergarten program" is actually a double proposition. The senior citizens' lunch program and the full-day kindergarten are totally separate issues.

Critical Thinking

Analyzing

If you wish to extend the Apply activity, give students these further propositions to analyze:

1. Resolved: Should there be a noise pollution law in our county?

2. Resolved: That schools should have no affiliations with advertisers.

3. Resolved: That students be required to perform two hours of community service a week and help keep Westcott Park clean.

REMEMBER:
Qualities of a Good Proposition

1. The proposition should be debatable.

2. The proposition should be worded so that the affirmative supports the change.

3. The proposition should be worded as a statement, not a question.

4. The proposition should contain only one issue.

APPLY

Look at the following propositions and decide which one does not fit the guidelines.

1. Resolved: That the Edgewater School District should create a student/faculty disciplinary board.

2. Resolved: That Kane County District 34 should provide free summer school for all students and day care for children of working parents.

3. Resolved: That Kenmore High-School students should be required to participate in one hundred hours of community service before graduation.

As you probably could tell, propositions 1 and 3 fit the guidelines for a good proposition. However, proposition 2 contains more than one problem. "Summer school for all students" and "day care for children of working parents" are two separate issues.

It takes time to discuss and work out a carefully worded proposition, but the time is well spent. A well-worded proposition sets the groundwork for a good debate.

❝It is a capital mistake to theorize before you have all the evidence. It biases the judgment.**❞**

SIR ARTHUR CONAN DOYLE
A Study in Scarlet

My partner, Cindy, and I are pleased to be here today to debate the proposition

<u>Resolved:</u> *That the Edgewater School should adopt a student-faculty disciplinary board.*

As students in Edgewater School we believe there is a need for new ways to handle disciplinary cases. A student-faculty board would be able to solve some of the problems with the current disciplinary process. We believe students, faculty, and parents would be more satisfied with a program that would increase morale, attendance, and student responsibility.

Let us describe the problems with the disciplinary code as they exist today. They are (1) unequal treatment for the same offense (2) confusion in interpreting the . . .

RESEARCHING THE TOPIC

Debate requires strong research skills. Debaters must be able to find evidence to support their positions and create arguments based on the evidence. Researching the topic takes time and effort but the research helps you develop your speech and respond to your opponent's speech. Debate researchers are held to the same ethical standards discussed in Chapter 10. This section on the research process will be based on the following debate topic:

Resolved: That the Molina City Council should ban smoking in all public restaurants.

Finding Evidence

What can we say about how smoking affects the bloodstream?

Can we find some doctors' opinions on the effects of secondary smoke?

Secondary smoke? What's that?

Exactly what is a public restaurant? Does it include country clubs?

These and many other questions could be asked by debaters who are starting to learn about the above debate topic. Although

Critical Thinking
Analyzing

● Have students decide on a debate topic and write out a plan for researching that topic. First have them write a proposal. Then encourage them to write questions they will need to answer through their research. Remind them that they must answer questions not only with regard to their proposal but also with regard to possible counter-arguments from the opposition.

455

Curricular Connection

Science

● You might tell students that a good way to test their debate evidence is to use their proposal in the same way a scientist uses a hypothesis. Once the hypothesis is developed, the scientist studies and tests it from various perspectives in an attempt to prove its basic truth. Applying this principle to the art of debate will help keep students from making faulty arguments.

debaters defend only one side of the argument, they need to know a great deal of information about the overall topic. A competent debater finds evidence, creates arguments, and is ethical in the use of evidence.

How much evidence is enough? There is no easy way to answer that question, but remember that you are not working on a persuasive speech. When you give a persuasive speech, you decide which points you will make. In a debate you never know for sure which points the opposition will raise. Therefore, you also need to have evidence to refute, or attack, the argument or evidence used by the other team. For this reason, you need much more evidence for debate than you will actually use.

To find information, you may follow the research guidelines and steps described in Chapter 10. You may need to use specialized periodicals or books. For example, to research the smoking topic, you may need to read medical books or city building codes for restaurants. Your reading will help you learn a great deal about the subject. It will also help you to learn the vocabulary words related to the topic. For example, secondary smoke refers to the smoke that affects a nonsmoker in a room with smokers. In your research, you will learn about the history of the subject, the main experts on the topic, and the important issues that could come up in a debate.

Debaters must be careful to verify their evidence, because their case will collapse if they use inaccurate or false evidence. For example, one speaker in a debate on state-required premarital counseling might say, "Professor John Gottman says, 'Conflict is bad for marriage.'" She might make this claim because she heard a comment about Gottman's research on the radio. Yet, if she went to Gottman's writings, such as *Why Marriages Succeed or Fail,* she would discover that Gottman talks about one stable type of couple as the "volatile couple," who have quite a bit of conflict and that he does not make a flat statement such as "conflict is bad for marriage." With some knowledge of his actual writings she could make a good case for teaching conflict management skills in premarital counseling.

Critical Thinking

Analyzing

Have students carefully read the "Speaking of . . ." article on page 457. Then ask students to identify situations in the article that would require John David Maurer to find and use evidence in dealing with individuals and groups.

SPEAKING OF . . .

JONATHAN DAVID MAURER

Jonathan Maurer's own words best explain his special communication situation. "I use unique communication skills in many aspects of my life, most notably as a student-council representative, as the editor of Maryville Academy's literary journal, and as a ward of the state of Illinois," he reports. As a student at John Hersey High School in Illinois and a resident of Maryville Academy, a residential facility for young people who are wards of the state, Jonathan must take charge of his own life and use his communication skills on his own behalf. It is his unusual personal responsibility to coordinate the people who can make decisions for him. "As a ward of the state," he explains, "I often find myself struggling to find the right person to sign certain forms, grant me permission for certain activities, and contact when an issue arises." He must interact with case workers, lawyers, officials of the Department of Children and Family Services, and immediate caretakers; sometimes he has to involve all these persons in one decision. This task requires Jonathan to have good self-esteem, strong interpersonal skills, and an ability to state his needs persuasively. His vocabulary includes terms such as "PRT or Placement Review Team Meeting," "pointcard," "homepass," and "privs."

Jonathan's skills have developed to the point where he can now help other state wards manage the system, instructing them about contacts and resources.

In addition to these responsibilities, Jonathan has other communication demands, such as conveying his classmates' concerns to the administration of his high school and giving speeches to the Maryville Academy Board to raise funds for the literary magazine, *On My Mind.*

In the future Jonathan may use his experiences and communication skills to serve as a counselor, a lawyer, a fund-raiser, or director of an educational institution.

❝'For example' is not proof.❞

JEWISH PROVERB

Skill Development

Research

Students might use the following checklist for evaluating evidence:

1. Is the source reliable?

2. Is the author an expert?

3. Is the evidence current?

4. Is the evidence consistent with other information?

Good research skills are crucial to debaters.

Competitive debaters often find that all the teams debating a topic have read much of the same evidence. If one speaker misinterprets evidence or misquotes a source, a speaker on the other team is likely to call attention to it. Experienced debaters are good critical listeners who are trained to find holes in the other side's evidence.

When you gather information, record it on note cards. Because you will use the cards during the debate, you need to group the cards in certain topic areas. For example, when debating smoking in public places, your topic areas may be "Medical Effects," "Personal Rights," "Economic Effects," and "Other Cities' Bans."

Creating Your Arguments

Your arguments are based on the evidence you find. In debate, an argument is created when you use your evidence to reach and defend a conclusion. As you build your arguments, be sure to test your evidence and types of reasoning, as discussed in Chapters 10 and 14. You can build arguments by using examples, expert testimony, statistics, logic, and analogies.

458

Critical Thinking

Evaluating

▼ Explain to students what is meant by **bias**—a tendency to show special favor to one person or group. Tell students that sometimes public figures, newspaper columnists, talk-show hosts, or call-in listeners to talk shows purport to be authorities or experts but they are really only expressing opinions, sometimes biased ones. Ask students how they might determine whether someone is an expert.

Examples You can give examples of similar situations to support your position. For example, you could use evidence based on medical studies of people who were exposed to secondary smoke. You could describe the effects on restaurants that banned smokers. You might say, "In a national survey of 100 restaurants that banned smoking in all areas, only 12 percent indicated a drop in customers. Sixteen percent reported an increase."

The examples you choose must be typical. If only one of eight restaurants had increased business as a result of banning smoking, the example is not typical.

Experts You can also support your position by using quotations from experts on the subject. You need to explain to the listeners why someone is considered an expert, why the person is qualified to speak on the subject, and why he or she is unbiased on the subject.

You might quote medical experts' opinions on the physical effects of secondary smoke. For example, you might say,

You can probably find evidence on the Internet to support your position.

66"Contrariwise," continued Tweedledee, "If it was so, it might be; and if it were so, it would be; but as it isn't, it ain't. That's logic."99

LEWIS CARROLL

Skills Development

Media Literacy

● Remind students that while the Internet can be a handy information source, it is a good idea to double-check all facts and data found there. Often information provided on the Internet is not attributed to a specific source and can't be proven. Discuss what other sources students might use to verify important facts.

459

Skill Development

Vocabulary

▲ Encourage students to write several analogies about various topics. Then have each student choose his or her best analogy and present it to the class.

Links to Past Learning

Remind students that statistics can be deceiving. Different studies show different results, and some sources are more convincing than others. Discuss with students what sources might be good references for statistics on the number of smoking-related cancer deaths.

Learning Styles

Visual Learning

● Some students could work together to create a poster or bulletin board that would identify and illustrate the five building blocks of debate.

"Dr. Alicia Chavez, a lung specialist, calls smoking by parents a form of child abuse because of the damage to the children's lungs."

A person such as the president of a cigarette company would be considered a biased source. You would not wish to quote this person's claim that secondary smoke is harmless.

Statistics You can use numerical information to show links between things. For example, you might discuss the link between the number of people who smoke and those who develop cancer. You might show a link between restaurants that banned smokers and an increase or decrease in their incomes. For example, a debater might say, "Over 50 percent of the Center City restaurants that banned smoking reported an increase in customers after three months. Many reported that new patrons stated a desire to eat in a smoke-free environment."

Logic You can also use reasoning to argue that if x happens, y might follow. For example, one team might argue, "If one person at a table becomes uncomfortable because of smoke, the entire table of people will leave early and reduce the income of the restaurant owner." The other side may respond, "If you don't allow people to smoke, certain people will never come into the restaurant."

Analogies You can create an argument by drawing an analogy, or describing likenesses between two things or ideas. A team might create a direct or literal analogy by suggesting eating in smoke-filled rooms is similar to eating in high-asbestos areas, and that no one would wish to do that. Another team may use a figurative analogy to highlight the problems of eating healthy food in a smoke-filled environment by saying, "There is no use cleaning the house when rats are swimming in the basement." A debater might say, "Eating a vegetarian meal in a smoke-filled restaurant is like painting a house that has rotting walls."

Links to Past Learning

Remind students that while they may have strong opinions about a case they are debating, opinions are not what win cases. Stress the importance of provable fact in every debated issue.

❝A few observations and much reasoning lead to error; many observations and a little reasoning to truth.❞

ALEXIS CARREL

Curricular Connection

Social Studies / Language Arts

Show segments of a videotape of the film version of *Inherit the Wind.* Encourage students to take notes on the debate techniques the two lawyers use in their handling of the case.

INTERACT

Debaters need to find information on very specific topics. Specialized magazines or journals are those with a narrow content focus. These are not general-interest magazines that cover many different topics. In teams of two or three, find two specialized magazines or journals that could be used to find evidence on three of the following topics.

Desktop Publishing	World Travel
Fishing Rights	Medical Education
Rifles	American Indian History
Water Pollution	Teenage Alcoholism
Extraterrestrial Beings	Child Abuse
Animal Rights	Illiteracy
Changing Roles of Women	Air Pollution

ARGUING THE ISSUES

The affirmative believes there is a serious problem in our community that must be changed. We fear that in two years . . .

The negative believes no serious harm will come to our community. In fact, our community is stronger . . .

When arguing the issues, affirmative and negative debaters perform two major jobs:

1. They build their own cases, using evidence and reasoning to support their position.

2. They respond to their opponent's case, using refutation and rebuttal.

Building a Case

Each side in a debate must build a **case**. A case consists of all of the arguments that will be made to support the affirmative or negative position. The arguments should be logically organized

Motivation

Tell students that because the rules of debate are so clear-cut, debating is in some ways easier than simply arguing. Following strict rules of debate etiquette can help debaters keep from getting flustered or angry at their opponents during critical moments of the presentation.

Critical Thinking

Synthesizing

Encourage students to use the refutation and rebuttal models on this page as guidelines for writing their own sample refutations and rebuttals. They can write on any topic. Make sure that their work shows comprehension of the difference between the two formats.

and supported by evidence. In debates based on propositions of policy, cases are built to answer the following questions:

1. Does a serious problem exist at present that makes a change necessary?

2. Will the suggested plan solve these problems?

3. Will the plan bring about new and greater benefits than those that exist at present?

The affirmative case tries to answer these questions with a yes, and the negative answers them with a no.

Debaters often organize their cases into outlines known as **briefs**. A brief contains arguments and evidence. Briefs are developed both to present cases and to defend against anticipated attacks from the opponent.

Responding to the Opponent

In addition to building a case, each side in the debate must argue against its opponent's case. Both the affirmative and the negative teams must also rebuild their own cases. This involves refutation and rebuttal.

Refutation **Refutation** is the process of attacking the opposing side's case. When you refute the case, you try to find fault with the team's evidence or reasoning. For example, you might say:

> "My opponent said, 'Secondary smoke does not cause serious harm.' He quoted an unknown person, Dr. Alvin Keefer, as saying 'Smoking only hurts the smoker.' Well, we maintain secondary smoke causes serious harm. I will read the evidence from three medical researchers in the Surgeon General's office. Dr. Martin Wheeler says, 'Secondary smoke presents great danger to people within fifteen feet of the smoker. . . .'"

Rebuttal **Rebuttal** is the process of rebuilding your own case after it has been attacked by the other team. A speaker might say: "We told you there was no serious harm from secondary smoke. We cited Dr. Alvin Keefer. The affirmative said there is great harm and

❝No one is listening until you make a mistake.❞
ANONYMOUS

Arguments in a case must be organized logically.

questioned Dr. Keefer's expertise. They quoted medical researchers. Well, Dr. Keefer is a director of a heart program at Boone Hospital. We have two other authorities who support his ideas. I will read the statement to you (the statements follow). Therefore our position still stands. Smoking harms only the smoker."

Effective debaters have enough evidence to rebuild their cases after their opponents have refuted them.

DEBATE FORMATS

There are two major types of debate formats. These are policy debate and Lincoln-Douglas debate. These formats may be used in the classroom, although classroom debaters may also create their own format. If you are a member of a school debate team, you will learn to debate using one or both of these formats.

Policy Debate

The **policy debate** format is similar to the type of debate discussed in this chapter. In policy debate, two teams debate a proposition of policy. Each team member speaks two or three times. The first speeches are designed to build the case; the second speeches involve refutation and rebuttal. There is a question

Curricular Connection

History

▲ Interested students could do library research to find out more about the origins of the Lincoln-Douglas style of debate.

Beyond the Classroom

Students might be interested in the following films, which feature courtroom scenes, including cross-examinations. You will be the best judge of which films you can safely suggest for your students in your community.

- *To Kill a Mockingbird*
- *Witness for the Prosecution*
- *Anatomy of a Murder*
- *The Verdict*
- *Midnight in the Garden of Good and Evil*

period, called cross-examination, during which the debaters may ask questions of the opposing team. The following are topics that could be debated in the policy format:

Resolved: That the United States Government should adopt environmental policies that lead to a significant increase in national parks and forests.

Resolved: That the federal government should establish national standards for the certification of elementary- and secondary-school teachers.

In the policy debate format, speeches are always given in the same order. Times vary, according to tournament rules. The usual speaker order and allotted times are as follows:

First affirmative speaker	8 minutes
Cross-examination	3 minutes
First negative speaker	8 minutes
Cross-examination	3 minutes
Second affirmative speaker	8 minutes
Cross-examination	3 minutes
Second negative speaker	8 minutes
Cross-examination	3 minutes
First negative rebuttal	5 minutes
First affirmative rebuttal	5 minutes
Second negative rebuttal	5 minutes
Second affirmative rebuttal	5 minutes

Lincoln-Douglas Debate

The **Lincoln-Douglas debate** format is named after the famous political campaign debates between Abraham Lincoln and Stephen Douglas. In Lincoln-Douglas debate, one speaker on each side debates a proposition of value. Each speaker delivers at least two speeches, building the case and supporting it. There is

Amazing Fact!

The Lincoln-Douglas debates were actually a series of seven debates held in various Illinois towns. Slavery was the primary issue.

usually a chance for each speaker to cross-examine the other. The following are topics that could be debated in the Lincoln-Douglas format:

Resolved: That capital punishment is morally wrong.

Resolved: That laws protecting citizens from themselves are justified.

The usual speaker order and allotted times for Lincoln-Douglas debate are as follows:

Affirmative constructive speech	6 minutes
Negative constructive speech	7 minutes
First Affirmative rebuttal	4 minutes
Negative rebuttal	6 minutes
Second Affirmative rebuttal	3 minutes

Cooperative Learning

Some students might enjoy presenting a Lincoln-Douglas debate for the class. Use the following proposition of value for the debate—Resolved: That destroying stray cats and dogs is morally wrong—or have students choose a proposition of value that interests them. Ask 4 or 5 volunteers to work together to prepare arguments for the affirmative side, and ask 4 or 5 volunteers to do the same for the negative side. Each group can select one speaker to present the group's arguments. The class can vote on which group presented the better arguments.

If cross-examination is used, there is a three-minute cross-examination period after the first two speeches. Therefore it would appear as follows:

Affirmative constructive speech	6 minutes
Negative cross-examination	3 minutes
Negative constructive speech	7 minutes
Affirmative cross-examination	3 minutes
First Affirmative rebuttal	4 minutes
Negative rebuttal	6 minutes
Second Affirmative rebuttal	3 minutes

Across the country there are slightly different styles and formats for debate.

CHAPTER 15 SUMMARY

This chapter presented an overview of a special type of persuasive communication called debate. Debate is a contest of persuasive argument between individuals or teams with rules, time limits, and a declared winner and loser. This chapter discussed the values of debate, how debate works, and the three types of debate propositions. It stressed the importance of researching the topic and arguing the issues. Two major forms of debate are policy debate and Lincoln-Douglas debate.

Cooperative Learning

● Expand on the Cooperative Learning activity suggested on page 466. Assign a debate topic and then divide the entire class into affirmative and negative sides. Allow them time to research and prepare their arguments. Each side can split up into subgroups responsible for specific portions of the debate. Encourage them to follow the preparation guidelines in the text. When both teams have prepared their arguments you will serve as the judge in a Lincoln-Douglas debate between the two teams. Individual volunteers from each team can alternate as speakers for each portion of the debate.

Answers

Think About It

Student answers will vary. Here are sample answers:

1. A debate is a formal argument that operates according to an organized set of rules. There are many different areas of debate: the classroom, competitive debate teams, and political debates between opposing candidates.

2. Research skills, organizational skills, critical listening skills, and speaking skills are all valuable adjuncts to debate.

3. The affirmative side argues in favor of an issue or change. The negative argues against the issue or change.

4. A proposition of fact is a statement that something is or is not true. The answers to these questions can be discovered and proved. Propositions of value are statements that something is good or bad, right or wrong, useful or useless. The teams debate which idea, thing, or person is better or more valuable. Propositions of policy are statements that center on change. This type of statement says something should or should not be done.

5. Examples, experts, statistics, logic, and analogies

6. Refutation is the process of attacking the opposing side's case. Rebuttal is the process of rebuilding your own case after it has been attacked by the other team.

7. Policy debate—two teams debate a proposition of policy. Each team member speaks two or three times. The speeches are designed to (1) build the case and (2) offer refutation and rebuttal. There is also a question period, called

CHAPTER REVIEW

Think About It

1. Define debate and describe three places where debates take place in everyday life.

2. What are the values of debate?

3. What are the differences between the affirmative side and the negative side?

4. What are the differences between propositions of fact, value, and policy?

5. List various types of evidence you may use to build an argument.

6. Define *refutation* and *rebuttal.* How are they different from one another?

7. Describe two debate formats.

Try It Out

1. Interview an adult who participated on a school debate team. Find out how that person's debate training helped him or her in a career. Report your findings to the class.

2. Write a debate proposition of fact, one of value, and one of policy. In a small group, discuss the propositions, using the criteria for good propositions discussed in class. Choose one of the propositions for a classroom debate.

3. Create arguments for each of the following situations and then, with a partner, role-play the situations in class:

You want a later curfew. Your parents say no.

You want an extension on your homework assignment. Your teacher says no.

Your brother or sister refuses to help you clean the room you share.

Class members should listen to the arguments you and your partner created. They should then discuss how each person used examples, experts, statistics, and logic to create the arguments and decide whether the evidence supported the conclusions each person drew.

4. Listen to a political or community debate. Identify the types of evidence used by each speaker. Decide which speaker or which side won the debate, and explain your decision.

Put It in Writing

1. Analyze a letter to the editor in your local paper. Record the use of examples, expert testimony, statistics, logical analysis, or analogies used by the writer to build an argument. Analyze two pieces of evidence by examining how well the evidence supports the writer's arguments.

2. Using the proposition "All public-school students should be required to wear school uniforms" or another proposition of your choice, write one affirmative argument and one negative argument.

cross-examination, during which the debaters may ask questions of the opposing team. Lincoln-Douglas debate—one speaker on each side debates a proposition of value. Each speaker delivers at least two speeches, building the case and supporting it. There is usually a chance for each speaker to cross-examine the other.

Quick Check

Ask students to find and define these Key Terms:

affirmative (446)

brief (462)

case (461)

debate (444)

flow sheet (450)

Lincoln-Douglas debate (464)

negative (446)

policy debate (463)

proposition (446)

proposition of fact (451)

proposition of policy (452)

proposition of value (451)

rebuttal (462)

refutation (462)

Speak About It

1. Present to the class the affirmative and the negative argument you developed for activity 2 of Put It in Writing.

2. As a class, choose a proposition of policy to debate. The proposition could be concerned with a school or community problem. Divide into affirmative and negative teams. Research the proposition and create arguments for your side. An affirmative speaker will present one argument, and a negative speaker will refute the argument. An affirmative and a negative speaker will then be given a chance for rebuttal. Discuss how your experience helped you understand the responsibilities of the affirmative and negative sides in a debate.

3. Using the following newspaper article as a springboard for discussion develop a class debate on this issue: Juvenile pranks without malicious intent should not be considered as grounds for manslaughter charges.

After 3 Die, Trio Get 15 Years for Taking Stop Signs
By Lisa Holewa
Associated Press 6/21/97

TAMPA, Fla.—Three friends were sentenced to 15 years in prison Friday for pulling up a stop sign as a prank and causing the deaths of three teens who drove into the path of an 8-ton truck.

"I understand your parents love you as much as these parents loved their children, there are no winners in this case," Circuit Judge Bob Mitcham told the young woman and two young men who were convicted last month of manslaughter.

Three 18-year-old buddies who were driving around listening to music after a night of bowling were killed when their car drove through the intersection and was hit by the truck. The stop sign was found lying on the roadside near the accident.

Turning to the sobbing families of those killed, Mitcham said: "My heart breaks for you."

Though a pre-sentence recommendation called for up to 50 years in prison, the judge, known as "Maximum Bob" for his harsh sentences, decided to give the defendants far less.

"I don't believe for one minute that you or the other two defendants pulled these signs up with the intent of causing the death of anyone," he told Christopher Cole, 20.

He then sentenced Cole to 30 years, suspending half, and did the same for Nissa Baillie, 21, and Thomas Miller, 20. The three could be eligible for parole after nearly 13 years.

All three cried and repeatedly wiped their eyes with tissue as each stood before the judge in orange jail jumpsuits, their hands cuffed. Their families and friends stood behind them and the families of the victims across the courtroom.

Randall White, Kevin Farr, and Brian Hernandez were killed on Feb. 7, 1996, the day after the stop sign was pulled up.

Cole testified that he and his friends stole as many as 19 signs along the rural roads east of Tampa the night before the accident. But he told jurors they didn't touch the stop sign at that intersection.

The defendants told investigators they panicked when they heard about the accident and threw the signs they had collected in a river.

"There's been many a night that I stayed up and cried . . . because your sons did not return home." Miller said, his face red and twisted by sobs, as he looked toward the victims' families.

Just before the sentencing, the judge refused a new trial request based on a witness' claim that a prosecutor forced him to lie.

Unit Focus

Unit 5 introduces oral interpretation and offers in-depth instruction and suggestions for selecting and performing. It also addresses the subjects of giving and receiving feedback on oral interpretation performances. And, finally, it discusses the process of group interpretation as an approach to building self-confidence, performance and analysis skills, and literary knowledge.

Unit Portfolios

Activities marked with this symbol are suitable for inclusion in speech portfolios.

Ability Key

▲ average and above-average students
● all students
▼ average and below-average students

Ancillary Resource Key

 = *Teacher's Resource Book*

 = Workbook

 = TRB Worksheets & Evaluation Forms

 = TRB Assessment and Testing

Performance Objectives

After completing this unit, students will be able to

1. define oral interpretation
2. describe how to find, select, and analyze literature for performance
3. prepare and mark a script
4. learn how to create mood and characters
5. evaluate oral interpretation, storytelling, and group-interpretation performances
6. prepare and perform choral-speaking and reader's theatre performances

UNIT FIVE

Interpretive Communication

Preparing for Oral Interpretation	16
Performing Oral Interpretation	17
Group Interpretation	18

Bibliography

Print

Baltuck, Naomi. *Apples from Heaven: Multicultural Folktales About Stories and Storytellers*. North Haven, Conn.: Linnet Books, 1995.

Cassady, Marshall. *The Art of Storytelling: Creative Ideas for Preparation and Performance*. Colorado Springs, Colo.: Meriwether,1994.

Lee, Charlotte I. *Oral Interpretation*, 8th ed. New York: Houghton Mifflin, 1991.

Porter, Steven, comp. and ed. *New Works for Reader's Theatre*. Studio City, Calif.: Phantom Publications in association with Players Press, 1994.

Shepard, Aaron. *Stories on Stage: Scripts for Reader's Theater*. Bronx, N.Y.: H.W. Wilson, 1993. A collection of 22 plays adapted from folk tales, short stories, myths, and novels.

Video

Jackie Torrence Presents—Latino Stories.
Jackie Torrence Presents—Native American Stories.
Jackie Torrence Presents—Asian-American Stories. (North Billerica, Mass.: Curriculum Associates, Inc., 1996) Videocassettes.

Web Site

Drew's Script-O-Rama
http://www.script-o-rama.com
A comprehensive index of movie and television scripts

You may wish to review the transcripts for readability and appropriate subject matter before sharing them with your students.

	Day 1	Day 2	Day 3	Day 4	Day 5
16 Preparing for Oral Interpretation					
Characteristics of Oral Interpretation	Selecting Material	Analyzing Literature	Pieces for Oral Interp.	Summary	
Appropriate Literature for Oral Interpretation					Chapter Review
Teacher's Resource Book					
Teaching Suggestions 16.1	16.2–16.3	16.4	16.5		
Worksheets & Evaluation Forms			46		
					Chapter Test 16
Workbook 16.1	16.2	16.3	16.4–16.5	16.6	

Week 16 / Chapter 16 Planner

Motivation

Ask students to come up with a list of words that describe the best storyteller they know. Ask: "What distinguishing characteristics do these people have? What makes them different from other storytellers?"

16

CHAPTER SIXTEEN

Preparing for Oral Interpretation

Chapter Objectives

After completing this chapter, you should be able to

1. define oral interpretation

2. list various sources of material for oral interpretation

3. describe the four standards for selecting literature

4. select quality literature for performance

5. describe the four key points for analyzing literature for performance

Links to Past Learning

Encourage students to talk about the very first stories they remember hearing. They might have had a relative who told them stories or read to them. Have students discuss why they think these early experiences have remained in their memories.

⚫ Key Terms

conflict	onomatopoeia	plot	setting
dramatic speaker	oral history	rhyme	style
mood	oral interpretation	rhythm	theme

❝When you perform . . . you are out of yourself— larger and more potent, more beautiful. You are for minutes heroic. This is power.**❞**

AGNES DE MILLE

Critical Thinking
Predicting

● Encourage students to look over the chapter objectives and the Key Words and predict what they will learn about in Chapter 16.

Skill Development
Quick Skill Opportunity

● Go through the list of Key Words and encourage volunteers to define any words they can. Write their definitions on the chalkboard.

473

Learning Styles

Audio Learning

● Bring in a copy of Dylan Thomas's *A Child's Christmas in Wales*, the Tevya stories by Sholem Aleichem, or a book of Native American legends and tales, and read brief excerpts to the class.

Learning Styles

Audio Learning

● Have students read aloud portions of any of the works you read to them. Encourage the class to offer feedback on the quality of each reading. Ask them to elaborate on what each speaker did that was interesting as well as those areas where he or she could use improvement.

474

Every night my father reads *The Cat in the Hat* to my youngest sister.

I love to listen to my grandmother read from her mother's diary.

At the Thanksgiving show our class read three poems about the founding of our country.

Our school has a Writers' Showcase in which students perform material written by other students.

Although the term *oral interpretation* may be new to you, the experience of interpreting literature orally is part of everyday life. A lawyer may read a piece of evidence to the jury. A religious leader may read prayers as part of a service. Parents read to their young children, and teachers read to their classes. An increasing number of stage presentations involve one or two performers interpreting a script directly to the audience.

You may remember how much you enjoyed being read to as a child. Or perhaps you heard stories told from memory around a campfire. Even now you probably find yourself enjoying another person's performance of some of your favorite authors' works.

In this chapter you will learn how to prepare for oral interpretation. You will learn the characteristics of oral interpretation, how to select material that is appropriate for oral interpretation, and how to analyze the material used in a performance.

CHARACTERISTICS OF ORAL INTERPRETATION

Oral interpretation involves the performing of literature aloud to communicate meaning to an audience. An interpreter analyzes the literature and uses his or her voice and body to communicate the results of the analysis. The interpreter is the connection between the literature and the audience. He or she shares the meaning of the literature with the listeners.

A performer may use many different writings for oral interpretation, including diaries, poems, stories, fables, essays, and plays. In addition to written literature, interpreters can use stories that have been handed down from generation to generation without

Multicultural Learning

● Encourage students to work in pairs to share stories from their family's or their ethnic culture's oral tradition.

Cooperative Learning

● Students might enjoy telling a group story. Ask one student to begin to tell a story from his or her imagination. When the student has talked for 30 seconds to a minute, point to a different student and ask him or her to continue the story. Continue in this way until each student has had a chance to add to the story. Remind students to listen carefully so that they can retain important details from the other speakers.

being written down. This is called the oral tradition and is the source of much of our literature today.

You may be wondering how oral interpretation is different from public speaking. Is oral interpretation a type of acting? There are major differences between oral interpretation and public speaking or acting. Understanding these differences will help you became successful at oral interpretation. When you prepare for an oral interpretation performance, you must be aware of the following:

1. *You are not the author.* When you do oral interpretation, you are performing literature written by another person. Therefore you are not sharing your own personal thoughts or feelings with the audience, as you would in public speaking. At times you may perform something you have written yourself, but this does not happen often.

2. *You perform the author's words, sometimes by direct reading.* As an interpreter, you bring to life the exact words of another person. In public speaking you speak from an outline or note cards. Your speech may change slightly from performance to performance. However, oral interpretation requires you to perform the literature exactly as it is written.

3. *You interpret a piece of literature.* In oral interpretation, you are not trying to create a message to inform or persuade your listeners. Instead, you are trying to help the listeners "see" the situations and images you are creating orally. Your goal is to share the meaning of the literature as you interpret it.

4. *You remain yourself during the performance.* When you are acting, you take on the role of a character in a play. When you interpret literature, you share your understanding of the writing. You use your voice and body to suggest the mood or the characters, but you do not become a character.

Oral interpretation helps you develop special connections to pieces of literature. As you work to bring literature to life through your analysis and performance, you will discover links between yourself and the author's writing. The connection will help you to recreate the literature for your listeners.

Cooperative Learning

Encourage students to break into small groups and share their impressions from the Observe activity.

Oral interpretation involves analyzing a piece of literature and sharing the meaning with listeners.

🔍 OBSERVE

For one week record all the examples of oral interpretation you hear. You may hear literature read through the media, in school, at home, or in some other setting. Note the situation, the interpreter, and the kind of material read.

APPROPRIATE LITERATURE FOR ORAL INTERPRETATION

Tamika read from a chapter of *Thirteen Ways to Sink a Sub,* a book about a substitute teacher in the classroom. I thought our substitute teacher would fall out of the chair, she laughed so hard.

Adam did a reading from the play *The Piano Lesson* by August Wilson. There are powerful family conflicts in that play.

Many pieces of good literature are appropriate for oral interpretation. You can find lists of short stories, plays, and poetry in literary indexes in most library reference rooms. Indexes such as the *Short Story Index, Grainger Index to Poetry,* and *Play Index* are

476

66[My stories] run up and bite me on the leg—I respond by writing down everything that goes on during the bite. When I finish, the idea lets go and runs off.**99**

RAY BRADBURY

good sources for finding literature for oral interpretation. This section describes some of the many kinds of literature you could use for oral interpretation.

Favorite Authors

Maybe you like the poetry of Shel Silverstein, Robert Frost, or Nikki Giovanni. Maybe you are a fan of Ray Bradbury's or Robert Fulgham's short stories or of the novels of Lois Lowrey, E. L. Konigsburg, Susan Cooper, Stephen King, or Madeleine L'Engle. If you have a favorite writer, you could choose his or her writings and share them with your listeners. Don't forget to consider a favorite magazine or newspaper columnist whose work you could interpret. You may wish to go back to the list of favorite fiction and nonfiction writings that you started when you read Chapter 5.

Literature Collections

You have probably read collections of literature, also called anthologies, in your English or reading classes. You can choose a short story, a poem, or an essay from one of these anthologies for your interpretation. You might also select from collections of folktales, particularly those from different cultures.

Biographies or Autobiographies

You may share the writing from a biography or autobiography of someone you admire. There are many biographies written about famous people. You could interpret Martin Luther King's words during his civil rights marches. You could describe Jackie Joyner-Kersee's Olympic performances or Dan Rather's career in journalism. You might read from Maya Angelou's autobiography, *I Know Why the Caged Bird Sings*.

Plays or Screenplays

You may enjoy dramatic literature, such as plays or screenplays. For example, if you like Neil Simon's comedies, you may read a section from *Barefoot in the Park*. You could perform from a children's play

Curricular Connection

Language Arts

● Encourage students to think about a favorite author and to write a paragraph on why they think this author's work would or would not be a good vehicle for oral interpretation.

477

Motivation

▼ Encourage students to think about their own family's rich cultural heritage. Have them discuss ways in which relatives tend to strengthen family ties with stories of the past. Have interested volunteers share a family story with the class.

for a young audience using *Amber Waves*, *Charlotte's Web*, or *Wiley and the Hairy Man*.

In recent years the actress Anna Deveare Smith has developed a special kind of one-person performance, sometimes referred to as a play. She combines acting, playwriting, and investigative reporting to explore race and community in America. She creates scripts based on interviews with different individuals who were involved in conflicts. She then interprets their comments, which reflect differing points of view, in a one-person performance. You could perform some of her characters from *Fires in the Mirror*.

Oral Histories

Perhaps you have a grandparent who tells you stories of his or her childhood. These stories are part of your oral history. **Oral histories** are stories that are told over and over and passed down through generations without being written down. With each retelling, the details may change, but the central ideas remain the same. For example, refugees often tell stories of leaving their country. Jewish refugees who lived through the concentration camps and Vietnamese refugees who escaped as boat people tell stories of how they survived.

Oral histories allow storytellers to make sense out of experiences and to pass on wisdom and ideas to the listeners. Often what the stories are about is not as important as why people tell them. Perhaps your grandparents like to tell you stories of their past because they enjoy reliving the experiences or because they want you to understand your cultural heritage.

OBSERVE

Listen carefully to the people around you who are telling personal stories. Perhaps it is your uncle describing his first dance or your mother telling about her childhood adventures. Keep a log for a week of the stories you hear. List the name and age of the storyteller, the subject of the story, and why you think the speaker told it.

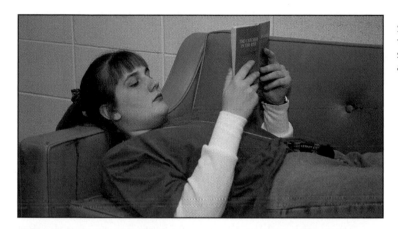

Selecting literature for interpretation should be enjoyable and challenging.

Curricular Connection

Language Arts

Students might like to write a draft of one of the personal stories they recorded in their log in the Observe activity. They may want to perform the story later.

✳ **INTERACT**

In small groups discuss some of your favorite authors and their writings. Make three suggestions for material that classmates might consider for their interpretations. Each person should bring at least one written selection to share with others. Read at least two pieces suggested by someone else and see whether you could develop one of the pieces in your performance.

Your Own or a Friend's Writing

Sometimes you may choose to read something you wrote, such as a story or poem. Or you might interpret a story written by another student and share it with the class. To hear a poem you have written recited by someone else could be very interesting. The poem "Whatcha Gonna Do?" on the next page was written by a junior-high-school student and has been used for oral interpretation by other people.

SELECTING MATERIAL

There are countless places to find material for oral interpretation. Enjoy yourself as you thumb through literature to find some possible pieces. Read the autobiography of someone you admire.

479

▲ Encourage students to write a paragraph or two discussing the theme of "Whatcha Gonna Do?"

Curricular Connection
Music

● Some students might want to set the poem "Whatcha Gonna Do?" to music. Encourage interested students to sing, talk-sing, or rap the poem. Encourage the class to comment on how these interpretations changed, detracted from, or enhanced the poem's meaning.

Listen carefully to the stories your great aunt tells at family gatherings. Once you find some material, you need to know how to select the best literature, or the best part for interpretation.

As you select your performance material, think about these standards: the quality of the literature, its audience appeal, the oral possibilities of the literature, and your feelings for the piece.

Quality of Material

Good literature has certain characteristics. It has a theme that connects the reader or listener to common human experiences. Most people have experienced love, anger, joy, and pain. They have felt scared, sad, or happy. Much good literature also has **conflict** the struggle between two opposing forces. All people have experienced conflicts. They may have had conflicts within themselves, with other individuals, with nature, or with a hostile environment. Many fables contain a moral or lesson that grows out of these conflicts.

Whatcha Gonna Do?

Whatcha gonna do
when the world
breaks down,
child,
Whatcha gonna do
when we all pull
that great big plug
of existence
out of its socket?
Whatcha gonna do
when the earth
stops turning,
and the sun
stops shining,
and the rain
stops falling?
Whatcha gonna do

when they drop
the bomb
on all
that you live for,
child,
Whatcha gonna do
when they blow up
all your dreams?
Whatcha gonna do
when all your ideals
crash in around you,
along with all
that you ever
thought
was right?
Whatcha gonna do
when a smile

becomes a rare thing
of the past,
child,
Whatcha gonna do
when the words
hope
and harmony
and endurance
get erased
from the human
dictionary of life?
Whatcha gonna do,
Whatcha gonna do . . .
I know
whatcha gotta do,
child,
I know . . .

480

Learning Styles
Audio Learning

● Bring in a recording of Laurence Olivier, Derek Jacobi, or Richard Burton performing a soliloquy from *Hamlet* or another Shakespearean play. Encourage students to point out places where the words seem to come alive through the actor's interpretation.

You gotta
hold on tightly
to the few
broken ideals
you're left with,
child,
you gotta
find new dreams
to dream
as soon as
the old ones die.
You gotta
always stop
to hug
the other soul
you meet,
and don't forget
to tell them
that you're praying
for them,
that you're fighting
for them.
You gotta
always remember
that someone,
somewhere
is pulling
for you too,
child,
you gotta
never forget

that courage
and determination
will forever fight
alongside you.
You gotta
understand
that there
are other forms
of sunshine
besides light,
that there
are other forms
of rain
besides water.
You gotta
push yourself always
as far
as you can go,
child,
and most of all,
you gotta
pick up
that great, big plug
of life
and pull it
along behind you,
until your muscles
ache,
until your heart
pains,
until your endurance

begins to wither
away,
until your standstill
hope
all together collapses.
Keep going,
keep dreaming,
'till
you reach
that lonely, empty
socket,
and thrust
that dusty plug into
it
with all
the fierce will
to live
you've built up
inside yourself.
Then,
child,
you gotta
get behind
this old, frail earth
and start pushing
it 'round
with all
your might . . .

— Kathleen (George)
Kearney

Performers should feel connected to the theme of their pieces. Good literature usually presents themes in new and different ways. The literature should help the reader see an ordinary idea in a new way. The material should excite the reader's imagination.

481

66Condense some daily experience into a glowing symbol, and an audience is electrified.99

RALPH WALDO EMERSON

Critical Thinking

Analyzing

● Write the following oral interpretation situations on the chalkboard:

- reading a fairy tale
- telling a joke
- reciting a poem about personal goals

Ask students to discuss the possible audiences for each.

The poem "Foul Shot," by Edwin Hoey, describes an ordinary scene in a special way. The poem gives a vivid picture of a young basketball player's struggle to sink a shot. Anyone who has tried to accomplish a goal under pressure can relate to this struggle. You may not play basketball, but you may have struggled to reach other goals. As you read the poem, you can imagine this scene and the tension of both the player and the spectators.

Audience Appeal

You need to ask yourself how your listeners will respond to the material you selected. You want to use a piece of literature that will appeal to your listeners. To analyze the audience, ask yourself whether the literature is appropriate to the age, concerns, and feelings of the audience members. Does the literature fit the occasion? A poem or essay that you like may not be the best piece for the senior-citizens' evening or the Sunday-school assembly. Read the poem "Mean Maxine" on page 484. Who would be the best audience for this poem? What might be an appropriate occasion?

Foul Shot

With two 60's stuck on the scoreboard
And two seconds hanging on the clock,
The solemn boy in the center of eyes,
Squeezed by silence,
Seeks out the line with his feet,
Soothes his hands along his uniform,
Gently drums the ball against the floor,
Then measures the waiting net,
Raises the ball on his right hand,
Balances it with his left,
Calms it with fingertips,
Breathes,
Crouches,
Waits,
And then through a stretching of stillness,
Nudges it upward.
The ball
Slides up and out,
Lands,
Leans,
Wobbles,
Wavers,
Hesitates,
Exasperates,
Plays it coy
Until every face begs with unsounding screams—

And then

          And then

                    And then,

Right before ROAR-UP,
Dives down and through.

                              —Edwin A. Hoey

Critical Thinking

Analyzing

Ask students to tell where the climax or point of greatest interest is in "Foul Shot." Then ask them to describe the best audience for the poem.

483

Curricular Connection

Language Arts

● Interested students might want to create their own poems on the subject of dealing with a sibling, using the rhythm of "Mean Maxine."

Critical Thinking

Analyzing

Ask students to identify the simile and hyperbole in stanza one of "Mean Maxine."

Skill Development

Vocabulary

▼ Ask students to brainstorm other words that we hear, see, taste, touch, or smell. Some suggestions are these: "rattle," "shiny," "licorice," "satiny," and "garlic."

Mean Maxine

There's no one mean as mean Maxine,
she smells like old cigars,
her brain is smaller than a bean,
I wish she'd move to Mars.

Some day I'll list the things I hate,
and that is where I'll list her,
I'd like to pack her in a crate—
too bad Maxine's my sister.

—Jack Prelutsky

Oral Possibilities

You also need to ask whether your listeners can grasp the meaning of your piece in just one reading. In oral interpretation, as in public speaking, you get only one chance to reach your audience. Your listeners cannot hear a certain line again or ask what a strange word means. When the language is too difficult or the sentence structure is too involved, that literature is not appropriate for reading aloud.

As you select your literature, look for words and ideas that can be clearly communicated to your listeners. As poet Ted Hughes says in his book *Poetry Is,* look for words that "live":

Words that live are those which we hear, like "click" or "chuckle," or which we see, like "freckled" or "veined," or which we taste, like "vinegar" or "sugar," or touch, like "prickle" or "oily," or smell, like "tar" or "onion." Words which belong directly to one of the five senses. Or words which act and seem to use their muscles, like "flick" or "balance."

Your Feelings

If you are going to communicate a piece of literature to other people, you must feel a connection to the material. Ask yourself: Have I ever had a feeling or experience similar to the ones

484

485

Links to Past Learning

Students may need some help understanding the concept of connecting to material. Remind them that their connection need not necessarily be based on the exact experience stated in the written piece. Tell them to try to find a connection to the *emotional* content of the material.

❝The cloning of humans is on most of the lists of things to worry about from Science, along with behavior control, genetic engineering, transplanted heads, computer poetry, and the unrestrained growth of plastic flowers.❞

LEWIS THOMAS

Motivation

Tell students that when they start to work on oral interpretation they will often use their sense memory to bring to mind details that will make their presentation come alive for listeners.

Limited English Proficiency

Assign LEP students to work with more-proficient students to create lists of words that "live."

described by the author? What can I bring to the performance? As an oral interpreter you cannot expect the audience to get excited over something that has no meaning for you. If you don't feel connected to the literature, you will have a hard time communicating its meaning to your audience. A place to start to consider your feelings is to look at your list of personal preferences in fiction and nonfiction and decide what drew you to these pieces.

The essay "Forget-Me-Not" was written by a high-school student. Another student chose to interpret it because it reminded her of feelings she had after her uncle's death.

Forget-Me-Not

It was the weekend and since I didn't have anything better to do, my mother had assigned me to clean the basement. I was glad to do it because my mom had this habit of keeping useless things: my old toys, outdated clothing, and various other old things. I, on the other hand, have to have everything in its proper place or I can't think straight. I had already cleaned away three shelves when I saw the box wedged between the toastmaster oven and my brother's old lava lamp. The memories of my father jumped back into my mind.

When it happened, I already knew that he was going to die. During those last weeks, I tore myself apart wondering whether I should still expect him to get well or whether to accept it. I remember feeling so helpless and depressed. I wondered when I could stop thinking about him, when my mind would clear of all the doctors and hospitals. Yet, my conscience wouldn't let him die. The inevitable call finally came. I thought that when I heard the news an incredible rush of emotions would flow out of me, but I just felt numb, cold, and very alone.

The next day, my mom and I went down to the hospital where my father had died. I didn't want to go, I never wanted to go near another hospital ever, but I could see that my mom needed me to help her, so I went. When we walked into the office, the first thing I noticed was the endless wall of white boxes. "These are the belongings of _____" was written in bold letters on each box.

66When we honestly ask ourselves which persons in our lives mean the most to us, we often find that it is those who, instead of giving advice, solutions, or cures, have chosen rather to share our pain and touch our wounds with a warm and tender hand.99

HENRI NOUWEN

Skill Development

Quick Skill Opportunity

● Call on volunteers to find examples of imagery that appeals to the senses in the essay "Forget-Me-Not." Write their responses on the chalkboard. Then ask students to think of an audience that this essay might *not* appeal to.

Each box represented a death. Each box represented a grieving man, woman, or child.

"Let me see," the nurse said as she groped in the corner for my father's box. "Watkiss, Watkiss, ah, here it is." She handed me the box. My mom finished the rest of the paper work and we went home.

I had forgotten all about the box. I didn't really want to know where it was or what was in it. I was angry that he was gone. I felt bitter towards him for leaving us.

Now here it was again: here he was again. I wondered what I would want to have with me when I died. I wondered what my box would contain. So, if nothing else, out of curiosity, I decided to open the box.

I gently pried the flaps of the box open. The first thing my eyes fell upon were his pajamas. They were his favorite pair. My mother had given them to him the last Christmas that he was well. They were made of flannel printed with little blue ducks. They were wrinkled from the years of wear. I folded them up and set them aside.

The next thing in the box was a brown paper bag filled with get-well cards. I remembered how he had stood the cards up all around his room, so he could see them all at a glance. I started to look through them and then I came to the Snoopy card that my brother had given him. It was his favorite card. It had been right next to his bed in every hospital room that he had been in. I read some of the other cards and then I looked in the box for the next item.

It was a small plastic bag containing two objects. The first was his slate black, square-framed glasses. It felt funny to look at them without seeing his face. They seemed so empty and ordinary. The other item was his wedding ring. I can't remember a time when it wasn't on his finger. His doctor wanted him to take it off for his operation, but he refused, so they had to sterilize it just before the surgery.

The next thing in the box was our family portrait. When I used to visit him, he would just sit and stare at it. I always wondered what

Substitute Teacher Tip

Call on individuals to tell the class which of the four selections—"Whatcha Gonna Do?" "Foul Shot," "Mean Maxine," or "Forget-Me-Not"—they felt most connected to and why.

Multicultural Learning

● Remind students that audiences will respond readily to literature from their own ethnic or religious background. Encourage students to look for possible oral-interpretation selections from countries, religious background, and ethnic groups different from their own.

he was thinking. Whatever it was, he would always be depressed after looking at it and he wouldn't talk for the rest of the visit.

The final item at the bottom of the box was his cup. He had had it from the first day he was in the hospital. I had brought it with me the first day I saw him there so that he would know that I was thinking about him. It was a light blue color with the words, "I LOVE DAD" in big bold letters. Part of the enamel on the handle had worn away from use. This was the one thing that I had given him that he had kept until his death.

I sat and looked at all of the things for a long time. I remembered all the things we had done together. I remembered his patience and his perseverance. I know now that he was only human, and that he didn't die on purpose. The pain I felt came from the destruction of his body, but no disease could destroy my memories of him and love for him.

I put everything back in the box except the cup, which I washed and filled with dirt. I planted the tiny seeds of the Forget-Me-Not and watched it struggle and stretch its way into existence.

—Carol Watkiss

Selecting the right piece of literature is the first step toward giving a fine performance. If you apply the standards you just read, you will find a piece that is worth your time and the time of your listeners.

CHECKLIST:
Selecting Material for Oral Interpretation

1. Does it connect with common human experiences?

2. Is it appropriate to the audience and to the occasion?

3. Will listeners be able to grasp the meaning in one reading?

4. Do you feel personally connected to the material?

487

> 66More than twenty thousand Dutch people helped to hide Jews and others in need of hiding during those years. I willingly did what I could to help. My husband did as well. It was not enough.99
>
> MIEP GIES

Curricular Connection

Language Arts

● Ask whether anyone in class has read Anne Frank's *Diary of a Young Girl* or the play based on the diary. If so, ask what the students know about Anne and her family, the setting of the diary and play, and the situation in Germany at the time.

Links to Past Learning

Ask students to think about the stories they heard when they were young children. Each story probably had a beginning, middle, and end. Tell them that when selecting material for oral interpretation they will be looking for these three structural elements, as well as for others.

✳ INTERACT

Select five of your favorite topic areas from the following list. Use the guidelines you just studied to find a piece of literature for each topic you chose.

With a group of four classmates, share your favorite reading topics and give each other examples of your favorite work under each topic.

love stories	automobiles
baseball	science fiction
murder mysteries	history
famous people	people of other lands
historical fiction	how to make things
mythology	teenagers' problems
true-life adventure	basketball
poetry	animal stories
scientific experiments	space travel

ANALYZING LITERATURE

Did you know that Katherine Paterson wrote *Bridge to Terabithia* as a way to help her own son understand the death of his friend? Did you know that Anne Frank actually was between twelve and fourteen years old when she wrote in her diary?

As you prepare for a performance, you must become very familiar with the literature you have selected. The better you understand the piece, the easier it will be to communicate its meaning to your audience. You must therefore analyze the piece carefully to understand its full meaning.

If your performance piece is part of a larger piece of literature, such as a section of a novel or a play, you need to first read the entire piece of literature. You have to understand the larger piece to understand how your section, or cutting, fits into the whole.

Interpreters
communicate with
the audience as
if they were the
dramatic speaker.

Curricular Connection

Language Arts

● Students can equate the dramatic
speaker with the term "narrator."
Both refer to the person telling a
story.

The cutting is the section you select or "cut" from the entire
work. Cutting is discussed in Chapter 17.

There are four keys to analyzing literature. When you analyze
a piece of literature for performance, you need to look at the dramatic speaker, the elements of the literature, the language, and
the author.

The Dramatic Speaker

The voice that is heard as you perform is the voice of the **dramatic
speaker**. This is the person telling the story or describing the
scene. It is not the author's voice but a voice created by the author.
The voice may belong to a character in the literature or to a
narrator who is not part of the action. As an interpreter, you
communicate with the audience as if you were the dramatic
speaker.

489

Skill Development

Quick Skill Opportunity

▼ Ask students to infer Dicey's age. Ask: who are Maybeth, James, and Sammy?

Curricular Connection

Language Arts

● Interested students could read and present book reports on *Dicey's Song, Dear Mr. Henshaw,* or other books by Cynthia Voight or Beverly Cleary. These reports might be audiotaped for inclusion in the students' portfolios.

In the two cuttings that follow you can examine the dramatic speaker. Cutting A is from *Dicey's Song,* and cutting B is from *Dear Mr. Henshaw.*

Cutting A

What a day, Dicey thought. What a summer, for that matter, but especially, What a day. She stood alone in the big old barn, in a patch of moonlight; stood looking at the sailboat resting on its sawhorse cradle, a darker patch among shadows. Behind her, the wind blew off the water, bringing the faint smell of salt and the rich, moist smell of the marshes. . . .

So. So they were going to live here, on the rundown farm, with Gram—Dicey's heart danced again, inside her, to say it to herself like that. Home. Home with their momma's momma, who was also a Tillerman. Home: a home with plenty of room for the four children in the shabby farmhouse, room inside, room outside, and the kind of room within Gram too—Dicey had seen Gram and how she listened when Maybeth sang, how she talked with James, how her eyes smiled at the things Sammy said and did—the kind of room that was what they really needed. One of the lessons the long summer had taught Dicey was how to figure out what they really needed.

—Cynthia Voigt, from *Dicey's Song*

Cutting B

Like I've been telling you, I am Leigh Botts. Leigh Marcus Botts. I don't like Leigh for a new name because some people don't know how to say it or think it's a girl's name. Mom says with a last name like Botts I need something fancy but not too fancy. My Dad's name is Bill and Mom's name is Bonnie. She says Bill and Bonnie Botts sounds like something out of a comic strip.

I am just a plain boy. This school doesn't say I am Gifted and Talented, and I don't like soccer very much the way everybody at this school is supposed to. I am not stupid either.

—Beverly Cleary, from *Dear Mr. Henshaw*

Skill Development

Media Literacy

● Have students give examples of books, television shows, films, or plays that have a very strong sense of place or setting. For example, most television soap operas and some situation comedies do not depend very much on setting for meaning. Conversely, setting is very important in shows or films set in the past or future or that focus on certain occupations, such as hospital personnel. Encourage students to analyze how setting is used to enhance meaning in each case.

In cutting A, it is clear that Dicey is not the dramatic speaker because Dicey would not say "Dicey thought" about herself. If you read the book, you would find that the dramatic speaker is an adult who knows Dicey well and cares about her.

In the book *Dear Mr. Henshaw,* the main character tells the story through letters to Mr. Henshaw. For example, cutting B is from a letter dated November 20. The dramatic speaker is a "plain boy" named Leigh Marcus Botts, an average kid. It certainly is not the adult female author.

The search for the dramatic speaker is your first step, because you are going to behave as that speaker during your performance. If your speaker is a "plain boy," you will not want to sound like a highly educated adult. If your speaker is a wise old woman, you will not want to sound like a bored teenager. In the pieces developed by Anna Deveare Smith, she impersonates each male and female character in the text. She uses their own words, which were recorded during her interviews with them. Thus, in *Fires in the Mirror,* she performs 24 monologues using the words of a rabbi, the brother of a murdered student, an African American minister, and others.

Elements of Literature

As you analyze a piece of literature, you will need to look for elements such as setting, plot, mood, theme, conflict, characters, and culture. Not every piece of literature will have all these elements, but understanding them can help you create a better performance.

Setting The time and place of the literature creates a **setting** for the performance. If the piece is set in a roller rink in 1992, the performance will be very different than if it is set in an English church in 1820. When you read *Anne Frank: The Diary of a Young Girl,* you can't understand Anne's desire for freedom during the twenty-five months her family hid from the Nazis unless you understand the setting. In the following excerpt, Anne brings that setting to life:

491

● Ask students to describe the mood of the excerpt from *The Diary of a Young Girl* and to determine whether this paragraph would be better read slowly or quickly.

I wander from one room to another, downstairs and up again, feeling like a songbird whose wings have been clipped and who is hurling himself in utter darkness against the bars of his cage. "Go outside, laugh, and take a breath of fresh air," a voice cries within me, but I don't even feel a response any more; I go and lie on the divan and sleep, to make the time pass more quickly, and the stillness and the terrible fear, because there is no way of killing them.

—Anne Frank, from *The Diary of a Young Girl*

Plot The **plot**, or story line of the piece, must be made clear to listeners. You must know the important events that move a story or play along. If you are doing a cutting, you need to know the entire plot and share the main points with the audience in your introduction. For example, if you are reading a cutting from Joseph Krumgold's *And Now Miguel,* you will need to tell your audience that the life of Miguel's family revolves around the life cycle of sheep. Thus, Miguel and his family must travel the mesa to the ranch and to the mountains. Little of the story will make sense to your audience if they do not understand this. If you are reading the whole story, you need to decide which moments are most important so that you can emphasize them for your listeners.

Mood The interpreter creates the **mood**, or the emotional feeling, of the literature. This is done through nonverbal messages. A humorous piece, such as Ina Friedman's *How My Parent Learned to Eat,* may require a fast pace, quick movements, and many smiles. A cutting from a book like *Scorpions* by Walter Dean Myers, in which a young boy faces problems with a gang, will need a slower pace and more serious facial expressions. Performers of horror writings by Stephen King or Christopher Pike will have to create a mood of fear and tension. Read the poem "Mending" and identify the mood you would create as its interpreter.

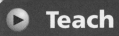

Interpreters must decide on the mood they want to create and how they will convey it.

Mending

A giant hand inside my chest
Stretches out and takes
My heart within its mighty grasp
And squeezes till it breaks.
A gentle hand inside my chest,
With mending tape and glue,
Patches up my heart until
It's almost good as new.
I ought to know by now that
Broken hearts will heal again.
But while I wait for glue and tape,
The pain!
The pain!
The pain!

—Judith Viorst

Theme Finding the **theme**, or main idea, helps you know what to emphasize in your performance. The theme may make a general statement about society, human nature, or the meaning of

Critical Thinking

Analyzing

Although the speaker in "Mending" does not really have a giant hand and a gentle hand inside her chest, ask students whether they think these are good metaphors for the speaker's feeling. What might have caused the speaker's broken heart?

493

Teach

Critical Thinking

Analyzing

● Ask students to think back to the essay "Forget-Me-Not" and try to state the theme. Tell them that a theme should be expressed as a sentence.

life. It may emphasize survival or peace at any price. Here are some examples of themes in literature:

Charlotte's Web by E. B. White—Friendship can be found in many places.

Dicey's Song by Cynthia Voigt—Home is where one is loved.

Bridge to Terabithia by Katherine Paterson—Death does not end the influence of someone in your life.

Mufaro's Beautiful Daughters: An African Tale by John Steptoe—Greed and selfishness are harmful.

The Planet of Junior Brown by Virginia Hamilton—Pride in individuality is important.

Dragonwings by Lawrence Yep—Prejudice is dangerous.

Tales from Gold Mountain: Stories of the Chinese in the New World by Paul Yee—Optimism overcomes prejudice and adversity.

Often an oral-interpretation performance includes a number of pieces of literature selected because they have a similar theme. For example, you might do a performance of five short poems or a performance of three cuttings from fiction. If you were to create a performance on the theme of "the immigrant as outsider," you might read selections including the poems "Apá" by Rosalinda Hernandez and "The Phone Booth at the Corner" by Juan Delgado, as well as a segment of the novel *The Joy Luck Club* by Amy Tan. You might introduce the presentation with a short story about your father's arrival in this country.

Conflict Conflict is at the heart of most literature. If no conflict existed in novels, stories, and plays, it would be hard to get involved in them. Conflicts can exist within individuals or between individuals. Conflicts can also exist between characters and the environment or nature.

Many stories about adolescents show internal conflict as the teenagers struggle to find their identity and to fit into the world. Often, struggles also exist between characters.

494

Skill Development

Quick Skill Opportunity

● Ask how many students have read the novels mentioned on this page or other novels by the same authors.

Motivation

● Ask students to think about some of the most interesting real or fictional characters they have read about. Ask what factors make a character interesting.

In some literature, the forces of good and evil fight one another to rule the world, as in *The Lord of the Rings*, J. R. R. Tolkien's epic trilogy.

An interpreter must understand plot, mood, theme, and conflict.

Individuals may be in conflict with society at large, as they are in *The Outsiders* by S. E. Hinton, or in *The Witch of Blackbird Pond* by Elizabeth George Speare, in which a young girl is accused of being a witch because she does not fit into the society around her.

Finally, characters may struggle against nature. In *Island of the Blue Dolphins* by Scott O'Dell, *Julie of the Wolves* by Jean Craighead George, or *Hatchet* by Gary Paulsen, the main characters try to survive in hostile environments.

Characters The interpreter needs to understand the characters who exist in the literature. You need to study the characters carefully to get a sense of how to suggest them in your performance. Your study should include their appearance, words and language,

495

Chapter 16 Preparing for Oral Interpretation

Beyond the Classroom

● Invite a storyteller to the class, or arrange for students to attend a storytelling session at a local library or other community setting.

Motivation

Students could investigate works by these Hispanic American writers: Judith Ortiz Cofer, Nicholasa Mohr, and Gary Soto.

actions, attitudes, and what others say about them. For example, in the novel *Anne of Green Gables,* by Lucy Maud Montgomery, the heroine is described as

> A child of about eleven, garbed in a very short, very tight, very ugly dress of yellowish gray wincey. She wore a faded brown sailor hat and beneath the hat, extending down her back, were two braids of very thick, decidedly red hair. Her face was small, white and thin, also much freckled; her mouth was large and so were her eyes, that looked green in some lights and moods and gray in others.

This pale young woman turns out to have quite a temper. It is described in the following scene from *Anne of Green Gables:*

> Gilbert reached across the aisle, picked up the end of Anne's long red braid, held it out at arm's length, and said in a piercing whisper,
>
> "Carrots! Carrots!"
>
> Then Anne looked at him with a vengeance!
>
> She did more than look back. She sprang to her feet, her bright fancies fallen into cureless ruin. She flashed one indignant glance at Gilbert from eyes whose angry sparkle was swiftly quenched in equally angry tears.
>
> "You mean, hateful boy!" she exclaimed passionately. "How dare you!"
>
> And then—Thwack! Anne had brought her slate down on Gilbert's head and cracked it—slate, not head—clear across.

The more you know about a character like Anne Shirley, the better you will interpret that character for an audience. As you read a piece of literature several times, you will find new ways of thinking about it or looking at its characters. These deeper meanings, found through your analysis, will strengthen your performance.

Culture Many of the works you are drawn to may be written from a cultural perspective. The authors may represent different ethnic backgrounds, using words that may be unfamiliar to you and writing in dialects that sound strange on your tongue. For example, in her powerful short story "How to Tame a Wild Tongue" Gloria Anzaldúa writes about being a Chicana entering a wider world. She uses English and Spanish as she explores the many changes in her own language. Poems by Maya Angelou and Gwendolyn Brooks are sometimes written in African American dialect. As you consider such pieces you will determine your own ability to use the language or dialect. In addition, you will need to be familiar with the culture reflected in the writings. Exploring new cultural works may provide opportunities for you and your classmates to teach each other words, songs, stories, and other aspects of your cultures.

In *The House on Mango Street* Sandra Cisneros writes about many aspects of growing up Spanish in her city neighborhood. Read the following selection about names aloud and learn to pronounce the names correctly, if they are unfamiliar to you.

My Name

In English my name means hope. In Spanish it means too many letters. It means sadness, it means waiting. It is like the number nine. A muddy color. It is the Mexican records my father plays on Sunday mornings when he is shaving, songs like sobbing.

It was my great-grandmother's name and now it is mine. She was a horse woman too, born like me in the Chinese year of the horse—which is supposed to be bad luck if you're born female—but I think this is a Chinese lie because the Chinese, like the Mexicans, don't like their women strong.

My great-grandmother. I would've liked to have known her, a wild horse of a woman, so wild she wouldn't marry. Until my great-grandfather threw a sack over her head and carried her off. Just like that, as if she were a fancy chandelier. That's the way he did it.

And the story goes she never forgave him. She looked out the window her whole life, the way so many women sit their sadness on an elbow. I wonder if she made the best with what she got or was she sorry because she couldn't be all the things she wanted to be.

Skill Development

Quick Skill Opportunity

● Ask students to point out the figurative language in the first paragraph of the excerpt from *The House on Mango Street*. What does the figurative language reveal about the narrator's mood?

497

> **❝**Words ought to be a little wild for they are the assaults of thought on the unthinking.**❞**
>
> JOHN MAYNARD KEYNES

Critical Thinking

Analyzing

● Ask why the narrator doesn't "want to inherit her [grandmother's] place by the window." Then ask whether students have ever wished for a new name.

Esperanza. I have inherited her name, but I don't want to inherit her place by the window.

At school they say my name funny as if the syllables were made out of tin and hurt the roof of your mouth. But in Spanish my name is made out of a softer something, like silver, not quite as thick as sister's name—Magdalena—which is uglier than mine. Magdalena who at least can come home and become Nenny. But I am always Esperanza.

I would like to baptize myself under a new name, a name more like the real me, the one nobody sees. Esperanza as Lisandra or Maritza or Zeze the X. Yes. Something like Zeze the X will do.

—Sandra Cisneros, from *The House on Mango Street*

Language

Writers create art with their words. A poet, playwright, or novelist works and reworks each sentence, struggling to find just the right words. Interpreters must respect the author's efforts. As an interpreter, you need to study the author's word choice, style, and rhythm and rhyme. If you do not understand what the author says or why something is expressed in a certain way, you cannot communicate the meaning of the literature to your listeners.

Word Choice As an interpreter you must make every effort to say exactly what the author means in the selection. Remember that the author chose a particular word for a reason. The word is not almost what the author wanted but exactly what the author wanted. If you are unfamiliar with any of the author's words, look them up so that you can understand their meaning.

As you probably remember from Chapter 2, words have two types of meanings. One type is the denotative meaning, which is the literal meaning or the dictionary definition. The other is the connotative meaning, which is your emotional or personal response to a word.

For example, the definition of rose is "any type of shrub with prickly stems and five-parted, usually fragrant flowers of red,

498

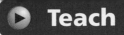

Learning Styles
Audio Learning

▼ Ask three students to say the sounds of the jackal, leopard, and frog. Then ask for volunteers to suggest sounds for a sparrow laughing, a fish jumping, and a deer leaping.

pink, white, or yellow." This is the denotative meaning of rose. It suggests no feeling or emotion. Roses may have a positive connotation to you because you think roses are beautiful. They may have a negative connotation if you are allergic to them.

Suppose you read the words "a blue rose." When you think about the word *blue*, you might realize that this color makes the rose unique and valuable. The choice to use blue in the description of a rose creates a connotative meaning because it suggests a unique or rare rose. You can see this in the following cutting from "The Blue Rose":

> You see, Jenny is different.
> Different?
> Yes, different from most other girls
> But surely, all people don't
> Have to be alike,
> think alike,
> act alike
> or look alike.
> To me Jenny is a blue rose.
>
> —Gerda Klein, from "The Blue Rose"

An author's use of language is extremely important. For example, in Verna Aardema's *Who's in Rabbit's House?* each animal has a sound associated with it. The jackal trots off "kpata, kpata," the leopard jumps "pa, pa, pa," and the frog laughs, "dgung, dgung, dgung." Such language makes this African folktale come alive for your listeners.

Style How the author says something may be as important as what the author says. The **style**, or the way a piece is written, helps you to create the mood or feeling for your listeners. Look at the following two descriptions of the same scene. The images created are very different. In version A, author Lloyd Alexander creates a setting and mood from another time and place, partly through the use of imagery. In this version, the imagery appeals to the senses of sight, hearing, and touch.

499

Skill Development

Quick Skill Opportunity

● Ask for volunteers to give brief examples of personification.

Version B has ordinary language, no appeal to the senses, and little indication of time and mood.

Version A

From the corridor, a faint sound grew louder. Taran hastened to press his ear against the slot in the portal. He heard the heavy tread of marching feet, the rattle of weapons. He straightened and stood with his back to the wall. The girl had betrayed him. He cast about for some means to defend himself, for he had determined they would not take him easily. For the sake of having something in his hands, Taran picked up the dirty straw and held it ready to fling; it was a pitiable defense, and he wished desperately for Gwydion's power to set it ablaze.

—Lloyd Alexander, from *The Book of Three*

Version B

The noise grew louder down the hall. Taran listened through a hole in the door. He heard a soldier and knew the girl had lied. "How can I defend myself?" he wondered. All Taran could find was loose straw.

A fine writer uses figurative language to appeal to the listeners' eyes and ears. (See Chapter 11 for a discussion of figures of speech.) For example, many poets use personification as they describe how "trees worry" or "chairs cheer." They may use hyperbole, as in, "Mean old Sarah shook the street as she pounded with her boots." You will find countless comparisons using metaphors and similes. Some writers also use **onomatopoeia**; that is, words that sound like their meanings, such as *hiss, crash, clang, roar, growl, slink, kerplop,* and *boing.*

Rhythm and Rhyme All poems have **rhythm**, the pattern of stressed and unstressed syllables. Some poems have **rhyme**, words that sound alike. As an interpreter, you must decide how you will read a rhymed poem. If you read the poem in a singsong rhythm, you will create a different message than if you read the lines naturally and thoughtfully. You can see the difference by

Some students might like to read "Macavity: The Mystery Cat" or other T. S. Eliot poems from *Old Possum's Book of Practical Cats.*

reading the first lines of Robert Frost's poem "Stopping by Woods on a Snowy Evening."

> Whose woods these are I think I know,
> His house is in the village, though;
> He will not see me stopping here
> To watch his woods fill up with snow.

Audience is an important consideration when you interpret rhyming poetry. When you read a poem in a singsong rhythm, adult listeners may tune you out because the rhythm will be boring. If you break the rhythm, your listeners will pay more attention. Yet if you are reading to children, they will enjoy the rhymes, and the rhythm will help keep them involved.

INTERACT

Select a children's poem, such as "The Duel" by Eugene Field, "The Little Boy and the Old Man" by Shel Silverstein, "The Cremation of Sam McGee" by Robert Service, or some rhyming stories such as those written by Dr. Seuss. In small groups read them according to the strict rhythm. Then read them breaking the rhythm. Discuss the differences in listening to each type.

Author

Sometimes you can understand more about a piece of literature by learning about its author. When researching the author, try to find out at what point in his or her life the selection was written. Was there a significance to the place, time, or title? Does the author have a theme he or she generally writes about?

You may think about what reason an author would have for writing the selection. For example, Virginia Hamilton is an African American writer who writes about black culture and history. Her characters are generally very sensitive, and often troubled, loners. They search for patterns to give meaning and order to their lives. In Hamilton's novel *M. C. Higgins, the Great,*

Skill Development

Active Listening

● Read the excerpt from *Working* aloud. Ask students to discuss what the selection reveals about setting, style, character, and theme.

Skill Development

Research

▲ Some students might want to read Studs Terkel's book *Working*. Encourage them to choose other material from the book to use for an oral interpretation for the class.

M. C. Higgins tries to come to terms with his past. He is in conflict with his father, and he wants to escape his Ohio home. If you were to interpret a section from this novel, you might find it valuable to know that the character and theme of the novel are typical of Hamilton's writing and that she has a strong belief in the importance of family relationships.

When you are interpreting an oral history, you will need to know about the author because you will be speaking for him or her. The following are the actual words of a newspaper publisher, Steven Simonyi-Gindele, as recorded by Studs Terkel in his book *Working*. In this section he describes his early working experiences and what they meant to him. If you were to interpret this orally you would speak as if you were the publisher.

I went to work when I was nine years old. I used to get up at three-thirty in the morning and deliver four hundred newspapers. I was bored by school and left in the last year. I was never afraid of working. I always enjoyed the challenge and I always enjoyed the reward. I did all kinds of things.

I was a busboy when I was thirteen. It took me six weeks of steadily looking for a job. It was high unemployment at that time in Canada. I realized then the only security a person has is what he himself can do. There's little security in a job working for somebody else. I like to control my fate as much as possible.

I don't believe the answer lies in making money. It didn't for me. By the time I was twenty-one I was driving a Cadillac and I could afford a fifteen-hundred-dollar-a-month seashore apartment in Florida, go to shows, and spend two hundred dollars a night and take my mother out, my grandfather, and live like a king. But I was more frustrated than when I was making thirty-four cents an hour delivering for a drugstore in Toronto.

I couldn't understand why I wasn't happy. Happiness is not related to money. Being successful at what you're doing is the measure of a man.

SPEAKING OF . . .

JUSTIN BRETT KLOSKY

Not many teenagers can sing songs from the 1940s and 1950s, but Justin Klosky of J. P. Taravella High School in Florida sings them regularly. In fact, he sings songs from the 1940s through the present for a very special audience—elderly men and women who live in nursing homes or assisted-living facilities. Justin has developed a one-hour show, targeted to the musical tastes of people between the ages of 65 and 100, which he performs at senior-citizen facilities. Although the heart of his performance is singing for and with the residents, he gets involved with the audience members between every song. He tells them about himself and his experiences and asks them to talk about themselves. According to Justin, "I talk to them about what they enjoy most in life, what hobbies they enjoy, and if they have children or grandchildren." He asks questions before singing certain songs in order to encourage comments and questions later. During each show, he encourages the listeners to sing along.

One of the most emotional songs in his repertoire is "The Greatest Love of All." When he sings it, Justin encourages the audience members to think about their loves and their greatest accomplishments. Justin takes these performances very seriously. He practices for an hour a day to keep his act fresh. When he performs, he wears a tuxedo to add to the professional image of the show.

Justin has a future in music as well as career possibilities in oral communication. He may build on these performance skills in careers such as a singer, talent agent, nursing-home administrator, recreation director, or a gerontologist.

Critical Thinking

Analyzing

After students have read the "Speaking of . . ." article on page 503, ask them to offer opinions on the ways in which Justin Brett Klosky might use style, rhythm, and rhyme in his performances.

Curricular Connection

Language Arts

▲ After reading the poem "Dreams," some students might wish to learn more about Langston Hughes. Encourage them to research Hughes and/or the Harlem Renaissance and to present their findings in a report to the class.

Cooperative Learning

● Have the class work together in small groups to create group poems. Have a group member come up with a line; the next group member adds a rhyming line, and so on until each group member has taken a turn. Students can rehearse their group poems a few times and then perform them for the rest of the class.

PIECES FOR ORAL INTERPRETATION

This chapter suggests ways to find material for oral interpretation. The following pages include some good choices for oral interpretation and for storytelling, a type of interpretive performance that is discussed in the next chapter. Reading and enjoying the literature on the next pages may help you decide what kinds of literature you would like to interpret.

Dreams

Hold fast to dreams
For if dreams die
Life is a broken-winged bird
That cannot fly.

Hold fast to dreams
For when dreams go
Life is a barren field
Frozen with snow.

       —Langston Hughes

The Day We Die

The day we die
the wind comes down
to take away
our footprints.

The wind makes dust
to cover up
the marks we left
while walking.

For otherwise
the thing would seem
as if we were
still living.

Therefore the wind
is he who comes
to blow away
our footprints.

— Kalahari origin (Africa),
Translated by Arthur Markowitz

Life Is So Full

Well, here I am! Seventeen years old today,
boy the clock's ticking fast.
Birthdays are a special time,
a day to celebrate your existence
and cherish the ones around you.

Life is so full,
abounding with wonders to be seen
and emotions to be experienced.
If we all just open our eyes and gaze
upon the subtleties and finer shadings of life
greater worlds unfold.
Worlds we rarely find time to look at.
But they're here and always will be
when we choose to find them.

I'm grateful to be a leaf
in the ever growing tree of life
and this leaf's not falling off
for nothing.

— Paul Garver (The author was terminally ill
when he wrote this poem.)

The Dog and the Shadow

A dog once walked across a bridge,
Carrying a cheese in his mouth.
When Dog was half-way over the bridge,
He saw another cheese down in the water.

Curricular Connection
Language Arts

● After reading "The Dog and His
Shadow," students might want to try
writing fables which could eventually
be prepared for oral interpretation.

505

Multicultural Learning

● Students might enjoy looking for Native American Coyote/Trickster tales that would be suitable for oral interpretation.

Critical Thinking

Analyzing

Ask students to think about the main character's age and probable appearance as they read "The Rice Puller of Chaohwa." Ask them also to think about any gestures they might use when interpreting the tale.

Dog was greedy.
He resolved to have both cheeses—
His cheese and its shadow.
Dog leaped in.
    He opened his mouth.
        He dropped his cheese.
Dog then recognized the shadow as a shadow.
For that shadow he had lost his cheese!

(To want too much may mean one loses everything.)

The Rice Puller of Chaohwa
A Chinese Tale

Near the village of Chaohwa, it is said, there lived a farmer by the name of Liu. He was not very different from the other farmers of Chaohwa, except that he was known as an impatient man. Some of his neighbors referred to him as Liu Always-in-a-hurry. When there was work to be done, he was always urging his wife and sons to go faster. If his wife had to go to the village for something or other, Liu practically pushed her out the door to get her started, and when she returned, he demanded to know what had kept her so long. When he was on the road himself, he was always stepping on the heels of anyone in front of him. He had an uncontrollable desire to be first in everything he did.

One day when Liu was in Chaohwa, he heard a group of farmers talking about their rice fields.

"My rice is sprouting very well," one of them said. "It is nearly two inches high."

Another farmer said, "Yes, my rice is doing well also. It is perhaps a little more than two inches high. In fact, nearly three."

"It is a good year for me, too," a third man said. "In some parts of my field the rice is nearly four inches tall already."

As Liu listened, he became very impatient with his own rice, which certainly wasn't four inches tall, or even three. Probably it wasn't even two.

506

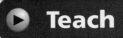
66With time and patience the mulberry leaf becomes a silk gown.99

CHINESE PROVERB

He hurried back to his fields, stepping on quite a few heels as he went. He even took a shortcut, trampling through the mud of a neighbor's rice field. When he saw the rice sprouts in his own fields, his heart fell. They were so short that he could hardly believe what he saw. Not one of them was more than two inches tall.

He hurried home thoughtfully and pondered rapidly over his problem. When his wife and sons spoke to him, he hardly heard them. All night long he rolled and tossed sleeplessly. But just before dawn, he sat upright suddenly, shouting, "I will help them!"

He went to his fields, reached down, and took hold of one of the sprouts with his fingers. Then he pulled ever so gently. The sprout came up a little. "Aha, that's better!" Liu said. Then he pulled the next stalk up a little, then the next. He went through the field this way and that, pulling on the stalks as fast as he could. All day he did this, and in the evening he came home weary and worn.

The next day he rushed again to his fields and began again at the beginning. When he returned home at nightfall, he told his family, "Oh, I am tired! I worked so hard today! But the rice is much taller now, and I am happy!"

Liu's family was surprised at the news, for rice grows ever so slowly. So in the morning they went out together to see the results of Liu's hard work.

What they found was sad to see, for the rice stalks lay withered and dead in the morning sun.

"Alas, is this gratitude?" Liu cried out to the ruined field. "Is this my reward for giving you a helping hand?"

As for the people of Chaohwa, when the news got around, they had to laugh at the outcome of Liu's impatience. And although Liu himself was forgotten as new generations were born and died in Chaohwa, people still say to someone who is overly eager, "Don't be a rice puller."

(Based on a translation by Hsin-Chih Lee and Cho-Feng L. Lee of a story recorded by Mencius (Meng-tse), who lived during the third and second centuries B.C.)

Skill Development

Quick Skill Opportunity

● Encourage students to experiment with interpreting the mood of the poem "Grasshopper Gumbo." Have volunteers read the poem aloud as if they are (1) a stodgy professor, (2) a zoologist, (3) a chef, and (4) a cafeteria customer. Remind them to articulate carefully.

Grasshopper Gumbo

Grasshopper gumbo
Iguana tail tarts
Toad à la mode
Pickled pelican parts
Elephant gelatin
Frog fricassee
Purée of platypus
Boiled bumblebee
Porcupine pudding
Steamed centipede skins
Squid sucker sundaes
Fried flying fish fins
Meadow mouse morsels
Cracked crocodile crunch

The school cafeteria
serves them for lunch.

　　　　　　—Jack Prelutsky

Two Haiku

On a leafless bough
　　In the gathering autumn dusk:
　　　　A solitary crow!

Listen! a frog
　　Jumping into the stillness
　　　　Of an ancient pond!

　　　　　—Translated by Dorothy Britton

Jazz Fantasia

Drum on your drums, batter on your banjoes,
sob on the long cool winding saxophones.
Go to it, O jazzmen.

Critical Thinking

Analyzing

● After they read "Jazz Fantasia," ask students to write a short paper in which they analyze the word choice, rhythm, and mood of the poem.

Sling your knuckles on the bottoms of the happy
tin pans, let your trombones ooze, and go husha-
husha-hush with the slippery sand-paper.

Moan like an autumn wind high in the lonesome
     treetops, moan soft like
you wanted somebody terrible, cry like a racing car
     slipping away from a
motorcycle cop, bang-bang! you jazzmen, bang altogether
     drums, traps,
banjoes, horns, tin cans—make two people fight on the
     top of a stairway
and scratch each other's eyes in a clinch tumbling down
     the stairs.
Can the rough stuff . . . now a Mississippi steamboat
     pushes up the night
river with a hoo-hoo-hoo-oo . . . and the green lanterns
     calling to the high
soft stars . . . a red moon rides on the humps of the low
     river hills . . .
go to it, O jazzmen.

     —Carl Sandburg

CHAPTER 16 SUMMARY

This chapter introduces oral interpretation, the art of reading literature aloud to communicate meaning to an audience. The chapter suggests a number of sources for finding literature for interpretation. When selecting your material, you need to consider four standards: the quality of the literature, audience appeal, oral possibilities, and your feelings for the piece. When analyzing material, you need to examine four key points: the dramatic speaker, the elements of literature, the language, and the author.

509

Answers

Think About It

Student answers will vary. Here are sample answers:

1. Oral interpretation involves performing literature aloud to communicate meaning to an audience. Typical places you might see oral interpretation in daily life are (1) parents reading to their children, (2) a religious leader reading prayers aloud, (3) a teacher reading aloud to a class.

2. Some sources of material for oral interpretation include favorite authors, literature collections, biographies or autobiographies, plays or screenplays, and oral histories.

3. (1) connection with human experiences, (2) appropriateness to audience and occasion, (3) ability of the audience to grasp the meaning in just one reading, (4) oral interpreter's personal connection to the material

4. (1) dramatic speaker, (2) elements of literature (3) language, (4) author

5. setting, plot, mood, theme, conflict, character, culture

CHAPTER REVIEW

Think About It

1. Define oral interpretation and describe three places you see it in everyday life.

2. List sources of material for oral interpretation.

3. What four standards are important when selecting material for oral interpretation?

4. Describe the four key points for analyzing literature for performance.

5. What are the elements of literature?

Try It Out

1. Interview a teacher, TV or radio announcer, or a minister, priest, or rabbi. Ask how they use oral interpretation in their work.

2. From an anthology of literature, select three pieces that meet the four standards for selecting material for oral interpretation. Share these with a partner and explain why each piece meets the standards.

3. Find a piece of literature that meets the standards for selecting material for oral interpretation and identify the characters, mood, setting, conflict, and plot.

4. With a partner, read "Foul Shot," "Mean Maxine," and "Mending." Identify the dramatic speaker in each piece.

Put It in Writing

1. List your three favorite authors and give an example of each person's work. Using a paragraph for each author, explain why you enjoy that person's writings, and decide whether the writing has possibilities for oral performance.

2. Read the poem "Mending." Write a short paper in which you analyze the language used. Consider word choice, style, and rhyme. Explain how the language helps create a mood.

3. Select a piece of literature that represents a distinct cultural background. Describe elements of the culture that are referred to in the text. Write down any words which are unfamiliar to you whether in terms of meaning or pronunciation. Write the meaning of the word and develop a pronunciation guide for your use during a performance.

Speak About It

1. Talk to a friend or neighbor who is at least seventy years old. With permission, record a story from the person's childhood. Play the tape to your class or retell the story.

2. Tell the class a fairy tale from your childhood.

Quick Check

Ask students to find and define these Key Terms:

conflict (480)

dramatic speaker (489)

mood (492)

onomatopoeia (500)

oral history (478)

oral interpretation (474)

plot (492)

rhyme (500)

rhythm (500)

setting (491)

style (499)

theme (493)

511

	Day 1	Day 2	Day 3	Day 4	Day 5
Week 17	**17** Performing Oral Interpretation				
	Preparing the Material	Using Your Voice & Body	Preparing a Perform. Script	Telling a Story	Summary
			Rehearsing Oral Interp.	Evaluating Oral Interp....	Chapter Review
Chapter 17 Planner	*Teacher's Resource Book*				
	Teaching Suggestions 17.1	17.2	17.3–17.6	17.7–17.11	
	Worksheets & Evaluation Forms		47–50	51–52	
					Chapter Test 17
	Workbook 17.1–17.2	17.3–17.4	17.5	17.6–17.7	

Motivation

Tell students that during study of this chapter they will have several opportunities to perform literature and learn how to give excellent performances for classmates, others in the school, and the public.

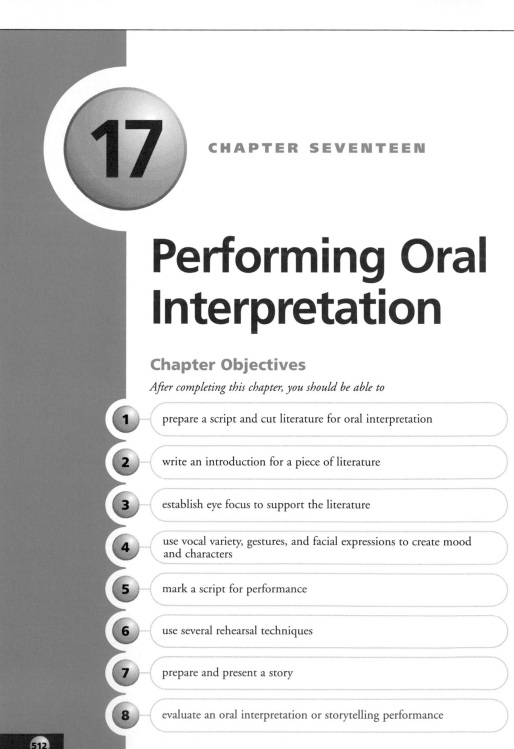

17

CHAPTER SEVENTEEN

Performing Oral Interpretation

Chapter Objectives

After completing this chapter, you should be able to

1. prepare a script and cut literature for oral interpretation

2. write an introduction for a piece of literature

3. establish eye focus to support the literature

4. use vocal variety, gestures, and facial expressions to create mood and characters

5. mark a script for performance

6. use several rehearsal techniques

7. prepare and present a story

8. evaluate an oral interpretation or storytelling performance

▼ Key Terms

body recall	eye focus	sense recall
cutting the literature	marking the script	storytelling

Critical Thinking

Predicting

● Have students read through the Key Words and predict what they will learn in the chapter.

Motivation

Read one of your favorite short selections from literature, including an introduction, to let students see and hear an oral interpretation performance.

513

Links to Past Learning

If you assigned a previous open-script exercise, remind students that they spoke ordinary dialogue and gave it emotional undercurrents. As an example, have two students read the following dialogue:

A: Hi.

B: Hi.

A: How are you?

B: Not bad. You?

A: Things are OK for me.

B: Really?

A: Yes. Great.

Then tell the two students (and the rest of the class) this scenario: A's brother has just been arrested and B knows who actually committed the crime for which the brother was arrested. Have the two students replay the scene with that information. Then tell students to create their own scripts and share their work with a partner.

> When Mr. Cole read Charles Dickens' *A Christmas Carol* to the class, I could see the Ghosts of Christmas Past, Present, and Future so clearly. It was a really spooky story.

> I saw a one-person show in which an actress created the life of Judy Blume through reading her books and letters.

As these comments demonstrate, well-performed oral interpretation can give listeners a different way of seeing the world. During a fine performance listeners become involved in the literature that the oral interpreter performs. The performance may lead listeners to understand the literature in a new way. Storytelling is closely related to oral interpretation. Like oral interpreters, storytellers weave magic from the words of an author.

How do you create such moments for listeners? Good performance skills plus good analysis plus a sense of creativity equals a fine performance. Before performing oral interpretation, you need to prepare the material, practice using your voice and body, mark and create a stage script, and rehearse. As part of your preparation for storytelling, you need to develop storytelling techniques. For both types of performance, you need to take risks and be creative in your approach. Also, you need to be able to critique your own performance and those of others.

PREPARING THE MATERIAL

> I found a great scene between the two main characters, but the maid comes into the scene for about four lines. This will get confusing. What should I do?

> I think the audience will get tired of all the "he saids" and "she saids" in the story. What should I do?

> Doesn't the audience need some background for this to make sense?

Two important steps in the preparation of your material are cutting the literature and creating an introduction. Each of these tasks is a special process.

514

66No passion in the world is equal to the passion to alter someone else's draft.99

H. G. WELLS

Learning Styles

Visual Learning

● Remind students to make copies of selections they wish to cut and not to mark library books.

Cutting a longer work is often necessary.

Cutting the Literature

Sometimes you find a piece of literature that you wish to perform, but it is too long. If so, the material must be cut. **Cutting the literature** means shortening it by taking out parts without changing its meaning. As you cut, you must try to save the sections that help the listeners understand the mood, the main conflict, and the characters. In shortening a piece, you can cut the following:

1. *Unnecessary descriptions.* A description of a house, mountains, or a dress, for example, may be interesting but unnecessary in presenting the main ideas or feelings.

2. *Descriptions of action or manner of speaking.* You can cut statements such as "Lee looked up angrily" because you can create this feeling with your voice and body. You could cut a sentence such as "She shook her fist at the dog" because you can substitute a gesture for it.

3. *Statements of "he said" or "she said."* Since you are creating the characters through vocal tones and nonverbal actions, you can leave out words that tell who is speaking.

4. *Words that might offend the listeners.* If a piece contains swear words or other words that could upset listeners, you can either substitute different words or leave out the offensive words altogether.

515

Learning Styles

Audio Learning

● Read the *Johnny Tremain* excerpt aloud using a different voice for when Rab speaks to the horse. Then have students try it.

5. *Unnecessary characters.* A minor character may enter the scene you are performing for only one or two lines. If so, you may wish to cut that person's lines. For example, a younger sibling may come into the scene to pester one of the main characters. Such an interruption can be cut if it does not change the meaning of the scene.

Look at the following example of cutting from the book *Johnny Tremain.* The reader wished to present the part in which Johnny learned to ride the skittish horse, Goblin. The reader was able to cut some of the landscape description and comments about the characters that did not relate to the riding lesson.

Rab had gone into one of the many stalls and backed out a tall, slender horse, so pale he was almost white, but flecked all over with tiny brown marks. The mane and tail were a rich, blackish mahogany. His eyes were glass blue.

~~Rab said: "I never saw a horse his color before. His sire was Yankee Hero, a white horse, fastest horse I ever saw run. Narragansett breed. We could no more afford to own one of Yankee Hero's sons than we could the Lytes' coach unless there was some little thing wrong with him. Eh, Goblin?"~~

The beautiful, wild, timid thing breathed softly, caressingly at Rab, but at the same time the queer, crystalline eyes watched Johnny as though sure that this was a boy who ate horses.

"Now you put on a bridle like this—see? And when winter comes, don't ever put a cold bit in a horse's mouth. Breath on it first. The saddle blanket—steady, steady, Goblin—it won't hurt you. And then the saddle. Now you lead him out in the yard. You hold the reins like this—left hand always and the thumb on the upper side, but down on the reins. And you put your left foot in the stirrup. If you get on from the right side and get kicked, it serves you right. There, see how easy? On and off just like that. You hold him a second."

Rab went into the tavern, and when he came back he had permission to take out the landlady's genteel nag. With Johnny on the nag and Rab on Goblin, they went to the Common.

~~Here were acres upon acres of meadow and cow pasture, hard ground cleared for the drilling of militia. The sun and the wind swept through them. Trees were turned to scarlet, gold, beefy red, blueberry bushes to crimson. Through one patch a white cow was plodding, seemingly up to her belly in blood. The cold, wild air was like wine in the veins. And across the vast, blue sky, white clouds hurried before the wind like sheep before invisible wolves.~~

"Easy, easy," cried Rab. "Easy does it." Goblin had been cavorting, blowing through his nostrils, begging to be let out. Rab kept him at a close canter. The landlady's sorrel flung himself after him. Now and then Rab would glance behind to see how Johnny was making out.

Creating an Introduction

Which of these two introductions would get your attention?

This is a cutting from the play *Step on a Crack*, by Susan Zeder, which tells about a girl's life in a stepfamily.

Ellie Murphy's mother died when she was four. Since that time Ellie and her father, Max, have been best friends. Until now. Ellie's father just married Lucille, and the three of them are figuring out how to be a stepfamily. Ellie finds great frustration in sharing her father; Max finds it hard to know how to react. In this scene from *Step on a Crack* by Susan Zeder, Ellie and Lucille are struggling for Max's attention.

The second introduction is more likely to gain attention. You learned the importance of the introduction to a speech in Chapter 11. Introductions are equally important for oral interpretation. Through the introduction, an interpreter gets the listeners' attention and prepares them for the literature to come. Successful introductions accomplish the following:

Capture the audience's attention

Tell the author and title

Give any necessary background information about the author or literature

Set the scene

Tie the selection to the audience's experience, if possible

Critical Thinking

Analyzing

▼ Have students note that the first introduction on this page fails to capture the audience's attention, gives little background, and does not set the scene.

517

Amazing Fact!

A. A. Milne's book *Winnie-the-Pooh* is considered a masterpiece of children's literature. Milne once revealed that he based the characters on his son, Christopher Robin, and his son's collection of stuffed animals.

Links to Past Learning

Encourage students to think of books they remember from when they were younger. Ask students to create a short introduction to a book they particularly enjoyed. Remind them to use the guidelines for successful introductions.

Motivation

Have students make a list of verbs, nouns, and adjectives that describe what it's like to be a child. Encourage them to think about their own impressions of childhood.

APPLY

Read the following introduction for a children's performance and find each of the necessary parts of an introduction.

One of the most famous stuffed animals in the world is a bear named Winnie the Pooh. He belongs to a boy named Christopher Robin. In the following selection from *The House at Pooh Corner* by A. A. Milne, Pooh and Christopher tell each other good-bye because Christopher must go to school and won't be able to play with Pooh very often anymore. Pooh and Christopher express feelings most of us have felt when we must say good-bye to a very close friend.

As you can see, this introduction meets all of the requirements listed above. It is a successful introduction.

You will need to create an introduction to your performance if it contains a number of short selections. This introduction should explain the theme of your performance to the audience so that they will understand the links among the selections. For example, if your theme is "A Child's View of the World" you might begin with this introduction: "What if the sky were pink, the trees were shaped like triangles, and horses had six legs? A child's world may be a riot of color, size, and shape. In the following pieces four authors present their child-eyed view of everyday life. As you listen, try to remember how you saw the world at age three or four."

If you are using a number of pieces in your performance, you may wish to prepare a short conclusion to the presentation that refers to remarks in your introduction. For example, you might conclude, "Dr. Seuss makes green eggs and ham delicious; Shel Silverstein reminds us of the dream creatures we had forgotten. We each need to hold on to ways to remember what it was like to see the world with young eyes."

Cooperative Learning

● Have one person from each group in the Interact exercise present the finished introduction to the class.

⚛ INTERACT

With a group of three or four classmates, select one of the following pieces: "Foul Shot," page 483, "Dreams," page 504, or "The Dog and the Shadow," page 505. Have each person prepare an introduction to the same piece. Share your introductions with one another. Combine the best parts of each introduction to create the final introduction to the piece.

USING YOUR VOICE AND BODY

When I perform "We Real Cool" by Gwendolyn Brooks, I use my voice to suggest different pool players saying the lines.

When I read "Foul Shot," I try to show the listeners the basketball hanging on the rim of the hoop by following an imaginary ball with my eyes.

After you have chosen, analyzed, and cut the selection, you are ready to decide how to use your voice and your body while presenting it. To begin, think of yourself as the dramatic speaker

There is a fine line between interpretation and acting.

Learning Styles

Kinesic Learning

● To get students to use their bodies in oral presentations, have volunteers present the following characters using only their bodies. Limited-English-proficiency students can probably succeed at presenting these or similar characters.

a very elderly person

a bus driver

a pig

a giraffe

a short-order cook

a doting mother

519

Amazing Fact!

Almost everybody is aware that humans have five external senses. Many people are not aware, however, that hunger, balance, thirst, and pain are known as internal senses.

Critical Thinking

Analyzing

● Ask students to write down their impressions from the Apply activity. Then have them compare their written reactions with a partner's. Tell them to focus on and discuss the similarities.

Skill Development

Media Literacy

● Have students keep a record for two days of television commercials they see that appeal to the senses. They should record whether these appeals are pleasant or unpleasant. Ask why advertisers would have an ad produced that many people find annoying or unpleasant.

talking to an audience and ask yourself, "How would I feel? How would I react in this situation?" If the dramatic speaker is an uninvolved observer, your voice and body should reflect this. If the dramatic speaker is a character in the middle of an argument, your voice and body need to show this anger.

Perhaps the most important thing to be aware of is that you will interpret the material, not act it out. You are sharing the story with your listeners. In order to look more carefully at the nonverbal part of your performance, you need to consider sense recall, use of voice, and use of body.

Sense Recall

As you begin to think about how to use your voice and body for oral interpretation, you can work with sense recall. **Sense recall**, or remembering physical experiences you have had, will help you suggest images or sense memories to your audience. You may recall sounds, tastes, smells, touch, and sights.

Suppose you want to interpret a piece in which a character bites into the perfect peach and sighs. You can communicate the sensation and action to your listeners more easily if you can recall a similar experience, such as biting into a beautiful, juicy strawberry. Use your sense recall to remember experiences that can help you interpret the meaning of literature.

 APPLY

Think about the following, in order to create your sense recall:

1. *Sound.* Imagine the sound of a car horn, airplane overhead, marching band, an unfamiliar sound when you're in the house alone, or chalk scraping across the board in a silent classroom.

2. *Taste.* Recall the taste of a lemon, chocolate candy bar, or bad tasting medicine.

continued

520

APPLY

3. *Touch.* Recall the feel of fur, hot sand under your bare feet, jumping into a cold swimming pool on a hot day, or the softness of a baby's hair.

4. *Smell.* Recall the smell of frying bacon, your favorite flower, a skunk, mothballs, or the air after a spring shower.

5. *Sight.* Imagine the details of your room, your favorite vacation spot, a severe thunderstorm, or your sister's face.

Each person's responses will be slightly different because everyone has unique experiences.

You may use a sense of **body recall** which means you remember your kinesthetic or bodily responses when you had certain feelings such as fear, anger, or anxiety. If you were interpreting a section of *One Eyed Cat* by Paula Fox, you would have to find ways to create the sense of guilt and anger Ned experiences after shooting out the eye of a wild cat. You would have to try to remember how your muscles tensed or your stomach ached at a time when you were very anxious and angry.

If you have moved from one home to another, you probably remember the experience well. Or you may have watched close

Learning Styles

Audio-Visual Learning

● Show a videotape of the opening few minutes of Alfred Hitchcock's thriller *Vertigo*. Have students discuss their sensory responses to James Stewart's chase across the rooftops.

Curricular Connection

Language Arts

▲ Encourage interested students to write a paragraph about something that makes them happy, sad, or afraid—something that wouldn't necessarily produce a similar reaction in another person. For example, someone who has been bitten by a dog will have different reactions to dogs than people who haven't been bitten.

Amazing Fact!

A voiceprint is a visual record of the sound waves of a particular voice. Voiceprints are made by running a tape recording of a voice through a special instrument. Voiceprints have been used as evidence in some court trials to identify a particular voice even though not everyone agrees that they are accurate enough to be used.

Substitute Teacher Tip

Have one or two volunteers read "Moving Day" aloud. Then lead a class discussion about what each reader brought to the material. Encourage constructive feedback.

Beyond the Classroom

● Encourage students to attend a poetry reading or other literary event. Ask them to describe their experience and to evaluate the oral interpretation skill of the reader or readers.

friends or relatives move away. In the following poem a student describes a moving day in her life. Think about sense experiences you can recall from your life to help you interpret this poem.

Moving Day

Crates
   full of my childhood
   stand by the door.
My mother's dishes are packed carefully;
   breaking them would mean losing part of our past.
The pale green curtains
   (the ones I picked out)
hang silently in the empty room.
Laughter—
   tears—
      talking—
the sounds of growing up
echo in the hallways.
Home.
New people will grow up here,
   will experience love and pain here;
this home will always be a home.
Our story will continue elsewhere;
We will still share laughter, tears, talking—
Love.
Boxes
   full of memories
   are being loaded into the car.
We will unpack these memories
   and use them to create
   a new Home.
But a part of me stays behind,
   watching my pale green curtains
   swaying in a warm breeze.

—Margaret Susan George

Unit 5 Interpretive Communication

Curricular Connection

Literature

▲ Interested students might want to read other lines spoken by the witches in Act IV, scene 1 of *Macbeth* to discover other possibilities for oral interpretation.

Use of Voice

How should your voice change to reflect the differences between the following two selections?

Selection A

Double, double, toil and trouble;
Fire burn, and cauldron bubble.
Fillet of a fenny snake,
In the cauldron boil and bake;
Eye of newt and toe of frog,
Wool of bat and tongue of dog,
Adder's fork and blindworm's sting,
Lizard's leg and howlet's wing,
For a charm of pow'rful trouble,
Like a hell-broth boil and bubble.

> — William Shakespeare,
> from *Macbeth,* Act IV, Sc. 1

Selection B

The sun had never been brighter. This was the day Sheila had waited for, and even the skies were cooperating. The trip to the state fair would take two hours, but she could spend that time just dreaming of the Ferris wheel and the square dancing. It was a downright sparkling day!

Your voice should sound different as you perform these pieces. Selection A calls for a spooky, mysterious reading. Selection B calls for a brighter, lighter reading. To interpret these two pieces, you would change your volume, pitch, rate, and vocal quality.

Volume can have great effect on your performance. You may speak more softly while portraying a shy person than a confident one. Your angry character may be louder than your sad character. If you describe a snowfall in the woods, you would probably speak softly to create a peaceful scene.

Your pitch should vary as you read male or female characters. Women and children have higher pitched voices than adult men.

Cooperative Learning

● Tell students that the first two lines of the excerpt from *Macbeth* are spoken in unison by three witches. The rest of the lines are spoken by the Second Witch. Ask for volunteers to present the excerpt to the class. Afterward, ask the performers to discuss how knowing they were playing witches added to their performance.

523

Motivation

Tell students that even small changes in volume and pitch during the course of oral interpretation can add great drama to the presentation.

Learning Styles

Audio Learning

▼ Recorded books on tape are sometimes good sources for students to hear dialect, especially when the setting is another country or a specific region of the United States.

An excited person's pitch will be higher than the pitch of someone who is depressed. The voice changes should suggest the difference but not exaggerate it.

If you are reading a playful poem, you can speak at a faster rate than if you are reading a sad story. Older characters may speak more slowly than younger ones. When you are shifting to a new character or changing the mood, you can use pauses to create the desired effect. Pauses also create suspense.

Your vocal quality should change to reflect different characters or different moods. For example, when telling a children's story you may use a raspy tone for the old queen and a nasal tone for the gnome.

There are many ways to create vocal effects. Therefore, you have to experiment with vocal changes. Tape your reading as you try different vocal sounds. These experiments will help you decide how you wish to sound.

Sometimes you may want to use an accent. If the dramatic speaker is an old Irish storyteller, you may want to use an Irish accent. If the main character is a Confederate soldier during the Civil War, you may want to use a southern accent. Performing with an accent requires extra time for practicing. Unless the accent is done well, it will distract or confuse listeners. People will pay attention to the accent rather than to the meaning of the literature. If you cannot speak easily with the accent, don't use it at all.

INTERACT

In groups of two or three, read the following selection from *Dicey's Song*. Try to create a voice for Gram, an old country woman. In this scene Gram tells Dicey about some regrets.

I didn't mind being alone, and I don't mind you living here. But that's not what I'm trying to say. I'm trying to say—I married John, and that wasn't a mistake. But the way we stayed married, the way we lived, there were lots of mistakes. He was a stiff and proud man, John—a hard man. . . .

continued

Links to Past Learning

Encourage students to recall what it feels like to receive a friendly smile, a mocking smirk, or an angry frown. Remind them that a large part of the information we take in from other people is nonverbal.

INTERACT

I stuck by him. But I got to thinking, after he died— whether there weren't things I should have done. He wasn't happy, not a happy man. I knew that, I got to know it. He wasn't happy to be himself. And I just let him be, let him sit there, high and proud, in his life. I let the children go away from him. And from me. I got to thinking—when it was too late—you have to reach out to people. To your family too. You can't just let them sit there, you should put your hand out. If they slap it back, well you reach out again if you care enough. If you don't care enough, you forget about them, if you can. I don't know, girl

Cynthia Voigt,
from *Dicey's Song*

Learning Styles

Kinesic Learning

● Have volunteers show physically how they might present the following in an oral interpretation:

disgust

excitement

suspicion

grief

impatience

boredom

anger

pain

Use of Body

As a performer, you use your body to bring characters to life and to convey the author's meaning. You must pay careful attention to movement, facial expression, and special ways to use your eyes, called eye focus.

Altering your vocal quality requires extra time for practice.

Skill Development

Quick Skill Opportunity

● Call on students to give brief facial expressions of grief, joy, fear, nervousness, embarrassment, and relief.

Movement Your gestures and posture help set the tone or create the characters for your listeners. As an interpreter, you will remain in one place most of the time, so you cannot use movements such as walking, falling, or touching others. There may be some performances when large movements are permitted in classrooms or contests. You will need to know what your listeners expect. Usually, you can suggest larger movements but you will not actually make them. Therefore, your gestures and posture take on great importance in communicating the meaning of the literature.

As an interpreter you may use gestures such as shrugging your shoulders, pointing your fingers, or scratching your head. You may throw a punch toward the audience to represent a fight, but you will not get into a fistfight with another character.

You can create a mood through your posture. For example, to suggest an embarrassed child, you might stand with your toes pointed in and your head turned toward your chest. Except when you are speaking as several characters, remember that you are taking on the role of the dramatic speaker. Try to imagine how this speaker would stand or move.

Facial Expression Your facial expression should quickly communicate the mood of the piece to your audience. A joyous mood can be shown with a smile, and a scary mood can be shown

Facial expression is important in conveying the mood of a piece.

526

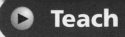 **Teach**

How can you write if you can't cry?

RING LARDNER

by tension in your face. If your character is frustrated, your face should show this. Because you do not use large body movements, you may wish to exaggerate your facial and eye expressions to communicate the meaning.

In the poem "It's All Right to Cry," Carol Hall creates many feelings. Try reading it and communicating the changes in mood to your audience.

It's All Right to Cry

It's all right to cry
Crying gets the sad out of you.
It's all right to cry
It might make you feel better.

Raindrops from your eyes
Washing all the mad out of you.
Raindrops from your eyes
It might make you feel better.

It's all right to feel things
Though the feelings may be strange.
Feelings are such real things
And they change and change
And change . . .
Sad and grumpy,
Down in the dumpy
Snuggly huggly,
Mean and ugly
Sloppy slappy,
Hoppy happy
Change and change and change . . .

It's all right to know
Feelings come and feelings go.
And it's all right to cry
It might make you feel better.

—Carol Hall

Skill Development
Feedback

● Encourage students to present their renditions of "It's All Right to Cry" to the class. Ask the other students for feedback on what they saw in each presentation.

Beyond the Classroom

● You might use the excerpts from *No Problem* to discuss again the importance of gauging the audience. Ask students to discuss the various audiences that might enjoy and relate to *No Problem*.

527

Cooperative Learning

Divide students into pairs. Give each pair either Scene 1 or Scene 2 from *No Problem* on pages 529–531. Have one member of each pair deliver the scene, incorporating proper eye focus to show the difference between the two characters. The other member of the pair can observe and comment on the speaker's effectiveness. Then have the pairs change roles.

OBSERVE

Think about an experience you have had that made you feel angry, happy, sad, sorry, or determined. Let your body respond to the feeling. If you tense up, do you feel it in your neck? stomach? chest? If you feel relieved, do you feel it in your stomach, arms, and legs? Concentrate on remembering the response of your body so you can use the body movements and gestures in your performance.

Eye Focus Although you usually look at the audience when performing, you may use your eyes differently when you are portraying a character. **Eye focus** is the place a performer looks while interpreting a piece of literature. Most interpreters show the difference between two or more characters by changing their eye focus. For example, you may look at one spot on the back wall when speaking as the first character, then shift your focus and look at a different spot when speaking as the second character. The audience should see your eyes and your head move slightly as you shift characters. You do not want to swing your head each time a new character speaks.

In the following figures you can see the way one interpreter places his characters from *Step on a Crack*. In Figure A you see the placement when reading a scene with only the two women, Ellie and Lucille. In Figure B you see the placement with the two women and Max. Because the two women are fighting for Max's attentions, Max is placed in the middle with the women on either side.

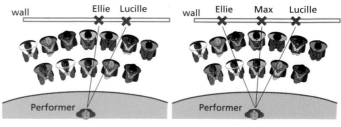

Figure A   Figure B

Learning Styles

Audio-Visual Learning

● To better monitor students' eye focus, videotape them performing segments of *No Problem*. Have the person playing Melissa use the camera as the focal point for narration; she should look slightly left of the camera when she is speaking to Mom and slightly right of the camera for her dialogue with Meredith and the sales clerk. Allow students to watch their videotaped performances and give self-feedback.

APPLY

Read aloud the following two short scenes from the play *No Problem* from Make It Live Productions. As you read, practice your eye focus. Melissa, a teenager from a wealthy family, struggles to gain attention from her parents. In the first scene she is talking with her mother; in the second scene she is shopping with her friend Meredith. If you wish to play male characters, you may write a similar set of situations from the male perspective.

Scene 1

Melissa: Shopping is a great way to relax and a great activity to do with friends. On a typical Saturday I go to the mall, have lunch, walk around, get a make-over, talk to friends, and try on the five-thousand-dollar dresses in the ritzy dress store on the top floor.

Mom: Melissa, remember, if you look good, you'll feel good!

Melissa: So, I started small . . . earrings. I have over two hundred pair. I try to pick up a new pair whenever I'm out.

(Melissa, by this point, is out of her chair. Jennifer, as Melissa's mom, has moved into Melissa's chair and begins to apply makeup. Melissa gets her bag from the prop table and begins to exit..)

Mom: Where are you going?

Melissa: Out!

Mom: You're not going anywhere. You're staying home with Max this afternoon. We discussed it last night.

Melissa: Mom . . . I told Meredith I'd meet her at the mall. I'll be home before dinner.

Mom: Well, you'll have to call her and tell her you can't make it.

Melissa: Why do I have to watch him?

Teach

Links to Past Learning

Remind students about the importance of taking a few moments to get calm and centered before a performance. Tell them that there is almost always enough time before a presentation to take a few deep breaths and try to get rid of excess body tension.

Cooperative Learning

● As students work in small groups to analyze and prepare *No Problem,* they might choose one group member as director. The director could watch several rehearsals and then give suggestions about performance. Encourage students to listen to one another carefully to avoid overly harsh criticism and hurt feelings.

Mom: Because I have an important meeting with a client and then your father and I have to be at that benefit downtown. *(She turns to Melissa.)* I thought I told you to throw those jeans away.

Melissa: They're my favorite pair.

Mom: Well, you look like a homeless person. What will people think?

Melissa: I don't care what people think!

Mom: Well, I do. Your father and I work too hard to have you traipsing around in ripped clothing.

Melissa: Fine Mom . . . I'll take them off!

Mom: Melissa, what has gotten into you lately? I don't know where you've picked up this attitude, but I will not tolerate it in my house. Do you understand?

Melissa: Fine.

Mom: Melissa, is there a problem? *(Pause.)*

Melissa: Well. I just don't see why I have to watch Max all the time. I'm not his mother.

Mom: Because this is a family. You can order a pizza. I'll leave some money on the counter. *(She freezes.)*

Melissa: At the mall you can always get people to help you . . . to pay attention to you . . . They have to. It's their job. . . .

Scene 2

(Melissa crosses to the prop table and picks up earrings.)

Melissa: Hey Mer', check out these earrings.

Meredith: Oh, Melissa, they're perfect. They're exactly what I need for my dress. Do you think they're real?

Melissa: Real? Let's see. *(She bites them.)*

Meredith: Melissa . . .

Melissa: What? This is how you figure out if they're real. You bite them.

Meredith: I don't think you're supposed to do that. You haven't paid for them.

Melissa: I have now. *(She looks at imaginary sales clerk.)*

Meredith: You can't buy a pair of $300 earrings.

Melissa: Who said anything about buying? *(She puts them into Meredith's pocket.)*

Meredith: Hey! Melissa! . . .

Melissa: Just act normal. Here he comes. *(She speaks to imaginary salesclerk.)* Oh, yes you can. Do you have those in silver? OK. We'll wait.

Meredith: If you want them, you take them!

Melissa: Fine. Whatever. You said you wanted to dress like me.

Meredith: I'll meet you outside.

Melissa: OK. *(She watches Meredith leave, sit, and freeze. She puts the earrings into her pocket. To salesclerk.)* No, I decided against that pair, they weren't what I wanted after all. I shop because in the mall I can be whatever I want, and that's very exciting.

PREPARING A PERFORMANCE SCRIPT

Several steps are necessary in the preparation of a performance script. First, you must order the literature pieces in the order in which you will perform them. Second, you mark the pieces to reflect your thinking about how you plan to use your voice and body during performances. Third, you create the overall structure of the performance, including transitions between pieces. Finally you create the actual script that you will use during your performance, including the introduction and any concluding remarks.

Critical Thinking
Organizing

● Encourage students to draw a diagram detailing their preparation for a performance script. They could start with "Ordering the Pieces" and, under that heading, write the pieces they chose and the numerical order in which the pieces will be presented. They could then continue through the rest of the steps in the preparation process.

531

Critical Thinking

Critical Thinking

Evaluating

● Encourage students to look for short pieces for performance throughout their daily lives. They may be surprised by how often they find interesting material from their other classes. Students could keep a log of the pieces they come across that might work for a presentation.

Ordering the Pieces

When performing several short pieces of literature, you need to put them in the order that will create the right mood or to keep your audience interested. For example, you could place a short story between two poems. Or you could shift moods by following up a sad piece with something funny. Take time to place your pieces in the order that will keep your listeners involved with the literature.

If you are preparing material for a class performance, you probably have great freedom in choosing, cutting, and arranging your pieces. If you are preparing for a contest performance, however, you may have to follow stricter rules.

Marking the Script

After you have practiced various vocal and nonverbal techniques and have decided which are best for your selection, you will want to mark your script. **Marking the script** involves writing symbols that will help you to remember how to read the script. The following guidelines are just suggestions. You can devise your own system. The system itself is unimportant—what is important is that you use marks that will help you remember how you want to read the selection.

Tips for Scriptmaking

Pauses: Use one diagonal line (/) to show a pause; two diagonal lines (//) to show a longer pause.

Emphasis: Use solid underlining (——) to indicate words to be stressed; wavy line (∿∿) to underline words that need a special tone or special emphasis.

Pronunciation: Write the letter x over a syllable that needs stress. (remémber)

Movement: Write cue (*cue*) to show a special movement.

Rate: Use colors to show changes in pace.

Learning Styles

Audio Learning

● Have a volunteer read "Let's Go Grandfather" aloud to the class using the scored version. Encourage all but the person presenting the poem to close their eyes. Afterward, have students talk about what they heard.

In the following poem, a student has made oral-interpretation markings on a poem written by a classmate.

Let's Go, Grandfather

	Let's <u>go,</u> Grandfather!
impatient	I don't want to sit on the beach
	<u>anymore</u>.
	Do you hear me?//
	Let's go back to the apartment
	to see Grandma,
anticipation	⎧ so I can try on her false teeth
	⎩ to see if they fit,
	⎧ and so I can lock my jacket
mischief	⎪ in the bathroom, on <u>purpose</u>,
	⎨ and make her pick the lock
	⎩ with her hair pin.
move forward	Do <u>you</u> <u>hear</u> me grandfather?
	Why don't you <u>speak</u>?
bend over	Your silence scares me./
	And why did you fall over like that?//
stand up straight	And then the ambulance came,
	but it was too late./
read slower	He had been dead
	for an hour.

—Carrie Kramer

✳ **INTERACT**

Obtain a copy of Abraham Lincoln's Gettysburg Address. With a small group, mark it in two different ways and try out the effect of each performance.

533

Links to Past Learning

Remind students that it is to their benefit to print their scripts neatly or to create typewritten or word processed scripts using a highly readable font. Discuss with students times when they may have seen speakers stumble over their notes or prepared speeches. Tell them that performing for an audience can be difficult enough without having to decipher an illegible script.

Creating the Structure

The overall structure includes the introduction, the transitions between pieces, and any concluding remarks. Your introduction should be written according to the guidelines suggested in the previous section (p. 517). In some cases, you may choose to use the introduction to each piece as your transition from one selection to another. In other cases you may wish to create a bridge between the pieces for your audience. For example, if you are preparing a performance on the theme of "Life Is Change" which includes "Moving Day" (p. 522) and "Let's Go Grandfather" (p. 533) you might link them together in the following way.

> Many of us will experience over and over again the changes Margaret George writes about in "Moving Day." We may move from one home to another; we will leave home to go to school or take a job. And we will often feel sadness as we undergo each change. Yet we will carry important things with us and stay in touch with the people we love. In "Let's Go Grandfather," Carrie Kramer writes about a different type of change—a permanent one which robs us of a life connection and leaves us more alone in the world.

Such a transition prepares the listeners for what they will hear. It establishes the tone of the presentation and indicates why the performer chose each piece to support the theme.

Creating the Stage Script

Once you know exactly what you are going to perform, type or write out the script. The script should be typed double-spaced or hand-written with a line of space between rows of words. The extra space will make the reading easier and give you room to mark the script.

Once the script is prepared, back it with dark construction paper or place it in a three-ring folder. Cut the script pages so that you do not need to turn the page in the middle of a paragraph or verse of poetry. The end of a page should be where you pause in the script.

Skill Development

Vocabulary

● Students should make sure they check the pronunciation (and definition) of any unfamiliar words in their scripts. Mispronouncing a word during a performance can be very embarrassing. Tell them that if they are having a hard time remembering how to pronounce one of the words in their script, they might try writing it out phonetically in the margin.

INTERACT

In groups of three or four, select a theme and develop the outline of a performance script on that theme, which must include a minimum of four pieces. The performance script should contain an introduction to the theme and performance, a list of the pieces selected (in full or in cut form), notes about transitions between each piece, and any concluding remarks. Indicate examples of material you considered but did not select for the final script.

REHEARSING ORAL INTERPRETATION

I'll just read it over before I give it. It's not much work because all the words are there.

Often beginning interpreters believe their work stops after finding and analyzing the piece of literature. They think, "I can read. Why do I need any more preparation?" Just as in public speaking, rehearsal is a very important part of preparing a performance. Reading your script silently to yourself as you lie in bed the night before the performance is not an effective way to practice. You need to carefully order the ideas in your mind and polish your delivery. You also need to learn to relax. The more relaxed you are, the more confident your reading will be.

After choosing the literature, read it silently several times, and then read it aloud.

Skill Development

On the Job

▲ Find out if any of your students do volunteer reading for children, the elderly, or the blind. Encourage these students to talk about any special techniques they might use to make their reading more effective.

Ordering the Piece in Your Mind

As you prepare to perform, you must make sure you have the main ideas of the piece fixed in your mind. The following simple steps will help you:

1. Read your entire piece silently two or three times. Go straight through. Don't stop and start over, and don't go back over any section.

2. Repeat step 1, but this time read the piece aloud.

3. Now try to give your performance while looking up at regular times. Stand up. Practice gestures and movement. Work with your script. Follow your markings. Try to complete the entire piece. Remember, this is a rehearsal, so it doesn't matter if you make mistakes. It is important that you go through the entire piece without stopping.

4. Continue giving the entire performance until you can complete the piece with the planned vocal tones and body movements.

In this part of your rehearsal, you should concentrate on the meaning of the ideas in your material. You are also getting to know the piece well enough so that you can look at your listeners. When the ideas are fixed in your mind, you will not get confused during the actual performance.

Polishing Your Delivery

Be sure your first rehearsal is not also your actual performance. Careful preparation time will pay off in a fine performance. The following steps can help you polish your delivery:

1. Imagine your audience in your mind. Set up chairs in front of yourself, talk to a mirror, or have one or two friends listen to you.

2. Always stand while practicing aloud to get used to gesturing and moving. Let your gestures flow from the literature—don't fake them.

3. Try to communicate with your real or imaginary audience. Look at your audience. Practice looking at each member.

536

Curricular Connection

Art

If students are giving performances for other classes or parents, assign several students to prepare flyers and posters announcing time and place of the performance and programs showing performers and their works.

4. If your practice audience is real rather than imaginary, adapt to your listeners. Watch for cues indicating a need to change your delivery. Ask your audience for feedback on points you can improve on and any movements you made that are effective or ineffective.

5. Give special practice to the introduction and any words or dialogue that must be carefully performed. You may wish to memorize these sections so that they sound exactly as you planned.

6. Use the script flexibly. You will need to look at it occasionally, but you must be able to maintain regular eye contact with your audience. Don't tie yourself to a word-for-word reading.

7. Try to record your performance on audiotape or videotape. That way you can hear or see exactly what your audience will hear or see.

8. Spread your rehearsal time over three or four days. If you wait until the last minute, you will only increase your nervousness. Leave yourself enough time so that you will be able to practice until you are comfortable.

9. Do not let your performance get stale. Vary your gestures, vocal tone, and facial expression. This will keep you thinking about the meaning of your piece.

Practicing Relaxation

Before you perform your selections, you may wish to use some relaxation techniques. These may help you feel less tense and more confident. Try some of the following strategies to see which work for you.

1. Clench your fists tightly for a count of ten. Release and let your whole body go limp.

2. Take a deep breath and hold it for a count of ten. Let it all out at once, letting your body go completely loose and limp.

3. Breathing normally, let your muscles relax more and more as you let out each breath.

537

❝Telling ourselves our own stories—interpreting the nature of our world to ourselves, . . . has as much as any single factor been responsible for the survival of African Americans and their culture.❞

HENRY LOUIS GATES, JR.
Talk That Talk

Limited English Proficiency

These students should be encouraged to take part in storytelling, perhaps in their native language. Nonverbal actions and expressions will help to make meaning clear even if not all the language is understood by others.

Motivation

Tell students that each of them has hundreds of stories to tell. After they read Janet Hudnut's story, have them give examples of various kinds of stories they could tell from their own lives.

4. Let your head hang down so your chin almost touches your chest. Slowly rotate your head in a circle, one way and then the other. Do this two or three times.

5. Imagine yourself on a warm beach, in a hot bath, or anywhere that seems relaxing to you. Breathe slowly and deeply.

Not all relaxation techniques (or mental-preparation techniques) work for everyone. Experiment. Try to find the methods that make you the best performer you can be.

TELLING A STORY

Whether you realize it or not, you are a storyteller. You tell informal stories every day. For example, when you tell your best friend about an argument you had with another friend, when you tell your brother about a movie you saw, or when you tell your parents about your day at school, you are telling a story. You also hear and tell more formal stories, ones that have been passed from person to person over a long time.

Storytelling is the art of sharing a tale or story with an audience. Storyteller William Brooke says, "The telling of a tale links you with everyone who has told it before. There are no new tales, only new tellers in their own way, and if you listen closely you can hear the voice of everyone who ever told the tale."

Storytelling is different from oral interpretation because you do not use a script. Instead, you rely on your memory to get all of the events in the right order. Composer Janet L. Hudnut tells this story:

> I remember one of my first lessons in anger. I was playing the piano one day at about age ten. I had just started practicing for a "gig" as we call it, which means playing for pay. Evidently the piano wasn't doing what I thought it should, so I started banging on it. My father reprimanded me, whereupon I said to him, "I am an artist, and artists do this all the time." He said, "Honey, the rest of us in this house are not 'artists,' so if you continue to need to do this, the piano will need to be removed."

Multicultural Learning

Encourage students to find out about the oral traditions of Native Americans and the role of the storyteller in Native American societies.

❝Facts are fine, as they go . . . but they's like water bugs skittering atop the water. Legends, now—they go deep down and bring up the heart of a story.❞

MARGUERITE HENRY
Misty of Chincoteague

Cooperative Learning

● Encourage the partners from the Interact exercise to exchange stories. Each person will tell his or her partner's story in a new way. Perhaps one partner will see humor where the other did not. Or the other partner might elaborate on a particular detail in the story. Have students report to the class about how their own stories struck them when told from another person's point of view.

When you were smaller, you may have heard many stories told to you at home or in school. These may have been fairy tales, fables, or stories adults made up. By now you may have told such stories to younger children. You may have told and listened to stories while sitting around a campfire at a Halloween party or while hanging around with friends.

Why is storytelling important? As one child says, "Life would be boring without stories." In addition, some authors suggest that the stories you tell communicate a lot about you to other people—what you believe, what you think is important, funny, or sad, and what you value. Storytelling helps to increase your vocabulary and improve your critical thinking, speaking, and listening skills as well as your imagination. Stories can help you cross the world or cross the street to see how other people live.

To become an effective storyteller, you need to practice storytelling techniques, including learning stories and developing your delivery skill.

Creating vivid images in your mind will help you express them to your listeners.

✳ INTERACT

Think about the events of the past week. What incident stands out in your mind? What makes it memorable? Tell the incident to a friend.

539

Beyond the Classroom

Encourage students to volunteer as storytellers at the public library, day-care center, or in elementary-school classrooms.

SPEAKING OF . . .

AMY RAO

For audience members in the WUSF-WSFP listening area of Tampa, Florida, the voice of Amy Rao is familiar and welcome. For four years Amy has worked on the Radio Reading Service, which brings printed material to those who cannot read because of blindness and other vision problems, illiteracy, or age. Amy creates a 30-minute children's show titled Small World, during which she performs children's stories, poems, and novels for a widespread audience. This show is hers from beginning to end. Amy is responsible for choosing material that is interesting and appropriate for an audience ranging from 7-12 years of age. In addition, she searches for material that will engage the listeners and sometimes contain a lesson. She then determines how to interpret the material to convey the author's meaning most effectively to young listeners and to hold their attention. According to Amy, "When I read children's stories, I try to vary my vocal patterns and use different accents." She works to create excitement in her voice to gain and hold the audience's attention. One way Amy does this is to involve her whole body in the presentation, even though she sits in a studio talking into a microphone. She describes this process, saying, "I am constantly gesturing with my hands and creating facial expressions so that their physicalizations carry into my voice."

Amy sees herself as a vocal performer who interprets literature so that young listeners may experience the story, poem, or novel and become caught up in its magic. In the future Amy may use her knowledge of children's literature and performing skills in careers that involve elementary teaching, children's theatre, library work, or radio announcing.

Beginning to Tell Stories

Narrative writing is writing that tells a story. When you choose a story for storytelling, look for a narrative that has suspense, excitement, simple language, a simple plot, a single theme, and a limited number of characters. Most importantly, choose a story that you really want to tell. You may wish to tell a story of your own or a story written by someone else.

Most beginning storytellers try to memorize the story word for word. Memorizing a story word for word is not a good idea because you can't make the story your own. When you tell a friend about an incident from your day, you don't tell it as if it is a speech you've committed to memory. You have an image of the event in your mind and a sequence of what happened. You create the words as you tell the story. The same idea applies to telling a story you have read. Remember the sequence of events and images created in your mind. The only words you might want to memorize are a repeated phrase (such as "Little pig, little pig, let me come in"). To make the story your own, you have to use your own words.

Learning Written Stories

When you are learning to tell a written story, follow these steps:

1. Read the story over several times.

2. Close the book and try to imagine the sequence of the story in your mind.

3. Open the book and read the story again, this time for the words that will add color to your telling. These include descriptive, concrete words that describe shape, color, and design.

4. Repeat the same process of imagining the story in your mind.

5. Now write out, draw, or outline the story (whatever works best for you).

6. Retell the story in your own words, out loud, so you can hear how it sounds.

7. Tell the story to a friend or record it.

8. Retell the story until you are pleased with your performance.

Limited English Proficiency

Have students with limited command of English work with partners to give them extra insight into their storytelling skills. Even students who do not read or write English particularly well may be capable of telling excellent stories in English.

Teach ◀

❝As a Chickasaw, I feel committed to the telling of Indian story, culling the lies out of history to find what is beneath them, and then speaking those found truths.**❞**

LINDA HOGAN

Beyond the Classroom

Students might enjoy writing narratives and then presenting them to a preschool or kindergarten class. Before students begin writing, review with them the essential elements of a good story—plot, character, and theme. Then have students write their stories. You might suggest that they base their stories on an historical or personal event. Encourage students to keep in mind their audience and their purpose as they write. When students have completed their narratives, have them prepare for their storytelling performances by using the Tips for Storytelling.

Tips for Storytelling

Now that you have prepared your story, it's time to tell it to an audience. As you speak, keep the following tips in mind:

1. *Capture your audience with a well-baited hook.* Make them eager to hear the story before you begin the telling. This can be accomplished by creating an interesting introduction. Here are some introductions other students have used:

   If you have trouble sleeping at night, maybe you'd better stop listening to this story right now. . . .

   In China, people do things differently. . . .

   Once, long ago, before yesterdays, before used-to-be's, back in the days when wishing did some good. . . .

2. *Be selective.* Remember, your audience wants to hear what happened. Choose words, events, and characters carefully, and don't get bogged down in lengthy description. The good storyteller remembers to keep it simple.

3. *Establish rapport with your listeners.* Rapport is everything! Eye contact is essential. Each listener should feel that the story is being told just for him or her.

4. *Create images.* As a storyteller, you must create vivid images in your mind if you want listeners to see them too. Visualize the pictures and people you are describing. Encourage your audience to imagine with all five senses how things feel, look, smell, taste, and sound.

5. *Use vocal variety.* Be sure to vary your vocal tone, rhythm, pitch, volume, and intensity. Use silences or pauses that will give your listeners time to imagine.

6. *Tell the story with zest.* Enthusiasm is contagious. If you enjoy your story, your audience will too.

7. *Make sure your audience knows when you are finished.* Your conclusion might be as simple as, "And that, my friends, is the story of `The Boastful Bullfrog,' " or as complex as, "If the story was beautiful, the beauty belongs to all of us; if it was not, the fault is only mine who told it."

Multicultural Learning

● If students are telling a tale with strong cultural roots, they should try to use music or sound effects appropriate to that culture. Flute, horn, drums, gourds, and stringed instruments could all provide effective transitions or emphasis during storytelling.

Learning Styles

Audio-Visual Learning

● Remind students to keep the size of their audience in mind when using props. For example, hand puppets will be most effective when used with small groups.

When telling a story, don't memorize it. Use your own words.

8. *Use props, if appropriate, to tell your stories.* Puppets, music, sound effects, posters, or objects that are mentioned in the story may be used to great effect. Be creative.

Remember, the most important thing about storytelling is that it should be fun. If you are enjoying yourself, your listeners will too.

EVALUATING ORAL INTERPRETATION AND STORYTELLING

The introduction did not prepare us for the piece. I understood Liza and Professor Higgins. I did not understand who the Pickering character was supposed to be.

Your use of a quiet tone and pauses really helped create the magic feeling of Terabithia.

Just as you learned to evaluate group discussions, public speaking, and debate, you need to be able to evaluate oral interpretation and storytelling performances. As a critic, you need to look at how effectively the performer communicates the meaning of a piece of literature. The purpose of a critique is to provide feedback to help the interpreter improve the next performance. The feedback you

Links to Past Learning

Have students use what they learned from this chapter and from Chapter 13 to create their own evaluation forms.

give and receive will help you improve your performance. Review the guidelines in Chapter 13 to help you critique effectively.

Different forms are used to evaluate the performance of various types of literature. You may find it interesting to experiment with creating your own critique forms. The sample critique forms shown here can be used to evaluate an oral interpretation or a storytelling performance.

Evaluation Form: Oral Interpretation Performance

Speaker's Name _____

Speaker's Topic _____

Evaluate each point as
S—Superior, **E**—Excellent, **G**—Good, or **F**—Fair.

_____ 1. **Choice of Selection** Is this selection appropriate to the speaker and occasion? Was the literature selected of high literary merit?

_____ 2. **Adequacy of Introduction** Did it give enough information about the author, time, place, characters, and action to arouse attention and interest? Was it compatible with the selection?

_____ 3. **Understanding** Did the interpreter appear to understand the feelings, thoughts, and attitudes of the dramatic speaker?

_____ 4. **Analysis** Did the interpreter appear to understand the theme, conflict, and characters of the piece?

_____ 5. **Bodily Action** Did the interpreter's gestures, posture, and facial expressions contribute to an understanding of the literature? Did any of the bodily actions distract from the meaning of the piece?

continued

_____ 6. **Vocal Work** Did the interpreter's voice contribute to an understanding of the literature? Were words pronounced clearly and correctly?

_____ 7. **Communication** Did the interpreter communicate the thoughts, emotions, attitudes, and intentions of the dramatic speaker? Did he or she share with rather than read to the audience? Was there sufficient eye contact with listeners?

8. **Additional Comments:** _____

_____

_____

_____

Evaluation Form: Storytelling Performance

Speaker's Name _____

Speaker's Topic _____

Evaluate each point as
S—Superior, **E**—Excellent, **G**—Good, or **F**—Fair.

_____ 1. **Choice of Story** Is the story appropriate for the occasion, audience? Does it fit the assignment? Is it a well-written or well-developed story?

_____ 2. **Effectiveness of Introduction** Did it give enough background on the development of the story? Did it motivate audience members to listen? Did it indicate who the usual listeners are (children, family members, tribal members . . .)

continued

545

continued

_____ 3. **Understanding** Did the interpreter set a mood or tone that matched the story? Did the interpreter convey the points of view of different characters?

_____ 4. **Analysis** Did the interpreter appear to understand the feelings, attitudes of the characters, or the culture of the story? Did the interpreter emphasize the theme and key points of the story?

_____ 5. **Bodily Action** How well did the interpreter's gestures, movements, facial expressions and appearance contribute to an understanding of the story? Did the nonverbal messages distract from the point of the story?

_____ 6. **Vocal work** How well did the interpreter's voice contribute to an understanding of the story's plot? characters? mood? Was the story told at a good pace? Were any characters developed well through vocal changes?

_____ 7. **Communication** Did the interpreter engage the audience members in the story? Did the audience respond as the interpreter wished? If the audience was supposed to participate, did they respond?

Critical Thinking
Synthesizing

● Encourage students to evaluate for themselves the areas of their storytelling that need improvement and the areas that they feel are particularly good. Then ask them to write a paragraph giving their reactions to what they learned in this chapter.

CHAPTER 17 SUMMARY

This chapter focuses on the performance of oral interpretation and storytelling. When preparing performance materials, interpreters often cut the literature selections and create introductions for them. Performers must use sense recall, voice, and body to bring literature to life. Oral interpreters arrange their pieces, mark their materials, and create scripts for performance use. Rehearsal includes practicing to ensure both a total understanding of the material and a polished delivery. Storytellers try to create visual images in their listeners' minds. They select stories they wish to tell and prepare them without actually memorizing. They work to engage the audience through their energy, language, and special techniques. Giving and receiving feedback helps improve both oral interpretation and storytelling performances.

547

Answers

Think About It

Student answers will vary. Here are sample answers:

1. (1) unnecessary descriptions, (2) descriptions of action or manner of speaking, (3) "he said" and "she said" statements, (4) words that offend the audience, (5) unnecessary characters

2. (1) ordering the pieces, (2) marking the script, (3) creating the structure, (4) creating the stage script

3. A good introduction should (1) capture the audience's attention, (2) tell the author and title, (3) give any necessary background information about the author or literature, (4) set the scene, (5) tie the selection to the audience's experience, if possible.

4. (1) Read the entire piece to yourself straight through two or three times. (2) Repeat step 1, but this time read the material aloud. (3) Give the performance while looking up at regular intervals.

5. (1) Capture the audience's attention with a great introduction. (2) Be selective; be choosy about wording and don't get bogged down in lengthy description. Keep it simple. (3) Build listener rapport. (4) Create vivid images. Encourage the audience to see, feel, smell, touch,

---

CHAPTER REVIEW

Think About It

1. When cutting a piece of literature for oral interpretation, what are some things you might delete?

2. List the steps for preparing a script for oral interpretation.

3. What are the characteristics of a good introduction?

4. What are the steps necessary to order the selection in your mind?

5. What are some of the tips for storytelling?

6. What is the purpose of an oral interpretation or storytelling evaluation?

Try It Out

1. Recite the alphabet, creating a happy mood by using only your voice. Recite it again, creating a sad or angry mood with your voice.

2. Use only facial expressions to create three different moods. Next use only posture to create the same three moods. Have class members identify the moods you are creating.

3. Choose a piece of literature you would like to interpret. Then cut the piece as necessary, write an introduction, and mark the script. Present the piece you prepared to the class. Use your body, gestures, voice, facial expressions, and eye focus to help you interpret the literature.

4. Work with a partner to discover many ways to present the same piece of literature. Each person should prepare a sample introduction, mark one copy of the script, and make any necessary cuts. Perform your versions for each other. Then combine your efforts and create a new presentation based on the best parts of each of your works.

Put It in Writing

1. Make journal entries listing suggestions and compliments you have received on the oral interpretations you have presented in class. At the end of the unit on oral interpretation, write a short paper that analyzes how you improved in your performance abilities.

2. In your journal, keep a record of your rehearsal techniques. Write a short paper in which you discuss which rehearsal techniques worked most effectively for you and which techniques did not help you. Make a note in your journal of those techniques that worked best for you.

3. Create a performance script. Select a theme and four to six pieces to support the theme. Develop an introduction, transition material, and a conclusion. Mark your script.

Speak About It

1. Listen to an oral interpretation performance outside the classroom, such as a tape or CD of a child's story, a religious reading, or a professional performance. Describe and evaluate the effectiveness of the performance for your class.

2. Present an oral critique of a classmate's oral interpretation.

3. In groups of four, perform pieces you prepared previously. Take turns being listeners and performers. The listeners should use an evaluation form to rate each performance and to give constructive criticism to the performer.

and taste the story. (5) Vary vocal tone, pitch, rhythm, volume, and intensity. (6) Make sure the audience knows when the story is finished. Give the story a closing. (7) Use props.

6. The purpose of an oral interpretation or storytelling evaluation is to provide the interpreter with feedback that will help the speaker improve his or her next performance.

Quick Check

Ask students to find and define these Key Terms:

body recall (521)

cutting the literature (515)

eye focus (528)

marking the script (532)

sense recall (520)

storytelling (538)

549

	Day 1	Day 2	Day 3	Day 4	Day 5
18 Group Interpretation					
Choral Speaking	Choral Speaking	Reader's Theatre	Reader's Theatre	Summary
					Chapter Review
Teacher's Resource Book					
Teaching Suggestions 18.1–18.2	18.3–18.5	18.6–18.7	18.8–18.9	
Worksheets & Evaluation Forms	53–54		55–56	
					Chapter Test 18
Workbook 18.1	18.2–18.3	18.4–18.5	18.6	

Week 18 · *Chapter 18 Planner*

Motivation

Ask students what it's like to work as a member of a team. Then tell them that group interpretation requires strong teamwork skills.

18

CHAPTER EIGHTEEN

Group Interpretation

Chapter Objectives

After completing this chapter, you should be able to

1   define *group interpretation, choral speaking,* and *reader's theatre*

2   list standards for selecting material for choral speaking and reader's theatre

3   describe a variety of performance techniques for choral speaking and reader's theatre

4   prepare and perform a choral-speaking presentation

5   prepare and perform a reader's-theatre presentation

6   evaluate group-interpretation performances

▼ Key Terms

choral speaking   script patterns

offstage focus   suggestion

reader's theatre

Critical Thinking

Predicting

● Have students read through the Key Words and objectives; ask whether anyone knows what choral speaking is or whether anyone has heard choral speaking or seen reader's theatre. Then ask students to predict what kinds of activities they will take part in while they study this chapter.

Cooperative Learning

● Read "The Adventures of Isabel" aloud to the class. Then call on two students to recite the poem. They will each read every other line. Let them decide who will read first. When they have finished reciting the poem, ask them to comment about the differences between speaking alternately with another person and speaking individually. Then have student groups read the poem as marked.

Motivation

Have students give examples of choral speaking in their daily lives. Suggestions might include saying the Pledge of Allegiance or taking part in group prayers at a religious service. Write students' examples on the chalk board.

The Adventures of Isabel

Group 1 { Isabel met an enormous bear
Isabel, Isabel, didn't care.

Group 2 { The bear was hungry, the bear was ravenous,
The bear's big mouth was cruel and cavernous.
The bear said, Isabel, glad to meet you,
How do, Isabel, now I'll eat you!

Group 3 { Isabel, Isabel, didn't worry
Isabel didn't scream or scurry.
She washed her hands and she straightened her hair up,

All   Then Isabel quietly ate the bear up.

—Ogden Nash

For centuries, human voices have been raised in choruses of song and speech. Group singing is more common than group speaking. Probably you have sung in groups since you were a small child, but you may not have spoken in groups. Many pieces of literature can best be brought to life through group interpretation.

This chapter introduces two types of group interpretation, choral speaking and reader's theatre. After mastering the material in this chapter, you will be able to use your preparation and performance skills to work creatively in a group.

CHORAL SPEAKING

Choral speaking is speaking in unison. Speakers blend and combine their individual voices to create a group voice. Good choral speaking involves more than saying the correct words at the same time. Choral speakers create a special type of performance to help listeners experience a piece of literature. Choral speaking works well with literature that has a strong rhythm. For this reason, choral-speaking groups frequently perform poetry.

Like the voices in a singing group, voices in a choral-speaking group have different ranges. In a school choir, there may be soprano, alto, tenor, and bass voices. In a choral-speaking group, the voices may be clustered into high, medium, and low; male

Links to Past Learning

Ask if any of the students have ever sung in a chorus or choir. Encourage them to describe their experiences at rehearsals. Tell students that choral speaking is much like singing in a group.

and female; or some other way. When choral speakers perform, they hold their scripts much like choir members hold their musical arrangements. When performing, the speakers stand, or sit on stools facing an audience.

Choral speaking has many benefits. It allows you to improve your oral-interpretation skills within a group and increase your self-confidence as a performer. Also, it is an enjoyable way to learn more about literature and interpretation. To become a choral speaker, you need to understand how to create script patterns, select the material, use performance techniques, and critique choral speaking.

Creating Script Patterns

Script patterns are the ways in which the speakers' parts are divided. Imagine that you are planning a performance by a group of five speakers. They will do an interpretation of the following lines from Ecclesiastes 1:1-8, a well-known piece of biblical literature:

1 To everything there is a season, and a time to every purpose under the heaven.

2 A time to be born, and a time to die;

3 A time to plant, and a time to pluck that which is planted;

4 A time to kill, and a time to heal;

5 A time to break down, and a time to build up;

6 A time to weep, and a time to laugh;

7 A time to mourn, and a time to dance;

8 A time to cast away stones, and a time to gather stones together;

9 A time to embrace, and a time to refrain from embracing;

10 A time to get, and a time to lose;

11 A time to keep, and a time to cast away;

12 A time to rend, and a time to sew;

continued

Learning Styles

Audio Learning

● To demonstrate why choral speaking works better with literature that has a strong rhythm, choose a paragraph from the text and call on two students to read it in unison. Encourage the rest of the class to discuss what they hear.

Limited English Proficiency

To further illustrate the point about individual voices and unison speaking, ask a volunteer to sing one sustained note. Before he or she begins, tell the rest of the students that you are going to point to individuals at random and they are to try to hit the same note and sustain it. Afterward ask for student feedback about the various vocal qualities.

Links to Past Learning

Remind students to think about what types of facial expressions, physical gestures, and posture might aid particular parts of their group interpretations.

13 A time to keep silent, and a time to speak;

14 A time to love, and a time to hate;

15 A time of war, and a time of peace;

16 To everything there is a season, and a time to every purpose under the heaven.

How would you divide the work of the speakers? Would you have all five voices say everything or would you let the speakers take turns? Depending on your script pattern, there are several ways to divide these lines. Here are some of the possibilities:

1. *Everyone speaks in unison.* All voices move through a piece together.

2. *Each person in the group reads one line.* If the piece is long, the first speaker starts the pattern again. For example, if there are five readers for the Ecclesiastes piece, person 1 reads lines 1, 6, and 11, plus the last line. Person 2 reads lines 2, 7, and 12, plus the last line. And so on. Everyone reads the last line.

3. *One person reads the first line or section; a second person reads the second line or section with the first person; and so on until everyone is reading in unison.* For example, since the full Ecclesiastes piece has sixteen lines, person 1 speaks the opening three lines, persons 1 and 2 the next three lines, and so on. The closing line is recited by the entire group.

4. *One person or group reads a line or section, and another person or group responds.* For example, in the Ecclesiastes piece, two groups respond to each other dividing each line. Group 1 says, "A time to be born." Group 2 responds, "A time to die."

5. *Several persons have solos and then are joined by the group. Individuals speak, and then the whole group speaks.* If the piece is long, this can be repeated several times. In the Ecclesiastes example, individual speakers might perform the first half of each line and the group could speak the rest in unison.

As you can see, there are many different ways to create a group script. Usually the entire group speaks together at some time during the performance. Look at the following examples of scripts for a chorus of voices:

Substitute Teacher Tip

Tell students that there are many different ways to interpret the same material. As an example, divide the class into three groups. Tell the first group to do their interpretation of "A Goblin Lives in Our House" giving it a dark, scary mood. Tell the second group to present a playful version. Then encourage students to discuss what each group did vocally and physically to express the assigned mood.

A Goblin Lives in Our House

Solo 1: A goblin lives in our house
High voices: in our house,
Low voices: in our house,
Unison: A goblin lives in our house all the year round.
Solo 2: He bumps
Solo 3: And he jumps
Solo 4: And he thumps
Solo 5: And he stumps
Solo 6: He knocks
Solo 7: And he rocks
Solo 8: And he rattles at the locks.
Solo 1: A goblin lives in our house.
Low voices: in our house,
High voices: in our house,
Unison: A goblin lives in our house all the year round.

     — From the French,
       adapted by Louise Abney

Reading in unison brings power to a piece.

Teach

66There never was a good
war, or a bad peace.99

BENJAMIN FRANKLIN

Critical Thinking

Analyzing

Ask students to read through "Battle
Won Is Lost" silently. Ask who is
speaking in the poem. What is the
theme of the poem? Tell them that
counting coup (koo) refers to the
Plains Indians' custom of touching a
live enemy and getting away, rather
than killing an enemy. The former act
was considered braver. Warriors

carried a coup stick with which to
touch an enemy.

Skill Development

Feedback

● Encourage students to take notes
on their classmates' readings during
the Interact presentation. Have them
refer to their notes as they offer
feedback. Remind them to use the
rules of constructive criticism by first
stating what they liked about the
presentation.

Skill Development

Research

▲ Remind students that there are
many sources of material for group
interpretation. After reading "Battle
Won Is Lost," they might be
interested in researching poetry about
other wars and battles. Encourage
them to do library research to find
examples of materials written during
the Civil War, World War I, World War
II, or the Vietnam War. They may wish
to present their findings to the class
or create a group-interpretation
performance.

556

Battle Won Is Lost

Unison: They said, "You are no longer a lad."
Solo 1: I nodded.
Unison: They said, "Enter the council lodge."
Solo 2: I sat.
Unison: They said, "Our lands are at stake."
Solo 3: I scowled.
Unison: They said, "We are at war."
Solo 4: I hated.
Unison: They said, "Prepare red war symbols."
Solo 5: I painted.
Unison: They said, "Count coups."
Solo 6: I scalped.
Unison: They said, "You'll see friends die."
Solo 7: I cringed.
Unison: They said, "Desperate warriors fight best."
Solo 8: I charged.
Unison: They said, "Some will be wounded."
Solo 1: I bled.
Unison: They said, "To die is glorious."
Solo 2: They lied.

— Phil George

INTERACT

With four or five classmates, select a piece of your choice and
plot out a speaker script. Then do a reading for the class and
explain the reasons for plotting out your script the way you did.

Selecting Material

Some literature demands to be read by a group in unison rather
than by a lone voice. The group reading will make the meaning
more easily understood. To select and analyze literature for
choral speaking, follow the same guidelines as you did for oral

Cooperative Learning

Encourage students to work together in small groups to rehearse and present a group interpretation of "Jigsaw Puzzle." When all groups have presented the poem, discuss what mood and theme each group emphasized.

Learning Styles

Kinesic Learning

● Have students play a rhythm game. You can either start the game yourself or choose a volunteer. Whoever starts must choose a rhythm and clap it, tap it, or stomp it. The rest of the class joins in as soon as they know the rhythm sequence. Then you will point to another student and that student must change the rhythm in some noticeable way. Continue in this way. Encourage students to come up with more and more complex rhythms.

interpretation in Chapter 16. In addition, literature for choral speaking must have these three qualities: strong rhythm, variety of moods, and a strong theme.

Rhythm In choral speaking the strong rhythm of the literature is extremely important. The rhythm helps keep the group members speaking together whenever necessary.

Variety of Moods Vocal tones, nonverbal expressions, and gestures are the primary instruments performers use to create mood. In choral speaking, various moods can easily be conveyed by different performers. The changes in mood in a piece of literature can be shown by the use of different types of voices. For example, a serious part may be spoken by low voices, while a playful part may be performed by high voices. Not all poems have frequent mood changes, but some variety within a poem is necessary for good choral speaking.

Theme When a group performs, the audience is watching and listening to a number of people at work. Therefore, the message must not be too complex or difficult to find. In some literature the theme is subtle, and the reader must search for the author's clues to bring it out. Sometimes an individual interpreter may be able to share such a theme with listeners, but in group performance, a subtle theme could be totally lost. Unless material is direct, the listeners will become confused.

Read the following poem and try to identify its theme. How would you emphasize the theme in choral speaking?

Jigsaw Puzzle

My beautiful picture of pirates and treasure
Is spoiled, and almost I don't want to start
To put it together; I've lost all the pleasure
I used to find in it: there's one missing part.

I know there's one missing—they lost it, the others,
The last time they played with my puzzle—and maybe

continued

Curricular Connection

Language Arts

● Interested students might want to try their hand at writing short comic, rhythmic poems. Then you might ask them to direct the class in a group interpretation of their work.

There's more than one missing: along with the brothers
And sisters who borrow my toys there's the baby.

There's a hole in the ship or the sea that it sails on,
And I said to my father, "Well, what shall I do? It isn't the same now that some of it's gone."
He said, "Put it together; the world's like that too."

—Russell Hoban

INTERACT

The following piece represents a work written by a college student to be performed by two voices. Its performance effectiveness will depend on the readers' abilities to create pictures with their voices, and to convey a reflective mood. Since the author creates two segments of each stanza by the use of italics, the second voice should comment on the words spoken by the first voice.

With a partner prepare this piece for choral speaking. You will have to find the meaning of "Charon" and discuss what the poet means by "remindful marigold," "waterfall-eyed widow," "indigoed edge," or "depuzzling." Then you will need to decide how to convey these complicated images to an audience. After trying out this difficult piece, discuss the pros and cons of performing it aloud. Consider how visual support, such as slides or the movement of one dancer, might enhance the performance. Present the poem to the class for discussion.

Remindful Marigold

1 Puddle-drowned grass bowed in a gravestone's shadow, fingering a remindful marigold:
2 *Placed there like a crystal egg on pins by a waterfall-eyed widow.*

1 Water singed the petals, cowering from cascades of alabaster:

❝Poetry is like fish: if it's fresh, it's good; if it's stale, it's bad; and if you're not certain, try it on the cat.**❞**

OSBERT SITWELL

2   *Wind wrinkled the indigoed edge*
    of a flower depuzzling.

1   Sunbeams stepped on the stem
    unshackling the rain-bruised petals:

2   *Shivering in the shadow—*
    Charon sailing in a moonless night.

1   Its stem slept alone
    in dark of day:

2   *Wind dancing through*
    its lost petals as its leaves lunged away.

1   Petals waltzed on a shadow
    as a stem shook in the ripples:

2   *Puddle, rocking*
    its lonely leaf asleep.

—Michael Gavin

Techniques for Choral Speaking

As a choral speaker, you will use many of the performance techniques you learned in Chapter 17. To be an effective choral speaker, you must also know how to speak precisely, use scripts uniformly, use space effectively, and use media supports.

Skill Development
Vocabulary

● Encourage students to look up all unfamiliar vocabulary they come across while exploring oral interpretation sources. They may wish to keep a journal of new words and their definitions and pronunciations.

Choral speaking requires that the team practice speaking with the same rhythms and speech patterns.

> **"**Great literature is simply language charged with meaning to the utmost possible degree.**"**
>
> EZRA POUND

Learning Styles

Kinesic Learning

● Have students work in small groups to practice moving and speaking in unison. Give them a set of instructions such as the following: "Open your books to page 560. Stand up. Slowly raise your books to within reading distance. Read the first sentence on page 560 aloud. Close your books. Sit down." Have each group perform the instructions until all members can perform in perfect unison.

Links to Past Learning

Remind students that when presenting material orally, it is important to use excellent diction and to pay particular attention to final consonants such as *d*'s and *t*'s. You might also want to stress to them that *-ing* endings should be fully pronounced and should rhyme with the word *sing*. Ask students to watch their pronunciations of "going to" and "wanting to."

Speaking Precisely Choral speaking requires teamwork. Like members of a basketball team, marching band, or cheerleading squad, the members of a choral-speaking group must cooperate if the group is to meet its goal. Choral speaking takes team effort. When people speak together, they have to start and stop at the same time, pronounce words in the same way, and speak clearly. They also have to learn to speak with the same rhythms and speech patterns, all of which takes a great deal of practice.

Using Scripts In your mind, picture four performers standing in a row. Person 1 is reading from a notebook. Person 2 is reading from a poetry book. Person 3 is holding a crumpled piece of paper but never looks at it. Person 4 reads from three note cards. What picture does this present to an audience?

To present a uniform group image, all performers must have identical scripts and handle their scripts in the same way. Most choral-speaking groups back their scripts with construction paper or place them in large folders. Usually each speaker knows the piece well and only needs to glance at the script rather than read it. When scripts are used they should be raised and lowered, and opened and closed, by all members of the group at the same time. Sometimes a group memorizes the literature and appears without scripts. This allows the group to move more easily.

Using Space Each member of a performing group needs to know where individuals are placed and how they will move. Sometimes the group sits or stands in a line in front of the audience, and often speakers with similar voices are placed together. In a large group, the stronger voices may be placed in the back and the softest voices in the front. The individuals who do solo speaking may step out in front of the group when performing.

The performance starts as the group enters the performance space and ends when they leave it. For this reason, members should plan an organized entrance and exit.

Usually the group members remain standing or sitting next to each other. If the literature contains action, the group may sway, point, wave their arms, or perform other movements to get a message across. Often, groups who perform for children will use movements to help keep the children's attention. Think about how a group of six might move to each of the following sets of lines.

Set A

And he huffed,
and he puffed,
and he blew the house down.

Set B

Double Dutch
Double Dutch
Ropes beat sidewalks clean.
Feet are jumping
Arms are pumping
One minute!
That's my dream.

Motivation

Encourage students to suggest other jump-rope rhymes or children's stories they can read with appropriate movements.

A solo speaker may move away from the group when speaking.

Cooperative Learning

Students might like to create a class performance project using the group interpretation techniques they are learning in this chapter. Encourage students to work together to choose appropriate materials. You might suggest books in the bibliography on page 585. Poetry by the following authors may also be suitable: Maya Angelou, Hilaire Belloc, Ana Castillo, Robert Frost, Nikki Giovanni, Joy Harjo, Langston Hughes, Edgar Lee Masters, Phyllis McGinley, Eve Merriam, Ogden Nash, Carl Sandburg, Leslie Marmon Silko, Luci Tapahonso, and Judith Viorst.

Learning Styles
Audio-Visual Learning

● Ask students to give examples of technologies other than slides that might be used to enhance the group interpretation source material discussed in this chapter.

It is possible to include some performers who do not speak but whose movements contribute to the meaning of the piece. One or two performers may playfully mime part of the poem. A dancer might create a set of movements for the piece.

Using Media Supports Some performers choose to use different media to help convey their message. You may project slides or computer graphics near the performers to make a point more strongly. For example, if you were to perform "Battle Won Is Lost," you might project two or three slides showing paintings of a battleground from the French and Indian War. You may select a piece of music to play as a background to the performance. These media supports must be chosen to enhance the meaning of the literature but not distract from the performance.

Critiquing Choral Speaking

Your voice was so loud it kept distracting me.

Be sure to keep your scripts at about the same level. I could not see Carol's face, and Nathan's script was moving up and down.

One of the pieces was so complicated that it was very difficult to find the meaning of the literature without a printed copy.

As a critic or listener, you may be called upon to give feedback on choral-speaking performances. The techniques you learned in Chapter 17 for critiquing interpretation also apply to choral speaking. In addition, you will want to consider criteria that relate specifically to group work. You might find the sample evaluation form useful in providing helpful feedback to choral speakers.

Evaluation Form: Choral Speaking

	Always	Sometimes	Never
Voice			
Members' voices blended in unison.	____	____	____
Members started and stopped together.	____	____	____
Members pronounced words in the same way.	____	____	____
Members varied vocal tone to show meaning.	____	____	____
Body			
Members adapted facial expressions to the material.	____	____	____
Members moved in unison.	____	____	____
Members looked at listeners regularly.	____	____	____
Members entered and exited in unison.	____	____	____
Scripts (if used)			
Members held scripts in similar ways.	____	____	____
Members' faces could be seen over their scripts.	____	____	____
Media Supports (if used)			
The meaning was conveyed more directly through media support.	____	____	____
The media support was integrated and not distracting.	____	____	____
Material and Script Patterns			
Material was well-suited for choral performance.	____	____	____
Material was appropriate to the audience.	____	____	____
Choice of script pattern helped communicate the meaning.	____	____	____

Motivation

Tell students that because reader's theatre doesn't depend on sets or costumes, it is much more portable than a typical theatre production. Reader's theatre can be performed equally well in a theatre, a classroom, a library, or the lobby of a building.

Beyond the Classroom

Students might enjoy listening to a member of your Theatre Department talk about his or her experiences onstage. Perhaps you can find someone who has even had experiences working in community or professional theatre like Jeff Seelbach has. Suggest that the speaker discuss how communication skills directly affect performance skills.

SPEAKING OF . . .

JEFF SEELBACH

Not many teens have the opportunity to appear in professional theatre productions, but Jeff Seelbach of Short Hills, New Jersey, is often on stage as part of a professional company. Jeff, a student at Milburn High School, has been involved in performing for ten years, starting at age ten in community theatre. These experiences opened the door to professional work with equity actors at New Jersey's State Theatre, Papermill Playhouse. At the age of 12 he performed the role of Young Herbert in *Great Expectations,* and at 14 he appeared as John Darling in *Peter Pan.*

According to Jeff, "Performance is the essence of theatre, and I am often asked to perform in singing and theatre groups." Yet Jeff has moved beyond his own acting career. Currently he uses his performing background to instruct elementary- and high-school students in theatre arts. Frequently, directors ask Jeff to teach stage blocking or musical numbers to other cast members. In order to serve this instructional role, Jeff tries to communicate in a very direct and clear manner and is careful to explain terms such as "equity" or "blocking." Trying to instruct or direct fellow students is not always easy. In describing his communication style, Jeff says, "I've found that the best way to work with peers and lead them is by example. . . . If I am respectful to them and to others around me, I've found they will at least listen to what I have to say. Most times they will follow my directions because they know I am straightforward and friendly."

Although Jeff's future career goals are not yet established, it is quite likely he will use some of his communication experience in positions such as theatre director, arts educator, recreation leader, or stage performer.

Beyond the Classroom

Many colleges and universities teach courses in reader's theatre. If possible, invite a college group to perform for your class.

READER'S THEATRE

Reader's theatre is a type of group interpretation in which speakers present literature in a dramatic form. Instead of acting out the literature as in a play, however, the speakers suggest the characters by using their voices, facial expressions, and some gestures. Reader's theatre may be performed with many kinds of literature, including short stories, plays, poetry, parts of novels, or material from newspapers or magazines. Reader's theatre brings many kinds of literature alive in creative ways. Although there are guidelines for performing reader's theatre, performers are encouraged to experiment with different ways to reach the audience.

The following short example shows how a piece of prose fiction might be scripted for a reader's theatre production. You can see how one speaker provides the narration, while others provide the dialogue.

Narrator: Amanda shuffled to the front of the room, avoiding the glances and snickers from those around her. She stared stone-faced at her unlaced shoes.

Speaker 2: Amanda.

Narrator: Ms. Parsons said, wagging her finger.

Speaker 2: How many times must I remind you, fighting will not be tolerated in this class?

Narrator: Keith, hiding behind his history book, snickered.

Speaker 3: Here we go again. This girl is on her way out. We did it.

Narrator: Amanda looked at her shoes as if tying them with her eyes.

Speaker 2: Young lady, have you nothing to say for yourself?

Narrator: Continued a frustrated Ms. Parsons. Amanda sniffled. A large tear, brimmed on her lower eyelid, spilled onto her cheek.

Links to Past Learning

Have four students read the excerpt on pages 565–566, using what they already know about oral interpretation techniques.

❝Not to go to the theatre is like making one's toilet without a mirror.❞

ARTHUR SCHOPENHAUER

Beyond the Classroom

Tell students that some theatre companies use a variety of reader's theatre techniques within their productions. City Lit Theatre Company, in Chicago, Illinois, for example, produces adaptations of literature, often performed on full sets with actors in full costume, yet using many of the reader's theatre techniques addressed in this chapter.

Speaker 4: No, ma'am.

Narrator: Che whispered. Keith fell out of his chair laughing. At this, Ms. Parsons turned to him.

As you can tell, in this example each person speaks one character's part of the dialogue. The narrator provides additional information to help the audience understand exactly what is happening.

To perform and appreciate reader's theatre, you need to understand the use of suggestion and imagination, performance techniques, selection of material, and ways to evaluate performances.

Suggestion and Imagination

Reader's theatre is sometimes called "theatre of the mind," because the action and scenery are created in the audience's mind, not on the stage. The key to this creation process is called **suggestion**. Suggestion is the way speakers create the action, props, and scenery in the audience's imagination. Imagine the scene with Amanda in the classroom. The reader who plays Amanda will not actually walk forward to show the meaning of the dialogue. She will remain in her place within the group of readers and look down. The reader who plays Keith may hold his script in front of his face to represent the history book.

Action in a play would be different. In a play, the actor playing Amanda would actually shuffle to the front of the room, and the actor playing Keith would hold a real history book. The use of suggestion in reader's theatre forces the audience members to use their imaginations. They may have to imagine a car chase or a funeral or a farmhouse in a tornado. The performers will suggest these scenes but will not play them out as they would in a theatre production. Reader's theatre performers do not become the characters; they only suggest the characters.

Performance Techniques for Reader's Theatre

The performance techniques of reader's theatre help performers to create this suggestion for the audience. These techniques include scripting, staging, eye focus, movement, and technical support.

Learning Styles
Audio Learning

● Have a pair of students improvise an argument between two characters using the reader's theatre technique of offstage focus. After they have finished the scene, ask them to share their responses to the activity with the rest of the class.

Scripting Usually one or two people act as narrators for reader's theatre. They may also read the parts of minor characters if there are not enough other performers. Although one speaker usually speaks for the same character, there may be times when all the performers become a crowd or perform the same motion, even if not all the characters are involved. For example, when performing the sentence, "Adam stepped back as the track team raced by," the person playing Adam may sit back on his stool while the rest of the cast may pump their arms to pantomime running by.

Staging The most common way of staging reader's theatre is to have the characters sit on stools in a line or semicircle facing the audience. Sometimes the stools may be arranged on platforms in various positions. The staging is always simple. Usually the performers use scripts, although sometimes they perform from memory. All characters remain on-stage during the performance. If an important character leaves or dies, that speaker could hang his or her head down or turn his or her back to the audience. If the character reenters, he or she can look up or turn toward the audience. In most productions, the cast members do not actually enter or exit.

Eye Focus During most reader's theatre performances, the cast members look toward the audience. The readers may look somewhere over the heads of the audience, perhaps at a spot on the back wall.

Another technique is called **offstage focus**. When using offstage focus, the speakers pretend there is a mirror behind the audience and that they are all reflected in it. When characters speak to each other, they speak to the imagined reflection. For example, when the second speaker, Ms. Parsons, talks to speaker 4, Amanda, she will look at the imagined reflection of Amanda on the back wall.

Even during a dialogue, the speakers usually look out over the audience. On occasion, characters will look at each other. During an important romantic scene or argument, two characters may talk directly to each other.

Skill Development
Quick Skill Opportunity

▼ Have students try to create, through suggestions, the following actions and scenes in the minds of their audience—their classmates. Be sure that LEP students participate in this exercise.

a car screeching to a halt

police arriving at the door

fishing from a bridge

a cold wind

a sudden shower

567

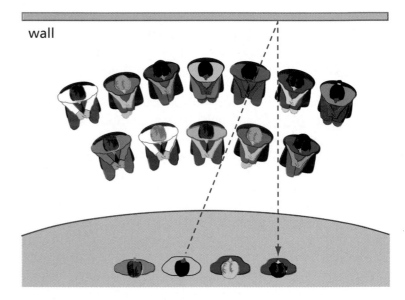

wall

Movement Usually reader's theatre involves little movement. The audience is to picture the movement in their minds. The speakers might suggest or pantomime some movement using changes in facial expressions, gestures, and posture. In our classroom scene, the speaker playing Keith will not try to fall out of the chair but will lean to one side. Mrs. Parsons will waggle her finger.

If important movement involves two characters, you can see them react to each other. If the script says, "Keith pulled Amanda's braid," Keith will pantomime a yanking action, and Amanda will grasp her head and gasp.

Technical Support Reader's theatre can be performed with very little technical support. Cast members rely on simple costumes, a few well-chosen props, lighting, or music to help create the suggestion. Scenery is rarely used. The cast usually performs in front of a curtain or solid-colored wall.

Cast members often wear well-coordinated everyday clothes, such as white shirts and dark pants. Special touches can be added. For example, a farmer may wear a straw hat, or a basketball player

"At least be sure that you go to the author to get at *his* meaning, not to find yours."

JOHN RUSKIN

may wear a team jersey. Props are seldom used, but if the piece being performed calls for a particular prop, such as a book or an umbrella, it may be used.

Lighting and music also help create the suggestion for the audience. Turning lights on and off can mark the beginning and end of a scene. In stage productions, spotlights might move from one speaker to another for dramatic effect. Sometimes a slide projector or computer is used to create pictures behind the performers. Music and sound effects may be added. However, reader's theatre performances should not rely too much on technical support. Such support must never limit the audience's imagination.

INTERACT

Find a copy of the book *The Little Prince,* by Antoine de Saint-Exupéry. In groups of four, discuss how you might stage a production of thirty to forty lines of this literature with five performers. In your plan, pay careful attention to who will speak, how your cast members will be arranged, important character movements, and eye focus. You need not worry about technical support.

Simple costumes and a very few props are usually all that are needed for reader's theatre.

Chapter 18 Group Interpretation

Skill Development

Research

▲ Interested students might want to do research to find out more about different kinds of theatre and performance techniques. To get them started, suggest that they find out about the following: fourth wall, proscenium arch, arena stage, Noh theatre, and puppet theatre. Some students might want to share their findings with the class by means of a report or a demonstration.

Selecting Literature

When performing reader's theatre, you may use one long piece of literature or several short pieces. When selecting literature for reader's theatre, you need to look for strong characters, a clear theme, picturesque language, and obvious conflict.

Characters Characters must stand out in reader's theatre. The audience must create these people in their minds. Therefore, characters must be easily pictured and remembered. Whether it's because of her language or because of her spunk, the main character of *Anne of Green Gables* stands out as a memorable character. Look for pieces with dialogue. This will make the characters more interesting for the audience. Look at the strong characters in the following scene from the play *Step on a Crack.*

> **Ellie:** (*Tentatively*) Hey Pop. Tell me about my real mother.
>
> **Max:** How come you want to hear about her all the time these days?
>
> *(Ellie sits at his feet and rests against his knees.)*
>
> **Ellie:** I just do. Hey do you remember the time it was my birthday and you brought Mom home from the hospital, and I didn't know she was coming that time? I remember I was already in bed and you guys wanted to surprise me. She just came into my room, kissed me goodnight and tucked me in, just like it was any other night.
>
> **Max:** (*Moved*) How could you remember that? You were just four years old.
>
> **Ellie:** I just remember.
>
> **Max:** Your mother was a wonderful person and I loved her very much.
>
> **Ellie:** As much as you . . . like Lucille?
>
> **Max:** Ellie.

Ellie: Was she pretty?

Max: She was beautiful.

Ellie: Do I look like her?

Max: Naw, you look more like me, you mug.

Ellie: *(Suddenly angry)* Why does everything have to change?

Max: Hey.

Ellie: How come Lucille is always so neat and everything?
I bet she never even burps.

Max: She does.

Ellie: HUH!

Max: I heard her once.

Ellie: Do you think I'd look cute with makeup on?

Max: You? You're just a kid.

Ellie: But Lucille wears makeup. Lots of it.

Max: Well, she's grown up.

Ellie: Hey, do you know how old she is?

Max: Sure. Thirty-five.

Ellie: How come you married such an old one?

Max: That's not old.

Ellie: Huh!

Max: Why, I am older than that myself.

Ellie: You are?

Max: Ellie, you know how you get to go to camp in the
summer. You get to go away all by yourself.

Ellie: Yeah, but I'm not going anymore.

Max: You're not?

Skill Development

Media Literacy

● Tell students that reader's theatre, like other kinds of performance, often depends upon stereotypes. For example, ask students to write down their impressions of the terms *used-car salesman* and *elderly unmarried aunt*. Encourage students to become aware of the various stereotypes they see in the media.

571

Critical Thinking

Synthesizing

● Encourage students to work in groups of three to perform the excerpt from *Step On a Crack*, using the reader's theatre techniques they have learned in this chapter.

Critical Thinking

Analyzing

● Ask students to decide on answers to the following questions as they look over the excerpt from *Step on a Crack*.

How old is Ellie?

How long have Max and Lucille been married?

Where are Max and Ellie?

How long has Ellie's mother been dead?

Why does Ellie dislike Lucille?

Ellie: Nope, look what happened the last time I went. You and Lucille got to be good friends, then as soon as I got back, you got married. Who knows, if I go away again I might get back and find out you moved to Alaska.

Max: We wouldn't do that.

Ellie: You might.

Max: Ellie, kids can't always go where parents go. Sometimes parents go away all by themselves.

Ellie: How come ever since you got married I am such a kid. You never used to say I was a kid. We did everything together. Now all I hear is, "Kids can't do this." "Kids can't do that." "Kids have to go to bed at eight-thirty." "Kids have to clean up their rooms." Why does everything have to change?

Max: Nothing's changed. I still love you the same. Now there's just two of us who love you.

Ellie: HUH!

Max: I just wish you'd try a little harder to . . .

Ellie: To like Lucille? Why should I? She doesn't like me. She likes cute little girls who play with dollies.

Max: Well she got herself a messy little mug that likes junk.

(Ellie pulls away.)

Max: I'm just kidding. She likes you fine the way you are.

Ellie: Oh yeah, well I don't like her.

Max: Why not?

(Lucille enters and overhears the following.)

Ellie: 'Cause . . . 'Cause . . . 'Cause she's a wicked stepmother. . . . *(Ellie giggles in spite of herself.)*

Skill Development

Making Conversation

● Encourage students to discuss with each other the theme and basic conflict in the excerpt from *Step On a Crack*.

66Drawing on my fine command of the English language, I said nothing.**99**
　　　　　ROBERT BENCHLEY

Learning Styles

Audio Learning

● After students have read and worked with the excerpt from *Step On a Crack*, call on volunteers to talk about the type of language used in the scene. Ask whether the characters have any individual characteristics or idiosyncrasies of speech. Write students' responses on the chalkboard.

Strong characters make reader's theatre interesting to the audience and fun for the performers.

Theme In order to hold an audience's interest, your literature must have a strong theme. Listeners should be able to identify the theme easily and follow it throughout the piece. If the theme is hidden, it will be difficult to bring it to the audience through reader's theatre.

Language Performers of reader's theatre rely on picturesque language to help create their suggestion. The language must be descriptive and exciting to hold the audience's interest. It must create mental pictures for the listener.

Conflict The best scenes for reader's theatre show conflict. It may be conflict within a person, between people, or between a person and the environment. The conflict holds the audience's attention. It makes people listen to find out how the conflict is resolved. You can see a good example of person-to-person conflict in the story "The Field."

573

Critical Thinking

Synthesizing

Encourage students to visualize the setting of the tale, decide on the theme, and identify the climax or point of greatest suspense as part of their preparation for performance.

The Field

Once there was a great field. At one edge of the field, there were trees and bushes and on the other a thin country road that curved about untraveled for many miles.

In the field were rocks, high gray piles of stone, good for the climbing, hiding, and exploring games of children.

In the middle of the field there was a tree, a single tree that had been growing for more than a hundred years. It was gnarled and its branches spread in many directions. The children from the neighboring villages would use the tree for home base in their games of tag and hide-and-go-seek.

The field lay just between the Kingdoms of Aura and Ghent. Both kings claimed the field even though it was bare except for the rocks and the tree and the children who played in it.

"Mine," said the King of Aura, politely.

"Mine," answered the King of Ghent in a louder voice.

Then the people of both countries began to say ugly things about each other.

And soon two armies gathered—one on each side of the field.

The battle began. The Aurians were camped by the bushes and the trees, and the Ghentians were over on the other side of the road.

In the tree in the middle of the field a robin had built her nest of twigs and grass. She had woven it together and now the nest hidden by the summer leaves held three blue eggs. Carefully, the mother sat on her eggs even though the arrows whizzed past the tree and the shotguns made sounds of thunder and there was the sound of screaming when soldiers were hurt or frightened. The bird stayed on her nest although there was crying and singing and shouting as the men moved up to the foot of the tree and then retreated.

One morning when the soldiers were starting to shoot at each other again, the robin flew down to the grass and unearthed a worm.

574

Learning Styles
Audio-Visual Learning

● Students might like to assign one member of their group to provide whatever media aids the group decides to use. For example, if they decide to use sound or lighting effects, this person would be in charge of finding or taping appropriate sounds and procuring simple lighting.

As she pulled it from the soil, the guns pounded the ground and the soldiers moved up and down, hiding and crawling in the thick grass, and there was smoke in the air and blood on the rocks where the children had played.

As the robin was flying back to her nest an arrow with a sharp tip flew past the crouching soldiers and pierced the throat of the bird. Her wings fluttered for a moment and then she fell like a heavy stone. Only one soldier saw her fall.

Then a shell from the king's prize cannon boomed across the field and landed not far from the tree.

The earth shook and the tree trembled and the branches wavered and the nest with the three small eggs fell down to the ground.

The young soldier watched the nest fall. He crawled over the rocks and the twigs and found the three small eggs unbroken. Not even a crack was on the shells.

The soldier put his shotgun down on the ground. He took off his iron gray helmet, and turning it over, he filled it with grass and a dandelion and some clover. He carefully placed the nest in the matted grass and cradled the helmet in his arms. He sat for a while watching the eggs in his helmet.

The commanding officer came by and saw one of his soldiers sitting down.

"Come on soldier, let's go . . . put your helmet on."

The young man, carrying his helmet, reached for his gun and started forward.

"Put your helmet on," the officer shouted.

There was a pause as the soldier looked down at the eggs.

"I can't, sir," he said.

"There's no such thing as can't in this man's army," yelled the officer. "Put your helmet on your head."

continued

Skill Development

Active Listening

Have students use the Evaluation Form on pages 577–578 to critique the reader's theatre performance of "The Field" suggested in the Interact activity on this page. Discuss the form with students before the performance.

The soldier put down his gun.

"I think," he said in a very quiet voice, "I think I'm going home now, sir." The commanding officer turned red in the face but the young man, carefully holding his helmet under his arm, turned around and walked off the field, past the bushes and trees.

On his way home the three eggs broke open and three small wet birds opened their tiny beaks for food. The soldier stopped. He gathered some berries from a nearby bush and offered them gently to each bird in turn. The soldier smiled. Then the birds settled down, resting on one another, and fell asleep.

—Anne Roiphe

INTERACT

Prepare the story "The Field" for a reader's theatre performance for four to six speakers. Present it for the class.

Critiquing Reader's Theatre

The commanding officer and the young soldier were talking at the same time.

There needs to be more use of facial expression to show emotions.

As a critic or listener, you may be called upon to give feedback after a reader's theatre performance. As with public speaking, effective feedback can help performers improve their skills. You may find the reader's theatre evaluation form useful in providing feedback.

Evaluation Form: Reader's Theatre		

Group members _____

_____

_____

Title of selection _____

	Always	Sometimes	Never
Voice			
Members blended in unison when appropriate.	____	____	____
Voices could be distinguished from each other easily.	____	____	____
Character voices remained the same throughout the performance.	____	____	____
Members made effective use of stress, pause, inflection, pitch, and volume.	____	____	____

continued

continued

Body

Members adapted facial expressions
    to the material.   ____   ____   ____

Members moved in unison
    when appropriate.   ____   ____   ____

Members looked at listeners regularly.   ____   ____   ____

Members entered and exited in unison.   ____   ____   ____

Scripts (if used)

Members held scripts in similar ways.   ____   ____   ____

Members' faces could be seen
    over scripts.   ____   ____   ____

Material

Material was suitable to the audience.   ____   ____   ____

Material was well scripted to
    show meaning.   ____   ____   ____

Material was suited to reader's theatre.   ____   ____   ____

Theme was communicated clearly.   ____   ____   ____

Staging

Costumes, props, and lights
    supported theme.   ____   ____   ____

Characters were consistently placed
    on wall by speakers.   ____   ____   ____

Movement held the interest
    of the audience.   ____   ____   ____

❝To this generation I would say: memorize some bit of verse of truth or beauty.**❞**

EDGAR LEE MASTERS

CHAPTER 18 SUMMARY

This chapter introduces group interpretation by discussing choral speaking and reader's theatre. To create a choral-speaking performance, you need to create script patterns that use voices in different ways and to select material that works well in group reading. As a performer you need to know how to speak precisely, use the scripts uniformly, and use space effectively. Finally, you need to be able to critique choral speaking. To create a reader's-theatre performance, you need to understand the use of suggestion. You also need to know the performance techniques of scripting, staging, eye focus, movement, and technical support. You must select your material carefully and know how to critique reader's theatre. Group interpretation will help you develop self-confidence, performance and analysis skills, and literary knowledge. It is an exciting way to approach literature.

Beyond the Classroom

With a partner, find a short story that has a theme, characters, and language that appeal to both of you and that would appeal to an audience of older adults. Cut and adapt the story for reader's theatre.

579

Answers

Think About It

Student answers will vary. Here are sample answers:

1. Choral speaking is speaking in unison; speakers blend and combine their individual voices to create a group voice. Reader's theatre is a type of group interpretation in which speakers present literature in a dramatic form. Rather than acting the story out, speakers suggest their characters by using their voices, facial expressions, and some gestures.

2. Selection criteria for choral speaking include rhythm, variety of moods, and theme.

3. Selections of literature for reader's theatre should be based upon interesting characters, a powerful theme, picturesque language, and a strong conflict.

4. It is so called because the action and scenery in reader's theatre are created in the audience's mind, not on the stage.

CHAPTER REVIEW

Think About It

1. Define choral speaking and reader's theatre.

2. What three criteria should you use for choosing a choral-speaking selection?

3. List three criteria for selecting literature for a reader's-theatre performance.

4. Why is reader's theatre sometimes called "the theater of the mind"?

5. Describe three performance techniques used in choral speaking and three used in reader's theatre.

Try It Out

1. With a small group of classmates, choose several pieces of literature appropriate for a group of elementary school children. You might use a book by Dr. Seuss or a group of poems by Shel Silverstein. Discuss why each piece of literature is appropriate for choral speaking. Use the selection criteria discussed in this chapter.

2. In small groups, brainstorm themes for a reader's-theatre presentation. Possible ideas might include world peace and growing up. Then brainstorm pieces of literature that could be used with each theme.

3. Cut and adapt a short story or a one-act play for reader's theatre. Rehearse and present the piece in class.

Put It in Writing

1. Choose a piece of literature for choral speaking or for reader's theatre. Analyze the literature according to the appropriate criteria discussed in the text. Explain why you believe the piece of literature would work well for reader's theatre or choral speaking. Describe what performance techniques you would use in presenting it. For example, would you use technical support? Include your analysis in your journal.

2. After performing a group interpretation, write a paper in which you discuss the performance techniques you used and how well they worked. For example, how did your group use space? How might the techniques change if you were to do the performance again?

3. As you prepare a group interpretation, create a one-page flyer to advertise the group's performance. The flyer should include the title of the performance, the list of pieces to be performed, and the performers. Indicate the time and place. Provide some visual images to convey the meaning of the selections. You may wish to do this on the computer in order to include graphics. Be sure spelling, punctuation, and grammar are correct.

Speak About It

1. Critique a choral-speaking or reader's-theatre performance given by your classmates. Use one of the forms in this chapter or create one of your own. Share your critique orally with the performers. Be sure to follow the guidelines discussed in this unit.

2. Choose one of the script patterns for choral speaking discussed in this chapter and use it for a piece of literature you chose from number 1 of the Try It Out. Rehearse the script with your group, and present it to an elementary classroom. Explain choral speaking to your audience.

5. Choral speaking techniques: (1) readers speak precisely; (2) all readers handle their scripts in the same way; (3) each individual is aware of where individuals are placed and how they move. Reader's theatre techniques: (1) all characters remain on stage during the entire performance, usually seated on stools; (2) readers usually look out over the audience, often at a particular spot on the back wall; (3) readers use stylized, suggestive movement when necessary, rather than acting out the scenes.

Quick Check

Ask students to find and define these Key Terms:

choral speaking (552)

offstage focus (567)

reader's theatre (565)

script patterns (553)

suggestion (566)

581

Afterword:

Conclusions About Competence

Now that you have reached the end of this text, we hope you consider yourself to be a more competent communicator. You have increased your knowledge of the communication process, and you have developed and practiced many different communication skills. To help you think about your progress over this course, we repeat the questions we asked you to answer in Chapter 1. At that time you were engaged in a self-diagnosis of your communication strengths, weaknesses, and concerns. Compare your answers at that time to your answers today. We hope you are satisfied with your progress. In addition, we believe you have the knowledge and tools to continue to improve in areas you identify as needing further improvement.

COMMUNICATION DIFFICULTIES

Use this checklist to examine situations in which you have experienced difficulties. When you compare your current answers to your answers at the beginning of the course, you may wish to think in the following categories:

S—Same response

I—Improved somewhat in this area

SI—Significantly improved in this area

The following questions refer to situations with which people often have problems. See whether you have ever found yourself in a similar situation. Do you ever have trouble

- telling a teacher that you do not understand the problem she just explained?

- talking to a friend about the problems you are having with your boyfriend or girlfriend?

- asking a stranger for directions if you are lost?

- convincing your parents to let you go out with friends even though you haven't finished your chores?

- explaining to your instructor or coach why you have to miss practice?

- expressing your opinion on a current-affairs topic?

- reading a poem or story aloud in class?

- understanding what a friend's facial expressions mean?

- telling a joke to a group?

- expressing feelings of anger, hurt, concern, or love?

- disagreeing with someone you like?

- looking people in the eye when you talk to them?

- arguing for your point of view?

PERSONAL COMMUNICATION CHECKLIST

Use this checklist to describe your communication strengths and weaknesses. Which statements never apply to you? Which statements sometimes apply to you? Which statements always apply?

1. When I'm introduced to people, I immediately forget their names.

2. I stumble over my words when I give an oral report.

3. I speak my mind when working in a group.

4. I tune out during a newscast or when hearing information I find boring.

5. I have trouble telling a friend that I'm upset or angry with him or her.

6. I have trouble carrying on a conversation with a person I just met.

7. I am uncomfortable when my friend expresses sadness or anger.

8. I find myself thinking about what I'm going to say instead of listening to other people.

9. I am afraid to join class discussion because I might say something silly.

10. I avoid making eye contact with people when I talk with them.

11. I tend to avoid taking a strong stand in an argument.

12. I wish I could find better ways to tell family members what concerns me.

13. I become uncomfortable when I have to relate to people from a cultural background different from mine.

14. I look forward to giving speeches on topics that interest me.

15. I find myself trying to structure the group tasks when we work on group projects.

CONSIDERATIONS OF COMPETENCE

By now you should have improved your communication competencies in a number of areas. When confronted with a situation, you should be more effective at

thinking of communication strategies you might use

selecting the best strategy for this situation

acting on that strategy

evaluating the effect of your actions

We hope you can think about the major sections of this text and identify areas in which you increased your competence so that you are considered "well qualified and capable." Becoming a competent communicator takes work. We encourage you to keep up the good work.

Communication is the centerpiece of everyday life. It is your means of connecting to the world around you. Commit yourself to improving your communication competence every day. Your life will be richer for this decision.

Bibliography

The following titles are useful sources for literature for oral interpretation, for additional help in researching and giving speeches, and for answering questions about parliamentary procedure.

Appleman, Deborah and Margaret Reed, eds. *Braided Lives: An Anthology of Multicultural American Writing.* St. Paul: Minnesota Humanities Commission, 1991.

Boyko, Carrie and Kimberly Colen. *Hold Fast to Your Dreams: Twenty Commencement Speeches.* New York: Scholastic, 1996.

Canfield, Jack, Mark V. Hansen, and Kimberly Kirberger, eds. *Chicken Soup for the Teenage Soul.* Deerfield Beach, Fla.: Health Communications Inc., 1997.

Cortina, Rodolfo, ed. *Hispanic American Literature: An Anthology.* Lincolnwood, Ill.: National Textbook, 1998.

Detz, Joan. *Can You Say a Few Words?* New York: St. Martin's, 1991.

Emra, Bruce, ed. *Coming of Age, Vol. 1,* rev. ed. Lincolnwood, Ill.: National Textbook, 1999. A collection of short stories about youth and adolescence.

_____. *Coming of Age, Volume 2.* Lincolnwood, Ill.: National Textbook, 1999. Poetry, short stories, essays, and memoirs by Gish Jen, Rita Dove, Simon Ortiz, Langston Hughes, Sandra Cisneros, and others.

Gallo, Donald, ed. *Short Circuits; Thirteen Shocking Stories by Outstanding Writers for Young Adults.* New York: Dell Laurel-Leaf, 1990.

_____. *Sixteen: Short Stories by Outstanding Writers for Young Adults.* New York: Delacorte, 1988. Chosen by the Young Adult Library Services Association as one of the 100 "Best of the Best" young adult books of the last 25 years.

George, Kristin O'Connell. *The Great Frog Race and Other Poems.* New York: Clarion, 1997.

Hopkins, Lee Bennett. *Opening Days: Poems About Sports.* San Diego: Harcourt Brace, 1996.

Kennedy, Dorothy M. ed. *I Thought I'd Take My Rat to School: Poems for September to June.* Boston: Little, Brown, 1993. Humorous poems about school.

King, Laurie, ed. *Hear My Voice: A Multicultural Anthology of Literature from the United States.* Reading, Mass.: Addison-Wesley, 1994.

Paterson, Katherine. *Jip.* New York: Lodestar / Dutton, 1996. Jip, who has been abandoned, lives at the poor farm where he helps with the chores, but when a mysterious stranger appears, who seems to know about his past, the novel takes some surprising twists. Set in the mid-nineteenth century, the novel explores the fugitive slave issue.

Paulsen, Gary. *Harris and Me: A Summer Remembered.* San Diego: Harcourt Brace, 1993. Amusing story of a city boy who goes to live in the country, where he and his cousin create considerable turmoil.

Prelutsky, Jack. *A Pizza the Size of the Sun.* New York: William Morrow, 1996.

Ridlon, Marci. *Sun Through the Window: Poems for Children.* Honesdale, Pa.: Boyds Mills Press, 1996.

Robert, Henry M. *Robert's Rules of Order, Newly Revised.* Glenview, Ill.: Scott, Foresman, 1981.

Silverstein, Shel. *Falling Up.* New York: HarperCollins, 1996. More poems to delight readers.

Sturgis, Alice. *Learning Parliamentary Procedure.* New York: McGraw-Hill, 1953.

Woodward, Jeannette A. *Writing Research Papers: Investigating Resources in Cyberspace.* Lincolnwood, Ill.: National Textbook, 1997.

Worley, Demetrice A. and Jesse Perry, Jr. *African American Literature: An Anthology of Nonfiction, Fiction, Poetry, and Drama.* Lincolnwood, Ill.: National Textbook, 1993.

Glossary

A

abstain: in parliamentary procedure, refrain from voting.

acquaintances: persons whom one knows but who are not close friends.

adjournment: closing of a meeting.

affirmative: in debate, the side that argues in favor of an issue or change.

agenda: list of subjects to be discussed at a meeting.

amendment: proposed change in a parliamentary motion.

argument: conversation in which two or more people express different points of view on a topic.

articulators: tongue, teeth, jaw, hard and soft palate, and lips, which form sound into words.

audience analysis: information about the audience that helps the speaker communicate with the members. It includes basic data, beliefs, and attitudes.

audience goal: speaker's description of what the listeners should be able to do after the speech is completed.

audiovisual aids: nonverbal supporting materials, such as graphs and diagrams, that help the speaker make his or her points more clearly and interest the audience.

B

bandwagon appeal: type of faulty reasoning that suggests a person should do something because everyone else is doing it.

body recall: remembering bodily responses to emotions such as fear or anger.

brainstorming: group discussion technique in which as many ideas as possible are listed aloud before group members give feedback to the ideas.

brief: outline of a debate case, containing arguments and evidence.

buzz group: small groups of audience members that discuss problems and report solutions to the larger group.

by-laws: rules that govern the procedures to be followed by a group.

C

call previous question: move to an immediate vote within parliamentary procedure.

card stacking: type of faulty reasoning that involves the piling up of information with very little support in favor of an idea.

case: all the arguments that will be made to support the affirmative or negative position in a debate.

cause-effect reasoning: an argument suggesting that one event produces a second event.

chairperson: name for the person who leads a meeting.

channel: means by which a message is transmitted.

choral speaking: type of group interpretation in which speakers blend and combine their voices to create a group voice.

chronological order: presentation of events in the order in which they happened.

clarity: clearness of a speaker's words.

clique: subgroup whose members tend to "stick" together and avoid other people.

committee: subgroup of a larger group, formed to carry out a specific task.

communication: process of sending and receiving messages to share meaning.

communication acts: major reasons for communicating, which include sharing information, discussing feelings, persuading, following social rituals, and using imagination.

communication strategies: verbal and nonverbal messages created to reach a specific goal.

competency steps: courses of action that competent communicators follow. They are these: thinking of strategies, selecting a strategy, acting on the strategy, and evaluating the strategy's effect.

competent communicator: person who develops a number of strategies for dealing with communication situations and follows the competencey steps to become more effective.

conclusion: final part of a speech that summarizes the main points, reminds the audience of the goal, and provides a clear ending.

conflict: a person's struggle with other individuals, nature, a hostile environment, or the self.

connected information: new information that is related to information the audience already knows.

connotative meaning: emotional or personal response to a word.

constitution: document that describes the nature and purpose of a group.

constructive criticism: feedback that tells a speaker what worked well, what could be improved, and how to improve.

context: setting and people that surround a message.

creative listening: type of listening in which one uses active imagination to interpret a message

criteria: standards that a solution has to meet in order to be acceptable.

critic: person who judges or evaluates.

critical listening: type of listening in which one examines a persuasive message and makes decisions about the findings.

critique: formal feedback given by a critic to a performer.

cutting the literature: shortening material for oral interpretation without drastically changing its meaning.

cyberspace resources: sources of information on the Internet.

D

debate: speech competition of spoken arguments between individuals or teams with rules, time limits, and a winner and loser.

deductive reasoning: using a general idea to reach conclusions about very specific instances.

delivery: way in which a speaker uses voice and body to present a speech. It includes speaker confidence, methods of delivery, personal delivery, rehearsing the speech, and use of audiovisual aids.

denotative meaning: dictionary meaning of a word.

diaphragm: muscle that separates the chest from the abdominal cavity.

dramatic speaker: voice that is heard telling the story or poem during a reading. Often the dramatic speaker is one of the main characters in the literary material.

E

empathic listening: type of listening that involves listening to another's feelings

empathy: ability to put oneself in another person's place to understand what that person is feeling.

ethical decisions: choices that have to do with questions of right and wrong.

eulogy: speech given at a funeral or memorial service to honor a person who died.

evaluating: third step in the listening process in which a listener examines the message and makes a judgment.

extemporaneous method: delivery in which the speaker uses a prepared outline but does not plan each word or sentence.

external barriers: situations in the environment that keep listeners from paying attention to the speaker.

eye focus: where a performer looks while interpreting a piece of literature.

F

fact: information based on evidence that can be proved or disproved.

faulty reasoning: incorrect or false reasoning.

feedback: other people's responses to a message that let the speaker know how he or she is doing.

first meetings: beginning stages of developing a relationship.

floor: name for the "right to speak" in parliamentary procedure.

flow sheet: in debate, a diagram of the arguments, listed in parallel columns across a page.

formal feedback: planned comments (written or oral) intended to affect the speaker's next speech.

forming: the first stage of the group life cycle during which members come together, figure out where each person fits, and try to establish leadership.

forum: discussion in which the audience participates.

G

gestures: movements of the head, shoulders, hands, or arms that speakers use to describe or emphasize a point.

glittering generalities: type of faulty reasoning involving vague statements that are not supported with specific information or linked to the main point.

group: small number of people who share a common purpose or interest, communicate easily and regularly among themselves, participate in planning and decision making, and feel connected to the other members.

group communication: type of communication that occurs when people participate in a group for social or work purposes.

group norms: ways in which people are expected to act as group members.

group problem solving: method group members use to solve problems. It involves the following steps: (1) identify the problem, (2) analyze the problem, (3) set criteria for a solution, (4) develop solutions, and (5) select a solution.

group purpose: group's reason for existing.

H

hearing: act of receiving sound.

hyperbole: figure of speech that consists of an intentional exaggeration.

I

impact: major effect.

impromptu method: delivery in which the speaker talks without notes and without much preparation.

inductive reasoning: using many specific pieces of information to reach a general conclusion.

informal feedback: verbal and nonverbal messages given spontaneously to the speaker.

informational listening: type of listening to gain information, directions, or news.

informative speech: speech that presents or describes information.

intellectual side of self: how a person handles ideas, values, and beliefs.

interpersonal communication: type of communication in which people (usually two persons) share meanings in order to build and maintain long-lasting and important relationships.

interpreting: second step in the listening process, in which a listener uses his or her own experience to give meaning to the message.

interpretive communication: type of communication in which a speaker brings literature to life for an audience.

interview: conversation with the purpose of obtaining information.

introduction: beginning of a presentation that gains attention, presents the topic, and connects the speaker to the audience.

J

Johari window: a four-part box diagram representing the awareness people have of themselves and others.

L

larynx: voice box that contains the vocal cords.

Lincoln-Douglas debate: type of debate in which one person on each side debates a proposition of value.

listener barriers: personal attitudes or behaviors that interfere with listening.

listening: process of receiving, interpreting, evaluating, and responding to messages.

M

majority: more than one-half of those people voting.

manuscript method: delivery in which a speaker writes out the entire speech and delivers it from this paper.

marking the script: writing symbols on the oral-interpretation script to help a speaker remember how to read it.

memorized method: delivery in which a speaker memorizes the speech and delivers it word for word.

metaphor: figure of speech that compares two things that are not usually thought to be alike. Metaphors do not use the words *like* and *as*.

minority: less than one-half of those people voting.

minutes: written report of what happens at a meeting.

moderator: person who keeps a panel or symposium discussion moving and makes sure everyone's ideas are heard.

mood: the emotional content of a piece of literature.

motion: proposed action for a group to consider for parliamentary action.

N

name calling: type of faulty reasoning that attacks the person rather than the person's ideas by using unpopular names or labels.

negative: in debate, the side that argues against an issue or change.

noise: anything that interferes with a listener's ability to receive a message.

nonverbal messages: communication expressed without words; it includes appearance, facial expression, eye contact, posture, gestures, voice, and space or time.

norming: the third stage in the group life cycle, during which members begin to develop a sense of identity and function well together with established norms.

O

offstage focus: focusing one's eyes on the imagined reflection of other performers.

onomatopoeia: figure of speech in which a word sounds like its meaning.

opinion: judgment based on beliefs or feelings.

oral history: story that is passed down through generations without being written.

oral interpretation: reading literature aloud to communicate meaning to an audience.

order of business: sequence in which a group will discuss topics.

P

panel discussion: discussion during which a subject is explored by the group members in front of an audience.

parliamentarian: person responsible for making sure parliamentary procedure is followed.

parliamentary procedure: set of rules based on *Robert's Rules of Order, Newly Revised* for running large group meetings.

perception: process of giving meaning to information learned through the five senses.

performing: the fourth and last stage in the group life cycle, during which the focus is on the task and members function together in completing the task.

personification: figure of speech that gives human characteristics to nonhuman things.

persuasion: process of changing a listener's beliefs or moving a listener to action.

persuasive speaking: type of speech in which a speaker attempts to convince an audience of certain beliefs or the need for certain actions.

pharynx: muscular sac between mouth and esophagus.

physical side of self: how a person looks and uses his or her body for physical activities.

pitch: highness or lowness of a speaker's voice.

plagiarism: representing the words or ideas of others as your own.

plot: storyline of a piece of literature.

policy debate: debate in which the affirmative and negative teams debate a proposition of policy.

PowerPoint: a computer program that allows you to create graphics.

problem-solution order: method of organizing the points of a speech based on two major areas: the problem and the solution.

process order: method of organizing the points of a speech based on the way something works.

proposition: statement of a problem, worded so there are clearly two sides to the argument.

proposition of fact: statement that says something is or is not true.

proposition of policy: statement that says something should or should not be done.

proposition of value: statement that says something is good or bad, right or wrong, useful or useless.

public communication: type of communication in which an individual communicates before a large audience. This includes public speaking.

public speaking: type of speaking in which one person addresses a group for a specific purpose.

purpose statement: sentence that summarizes the main idea or purpose of the speech.

Q

quorum: number of members who must be at a meeting in order to conduct the meeting and make binding decisions.

R

rate: speed at which the speaker talks.

reader's theatre: type of group interpretation in which speakers present literature in a dramatic form.

rebuttal: in debate, the process of rebuilding one's case after it has been attacked by the other team.

receiving: first step in the listening process, which involves hearing and seeing messages.

recess: to take a break from a meeting for a set period of time.

refutation: process of attacking the opposing side's argument in a debate.

research: everyday process of investigation.

resonators: hollow chambers, such as the mouth, pharynx, and nasal cavities, that increase sound.

responding: fourth step in the listening process, which involves giving verbal or nonverbal feedback to the speaker.

rhyme: words that sound alike.

rituals: informal rules or patterns for interaction.

role: personal pattern of communication that characterizes one's place in a group.

S

script patterns: ways in which the speakers' parts are divided in group interpretation.

second a motion: show support for a parliamentary motion.

secret ballot: written vote used for nominations and controversial topics.

self-concept: one's picture of oneself formed from personal beliefs and attitudes.

self-esteem: one's opinion of oneself based on personal self-concept.

sense recall: remembering experiences a performer has had that will help him or her suggest images to the audience.

setting: time and place in which a piece of literature is set.

simile: figure of speech that compares two things that are not usually thought to be alike, using words such as *like* or *as*.

slang: informal language that is unique to a particular group.

social rituals: rules for interaction in a culture or society.

social-ritual speech: short, informative speech that follows the same pattern every time it occurs.

social side of self: how a person relates to other people.

space order: method of organizing the points of a speech based on the physical relationship of people, places, or objects.

speaker barriers: characteristics of the speaker that interfere with the audience's listening.

speech to inform: speech in which the speaker's purpose is to increase the knowledge of the listeners.

speech to persuade: speech in which the speaker's purpose is to convince the listeners to hold a certain belief or to act in a certain way.

stage fright: nervousness when addressing an audience.

stereotyping: labeling people as part of a group and treating them as if they possessed only the characteristics of that group.

storytelling: the art of reciting to an audience.

style: way that a piece of literature is written.

subgroup: smaller group within a group.

suggestion: way in which speakers in reader's theatre create most of the action, props, and scenery in the audience's imagination through their performance skills.

support: messages that make people feel good about themselves.

supporting material: material that develops the main points of the speech.

survey: method of gathering information and opinions from a large number of people.

symposium: group discussion during which members give short speeches to an audience.

T

table a motion: in parliamentary procedure, to put a motion aside to be discussed at another time.

testimonials: using expert opinion or statements to create positive feelings for a person, thing, idea, or event.

theme: main idea of a piece of literature.

thought speed: the extra time listeners gain because they can process words faster than speakers can produce them.

time order: method of organizing the points of a speech by placing them in a chronological pattern.

topical order: method of organizing the points of a speech by breaking a whole topic into its natural parts.

trachea: windpipe through which air passes in and out of lungs.

transition: words or phrases that form links between ideas.

U

unrelated testimonials: type of faulty reasoning that involves using statements from a person who is not an expert to create positive feelings for a person, thing, idea, or event.

V

verbal messages: words one uses when communicating.

visualize: process of imagining every move in one's mind before actually performing the act.

vocal cords: two elastic folds of membrane, with a slit between them, that produce sound when they vibrate.

vocal quality: sound or tone of a speaker's voice.

volume: loudness or softness of a speaker's voice.

Index

Critical listening, 63–65
  skills of, in debate, 445
Criticism, constructive, 174–177,
  396–399
Critique, 395. *See also* Evaluation;
  Feedback
  of choral speaking, 562–563
  learning to, 395
  of oral interpretation, 543–546
  of reader's theatre, 576–578
Cross-examination in debate, 449,
  464–466
Culture
  in nonverbal communication, 36
  in oral interpretation, 496–498
Cutting literature in oral interpretation, 515–517
Cyberspace resources, doing
  research with, 292–293

D

Data. *See also* Information; Research
  in audience analysis, 267
  on electronic sources, 293
Davila, Roger, 124
"The Day We Die" (Markowitz),
  504–505
Dear Mr. Henshaw (Cleary), 490,
  491
Debate, 442–467
  affirmative position in, 446,
    447–448
  building case in, 461–462
  creating arguments in, 458–462
  creating propositions in, 446,
    450–455
  critical listening skills in, 445
  cross-examination in, 449,
    464–466
  ethics in, 455
  flow sheet in, 450
  formats for, 463–466
  negative position in, 446, 448
  notetaking in, 449–450
  organizational skills in, 445
  process in, 446–450
  rebuttal in, 462–463
  refutation in, 462
  research skills in, 445, 455–456,
    458–463
  resolutions in, 447
  responding to opponent in,
    462–463

speaking skills in, 446
  values of, 444–446
Deductive reasoning, 422–423
Definition in informative speech,
  381
Delgado, Juan, 494
Delivery. *See* Speech delivery
Democracy, 17–19
Demonstration in informative
  speech, 381–382
Denotative meaning, 28, 498–499
Description
  in constructive criticism, 396
  in informative speech, 381
  in supporting material, 302–303
Diagrams as media aids, 369
Dialect in oral interpretation, 497
Diaphragm, 53
Dicey's Song (Voigt), 490, 494,
  524–525
Dictionaries, 290, 291
Dictionary of American Biography,
  291
Digate, Natalie, 68
Direct analogy, 460
Direct quotation cards, 297
Disconfirming message, 60
Discussion
  group, 192, 212–216, 220–231
  in parliamentary procedures,
    246, 247
Distractions in listening, 69–74
"The Dog and the Shadow,"
  505–506
Douglas, Stephen, 464
Dragonwings (Yep), 494
Dramatic speaker, 489–491
"Dreams" (Hughes), 504
Dunbar, Paul Laurence, 327

E

Ecclesiastes 1:1-8, 553–554
Education Index, 289
Elected leaders, 209
Electronic media resources, doing
  research with, 291–292
Elizabeth, Queen of England, 410
Emerging leaders, 209
Emotional appeal, 424
Emotions. *See* Feelings
Empathic listening, 67–68
Empathizing, 170–171
Empathy, 171

Emphasis
  marking script for, 532–533
  repetition in, 380
Ethical decisions, 409
Ethics
  in debate, 455
  in persuasive speaking, 409
  in research, 300–301
Eulogies in social-ritual speeches,
  390
Evaluation. *See also* Critique;
  Feedback
  of choral speaking, 562–563
  of communication strategy,
    112–113
  forms for, 216, 400–402,
    544–546, 563, 577–578
  of group discussion, 212–216
  honesty in, 142
  of informative speeches, 391–402
  in listening process, 60
  of oral interpretation, 543–546
  of persuasive speech, 433–435
  of reader's theatre, 577–578
  self, 43–44
  of supporting materials, 306–308
Evidence
  finding, for debate, 455–456, 458
  in inductive reasoning, 421–422
  in supporting ideas, 419
Examples
  in debate, 459
  in introduction, 332
  as supporting materials, 303–304
Expectations in audience analysis,
  269–270
Experiences, impact on
  perceptions, 39
Experts
  in debate, 459–460
  role of, 189
Expository writing. *See*
  Informative Speech
Extemporaneous method of speech
  delivery, 346–348
External barriers to listening, 69
Eye contact
  in nonverbal message, 31–32
  in oral interpretation, 528–531
  in personal delivery, 361
  in reader's theatre, 567
  in speech delivery, 361

Credits

Photo Credits

Page abbreviations are as follows: (T) top, (C) center, (B) bottom, (L) left, (R) right.

CHAPTER 1
xviiii, © 1993 Ron Chapple/FPG International LLC; **3, 21,** © 1996 Mike Malyszko/FPG International LLC; **6,** Skjold Photographs; **14,** Skjold Photographs; **17,** Skjold Photographs; **19,** © Jeff Ellis Photography

CHAPTER 2
25, 47, Roger Tully/Tony Stone Images; **29,** Ian Shaw/Tony Stone Images; **31,** © Jeff Ellis Photography; **33,** © Jeff Ellis Photography; **38,** © Jeff Ellis Photography; **41,** © Jeff Ellis Photography; **42,** © Jeff Ellis Photography; **47,** © Jeff Ellis Photography

CHAPTER 3
51, 81, © The Stock Market/Ariel Skelley, 1994; **52,** © Jeff Ellis Photography; **54,** Skjold Photographs; **59,** © Jeff Ellis Photography; **61,** © Jeff Ellis Photography; **64,** © Jeff Ellis Photography ; **66,** Skjold Photographs; **68,** © Jeff Ellis Photography; **71,** Dan Bosler/Tony Stone Images; **72,** © Jeff Ellis Photography; **75,** Skjold Photographs; **77,** © 1989 Peter Gould/FPG International LLC; **78,** © Jeff Ellis Photography

CHAPTER 4
85, 115, David Young Wolff/Tony Stone Images; **88,** © Jeff Ellis Photography; **91,** Skjold Photographs; **94,** © Jeff Ellis Photography; **97,** (L) R. Frerck/Odyssey Productions/Chicago; (R) Unicorn/Margaret Finefrock; **99,** © Jeff Ellis Photography; **100,** Skjold Photographs; **103,** © Jeff Ellis Photography; **105,** © Jeff Ellis Photography;

107, © Jeff Ellis Photography **110,** Skjold Photographs; **111,** David Madison/Tony Stone Images

CHAPTER 5
118, © The Stock Market/Ariel Skelley, 1996; **121, 145,** © 1995 Ron Chapple/FPG International LLC; **123,** © Jeff Ellis Photography; **125,** Skjold Photographs; **127,** Skjold Photographs; **132,** © Jeff Ellis Photography; **141,** © Jeff Ellis Photography

CHAPTER 6
149, 177 (B), © 1996 Stephen Simpson/FPG International LLC; **152,** © Jeff Ellis Photography; **154,** © Jeff Ellis Photography; **160,** © Jeff Ellis Photography; **162,** Skjold Photographs; **164,** Penny Tweedie/Tony Stone Images; **168,** Skjold Photographs; **167,** © Jeff Ellis Photography; **173,** © Jeff Ellis Photography; **177,** (T) © Jeff Ellis Photography

CHAPTER 7
180, © 1996 Gary Buss/FPG International LLC; **183, 217,** Scott Robinson/Tony Stone Images; **187,** © Jeff Ellis Photography; **196,** © Jeff Ellis Photography; **197,** © Jeff Ellis Photography; **201,** © Jeff Ellis Photography; **204,** © Jeff Ellis Photography; **207,** © Jeff Ellis Photography; **215,** © Ron Chapple/FPG International LLC

CHAPTER 8
221, 251, © The Stock Market/Jose Pelaez, 1996; **224,** © Jeff Ellis Photography; **226,** © Jeff Ellis Photography; **230,** George A. Robinson/Tony Stone Images; **232,** Unicorn/Aneal Vohra; **233,** © Jeff Ellis Photography; **236,** © Jeff Ellis Photography; **239,** © Jeff Ellis Photography; **241,** © Jeff Ellis Photography; **246,** © Jeff Ellis Photography

Literary Acknowledgments

Every effort has been made to locate and contact copyright holders. In some cases, this has proved difficult. The publisher will correct any omissions or errors upon notification.

CHAPTER 2
45 "A Coup for the University" from "A New Football Team Learns a New Set of Signals," by Lisa Guernsey, *The Chronicle of Higher Education,* August 8, 1997. Copyright 1997 The Chronicle of Higher Education. Reprinted with permission.

CHAPTER 3
76 "I Have a Dream" by Martin Luther King, Jr. Reprinted by arrangement with The Heirs to the Estate of Martin Luther King, Jr., c/o Writers House, Inc. as agent for the proprietor. Copyright 1963 by Martin Luther King, Jr., copyright renewed 1991 by Coretta Scott King.

CHAPTER 4
114 From *How to Say No and Keep Your Friends: Peer Pressure Reversal for Teens and Preteens* by Sharon Scott. Reprinted by permission of HRD Press, Inc., 22 Amherst Rd., Amherst, MA 01002, 1-800-822-2801 (U.S. and Canada) or (413) 253-3488.

CHAPTER 5
138 Johari Window from *Group Processes: An Introduction to Group Dynamics,* Third Edition by Joseph Luft. copyright ©1984, 1970, 1963 by Joseph Luft. Reprinted by permission of Mayfield Publishing Company.

CHAPTER 6
156 "Knowing how to Play the Friendship Game" by Julie Buchwald. Reprinted by permission of the author.

CHAPTER 10
288 From *Readers' Guide to Periodical Literature.* Reprinted by permission of H.W. Wilson Company.
296 Excerpt from "The High Frontier of the Rain Forest Canopy" by Edward O. Wilson, *National Geographic* 180, no. 6 (December 1991): 102ff. Reprinted by permission of the National Geographic Society.
299 "CHA Kids Follow a Path of Safety" by Jerry Thornton, © Copyrighted Chicago Tribune Company. All rights reserved. Used with permission.

CHAPTER 13
404 "533-12 Freeze" by Matthew Wilkinson, by permission of Matthew N. Wilkinson.

CHAPTER 14
430 "I Think the Best—Expect the Best" by Kenyatta Wilson
436 "Meeting America's Challenge" by permission of Aliya Esmail.
439 "It's All Arabic to Me" by Mona M. Abo-Zena. Reprinted by permission of the author.

CHAPTER 15
446 From "High school students can't say enough about debate experience" by Connie Sowa-Jamrok, as appeared in the *Chicago Tribune,* April 24, 1994. Reprinted by permission of the author, Connie Sowa-Wachala.
469 "After 3 died, trio get 15 years for taking stop signs" by Lisa Holewa, as appeared in the *Chicago Sun-Times,* June 21, 1997. Reprinted by permission of Associated Press.

CHAPTER 16

480 "Watcha Gonna Do?"by Kathleen (George) Kearney.

483 "Foul Shot" by Edwin A. Hoey. Special reprint permission granted from READ® *Magazine* and published by Weekly Reader Corporation. Copyright © renewed 1989, 1962 by Weekly Reader Corporation. All rights reserved.

484 "Mean Maxine"by Jack Prelutsky from *The New Kid on the Block* by Jack Prelutsky. Copyright © 1984 by Jack Prelutsky. Reprinted by permission of Greenwillow Books, a division of William Morrow & Company, Inc.

485 "Forget-Me-Not" by Carol Anne Watkiss, originally published in *Edda Literary Magazine,* Homewood-Flossmoor H.S., Chicago, 1984. Reprinted by permission of the author.

490 From *Dicey's Song* by Cynthia Voight. Reprinted with the permission of Atheneum Books for Young Readers, an imprint of Simon & Schuster Children's Publishing Division. Copyright © 1982 Cynthia Voigt.

490 From *Dear Mr. Henshaw* by Beverly Cleary. Copyright © 1983 by Beverly Cleary. Reprinted by permission of Morrow Junior Books, a division of William Morrow & Company, Inc.

493 "Mending" by Judith Viorst. Reprinted with the permission of Atheneum Books for Young Readers, an imprint of Simon & Schuster Children's Publishing Division from *If I Were in Charge of the World and Other Worries* by Judith Viorst. Text copyright © 1981 by Judith Viorst.

497 From *The House on Mango Street.* Copyright © 1984 by Sandra Cisneros. Published by Vintage Books, a division of Random House, Inc., New York and in hardcover by Alfred A. Knopf in 1994. Reprinted by permission of Susan Bergholz Literary Seravices, New York. All rights reserved.

499 From *The Blue Rose* by Gerda Klein. Reprinted by permission of the author.

500 From *The Book of Three* by Lloyd Alexander, © 1964 by Lloyd Alexander. Reprinted by permission of Henry Holt and Company, Inc.

501 From "Stopping by Woods on a Snowy Evening" by Robert Frost. From *The Poetry of Robert Frost,* edited by Edward Connery Lathem, Copyright 1951 by Robert Frost, Copyright 1923, © 1969 by Henry Holt and Company, Inc. Reprinted by permission of Henry Holt and Company, Inc.

502 From *Working* by Studs Terkel. Reprinted by permission of Donadio & Ashworth, Inc. Copyright © 1972, 1974 by Studs Terkel.

504 "Dreams" by Langston Hughes from Collected Poems by Langston Hughes. Copyright © 1994 by the Estate of Langston Hughes. Reprinted by permission of Alfred A. Knopf, Inc.

504 "The Day We Die," anonymous Kalahari Bushman song from *The Rebirth of the Ostrich* by Arthur Markowitz. Reprinted by permission of the National Museum, Monuments and Art Gallery P/Bag 00114, Gabarone, Botswana, Africa.

506 "The Rice Puller of Chaowha" from *The Tiger's Whisker* by Harold Courlander, copyright 1959, 1987 by Harold Courlander. Reprinted by permission.

508 "Grasshopper Gumbo" by Jack Prelutsky from *Something Big Has Been Here* by Jack Prelutsky. Copyright © 1990 by Jack Prelutsky. Reprinted by permission of Greenwillow Books, a division of William Morrow & Company, Inc.

508 Haiku from *A Haiku Journey: Basho's Narrow Road to a Far Province.* Translated by Dorothy Britton. Published by Kodansha International Ltd. Copyright © 1974 by Kodansha International Ltd. Reprinted by permission. All rights reserved.

508 "Jazz Fantasia" from *Smoke and Steel* by Carl Sandburg, copyright 1920 by Harcourt, Brace and Company and renewed 1948 by Carl Sandburg. Reprinted by permission of the publisher.

CHAPTER 17

516 Abridged from *Johnny Tremain* by Esther Forbes. Copyright © 1943 by Esther Forbes Hoskins, © renewed 1971 by Linwood M. Erskine, Jr., Executor of the Estate of Esther Forbes Hoskins. Reprinted by permission of Houghton Mifflin Co. All Rights reserved.

Notes

Notes